MOON HANDBOOKS

RETIRÉ DE LA COLLECTION UNIVERSELLE
Bibliothèque et Archives nationales du Québec

YUCATÁN PENINSULA

LIZA PRADO & GARY CHANDLER

YUCATÁN PENINSULA, TABASCO, AND CHIAPAS

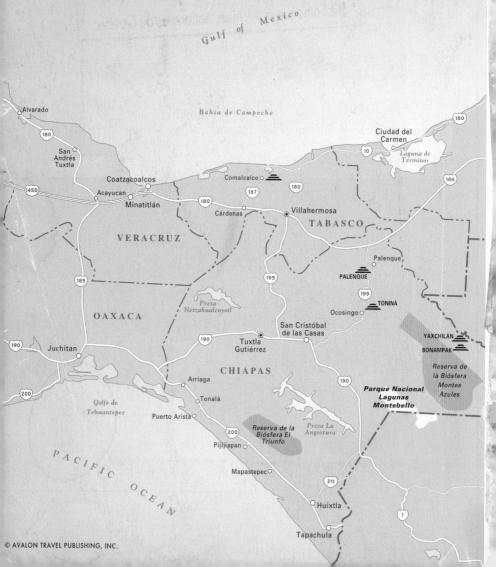

Gulf of Mexico

Bahía de Campeche

Alvarado

San Andrés Tuxtla

Coatzacoalcos

Acayucan

Minatitlán

Cárdenas

Comalcalco

Villahermosa

TABASCO

Ciudad del Carmen

Laguna de Términos

VERACRUZ

Palenque

PALENQUE

Presa Netzahualcoyotl

OAXACA

195

199

TONINÁ

Ocosingo

San Cristóbal de las Casas

Juchitan

Tuxtla Gutiérrez

YAXCHILÁN

BONAMPAK

Reserva de la Biósfera Montes Azules

CHIAPAS

Arriaga

Tonalá

Parque Nacional Lagunas Montebello

Golfo de Tehuantepec

Puerto Arista

Reserva de la Biósfera El Triunfo

Presa La Angostura

Pijijiapan

PACIFIC OCEAN

Mapastepec

Huixtla

Tapachula

© AVALON TRAVEL PUBLISHING, INC.

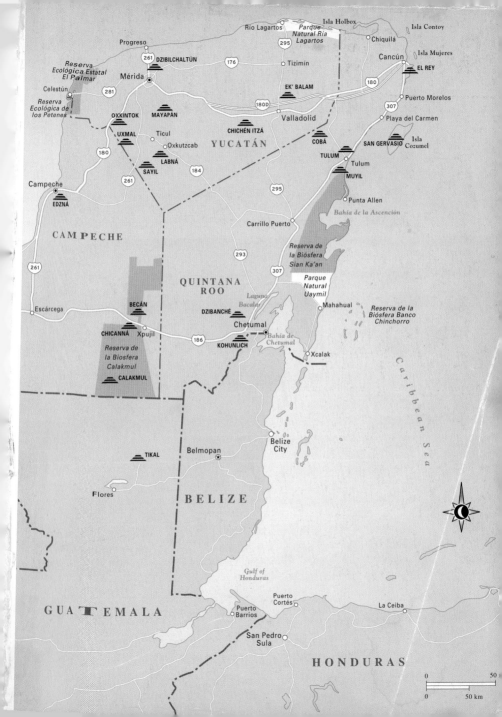

DISCOVER
THE YUCATÁN

On the northern coast of the Yucatán Peninsula
is a place called Uaymitún, where swampy coastal wetlands reach almost
to the ocean. A thin strip of land separates the two, just wide enough
for a two-lane highway and a few houses. On the inland side of the
road stands a high platform with a set of stairs winding up the center.
Climbing to the top, you discover that the swamp – rather unappealing
from below – is in fact filled with tens of thousands of flamingos, their
bright pink feathers a stark contrast to the gray-green surroundings.

Behind you are the emerald waters of the Gulf of Mexico. To the
east is a small Maya ruin called Xcambó – the coastal wetlands were
a major salt production area for ancient Mayas and they remain so
today, more than a thousand years later. Some 40 kilometers south
is the great colonial city of Mérida, known as the "White City" for the
traditional white cotton dresses and suits its residents used to wear.

A majestic archeological site, Uxmal is a must-see for any traveler who's
interested in the Maya world.

And just down the road from Uaymitún is the quiet town of Chicxilub, built near the place where a massive meteor smashed into the earth 65 million years ago, gouging a crater 2.5 kilometers deep and 200 kilometers wide. Scientists believe the impact and its aftermath wiped out the dinosaurs and ushered in the age of humankind, making this, in a sense, the very spot where the world as we know it began.

Uaymitún is not a major tourist destination – were it not for the flamingos, it probably wouldn't rate a mention. But in a way that's what makes it all the more amazing. The Yucatán Peninsula has so much history, culture, wildlife, so many natural wonders and outdoor opportunities, that even a dusty roadside town seems rich with stories and possibilities.

For many travelers, the area's Maya ruins are the biggest draw. Mérida is within easy reach of these spectacular archaeological

A cultural supernova, Mérida can't help but shine.

zones, from the soaring pyramids of Chichén Itzá and Uxmal to the more intimate sites of Labná and Ek' Balam. Farther away are even more ruins, including the famously beautiful temples at Palenque, Chiapas, and the impressive yet virtually unknown ruins in southern Campeche. It would take weeks to visit all of the Yucatán's archaeological sites, but no more than one to leave you awed by the artistry and ingeniousness of the ancient Maya.

There's more – a lot more. Mérida is just one of numerous beautiful colonial cities in the Yucatán Peninsula that boast distinctive architecture, broad plazas, and soaring churches. In San Cristóbal, a strong indigenous influence is palpable to this day; in Izamal, a grand cathedral and convent built atop an ancient Maya temple belie a complicated history of conquest, both physical and spiritual.

If you are a snorkeler or diver, Isla Cozumel is internationally known for its pristine coral reefs, varied sealife, and near perfect visibility, while the mainland hides the longest underground river system in the world, filled with crystalline water and spectacular cave formations.

A small but special site, Ek' Balam is just a stone's throw away from Cancún.

The Yucatán also is a world-class bird-watching area, and the northern wetlands from Celestún clear around to Isla Holbox teem with flamingos, herons, egrets, cormorants, spoonbills, pelicans, and more. Sian Ka'an Biosphere Reserve, south of Tulum, also has terrific bird-watching, and is one of several outstanding sport fishing areas in the Yucatán Peninsula. Another biosphere reserve in Campeche State – Calakmul – is home to howler and spider monkeys, elusive jaguars, and mountain lions.

Isla Cozumel and the Yucatán's northern coast have long been known as first-rate windsurfing and sailing destinations, and are becoming favorites for practitioners of a new wind sport: kiteboarding. And if you love beaches... well, you know that you've come to the right place. Cancún and the Riviera Maya are as famous for their white sand beaches and clear, turquoise waters as they are for their vibrant nightlife.

The Yucatán is a place of many stories, and it has been for millennia. The monuments and platforms at Maya temples are inscribed with hieroglyphics that tell complicated tales of kings and succession, war and conquest, gods and rituals. The Yucatán was a favorite haunt of

Regional dance performances in downtown Mérida are well attended by locals and travelers alike.

pirates and buccaneers, whose exploits are still the subject of fairy tales and feature films. The Yucatán's colonial era was rife with boom and bust, following the rise and fall of products such as Campeche wood, henequen, and chicle. The same tales include (or should include) the misery and exploitation of indigenous workers, and of the Caste War, in which Mayas rose up against the colonialists and nearly succeeded in driving them off the peninsula for good. More recently is the remarkable story of Cancún, which only 30 years ago was a mosquito-infested sandbar in an isolated corner of Mexico and is now one the world's top vacation destinations.

The Yucatán Peninsula is one of those places everyone ought to visit in his or her life. It is a place of beauty and mystery, with endless opportunities for exploration, learning, and enlightenment. It's also a fun place to visit and home to a diverse and gracious population. For us it has been a joy to explore the region, and it is our sincere hope that the Yucatán not only meets your expectations but reveals, as it has to us again and again, places and people and stories beyond your imagination.

The murals at Bonampak in Chiapas are a rarity in the Maya world.

Contents

The Lay of the Land 14
Planning Your Trip 18
Explore the Yucatán Peninsula 20
The Best of the Yucatán... 20
Pyramids and Palaces 22
A 10-Day Eco-Adventure 24
Diving and Snorkeling... 26
A Family Affair... 27

Cancún... 29
Sights.. 32
Entertainment and Events 40
Shopping 44
Sports and Recreation 45
Accommodations 50
Food... 56
Information and Services.. 61
Getting There and Around 65
Isla Mujeres 69
Isla Holbox 89

Isla Cozumel.. 98
Sights... 103
Entertainment and Events 111
Shopping 113
Sports and Recreation 114
Accommodations 118
Food.. 122
Information and Services... 125
Getting There and Around 126

The Riviera Maya... 129
Puerto Morelos 130
Punta Bete and Playa Xcalacoco 138
Playa del Carmen 139

Paamul 160
Puerto Aventuras 161
Xpu-Há 165
Akumal 167
Tankah Tres 175

Tulum and Southern Quintana Roo 178

Tulum 181
Cobá 197
Sian Ka'an Biosphere Reserve 202
Carrillo Puerto 206
La Costa Maya 209
Laguna Bacalar 220
Chetumal 224

The State of Yucatán 232

Mérida 235
The Puuc Route and Around 263
Celestún 286
Dzibilchaltún 290
Progreso 291
East of Progreso 296
Izamal 298
Chichén Itzá and Pisté 304
Valladolid 313
Ek' Balam 319
Río Lagartos and San Felipe 323

The State of Campeche 327

Campeche City 328
Archaeological Zones near Campeche City 344
Río Bec Region 348

The State of Tabasco 364

Villahermosa 366
Comalcalco 375

The State of Chiapas 379

Palenque Archaeological Zone and Town 382

The Río Usumacinta Valley... 393
Ocosingo.. 400
San Cristóbal de las Casas.. 403
Villages Around San Cristóbal... 419
South of San Cristóbal.. 422
Tuxtla Gutiérrez.. 426
Around Tuxtla Gutiérrez... 433
The Pacific Coast... 438

Background.. 440
The Land.. 440
Flora... 442
Fauna... 443
Environmental Issues.. 449
History... 449
Government.. 456
Economy... 458
People and Culture.. 459

Essentials.. 461
Getting There... 461
Getting Around.. 463
Visas and Officialdom... 469
Food.. 470
Tips for Travelers.. 471
Health and Safety... 473
Information and Services.. 475

Resources... 478
Maya Glossary... 478
Spanish Glossary.. 480
Spanish Phrasebook.. 482
Suggested Reading... 488
Internet Resources.. 489

Index... 491

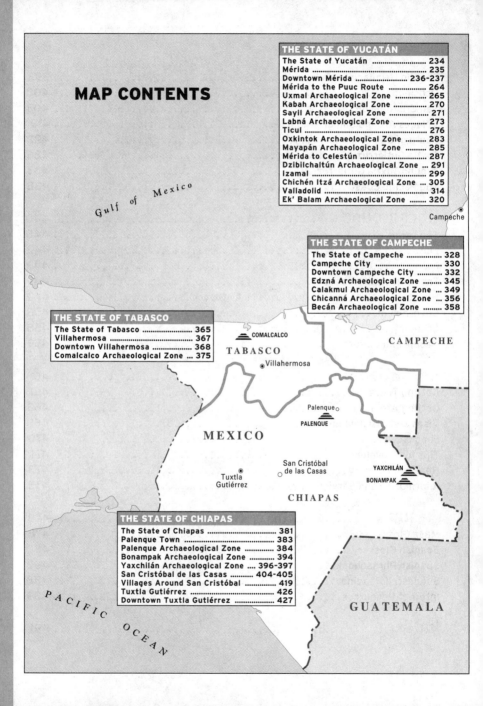

MAP CONTENTS

THE STATE OF YUCATÁN

The State of Yucatán 234
Mérida 235
Downtown Mérida 236-237
Mérida to the Puuc Route 264
Uxmal Archaeological Zone 265
Kabah Archaeological Zone 270
Sayil Archaeological Zone 271
Labná Archaeological Zone 273
Ticul 276
Oxkintok Archaeological Zone 283
Mayapán Archaeological Zone 285
Mérida to Celestún 287
Dzibilchaltún Archaeological Zone ... 291
Izamal 299
Chichén Itzá Archaeological Zone ... 305
Valladolid 314
Ek' Balam Archaeological Zone 320

THE STATE OF CAMPECHE

The State of Campeche 328
Campeche City 330
Downtown Campeche City 332
Edzná Archaeological Zone 345
Calakmul Archaeological Zone ... 349
Chicanná Archaeological Zone ... 356
Becán Archaeological Zone 358

THE STATE OF TABASCO

The State of Tabasco 365
Villahermosa 367
Downtown Villahermosa 368
Comalcalco Archaeological Zone ... 375

THE STATE OF CHIAPAS

The State of Chiapas 381
Palenque Town 383
Palenque Archaeological Zone 384
Bonampak Archaeological Zone 394
Yaxchilán Archaeological Zone 396-397
San Cristóbal de las Casas 404-405
Villages Around San Cristóbal 419
Tuxtla Gutiérrez 426
Downtown Tuxtla Gutiérrez 427

Gulf of Mexico

Campeche

COMALCALCO

TABASCO

CAMPECHE

Villahermosa

Palenque
PALENQUE

MEXICO

San Cristóbal
de las Casas

YAXCHILÁN

Tuxtla
Gutiérrez

BONAMPAK

CHIAPAS

GUATEMALA

PACIFIC OCEAN

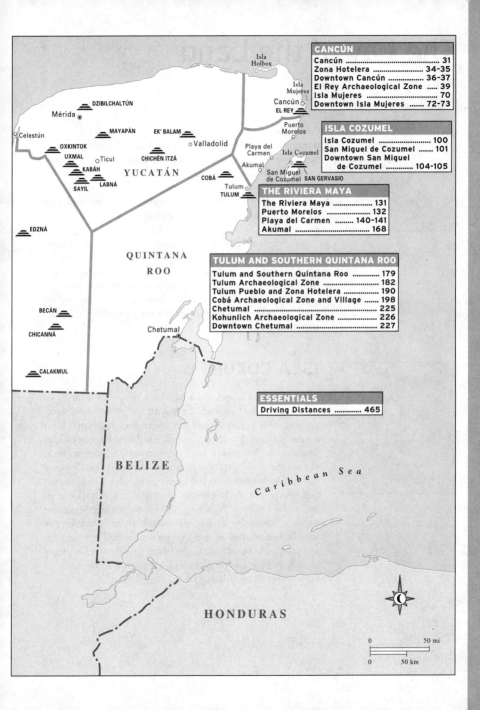

CANCÚN

Cancún 31
Zona Hotelera 34-35
Downtown Cancún 36-37
El Rey Archaeological Zone 39
Isla Mujeres 70
Downtown Isla Mujeres 72-73

ISLA COZUMEL

Isla Cozumel 100
San Miguel de Cozumel 101
Downtown San Miguel
de Cozumel 104-105

THE RIVIERA MAYA

The Riviera Maya 131
Puerto Morelos 132
Playa del Carmen 140-141
Akumal 168

TULUM AND SOUTHERN QUINTANA ROO

Tulum and Southern Quintana Roo 179
Tulum Archaeological Zone 182
Tulum Pueblo and Zona Hotelera 190
Cobá Archaeological Zone and Village 198
Chetumal 225
Kohunlich Archaeological Zone 226
Downtown Chetumal 227

ESSENTIALS

Driving Distances 465

The Lay of the Land

CANCÚN

Cancún has two parts: the Zona Hotelera (Hotel Zone) and downtown. The Zona Hotelera has Cancún's top resorts and nightclubs, and miles of spectacular beaches. It's also quite commercialized—come here for maximum R&R and partying. Cancún's downtown area has a surprisingly rich cultural scene, including jazz bars and bohemian cafés. The hotels and restaurants are cheaper and the beaches are an easy bus or cab ride away.

Isla Mujeres is a long thin island just offshore from Cancún. Everything is mellower here—the people, the nightlife, even the waves. Many come just for the day, but good hotels and a small-town ambiance make it a tempting place to linger for awhile.

Even smaller is Isla Holbox, which has sand roads and no cars. The beaches aren't glorious, but the tranquility and isolation more than make up for it.

ISLA COZUMEL

Mexico's largest island and a half-hour ferry ride from Playa del Carmen, Isla Cozumel is a diving and snorkeling wonderland, with a pristine coral reef and crystal-clear water. With over a hundred dive shops, and an equal number of excellent dive and snorkel sites, it attracts underwater enthusiasts from around the world. But there's more to do than dive: Cozumel has two eco-parks, several beach clubs, plus a tournament golf course and world-class kiteboarding. Cozumel was an important religious pilgrimage site for the ancient Maya and there's a fascinating ruin in the middle of the island; on the island's undeveloped eastern side are little-visited beaches with soft sand and dramatic surf. The island's main town has plenty of taxis and car and moped rental agencies, making it easy to explore this diverse island.

THE RIVIERA MAYA

The Riviera Maya is the 130-kilometer-long (81 miles) coastal area between Cancún and Tulum. Its biggest city, **Playa del Carmen,** has hotels of all categories, plus great restaurants and shopping, and an active nightlife. However, with a more laid-back atmosphere and fewer large resorts, Playa del Carmen is no Cancún. **Puerto Morelos** and **Akumal** are smaller, but still have ATMs, Internet, and many appealing places to sleep and eat. Along the coast are various private developments, from mega-resorts to modest hotels clustered around a small beach.

The Riviera Maya's best public **beaches** are at Playa del Carmen, Akumal, and **Xpu-Há.** There is terrific snorkeling and diving, not only on the coral reef offshore but in numerous **cenotes** (freshwater sinkholes) that line the inland areas.

Highway 307 runs the length of the Riviera Maya, and can be explored by frequent buses and shuttles, or by taxi or rental car.

TULUM AND SOUTHERN QUINTANA ROO

At the southern end of the Riviera Maya, Tulum is famous for its stunning beaches and bungalow-style accommodations. A nearby **Maya ruin** of the same name is perched on a bluff, with a dramatic view of the Caribbean (and a beach of its own). For many, Tulum is Mexico's Caribbean at its best.

Southern Quintana Roo is the least developed stretch on this coastline. Just south of Tulum, the **Sian Ka'an Biosphere Reserve** is a huge nature reserve with bays, lagoons, and tangled mangrove islands that are not only beautiful but also ideal for bird-watching and fly-fishing. Farther south, the isolated area known as the **Costa Maya** has two small towns with appealingly isolated bed-and-breakfasts and a rather incongruous cruise ship port. **Laguna Bacalar** is a lovely freshwater lagoon a short distance from **Chetumal,** the busy state capital and gateway to Belize.

THE STATE OF YUCATÁN

If Quintana Roo is the place to go for beaches, Yucatán is the place to go for Maya ruins and colonial charm. Mérida, the largest city, has beautiful colonial architecture and excellent museums, and hosts free music and dance performances every single day of the year. Other fine colonial cities include Izamal and Valladolid.

But Yucatán's ancient Maya ruins may be its biggest draw. The huge pyramid and ball court of Chichén Itzá are world famous. Uxmal archaeological zone is arguably more beautiful, and as part of the Puuc Route, has four smaller but worthwhile sites nearby.

As if colonial cities and Maya ruins weren't enough, Yucatán also has world-class bird-watching in places like Río Lagartos and Celestún, plus many opportunities for biking, caving, and swimming in cenotes.

THE STATE OF CAMPECHE

Centuries ago when Campeche was a major port, a massive wall with fortified bastions was built around the city to ward off frequent pirate attacks. Today, the walls encircle a beautiful colonial center, with brightly painted buildings and beautiful churches. The bastions have been converted into museums; one, Fuerte de San Miguel, has a remarkable collection of Maya artifacts, including 1000-year-old jade funerary masks.

The artifacts come from Campeche's archaeological sites, which are as impressive as they are little visited. In southern Campeche, Calakmul is home to the largest known Maya structure and is now thought to have been one of the largest of all Maya cities. It is ensconced in a protected forest reserve, and it is not uncommon to see parrots and howler monkeys lounging in the trees. Nearby are a half-dozen smaller but equally intriguing sites.

THE STATE OF TABASCO

Mesoamerica's first major civilization, the Olmecs, flourished in present-day Tabasco. At an outdoor museum in the state capital, Villahermosa, you can marvel at the immense carved stone heads left by this intriguing and little-understood culture. Tabasco boasts another unique ancient site, the Maya ruins of Comalcalco, which are notable for being made of adobe-like brick instead of stone.

Comalcalco also is famous for its chocolate. Cacao has been cultivated here for centuries—and it was here that Columbus first tasted it. It would have been extremely bitter, in keeping with the traditional Maya preparation, but Columbus thought enough of the drink to bring some back to Europe, where milk and sugar were added to create the chocolate we know today. Visitors here can take tours of area farms to learn how cacao is grown and processed.

THE STATE OF CHIAPAS

No tour of the Maya ruins is complete without a visit to Palenque. Its grand pyramids, extensive inscriptions, and superb museum make it among the most elegant and compelling of all Maya archaeological zones. Other important—and impressive—archaeological sites in Chiapas include Yaxchilán, Bonampak, and Toniná.

In the center of the state is San Cristóbal, another of Mexico's great colonial cities. Its colorfully painted streets, bohemian atmosphere, and strong indigenous presence and influence make it a perennial favorite for travelers. Nearby are autonomous indigenous villages, which can be visited with approved guides, and Sumidero Canyon, a winding river gorge with stone walls that climb 1,000 meters (3,281 feet) toward the sky. A new highway connects San Cristóbal to the state capital, Tuxtla Gutierrez, which has an excellent zoo but not much else.

Planning Your Trip

Deciding how long to visit the Yucatán Peninsula is one of your first decisions, and is ultimately a very personal one. The fact is, for some people, a week is all the time they want or need to enjoy the beach and see a few ruins; any more time and they'd start getting antsy. For others, a week is barely enough time to settle into the rhythm of a place, let alone do and see everything it has to offer. Indeed, the Yucatán Peninsula has so much to offer, you'd have to stay for two months or more to really see it all. Of course, the length of any trip or vacation is most often determined by unrelated criteria, like how much time off work you have, how much you care to spend, when the kids have to start soccer camp, and so forth.

Ten to fourteen days is a reasonable amount of time to allow you to see a little of everything. Most people planning a trip through the Yucatán Peninsula (as opposed to just Cancún and the Riviera Maya) aren't too keen on the big resorts, but you can still enjoy the beach—try the bungalows at Tulum, or the small hotels and B&Bs in Playa del Carmen, Akumal, Xpu-Há, or even Isla Holbox. You'll want at least five days in Mérida and its surroundings to enjoy the countless cultural events the city has to offer, plus the Maya ruins and smaller colonial towns nearby. Add another 3–6 days for more remote destinations, like southern Quintana Roo or the Río Bec region of southern Campeche, not to mention Tabasco and Chiapas.

If you have a week or less, don't try to see too much—you'll just chew up a lot of time getting from place to place, and checking in and out of hotels. Rather, pick one or two places to really experience and enjoy—Mérida and Xpu-Há, say—and save the rest for your next trip.

No matter how much time you have, when planning your trip be sure to account for the time it takes to travel from one place to the next. Distances are not short in the Yucatán Peninsula, especially if you plan to visit Chiapas and Tabasco.

WHEN TO GO

The best time to visit the Yucatán Peninsula has a lot to do with why you're going and what you hope to see and do. Weather is a major consideration for any sort of trip. Cloudless skies are a priority if you plan on spending some or most of your visit on the beach. But you can have too much of a good thing—in the interior regions of the Yucatán Peninsula, a little rain or cloud cover can keep the temperature down and be a welcome relief. Equally important is how much money you're willing to spend, especially on accommodations, which can vary dramatically depending on the month and day you visit. If you're on a tight budget, you may consider coming in the low season, but you'll be taking a gamble on the weather. Another consideration is that some activities can only be done during certain times of the year, like bird-watching or snorkeling with whale sharks. Finally, be mindful of holiday and vacation periods, especially Christmas, spring break, July and August (when most of Europe is on vacation), and *Semana Santa* (Holy Week, the week before Easter and the main vacation period in Mexico). Prices can skyrocket, along with the number of tourists, both foreign and Mexican. Of course, if partying is high on your priority list, there is no better time to visit.

For most independent, guidebook-toting travelers, the best time to come to the Yucatán Peninsula is from mid-January until the beginning of May. The winter rains ought to have long passed (they typically end in early November, but sometimes stretch into the new year), yet the summer humidity and high temperatures have yet to set in. Temperatures definitely will be on the rise, however, peaking in May to August. The Yucatán Peninsula, and Mérida in particular, are infamous for being brutally hot during the late spring and summer—if the heat really gets you, consider coming earlier rather than later. You may get the occasional *norte* (rainy cold front from the north) during this period but that's the luck of the draw. This period does include spring break and *Semana Santa* (the best or worst time to come, depending on your point of view), but otherwise crowds are thinner and prices are lower compared with the Christmas and summer periods. You'll miss the whale sharks in Isla Holbox (June–September) but will still be able to catch the flamingo mating season (November–February).

Late November and early December are another pocket of relatively reliable weather, reasonable prices, and light visitation. But expect prices to jump on December 15, like clockwork. July and August can be especially busy on the Riviera Maya and around Mérida, which are preferred by European vacationers.

WHAT TO TAKE

Mérida, Campeche, Cancún, Cozumel, and Playa del Carmen all have modern stores, supermarkets, and malls, so you don't have to be concerned about not being able to find the basics, and then some. However, prices on the coast can be exorbitant on items that shop owners know you can't do without. Sunscreen, bug repellant, billed hats, and swimsuits are the most notable examples; if you think these items are pricey at home, the hotel gift shop will leave you floored (and broke!). Mérida, Cancún and Playa del Carmen all have Wal-Marts now, which means somewhat lower prices and a better selection than before. It's still best to bring those items from home, however, and a little more than you think you'll need.

A few other items to remember when you're packing: An extra set of contacts or glasses in case the ones you have get lost, broken, or washed away while swimming or snorkeling. Bring a supply of your preferred birth control, condoms, and feminine products—all are readily available in the region (and Mexico, in general), but you may have trouble finding the brand you prefer. Same goes for any prescription medications; many people, especially seniors, come to Mexico partly to take advantage of much lower prices on pharmaceuticals, but always bring enough for your whole trip in case what you're looking for isn't available. Also, pharmacists in Mexico receive far less formal training (if any) than elsewhere; be sure you know the exact dosage and ingredient you require, and always double-check that you are getting the correct amount. A travel clock is useful, too, because many hotels don't have reliable wake-up call systems.

Finally, a good pair of shoes—or at least Teva-style sandals—are essential for visiting the archaeological zones. Never climb the ruins in flip-flops. The vast majority of accidents and injuries that occur at archaeological sites are from people slipping and falling, so you'll want shoes that give you plenty of balance and traction.

Explore the Yucatán Peninsula

THE BEST OF THE YUCATÁN

This is the biggie—see and do a little of everything in the Yucatán Peninsula in just two weeks. There are beaches to enjoy, ruins to explore, museums to visit, cenotes to snorkel in, and cities to discover—this is a trip for travelers with plenty of energy and a hankering to see it all. Renting a car for the entire trip will give you added speed and flexibility and ensure you have time to enjoy every stop. But if a rental car is out of your budget, most of the route can be done easily enough by bus. A good compromise is to rent a car for a few key days—we've mentioned where you should do this. Here goes:

Day 1

Arrive in Cancún but head south to **Playa del Carmen,** which is a better base for exploring the Riviera Maya. (**Akumal** or **Xpu-Há** are other good choices). If you're planning on diving, consider heading straight to **Isla Cozumel** to save yourself the ferry ride the next day.

Day 2

Spend your first full day exploring the Riviera Maya underwater. Numerous shops in Playa del Carmen, Akumal, **Puerto Morelos,** Cozumel, and elsewhere offer great **snorkeling tours** on the ocean reef. Or try snorkeling in the **cenotes,** either at a park like **Hidden Worlds** or **Dos Ojos,** or on your own. Budget some beach time for the afternoon.

Day 3

Time to head inland. Get an early start and head straight for **Chichén Itzá,** getting there as close to opening time as possible. That way you'll have a jump on the big tour buses, and can enjoy these magnificent ruins with fewer people to weave around. Budget several hours there, and when you're done head to Mérida.

Day 4

Spend the whole day exploring **Mérida,** one of Mexico's great colonial cities. Go to the **anthropology museum** or the **modern art museum,** the market, or just visit the

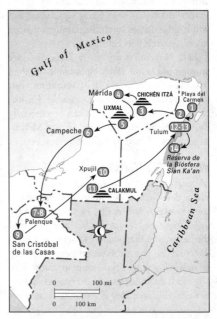

church, murals in the government buildings, and the plaza. See what's happening that night—there's a free cultural performance every night of the year.

Day 5

You can spend this day in a couple different ways. There are a number of great day trips from Mérida, including a **flamingo tour** in the town of Celestún, or visiting the colonial town of Izamal and swimming in cenotes near Cuzamá. Then again, if you especially love the Maya ruins, you won't want to miss those along the Puuc Route. To do this, get an early start and visit Uxmal first—it is the biggest and the best of the sites here, and you don't want to shortchange your time there. Time permitting, visit one or two of the smaller Puuc ruins as well. Check into a hotel in Ticul or Santa Elena, have dinner, then go to the sound and light show at Uxmal that night.

Day 6

Plan on driving to Campeche City this morning. Check into a hotel and then pick a few of the sights to take in. The archaeology museums at Puerta del Mar and Fuerte de San Miguel are especially good. If it's a Saturday or Sunday, spend the evening in the park, where free musical performances are held and street carts sell food.

Day 7

Start early for a long drive to Palenque. Check into your hotel.

Day 8

Spend the day visiting Palenque Archaeological Zone. If you only hire a guide at one set of ruins, make it this one. Be sure to leave time for the terrific museum.

Day 9

Stay another day in Palenque to see some of the nearby sites. If you still haven't gotten enough of the Maya ruins, consider booking an all-day tour (or going on your own) to Yaxchilán and Bonampak. Or visit the nearer site of Toniná, with a stop at Misol Ha, Agua Clara, and Agua Azul for a bit of outdoorsy fun.

Alternatively, take this day to drive south to San Cristóbal, a remarkable colonial city. Doing this will force you to adjust much of the rest of the itinerary—and involves backtracking through Palenque again, a four-hour drive each way—but San Cristóbal is a magical place for many, with beautiful architecture, cool mountain air, and a strong indigenous presence.

Day 10

From Palenque, drive to the southern Campeche town of Xpujil. Depending on your time and energy, visit one of the many small Maya ruins clustered along Highway 186.

Day 11

If you want to see even more ruins, a day-long trip into Calakmul is a terrific experience, albeit tiring. Otherwise, jump ahead in the itinerary—you can always use the extra day at Tulum, either for more beach time or for exploring more of the Sian Ka'an Biosphere Reserve.

Day 12

Drive to Tulum, where you can treat yourself to a beachside bungalow on one of Tulum's glorious beaches. Spend the afternoon relaxing.

Day 13

Another beach day on Tulum's quiet and dreamy southern beaches. If you get restless, sample some of the great cenote snorkeling around Tulum.

Day 14

Take a tour of the Sian Ka'an Biosphere Reserve, an ideal place for fishing, bird-watching, and snorkeling.

PYRAMIDS AND PALACES

For many, the Maya ruins are the Yucatán Peninsula's greatest attraction, with their massive pyramids and palaces, and amazing artistic and astronomical features. Few visitors have time to visit every site in a single trip; below is a description of each state's best Maya ruins to help you decide which ones to add to your itinerary—and which to save for next time!

State of Yucatán

There is no better state to see Maya ruins than Yucatán in terms of number, quality, and ease of access. Mérida, the lively state capital, also has an excellent Maya archaeology museum.

Chichén Itzá is a must-see, with the largest ball court of any Maya ruin and a pyramid recognizable the world over. Come early to beat the tour groups that arrive by the dozen from Cancún, and plan on spending several hours—it's huge. The evening sound and light show is worth attending.

Uxmal may be the state's most beautiful site, with intricate palaces and a massive pyramid with rounded corners—another must-see. The sound and light show here also is recommended.

The Ruta Puuc (Puuc Route) is a series of four smaller ruins near Uxmal. Kabah and Labná are especially memorable, including beautiful archways and facades decorated with scores of identical rain-god masks. A roundtrip bus from Mérida hits all four plus Uxmal, but visiting by car will give you the freedom to appreciate them longer.

Ek' Balam, near the city of Valladolid, boasts one of the best-preserved stucco friezes in the Maya world and a terrific view from atop its main pyramid.

Other sites in the state include the neatly organized Mayapán, the little-visited Oxkintok with a great cave system nearby, and Dzibilchaltún with its first-rate museum and intriguing main temple.

State of Campeche

Campeche has a rich collection of archaeological sites, made all the more appealing because so few tourists visit them. The attractive state capital, Campeche City, has two highly recommended archaeology museums too.

Calakmul, in an area of southern Campeche known as the Río Bec region, was one of the most powerful Maya cites in its time and contains the largest known Maya pyramid. Even better, the site is ensconced in a biosphere reserve, where you can usually spot monkeys and tropical birds.

Becán and Chicanná are also in the Río Bec region. Becán's many structures include two huge pyramids and an impressive multi-room palace, while Chicanná has gorgeously decorated temples and residential buildings.

Edzná is located less than an hour's drive or bus ride from Campeche City, but you still may be the only one there when you visit. A peaceful site, its Temple of Five Stories looks over a small acrópolis and broad main plaza.

Other excellent sites in Campeche include Balamkú, Hormiguero, and Río Bec in southern Campeche, and Santa Rosa Xtampak in northeastern Campeche. All but Balamkú can be very hard to reach, however.

State of Quintana Roo

Quintana Roo is better known for its beaches and resorts than for its Maya ruins, but the state does has a few sites worth visiting. The capital, Chetumal, near the Belize border, has an excellent museum on Maya culture that is well worth a visit.

Cobá has the second-highest pyramid on the peninsula, offering a great view of the pancake-flat countryside. Nestled in a forest near several small lakes, Cobá is also a good place to spot birds, including herons, parrots and toucans.

Tulum, the subject of innumerable postcards, is perched on a bluff overlooking the turquoise Caribbean Sea. The structures themselves are quite decayed, but a visit here is still worthwhile. Come early, as the site is often mobbed by day-trippers from resorts near and far.

Kohunlich, in southern Quintana Roo, is best known for a series of imposing stucco masks. Nearby is a unique luxury resort operated by Fiesta Americana, with guided trips to the ruins and surrounding forest and river areas.

San Gervasio is Isla Cozumel's main archaeological site, with several modest temples connected by forest paths. Dedicated to the goddess of fertility, San Gervasio was an important pilgrimage site for ancient Maya women.

El Rey and **Yamil Lu'um** are two small ruins right in Cancún's hotel zone. El Rey is larger and better preserved, and is also home to hundreds of iguanas, as interesting to see as the structures themselves.

State of Chiapas

Chiapas doesn't have as many ruins as other states, but the ones it has are magnificent. Most are in the northern part of the state, making them relatively easy to reach from the Yucatán Peninsula proper.

Palenque is the all-time favorite ruin of many travelers, thanks to its elegant design, intricate carvings, and superlative museum. Much of what archaeologists know about the Maya calendar, hieroglyphics, and astronomy emerged from studies conducted here.

Bonampak and **Yaxchilán** are sister cities located along the Guatemalan border, commonly reached on tours from Palenque. The former contains brilliantly colored murals, while the latter has beautifully carved stone panels and monoliths.

Toniná was one of the last major Maya cities to fall, and its statues and carvings are dominated by images of death and desperate ritual sacrifice. The site is seldom visited, though it has a great museum and is only a couple hours from Palenque.

State of Tabasco

Tabasco has only one major Maya site. It is much better known as the birthplace of the Olmecs, the first civilization in Mesoamerica.

Comalcalco was built in an area of swampy coastal wetlands where very little stone was available. Instead, the pyramids were built of packed earth, with oyster shells mixed in for strength, and covered with baked bricks. It is the only Maya ruin to be built in such a way.

A 10-DAY ECO-ADVENTURE

Lazing on a beach or contemplating museum displays is all right, but some travelers crave a little more action. The Yucatán has plenty to offer active, outdoorsy travelers, including sports such as scuba diving and kiteboarding, and activities such as bird-watching and snorkeling with whale sharks. This tour is a workout for the eyes, too, taking you to some of the peninsula's most stunning (and little-visited) natural areas, from deserted windswept shores to tangled mangrove forests to limestone caverns filled with the clearest, bluest water you've ever seen.

Day 1

Arrive in Cancún but plan on basing yourself along the Riviera Maya. Playa del Carmen and Akumal have the most lodging options, but are by no means the only choices. If you're planning on diving, consider heading straight to Isla Cozumel to save yourself the ferry ride tomorrow.

Day 2

Spend your first full day exploring the Riviera Maya. You've got plenty of options: for divers, there's no shortage of world-class diving at Isla Cozumel. You can book two-tank dive trips on the island or at dive shops at Playa del Carmen. Or try cenote diving on the mainland; shops in Playa del Carmen and Tulum have the most experience, or you can head to Hidden Worlds or Dos Ojos, both of which offer full-service guided dive trips at privately managed cavern systems. You also can snorkel at any of the previously mentioned places, as well as on the coral reef at Puerto Morelos or at Laguna Yal-Ku in Akumal.

Day 3

Get up early and head straight to Chiquilá to catch the ferry to Isla Holbox. Leave your car in one of several lots near the ferry pier.

Day 4

Go snorkeling with whale sharks in the morning and kayaking through the mangroves in the afternoon—the bird-watching is excellent here. Or just go snorkeling, and take some time after lunch to relax on the island's rustic beach. If you know how to kiteboard, rent equipment for the afternoon; if you don't, learning the basics usually takes about three days.

Day 5

Return to Chiquilá and drive to Mérida. If you get an early start, you may have time to stop over at the beautiful colonial town of Izamal or the cenotes of Cuzamá, where a horse-drawn cart takes you through abandoned henequen fields to ladders that lead into underground caverns for a cool swim.

Day 6

Drive to Celestún and take a flamingo tour.

You can get there on your own or book a tour at one of Mérida's many tour operators. Head back to Mérida and check out a museum and one of the nightly cultural performances.

Day 7

Spend the next day visiting some of the *grutas* (caves) along the Puuc Route south of Mérida. Calcehtok is the most adventuresome, with local guides offering two- to five-hour tours of this huge cave system. The longest tours go about four kilometers (2.5 miles) and reach a tiny chamber where human bones were left from ancient Maya ceremonies. Not far away, Loltún caves have paths and lighting, but are fascinating nonetheless. Drive to Valladolid.

Day 8

Get up bright and early to be at the entrance of Cobá Archaeological Zone by 7 A.M., or earlier. Of all the nearby Maya ruins, this one is the best for bird-watching. It's not uncommon to spot toucans and parrots, among many other species. Cobá is also an impressive ancient ruin, with the second-highest pyramid in the Yucatán Peninsula, affording awesome views of the countryside. The structures are set in a thick forest—hence the first-rate bird-watching—and are quite spread out. You can rent bikes near the entrance and explore the ruins on wheels, also unique among the Maya ruins. There's a monkey park a short distance from Cobá, a great place to see howler and spider monkeys. Treat yourself to a night at one of the beach cabañas in Tulum.

Day 9

Spend your last day enjoying the Yucatán's other great natural wonder: the beach. Tulum has the best of the best—white sand lapped by turquoise water and backed by palm trees. Hey, even eco-adventurers can use some sand time. If you get restless, rent some snorkel gear and check out some of the cenotes near Tulum village.

Day 10

Fly home.

DIVING AND SNORKELING

For all its terrestrial wonders, the Yucatán Peninsula's underwater treasures are no less compelling, including the world's longest underground river system, the second-longest coral reef, and the Northern Hemisphere's largest coral atoll. Isla Cozumel, fringed by pristine coral reefs and remarkably clear water, is one of the world's top scuba diving and snorkeling destinations, while Isla Holbox is a favorite feeding ground of manta rays and huge (but harmless) whale sharks. But you need not leave the mainland to appreciate the Yucatán's underwater realm—eerily beautiful cenotes and healthy coral reefs all along the Caribbean coast offer fantastic views and unforgettable experiences and can be enjoyed either on an organized tour or on your own.

Day 1
Arrive at Cancún's International Airport and take a bus or taxi to **Playa del Carmen.** Spend the afternoon at **Playa Tukán**—the white sand and turquoise water will be a welcome sight after hours on a plane. If you don't have your own snorkeling equipment, arrange an extended rental at any of the dive shops in town. You'll want to book a car rental too. Have dinner at one of the eateries along Quinta Avenida.

Day 2
Explore the Riviera Maya—there's great snorkeling on the reefs at **Puerto Morelos,** in the lagoon at **Akumal,** and in the caverns at **Hidden Worlds.** Divers can sign up for a cavern dive at Hidden Worlds, or at any of the shops in Tulum, where underground diving is the specialty.

Day 3
Go cenote-hopping in your rental car. Great options for snorkelers and divers are **Cenote Tankah** in Tankah Tres, **Cenote Azul** and **Cristalina** (both on Highway 307 across from Xpu-Há), and the string of cenotes just west of Tulum on the road to Cobá, including **Car Wash, Kolimba/Kin-Ha, Cenote Grande,** and **Calavera Cenote.**

Day 4
Take the ferry to **Isla Cozumel.** Arrange a snorkeling trip or a set of dives for the next two days. Spend the rest of the day at a beach club south of town or check out the small town of **San Miguel.**

Day 5
Go on a snorkel or dive trip. Ask to take a break or stop for your surface interval at **Playa Palancar.**

Day 6
Go on another snorkel or dive trip in the morning. **Parque Nacional Chankanaab** and **Parque Ecológico Punta Sur** both offer snorkeling. In the evening, take the ferry back to Playa del Carmen, return the snorkel equipment, and check out the nightlife on Quinta Avenida.

Day 7

Head south to **Mahahual** or **Xcalak**, two small towns near the Belize border with fantastic snorkeling and diving right from the shore. Xcalak is the best jumping-off point for Chinchorro Bank, a spectacular coral atoll a two-hour boat ride away.

Day 8

Spend this day snorkeling from the shore or taking a dive trip, either on the reef or at **Chinchorro Bank.**

Day 9

Head back to **Playa del Carmen** or **Cancún.** Be sure to enjoy your last afternoon on one of the beautiful beaches. Remember, you shouldn't dive for at least 24 hours before flying.

A FAMILY AFFAIR

The Yucatán Peninsula is an excellent family destination, with sights and activities that are fun for kids as well as parents. The Caribbean coast has terrific beaches, easy snorkeling, and numerous family-friendly eco-parks. Inland, the Maya ruins are fascinating to visitors of all ages, as are outings like bird-watching and swimming in cenotes. The region also has excellent lodging, eating, and transportation options, making it suitable for family trips of every size and budget. And the people of the Yucatán Peninsula, as everywhere in Mexico, are open and welcoming to children and families.

Day 1

Arrive in **Cancún** and check into your hotel. If you're in the Zona Hotelera, you won't be able to resist the beach—the afternoon sun is great and the water is warm. If you're downtown, take a bus or taxi to the beach or stroll through **Parque Las Palapas.** In the evenings, lots of local kids play games in the central plaza or ride the small Ferris wheel and kiddy rides. Be sure to buy some churros filled with *cajeta* (similar to caramel syrup).

Day 2

Spend the day on the beach. Head to **Playa Chac-Mool,** where you can rent boogie boards, parasail, or just build sand castles. Have lunch at the Rainforest Café in the Forum by the Sea Mall. After an afternoon break, go to La Isla Shopping Village, where you and the kids can choose from among swimming with dolphins or sharks at the **Interactive Aquarium,** playing video games, or watching a movie. Book a tour to Xcaret or plan on taking a taxi or bus to the entrance.

Day 3

Spend the day at the mega eco-park **Xcaret.** Get there at opening to enjoy it to the hilt.

Day 4

Rent a car and head inland to the Maya ruins of **Chichén Itzá.** Either stay at one of the hotels near the archaeological site—most have swimming pools, which are nice after a hot stay at the ruins—or at one of the more modest accommodations in the adjacent town of **Pisté.** Another option is to stay in the nearby city of **Valladolid,** which is more pleasant than Pisté and has three easy-to-reach **cenotes,** where kids are sure to delight in the cool water and eerie, otherworldly environment. At night, go to the sound and light show at the ruins.

Day 5

Spend the day at the **Chichén Itzá** ruins. It's a huge site, and you may not be able to see everything with little ones in tow. There are snack shops at the entrance, and another one inside the site; better yet, pack a lunch and plan on stopping at a shady spot for a mid-visit picnic. Return to the hotel for an afternoon swim. If you're staying in Valladolid, check out the cenotes or see what's playing at the movie theater.

Day 6

Make your way back to Cancún or Playa del Carmen. Starting early, you'll have plenty of time to spend one last afternoon on the beach. If Chichén Itzá was a real hit, consider stopping on the way at **Ek' Balam,** a small ruin just north of Valladolid. It has a huge pyramid—which you can climb, unlike the one at Chichén Itzá—and a spectacular stucco frieze.

CANCÚN

Cancún is a big, beautiful, contradictory place. For many people, it is the ultimate vacation destination, with five-star hotels, white sand, impossibly blue waters, and a nightlife that never stops. Others dismiss Cancún as "inauthentic," a place where you can spend a week and never speak Spanish, never convert your dollars into pesos, and never eat at a restaurant you don't recognize from malls back home.

Both perspectives are true, but one-sided. It's hard not to cringe at those loud tourists who don't bother to explore—or even care about—any part of Mexico beyond their beach chairs. Yet those who pooh-pooh Cancún are also selling the city short. Cancún makes no apologies for being a mega-destination, for bending over backward to please travelers, no matter how obtuse. At the same time, Cancún is a working, breathing city with a fascinating history and plenty of "real" Mexican culture: a charming central plaza, friendly hardworking residents, and quesadilla stands you wish you could resist.

Why not take advantage of both sides of Cancún? The beaches and nightclubs will blow your mind—don't miss them! But be sure not to miss out on Cancún's more subtle side, from live music in a bohemian downtown café to munching on corn on the cob sold from a cart on the street.

And when you need to, just get away. A 15-minute ferry ride delivers you to the slow-paced island of Isla Mujeres, a sliver of sand surrounded by breathtaking blue waters. Farther north and even more mellow is Isla Holbox; no cars, no banks, no post office, it's a world away from Cancún, yet reachable in a morning.

© LIZA PRADO

HIGHLIGHTS

◖ **Zona Hotelera Beaches:** With deep white sand and impossibly blue water that extends for miles, it's no wonder Cancún's beaches are considered some of the best in the world (page 32).

◖ **La Casa de Arte Popular Mexicano:** A small museum with a truly amazing collection of Mexican folk art from around the country (page 39).

◖ **Playa Norte:** While away the day on Isla Mujeres' best beach, where soft white sand is gently lapped by a waveless azure sea (page 71).

◖ **Isla Contoy:** Go snorkeling, hiking, and bird-watching on a day trip from Isla Mujeres to this protected island preserve (page 74).

◖ **Whale Shark Feeding Grounds:** Snorkel alongside the world's biggest fish – up to 9 meters (30 feet) long and weighing in at 10 tons – when they congregate off Isla Holbox June-September (page 90).

LOOK FOR ◖ TO FIND RECOMMENDED SIGHTS, ACTIVITIES, DINING, AND LODGING.

PLANNING YOUR TIME

A week will do just fine in Cancún, time enough to get your tan on, plus take a day trip or two, like visiting Isla Mujeres or one of the nearby Maya ruins. Ten days gives you time to explore deeper and farther, turning a day trip to Isla Mujeres or the Maya ruins into an overnighter, or venturing north to the remote island of Isla Holbox. Isla Mujeres and Isla Holbox are quite small but wonderfully relaxing; if either is your main destination, budget three or four days to experience them fully, but don't be surprised if you end up staying longer.

Cancún, Isla Mujeres, and Isla Holbox can all be reached and navigated by bus, ferry, taxi, and on foot—no need to rent a car. Same for destinations along the Riviera Maya, although

a car will help you maximize your time there. You should definitely consider getting a rental car, however, to see the Maya ruins near Cancún. Being able to arrive early and visit some of the smaller ruins makes an inland excursion significantly more rewarding.

HISTORY

Cancún is a new city in a new state. In the 1960s, the Mexican government set out to create the next Acapulco; in 1967 a data-crunching computer selected a small, swampy Caribbean island ringed with sparkling white sand as the country's most promising tourist town. The area was a backwater—not even a state yet. Nevertheless, thousands of mangroves were torn out to make room for an international

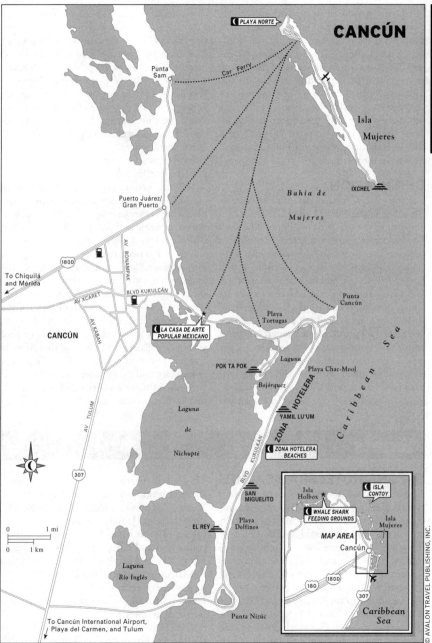

PLAYA NORTE

CANCÚN

Punta
Sam

Car Ferry

Isla
Mujeres

IXCHEL

Bahía de

Mujeres

Puerto Juárez/
Gran Puerto

AV. BONAMPAK

To Chiquilá
and Mérida

180D

AV. XCARET

BLVD KULKULCÁN

Punta
Cancún

Playa
Tortugas

Caribbean Sea

LA CASA DE ARTE
POPULAR MEXICANO

CANCÚN

AV. KABAH

POK TA POK

Laguna

Bojórquez

Playa Chac-Mool

ZONA HOTELERA

YAMIL LU'UM

AV. TULUM

Laguna

de

Nichupté

BLVD. KULKULCÁN

ZONA HOTELERA
BEACHES

307

SAN
MIGUELITO

EL REY

Playa
Delfines

Laguna
Río Inglés

To Cancún International Airport,
Playa del Carmen, and Tulum

Punta Nizúc

0   1 mi
0   1 km

Isla
Holbox

ISLA
CONTOY

WHALE SHARK
FEEDING GROUNDS

MAP AREA

Isla
Mujeres

Cancún

180   180D

307

Caribbean
Sea

© AVALON TRAVEL PUBLISHING, INC.

beach destination, with new infrastructure, electrical plants, purified tap water, and paved avenues lined with trees. A nearby fishing village was expanded to house workers for the new hotels—it is now downtown Cancún and serves much the same purpose. Cancún was officially "opened" in 1974, the same year the territory was elevated to statehood. (The state was named after army general Andrés Quintana Roo, and is pronounced "keen-TA-nah Roh".) Today, it is one of the top beach destinations in the world.

ORIENTATION

Cancún's Zona Hotelera lies on a large narrow island in the shape of a number "7." The southern foot of the "7" is called Punta Nizúc—a few hotels and clubs are there. The bend or corner of the "7" is Punta Cancún—this is the heart of the Zona Hotelera and is crowded with hotels, restaurants, and most of the nightclubs and malls. Between Punta Nizúc and Punta Cancún is the island's long (13 kilometers/eight miles) "leg," lined with high-end hotels and resorts on the ocean side, and restaurants, clubs, and some water-sport agencies on the other. (The latter overlook Laguna Nichupté, the lagoon formed between the island and the mainland.) Boulevard Kukulcán is the island's busy main drag—it runs the entire length and

care should be taken whenever crossing it as cars and buses race by without seeming to notice the tourists in the crosswalks. Boulevard Kukulcán is marked off by kilometers and most addresses in the Zona Hotelera include a kilometer number (e.g., Boulevard Kukulcán Km. 5.5). There are spectacular beaches up and down the island. Public buses run the length of Boulevard Kukulcán and into downtown Cancún all day and well into the night. Service is cheap and frequent.

Downtown Cancún is on the mainland, near the northwestern tip of the "7." It is divided into various *super manzanas* (square blocks) and most addresses include the particular *super manzana* (e.g., S.M. 4) along with the street name and number. Avenida Tulum is downtown's main throughway. Boulevard Kukulcán intersects Avenida Tulum (and turns into Avenida Cobá) just south of the downtown center—look for a roundabout with huge shells and starfish stood on end. Cancún's bus terminal is a few blocks north of there, at the intersection of Avenida Tulum and Avenida Uxmal. West of Avenida Tulum is a large park (Parque Las Palapas) and beyond that Avenida Yaxchilán. Most of downtown Cancún's hotels, restaurants, and music venues are on or around Parque Las Palapas and Avenida Yaxchilán, primarily in Super Manzanas (S.M.) 22–25.

Sights

◖ ZONA HOTELERA BEACHES

The beaches in Cancún are among the most spectacular in the world. You see postcards of them and you think they must be digitally enhanced—the sand could not be *so* white or the sea *so* aquamarine. But a combination of clear Caribbean water, a shallow sandy seafloor, and a high bright sun make for incredible colors. At high noon, even the postcards don't compare to the living picture show that is Cancún's coastline.

There is a notion that the high-rise hotels have monopolized Cancún's best beaches.

This is only partly true. While most hotels *do* front prime real estate, all beach areas in Mexico are public (except for those used by the military). Hotels cannot, by law, prohibit you or anyone else from lying out on your towel and enjoying the sun and water. Many high-end hotels subvert this by making it difficult or uncomfortable for non-guests to use their beaches: very few maintain exterior paths and others spread guest-only beach chairs over the best parts. (In the hotels' defense, they do a good job of keeping their areas clear of trash and seaweed, which can mar otherwise beautiful beaches.) If your hotel has a nice beach area, you're all set. If not, you can just walk through a hotel lobby to the beach—as a foreigner you are very unlikely to be stopped. (The real shame is that hotel employees seem much more apt to nab locals doing the same thing.) But even that is unnecessary if you don't mind a little extra walking. The city maintains several public access points, marked with large white signs along Boulevard Kukulcán. The area right around the access point is often crowded, but you can walk 100 meters (328 feet) or so to less crowded areas. Also, some fantastic beaches (Playa Delfines, especially) are totally hotel-free and have a refreshing mix of both Mexican and foreign beachgoers.

Be aware that the surf along the Zona Hotelera's long east-facing leg can be heavy. You should pay attention to the colored flags on the beach: green is Safe, yellow is Caution, red is Closed. There are lifeguards near all public access points, but instances of drowning (and near-drowning) do occur occasionally. The beaches along the short north-facing leg are much calmer. For really calm waters head to Isla Mujeres, where the water can be waist deep more than 75 meters (246 feet) from shore. The Laguna Nichupté is not recommended for swimming because of pollution and crocodiles.

Playa Caracol

Playa Caracol (Blvd. Kukulcán Km. 8.5) has a small stretch of beach right at the public access point, but it's not too pleasant and often very crowded. The beach is much better just east of there, in front of the Fiesta Americana Coral Beach. Unfortunately, it's difficult to access without cutting through the hotel.

Playa Chac-Mool

Playa Chac-Mool (Blvd. Kukulcán Km. 10) is the beach you see from Forum by the Sea mall. The beach and water are a bit rocky right at the access point, but wide and beautiful just a few hundred meters south, in front of the Hotel Sierra and Hyatt Cancún Caribe. There

is parasailing here, and the hotels cast afternoon shadows on the beach, in case you forgot your umbrella.

The beach club **Playa Cabana** (tel. 998/848-8380 ext. 113, www.playacabana .com, 10 A.M.–6 P.M. daily, US$10) also is here. Tahiti-esque in style—dark wood cabanas have billowing curtains, queen-size beach loungers, and incredible views of the turquoise sea just a few feet away (US$20 extra). There's a DJ who spins cool tunes, a split-level infinity pool, plus a full bar and restaurant. It's definitely a scene. But then again, it's in the heart of the Zona Hotelera—kind of goes with the territory.

Playa Marlín

Playa Marlín (Blvd. Kukulcán Km. 12.5) is a wide and clean beach. There is parking and Plaza Kukulcán, with a bowling alley and restaurants, is nearby. The public access here is unappealing, through an unused parking lot and past the gutted shell of a former beach club—a victim of Hurricane Wilma. But if

© LIZA PRADO

Playa Delfines is a popular beach for both locals and travelers.

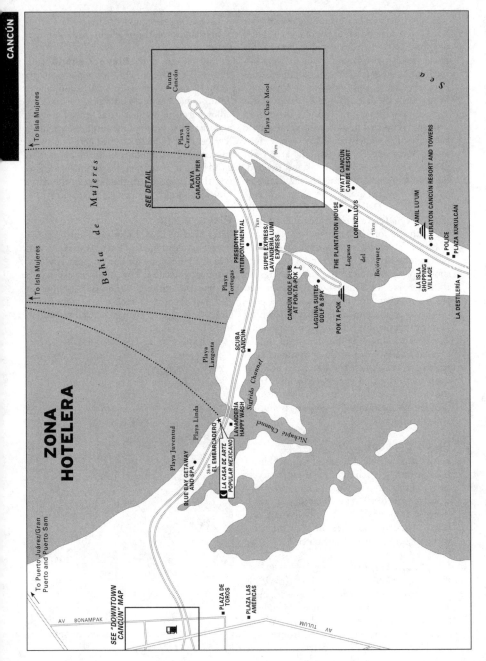

CANCÚN

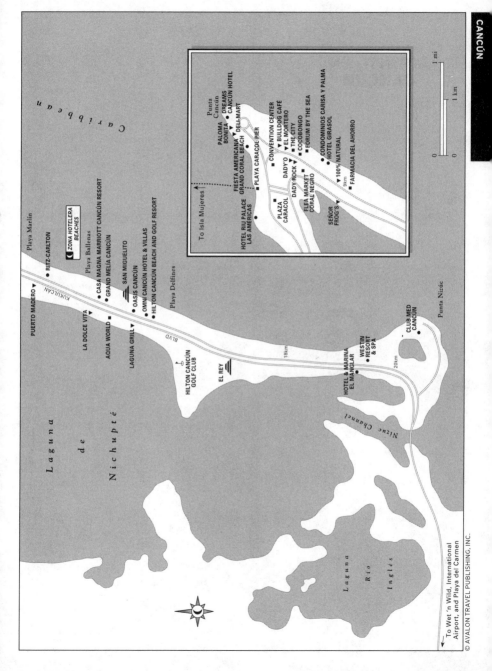

Caribbean

Playa Marlin

RITZ-CARLTON ▼

Playa Ballenas

CASA MAGNA MARRIOTT CANCÚN RESORT ■

GRAND MELIA CANCÚN ■

SAN MIGUELITO

OASIS CANCÚN ●

OMNI CANCÚN HOTEL & VILLAS ●

HILTON CANCÚN BEACH AND GOLF RESORT ●

Playa Delfines

PUERTO MADERO ▼

LA DOLCE VITA ▼

AGUA WORLD ■

LAGUNA GRILL ▼

KUKULCÁN BLVD

HILTON CANCÚN GOLF CLUB ⚑

EL REY

18km

20m

HOTEL & MARINA EL MANGLAR ●

WESTIN RESORT & SPA ●

CLUB MED CANCÚN ●

Punta Nizúc

Laguna

de

Nichupté

Nizuc Channel

Laguna

Río

Inglés

To Wet 'n Wild, International Airport, and Playa del Carmen

ZONA HOTELERA BEACHES

© AVALON TRAVEL PUBLISHING, INC.

Inset map

Punta Cancún

PALOMA BONITA ▼

DREAMS CANCÚN HOTEL ●

DELI-MART ●

FIESTA AMERICANA GRAND CORAL BEACH ▼

PLAYA CARACOL PIER

CONVENTION CENTER ■

BULLDOG CAFÉ ▼

EL MORTERO ▼

THE CITY ■

COCOBONGO ■

FORUM BY THE SEA ■

DADY'O ▼

DADY ROCK ▼

CONDOMINIOS CARISA Y PALMA ●

HOTEL GIRASOL ●

100% NATURAL ▼

FARMACIA DEL AHORRO ■

FLEA MARKET CORAL NEGRO ■

PLAZA CARACOL ■

HOTEL RIU PALACE LAS AMÉRICAS ●

SEÑOR FROG'S ▼

9km

To Isla Mujeres

1 mi

1 km

0

© AVALON TRAVEL PUBLISHING, INC.

CANCÚN

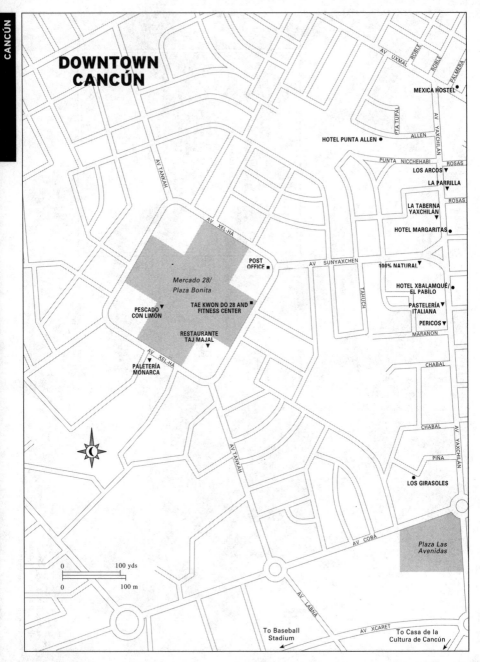

DOWNTOWN CANCÚN

AV UXMAL
ROBLE
ROBLE
PRIMERA

MEXICA HOSTEL ●

PTA TUPAL
AV YAXCHILÁN

HOTEL PUNTA ALLEN ● ALLEN

PUNTA NICCHEHABI
ROSAS

LOS ARCOS ▼

LA PARRILLA ▼

ROSAS

LA TABERNA YAXCHILÁN ▼

HOTEL MARGARITAS ●

AV XEL-HA

AV TANKAH

AV SUNYAXCHEN

POST OFFICE ■

100% NATURAL ▼

Mercado 28/
Plaza Bonita

HOTEL XBALAMQUÉ/ EL PABILO ●

TAHUCH

PESCADO CON LIMÓN ▼

TAE KWON DO 28 AND FITNESS CENTER ■

PASTELERÍA ▼ ITALIANA

PERICOS ▼

MARAÑON

RESTAURANTE TAJ MAJAL ▼

CHABAL

AV XEL-HA

PALETERÍA MONARCA ▼

CHABAL

AV YAXCHILÁN

PINA

AV TANKAH

LOS GIRASOLES ●

0   100 yds

0   100 m

AV COBA

Plaza Las Avenidas

AV LABNA

To Baseball Stadium

AV XCARET

To Casa de la Cultura de Cancún

CANCÚN

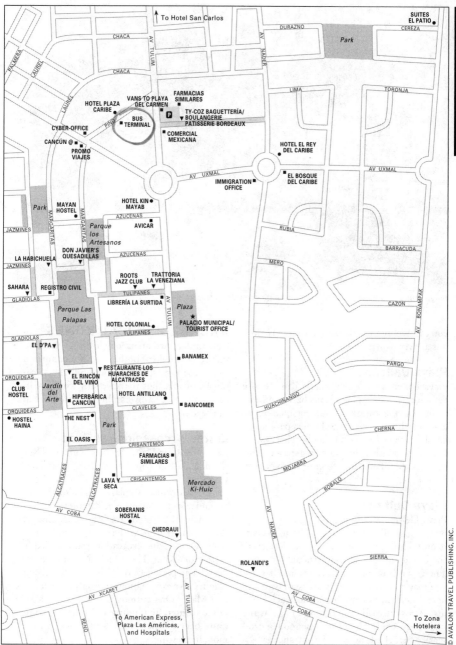

© AVALON TRAVEL PUBLISHING, INC.

© LIZA PRADO

Maya ruins and high-rise hotels stand side-by-side in the Zona Hotelera.

you can ignore that, the beach itself is as glorious as everywhere else.

Playa Ballenas

Playa Ballenas (Blvd. Kukulcán Km. 14.5) is yet another wide and gorgeous beach. A kiosk right near the entrance rents personal watercraft and boogie boards and offers parasailing and banana boats. As at other beaches, walk a little way in either direction to get away from the crowds. There is no food or drink service here. Parking is at the entrance.

Playa Delfines

Playa Delfines (Blvd. Kukulcán Km. 17.5) is our favorite, if we had to pick. The access path is on a bluff, affording a panoramic view of the beach and water, unobstructed by hotels. There's a mix of tourists and local families, and you may see surfers. (The waves can be strong here—take care swimming.) The beach is also just across the road from Ruínas El Rey, which makes a nice side trip. There is no food or drink service here. Parking is at the entrance.

ARCHAEOLOGICAL ZONES

Cancún has two archaeological sites, both in the Zona Hotelera. Both are minor compared to the big sites spread throughout the Yucatán Peninsula, but they are still worth visiting and can be easily combined with a day at the beach.

El Rey Archaeological Zone

Just across from Playa Delfines, Ruínas El Rey (Blvd. Kukulcán Km. 17.5, 8 A.M.–5 P.M. daily, US$3, use of video camera US$3) consist of several platforms, two plazas, and a small temple and pyramid, all arranged along an ancient 500-meter (1,640-foot) roadway. The ruins get their name (Ruins of the King) from a skeleton found during excavation and believed to be that of a king. The ruins date from the late Postclassic period (A.D. 1200–1400); various plaques give explanations in English, Spanish, and Maya. One curious note—the ruins are home to literally hundreds of iguanas, some quite beefy, which make a visit here all the more interesting.

CANCÚN

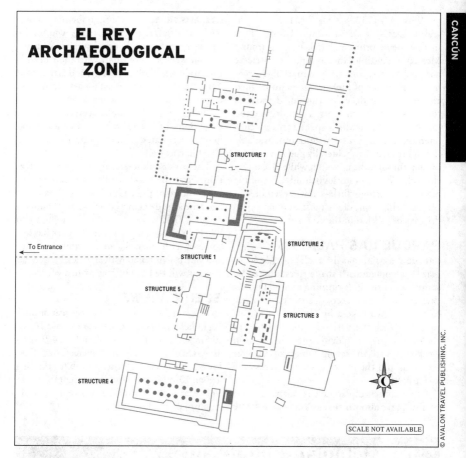

EL REY ARCHAEOLOGICAL ZONE

STRUCTURE 7

To Entrance

STRUCTURE 1

STRUCTURE 2

STRUCTURE 5

STRUCTURE 3

STRUCTURE 4

SCALE NOT AVAILABLE

© AVALON TRAVEL PUBLISHING, INC.

Yamil Lu'um Archaeological Zone

Lodged between the Westin Laguna Mar and the Park Royal Pirámides, Yamil Lu'um (Blvd. Kukulcán Km. 12.5, free) consists of two small temples that were built between A.D. 1200 and 1550: the **Templo del Alacrán** (Temple of the Scorpion), owing its name to the remains of a scorpion sculpture on one of its walls, and the **Templo de la Huella** (Temple of the Hand-print), named so because of a handprint in the stucco. Unfortunately, neither the scorpion sculpture nor the handprint is visible these days. The ruins are well above the beach on Cancún's highest point, suggesting that the two small temples were used as watchtowers, lighthouses, and navigational aids. To see the ruins, go to the concierge at either the Westin or the Park Royal Pirámides and ask if you can walk through to the site. If you are refused, head to Playa Marlín—at the very least, you can see them from afar.

◖ LA CASA DE ARTE POPULAR MEXICANO

If you have any doubts about the genius of Mexican art, put them permanently to rest at La Casa de Arte Popular Mexicano (El Embarcadero, Blvd. Kukulcán Km. 4, tel. 998/849-4332, 9 A.M.–7 P.M. Mon.–Fri. and 11 A.M.–7 P.M. Sat.–Sun, US$5). This small museum brims with folk art from around Mexico, including fantastic masks, intricate nativity scenes, and truly remarkable *árboles de vida* (trees of life)—large hand-painted clay pieces that defy description. If there's a flaw, it's that the curators try to display too much, and the smallish space can feel cluttered. Fortunately, a free audio tour, available in English or Spanish, literally guides you step-by-step through the museum, while explaining the techniques and stories behind many of the pieces. Surprisingly little-known, even here in Cancún, this is one of the most comprehensive displays of its kind in the country.

PARQUE LAS PALAPAS

Parque Las Palapas is a classic Mexican plaza—complete with shade trees, quesadilla stands, and little girls running around in frilly dresses and big sneakers. It's the place where locals come to take a break from the heat, to gossip with their friends, and to listen to the local teenagers playing their guitars. On weekends, artisans set up tables to sell their creations and the merry-go-round across the street lights up.

At the corners of Parque Las Palapas are two smaller parks also worth checking out. **Parque**

Los Artesanos is a young bohemian hangout, with disaffected young artists who fill the small park with their bongo drum jam sessions, and on weekend evenings, with their beautiful handmade clothes, jewelry, and art. **Jardín del Arte** is a space reserved for art expositions (artwork is displayed under a series of stationary white umbrellas) and concerts on its small stage. Some of downtown's best restaurants and hotels are situated here or on nearby Avenida Yaxchilán as well.

The park could certainly use some renovation: First the band shell's huge *palapa* roof burned down, then Hurricane Wilma damaged the already aging sidewalks and common squares. Oddly, the city seems in no hurry to make the needed repairs, and the park has lost some of its former charm and ambiance. It's still worth a visit, and with any luck Parque Las Palapas will be back in shape when you do.

SCENIC VIEWS

In case you got stuck with the aisle seat on your flight here, **La Torre Escénica** (Scenic Tower, El Embarcadero, Blvd. Kukulcán Km. 4, 9 A.M.–10 P.M. daily, US$9) is an 80-meter (262.5-foot) tower with a rotating passenger cabin, affording a good 10-minute view of this part of the coastline. Audio description is available in Spanish, English, German, and French.

Entertainment and Events

Cancún is justly famous for its nightlife, with a dozen or more world-class clubs throbbing with music of all sorts and filled with revelers of all ages and nationalities every single night of the week. The partying is especially manic during spring break, summer, Christmas, and New Year's Eve. The city also offers a good mix of small music venues, theaters and cultural centers, bars, and cinemas.

LIVE MUSIC

As the name suggests, **Hard Rock Cafe** (Forum by the Sea mall, Blvd. Kukulcán Km. 9, tel.

998/881-2020, 11 A.M.–2 A.M. daily) is the place to go for live rock. Bands play at 10 P.M. every night except Sunday when the tunes start at 9 P.M.

For soft jazz, head to **Cassis Jazz Bar** (Hyatt Cancún Caribe Resort, Blvd. Kukulcán Km. 10.5, 998/884-7800 ext. 7270) a chic lounge bar where musicians serenade guests from 6 P.M.–1 A.M. every night.

A lively jazz and blues joint, **Roots Jazz Club** (Tulipanes 26, tel. 998/884-2437, 6 P.M.–1 A.M. Tues.–Sat.) is arguably the best music venue in town. Get there early for a quality dinner and—almost more importantly—a seat near the small stage. Music starts at around 10 P.M. and a US$3–5 cover may apply.

El Pabilo (Hotel Xbalamqué, Av. Yaxchilán 31, tel. 998/892-4553, 8 A.M.–midnight daily, free) is a small artsy café with great live music Monday–Saturday. Music featured includes *bohemia cubana*, fusion jazz, classical guitar, and flamenco. Shows start at 9 P.M.

At the corner of Parque Las Palapas, **El Rincón del Vino** (Alcatraces 29, tel. 998/898-3187, 6 P.M.–1 A.M. Mon.–Sat.) is a lively wine bar that carries labels from all over the world, including Mexico, Chile, South Africa, Italy, Spain, and the United States (US$5–7/glass). The friendly staff can provide recommendations, and a short menu of baguettes, salads, and tapas help keep you thirsty. Live music, usually a guitar soloist, begins at 9:30 P.M. every night but Sunday and Monday.

For bongo drum jam sessions, wandering guitarists, and other street musicians, head to **Parque Las Palapas** on weekend evenings where you're likely to catch one or all of these performers.

PERFORMING ARTS

Teatro Cancún (El Embarcadero, Blvd. Kukulcán Km. 4, 998/849-5580, ticket office on ground level open 11 A.M.–7 P.M. Mon.–Sat., cash only) stages shows by a variety of performers, from dance schools to professional musicians, several times a year. The theater is large and has some interesting murals, though overall it's a bit auditorium-like. Ticket prices vary depending on the event, but range US$10–25.

For *ballet folklórico* (traditional dances from around Mexico) head to **La Joya** restaurant at the Fiesta Americana Coral Beach for colorful live performances (7:30 P.M. Tue., Thu., Fri., and Sat., US$5).

Casa de la Cultura de Cancún (Av. Yaxchilán s/n, S.M. 21, 998/884-8364, casaculturacancun@prodigy.net.mx) is a state-funded institute that offers an incredible gamut of artistic workshops, performances, and expositions (free–US$3.50). While the institute has

an ever-changing schedule, which often includes dance, dramatic, and visual art presentations, some events are fixed: Monday is movie night, with films falling into a monthly theme (8 P.M., US$2); Tuesday is open-mike night, when artists are invited to share their poetic, musical, and story-telling talents (8 P.M.); on Thursdays a live concert—varying from folk to classical—is presented (8:30 P.M., US$5); and Saturday mornings are dedicated to children in what is called "Sábados de Minicultura" with offerings including puppet shows, educational movies, and theater (no admission fee). Be sure to call for weekly listings, as the calendar is packed with programming.

DISCOTHEQUES AND BARS

Most of Cancún's biggest, most popular nightclubs are near the Forum by the Sea mall in the **Zona Hotelera,** with a few a bit farther afield. Each club has a different "on" night—Monday is Dady-O, Tuesday is Fat Tuesday, etc. These don't seem to change much, but definitely ask around before buying your tickets. Dress code is casual but don't wear flip-flops, Tevas, or bathing suits (unless, of course, it's Speedo Night).

Some hotels organize clubbing trips—this may seem lame, but it can mean priority admission, reserved tables inside, and a shuttle there (but typically not back). And the organizers head to the same nightly hotspots you're probably looking for anyway. **Downtown** venues are definitely on the quieter side, lacking the bells and whistles you'll find in the Zona Hotelera.

BULLFIGHTS

If you're curious about bullfighting, head to Cancún's **Plaza de Toros** (Av. Bonampak at Sayíl, tel. 998/884-8372, US$33, children under 6 free) where every Wednesday at 3:30 P.M. you can get a glimpse of what makes this sport so popular in Latin America. Cancún's bullfights differ from traditional *corridas* (runnings) in that only four bulls are fought (versus five or six) and a mini-*charrería* (rodeo) and a *ballet folklórico* performance are also

PARTYING IN CANCÚN

Travelers flock to Cancún as much for its vibrant nightlife as for its white sand beaches. Hands down, it's the hottest – and some say, wildest – scene on the Riviera.

ZONA HOTELERA

Dady-O (Blvd. Kukulcán Km 9.5, tel. 998/883-1626, www.dadyo.com.mx, 10 P.M.–6 A.M. nightly, US$16 cover, US$37 with open bar and entrance to both Dady-O and Dady Rock) is, well, the daddy of Cancún's nightclubs, with seven different "environments," including CO2 blasts, laser shows, and theme parties on several different levels.

Next door, **Dady Rock** (Blvd. Kukulcán Km 9.5, tel. 998/883-1626, 6 P.M.–4 A.M. nightly, US$16 cover, US$37 with open bar and entrance to both Dady-O and Dady Rock) is technically a restaurant and bar – there is no dance floor – but popular rock music, sometimes live, has partiers dancing every place possible, including on the bar. Dady Rock also hosts some contests: "Hot Male," "Hot Legs," "Wet Body," etc. (Gary was the runner-up – again – in the "Hot Legs" contest.)

Bulldog Cafè (Blvd. Kukulcán Km 9.5, tel. 998/848-9850, www.bulldogcafe.com, 10 P.M.–6 A.M. daily high season, Fri.-Sat. only in low season, US$20 cover, US$40 with open bar high season, US$30 low season), features hip-hop, rock, and Latin dance music. Friday and Saturday are the big nights. Five enormous bars and a private VIP lounge with a whirlpool tub are the highlights.

The City (Blvd. Kukulcán Km 9, tel. 998/848-8380, www.thecitycancun.com, 10 A.M.–6 P.M. daily, beach club US$10, 10 P.M.–5 A.M. daily, nightclub US$30 cover with open bar, no cover Mon.-Tues., women drink free Wed. and Sun.) is a mega-club with a total capacity of 15,000. During the day, you can hang out at its beach club, **Playa Cabaña,** with its split-level infinity pool, queen-size lounge chairs, and DJed tunes (see *Playa Chac-Mool*). At night, party inside, with your eyes on the cinema-size screen, and under what's claimed to be the biggest disco ball in the world (it's pretty big). Be sure to break loose on the movable dance floor, which travels from the third floor to the center of the club below.

CocoBongo (Blvd. Kukulcán Km. 9, tel. 998/883-5061, www.cocobongo.com.mx,

---

held. Because of this, you won't see bullfighting aficionados here—which changes the experience dramatically—but it's a good cultural sampler. Tickets are available at the box office or through most travel agencies in Cancún.

PROFESSIONAL BASEBALL

Baseball is huge in Mexico, particularly in the north, where you'll see as many baseball diamonds as you will soccer fields. While still not having the pull in the Yucatán as it does elsewhere, it is a sport on the rise. The local team **Los Langosteros** (The Lobstermen) are one of the 18 teams that make up Mexico's professional baseball league, the Liga Mexicana de Beisbol. You can catch a game from the beginning of March through the end of June at the **Estadio Beto Avilá** (Avenida Xcaret s/n, behind Wal-Mart, US$2–7), which was remodeled in 2007.

FESTIVALS

Held annually since 1991, the **Cancún Jazz Festival** is a weeklong event held in mid- to late May, drawing top jazz musicians from around the world. This is a huge crowd-drawing event so be sure to reserve tickets early. Prices and venues vary—ask your hotel concierge or call the city's tourist information office for details.

CINEMA

Cancun has several major movie theaters, all offering the latest American and Mexican releases. Make sure you see *subtitulada* after the listed titles unless, of course, you want to hear Arnold Schwarzenegger dubbed. Also, if you can, go on a Wednesday, when most movie theaters throughout the country feature discounted ticket prices.

Cinemark (La Isla Shopping Village, 2nd

US$40 with open bar, US$45 Fri.-Sat., 10 P.M.-4 A.M. daily) is a spectacular club featuring live rock and salsa bands, flying acrobats, and rotating impersonator shows of The Mask, Beetle Juice, Madonna, and Spiderman. Not only will you see them on stage, but you'll also find them on the bar and swinging in the air. Movie clips are also projected onto huge high-tech screens.

Old standbys **Carlos'n Charlie's** (Forum by the Sea mall, Blvd. Kukulcán Km. 9, tel. 998/883-1862) and **Señor Frog's** (Blvd. Kukulcán Km. 9.5, tel. 998/883-3454) both open at noon for meals and stay open until 2 A.M. for drinking, dancing, and general mayhem.

If you're looking for a sports bar, a popular one is **Champions** (Marriott Casa Magna, Blvd. Kukulcán Km. 14.5, tel. 998/881-2000, 5 P.M.-2 A.M. daily). It's got 40 screens, including a giant wide-screen TV, which play nonstop live sports. A few pool tables and a DJ also add to the mix.

DOWNTOWN CANCÚN

Located inside Plaza Las Américas, **Mambo-café** (Av. Tulum at Av. Sayil, tel. 998/887-7891, www.mambocafe.com.mx, 10 P.M.-4 A.M. Wed.-Sun., cover US$4-5, free some nights) is one of the hottest spots in the downtown Cancún scene. Popular with locals and expats, you'll be assured of spinning to the sounds of salsa, *cumbia*, and merengue.

La Taberna Yaxchilán (Av. Yaxchilán 23, tel. 998/887-5433, 1 P.M.-6 A.M. daily) is a game-themed bar with pool tables, darts, dominoes, cards, backgammon, chess...more games than you probably saw at your last sleepover. Excellent two-for-one drink specials typically run 6 P.M.-9 P.M. and again 2 A.M.-4 A.M. The only real downside of the place is the cloud of cigarette smoke – prepare to inhale lots of it whether you're puffing or not.

Across the street, **Los Arcos** (Av. Yaxchilán 57, 10 A.M.-3 A.M. daily) doesn't do much business as a restaurant – La Parilla a few doors down is better – but it gets packed at night with a young mix of locals and tourists. At last check, national beers were two-for-one all day and night.

Fl., Blvd. Kukulcán Km. 12.5, tel. 998/883-5604, US$4.50 general, US$3 matinee, US$2 Wed.) has five screens showing fairly recent Hollywood films, plus a Mexican or Latin American option now and again.

In Plaza Las Américas, **Cinépolis** (Av. Tulum at Av. Sayil, 1st Fl., tel. 998/884-0403, US$4.50 general, US$3–4 matinee, US$2 Wed.) is a popular choice among locals.

Upstairs, treat yourself to a first-class movie experience at **Cinépolis VIP** (Plaza Las Américas, Av. Tulum at Av. Sayil, 2nd Fl., tel. 998/884-4056, US$7 general, US$5–6 matinee, US$5 Wed.). Inside you'll find overstuffed leather seats with extra leg room, side tables for your munchies, and waiters who will bring you sushi, crepes, gourmet baguettes, cappuccinos, cocktails and—oh, yeah—buttered popcorn too.

Shopping

With five major malls, several smaller ones, and hundreds of independent shops, you can buy just about anything in Cancún. The malls are large, modern, and busy, with name-brand clothes, jewelry and watches, movies, arcades, bowling, aquariums, and a full range of restaurants. The malls also have T-shirts, souvenirs, and handicrafts, but you may find better prices at **Flea Market Coral Negro** (Zona Hotelera, across from Forum by the Sea, 8 A.M.–midnight daily) or **Mercado Ki-Huic** (downtown, Av. Tulum at Av. Cobá, 9 A.M.–9 P.M. Mon.–Sat., 10 A.M.–8 P.M. Sun.), both easy to reach by bus or on foot. There are many more shops north of Ki-Huic on Avenida Tulum (the other side of the street is best) and a couple of open-air markets are nearby. Most mall and independent shops accept credit cards, but plan on paying in cash at the markets.

OPEN-AIR MARKETS
Mercado 28 (Av. Sunyaxchen at Av. Xel-Ha, 9 A.M.– 8 P.M. daily) is a large open-air market featuring a wide variety of Mexican handicrafts: ceramics from Tonalá, silver from Taxco, hammocks from Mérida, *alebrijes* (wooden creatures) from Oaxaca, hand-woven shirts from Chiapas. You'll also find a fair share of T-shirts, key chains, coconut monkeys, and women offering to braid your hair. Basically, you'll find a little of everything. If you're hungry, head toward the center of the complex, where a handful of restaurants offer traditional Mexican fare.

On weekend evenings, stroll through **Parque Las Palapas** and **Parque Los Artesanos,** both great spots to pick up local handicrafts, Chiapanecan clothing, bohemian jewelry, and art.

Since 2001, the **Concurso Municipal de Artesanías,** a city-wide handicraft competition, has been held annually the first week in November in Cancún's Palacio Municipal. In addition to showcasing the city's best artisans, many participants also sell their work just in front of the building. Look for the large white tents—and the crowds—on Avenida Tulum.

ARTESANÍA
Next to Mercado 28, **Plaza Bonita** (Av. Sunyaxchen at Av. Xel-Ha, 9 A.M.–8 P.M. daily) is a multileveled shopping center built to look like a colonial village—bright courtyards, fountains, greenery, and all. Items are a little more expensive than those found in the market next door, but the quality is almost always better.

In the Zona Hotelera, the gift shop at **La Casa de Arte Popular Mexicano** (El Embarcadero, Blvd. Kukulcán Km. 4, tel. 998/849-4332, 9 A.M.–7 P.M. Mon.–Fri. and 11 A.M.–7 P.M. Sat.–Sun,) has a quality—and pricey—selection of authentic Mexican folk art from around the country. If you can get past the price tag, the challenge becomes getting the stuff home in one piece!

BOOKSTORES
For a serious bookstore, head to Alma Libre books in Puerto Morelos (see *Riviera Maya* chapter), which has 20,000 titles in numerous languages. In Cancún, your best bet is **Librería La Surtida** (Av. Tulum directly across from Palacio Municipal, tel. 998/887-1428, 9 A.M.–10 P.M. daily) which has one shelf of English-language guidebooks to the Yucatán Peninsula, Central America and Cuba, plus a number of maps and Spanish phrasebooks. The prices are jaw-dropping—US$35–50!—but the store does a decent job of stocking at least one copy of the most relevant titles. You can also get a copy of *USA Today* for the bargain price of US$3.50.

MALLS
Plaza Caracol (Blvd. Kukulcán Km. 8.5, tel. 998/883-1038, www.caracolplaza.com, 8 A.M.–10 P.M. daily) is a modern mall with narrow, winding corridors that somehow never lead you out, kind of like a Vegas casino without the gambling. Shops mostly sell cloth-

ing and kitschy souvenirs and the main food court fails to inspire. At best, it's an option on a rainy day.

Forum by the Sea (Blvd. Kukulcán Km. 9, tel. 998/883-4425, www.forumbythesea.com.mx, 10 A.M.–11:30 P.M. daily) is a doughnut-shaped building with its three floors opening onto the airy main lobby. The stores offer mid- to high-end goods varying from nice T-shirts to expensive jewelry. The best reason to come, however, is the spectacular view of the Caribbean from the third-floor balcony, which has tables and chairs set up for food court customers. The view is so good, you almost forget you're in a mall.

La Isla Shopping Village (Blvd. Kukulcán Km. 12.5, tel. 998/883-5025, www.laislacancun.com.mx, 9 A.M.–8 P.M. daily) is the most pleasant of the Zona Hotelera malls, and the only one set outdoors. Arranged around an artificial river, it has wide airy passageways and plenty of genuinely good shops and restaurants. There are also the popular Interactive Aquarium and a five-screen movie theater.

Plaza Kukulcán (Blvd. Kukulcán Km. 12.5, just past La Destilería, tel. 998/885-2200, www.kukulcanplaza.com, 9 A.M.–10 P.M. daily) underwent extensive renovation in 2005 and is now anchored by Maraf Jewelry and a handful of upscale shops dubbed "Luxury Avenue." Some usual suspects can also be found here, including Señor Frog's, Sunglass Island, MixUp music store, and a Sergio Bustamante gallery. Ruth's Chris Steak House is on the 1st floor and an innovative bar/bowling alley is on the 2nd floor.

You don't have to go to the Zona Hotelera for your mall fix. **Plaza Las Américas** (Av. Tulum at Av. Sayil, tel. 998/887-4839, 9 A.M.–midnight daily) stretches almost a block and includes dozens of mid- to upscale shops, a discotheque, and two movie theaters. Unlike the Zona Hotelera, here you'll be among mostly Mexican shoppers.

Sports and Recreation

While relaxing by the pool or on the beach is more than enough sports and recreation for many of Cancún's visitors—and who can blame them?—there *are* a number of options for those looking for a bit more action. From golf and fishing to scuba diving and kiteboarding (and a whole bunch of things in between), Cancún has something for everyone.

BEACH ACTIVITIES

Parasailing (*paracaídas* in Spanish) is that classic beach thrill ride in which you don a parachute and are pulled behind a boat to a dizzying height. If you do it only once, do it in Cancún for views of the endless white beaches and impossibly turquoise sea. You can choose a traditional one-person ride (with takeoff from the shore) or a two-person ride, in which you sit in a small raft and take off from the boat or the water. Price and duration are fairly uniform: US$45–55 per person for a 10- to 12-minute ride. Look for independent operators at most public beaches, especially **Playa Ballenas** (Blvd. Kukulcán Km. 14.5, Cancún Palace Hotel), **Playa Chac-Mool** (Blvd. Kukulcán Km. 10, near the Hotel Sierra), and **Playa Delfines** (Blvd. Kukulcán Km. 17.5, near the Hilton) roughly 10 A.M.–6 P.M. daily. Or sign up at friendly **Solo Buceo** or **Aqua World** (Blvd. Kukulcán Km. 15.2, tel. 998/848-8300, www.aquaworld.com.mx), both of which offer many other activities as well.

Personal watercraft (aka wave runners) are rented at various places along the beach, including all the same places that offer parasailing. Prices are US$50 for 30 minutes or US$90 for an hour; one or two people can ride at a time. **Banana boats** (those big yellow rafts pulled behind a motorboat) are somewhat less common but are definitely available at Playa Ballenas. The cost there is US$20 per person for a 20-minute ride.

SNORKELING AND SCUBA DIVING

For experienced snorkelers and divers, Cancún proper is less interesting than Isla Mujeres and doesn't even compare to Cozumel. Cancún's sandy seafloor simply doesn't have the coral and rock formations that make for great underwater excursions. Where there are large reefs, as at Punta Nizúc, neglect and heavy boat traffic have left much of the coral dead. If you're aching for a fix, there are a few good sites, including a ship intentionally sunk 24 meters (80 feet) down. Most local shops also offer diving and snorkeling trips to Cozumel and the cenotes—inland freshwater sinkholes south of Cancún offering superb cavern and cave diving.

For the best **open-water snorkeling,** talk to a scuba diving shop. All those listed here offer guided snorkeling trips, and are invariably better than the ubiquitous "jungle trips" hawked around Cancún, even for beginners. For something different altogether, arrange a **cenote snorkeling** trip. The water is unbelievably clear and swimming through and among the cave formations is otherworldly. Perhaps the best introduction to cenotes is at Hidden Worlds Cenote Park, which offers several guided trips daily through its own cenote system just north of Tulum.

For **diving,** a number of shops offer fun dives as well as certification courses at all levels. Again, the diving in Cancún is okay for a quick fix on a tight schedule, but you'll find better conditions and smaller groups just about anywhere else on the Riviera Maya or Isla Cozumel.

Solo Buceo (Dreams Cancún Hotel, Blvd. Kukulkán Km. 9.5, tel. 998/883-3979, www .solobuceo.com, 9 A.M.–4:30 P.M. daily) is a friendly shop at the Dreams Cancún hotel with a strong reputation for service, and where most dives are led by instructors rather than dive masters. Two-tank reef dives run US$70, while two-tank Cozumel or cenote trips cost US$145, including lunch; prices include all gear except a wetsuit (US$10, recommended for cenote trips). Open-water certification classes (US$370, 2–4 days) can also be arranged. Despite its name, Solo Buceo offers more than "only diving," including snorkeling, parasailing, and Hobie Cat rides.

Scuba Cancún (Playa Langosta, Blvd. Kukulcán Km. 4.5) tel. 998/849-4736, www .scubacancun.com.mx, 7 A.M.–8 P.M. daily) is one of Cancún's oldest dive shops, founded in 1980 and still run by the same family. It offers the standard selection of dives, including one-tank (US$54), two-tank (US$68), night (US$56; Thurs. only), and two-tank cavern and Cozumel dives (US$135, including lunch); all prices include equipment. Snorkel trips are offered in Cancún (2 P.M. daily, US$29) and Cozumel (US$95). This is a popular shop and dives can sometimes get crowded—ask ahead.

Aqua World (Blvd. Kukulcán Km. 15.2, tel. 998/848-8300, www.aquaworld.com.mx) is Cancún's biggest, most commercialized water sports outfit, of which scuba diving is only a small part. Come here if you are looking for activities for the whole family, divers and non-divers alike, all in one spot. Otherwise, head to smaller shops for more personal attention.

Many hotels are affiliated with independent shops that cater exclusively to guests there. Ask your concierge if that's the case at the hotel you're in.

WIND SPORTS

Ikarus Kiteboarding School (tel. 984/803-3490, www.kiteboardmexico.com) is based in Playa del Carmen but opened a new kiteboarding camp at Isla Blanca, a huge saltwater lagoon north of Cancún. Conditions for learning to kiteboard don't get much better than this: steady wind, kilometers of flat water with few boats or other obstacles, and the water's never more than waist deep. Private classes are US$75 an hour, while groups are US$45–55 an hour per person (maximum three to a group). Most first-timers need 3–6 hours of instruction to learn the basics.

Solo Buceo offers one-hour Hobie Cat sailboat trips for US$50 (up to four people).

WATERSKIING, WAKEBOARDING, AND SURFING

Waterski Cancún and Wakeboard (Marina Manglar, Blvd. Kukulcán Km. 20, cell tel. 044-998/874-4816, toll-free USA tel. 800/697-1517, www.waterskicancun.com) has three slalom courses and a number of ski sites at the far southern end of Laguna de Nichupté and the Zona Hotelera, opposite the Sun Palace Resort. Free skiing and wakeboarding cost US$120 an hour, while the slalom course is US$40 for six runs.

The **Asociación de Surf de Quintana Roo** (Quintana Roo Surf Association, Blvd. Kukulcán Km. 13, tel. 998/847-7006, surf-cancunmex@hotmail.com) offers surf classes and rentals and hosts occasional surf competitions. The group has a kiosk on Playa Delfines, which is generally the best surf beach.

SWIMMING WITH DOLPHINS

The **Interactive Aquarium** (Plaza La Isla, Blvd. Kukulcán Km. 12.5, tel. 998/883-0411, toll-free Mex. tel. 800/812-0856, 9 A.M.–7 P.M. daily, adults US$13, children US$10) has a disappointingly small display of fish and other sea creatures, but its main raison d'être are the interactive dolphin and shark exhibits. A 20-minute dolphin show is held daily at 6 and 7 P.M. (free with admission) and definitely makes a visit here more worthwhile. Interactive programs for kids and adults range from petting and swimming with the dolphins (US$66–130) to being "trainer for a day" (US$240); reserve well in advance. You can climb into an acrylic phone booth and be lowered into the aquarium's huge shark tank, and feed bull, brown, and nurse sharks from small slots (US$65 one person, US$100 two, US$120 three; 30 minutes).

Other dolphin interaction programs include those at Cancún's **Wet 'n Wild** (see *Eco- and Water Parks*), Isla Mujeres' **Dolphin Discovery** (tel. 998/877-0875, reservations 998/849-4748, www.dolphindiscovery.com), and the Riviera Maya's **Delphinus** (toll-free Mex. tel. 800/335-3461, www.delphinus.com.mx). Visi-

tors can go to the parks directly but most sign up at their hotels or online.

ECO- AND WATER PARKS

Visitors to Cancún have three major eco-parks to choose from: **Xcaret, Xel-Ha,** and **Parque Garrafón.** Good for both kids and adults, all offer a combination of outdoor activities, including snorkeling and tubing, plus optional add-ons such as dolphin-interaction programs and modified scuba diving. Admission is far from cheap, especially the all-inclusive packages that come with meals and extra activities. Still, each park is unique and interesting in its own way, and many people list a visit as the highlight of their vacation.

Despite the deluge of advertising you'll see downtown and in the Zona Hotelera, none of the three parks is actually in Cancún. Parque Garrafón is the closest, situated on the southern tip of Isla Mujeres. The others are 60–90 minutes south of Cancún, near Playa del Carmen and Tulum. You can buy tickets at the gates, though most people buy them at their hotels or in a travel agency in Cancún so that bus transportation is included in the cost; discounted park tickets also are popular giveaways for taking part in a time-share presentation. For more detailed information about each park, see the *Isla Mujeres* section, the *Riviera Maya* chapter, or the *Tulum and Southern Quintana Roo* chapter.

If you're tired of the hotel pool, check out the **Wet 'n Wild** water park (aka Parque Nizuc, Blvd. Kukulcán Km. 25, tel. 998/881-8000, US$28 Mon.–Sat., US$15 Sun. 10 A.M.–5 P.M. daily). As the name suggests, it offers classics like twisting slippery slides, high-speed water toboggans, and family-size inner tubing—a great way to cool off. The park also has dolphin and sea lion interaction programs (US$70–130 pp) which includes entry to the park. Beware of some hidden charges—inner tubes, lockers, towels—as well as pricey snacks.

SPORT FISHING

More than a dozen species of sport fish ply the waters off Cancún, including blue and white marlin, blackfin tuna, barracuda, dolphin dorado, wahoo, grouper, and more. **Fishing Charters Cancún** (Blvd. Kukulcán Km. 7.5, tel. 998/883-2517, www.fishingcharters.com.mx, 6:30 A.M.–9 P.M. daily) operates a fleet of custom fishing boats, ranging 30–38 feet. Expert anglers can reserve the type and size boat they like and request particular captains; a chart on the website gives peak seasons for 10 species of fish. The boats hold 4–8 people and go out for 4–8 hours; prices range US$385–595 for four hours, and US$585–795 for all day. Individual anglers can sign up for "shared" trips for US$99 pp for four hours or US$115 for six hours. All trips include captain, mates, gear, bait, tackle, drinks, and, in some cases, lunch. Hotel pickup by SUV or boat can be arranged, and the crew will fillet your catch upon return. Reservations required.

Fly-fishing for bonefish, tarpon, snook, and permit is also good in this part of the world. **Villas El Manglar** (Blvd. Kukulcán Km. 19.8, tel. 998/885-1808, www.villasmanglar.com) organizes trips to the shallow waters surrounding Isla Blanca, about 40 minutes away, north of Cancún. The trip costs US$375 for two anglers, runs 5:30 A.M.–4 P.M., and includes equipment, box lunch, and drinks. The hotel will also provide free door-to-door service.

GOLF

With a recent US$6 million face-lift, the **Hilton Cancún Golf Club** (Blvd. Kukulcán Km. 17.5, tel. 998/881-8016, www.hiltoncancun.com) is considered one of the finer courses in the region. This 18-hole par-72 course hugs Laguna Nichupté and boasts Paspalum Sea Isle turf, new landscaping, and even a great view of the Maya ruins El Rey from the 16th hole. Alligators also are rumored to be in one of the water hazards so consider leaving those waterbound balls behind. Green fees are US$199; after 2 P.M. they're US$149. Both rates include a shared golf cart. There's a driving range and putting green to practice all of your strokes. Equipment rental also is available.

The **Cancún Golf Club at Pok-ta-Pok** (Blvd. Kukulcán Km. 7.5, tel. 998/883-1230,

www.cancungolfclub.com) is an 18-hole championship golf course designed by Robert Trent Jones, Jr. The course runs along the Caribbean and the Laguna Nichupté and features its own Maya ruin near the 12th hole, discovered when the course was built. Green fees are US$140 and drop to US$90 after 2 P.M. Rates include a shared golf-cart rental. Clubs and shoes can be rented at the pro shop. Some Zona Hotelera hotels receive discounts—ask your concierge for details.

If you feel like a short round of golf but don't want to shell out the big bucks, there are also two par-3 courses in the Zona Hotelera: **Grand Melia Golf Club** (Blvd. Kukulcán Km. 16.5, tel. 998/881-1100, US$28 green fees) and **Oasis Cancún Golf Club** (Blvd. Kukulcán Km. 16, tel. 998/885-0867, ext. 6277, US$22 green fees). Club rentals are available at both courses too.

If you're willing to travel a bit, you'll find the only Jack Nicklaus course in the region at **Moon Palace Golf & Spa Resort** (Carretera Cancún-Chetumal Km. 340, tel. 998/881-6088, www.palaceresorts.com). Just 15 minutes south of the Zona Hotelera, this resort has three 9-hole courses—each par 36—that make up its impressive 9.9 kilometers (10,798 yards). Green fees are US$260 and include a shared golf cart, snacks, drinks, and a round-trip transfer to the Golf Club. After 2:30 P.M., the green fee drops to US$170 with no perks included. There's also a driving range, a green side bunker, and putting and chipping greens. Club rentals also are available at the pro shop.

TENNIS

Many of the hotels in the Zona Hotelera have their own tennis courts. Most are lit for night play and many are open to nonguests for a fee. Good choices include the **Fiesta Americana Coral Beach** (Blvd. Kukulcán Km. 9.5, tel. 998/881-3200, US$22/hr. indoor clay courts, 7 A.M.–7 P.M. daily, until 9 P.M. Mon.–Fri. high season) and the **Hilton Cancún Beach and Golf Resort** (Retornos Lacandones Km. 17, tel. 998/881-8000, US$20/hr. daytime US$40/hr. after dark). Both have rackets for rent.

JUNGLE TOURS

It sure *looks* as if it would be fun: driving your own personal watercraft or two-person speedboat across the lagoon and through the mangroves to a national marine park where you snorkel with the fishes before returning home. Unfortunately, the rules—Stay in line! Don't go too fast! Don't pass!—keep the boat part pretty predictable and you see very few birds in the mangroves. The snorkeling is also disappointing, with dozens of tourists swarming a dead coral reef that is home to few fish. We don't recommend this sort of trip, but dozens of agencies will gladly take your money (US$55 pp, 2–2.5 hours).

HORSEBACK RIDING

Rancho Loma Bonita (Carretera Cancún-Chetumal, four km/2.5 mi south of Puerto Morelos, tel. 998/887-1708, US$66 adults, US$60 children) is the place to go to ride horses. Tours last two hours and include horseback riding along the beach or into the jungle. Drinks and lunch are included in the rate. Tours start at 9 A.M., noon, and 3 P.M.; there's a free shuttle from Plaza Kukulcán (Blvd. Kukulcán Km. 12.5) at 8 A.M., 10:30 A.M. and 1:30 P.M.—reservations required.

BOWLING AND ARCADES

There's nothing like a couple games of *boliche* (bowling) or *billar* (billiards) in an air-conditioned mall to take the edge off the midday heat and humidity. This one doubles as a bar at night, a unique alternative to Cancún's more frenetic nightlife options. Arcades are in most malls and most are kid-oriented.

This is not your father's bowling alley: **2.02 South** (Plaza Kukulcán, Blvd. Kukulcán Km. 12.5, tel. 998/885-0441, open 11 A.M.–2 A.M. daily) has eight lanes with neon lighting along the medians, several red-carpeted pool tables, a full bar serving every mixed drink imaginable, even a DJ and small dance floor. During the day, kids and adults alike can enjoy bowling (US$6/lane, US$1 shoes) and pool (US$10/hr.), plus a hamburger or half-rack at the Houlihan's-style restaurant.

© LIZA PRADO

Horseback riding on deserted beaches is just one of many excursions available.

Above the food court in Plaza Las Américas, **Recórcholis!** (Av. Tulum at Av. Sayil, 11 A.M.– 11 P.M. daily) offers a fully loaded kids' zone, with video games, air hockey, skeet ball, and other carnival games. There is also an area reserved for children ages 4–10 that has—among other things—jungle gyms, playhouses, and an arts and crafts section.

BODY WORK

The **Centro Naturista Xbalamqué** (Hotel Xbalamqué, Calle Jazmines near Av. Yaxchilán, tel. 998/887-7853, 9 A.M.–8:30 P.M. Mon.–Fri.) offers a full line of massages (US$36–42), body wraps (US$42), and spiritual treatments like Reiki and crystal therapy (US$36–42) in its downtown location. If you prefer to stay in the Zona Hotelera, most hotels either have their own spa or can arrange for an on-site treatment.

Next to Mercado 28, **Tae Kwon Do 28 and Fitness Center** (Av. Xel-Ha 5, tel. 998/884-6765, 6 A.M.–10 P.M. Mon.–Fri.) offers a wide variety of classes, including yoga, spinning, Pilates, kick boxing, and capoeira. Classes cost US$3 per session, but if you're staying longer than a couple of weeks, ask about the monthly rates.

SPANISH CLASSES

El Bosque del Caribe (Av. Nader 52, tel. 998/884-1065, www.cancunlanguage.com, 7:30 A.M.–2 P.M., and 5–7 P.M. Mon.–Fri.) is Cancún's best Spanish language school, with experienced instructors and individual attention. Group classes never exceed six students, and often have just two or three. Group courses are US$195 a week for 25 hours of class (five hours/day Mon.–Fri. mornings), or US$145 a week for 15 hours. Either can be combined with a four-day open-water diving certification course for US$545 or US$495, respectively. Private classes run US$20 an hour or US$340 for 20 hours a week, and are typically held in the afternoon. A US$100 registration fee includes airport pickup and materials, but you can cut it to just US$20 (for books) if you come directly instead of signing up on the Internet. The school can arrange lodging at a great price, whether at the center itself (US$20/night), at a nearby eight-room student house (US$15/night), or with local families (US$23/night with breakfast). Lodgings can fill up in the summer months, so reserve in advance.

Accommodations

Cancún has scores of hotels, varying from backpacker hostels to ultra-high-end resorts. Price usually dictates where people stay, but definitely consider the type of experience you want as well. The most important decision is whether to stay in the Zona Hotelera or downtown. The Zona Hotelera has spectacular views, easy access to glorious beaches, excellent familiar foods, but not much "authentic" interaction with local people. Expect to pay U.S. prices or higher. Downtown Cancún is culturally rich—offering good hotels, varied culinary treats, bohemian music venues, and a great central park. It's less expensive in almost every way from the Zona Hotelera (hotels, restaurants, telephone, Internet) but staying here means taking a bus to the beach and not hav-

ing access to hotel pools and beach clubs. Many locals live and shop in this area, and Mexicans generally outnumber tourists.

Hotel rates are lowest in late spring and early fall; they rise in July and August when Mexicans and Europeans typically take long vacations, and from December to April when many Americans travel. Prices often double between December 15 and New Year's Day, and the week before Easter (*Semana Santa*). The Internet is the best place to find a bargain, especially in the Zona Hotelera—there are some amazing deals in the off-season. Package deals are worth investigating too, but be aware of pseudo-perks such as welcome cocktails or "free" excursions. Most of that stuff you can arrange when you arrive for a fraction of the cost. On the other hand, car rentals, airport pickup, or a free meal or two can be convenient.

ZONA HOTELERA
Under US$150

Although it doesn't appear to have changed much since the mid-1980s, **Hotel Girasol** (Blvd. Kukulcán Km. 9.3, tel. 998/883-5045, hgirasolcun@hotmail.com, US$100 s/d with a/c, US$116 s/d with a/c and kitchenette) offers clean and comfortable rooms with fantastic views of the Caribbean. The beach in front is spectacular and a well-maintained infinity pool does the trick if you want to relax off the sand. Probably the best aspect about this place is its location—just at the end of the nightclub strip—perfect for partying.

Next door, **Condominios Carisa y Palma** (Blvd. Kukulcán Km. 9.4, tel. 998/883-0287 or U.S./Canada tel. 866/521-1787, www.carisaypalma.com, US$106 s/d with a/c) rents out private condominiums with fully equipped kitchenettes. Accommodations vary significantly in style but all are clean and have mag-

nificent views of the ocean or the lagoon. Strangely, some condos feature kitchenettes within a few inches of the bed so make sure you look at your room before moving in. A tennis court and large pool also are on-site.

As the name suggests, **Laguna Suites Golf & Spa** (Paseo Pok-Ta-Pok No. 3, tel. 998/891-5252, toll-free U.S. tel. 800/690-8590, www.lagunasuites.com.mx, US$102 s/d with a/c) is located off the strip, on the Laguna de Nichupté. A restful place, it offers simple but modern rooms with tile floors, cable TV, and air-conditioning. There's a small pool with a chic *palapa* lounge in the center of the property. For quality pool and beach time, guests are better off taking the free shuttle to Laguna Suites' sister hotels—Sunset Royal and Sunset Laguna—both just minutes away. Discounts for the Pok-Ta-Pok golf course and spa also are available.

On the lagoon side of the strip, the quiet **Hotel & Marina El Manglar** (Blvd. Kukulcán Km. 19.8, tel. 998/885-1808, www.villasmanglar.com, US$120 s/d with a/c) has spacious and

© LIZA PRADO

Wake up to impossibly turquoise waters in the Zona Hotelera.

nicely appointed rooms. Each one has a king-size bed and two couches that can double as twin beds—perfect for a family with children. There is a well-maintained pool on-site and daily continental breakfast is served under a *palapa*. If you're interested in fly-fishing or diving, ask at the front desk about booking a trip.

US$150-250

Located on a spectacular beach, ◖ **Omni Cancún Hotel & Villas** (Blvd. Kukulcán Km. 16.2, tel. 998/881-0600, toll-free U.S. tel. 888/444-6664, www.omnihotels.com, US$214–249 s/d with a/c, US$560 suite) has newly renovated rooms, all decorated in a contemporary style with muted colors, marble floors, luxurious linens, and amenities like flat-screen TVs, extra large safes, and minibars. A series of refreshing pools and a mega-Jacuzzi (seating 35) lead to the beach with plenty of *palapa* sunshades. All-inclusive packages are available, though many guests prefer to just eat à la carte at one of the four restaurants and snack bars. Service is top notch—the only downers are the "customer service" agents near the lobby bar who try to rope guests into time-share presentations.

Renovated in 2006, **Casa Magna Marriott Cancun Resort** (Blvd. Kukulcán Km. 14.8, tel. 998/881-2000, toll-free U.S./Canada tel. 800/228-9290, www.marriott.com, US$149–219 s/d with a/c, US$319–339 suite) offers over 400 rooms, all with private terraces, sleek decor, and modern amenities. Guests can choose from five eateries including an Argentinean steak house and a Japanese and Thai restaurant. There's also a full-service spa, two tennis courts with lights, and a gym with separate men's and women's saunas. The main drawback of the hotel is the pool—it's well-maintained but too small; fortunately, it's just steps from the Caribbean, where there's plenty of room to swim. All-inclusive packages are also available.

The **Westin Resort & Spa** (Blvd. Kukulcán Km. 20.2, tel. 998/848-7400, www.westin.com, US$240–289 s/d with a/c) is a minimalist-style hotel with clean lines, square windows, stark white walls, and a splash of color here and there. It's breathtaking. Situated at the southernmost end of the Zona Hotelera, the Westin also is in a prime location—with a beach on the Caribbean, and another on Laguna Nichupté, both lined with *palapas*. There are three impressive pools: two infinity ones ocean-side and one "normal" pool lagoon-side. A full-service spa and two tennis courts also are on-site.

Over US$250

The **Hilton Cancún Beach and Golf Resort** (Blvd. Kukulcán Km. 17, tel. 998/881-8000, www.hilton.com, US$249–299 s/d with a/c, US$319–349 s/d villa) is a classy resort spread luxuriously over 250 acres of land. Cascades encircle the grounds, pools upon pools stretch to the ocean, and seemingly endless windows look out onto the Caribbean and Laguna Nichupté. Rooms range from deluxe standards to ocean front villas. All are decorated similarly in cool blues and whites and feature top-of-the-line amenities. Villas include a light breakfast and a complimentary cocktail hour. Two tennis courts, an 18-hole golf course, a modern gym, and a full-service spa also are open to all guests.

Considered the epitome of luxury, **The Ritz-Carlton** (Blvd. Kukulcán Km.13.9, tel. 998/881-0808, www.ritzcarlton.com, US$459 s/d with a/c, US$679 suite) is unparalleled in its elegance. Fine art, chandeliers, and marble floors greet you the moment the white-gloved porter opens the door for you. Although you may feel like you've entered an ultra-conservative country club, the staff is attentive and friendly, striving to make you feel at home. All 365 rooms have ocean views and balconies and while tastefully appointed, lack the presence that the lobby evokes—it feels like just another high-end hotel room. The two pool areas are nice but unremarkable—the beach, however, is beautifully maintained. The gym is definitely another highlight—kids are even allowed to work out, an unusual plus.

Well located at Punta Cancún, ◖ **Fiesta Americana Grand Coral Beach** (Blvd. Kukulcán Km. 9.5, tel. 998/881-3200, www.fiesta

mericana.com/grand-coralbeach-cancun, US$492–514 s/d junior suites, US$626 s/d Grand Club) is an elegant hotel offering 602 spacious and comfortable suites all with ocean-view balconies. It features a spectacular series of infinity pools, lush and manicured gardens, and views that will leave you breathless. It's set on one of the calmest beaches of the Zona Hotelera, and guests can lounge under one of the many *palapas,* wade into the impossibly clear turquoise water, and enjoy service at one of its five restaurants. Activities such as Spanish lessons, tennis, and free use of a par-72 golf course also are available. Catering to families and older couples, this hotel feels calm and soothing in a sea of rowdy hotels.

All-Inclusive Resorts

The current trend is toward all-inclusive packages, which often include all meals, drinks, activities, taxes, and tips. The deal is a great one if you plan on spending most of your time at your hotel, but if you stay for more than a few days, it can get tiresome.

The adults-only **Blue Bay Getaway and Spa** (Blvd. Kukulcán 3.5, tel. 998/848-7900, www.bluebayscancun.com, US$143–158 pp) is a perfect place for 20- and 30-somethings looking to be in a racy atmosphere. Along with five restaurants to choose from, three pools to play in, and a discotheque and spa on-site, Blue Bay also offers daily games in which losers have to give up most of their clothes, kissing games in which the most outrageous kiss wins, and inventive sexual position games (with swimsuits on, of course). Toplessness also is invited on the premises. The resort itself is basic but nice enough—the rooms are simple, the pools are well maintained, and the stretch of beach, though nowhere near the nicest on the strip, is decent. The biggest complaint? Weak drinks. Ask for them strong.

Hotel Riu Palace Las Americas (Blvd. Kukulcán Km. 8.5, tel. 998/891-4300, www .riu.com, US$197–274 pp) is the most elegant of the three Riu hotels in the Zona Hotelera. A starkly white complex, you'll feel as if you've been transported to a Victorian-age hotel: crys-

tal chandeliers, gilt-framed mirrors, mahogany detailing, bronze statutes, and an enormous stained-glass ceiling. The 368 junior and full suites are not quite as impressive but nice nonetheless; each has a separate sitting area, a minibar that's restocked every day, and amenities that you'd expect from a high-end hotel (e.g., satellite TV, air-conditioning, hair dryer, in-room safe). The biggest complaint guests seem to have with the rooms are the ultra-firm beds—be sure to ask for a foam topper if it's an issue. Outside of the rooms, the beach is narrow but the two infinity pools, endless water activities, six restaurants, and five bars make for many repeat customers.

Occupying the southernmost tip of the Zona Hotelera's long ocean-facing leg, **Club Med Cancún** (Blvd. Kukulcán Km. 20.6, tel. 998/881-8200, toll-free U.S. tel. 888/932-2582, www.clubmed.com, US$685 s, US$830 d, club membership required, US$60/year adult, US$30/year child) has a secluded feel that is rare on the strip. Secluded, however, does not mean boring. A huge variety of activities ranging from sailboarding and water skiing to learning to trapeze to salsa dancing, with instruction if you need it, are included. And if you've got kids, the Mini-club keeps the little ones happy and busy all day long with things like tennis lessons, tie-dying, and performing in variety shows. Two excellent restaurants, a snack bar, and free-flowing drinks assure that all guests are kept full and happy.

DOWNTOWN HOTELS
Under US$25

Opened in 2005, **⬤ Hostal Haina** (Orquídeas 13, tel. 998/898-2081, www.hainahostal.com, US$11 dorm, US$39 s/d with a/c)is the best budget option in town. Dorms are spotless and have bunks with thick mattresses, plenty of fans, and gleaming bathrooms. Private lockers, linens, towels, and soap are included. Private rooms are equally as comfortable but with the added features of mini-split air-conditioning, cable TV, and small fridges. All guests receive a hearty continental breakfast, and have access to a fully equipped Mexican-tile kitchen.

Common lounge areas are welcoming too—a leafy, well-tended garden as well as two TV rooms. All in all, a sure thing.

Mexica Hostel (formerly Mexico Hostel, Palmera 30, 998/887-0191, www.mexicohostels .com.mx, US$10 dorm, US$32.50 d) is the new name of Cancún's longest-running hostel, still the go-to spot for backpackers here. The hostel was bought and renamed by, of all people, the owner of The Weary Traveler in Tulum, and basic features like free hearty breakfasts, a fully equipped kitchen, and storage lockers haven't changed a bit. The hostel's interior is as labyrinthine as ever, with dorm rooms, large and small, all with heavy-duty fans, squeezed into every nook and cranny. That doesn't leave much room for common space, but a bar is being built alongside the rooftop kitchen and dining area. What the hostel doesn't lack—and what keeps travelers coming—is that worldly, outgoing, traveler-friendly ambiance that you just can't get in a hotel.

Run by a friendly family from Veracruz, **The Nest** (Alcatraces at Margaritas, tel. 998/884-8967, mjkglobal@yahoo.com, US$12 dorm, US$14 dorm with a/c, US$37 s/d with a/c) is a remodeled one-story house, offering single-sex and mixed dorms as well as one private room. In the summertime, the dorms with air-conditioning are worth the extra two bucks—your sweat glands will thank you. The Nest also has a huge and well-equipped kitchen, a TV room, wireless Internet access, and laundry service. Lockers and a hearty continental breakfast are included in the rates.

Club Hostel (Orquídeas 7, tel. 998/892-3384, US$11 dorm with a/c, US$23 s/d with shared bathroom and a/c, US$33–37 s/d with a/c) is the perfect name for this hostel, which feels more like a frat house than a guest house: X-box tournaments in the TV room, guys lounging on couches, an empty pool in back, a messy kitchen. The rooms themselves are pretty comfortable though—even the dorms have thick beds, mini-split air-conditioning, and hot water. Everyone gets a continental breakfast during the high season

too. An excellent deal, especially if this feels like home.

Run by a friendly family, **Mayan Hostel** (Margaritas 17, tel. 998/892-0103, www.cancunhostel. com, US$11 dorm, US$35 s/d, US$40 s/d with a/c) offers dorms and private rooms, most with *palapa* roofs and direct access to a leafy rooftop lounge, creating a beachy feel in the middle of downtown Cancún. The accommodations are very clean—dorms have bunks and include sheets and a locker—though bathrooms are showing some wear. A common rooftop kitchen is fully equipped and kept up nicely. Purified water and continental breakfast are included in the rate. English and German spoken.

For a proper hotel, the **Hotel San Carlos** (Cedro 28, tel. 998/884-0602, www.hotelsan-carloscancun.com, US$18.50 s, US$28 s with TV, US$32.50 s/d with a/c, US$35 t with fan) offers perfectly adequate rooms, with clean private bathrooms and tiny balconies looking onto the market below. The balconies have flowers—all right, they're fake—and bright paint to cheer up the otherwise aging walls. The beds are a bit hard, and the cheapest rooms have no windows (avoid those if you can) but this isn't a bad option, all in all. Located five blocks north of the bus terminal; an Internet café on the ground level charges US$1 an hour.

US$25-50

A great little hotel on a quiet street, **⟨ Los Girasoles** (Piña 20, tel. 998/887-3990, los-girasolescancun@hotmail.com, US$37 s/d with kitchenette and a/c) offers 18 spotless and colorful rooms with kitchenettes. Rooms are sunny and have wood and ironwork furnishings. Air-conditioning, cable TV, wireless Internet, and friendly service make it an especially pleasant place to stay.

Once a solid option for budget travelers, **Hotel Punta Allen** (Punta Allen 8, tel. 998/884-0225, www.puntaallen.da.ru, US$45 s/d with a/c) is now a hit-or-miss experience. Rooms are basically clean but some are missing toilet seats, have chipping walls, and worn floors. The ones in back, while dark, are better maintained—it's amazing what a coat of paint and new curtains can do to a room. The biggest plus about the place is its location—just half a block from the bar and restaurant scene.

Opening onto a lively pedestrian walkway lined with shops and restaurants, **Hotel Colonial** (Tulipanes 22, tel. 998/884-1535, hotel-colonialcancun@hotmail.com, www.hotelcolonial.com, US$32.50 s/d with fan, US$37 s/d with a/c) is a decent option if every penny counts. The rooms are dark and no frills, but they're clean, have hot water, and the bright bedspreads cheer up the place just a bit. Besides the nightly rate, the location is, without a doubt, its biggest draw.

Next to Chedraui supermarket, **Soberanis Hostal** (Av. Cobá near Av. Tulum, tel. 998/884-4564, www.soberanis.com.mx, US$49 s/d with a/c, US$12 dorm with a/c) offers minimalist-style rooms with sleek wood furnishings and tile floors. All have cable TV, telephone, and security boxes. Four small single-sex dorms are a steal, with two bunk beds apiece, lockers, and private bathrooms. Be sure to ask for a room toward the back of the building as street noise can border on unbearable. Continental breakfast is included in all the rates. A discount is available by showing this guidebook or your ISIC card.

Suites El Patio (Av. Bonampak 51, tel. 998/884-3500, www.cancun-suites.com, US$50 s, US$62 d) is a charming colonial hotel with clean, airy rooms decorated with Mexican tiles and hand-carved wardrobes. Although it's seemingly in the middle of nowhere, the bus headed directly to the Zona Hotelera stops a few blocks from its front door and downtown Cancún is only minutes away by foot. Continental breakfast is served in the lush outdoor patio or in the common room, which has board games, books, and several decks of cards.

US$50-100

Bougainvillea and a gurgling fountain welcome you to the excellent C **Hotel El Rey del Caribe** (Av. Uxmal at Nader, tel. 998/884-2028, www.reycaribe.com, US$53 s, 63 d, most with kitchenette), an eco-friendly hotel two blocks east of the bus terminal. Rooms are clean and comfortable (if a bit plain), but it's the verdant tropical garden with hammocks, pool, and an outdoor dining area with beautiful hardwood flooring that make this such a memorable place—you might even forget for a moment you're in the city. The hotel employs solar heating, rainwater recovery, and organic waste composting. Definitely think about treating yourself to a milk-and-honey massage offered poolside.

Conveniently located kitty-corner to the bus station, **Hotel Kin Mayab** (Av. Tulum 75, tel. 998/884-2999, www.hotelkinmayab.com, US$45–51 s/d with a/c) offers 45 rooms in two buildings. All are clean and air-conditioned, with heavy wood furnishings, stenciled walls, and tile floors. The ones in the main building are a bit bigger and open onto a bright interior courtyard with lots of hanging plants and comfy chairs; the rooms in the adjacent building are set up like a motel, opening directly onto the hotel's T-shaped pool, garden, and *palapa*. Either way, be sure to ask for a room facing away from Avenida Tulum—the street noise can get pretty loud, especially in the early morning.

Located in the heart of downtown, **Hotel Antillano** (Claveles at Av. Tulum, tel. 998/884-1132, www.hotelantillano.com, US$55 s, US$72 d) offers 48 air-conditioned, very 1980s-style rooms. Though all are reasonably comfortable, rooms facing the interior courtyard are much quieter. A well-maintained pool is a bonus, as is the daily continental breakfast. Seniors: be sure to ask for a discount.

The **Hotel Xbalamqué** (Av. Yaxchilán 31, tel. 998/884-0699, www.xbalamque.com, US$60 s/d with a/c, US$80 suite, including light breakfast) goes further than any other to remind you you're in Maya country: imposing replicas of Maya statues and stelae decorate the common areas and complement the impressive mural in the main lobby and many corridors. Rooms are showing their age, but still comfortable and decorated in traditional Mexican decor and tile inlaid floors. In back, a lush pool complete with waterfall makes for a restful escape, and a small spa offers a variety of massages and treatments (guests receive 10 percent off). A bohemian coffeehouse is also on the premises, offering nightly live music. Contrary to some travelers' expectations, the hotel does not have a beach club in the Zona Hotelera, but has half-off passes for The City's beach club.

Over US$100

Directly across from the bus station, **Hotel Plaza Caribe** (Av. Tulum at Av. Uxmal, tel. 998/884-1377, www.hotelplazacaribe.com, US$102 s/d with a/c) offers comfortable, somewhat characterless rooms with air-conditioning, cable TV, and wireless Internet. All open onto two lush court-yards—one with a pool, the other with a playground—plus a reliable *palapa*-roofed restaurant. Ultimately, you'll get more bang from your buck elsewhere, but the Plaza Caribe's location can't be beat if you're traveling by bus, especially if you arrive late or have an early morning departure.

In the middle of the Yaxchilán strip, **Hotel Margaritas** (Av. Yaxchilán 41, tel. 998/884-9333, ventashic@sybcom.com, US$104 s/d with a/c) offers dated though sunny rooms with bright bedspreads and marble floors. Some are a bit musty, but once you get the air-conditioning running, the smell should diminish. The hotel also offers a pleasant pool and an open-air restaurant. Well-located for the action downtown.

Food

Cancún has dozens of excellent restaurants. Seafood is the area specialty, but you'll find a full range of options, from Cajun to Japanese, vegetarian to Argentinean steak houses. The finest restaurants are in the Zona Hotelera, mostly along the west side of Boulevard Kukulcán or in the high-end hotels. You'll also find several very good restaurants in the malls, believe it or not. Eating out in the Zona Hotelera is by no means cheap—lobster fetches U.S. prices or higher. The malls have some cheapish eats, mostly fast food such as Subway, McDonald's, and Burger King, and we've included a few budget restaurants as well. Downtown Cancún, just a short cab or bus ride away, is the place to go for good sit-down restaurants that won't blow your budget, though up-scale diners will find a number of satisfying places to eat there as well.

MEXICAN

This is the category where you will find the widest price range, from upscale restaurants to good cheap eateries.

Zona Hotelera

With great views of the lagoon, especially at sunset, **(La Destilería** (Blvd. Kukulcán Km. 12.5, tel. 998/885-1086, 2 P.M.–11 daily, US$11–25) serves inventive Mexican food, including cilantro fish fillet, tenderloin medallions in chipotle sauce, and shrimp cooked with tequila and lime. Speaking of tequila, the restaurant has more than 150 types of the agave-derived drink and even offers a guided "tequila tour" (5:30 P.M. Mon., Wed., Fri., US$5), with an explanation of tequila brewing and an option to order sample tastings (at additional cost). Dinner, appetizers, and drinks can add up to a hefty outlay here, but it's worth the expense. Reservations recommended.

El Mortero (Blvd. Kukulcán Km. 8.9, tel. 998/848-9800, 6–11 P.M. daily, US$18–35) is a replica of an 18th-century hacienda, complete with a fountain on the patio and roving mariachis. Grilled dishes are the specialty, from huge steaks for two to *camaron al pastor*—literally "shepherd's shrimp," a tasty recipe using red adobo chili that has been adapted from a perennial favorite at roadside taco stands. Served, as it should be, with pineapple slices.

Overlooking Playa Caracol, **Paloma Bonita** (Punta Cancún, Blvd. Kukulcán Km. 8.8, tel. 998/848-7082, 6:30 P.M.–11:30 P.M. Mon.–Sat, noon–11:30 P.M. Sun., US$12–35) is a real find, serving creative Mexican dishes in three lovely dining rooms. Try the quail in rose-petal sauce or pork loin wrapped in banana leaf, seasoned with *achiote* seed, a spice used by the Mayas. There are also a dozen different types of homemade *mole,* a classic Mexican sauce originally made from chocolate and served over chicken, pork, or beef. The restaurant has live music, usually mariachi or marimba, 6:45–10:30 P.M. daily.

Downtown

On the southeast corner of Parque Las Palapas, **Restaurante Los Huaraches de Alcatraces** (Alcatraces 31, tel. 998/884-3918, 8 A.M.–6:30 P.M. Tues.–Sun., entrées US$3–5) is a nice place for lunch or early dinner. Served cafeteria-style, traditional Mexican dishes, such as garlic-baked fish or chicken in homemade mole, come with a choice of two sides, such as veggies or beans. There are some pre-Hispanic options, too, such as quesadillas made with blue-corn tortillas.

If Disneyland ever created a Mexican Revolution ride, it would surely look like **Pericos** (Av. Yaxchilán 61, tel. 998/884-3152, open noon–midnight daily, US$13–25), one of downtown Cancún's most well-known restaurants. In a huge eating area bedecked in Revolution-era photos and classic Mexican artwork, *bandito* waiters sport headbands and criss-crossed ammo belts, the bar has saddles instead of stools, there are not one but two gift shops, and kids may get a rubber chicken on their plates as a joke. Low-key it's not, but Pericos has a solid reputation for serving good grilled meats, seafood, and fish in a boisterous, family-friendly atmosphere. Daily live music includes marimba that plays 7:30–10:30 P.M. and a roving mariachi band that begins playing at 10:30 P.M.

El Oasis (Alcatraces 57, no phone, 7 A.M.–4 P.M. Mon.–Sat.) is a simple downtown eatery operated out of the front yard of the cook's home. Tasty *tortas* and hamburgers run US$1–2, main dishes with chicken or pork are US$3–4.

Your heart won't be pleased, but your belly sure will be at **◖ Don Javier's Quesadillas** (Parque Las Palapas, 8 A.M.–midnight daily), a street-corner institution in Cancún's appealing central plaza. Day or night you can get Yucatecan snacks like *sopes, panuchos, salbutes,* tostadas, and—of course—quesadillas. All items come with your choice of a dozen stuffings, including *nopales* (cactus), *rajas* (sautéed chile), mushrooms, or potatoes. All items cost just under a buck. Two items will satisfy a small appetite, four might push you over the edge.

SEAFOOD

Almost every restaurant in Cancún serves seafood, regardless of the particular genre. The following are ones that specialize in seafood, especially lobster.

Zona Hotelera

At **Lorenzillo's** (Blvd. Kukulcán Km. 10.5, tel. 998/883-1254, www.lorenzillos.com.mx, 1 P.M.–midnight daily, US$18–45), live lobster is kept in an adapted rowboat at the entrance—select the one you want, weigh it on an old-time scale, and before long, dinner is served. Smaller tables line the narrow patio overlooking the lagoon and have small bowls with pellets to throw to the blue trumpet fish schooling below you. More upscale than its sister restaurant next door, Lorenzillo's doesn't have a kid's menu and isn't great for families. Prices are steep, especially on wine and specials.

The owners of **The Plantation House** (Blvd. Kukulcán Km. 10.5, tel. 998/883-1433, www.plantationhouse.com.mx, 1 P.M.–midnight daily, US$16–33) could have picked a more sensitive name, but they could hardly do better with the island-style seafood and ambience. The house specialty is the seafood *sabre* (sable): lobster or shrimp grilled on a small sword, kabob-like. As if that weren't enough, the grill is in a kiosk in the lagoon—live fish or lobster are rowed over in a little boat, and rowed back to your table when cooked. Lorenzillo's, a slightly more upscale sister restaurant, is next door.

Downtown

One of downtown's finest restaurants, **◖ La Habichuela** (Calle Margaritas 25 at Parque Las

Palapas, tel. 998/884-3158, www.lahabichuela. com, noon–midnight daily) has been serving excellent Caribbean and Mexican dishes since 1977. The seafood here is especially good—try the giant shrimp in tamarind sauce or *cocobichuela,* the house specialty, with lobster and shrimp in a sweet Caribbean curry. For dessert, the Maya coffee flambé is a treat. Dishes range US$13–27.

Facing the Mercado 28 parking lot, (**Pescado Con Limón** (Mercado 28, tel. 887-2436, 11:30 A.M.–7:30 P.M. daily, US$5–9) is a popular stop. Not a fancy place—patrons sit at plastic tables and chairs—the seafood is as fresh and good as it comes. Try a shrimp dish or one of the fried fish platters for a taste treat that has locals and expatriates returning regularly.

ITALIAN
Zona Hotelera

(**La Dolce Vita** (Blvd. Kukulcán Km. 14.6 across from the Marriott Hotel, tel. 998/885-0161, www.cancunitalianrestaurant.com, noon–11:30 P.M., US$14–26) was the first stop in a January 2006 *New York Times* article called "36 Hours in Cancun." No surprise: this award-winning Italian restaurant and Cancún institution has excellent service and inventive dishes, including veal ravioli in rosemary sauce and *boquinete Dolce Vita:* white snapper stuffed with shrimp and mushrooms and baked in light golden pastry. The atmosphere is casual but elegant, and there's live jazz nightly except Sunday. It can get busy, so reservations are recommended. La Dolce Vita Centro, a downtown location (Av. Cobá 87 at Av. Nader, tel. 998/884-3393, noon–midnight), has similar prices and dishes.

Fantino's, at the Ritz Carlton Hotel (Retorno del Rey 36, tel. 988/881-0808, 7 A.M.–11 P.M. Mon.–Sat., US$30–60) is an extremely refined Italian-Mediterranean restaurant, and one of few places in laid-back Cancún with a dress code: slacks, collared shirt, and dress shoes for men. The intimate room—it has only 16 tables—is the epitome of elegance with plush chairs, gilt mirrors, heavy curtains, and a spectacular ocean view (get here before the sunset to

see it!). Choose a main dish (such as Chilean sea bass in caramelized onions or lamb with basil risotto) or order a four-, six-, or nine-course tasting menu. It's not cheap: the nine-course menu with wines runs a cool US$208.

The chic decor and terrific food at **La Madonna** (Plaza La Isla, Blvd. Kukulcán Km. 12.5, tel. 998/883-2222, noon–midnight, US$15–25, US$28–42) will have you wondering "Are we really in a mall?" A huge modern replica of the Mona Lisa peers over a classy dining room with fine fixtures and settings. The Swiss and Italian menu includes veal, shrimp fettuccini, and risotto, plus specials such as live lobster and New Zealand lamb. Doubling as a martini bar (with 150 different martinis to choose from), this is also a nice place to stop for a mid-mall drink.

Downtown

Rolandi's (Av. Cobá 12, tel. 988/884-4047, 1 P.M.–midnight, US$6.50–13) is a Cancún institution, with sister pizzerias in the Zona Hotelera and Isla Mujeres. The food here—and at all of them—is consistently good; choose among thin-crust pizzas, calzones, and great homemade pastas. Pocket bread, warm and inflated right from the oven, and a dish of olive oil comes with every order—a nice touch. The atmosphere is casual; an easy-to-miss veranda in the rear has trellises draped in ivy, blocking out street noise.

Just half a block from Parque Palapas, **Trattoria La Veneziana** (Tulipanes near Av Tulum, tel. 998/860-5863, 4 P.M.–1 A.M. Mon.–Sat., 2 P.M.–1 A.M. Sun., US$5–11) offers authentic Italian cuisine—over 15 pasta dishes and 20 pizza combinations—with authentic Italian spirit. Service is boisterous and friendly and the setup is sidewalk casual. A tasty, affordable alternative on a balmy night.

MEAT LOVERS
Zona Hotelera

Puerto Madero (Blvd. Kukulcán Km. 14.1, tel. 998/885-2829, www.puertomaderocancun.com, 1 P.M.–1 A.M. daily, US$15–45) is a cool, classy place serving extremely fresh and carefully prepared meats in huge Argentinean-style portions. The dining rooms have dark bricks and exposed iron beams, reminiscent of a shipyard warehouse (in a good way), and there's an elegant half-moon patio. The menu includes salads, pastas, and grilled fish, in addition to the many cuts of beef, some of which serve two.

The name of the place says it all— **Cambalanche Argentinean Big Steak House** (Forum by the Sea, 2nd Fl., Blvd. Kukulcán Km. 9, tel. 998/883-0902, 1 P.M.–1 A.M. daily, US$20–30). Excellent, huge cuts of beef serve two or more; the rib eye and top sirloin likely will leave you panting. The subdued ambience, frosted glass, and tuxedoed waiters help you forget the fact that, yes, you're in a mall. Pricey but worth it.

Ruth's Chris Steak House (Plaza Kukulcán, Blvd. Kukulcán Km. 12.5, tel. 988/885-0500, 1–11:30 P.M. daily, US$28–50) will already be familiar to steak aficionados, serving its signature USDA corn-fed Midwestern beef. Plaza Kukulcán underwent a major renovation in 2005, and Ruth's got dolled up too: guests now sip drinks in a demure lounge while waiting for a table in the sunken dining area.

Downtown

La Parrilla (Av. Yaxchilán 51, tel. 998/287-8118, 12:30 P.M.–2 A.M. Mon.–Thurs., 12:30 P.M.–4 A.M. Fri.–Sat., 12:30 P.M.–1 A.M. Sun., US$8.50–25) is one of the most popular of the restaurant-bars on this busy street, grilling a variety of delicious beef fillets, plus shrimp and lobster brochettes, chicken, fajitas, and tacos—the fiery spit in front is for *taquitos al pastor,* a Mexican classic. The breezy streetside eating area is comfortable and casual—good for families.

LIGHT FARE
Zona Hotelera

Deli-mart (Punta Cancún, Blvd. Kukulcán Km. 8.8, tel. 998/883-3818, 7 A.M.–11 P.M. daily, US$5–11) serves basic, affordable meals, from sandwiches and fries to fajitas and pasta dishes. A small outdoor eating area usually has a soccer game on the TV, and there's a full bar with a happy hour that runs from 6 P.M. to 8 P.M. The market has pre-made sandwiches, plus basics like chips, soda, water, and sunscreen. Nothing too memorable, but it's one of few genuinely cheap places to eat in the Zona Hotelera.

With locations in the Zona Hotelera and downtown, **100% Natural** (Blvd. Kukulcán Km. 9.5, tel. 998/883-1580, 8 A.M.–midnight daily, entrées US$5–11) is a well-known stop for travelers and locals alike. Popular for its fruit salads, veggie sandwiches, and freshly squeezed juices, it makes a great option for those seeking vegetarian meals. The downtown branch is located on Avenida Sunyaxchén at Avenida Yaxchilán (tel. 998/884-3617, 7 A.M.–10:30 P.M. daily).

Downtown

Part of the Hotel Xbalamqué downtown, **El Pabilo** (Av. Yaxchilán 31, tel. 998/892-4553, 8 A.M.–midnight, US$3.50–8), describes itself as a *cafebrería,* a classy but unassuming combination café, bookstore, and art gallery. Indeed, you can get excellent coffee and light meals here, and enjoy rotating exhibits and books in various languages, many for sale. Better still, every night but Sunday starting at 9 P.M., you're treated to great live music, a different genre each night from *bohemia cubana* to fusion jazz.

In nearby Parque Las Palapas, **El D'Pa** (Margaritas at Gladiolas, tel. 998/884-7615, 1 P.M.–1 A.M. Tue.–Sun., US$4–10) is an eclectic French-inspired restaurant offering creative crepes, baguettes, quiches, and salads. While the outdoor seating is great for people watching, the charming interior is worth a look—turn-of-the-20th-century prints, antiques, lamps with feathers, and even a pink sofa might just lure you in.

Also downtown, get a great baguette sandwich at **Ty-Coz Baguettería** (Av. Tulum at Av. Uxmal, tel. 998/884-6060, 8 A.M.–9 P.M. Mon.–Sat.), a small agreeable shop tucked behind the Comercial Mexicana supermarket opposite the bus terminal. Popular with local professionals and students, the menu includes

French- and German-inspired baguette sandwiches and *cuernos* (literally horns, they're large stuffed croissants). Most are US$3–5, but you can always order the *económica* with ham, salami and cheese for just US$1.25.

OTHER SPECIALTIES
Zona Hotelera

Classy but unassuming, **⟨ Laguna Grill** (Blvd. Kukulcán Km. 15.6, tel. 998/885-0267, www.lagunagrill.com.mx, 2 P.M.–midnight, bar area 6 P.M.–1:30 A.M., US$15–30) has an excellent lagoon-side patio with tables set well apart, diminishing the bustle found at other Zona Hotelera restaurants. The tables themselves are made of varnished tree trunks, with iron chairs and attractive glass candleholders. Contemporary gourmet offerings include sesame blackened ahi tuna with asparagus, and grilled lamb chops with pasta, grapes, and goat cheese. The bar has old-time armchairs and sofas set on a breezy deck.

Blue Bayou (Hyatt Cancún, Blvd. Kukulcán Km. 10.5, tel. 998/884-7800, 6:30–10:30 P.M. daily, US$12–30) is an award-winning Cajun restaurant, with dishes such as blackened grouper and "sailfish Mississippi"—grilled sailfish with mushroom-sauce risotto and vegetables. Chicken and meat dishes are also available. The space has dozens of hanging plants, and tables are set along a circular slow-sloping ramp, allowing maximum intimacy in the relatively small space. Enjoy great live jazz starting at 8 P.M. nightly; reservations recommended.

Hard Rock Café (Forum by the Sea mall, Blvd. Kukulcán Km. 9, tel. 998/881-2020, 11 A.M.–2 A.M. daily, US$10–20) has a dress code, which is that you must wear a shirt *and* shoes after 10 P.M. Otherwise, the place is pretty casual. Burgers, big sandwiches, and chicken-fried-chicken are popular, served with fries in a two-level circular eating area. Most tables have a view of the stage, where live rock bands play nightly. During the day, eat out on the outdoor deck, which overlooks the beach.

Rainforest Cafe (Forum by the Sea mall, Blvd. Kukulcán Km. 9, tel. 998/881-8130, 10 A.M.–1:30 A.M. daily, US$10–22) doesn't offer the best American fare in town but it is a fantastic place to take your kids. Trumpeting elephants, giant flapping butterflies, and life-sized gorillas set in a rainforest-themed room will have your children giggling within minutes. Be sure to keep an eye out for the resident clown, who entertains the young clientele while they're waiting for their burgers and shakes.

Downtown

⟨ Roots Jazz Club (Tulipanes 26, tel. 998/884-2437, 6 P.M.–1 A.M. Tues.–Sat., US$6–15) has good service and a varied menu with anything from hearty green salads to squid stuffed with cheese in a tomato and mango sauce. But the best reason to come is the great live jazz played from a small stage.

Great for a change of pace, **Sahara** (Calle Gladiolas, tel. 998/149-1492, noon–midnight Tue.–Sun, US$5–12) offers authentic Lebanese food in a casual setting. Traditional favorites like hummus, falafel, and tabbouleh are featured front and center but consider ordering a hookah hookup (so to speak, US$7) or having your coffee grounds read (US$10, including the coffee).

On the edge of Mercado 28, **Restaurante Taj Majal** (2nd Fl., tel. 998/887-6758, noon–10 P.M. daily, entrées US$7–11) has a good sampling of dishes from around India. While connoisseurs of Indian fare won't be blown away, the selection is tasty and especially ample for vegetarians.

SWEETS
Downtown

Pastelería Italiana (Av. Yaxchilán 67, tel. 998/884-0796, 8:30 A.M.–10 P.M. Mon.–Sat., 1–8 P.M. Sun.) offers good coffee and a large selection of fresh cakes—US$2 a slice, US$13–17 whole cakes—served at comfortable outdoor tables. Yaxchilán is a busy avenue, but a long awning and tall plants help block out the noise.

Boulangerie Patisserie Bordeaux (Av. Tulum at Av. Uxmal, tel. 998/887 6219, 9 A.M.–5 P.M. Mon.–Sat., 8 A.M.–4 P.M. Sun.) offers fresh-baked Danish pastries, cakes, and homemade chocolates, most for around US$0.50 apiece. There are no tables, so you have to take it to go. It's a bit hidden, on a narrow street behind Comercial Mexicana, a few doors past Ty-Coz sandwich shop.

GROCERIES
Zona Hotelera
If you just want to stock up for a picnic on the beach, numerous small markets along Boulevard Kukulcán in the Zona Hotelera have chips, water, and sunscreen and other basics. For a more complete grocery, head to **Super Express** (Plaza Quetzal, just west of Hotel Presidente-Intercontinental, Blvd. Kukulcán Km. 8, tel. 998/883-3654, 8 A.M.–11 P.M. daily), which has canned food, meats, fruit and veggies, bread, chips, drinks, and more.

Downtown
For mega-supermarkets with everything from in-house bakeries to snorkel gear, head to the downtown locales of **Chedraui** (Blvd. Kukulcán at Av. Tulum, 7 A.M.–11 P.M. daily) and **Comercial Mexicana** (Av. Tulum at Uxmal, 7 A.M.–midnight daily). Both supermarkets have ATMs just inside their doors.

Just a couple of blocks from the bus station, **Mercado 23** (Calles Ciricote and Cedro, three blocks north of Av. Uxmal via Calle Palmeras, 6 A.M.–6 P.M.) has stands of fresh fruits and vegetables, and almost none of the touristy trinkets that Mercado 28 has. The selection is somewhat limited, but the produce is the freshest around.

DINNER CRUISES
Operated by Dolphin Discovery, the **Lobster Dinner Cruise** (tel. 998/849-4748, www.the lobsterdinner.com, US$79 dinner and open bar, no children under 12 years, departures 5 P.M. and 8 P.M. nightly) serves three-course lobster and steak dinners aboard an 18.3-meter (60-foot) galleon. The ship cruises the lagoon at sunset or under a starry night sky, while diners enjoy the sounds of a soft jazz saxophone. Reservations required.

If the Lobster Dinner cruise sounds too staid, the **Galleon of Captain Hook** (El Embarcadero, Blvd. Kukulcán Km. 4.5, tel. 998/849-4451, www.capitanhook.com, US$67 steak, US$77 lobster or surf-and-turf, children ages 5–12 half price, under five free, 7–10:30 P.M. nightly) offers a larger, more boisterous alternative, including costumed crew members and a pitched pirate "battle" against an enemy galleon while cruising the bay.

Operated by AquaWorld, the **Cancún Queen** (Blvd. Kukulcán Km. 15.5, tel. 998/848-8300, www.aquaworld.com.mx, US$43 fish or chicken, US$65 surf & turf, including open bar) is the only dinner cruise aboard a paddle steamer. Meals are served in an air-conditioned dining room, and there's live music and dancing on the deck, all while the old-time river boat makes a three-hour tour of Laguna Nichupté. Departures are Wednesdays and Fridays at 5 P.M., or 6 P.M. in the summer. Reservations recommended.

Information and Services

TOURIST INFORMATION
Downtown, the **Tourist Office** (Palacio Municipal, Av. Tulum 5, tel. 998/881-2800 ext. 2175, www.cancun.gob.mx, 9 A.M.–4 P.M. Mon.–Fri.) is a bustling office with staffers who happily provide information on city and regional sights. A kiosk just outside of the office has brochures and maps. English spoken.

In the Zona Hotelera, try your luck with the **Secretaría Estatal de Turismo** (State Tourism Department, Convention Center, 1st Fl., tel. 988/881-9000, 9 A.M.–5 P.M. Mon.–Fri., 9 A.M.–1 P.M. Sat.)—it's tough to get useful information but occasionally it has maps and tourist magazines.

There are also several excellent publications that are worth picking up to supplement the information in this book: *Cancún Tips* is a free tourist information booklet available in many hotels and shops; *Restaurante Menu Mapa* is one of several ubiquitous brochures put out by

GETTING MARRIED IN CANCÚN

If you are thinking of getting married in Cancún – congratulations! In México, most weddings have two parts: a religious ceremony, which traditionally takes place in church – but can really take place anywhere – and a civil ceremony, which must be conducted by a judge. You can have the civil ceremony at the judge's office, or pay extra for him to come to the wedding site. The two ceremonies don't have to be on the same day, though the civil, not the religious, marks your "official" marriage date. The paperwork can be a bit time-consuming – definitely plan ahead – but many foreign couples come away having unexpectedly enjoyed the process. As weddings get more creative – on the beach, officiated by your best friend, with vows you wrote yourself and set to music – a civil wedding can provide a reassuring stamp of officialdom to the undertaking. If nothing else, your folks will appreciate it, and it's another chance to say "I do." Here's what's involved:

Go to a Registro Civil office (Calle Margaritas at Parque Las Palapas, tel. 998/884-9522, 9 A.M.–1 P.M. and 1-4 P.M. Mon.-Fri.) and request a list of the documents you will both need to submit. In Cancún, as in most cities, these include:

- Copies of your passport and valid visa (tourist visa is okay).

- Copies of the passports and valid visas (if not Mexican citizens) of two witnesses who will attend the service.

- A recently issued copy (six months or less) of your birth certificate plus an *apostille*, an internationally recognized certification. You typically obtain new birth certificates from the city you were born in, and then send it to a state office for the *apos-*

tille. Both must be translated into Spanish by an official translator; the Registro Civil will give you a list of its approved translators. Bring the originals and one copy of each. (There are a few special rules if either of you is divorced, widowed, or a Mexican citizen; ask the Registro Civil for details.)

- Certified blood test, which checks for reproductive compatibility and several infectious diseases, including HIV/AIDS. The Registro Civil has a list of clinics that perform prenuptial exams, which must be done no more than 15 days before the ceremony.

The Registro Civil needs at least three days to process your documents once they are all in order. Then make an appointment for the civil service. You can get married at the office (US$285), or have the judge come to your hotel or ceremony site (US$305); if one of you is a Mexican citizen, the costs are US$93 and US$103, respectively. Hold off on the champagne – neither you nor the witnesses are allowed to have consumed alcohol before the ceremony (and you cannot change witnesses once the forms are submitted). The ceremony takes around 30 minutes and consists mostly of the judge making declarations, and you, your witnesses, and your parents (if present) signing numerous forms, even taking fingerprints.

Once you're married, there's just one last hoop to jump through. After your ceremony, stop at the Registro Civil and order a few copies of your marriage certificate. Be sure to ask about getting *apostilles* – you'll need them back home to prove your marriage was genuine.

¡Felicidades!

Cancún Travel (www.cancuntravel.com); this one has maps, restaurant menus, and reviews and discount coupons. *Map@migo* also has maps and coupons. The state cultural institute publishes the *Agenda Cultural* with listings of upcoming events, exhibitions, and workshops. It can be hard to find—ask at the Casa de la Cultura.

Booths with tourist information signs abound along Avenida Tulum and Boulevard Kukulcán, but they are virtually all operated by hotel and condo companies offering free tours and meals in exchange for attending a time-share presentation. Unless you are willing to spend a morning or afternoon in a hard-line sales pitch, stay clear of these kiosks.

NEWSPAPERS

In Spanish, *Novedades de Quintana Roo* is the state's oldest newspaper, centrist in coverage, with a good classified section. *¡Por Esto!* is a left-of-center Quintana Roo paper, while *Diario de Yucatán* is more conservative and covers the entire region. The Cancún version of the *Miami Herald Tribune* (US$1) is a good English-language alternative.

HOSPITALS

Although there is no hospital in the Zona Hotelera, there are several recommended private hospitals within a few blocks of each other in downtown Cancún. All have emergency rooms and English-speaking doctors: **Hospital de las Américas** (Av. Bonampak, behind Las Américas mall, tel. 998/881-3434), **Hospitén Cancún** (Av. Bonampak Lote 7, tel. 998/881-3700), and **Hospital Americano** (Retorno Viento 15, tel. 998/884-6133).

For diving-related injuries, try the **Hiperbárica Cancún** (Alcatraces 44, tel. 998/892-7680, www.hiperbarica-cancun.com)—it has a hyperbaric chamber. English spoken.

PHARMACIES

In the Zona Hotelera, try any of the malls or head directly to **Farmacia del Ahorro** (Blvd. Kukulcán Km. 9.5, tel. 998/892-7291, 24 hours). Downtown, **Farmacias Similares** (Av. Tulum at Calle Crisantemos, tel. 998/898-0190, 24 hours) is a reliable national chain offering discounted generic medications.

POLICE

For **24-hour emergency assistance**—police department, fire station, and ambulance—dial toll-free **060** or **066** from any phone.

In the Zona Hotelera, the tourist police, ambulance, and fire station (Blvd. Kukulcán Km. 12.5, 998/885-2277, 24 hours daily) are in the same building, next to Plaza Kukulcán.

Downtown, the police station (Av. Xcaret at Av. Kabah, 998/884-1913, 24 hours daily) faces the Carrefour supermarket.

MONEY

In a town as popular as Cancún, you'll have no problem accessing or exchanging your money—banks, ATMs, and *casas de cambio* (exchange houses) are everywhere tourists are. In the Zona Hotelera, shopping centers are the easiest place to find them. Downtown, money services line Avenida Tulum and, to a lesser extent, Avenida Uxmal. Often, hotels will exchange your money, too (at pitiful rates, however).

For the best *casa de cambio* rates, head to the full-service **American Express** (Av. Tulum 208 at Calle Agua, tel. 998/881-4000, 9 A.M.–6 P.M. Mon.–Fri., 9 A.M.–1 P.M. Sat.). American Express also has a kiosk in the Plaza La Isla open 9 A.M.–3 P.M., 4–6 P.M., and 7–10 P.M. daily.

For a bank in the Zona Hotelera, head to Plaza Caracol (Blvd. Kukulcán Km. 8.5) where you'll find **Bancomer** (tel. 998/883-0834), **HSBC** (998/883-4652), and **Banamex** (998/883-3100), or Plaza Kukulcán (Blvd. Kukulcán Km. 12.5) where there's a **Banco Serfín** (998/881-4809). All have ATMs that accept foreign cards, and are open roughly 9 A.M.–4 P.M. Mon.–Fri.

Downtown, the best-located banks are on Avenida Tulum between Boulevard Kukulcán and Avenida Uxmal: **Bancomer** (Av. Tulum 20, tel. 998/881-6210, 8:30 A.M.–4 P.M. Mon.–Fri., 10 A.M.–2 P.M. Sat.) and **Banamex** (Av. Tulum 19, tel. 998/881-6403, 9 A.M.–4 P.M. Mon.–Fri., 10 A.M.–2 P.M. Sat.).

INTERNET AND TELEPHONE

Downtown Internet cafés charge around US$1–1.50 an hour, while those in the Zona Hotelera charge 5–10 times as much. Downtown, look for Internet cafés on Avenida Uxmal near the bus terminal; most offer reasonable national and international phone service as well. In the Zona Hotelera, all the malls have at least one place to check your email. Most of the cafés listed here can also download digital photos and burn them onto CDs (bring your own cables).

Cancún @ (Av. Uxmal 22-D, tel. 998/892-3484, 8 a.m.–2 a.m. daily) is a quiet, friendly downtown shop with fast Internet for under US$1 an hour; CD-burning US$4. Across the street, **Cyber-Office** (Av. Uxmal at Calle Pino, tel. 998/892-3854, 8 a.m.–midnight daily) has reliable Internet and cheap international phone service—under US$0.15 a minute to the United States and Canada.

In the Zona Hotelera, **Internet cafés** are located at Plaza Kukulcán (10 a.m.–10 p.m. daily, US$7.50/hr.) and Forum by the Sea (10 a.m.–10 p.m. Mon.–Sat., US$6/hr.).

POST OFFICE

The downtown post office is in front of Mercado 28 (Av. Sunyaxchen at Av. Xel-Ha, tel. 998/834-1418, 9 a.m.–6 p.m. Mon.–Fri., 8 a.m.–1 p.m. Sat.—stamps only). There is no post office in the Zona Hotelera, but your hotel may be able to send mail for you.

IMMIGRATION

Cancún's immigration office (Av. Nader at Av. Uxmal, tel. 998/884-1749, 8 a.m.–1 p.m. Mon.–Fri.) is an efficient, welcoming office—worlds better than the one in Playa del Carmen. For information on visa extensions and other immigration matters, see *Visas and Officialdom* in the *Essentials* chapter.

TRAVEL AGENCIES

There are literally scores of travel agencies in Cancún. Most prices are pretty uniform, both for area trips and international and domestic flights. In the Zona Hotelera, most large hotels have reliable in-house travel agencies. Downtown, there are numerous agencies on Avenida Tulum and Avenida Uxmal, including **American Express** (Av. Tulum 208 at Calle Agua, tel. 998/881-4000, 9 a.m.–6 p.m. Mon.–Fri., 9 a.m.–1 p.m. Sat.) and **PromoViajes** (Av. Uxmal 26, tel. 998/884-3128, www.promoviajesmexico.com, 9 a.m.–7 p.m., Mon.–Sat.). **Nómadas Travel Agency** (Hostal Soberanis, Av. Cobá near Av. Tulum, tel. 998/892-2320, www.nomadastravel.com, 10 a.m.–7 p.m. Mon.–Fri.) specializes in youth travel services, including international hostel cards and student air tickets, but it is still a full-service travel agency with professional service and good fares for all travelers.

LAUNDERETTE

Downtown, there are several launderettes on Av. Uxmal west of the bus terminal. On the other side of Parque Las Palapas, **Lava y Seca** (Retorno Crisantemos 22, tel. 998/892-4789, 10 a.m.–6:30 p.m. Mon.–Fri., 10 a.m.–6 p.m. Sat.) charges US$4.25 per three kilograms (6.6 pounds). Same-day service available if you drop off your laundry early.

In the Zona Hotelera, **Lavandería Lumi** (Plaza Quetzal, Blvd. Kukulcán Km. 7.4, tel. 998/883-3874, 8 a.m.–7 p.m. Mon.–Sat., 9 a.m.–3 p.m.) will wash, dry and fold your dirty clothes for US$10 for four kilograms (8.8 pounds) in 2–3 hours, or you can do it yourself for US$7, including soap. A cheaper but less central option is **Lavandería Happy Wash** (Blvd. Kukulcán Km. 3.5, tel. 998/155-4377), which charges US$3 for three kilograms (6.6 pounds).

STORAGE

On the 2nd floor of the bus station, **Guarda Volumen** (tel. 998/884-4352, ext. 2851, 7 a.m.–9:30 p.m. daily) is the only place to store your belongings, charging US$0.35–1 an hour, depending on the size.

Getting There and Around

GETTING THERE
Air

The Cancún International Airport (CUN) is 20 kilometers (12 miles) south of Cancún. Most flights arrive and depart from the airport's Terminal 2 (tel. 998/848-7200, ext. 107), which also has the airline, taxi, bus, and car rental desks, and ATMs. Charter flights, plus Spirit Airlines, use Terminal 1 (tel. 998/886-0341); a free shuttle van ferries travelers between the two.

FLYING TO CANCÚN

The following airlines service Cancún International Airport (CUN):

- **Aerocosta** (Av. Tulum at Av. Uxmal, tel. 998/884-0383)

- **Aerocozumel** (airport tel. 998/886-0083)

- **Aeroméxico** (Av. Cobá at Av. Bonampák, tel. 998/287-1860, airport tel. 998/287-1820, toll-free Mex. tel. 800/021-4010, www.aeromexico.com)

- **Air Canada** (airport tel. 998/886-0883, www.aircanada.com)

- **Alaska Airlines** (airport tel. 998/886-0803, toll-free Mex. tel. 800/426-0333, www.alaskaair.com)

- **American Airlines** (airport tel. 998/886-0086, toll-free Mex. tel. 800/904-6000, www.aa.com)

- **Asur** (airport tel. 998/886-0183)

- **Aviacsa** (Av. Cobá 37, tel. 998/887-4211, airport tel. 998/886-0093, toll-free Mex. tel. 800/006-2200, www.aviacsa.com)

- **Click Mexicana** (Av. Cobá 5, tel. 998/884-2000, airport tel. 998/886-0083, toll-free Mex. tel. 800/112-5425, www.clickmx.com)

- **Continental** (airport tel. 998/886-0006, toll-free Mex. tel. 800/900-5000, www.continental.com)

- **Copa Airlines** (airport tel. 998/886-0652, www.copaair.com)

- **Cubana de Aviación** (Av. Tulum 232, tel. 998/887-7210, airport tel. 998/886-0355, www.cubana.cu)

- **Delta** (airport tel. 998/886-0668, toll-free Mex. tel. 800/123-4710, www.delta.com)

- **Grupo TACA** (airport tel. 998/886-0008, www.taca.com)

- **LanChile** (airport tel. 998/887-9012, www.lanchile.com)

- **Líneas Aéreas Azteca** (Av. Cobá 5, tel. 998/892-3126, airport tel. 998/886-0831, www.aazteca.com.mx)

- **Lufthansa** (airport tel. 998/886-0122, www.lufthansa.com)

- **Magnicharters** (Av. Nader 93, tel. 998/886-0600, airport tel. 998/886-0833, www.magnicharters.com.mx)

- **Mexicana** (Av. Tulum 269, tel. 998/881-9093, airport tel. 998/886-0042, toll-free Mex. tel. 800/502-2000, www.mexicana.com)

- **Northwest Airlines** (airport tel. 998/886-0044, www.nwa.com)

- **Spirit Airlines** (Retorno Jazmines at Av. Yaxchilán, tel. 998/886-0708, airport tel. 998/887-1862, www.spiritair.com)

- **United Airlines** (toll-free Mex. tel. 800/003-0777, www.united.com)

- **US Airways** (airport tel. 998/886-0373, toll-free Mex. tel. 800/428-4322, www.usairways.com)

CANCÚN BUS SCHEDULES

Cancún's **main bus station** is located downtown at Avs. Tulum and Uxmal; call toll free 01-800-702-8000 for up-to-date schedules and prices.

DESTINATION	PRICE	DURATION	SCHEDULE
Campeche City	US$29-33*	7 hrs	7:45 A.M., 11:30 A.M., 3 P.M.*, and 10:30 P.M.
Cancún Int'l Airport	US$3.25	20 min.	every 30 min. 6:30 A.M.-8:30 P.M.; every 60 min. 4:30 A.M.-6:30 A.M. and 8:30 P.M.-11:30 P.M.
Chetumal	US$19-23*	5.5 hrs	every 1-2 hrs 5 A.M.-8 P.M., plus 11 P.M. and 12:30 A.M.
Chichén Itzá	US$12.50	3 hrs	9 A.M. or take any Pisté bus
Chiquilá	US$6.50	3 hrs	7:50 A.M. and 12:40 P.M.
Mahahual	US$15.50	5 hrs	7 A.M. and 11:30 P.M.
Mérida	US$20-32*	4 hrs	hourly 5 A.M.-7:30 P.M.; 10 P.M.; and midnight-2 A.M.
Mexico City	US$95-110*	24 hrs	eight departures 6:15 A.M.-8 P.M.
Palenque	US$44-51*	12 hrs	4:15 A.M., 3:45 P.M., and 5:45 P.M.*
Pisté	US$8.50	4 hrs	hourly 5 A.M.-12:30 A.M.

Bus

Buses leave Cancún's clean and modern bus terminal (Av. Tulum at Av. Uxmal) for destinations in the Yucatán Peninsula and throughout the interior of Mexico.

Shuttle vans also are a way to get from Cancún to Playa del Carmen. They queue up directly across Av. Tulum from the bus terminal, near the Comercial Mexicana, and depart every 10–15 minutes, 24 hours a day. The fare is US$2 to Puerto Morelos and US$3 to Playa del Carmen.

GETTING AROUND
To and From the Airport

Cancún's airport is served by taxi, shuttle, and bus. A taxi from the airport costs US$40, whether you're headed downtown or to the Zona Hotelera. It's the same to return to the airport from the Zona Hotelera, but much less from downtown, around US$15. A taxi to Playa del Carmen from the airport is US$62, and US$40 the other way around.

Shuttles can be booked at the service windows as you exit the airport; it's US$9 to Can-

DESTINATION	PRICE	DURATION	SCHEDULE
Playa del Carmen	US$3.25	1 hr	every 15 min. 4:30 A.M.–midnight
Puerto Morelos	US$2	30 min.	every 15 min. 4:30 A.M.–midnight
Río Lagartos	–	–	No direct service; connect through Tizimín
Tizimín	US$7.50-9	3-4 hrs	7:30 A.M., 1 P.M., and 1:30 P.M.
San Cristóbal (Chiapas)	US$54-63	18 hrs	2:15 P.M., 3:45 P.M., and 5:45 P.M.*
Tulum	US$5-6.50	2 hrs	nine departures 6 A.M.–2 P.M., plus 8 P.M.
Valladolid	US$7-11	2-3 hrs	six direct departures 5 A.M.-5:30 P.M., second-class hourly 1:15 A.M.–midnight
Villahermosa	US$48-60	12 hrs	seven departures 7 P.M.–11:30 P.M., plus 10 A.M. and 1 P.M.
Xpujil	US$26.50	7 hrs	seven departures 6:15 A.M.-11:30 P.M.

*Denotes deluxe service; not available for all departures

cún and US$18 to Playa del Carmen. You may have to wait a short time for the shuttle to fill up. There is no return shuttle service.

ADO's Riviera line has comfortable bus service every 20–30 minutes to and from the downtown bus station and the airport; service to Playa del Carmen is less frequent, but still convenient and affordable.

Bus

Frequent buses (US$0.60) run between downtown Cancún and the Zona Hotelera—you'll rarely have to wait more than five minutes for one to pass. These buses are red and have "R-1," "Hoteles," or "Zona Hotelera" printed on the front, and stop at or near most major hotels, beaches, the bus station, and ferry ports.

Taxi

You'll have no trouble finding a taxi around town or in the Zona Hotelera—they are everywhere tourists are. Before getting into one, however, make sure to agree upon a price—meters are often not used and drivers sometimes

TAXI SCAM

Beware of taxi drivers that try to convince you that the hotel you're going to is closed, roach-infested, flooded, burned down, has no running water, was destroyed by a hurricane, (add your disaster of choice). As sincere as the drivers might seem, they are more often than not retaliating against hotels that refuse to pay a finders fee. Taxi drivers in Cancún and throughout the Riviera Maya earn significant commissions – as much as US$10 per person *per night* – for bringing guests to certain establishments. Some hotels refuse to pay the fee and taxi drivers, in turn, try to take their clients to "cooperative" hotels instead. Don't fall for it. You may have to be firm, but insist that the driver take you to the hotel of your choice. Your best option is to call ahead for a room reservation, which also serves to confirm that the hotel actually is open and operational.

DRIVING DISTANCES FROM CANCÚN

LOCATION	DISTANCE
Airport	20 km (12.5 mi)
Akumal	105 km (65 mi)
Bacalar	320 km (199 mi)
Campeche	487 km (302.5 mi)
Chetumal	382 km (237.5 mi)
Chichén Itzá	178 km (110.5 mi)
Cobá	173 km (107.5 mi)
Izamal	266 km (166 mi)
Mahahual	351 km (218 mi)
Mérida	320 km (199 mi)
Paamul	82 km (51 mi)
Playa del Carmen	68 km (42.5 mi)
Puerto Aventuras	87 km (54 mi)
Puerto Juárez	5 km (3 mi)
Puerto Morelos	36 km (22.5 mi)
Punta Allen	182 km (114km)
Tulum	130 km (81 mi)
Valladolid	158 km (98 mi)
Xcalak	411 km (255.5 mi)
Xcaret	74 km (46 mi)
Xel-Há	122 km (76 mi)
Xpu-Há	101 km (63 mi)
Xpujil	501 km (311 mi)

overcharge. When we were here, the rate around downtown was US$1.60, from downtown to Isla Mujeres ferries was US$1.60, and from downtown to the Zona Hotelera was US$6–14, depending on the destination. Rates within the Zona Hotelera jump dramatically, and depend on how far you're going. Ask your hotel concierge for specific rates, but expect to pay US$4–12.

Car Rental

Although you won't need a car to visit Cancún proper, renting one is a great way to visit the nearest archaeological sites (i.e., Tulum, Cobá, Ek' Balam, and Chichén Itzá) without being part of a huge tour group. A rental also makes exploring the Riviera Maya a little easier, though buses cover that route fairly well. Driving in the Cancún area is relatively pain-free—unexpected speed bumps and impatient bus drivers are the biggest concern.

Car rentals are available at the airport, on Avenida Tulum and Avenida Uxmal, and at hotels and malls in the Zona Hotelera. Various sizes and types are available, from SUVs to Volkswagen bugs (optimistically dubbed VW "sedans"); prices with insurance and taxes start at around US$50 a day. The best rates are usually with online reservations, though some of the small agencies offer great deals during the low season. You also can get discounted rates if you can stomach spending half a day in a time-share presentation.

Most of the international chains have offices at the airport and in town; **Avicar** (Azucenas 1, tel. 998/884-9635, www.avicar.com. mx, 8 A.M.–1 P.M. and 4 P.M.–7 P.M. daily) and **Zipp Rent-A-Car** (Blvd. Kukulcán Km. 4 across from El Embarcadero, tel. 998/849-4193, or Avalon Grand Hotel, Blvd. Kukulcán Km. 11.5, tel. 998/848-9350, www .zipp.com.mx) are good local options.

Isla Mujeres

Just eight kilometers (five miles) long and no more than a quarter-mile wide, Isla Mujeres is a sliver of land fringed by white sand beaches amid the wide turquoise sea. It was actually one of the first places in the Mexican Caribbean to have hotels and other tourist developments, but attention quickly shifted to Isla Cozumel and then Cancún proper. It may have been a blessing in disguise: as those areas exploded, rushing to build high-rise hotels and cruise ship ports, Isla Mujeres developed more slowly, attracting backpackers, bohemians, and the occasional B&B, while remaining pretty much what it always was—a quiet, picturesque fishing community.

But even slow change adds up, and today Isla Mujeres is a well-established tourist destination. Thousands of day-trippers come from Cancún to shop, eat, and relax on the island's calm beaches. While still popular with backpackers, Isla Mujeres also attracts mid-range and upscale travelers with an ever-expanding selection of boutique hotels and B&Bs.

Despite higher hotel prices, and many more T-shirt shops, golf carts, and pushy tour operators, Isla Mujeres remains at its core a mellow tropical island, with a friendly and laid-back population. Passersby greet one another, people stroll in the middle of streets, and many businesses close for long lunches. Add that to beautiful beaches, and numerous options for snorkeling, biking, and other outdoor excursions, and it's no wonder so many visitors find themselves extending (and re-extending) their time here.

HISTORY

The history behind the name *Isla Mujeres* (Island of Women) depends on whom you ask or what book you read. One version is that pirates who trolled these waters kept their female captives here while they ransacked boats on the high seas. The other story is that when the Spaniards—ransackers of a different ilk—arrived they found a large number of female-shaped clay idols and named the island after them. The latter is the more likely story, and the one to which most archaeologists subscribe. It is thought that the idols were left behind by the Mayas using the island as a stopover on their pilgrimages to Cozumel to worship Ix Chel, the female goddess of fertility.

ORIENTATION

The town of Isla Mujeres (known as the *centro* or center) is at the far northwestern tip of the island, and at just eight blocks long and five blocks deep, is very walkable. This is where most of the hotels, restaurants, shops, and services are. There is no real "main" street, though Avenida Matamoros is notable for its bohemian shops and atmosphere, while Avenida Hidalgo has a busy pedestrian-only section and intersects with the town *zócalo* (central plaza) and city hall. Avenida Rueda Medina is a busy street that runs along the south side of the *centro* past the ferry piers and continues all the way to the island's other end, becoming Carretera Punta Sur at Parque Garrafón (for that reason it is also known as Carretera Garrafón). The road

CANCÚN

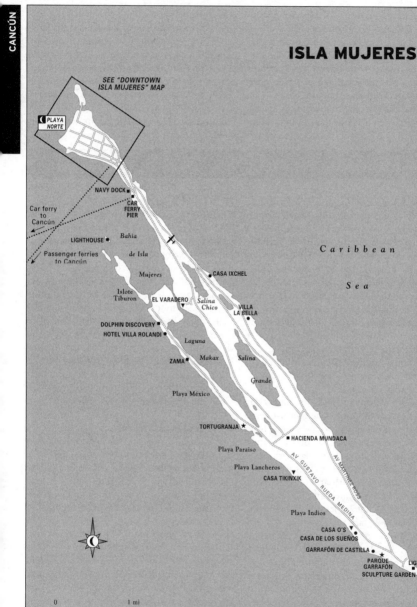

ISLA MUJERES

SEE "DOWNTOWN ISLA MUJERES" MAP

PLAYA NORTE

NAVY DOCK ■

CAR FERRY PIER

Car ferry to Cancún

LIGHTHOUSE ■ *Bahía*

de Isla

Passenger ferries to Cancún

Mujeres

● CASA IXCHEL

C a r i b b e a n

Islote Tiburon

EL VARADERO ▼

Salina Chico

S e a

VILLA LA BELLA ●

DOLPHIN DISCOVERY ■
HOTEL VILLA ROLANDI

Laguna

ZAMA ■ *Makax*

Salina

Grande

Playa México

TORTUGRANJA ★

■ HACIENDA MUNDACA

Playa Paraiso

Playa Lancheros

CASA TIKINXIK ▼

AV. GUSTAVO RUEDA MEDINA

AV. MARTÍNEZ ROSS

Playa Indios

CASA O'S ●
CASA DE LOS SUEÑOS

GARRAFÓN DE CASTILLA ●

PARQUE GARRAFÓN
SCULPTURE GARDEN

LIGHTHOUSE

IXCHEL

0   1 mi

0   1 km

© AVALON TRAVEL PUBLISHING, INC.

that runs the length of the upper edge of the island is Avenida Martínez Ross.

SIGHTS
◖ Playa Norte

The closest downtown beach—and arguably the most beautiful on the island—is Playa Norte. It runs the width of the island on the northernmost edge of town. Here you'll find people sunning themselves on colorful beach towels, sipping margaritas at beachside restaurants, and relaxing under huge umbrellas. You'll also find plenty of people playing in the calm turquoise sea that is so shallow you can wade 35 meters (115 feet) and still be only waist deep.

At the north end of the beach **Buho's** (end of Av Carlos Lazos) rents beach chairs and umbrellas for US$5 apiece. Near the middle of the beach, **Water Sports Playa Norte** (end of Av. Guerrero at Playa Norte, 9 A.M.–5 P.M. daily) also rents chairs and umbrellas (US$15/day for a pair) plus snorkel gear (US$15/day), kayaks (US$10–20/hr.) and Hobie Cats (US$35/hr.). They also offer daily snorkel tours (US$25 pp, 2 hrs.) at 10 A.M., noon, and 2 P.M.

Other Beaches

Zama (Carretera Sac Bajo, near Hotel Villas Rolandi, tel. 998/877-0739, 10 A.M.–6 P.M. daily) is a small, very pleasant beach club and spa on the island's calm southwest shore. You can relax in a comfy beach-bed on the large clean beach or in a hammock in the shady garden. The water here has a fair amount of sea grass, but you can always swim from the pier or in one of the two appealing midsize pools. And it's all free, amazingly enough, if you eat at the small outdoor restaurant. Prices and selection are perfectly reasonable, including a kid's menu and everything from burritos to chicken fajitas to shrimp any way you like (US$5–20).

At the south end of the island, **Playa Lancheros** is less-manicured than Playa Norte, but has incredible views over the Caribbean to Cancún. The main feature of the beach is **Casa Tikinxik** (11 A.M.–6 P.M. daily, US$5–8), an Isla Mujeres institution whose specially grilled fish gives the restaurant its name. Playa Lancheros can get rowdy, especially on weekends when Cancúnenses and foreign tourists pack

© LIZ A PRADO

Kick back under a palm tree at any of Isla Mujeres's mellow beaches.

the beach clubs on either side of the restaurant, but it's a good place for a leisurely lunch.

Hacienda Mundaca

The ruins of a hacienda with a few paths and a sad little zoo is what you'll find if you stop at the **Hacienda Mundaca** (Av. Rueda Medina at Carretera Garrafón Km. 3.5, 9 A.M.–5 P.M. daily, US$2). It was built in the mid-1800s by Fermín Antonio Mundaca de Marechaga, a former African slave trader and pirate, to woo an islander with whom he'd fallen in love. Called La Trigueña because of her dark blond hair, the woman did not return his affections and instead, married another man before the hacienda was completed. It's said that Mundaca was left despondent and a bit crazed with the news, leaving his property to decay, the crops to rot, and the animals to die. He eventually left the island and died in Mérida. (Though Mundaca isn't buried on the Isla Mujeres, his tombstone, which he carved himself, is in the island's downtown cemetery—look for the skull and crossbones and the inscription *Como tú eres yo fui, y yo como soy, tu séras* (As you are, I was, and as I am, you will be). Hardly worth the admission fee, the most impressive aspect about the hacienda is that it somehow manages to attract enough visitors to stay open. It's the legend behind it, perhaps, that keeps people coming.

Sea Turtle Sanctuary

Commonly referred to as the **Tortugranja** (Turtle Farm; Carretera Sac Bajo, 5, tel. 998/888-0507, 9 A.M.–5 P.M. daily, US$2) this modest sea turtle sanctuary on the island's southwestern shore makes for a fascinating stop on your golf-cart tour of the island. The one-room cement structure contains several enclosures with sea turtles of different ages and species. The tank of just-hatched *tortuguitas* is always a hit; please respect the rules (and huge signs) and refrain from touching or picking them up. During the nesting season, one section of sand is fenced off, and eggs collected from nests are transplanted here for protection. Small aquariums along the walls contain sea anemones, sea horses, and the deadly rockfish, among others.

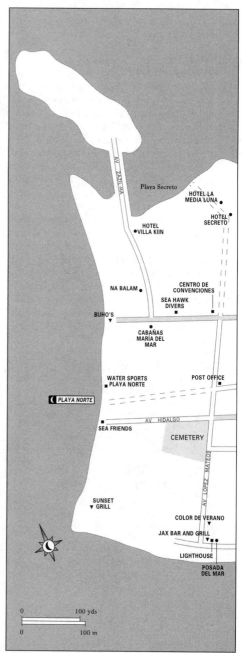

CANCÚN

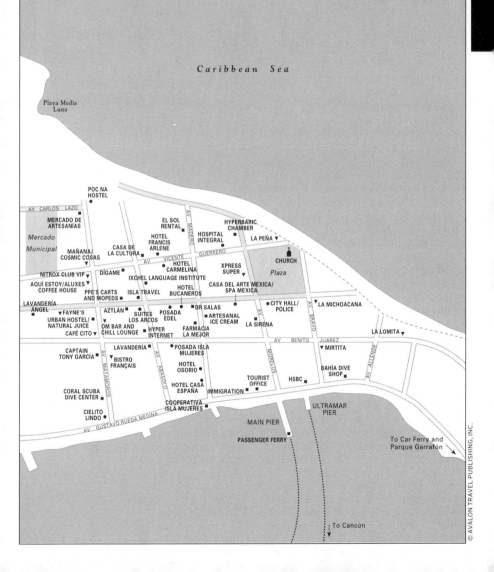

DOWNTOWN ISLA MUJERES

Caribbean Sea

Playa Media Luna

AV CARLOS LAZO

POC NA HOSTEL

MERCADO DE ARTESANÍAS

Mercado Municipal

EL SOL RENTAL

AV MADERO

HYPERBARIC CHAMBER

HOSPITAL INTEGRAL

LA PEÑA

HOTEL FRANCIS ARLENE

MAÑANA/ COSMIC COSAS

CASA DE LA CULTURA

AV VICENTE GUERRERO

HOTEL CARMELINA

XPRESS SUPER

CHURCH

Plaza

NITROX CLUB VIP

DÍGAME

IXCHEL LANGUAGE INSTITUTE

AQUÍ ESTOY/ALUXES COFFEE HOUSE

PPE'S CARTS AND MOPEDS

ISLA TRAVEL

HOTEL BUCANEROS

CASA DEL ARTE MEXICA/ SPA MEXICA

LAVANDERÍA ANGEL

DR SALAS

CITY HALL/ POLICE

AV BRAVO

LA MICHOACANA

FAYNE'S

AZTLÁN

SUITES LOS ARCOS

POSADA EDEL

ARTESANAL ICE CREAM

LA SIRENA

URBAN HOSTEL/ NATURAL JUICE

OM BAR AND CHILL LOUNGE

HYPER INTERNET

FARMACIA LA MEJOR

LA LOMITA

CAFÉ CITO

AV BENITO JUAREZ

CAPTAIN TONY GARCÍA

LAVANDERÍA

AV MATAMOROS

POSADA ISLA MUJERES

AV ABASOLO

MORELOS

MIRTITA

BISTRO FRANÇAIS

HOTEL OSORIO

AV ALLENDE

BAHÍA DIVE SHOP

CORAL SCUBA DIVE CENTER

HOTEL CASA ESPAÑA

IMMIGRATION

TOURIST OFFICE

HSBC

CIELITO LINDO

COOPERATIVA ISLA MUJERES

AV GUSTAVO RUEDA MEDINA

ULTRAMAR PIER

MAIN PIER

PASSENGER FERRY

To Car Ferry and Parque Garrafón

To Cancún

© AVALON TRAVEL PUBLISHING, INC.

© LIZA PRADO

Various organizations along the Riviera Maya protect sea turtles.

Between May and August, travelers may be able to accompany the center's workers in looking for fresh sea turtle nests on the island's eastern shore and re-locating eggs to protected areas, and, until October, helping release hatchlings into the sea. Both activities take place in the evening several nights a week, but are not formal tours. Those interested should inquire at the center, and having basic Spanish (and possibly your own vehicle) will make participating much easier. There's no charge, but a tip is customary.

Ixchel Ruins and Sculpture Garden

At the southern tip of the island, a crumbling Maya temple stands on a cliff overlooking the sea. Thought to be dedicated to Ixchel—the goddess of the moon, fertility, weaving, and childbirth—the ruins are believed to have been a pilgrimage site that also may have doubled as an observation post or as an astronomical observatory. In any case, when Francisco Hernández de Córdoba first reported their existence in 1517, they had been long abandoned.

By themselves, the ruins aren't too exciting—hurricanes have all but destroyed them—but a visit here also includes stopping in a tiny museum, climbing a renovated lighthouse, and enjoying the sculpture garden—a dozen or so multicolored modern sculptures lining the path to the ruins. Just past the ruins, the trail continues to the very tip of the island—the easternmost point of Mexico actually—before looping back along the craggy waterfront to the entrance. A decent side trip, especially if you have a golf cart at your disposal.

Admission to the site is included in the ticket price to Parque Garrafón; all others must pay US$3 (open 10 A.M.–5 P.M. daily). There is also a kitschy Caribbean "village" with shops and a restaurant. No buses go there, unfortunately. By moped or golf cart, continue south on the main road past Parque Garrafón. The road bends and you'll see the lighthouse down a small dead-end road.

Isla Contoy

Decreed a national park in 1998, bird and nature lovers will enjoy a trip to Isla Con-

LIZA PRADO

The path along the southernmost point of Isla Mujeres affords beautiful views of the Caribbean.

toy, a small island located just 24 kilometers (14 miles) north of Isla Mujeres. Surrounded by crystal-clear water, Contoy's saltwater lagoons, mangrove trees, and coconut palms make a perfect home to over 150 species of birds including herons, brown pelicans, frigates, and cormorants. In the summertime, you might also catch a glimpse of one of the three species of sea turtles that comes to lay its eggs on its shores. The island's only structures are a three-story viewing tower and a visitor's center, which houses a small museum. The rest of the island is tropical jungle that is accessible by hiking trails and the beach. To protect the local ecology, visitors can enter the park between 9 A.M. and 5 P.M. and are limited to 200 per day. The entrance fee is US$5 per visitor.

Isla Mujeres has lots of tour operators that offer the same basic trip to Isla Contoy for approximately US$50 (plus US$5 park entrance fee): bread and juice at the office between 8:30 and 9 A.M.; a departure shortly thereafter with nonalcoholic drinks served on the boat trip; snorkeling on the Ixlache reef a few minutes before arriving at Contoy; a walking tour of the island, including a trip to the museum and observation tower while lunch is prepared; lunch on the beach, which typically consists of barbecued chicken and grilled fish, rice, salad, guacamole, beer, and nonalcoholic drinks; afterward sunbathing, swimming, snorkeling, and general exploring are encouraged before the boat sets off at 3 P.M., arriving at Isla Mujeres around 4 P.M. What typically distinguishes one trip from another are the size of the boat, the number of tourists taken on each tour, the knowledge of the guide who takes you, the quality of the food, and whether there is an open bar. Tour operators or agencies that offer the trip include: **Captain Tony García,** (Av. Matamoros near Av Benito Juárez, 998/877-0227) a friendly, English-speaking guide with over 20 years' experience, whose house doubles as his office—swing by to see if he's got a tour going; the local fishermen's coop, **Cooperativa Isla Mujeres** (Av. Madero pier, no tel., 8 A.M.– 8 P.M. daily); and **Isla Travel** (Hidalgo 15, tel. 998/877-0845, 9 A.M.–2 P.M. and 4–7 P.M. Mon.–Fri., 9 A.M.–4 P.M. Sat).

ENTERTAINMENT AND EVENTS

Given Isla Mujeres' popularity with backpackers and people with generally laid-back attitudes, it's not surprising to find that the nightlife here tends strongly toward the bohemian, live-music and bar scene, rather than the pulsating nightclubs popular in Cancún.

Live Music

The Texan-owned **Jax Bar and Grill** (Av. Lopez Mateos at Av. Rueda Medina, tel. 998/877-1218, 8 A.M.–2 A.M. daily, drinks US$1–3) is known as a yacht crew hangout. In the high season, live country blues and classic rock fill the air 9–11 P.M. almost every night, and the partying continues until late into the night. Utilitarian breakfasts and burgers (US$4–7) are served until 10 P.M. Not everyone's scene, but those who like it come back again and again.

Fayne's (Hidalgo 12, tel. 998/877-0528, 5 P.M.–midnight daily, no cover, drinks US$1.50–3.50, food US$7–13) is a popular spot to listen to live and DJ music 9 P.M.–midnight daily. Music ranges from rock to salsa to reggae. The menu is likewise varied, from pasta to seafood.

Next door, **La Adelita** mixes tequila with revolution, with photos of Pancho Villa on the walls and an array of Mexican moonshine on shelves around the small bar and sitting area.

Bars

On the central plaza, **La Peña** (Av. Guerrero at Av. Bravo, tel. 998/845-7384, 7:30 P.M.–3 A.M. daily) is a hip beach bar without the attitude, featuring low lighting and mammoth *roble* chairs imported from Thailand. A rambling place, with nooks here and there, the back deck has swings that overlook the ocean while the front room has shutters that transform into tables. Perfect for kicking back with a few friends or for meeting some new ones. There also are a few billiards tables if you feel like shooting some pool. The place gets going after midnight.

Om Bar and Chill Lounge (Matamoros 30, tel. 998/820-4876, 7 P.M.–1:30 A.M. Mon.–Sat.) is a bohemian bar with cool tunes, dim lighting, and low seating. Three tables have beer taps: Customers order the type of brew they want hooked up, drink their fill, and when they're ready for the tab, the keg's meter is measured for consumption. If you prefer harder stuff, kick off your night with the house specialty—*la viuda express* (the widow express)—which includes a shot of espresso, tequila, Baileys, Kahlua, and a little sugar.

Overlooking Playa Norte, **Buho's** (Av. Carlos Lazo at Playa Norte, 9 A.M.–1 A.M. daily) is a popular beach bar, with swings surrounding the bar, shells and buoys serving as decor, and hammocks well within reach. Happy hour runs 2–5 P.M. daily and features two-for-one beers and cocktails.

Discotheques

Nitrox Club V.I.P. (Av. Matamoros near Av. Guerrero, tel. 998/887-050568, 9 P.M.–3 A.M. Wed.–Sun., no cover) is the only dance club downtown and features mostly techno and reggae, although Fridays is Latin night. Unfortunately, it has a tiny dance floor but with two-for-one beer, you may end up spending most of your time at a table.

SHOPPING

As soon as you step off of the ferry, you will be surrounded by kitschy souvenirs and cheap T-shirts. Don't be discouraged! Isla Mujeres has a burgeoning market of specialty stores, most of which showcase the talents of Mexican artists. Poke around a bit, and you'll run into the following trailblazers and probably a few new ones.

A jewel hidden in a street of T-shirt shops, **Aztlán** (Hidalgo near Abasolo, tel. 998/887-0419, 9 A.M.–9 P.M. Mon.–Sat.; credit cards accepted) specializes in Mexican masks brought from every corner of the country. The owners, transplants from Mexico City, also make popular religious art that fills one corner of the shop.

La Sirena (Av. Morelos near Av. Hidalgo,

tel. 998/877-0223, 10 A.M.–6 P.M. Mon.–Sat.) is a tiny shop that's jam-packed with high-quality handicrafts from all over Mexico: beautiful textiles from Chiapas, masks from Guerrero, skeleton art from Mexico City, *alebrijes* from Oaxaca…you'll find a fine sampling of Mexican art here. The prices are a bit inflated but no worries, bargaining is welcome.

A bit kitschy around the edges, **Casa del Arte Mexica** (Hidalgo 6, tel. 998/877-1679, 10 A.M.–9 P.M. Mon.–Sat.) sells good Maya replicas as well as beautiful batik work made by islanders.

If you're in the market for decent diving or fishing gear, **Bahía Dive Shop** (Av. Rueda Medina 166, tel. 998/877-0340, bahiaisla mujeres@hotmail.com, 9:30 A.M.–7 P.M. Mon.–Sat., 8 A.M.–2 P.M. Sun.) has a wide—and pricey—range of equipment. A good source if you forgot your equipment at home.

Located in Mañana café, **Cosmic Cosas** (Av. Matamoros at Av. Guerrero, 9 A.M.–5 P.M. Mon.–Sat.) has long been one of the area's best foreign-language bookstores. You can buy, sell, and trade everything from beach trash to guidebooks to Maya history, with titles in English, German, Hebrew, and Spanish and ranging in price US$2–12. If you're hungry and out of pesos, trade-ins can also be used as credit at the café.

SPORTS AND RECREATION
Scuba Diving

Beginner divers will appreciate the still water and vibrant sealife on Isla Mujeres's western side, while the east side presents advanced divers more challenging options, with deeper water (up to 40 m./131 ft.), more varied terrain, and even a couple of shipwrecks. Favorite sites include **La Bandera** (a reef dive), **Media Luna** (a drift dive), **Ultrafreeze** (a shipwreck, in notoriously chilly water), and the famous **Sleeping Shark Cave**—a deep cave known to attract sharks where they fall into a strangely lethargic and nonaggressive state. The reason behind this phenomenon varies by the teller: salinity of the water, low carbon dioxide, or the flow of the water. Unfortunately, overfishing and overdiving has disrupted the slumber

© LIZA PRADO

Dive and snorkel boats use the same dock as many anglers.

party and there's only a 30–50 percent chance of seeing sharks there. Some guides say the chances of seeing the sharks increase in September, but you'll always find someone to disagree with that.

Isla Mujeres has a handful of dive operations. Rates are fairly uniform: around US$45 for one tank, US$50 for two, and US$5–10 for equipment if you need it. The sleeping shark cave and deep dives run a little higher. Open water certification courses are US$320–340, including equipment and materials.

Sea Hawk Divers (Av. Carlos Lazo at Av. Lopez Mateos, tel. 998/877-1233, www.islamujeres.net/seahawkdivers, 9 A.M.–10 P.M. daily) is a highly recommended dive shop owned and run by Ariel Barandica, a PADI-certified instructor. Service is friendly, professional, and dive groups are never larger than six. Sea Hawk also has a number of excellent rooms above and behind the shop; they're usually booked well in advance, but are definitely worth asking about.

At the end of Avenida Hidalgo on Playa Norte, **Sea Friends** (Playa Norte, tel. 998/860-1589, seafriendsisla@yahoo.com.mx, 8 A.M.–5 P.M. daily) is a professional and welcoming shop that has been in operation since 1974. It offers small groups—six or fewer—and most dives are led by instructors rather than dive masters.

Coral Scuba Dive Center (Matamoros 13-A, tel. 998/877-0763, www.coralscubadivecenter.com, 9 A.M.–10 P.M. daily) the island's largest dive shop, though that isn't always a good thing: On busy days boats carry 12–14 divers at a time and diving here can have a party-like feel. Then again, the shop has plenty of repeat customers, so they must be doing something right. Equipment is in top condition and prices are somewhat lower.

Snorkeling

Isla Mujeres's western side has calm shallow water (7–10 m./23–33 ft.) that's ideal for snorkeling. Tours can be booked at many hotels, on Playa Norte and at kiosks near the ferry pier, and typically cost US$25 per person for 1.5–2 hours. Most groups go to **Lighthouse** (by the ferry piers) and **Manchones** (off the southern end of the island), where the coral and sealife there are in relatively good shape despite the heavy traffic. Dive shops also offer snorkel trips, and are more apt to take you to a less-visited area. Another option is to take a trip to **Isla Contoy**, which usually includes an hour or more of snorkeling in addition to exploring the island.

You can snorkel on your own at **Garrafón de Castilla** (Carr. Punta Sur Km. 6, tel. 998/877-0107, 9 A.M.–5 P.M. daily, US$3.75), a modest beach club at the southern tip of the island. The club itself is a bit desultory, but you can explore over 300 meters (894.3 feet) of coral reef, including the part used by its much-hyped neighbor, Parque Garrafón. Snorkel gear rents for US$5.50, and lockers and towels are US$2 apiece. Hour-long tours to nearby Manchones reef can also be arranged (US$20 pp, including equipment).

Dolphin Discovery

Dolphin Discovery (Carretera Sac Bajo, just past Hotel Villas Rolandi, Isla Mujeres tel. 998/877-0875, reservations 998/849-4748, www.dolphindiscovery.com) offers various dolphin interaction programs at its large facility on the island's calm western shore. Programs vary in price according to the amount and type of direct interaction; the Royal Swim (US$139 pp; 30-minute orientation, 30 minutes in water) is the most interactive, with two dolphins per group of eight people doing a "dorsal tow," "footpush," and "kiss," plus some free swim time. Programs typically begin at 10:30 A.M., noon, 2 P.M., and 3:30 P.M. Most people come from Cancún, either on Dolphin Discovery's private ferry or on an all-day cruise/dolphin package. Oddly, there is no Dolphin Discovery kiosk in Isla Mujeres *centro,* but most hotels can arrange your visit or you can just go yourself. Taxi fare is US$5 from the center and US$7 from Playa Norte. Reservations required.

Eco-Parks

Built on a sloping bluff at the southern end

of Isla Mujeres, **Parque Garrafón** (Carretera Garrafón Km. 6, tel. 998/849-4748, 10 A.M.–5 P.M. Sun.–Fri., US$65 adults, US$49 child; or US$89 adult, US$65 child, all-inclusive) is a combination eco- and water park that sells itself as one of the best in the Riviera. It falls short. While visitors do have a variety of activities to choose from—snorkeling, kayaking, snubaing (like scuba diving, but with a long tube instead of an air tank), or sea treking (a short underwater walking tour using a Martian-like helmet and breathing device)—it's hard to mask the damaged reef. The long curving infinity pool and zip lines are nice but for the price, you might as well swim at your hotel.

Sport Fishing

The fishermen's cooperative, **Cooperativa Isla Mujeres** (Av. Madero pier, no tel., 8 A.M.–8 P.M. daily) offer *pesca deportiva* (sport fishing). Boats typically carry up to six people for the same price, and include nonalcoholic drinks, sandwiches, and bait. Two trips are usually available, depending on the season: Pesca Mediana (US$50 per hour, 3–4 hours minimum) focuses on midsize fish, including snapper, grouper, and barracuda; and Pesca Mayor (US$250, four hours or US$600, eight hours) goes after large catch such as marlin and sailfish. Reserve directly at the pier. Alternatively, many dive shops, including Sea Hawk Divers and Sea Friends, also offer fishing trips for comparable prices.

Body Work

In downtown Isla, **Spa Mexica** (Hidalgo 6, tel. 998/877-1679, 9 A.M.–10 P.M. Mon.–Sat.) offers a range of massages in a recently renovated spa. Massages begin at US$45 an hour and are given by certified masseuses. A great way to ease yourself into the island's rhythm.

The boutique resort, **Casa de los Sueños** (Carretera Garrafón Km. 9, tel. 998/877-0651, www.casadelossuenosresort.com, 9 A.M.–6 P.M. daily) has a beautiful feng shui spa where clients can choose from a number of massages (US$89–149) and body treatments (US$70–115). For a treat, book the Day Escape

(US$140), which includes a welcome drink, a flower petal footbath, a 50-minute massage, a two-course meal at the hotel restaurant, and the use of many of the hotel's facilities for the day. Private yoga instruction also is offered for US$40 per person (two people minimum).

Yoga classes are offered at **Hotel Na Balam** (Calle Zazil-Ha #118, tel. 998/877-0279) at 9 A.M. Mon.–Fri. Classes are free for guests of the hotel, or US$14 per session for everyone else. Ask about monthly rates if you plan to stay awhile.

Spanish Classes

Opened in 2001, **Ixchel Language Institute** (Av. Abasolo near Av. Hidalgo, cell tel. 044-998/82-12-21-86, www.stormpages.com/ixchel) offers Spanish lessons to travelers of all levels. Classes are taught by Laura Hernández, an experienced language teacher from Mexico City, and are scheduled around your day so that you can enjoy the island as much as possible. Standard offerings include "Survival Spanish" to learn basic phrases and vocabulary for traveling, beginner Spanish, and private tutoring where the course is tailored to the student's needs. Set courses are geared for one or two students and the rates are reasonable—US$11 per hour for one person, US$10 for two (minimum five hours). Tailored courses run US$18.50 per hour.

Art and Performance Classes

The **Casa de la Cultura** (Av. Guerrero at Av. Abasolo, tel. 998/877-0639, 9 A.M.–9 P.M. Mon.–Fri.) is a publicly funded organization that offers free or subsidized artistic workshops. Geared toward children and adolescents, classes include dance, painting, ceramics, and singing. Travelers are welcome.

ACCOMMODATIONS

Isla Mujeres has wide variety of lodging options, from youth hostels to upscale boutique hotels. Most budget and mid-range places are in the center, while higher-end resorts occupy secluded areas farther down the island. The latter means renting a golf cart or taking taxis (or else never leaving the hotel grounds, which may be just what you're looking for!).

Under US$50

For all the high-end hotels and day-trippers from Cancún, Isla Mujeres is still a backpacker's haven, the heart of which is the (**Poc Na Hostel** (Av. Matamoros 15, tel. 998/877-0090, www.pocna.com, US$6 pp camping, US$8.50–11.50 dorm, US$22–30 s/d, all with continental breakfast). In this large, labyrinthine hostel, dorms (including one for women only) have 6–10 comfy bunks and a small bathroom, while private rooms are simple and clean, with cement floors and whitewashed walls. Dorm and room prices vary by amenity: fan or a/c, private or shared bathroom, TV or no TV. The airy common area has food service and Internet; another room has Foosball and a pool table. The hostel hosts live music on Sundays and organizes daily activities, from volleyball tournaments to trips to Isla Contoy. The island's best beach is a three-minute walk away. The drawbacks are no kitchen access and the risk you'll never see Maya ruins because you couldn't bring yourself to leave. Visa and MasterCard accepted.

The new owners of **Urban Hostel** (Av. Matamoros at Calle Hidalgo, 2nd Fl., tel. 998/196-3824, US$10 dorm, US$17 s/d) have big plans for their little hostel: new kitchen, new patio bar and grill, new lockers, and new paint, plus a flat-screen TV, satellite Internet, even a massage area. The four dorm areas will continue to have 6–10 bunks apiece and ample space to move around. Private rooms with a shared bathroom have strong fans and are getting new beds. Although well located, Urban Hostel has never managed to reach its full potential as an alternative to Poc Na; completing even half these renovations would be a great start.

If you want a private bathroom but can't swing a mid-range room, consider the low-key **Posada Isla Mujeres** (Av. Juárez near Av. Abasolo, tel. 044-998/191-1531, US$18.50 s/d, US$28 s/d with a/c and TV). Less of a scene than the hostels, rooms are no frills and cramped, but they're clean enough. No charm here but then again, they're not charging for it.

Don't let the reluctant service at the **Hotel Osorio** (Av. Madero near Calle Juárez, tel. 998/877-0294, US$14 s, US$20 d, US$32.50 s/d with a/c and TV) dissuade you from staying here. Mint green floors, peach-colored walls, and flower bedspreads, the rooms not only have old-school character but are super clean and close to the ferry terminal too. Ask for one on the top floor—they open onto an outdoor corridor with decent light and get the best breezes.

If you've outgrown hostels but your wallet hasn't, the bright purple **Hotel Carmelina** (Av. Guerrero 4, tel. 998/877-0006, US$25.50–35 s/d with fan, US$45 s/d with a/c) is a decent choice. The exterior has a slight weekly-motel feel (the managers live in a few ground-floor rooms and another room houses a manicure shop), but the rooms are large, clean, have hot water, and get a good breeze from the open-air corridors. There's only one room with air-conditioning so be sure to call ahead if you want dibs.

Not only a fantastic deal but also perfectly located on Isla's pedestrian walkway, (**Posada Edel** (Av. Hidalgo 12-A, tel. 998/877-0474, hp_edelmar@hotmail.com, US$35 s with a/c, US$45 d with a/c) offers simple, clean rooms with tile floors, cable TV, mini-fridge, and coffeemakers. Doubles also have small kitchenettes—a major plus if you want to save a little money on food. There's no reception desk but the owner typically is around until 2 P.M. If you stop in and find no one, ask for assistance at the gift shop next door.

US$50-100

(**Suites Los Arcos** (Av. Hidalgo 58, tel. 998/877-1343, www.suiteslosarcos.com, US$65–80 s/d) offers large, colorful rooms with gleaming bathrooms and wood furnishings. All have a small fridge and microwave for snacks and leftovers. Four of the 12 rooms have balconies—those overlooking Avenida Hidalgo are great for people watching, while those on the opposite side of the building are huge—perfect for relaxing in the sun.

Down the street, **Hotel Bucaneros** (Calle

Hidalgo 11, tel. 998/877-1222, www.bucaneros .com, US$40–55 s/d, US$65–72 s/d with kitchenette) has 16 nicely appointed rooms, all with modern bathrooms and air-conditioning. Basic rooms can be a bit stuffy, but those with a "kitchenette" (i.e., hot plate, mini-fridge, and toaster) are larger, often with a balcony and a separate dining area. Both are decent deals, considering the market.

(Hotel Casa España (Calle Madero near Av. Medina, tel. 998/877-1675, www.hotelcasa espanaislamujeres.com.mx, US$55–65 s/d with a/c, US$75 with a/c and kitchenette, US$100–110 suite with a/c) is a colorful hotel with a lush central garden and well-maintained pool. The rooms are airy and bright with rustic Mexican wood furnishings and small balconies. Some also come equipped with kitchenettes. As expected, suites are a step up—if you're want to treat yourself, ask for the one with the tub overlooking the Caribbean. The view is spectacular.

Posada del Mar (Av. Rueda Medina 15-A, tel. 998/877-0770, www.posadadelmar.com, US$80–100 s/d) is a friendly, longtime favorite. Spacious, modern rooms have spotless bathrooms, a balcony, air-conditioning, and cable TV. The pool is decent, fed by an attractive stone aqueduct; try a Maya Sacrifice cocktail at the adjoining bar. The advantage here is the location, near restaurants and the ferry terminal, and just across from a pleasant, active beach, where hotel guests have free use of the beach chairs, umbrellas, and kayaks.

Somewhat overpriced for the amenities and locale, the **Hotel Francis Arlene** (Av. Guerrero 7, tel. 998/877-0310, www.francisarlene.com, US$55–60 s/d with fan, US$60–65 s/d with a/c) can still hold its own with its 26 simple and spotless rooms. The decor is dated and only some have cable TV but all open onto a peaceful plant-filled courtyard. Larger, top-floor rooms have ocean views, which is a plus.

(Hotel Villa Kiin (Calle Zazil-Ha 129, tel. 998/877-0045, US$50–135 s/d, US$99–179 suite, including continental breakfast) has an eclectic combination of rooms, from thatch-roof bungalows, to hotel-like rooms with a/c,

to spacious suites with king-size bed and ocean views. The location can't be beat: walking distance to town, a semi-private beach (with no waves—perfect for kids), and Playa Norte just steps away. The hotel has two community kitchens, a TV room, and a leafy garden with hammocks. Rooms are a bit overpriced for what you get, although cooking a few meals will save you a bundle, and the seclusion, location, and family-friendly environment will prove priceless to some.

For a very homey place, **Cielito Lindo** (Av. Rueda Medina at Av. Matamoros, tel. 998/877-0585, joyw@prodigy.net.mx, US$80–90 s, US$100–112) is a great option. There are just two studio apartments, both charmingly decorated with Mexican bedspreads and artwork, tile floors, shelves of used books, and kitchenettes (fridge, coffeemaker, microwave, sink, and dishes in both; gas stove in one only). Both have air-conditioning—but can be rented with fan only, for US$10 a night less—and share a balcony overlooking a busy street. The owner, New York transplant Joy Williams Jones, has lived on the island since 1987. Three-day minimum and adults-only preferred. Reservations recommended.

US$100-300

The best hotel in the *centro* is **(Hotel Secreto** (Sección Rocas 11, tel. 998/877-1039, www.hotelsecreto.com, US$250–280 s/d), an angular glass and stucco hotel exuding discreet, understated class. Modern rooms have stone floors, CD players, thick mattresses, and huge private balconies with lounge chairs and excellent ocean views, especially from the 2nd and 3rd floors. A long curving infinity pool is framed by wide wooden patio, with comfortable deck chairs and a small bar. The rooms and pool overlook the attractive (though often very rough) Playa Media Luna. The hotel does not have a restaurant, but town is a short walk away, and a number of top restaurants deliver here. Continental breakfast included.

Next door to Hotel Secreto, **Hotel la Media Luna** (Sección Rocas 9–10, tel. 998/877 0759, www.playamedialuna.com, US$110–180 s/d) offers clean, classic rooms, many with the same excellent ocean view as the Hotel Secreto. Although not as cool as its neighbor—decor is a bit dated and air-conditioners are the boxy, old-school kind—the Media Luna is still one of the *centro*'s top hotels. Suites have a large balcony and whirlpool tub, and go for US$150 in the low season.

Right on Playa Norte, **Na Balam** (Calle Zazil-Ha 118, tel. 998/877-0279, www.na balam.com, US$180–340) used to be one of Isla Mujeres's top hotels and is still one of the most popular. The restaurant and beach area are excellent—worth visiting even if you don't stay here—and there are daily meditation, yoga, and relaxation sessions for guests. (The hotel receives many yoga tour groups.) But the rooms and grounds leave something to be desired, especially the poolside rooms, which are dreary and not worth the price. Beachside and beachfront rooms have attractive whitewashed walls, stone floors, recessed lights, and (some) private whirlpool tubs. But it's the little insults—scum in the whirlpool tub, broken in-room safes, sometimes surly service, especially at reception—that guests consistently complain about. Not the end of the world, but certainly not what you expect for US$200-plus a night.

A block from Playa Norte, **Cabañas María del Mar** (Av. Carlos Lazo on Playa Norte, tel. 987/877-0179, www.cabanasdelmar.com, US$99–132) has three types of rooms: The cheapest ones are dated and have small bathrooms—there are better options in this range elsewhere. Middle-priced rooms, near the hotel's garden swimming pool, are larger and more comfortable with tile bathrooms and some patio space. The priciest rooms are smallish, but sleek and modern with king-size beds and good ocean views.

Casa Ixchel (Av. Martínez Ross s/n, tel. 998/888-0107, www.casaixchelisla.com, US$89–229) is one of the newer additions to a growing list of boutique hotels in Isla Mujeres. It has just nine rooms, all with names like Grace, Karma, and Serenity. Standard rooms are tiny, suites have a bit more breathing room, and you can actually unpack your bags in the

apartments. But even in the small quarters, each room has a toy kitchenette, deep bathtub, luxurious beds, and classy decor. There are great ocean views from the pool and patio area, though for swimming—and eating—you'll have to head into town. The hotel has a few bikes (and snorkel gear) for guests to borrow, but you may want to rent a golf cart during your stay.

Villa La Bella (formerly Villa Las Brisas, tel.998/888-0342, www.villalabella.com; US$132–165) is run by an amiable American couple, who take pride in personalized service. Having just five rooms and one honeymoon suite certainly helps, and the owners have plenty of honest recommendations of things to do and places to eat, if you ask. Ground-floor rooms have bright paint and whimsical decor (and a/c), and are more cheerful than the *palapa*-roofed units upstairs. The pool is meticulously maintained, and a large, creative breakfast is included; the bar serves outstanding margaritas and other drinks. Taxis pass frequently, though many guests rent golf carts for their stay.

Over US$300

◖ **Hotel Villa Rolandi** (Carretera Sac-Bajo No. 15–16, tel. 998/877-0500, www.villa rolandi.com, US$390–550 s/d) is one of two gorgeous boutique hotels on Isla Mujeres's calm, southwestern shore. Here, every suite has a private terrace with whirlpool tub, deep comfortable beds, two-person shower and steam bath, plus robes, slippers, and breakfast and one meal at the hotel's excellent ocean-front restaurant. An attractive infinity pool overlooks a small beach with umbrellas and beach chairs. The hotel can arrange personalized snorkel, scuba, and other activities, and delivers guests to and from Cancún in a private yacht. No children under 14. A taxi from town costs around US$4.

The boutique hotel, ◖ **Casa de los Sueños** (Carretera Garrafón Km. 9, tel. 998/877-0651, www.casadelossuenosresort.com, US$350–400 s/d, US$450–500 suite) has eight luxurious rooms, most with breathtaking views of the

Caribbean and Cancún beyond. Each is decorated differently but all have high-end Mexican art and furnishings, marble bathrooms, large terraces, and feng shui touches like small gurgling fountains. The hotel also has a swank full-service spa and a meditation room. There's no beach—a drawback for sure—but then again, guests can swim from the hotel's pier or in the small infinity pool. Rates include continental breakfast, roundtrip ferry transportation, minibar consumption, and use of kayaks, bicycles, and snorkel gear. Adults only.

Long-Term Rentals

For weekly rentals, try the apartments at **Color de Verano** (Av. López Mateos at Rueda Medina, tel. 998/877-1264, colordeverano@prodigy.net.mx, www.colordeverano.com, one bedroom US$720–820/week, studio penthouse US$900/week). Over a classy boutique café, the apartments are attractive and fully furnished, with full-size kitchens and large modern bathrooms. All three have air-conditioning and large patios; two have outdoor whirlpool tubs. The studio penthouse is smaller than the one-bedrooms (queen bed instead of king) but has a larger terrace and better ocean view. There's maid service six days a week, and guests have free use of a washer/dryer, and two bicycles per apartment. In-room satellite Internet charged per minute.

FOOD

Seafood is the specialty in Isla Mujeres, even more so than in Cancún. In fact, much of the lobster and fish served on the Riviera Maya is caught near Isla Mujeres, so it stands to reason that it's freshest here. The island's popularity among backpackers, especially Europeans, means you'll also find a number of artsy bistros—look on Avenida Matamoros especially.

Mexican and Seafood

On Playa Lancheros, **❰ Casa Tikinxik** (11 A.M.–6 P.M. daily, US$5–8) is a classic Mexican beach restaurant, with metal tables, cold beer, and finger-licking portions that make the long wait worth it. Be sure to try the specialty,

pescado tikinxik (TEEK'n-cheek), a whole grilled fish prepared in the parking lot grill using a spicy red sauce that dates to Maya times.

❰ La Lomita (Av. Juárez Sur 25-B, tel. 998/826-6335, 9 A.M.–11 P.M. Mon.–Sat., US$4.25–6), a brightly painted restaurant frequented by locals, offers standard, solid Mexican fare. *Comida corrida*—a two-course special with drink—is offered daily and often includes *chiles rellenos,* tacos, and stews. Ceviche, grilled whole fish, and other seafood meals are also featured at reasonable prices.

The **Zazil Ha** restaurant, part of the Na Balam hotel, (Calle Zazil-Ha 118, tel. 998/877-0279, 7 A.M.–11 P.M. daily, US$8–14) has a spacious indoor dining area, with a high *palapa* roof and moody lighting, and smaller beach area that is especially good for watching the sunset. The menu, available in both areas, includes excellent lunch items like ceviche and fish tacos, and equally tasty dinner entrées, like black pasta with calamari and tofu-and-veggie skewers, all in generous portions. Get here from along the beach or from Avenida Zazil-Ha.

A convenient, reliable place to get a meal, **Pinguino** (Rueda Medina 15-A, tel. 998/877-0044, 7 A.M.–11 P.M. daily, US$4–11) is part of Posada Del Mar, but is separated from the reception area so you don't feel like you're at a hotel restaurant. It offers three meals a day: Breakfasts are huge and the chef prepares excellent seafood dishes for lunch and dinner. With a view of the ocean, this is an especially good place to watch the sunset.

Italian

❰ Casa Rolandi at Hotel Villa Rolandi (Carretera Sac-Bajo No. 15–16, tel. 998/877-0500, noon–11 P.M. daily, US$10–20) is arguably the best restaurant on the island. With candlelit tables overlooking the calm southwest-facing shore, the restaurant has impeccable service and a creative Italian-Swiss menu. Everything sounds good, from seafood risotto to pumpkin-stuffed ravioli, plus many more pasta, meat, and fish dishes. The wine and drink selection is large—try a *mojito,* a classic Caribbean drink made of rum, lime, sugar, and fresh mint. Rolandi's also has a popular pizzeria in town (Av. Hidalgo between Avs. Abasolo and Madero) and two in Cancún.

Aquí Estoy (Av. Matamoros at Av. Hidalgo, noon–10 P.M. Mon.–Sat.) serves slices (US$1.50–3) and whole pizzas (US$8.50–10) from its appealing hole-in-the-wall on busy Av. Matamoros. Pesto, veggie, and Hawaiian pizzas are favorites, or try a specialty, like spinach and goat cheese pizza, for a taste treat. Other than a few high stools, it's takeout and standing-room only.

Cafés and Bistros

Operated by three Israelis and a Chilean, **Mañana** (Av. Matamoros at Av. Guerrero, 9 A.M.–5 P.M. Tues.–Sat., US$2–3) is a hip café with an eclectic menu, from kabobs and homemade hummus on pita to cheeseburgers and schnitzel. Great breakfast options include bagels, omelets, fruit, and granola. Half the dining area houses the Cosmic Cosas bookstore, which, along with the good food, cheerful decor and youthful ambiance, make this a natural hub for travelers. Opening and closing hours are somewhat flexible.

The preppy boutique café **Color de Verano** (Av. Lopez Mateos at Rueda Medina, 8–noon and 4–11 P.M. Mon.–Sat.) specializes in light sophisticated fare like quiche, pâté, and banana-flambé crepes, with which you'll feel almost duty bound to order a homemade dessert, glass of wine, or espresso. Three fully furnished apartments also are on the premises for long- and short-term rental.

Café Cito (Matamoros 42, tel. 998/888-0351, 7 A.M.–2 P.M. Mon.–Sat., 8 A.M.–2 P.M. Sun., US$2–6) is reminiscent of a Cape Cod eatery with its breezy blue and white decor and tables with sea shells beneath the glass. It's perfect for breakfast, serving tasty crepes, waffles, coffee, and big creamy *licuados* (milk- or water-based fruit shakes).

Bistro Françáis (Matamoros 29, 8 A.M.–noon and 6–10 P.M. daily, US$5–14) offers fantastic food in a quirky dining area decorated with bright bubble writing, cartoonish drawings, and Mexican hand-painted tiles. French toast is a must for breakfast, while the *coq au vin,* beef kabobs, and lime and caper fish all make terrific dinners, and at surprisingly affordable prices. If vegetables are your thing, the veggie kabob is top-notch and features unforgettable portabella mushrooms. Instead of a beer, wash it down with wine, served by the glass for just US$2–4.

Other Specialties

Another of Isla Mujeres's best and favorite restaurants, **⊂ Casa O's** (Carretera Garrafón 9, tel. 998/888-0170, www.casaos.com, 1–10 P.M. daily, US$9–20) has a romantic *palapa*-covered dining area, with gorgeous views over the turquoise waters all the way to Cancún. The menu is varied and features some of the finest catches and cuts on the island; the filet mignon and shrimp kabobs are especially tasty. Portions are large, but don't miss out on the excellent appetizers and starters, like ceviche, heart of palm salad, and lobster bisque. Located one street below Casa de los Sueños; coming from town, the turnoff is just before the hotel entrance.

In a clapboard house facing the lagoon, with fishing boats crowded up next to it, **El Varadero** (noon–10 P.M. Tue.–Sun., US$7–14) doesn't really evoke the famous white-sand beach east of Havana that it's named for, but good food—and even better mojitos—have a way of trumping geography. Dig into classic Cuban fare while sitting at aluminum tables on an outdoor patio decorated with shipping buoys. Located at the mouth of Laguna Makax, near Puerto Isla Mujeres.

On Playa Norte, **Sunset Grill** (Av. Rueda Medina, tel. 998/877-0785, 10 A.M.–9 P.M. Mon.–Fri., 8 A.M.–9 P.M. Sat.–Sun., US$8–20) offers a great view with cool music on one of the best beaches on the island. Beachside chairs and umbrellas are also available for the day if you order from the menu. Food is standard but good, including grilled fish, ceviche, hamburgers, plus specials like rib eye and BBQ ribs.

Sweets

Aluxes Coffee House (Matamoros at Hidalgo, 7 A.M.–10 P.M. Mon.–Sat., US$1–3) is a great place to hang out with jazz playing in the background, comfy chairs, and artsy decor. Have a cup of caffeine, nibble on homemade brownies, muffins, and cheesecake, and catch up on your postcards. Milk shakes, ice cream sundaes, and smoothies are also offered.

La Michoacana (Av. Bravo at Av. Hidalgo, 9 A.M.–10 P.M. daily, US$0.60–1.50) offers homemade *aguas, paletas,* and *helados* (juices, popsicles, and ice cream). Choose from seasonal fruits including passion fruit, watermelon, pineapple, and mamey. Of course, chocolate- and vanilla-flavored treats are available too.

If you don't mind spending a bit extra on your frozen treats, try **Artesanal Ice Cream** (Av. Madero near Av. Hidalgo, 2–10 P.M. Tues.–Sat., 4–10 P.M. Sun.), a hipsterish ice cream parlor selling a variety of handcrafted ice creams at Häagen-Dazs prices.

Groceries

If you want to take snacks to the beach or prefer to cook your own meals, you can find a good selection of foodstuffs at several markets. **Mirtita** (Av. Juárez 14, tel. 998/887-0157, 7 A.M.–8:30 P.M. Mon.–Sat., 7 A.M.–4:30 P.M. Sun.) is a mom-and-pop grocery store run by the Magaña Family since 1965. **Xpress Super** (central plaza, Av. Morelos, 7 A.M.–10 P.M. Mon.–Sat., 7 A.M.–9 P.M. Sun.) is a chain supermarket offering a variety of all the usual suspects. Just inside the front door, you'll also find a small pharmacy. The **Mercado Municipal** (Av. Guerrero at Av. Matamoros, 6 A.M.–4 P.M. daily) is the place to go for fresh fruits and vegetables on the island, though selection can be slim depending on the season. There are also a handful of restaurants outside the market that serve cheap eats.

INFORMATION
Tourist Information

Across from the ferry docks, the **Oficina de Turismo** (Av. Rueda Medina 130, tel. 998/877-0307, www.isla-mujeres.com.mx, 9 A.M.–4 P.M. Mon.–Fri.) offers general information on the island, including hotel, restaurant, and tour options. It also gives out free brochures, maps, and copies of *Islander,* a twice-yearly tourist magazine.

Can-Do Isla Mujeres (www.cancunmap .com, US$8) is a series of fantastic professional-quality color **maps** of Isla Mujeres. It is extremely detailed, including annotated listings of almost every restaurant, hotel, and point of interest on the island. It is available at many restaurants and hotels or can be ordered online.

Hospitals

The general practitioner physician **Dr. Antonio E. Salas** (Hidalgo 18-D, tel. 998/ 877-0021, 24 hours tel. 998/877-0477, dr salas@prodigy.net.mx, 9 A.M.–3 P.M. and 4–9 pm daily) is highly recommended by islanders. He works directly with the Centro de Salud in town and has connections at most of Cancún's hospitals. He speaks fluent English and basic German.

Hospital Integral Isla Mujeres (Guerrero 7, tel. 998/877-0117, 24 hours daily) is equipped to handle walk-in consultations, simple surgeries, and basic emergencies. In case of a serious injury or illness, patients are taken to a Cancún hospital by boat. Cash only.

Isla Mujeres's primary **hyperbaric chamber** (tel. 998/877-0819, 9 A.M.–4 P.M.), or *cámera hiberbárica* in Spanish, is on the pedestrian-only extension of Avenida Morelos, just north of the center square. Recreational divers use it only very rarely; the main patents here are bent lobstermen, whose association collects monthly dues to help pay for the unit's operation and upkeep.

Pharmacies

Farmacia La Mejor (Madero 17, tel. 998/877-0116, 9 A.M.–10:30 P.M. Mon.–Sat., 9 A.M.–3:30 P.M. Sun.) has a fully stocked pharmacy. It also carries film, toiletries, sunscreen, and other personal items.

Police

The police (central plaza, tel. 998/877-0082) are available 24 hours daily.

FERRIES TO ISLA MUJERES

© LIZA PRADO

The ferry between Isla Mujeres and Cancún is known for its spectacular views of both destinations.

Various passenger ferries (and also a car ferry) leave for Isla Mujeres from Cancún every day. Those leaving from the Zona Hotelera are more expensive and take longer, but may be more convenient.

ZONA HOTELERA

Barcos Mexicanos (El Embarcadero/Playa Linda, Blvd. Kukulcán Km. 4, tel. 998/849-7515, US$10 one way, US$15 round-trip, 30 minutes each way). Departure: 9 A.M.*, 9:30 A.M., 10:30 A.M.*, 11 A.M., 11:30 A.M.*, 12:30 P.M., 2 P.M., and 2:45 P.M.* Return: 10:15 A.M.*, 11:50 A.M., 2 P.M.*, 3:30 P.M. and 5:30 P.M., and 6:15 P.M.* (Departures with an asterisk are available in the high season only.)

Playa Caracol Ferry (Blvd. Kukulcán Km. 8.5, no phone, US$15 round-trip, 30 minutes). Departure: 9 A.M., 11 A.M., and 1 P.M. Return: 11:50 A.M., 3:20 P.M., 5 P.M., and 6:15 P.M.

UltraMar/Playa Tortugas (Blvd. Kukulcán Km. 6.5, tel. 998/843-2011, US$15 round-trip, 30

SERVICES
Money
Immediately in front of the passenger ferry pier, **HSBC Bank** (Av. Rueda Medina between Av. Madero and Av. Morelos, tel. 998/877-0005, 8 A.M.–7 P.M. Mon.–Sat.) provides currency-exchange services and has 24-hour ATMs.

Internet and Telephone
A smattering of Internet and telephone places have popped up around the *centro*, which has helped to reduce the once-exorbitant prices. A couple of reliable and air-conditioned shops include: **IslaMujeres.com** (Madero 17, 8 A.M.–10 P.M. daily, US$1.50/hr.) and **Ciberco Lichos** (Av. Abasolo, between Av.

Hidalgo and Av. Juárez, 10 A.M.–11 P.M. daily, US$1.50/hr.).

For telephone calls, **DígaMe** (Av. Guerrero between Avs. Matamoros and Abasolo, 8 A.M.–10 P.M. Tue.–Sun.) had the best rates on the island at the time of research: US$0.27 per minute to the United States and Canada, US$0.37–65 per minute to Europe and Israel.

Post Office
The post office (Av. Guerrero at Av. Lopez Mateos, tel. 998/877-0085) is open 9 A.M.–4 P.M. Monday–Friday.

Immigration
The immigration office (Av. Medina near Av.

minutes). Departure: 9 A.M., 10 A.M., 11 A.M., noon, 1 P.M., and 4 P.M. Return: 9:30 A.M., 10:30 A.M., 11:30 A.M., 12:30 P.M., 3:30 P.M., and 5:30 P.M.

GRAN PUERTO
Passenger ferries operating from this pier (and neighboring Puerto Juárez) are faster, more frequent, and cost half as much as ferries in the Zona Hotelera. To get here, take the red R-1 bus (US$0.70, 20 minutes) on Blvd. Kukulcán or Av. Tulum; continue past the downtown bus terminal and north out of the city; you'll know Gran Puerto by its tall observation tower. The modern outdoor waiting area has two ATMs, a convenience store, gift shop, and even a McDonalds. Be aware that you may be approached by people dressed in UltraMar uniforms who are in fact selling timeshares.

UltraMar (tel. 998/843-2011, www.granpuerto.com.mx, US$3.50 each way, 15 minutes) boats feature comfy seats in an air-conditioned cabin, an open-air deck, and televisions playing a short promotional program on Isla Mujeres. Departure: every 30 minutes 5 A.M.-10 P.M., plus 11 P.M. and midnight. Return: every 30 minutes 5:30 A.M.-10:30 P.M., plus 11:30 P.M. and 12:30 A.M.

PUERTO JUÁREZ
Two blocks past Gran Puerto, Puerto Juárez is the original Isla Mujeres ferry pier, but the boats and waiting area are older and less comfy than at Gran Puerto.

Transportes Maritimos Magaña (Puerto Juárez, tel. 998/884-5479, US$3.50 each way, 15 minutes). Departure: every 30 minutes 6:30 A.M.-11:30 P.M. daily. Return: every 30 minutes 6 A.M.-8:30 P.M. daily.

PUNTA SAM VEHICLE FERRY
This lumbering vehicle ferry takes 45-60 minutes to cross between Punta Sam, on the mainland, and Isla Mujeres. Rates are according to your vehicle: US$17 for cars, $21 for SUVs, US$6.50 motorcycles, and US$5.50 for bicycles. Rates include the driver only – passengers (including walk-ons) are US$1.50 each way. On Isla Mujeres, the car ferry pier is a few hundred meters south of the passenger piers, past the naval dock. To get to Punta Sam, drive north on Av. Tulum, turn right on López Portillo and follow it to the pier, about five kilometers (3.1 miles) past Gran Puerto. The red R-1 bus also goes there (US$0.50, 30 minutes from downtown). Arrive an hour before your departure to get in line; tickets go on sale 30 minutes prior. Departure: 8 A.M., 11 A.M., 2:45 P.M., 5:30 P.M., and 8:15 P.M. Return: 6:30 A.M., 9:30 A.M., 12:45 P.M., 4:15 P.M., and 7:15 P.M.

Morelos, tel. 998/877-0189, 9 A.M.–3 P.M. Mon.–Fri., 9 A.M.–noon Sat.–Sun.) issues tourist cards to those arriving by boat from another country; for all other matters, including extending your visa, visitors must go to the Cancún office.

Travel Agencies
Isla Travel (Hidalgo 15, tel. 998/877-0805, islatravel@hotmail.com, 9 A.M.–7 P.M. Mon.–Sat., 10 A.M.–2 P.M. Sat.) is a good booking agency for tours—snorkeling, diving, Isla Contoy—on and off Isla Mujeres. Trips to Chichén Itzá, Xcaret, and Cuba also can be arranged. Travel services such as changing flights reservations or purchasing ADO bus tickets are provided as well.

Launderette
Tucked into Plaza Isla Mujeres, **Lavandería Ángel** (Av. Hidalgo, Local A3, tel. 998/151-3774, 8 A.M.–midnight daily) provides cheap laundry service with a smile. Same-day service is US$1 per kilogram (2.2 pounds), with a four-kilogram (8.8-pound) minimum. Express service is US$20 per kilogram, with the same four-kilogram minimum. If you call, they'll pick up and drop off your clothes at your hotel for no extra charge (though a tip to the driver is customary).

Lavandería (Av. Juárez at Abasolo, no tel. 7 A.M.–9 P.M. Mon.–Sat., 8 A.M.–2 P.M. Sun.) is a full-service launderette offering same-day service with a two-hour wait. Loads cost US$4.75 per four kilograms (8.8 pounds).

GETTING THERE

Isla Mujeres has a small airstrip but almost everyone takes the ferry—an inexpensive, quick, and scenic ride through the turquoise *Bahía de Mujeres* (Bay of Women).

Passenger Ferries

Passenger-only ferries leave for Isla Mujeres from Cancún in the Zona Hotelera and Puerto Juárez, about three kilometers (1.9 miles) north of downtown Cancún. If you are just going for the day, reconfirm the return times and remember that late-night ferries go to Puerto Juárez, not the Zona Hotelera.

Car Ferries

A vehicle ferry operates from Punta Sam, about five kilometers (3.1 miles) north of Puerto Juárez in Cancún. (See the *Ferries to Isla Mujeres* sidebar in this chapter for more details.)

GETTING AROUND

Isla Mujeres is a small and mostly flat island. In town you can easily walk everywhere. You could conceivably cover the length of the island on foot, but it's a long, hot walk with no sidewalks. Consider taking the bus, a taxi, or—better yet—rent a bike, moped, or golf cart for a little bit more adventure.

Bus

The bus is the cheapest way to get around Isla Mujeres—US$0.40 a ride. Unfortunately, it runs only between downtown and Playa Lancheros, about halfway down the island. Theoretically it runs every 30 minutes, but be prepared to wait from 45 minutes to forever (gas on the island is limited and sometimes runs out—ask at your hotel about the current situation). Bus stops are every couple of blocks on Rueda Medina and Avenida Martínez Ross

and are well marked with big blue and white signs—they're hard to miss.

Taxi

Isla Mujeres has many more taxis than seem necessary—in town, the danger isn't that you won't be able to hail a cab, but that you might get hit by one. They are especially numerous near the piers. Out of town, you shouldn't have to wait too long for a taxi to pass, and Parque Garrafón, Dolphin Discovery, and Playa Lancheros all have fixed taxi stands. From downtown, rates are US$1.25 around town or to Playa Norte, US$2 to Parque Garrafón, and US$4 to Playa Lancheros or Tortugranja or Punta Sur. Taxis are per trip, not per person, and drivers may pick up other passengers headed the same direction. You can also get a private driving tour of the island for US$13 per hour.

Bicycle, Golf Cart, and Moped Rental

Most rental operations on the island have fixed rates: golf carts—US$14 per hour, US$40 per day (store hours), and US$46 per 24 hours; mopeds US$9 per hour, US$22 per day, US$30 for 24 hours; and bicycles—US$2 per hour, US$8 per day. A word of caution: There are many road accidents, some very serious, involving tourists driving mopeds. Two people on a moped make it significantly less stable, especially for novice drivers, while renting separate mopeds will cost you more than a single golf cart, which carries four or more and is much safer.

Agencies right at the ferry pier may charge slightly more than those a few blocks away. Try **Ppe's Carts and Mopeds** (Hidalgo 19, tel. 998/877-0019, 9 A.M.–5 P.M. daily) or **El Sol Rental** (Av. Madero between Av. Guerrero and the ocean, 998/877-0791, 9 A.M.–5 P.M. daily).

Isla Holbox

At the northeastern tip of Quintana Roo where the Caribbean Sea mingles with the Gulf of Mexico, and completely within the Yum Balam national reserve, Isla Holbox (ohl-BOASH or hole-BOASH) is one of the last obscure islands in the Yucatán Peninsula. The town of Holbox is a fishing village (pop. 2,000) with sand roads, golf carts instead of cars, no ATMs, no cell phone service, no hospital, and no post office. Instead, you'll find brightly painted homes, *palapa*-roofed hotels, and a handful of Italian and Spanish expats who have opened B&Bs. The beaches are loaded with shells of all sorts but don't have the thick sand and reliably crystalline waters that Cancún has (though they are still awfully nice). In the summer, mosquitoes, sand flies, and horseflies can be vicious (come prepared with repellant!). Above all, Holbox offers a sense of peace and tranquility that is increasingly hard to find on Mexico's Caribbean coast, and the feeling of a place as yet untouched by big business. Holbox also offers great opportunities for sport fishing and bird-watching, and from June–September you can snorkel with whale sharks. Whale shark tours are monitored by the government and environmental groups to protect these creatures from harm. Sea turtles nest on Holbox as well, but tours are restricted to avoid disturbing them.

HISTORY

Mayas inhabited Holbox but abandoned the island more than 300 years before the first Europeans—wayward pirates—arrived. The name of the island and town is a matter of some dispute. Some say that "Holbox" means "black water" in a reference to the Maya founders who settled beside a spring whose water appeared to run black. A more popular story is that the pirate Francisco de Molas buried a treasure on the island and cut off the head of his African bodyguard to watch over the spot for eternity. De Molas was promptly killed by a snakebite, but the disembodied head of his bodyguard

appears occasionally to islanders, trying to divulge the treasure's location but succeeding only in scaring everyone away. By this latter account, the island was originally called "Pool-box," meaning "black head," and was apparently bastardized by subsequent Dutch arrivals.

Whatever the reason behind the name, this much is certain—the original town, located farther west, was destroyed by a hurricane and was rebuilt in the current location about 150 years ago. Storms are serious business on this

SEA TURTLES

At one time, sea turtles were plentiful and an important supplement to the regional diet. They were easy prey: Sea turtles were captured and killed as they clambered onto shore to lay eggs. The meat was sun-dried so that it could be eaten over time and the fat saved for soups and stews. The eggs – gathered from the nest or cut from the turtle – were eaten or saved for medicinal purposes.

Today, overfishing has placed all species of sea turtles on the endangered species list. Four of these eight – hawksbill, Kemp's ridley, green, and loggerhead – nest on the shores of the Yucatán Peninsula. Various environmental protection organizations in the Yucatán have joined forces with the Mexican government to save these ancient creatures; they have developed breeding programs and maintain strict surveillance of known nesting beaches to stop poaching.

It is strictly prohibited to capture and trade sea turtles or their products in Mexico. Do not buy their eggs, meat, or products like leather, oils, or tortoiseshell combs. By not participating in the trade of turtle products, you will help to promote the protection of these noble sea creatures.

low, flat island, which is buffeted by tropical conflagrations with some regularity; the most recent hurricane to strike was Wilma in 2005. *Nortes* are fall and winter storms that sweep down the Gulf coast bringing rain and turbid seas. *Maja' che* is the Maya name for sudden winds that can knock over trees; they are most common in April and May. In major storms, the whole island is evacuated.

Storms, however, have not managed to destroy Holbox's oldest house—a red wooden building with a *palapa* roof on the north (beach) side of the park. It belongs to Doña Trini, whose father bought it from the original owner almost a century ago. Doña Trini is a well-known hammock weaver; you can knock on the door to see her work or buy one of the finished products (Igualdad in front of the park, tel. 984/875-2262). Most of the town lives by fishing, though, and Holbox has almost 400 fishing boats and several fishing cooperatives. The town holds a land-and-sea parade on April 14 in honor of Saint Thelmo, patron saint of fishermen.

Other festivals include Environmental Week (July 1–5), when a group of local residents leads activities and presentations at local schools. Tourists can join the kids in one of the week's biggest events: picking up trash from the beach.

SIGHTS
◖ Whale Shark Feeding Grounds

Whale sharks congregate in shallow waters about 10 miles east of the village June–September. Snorkeling with whale sharks is a unique and (to some) nerve-wracking experience. The sharks themselves are harmless—like baleen whales, they eat plankton, krill, and other tiny organisms. But they are big: at 6–7.6 meters (20–25 feet) and more than 10 tons, they're the biggest fish in the world. The captain pulls the boat alongside a shark (at Holbox they tend to feed on the surface) and two guests and a guide slip into the water with life jackets, masks, snorkels, and fins. The water tends to be murky—it's all the sealife in the water that attracts the sharks

Snorkel with whale sharks, gentle giants that feed in these waters.

© LIZA PRADO

in the first place—and the sharks are surprisingly fast. Still, you get a good view of these enormous, gentle animals, with their tiny eyes, bizarre shovel-mouths, and dark spotted skin. It's best to be on a small tour—since you go in two by two, you'll get more time in the water. Tours cost around US$80–90 a person, last 4–6 hours, and typically include snorkel gear, a life preserver, a box lunch, and nonalcoholic beverages. If there is time at the end of the tour, ask to stop off Cabo Catoche for a little snorkeling.

Isla Pájaros

Located in Yalahau Lagoon, **Isla Pájaros** (literally, Bird Island), is a wildlife sanctuary that is home to more than 150 species of birds throughout the year. Frigate birds, white ibis, double-crested cormorants, roseate spoonbills, and boat-billed herons are among the most frequently seen. In addition, between May and September, 40,000 flamingoes typically nest (and rest) here before they migrate to South America. Visitors are not allowed to wander on the island but two observation towers and walkways make spotting birds easy.

Town Beach

The town's main beach has no name but you can't miss it, extending eastward from town and fronted by a few hotels and private homes. It's ideal for beachcombing and shell-collecting, and only somewhat less-so for sunbathing, thanks to wind and a fair amount of dune grass. If you do swim, be sure to dry off immediately: horseflies (*tábanos* in Spanish) love skin still moist with seawater and they pack a mean bite.

Holbox's steady winds and shallow, waveless shore also make it ideal for kiteboarding and other wind sports. The strongest winds are September–March, while July and August tend to have lighter, novice-friendly breezes. Watching the kiteboarders zip and soar over the emerald waters is a sight unto itself. Holbox has a one-person kiteboarding operation if you want to try it for yourself.

© LIZA PRADO

The town beach caters to anglers and travelers alike.

Yalahau Spring

Said to have been used by pirates to fill their water barrels, **Yalahau Spring** is an *ojo de agua* (natural spring) on the edge of the mainland. Today, it is a picturesque swimming hole complete with a large *palapa*, picnic area, and pier. A trip here typically is combined with a stop to Isla Pájaros.

Isla de la Pasión

Just 15 minutes from town by boat, **Isla de la Pasíon** is a tiny deserted island just 50 meters (164 feet) wide. It's known for its white sand beach and beautiful emerald waters—perfect for a relaxing day at the beach. There are trees and a large *palapa* for shade. Be sure to bring plenty of water and snacks—there are no services on the island.

SHOPPING

La Bambina II(Av. Pedro Joaquín Coldwell, besomirosy@hotmail.com, tel. 984/875-2420, 10 A.M.–2 P.M. and 4–8 P.M. Tue.–Sun.) is an artsy shop run by a friendly multilingual Swiss expat named Rosy. Most of the items sold are handmade by locals or artists passing through town. Silver jewelry, bohemian clothes, handbags, and coconut objets d'art decorate this tiny shop. Located behind Hotel Faro Viejo; ask here about whale shark trips as well.

If you're into shells, **Lalo.com** (Abasolo 139, tel. 984/875-2118) is the place to go—it's filled with beautifully polished samples from all over the world. The owner—Maestro Lalo—lives below the shop so if you'd like to see his goods, ring the doorbell, and he'll open up.

If you're interested in buying a hammock or just seeing how they're made, wander over to **Doña Trini's** house (Igualdad in front of the park, tel. 984/875-2262). There, Doña Trini makes hammocks in endless colors and varying sizes. She also welcomes onlookers—whether they buy or not—and enjoys talking about her trade and her island. It takes Doña Trini about a month to complete a hammock so she often is steadily working away at one of her creations; if you want to be sure to see her at work, however, give her a call the night before to let her know

when you'll be stopping by. Hammocks cost US$45–80, depending on the size and material, and can be custom-ordered.

SPORTS AND RECREATION

There is a lot to do on Holbox, and lying in a hammock is one of the most popular activities. If you want to stretch your legs, hotels can arrange various tours, and there are a number of independent tour operators looking for your business. Either way, be clear on what you're getting before you sign up. Ask how many people will be on the tour, how long you will spend at the various sites (as opposed to getting there and back), whether any meals are included, whether the boat has shade from the sun, and whether the guide speaks your language (remembering that the person selling you the trip may not be the guide). You can also see about combining activities, such as going snorkeling before or after bird-watching or visiting the whale sharks. Although there are a handful of tour operators (and more certainly on the way), the following are well recommended: Carmelo at **Posada Mawimbi** (Av. Igualdad on the beach, tel. 984/875-2003, www.mawimbi .net) and Alberto at **Banana Tours** (Av. Igualdad between Avs. Palomino and Bravo, tel. 984/875-2366, 8 A.M.–9 P.M. daily, may close 1–4 P.M. in low season).

Snorkeling and Scuba Diving

Cabo Catoche, a coral reef in about 2–4 meters (6.5–13 feet) of water at the far eastern end of Isla Holbox, is the go-to spot for snorkeling. The water isn't as clear as in Isla Mujeres or Cancún, but the reef here is more pristine, and the animal life more abundant, including stingrays, moray eels, nurse sharks, sea stars, conch, and myriad fish. Because it is so far from town, tour operators usually prefer to combine it with another outing, such as an island tour or visiting the whale sharks. Posada Mawimbi and Banana Tours both offer snorkeling trips to Cabo Catoche for US$50–60 per person, lasting 4–5 hours. Less expensive tours (to nearer areas) can sometimes be arranged.

Posada Mawimbi also offers diving, though

Holbox is not known as a diving destination. The island lies on a huge shallow shelf, surrounded by sand. The best dive sites are a whopping 40–80 kilometers (25–50 miles) away, typically straight into the Gulf of Mexico. The effort is rewarding—shipwrecks, coral reefs, walls, and drift dives—but the long trip there and back is tiring and costly. Visibility is lower than in the Caribbean, although animal life is often more abundant. Posada Mawimbi offers two-tank dives for US$150–200 per person. Trips are small—maximum four divers—but cannot be arranged more than a day in advance because of variable weather in the gulf. Trips include lunch and all equipment.

Wind Sports

Take Off International (www.takeoff.nl/html-nieuw/mexico/index-mexico.htm) offers a three-day (three hours a day) introductory kiteboarding course for around US$335, all equipment included. If you want to improve your jumps, back loops, or just want a refresher, you can take a private two-hour lesson for US$135.

Certified kiters can rent kite and board for US$90 a day or US$350 a week. Take Off is a one-man operation with no fixed office, so you should email in advance to arrange a class; otherwise, ask at Hotel Faro Viejo for more information. Ask about windsurfing or sailing classes, as well, if those are more your style.

Bird-Watching

Holbox has more than 30 species of birds, including herons, white and brown pelicans, double-crested cormorants, roseate spoonbills, and greater flamingos (the brightest pink of the five flamingo species). A bird-watching tour (US$20–40 pp, 3–4 hours) generally includes taking a boat through the mangroves, to Isla Pájaros, and finally, to the flamingo nesting grounds. Most hotels can arrange a standard trip; Xaloc Resort has an island tour for US$25 per person that includes visiting Bird Island and Yalahau Spring, for swimming. Posada Mawimbi has bird-watching tours by kayak—you visit only the mangroves but typically succeed in seeing more birds since there is no motor

© LIZA PRADO

Fly high over the emerald waters of Isla Holbox, one of the best places in the region to kiteboard.

to scare them off (US$40 pp, 3–4 hours). More specialized bird-watchers may want to contact Juan Rico Santana (tel. 984/875-2021)—he leads many of the hotel trips, but he can arrange separate, more focused trips that are tailored to your interests.

Sport Fishing

Holbox is a good spot for sport fishing and still not very well known. A deep-sea fishing tour costs US$250–400, depending on how long you go out. A tour with a local fisherman, going after smaller and more plentiful catch, lasts 4–5 hours and costs around US$100. If you know how to fly-fish, a four- to six-hour tour in search of tarpon runs US$250–350. Most hotels can arrange trips, including Xaloc Resort, Faro Viejo, and Posada Mawimbi.

Baseball

Holbox has an amateur baseball team, known simply as *Selección Holbox* (Team Holbox). The season lasts all summer, and games against visiting teams are held most Sundays at noon at the baseball "stadium" on Avenida Benito Juárez a few blocks from the pier. It's a popular outing for island families, who typically bring tostadas and huge bowls of fresh homemade ceviche to go with the cold beer and soda on sale in the stands. Admission is US$1–2; bring a hat as there is little shade.

ACCOMMODATIONS

For many travelers, a big part of Holbox's charm is staying in one of the bungalow-style hotels that dot the island's long beach. The lodgings vary somewhat in style, amenities, and price, but all aim to offer simple rest and relaxation in a peaceful seaside setting. In town, hotels offer comfortable rooms a short distance from the beach, but at more accessible rates.

Under US$50

It is usually possible to camp on the beach, but **Ida y Vuelta Camping** (Calle Plutarco Elias Calles between Róbalo & Chacchi, tel. 984/875-2358, idayvueltacamping@yahoo .com, www.camping-mexico.com, US$8 per adult, US$5 per child) is a much better option. About 200 meters (650 feet) from the beach, the "campground" has five large *palapas* with sand floors and mosquito screens where you can hang hammocks or pitch a tent—the Italian owners will loan you either one, plus a pad and sheet, if you don't have them. There's a clean colorfully tiled common bathroom and a full kitchen for guests too.

Posada Los Arcos (Av. Benito Juárez at the park, tel. 984/875-2043, US$18.50 s, US$28 s with a/c, US$32.50 d with a/c, US$37 d with a/c and kitchenette) has long been a cheap, reliable option for budget travelers. The place is definitely starting to show its age in peeling paint, saggy mattresses, and so on. Rooms upstairs are better, brighter, and have a patio overlooking an interior garden. Good location and a friendly owner.

A few blocks from the park, **Posada Anhelyng** (Av. Porfirio Díaz s/n, kitty-corner from the soccer field, tel. 998/875-2006, US$37 s/d) has just five units; all have air-conditioning, TV, two beds, and are clean and spacious enough to make up for the somewhat sterile decor. Some rooms have a separate kitchen/eating area with a fridge, though you may have to borrow an electric stove and dishes from the owners. Reception is at the family's blue house on Avenida Porfirio Díaz nearer the park—look for the sign.

Rooms at **Posada D'Ingrid** (Av. Morelos at Av. Pedro Joaquín Coldwell, tel. 984/875-2070, US$32.50–46) are clean and comfortable, though rather small. Each has either a fan or air-conditioning, and either a queen and twin bed, and or two queens. The prices are a bit high for what you get, but there are a full common kitchen and *palapa*-covered eating area in the courtyard. Friendly owner.

US$50-100

⬛ Hotel Posada Mawimbi (Av. Igualdad at the beach, tel. 984/875-2003, www.mawimbi .net, US$50 s/d with fan, US$60 s/d with a/c, US$60–80 bungalow with kitchenette, US$90 suite with a/c) is an upscale *palapa*-roofed posada with modern, comfortable rooms and bungalows that have lots of boho flair. Details like Guatemalan bedspreads, inlaid stones, colorful tile work, and exposed wood beams combine to give the rooms a personalized touch. There's a shady garden with plenty of hammocks and chairs, and the well-tended beach is just steps away. Italian owners Onny and Carmelo maintain a low-key friendly atmosphere, and offer recommended excursions, including whale shark tours, snorkeling, and scuba diving.

Each of the five colorful cabañas at **Villas Los Mapaches** (Av. Pedro Joaquín Coldwell s/n, tel. 984/875-2090, www.losmapaches .com, US$50 bungalow, US$50–75 bungalow with kitchenette) is decorated differently though all have a beachy, homey feel. All have solid wood frames and most have a large bedroom and bathroom, a loft with a queen-size bed, and a fully equipped kitchen and patio. The cabañas are set in a large palm-shaded garden that fronts the beach. It's about five blocks into town and a bit farther to the best swimming and beach areas. Use of the hotel's bicycles is included in the rate.

Opened in 1999, **Hotel La Palapa** (Av. Morelos at the beach, tel. 984/875-2121, www .hotellapalapa.com, US$60 s/d with a/c, US$80 suite with kitchenette) is owned and operated by an Italian family that's been on the island since 1989. Rooms vary in size and quality— some are a bit dim, but the ones facing the Gulf of Mexico have beautiful views. The hotel has a nice garden and small beach area, which the owners keep clean and free of boats (though boats pull up onshore on either side).

Over US$100

Xaloc Resort (Calle Chacchí s/n, Playa Norte, tel. 984/875-2160, www.holbox-xalocresort .com, US$111–165 s/d) is a classy, understated eco-resort about a 15-minute walk from town. It has 18 *palapa*-roofed cabañas sprinkled around two pools; each is large with thick beds, mosquito nets, red-tile floors, and large bathrooms. Though the grounds are nice, they're crowded—too many bungalows on the lot. Also, the beach-front units—definitely

the nicest—get noise from the sand street in front. Nevertheless, service here is excellent, which goes a long way toward a good experience. A full breakfast is included in the rate and is served in the hotel's bright Yucatecan restaurant. If you're interested in booking a tour, Xaloc also offers quality trips, often led by a working biologist.

For quality, amenities, and location, **Villas Delfines** (Playa Norte, tel. 984/875-2196, www.holbox.com, US$90–150) gets our vote. Deluxe beachfront cabañas are spacious and attractive, with wood floors, two comfortable queen-size beds, fridge, and a large patio perfect for morning coffee. The pool and beach areas are often better maintained here than elsewhere, and the restaurant serves good, standard meals. About a 25-minute walk from town, the beach is large and boat-free, and there is less golf cart and moped traffic. Delfines is also an eco-friendly hotel, with waterless composting toilets (nicer than they sound), solar power, and fans only. Garden units are smaller, have concrete floors, and are missing the details that make the beachfront cabañas special.

FOOD

There are only a handful of restaurants on Isla Holbox—some at the beachfront hotels but most on or near the central park. If you stay for more than a couple days, don't stress about where to eat; by the end of your visit, you'll likely end up eating at every place in town.

Restaurants

Antojitos Los Chivos (Av. Benito Juárez at Av. Igualdad, 8 P.M.–midnight daily) is a classic snack shack serving good cheap Mexican food at plastic tables set up on the street. Everything is US$0.50, including Quintana Rooan staples such as *salbutes* and *panuchos,* variations of tostadas.

La Isla del Colibrí (central plaza, Benito Juárez at Av. Porfirio Díaz, 8 A.M.–1 P.M. and 6–11 P.M. daily, US$3.50–8) is especially good for breakfast, with big fruit juices and *licuados.* The fish dishes in the evening aren't bad.

A sister restaurant just down the street is a bit fancier and quite good, but it is open only in the high season.

The popular **Pizzería Edelín** (central park, Av. Palomino at Porfirio Díaz, tel. 984/875-2024, 11 A.M.–midnight daily, US$3.50–10) has decent thin-crust pizza—try the lobster or olive-and-caper toppings. Other options include fish, pasta, and Mexican finger foods. If you can, sit on the porch, as the tables there are much cooler.

Enjoy the breeze on the veranda of **Viva Zapata!** (Igualdad at Av. Benito Juárez, tel. 984/875-2204, 5 P.M.–11 P.M. daily, US$4–10). Specializing in grilled meat and seafood, this is a popular place with travelers. Be sure to check out the homage to Latin American revolutionary leaders inside.

Overlooking the park, **Cueva del Pirata** (central plaza, Av. Benito Juárez at Porfirio Díaz, tel. 984/875-2183, 8 A.M.–11 P.M. Mon.–Sat., US$5–16) is one of the classiest places in town. Soft jazz fills the room and spills out to the candlelit tables on the front porch. Offering a handful of homemade pastas, a dozen sauces to choose from, and imported wine—this is the place to go all-out. Try the lobster marinara sauce—it's worth the premium price. Meat, poultry, and seafood dishes are also offered.

Baked Goods and Ice Cream

A great local bakery, **Panadería La Conchita** (Av. Palomino at López Mateos, 7 A.M.–10 A.M. and 5–9 P.M. daily) makes bread, cookies, cakes, and other baked goods for the entire island's population. Even if you don't buy directly from the store, you're sure to eat some of its products in the town's restaurants and hotels.

Cool off with a homemade treat from **Paletería Ancona** (Morelos between Díaz and Igualdad, 9 A.M.–9 P.M. daily), which makes juices, popsicles, and ice cream from such varied flavors as coconut, peanut, tamarind, rice, and corn.

Groceries

Supplies ebb and flow in Isla Holbox, so you might have to go to more than one store to find everything you're looking for.

Super Monkey's (half a block south of the park on Av. Benito Juárez, 7 A.M.–11 P.M. daily) has canned and packaged food, bug repellent, sunscreen, and toiletries.

Frutas y Verduras (in front of Super Monkey's on Av. Benito Juárez, 7 A.M.–3 P.M. and 4–8 P.M. daily) has the best selection of fruits and vegetables on the island. You'll also find beans, pastas, and spices. Another option is **Frutería Ruby** (Av. Palomino at López Mateos), open daily 7 A.M.–10 P.M.

INFORMATION AND SERVICES

Holbox has no bank, no ATM, and no post office. Few hotels, restaurants, or tour operators take credit cards, so definitely bring enough cash for your stay and in case you decide to stay an extra day or two. (In a pinch, try buying your tours through the top-end hotels, where credit cards are accepted.) Hours of operation on the island are decidedly flexible—"open all day" usually means "closed for a couple of hours in the middle of the day for lunch."

Hospitals

The only health center on the island, **Centro de Salud** (Av. Benito Juárez between Oceano Atlántico and Adolfo López Mateos, 8 A.M.–2 P.M. and 5–7 P.M. Mon.–Sat., 9 A.M.–1 P.M. Sun.) has no phone, occasionally runs out of medicine, and is equipped to handle only minor injuries and illness. For more advanced medical attention, head to Cancún or Mérida; in emergencies you may be able to charter a small plane.

Pharmacies

Farmacia Pepe's (next to Super Monkey's on Av. Benito Juárez, tel. 998/875-2084, 8 A.M.–2:30 P.M. and 5–11 P.M. daily) is the only pharmacy on Holbox. The owners live on-site, so you can always ring if it's urgent.

Internet and Telephone

Facing the park and open late, **Internet El**

Parque (Av. Benito Juárez, 9 A.M.–midnight daily) charges US$1.50 per hour for reasonably fast Internet, and US$0.40 per minute for calls to the United States and Canada and US$0.80 per minute for calls to Europe.

Launderette

A number of women offer laundry service out of their homes, most charging around US$5 for three kilograms (6.6 pounds). Look for signs around town or ask at your hotel.

GETTING THERE
Car, Bus, and Ferry

To get to Holbox, you first need to get to the small coastal village of Chiquilá. There are direct buses from Cancún and Mérida (see those sections for fares and schedules). If you're driving, take old Highway 180 (not the *autopista*) to El Ideal, about 100 kilometers (62 miles) west of Cancún. Turn north onto Highway 5 and follow that about 140 kilometers (87 miles) to Chiquilá, passing though the town of Kantunilkín. (There are shortcuts from both Mérida and Cancún, but they follow smaller, less-maintained roads). You'll have to leave your car in Chiquilá. Several families run small overnight parking operations, charging US$4–5 a day.

The **9 Hermanos** (US$3.75; 25 minutes) ferry to Isla Holbox leave Chiquilá at 6 A.M., 8 A.M., 10 A.M., 11 A.M., noon, 2 P.M., 4 P.M., 5 P.M., and 7 P.M. Returning boats leave Holbox at 5 A.M., 7 A.M., 9 A.M., 10 A.M., 11 A.M., 1 P.M., 3 P.M., 4 P.M. and 6 P.M. Going to Holbox, it's a good idea to get to the dock a half hour early as the boat occasionally leaves ahead of schedule. Private boatmen make the trip in either direction for approximately US$23.50–32.50 for up to six people; ask at the dock.

From Chiquilá, second-class buses to Cancún (US$6.50) leave the dock parking area at 5:30 A.M., 7:30 A.M., and 1:30 P.M.; all wait for the boat arriving from Holbox. To Mérida, there's just one bus at 5:30 A.M. (US$14).

If you get stuck in Chiquilá, the **Hotel Puerta del Sol** (US$22 s/d with fan, US$30 with a/c) is your only option, located a short distance back down the main road from the dock. Rooms here are very simple, all with TV and private bath. Fan rooms are fairly dumpy, but those with air-conditioning are newer and nicer. There are several basic restaurants facing the dock parking area.

Air

Aerosaab (tel. 984/873-0804, www.aerosaab .com) offers a popular full-day tour to Isla Holbox from its home base in Playa del Carmen. Using one of two 4- to 5-passenger Cessna airplanes, the trip includes a scenic flight up the coast to Holbox, plus a tour of Isla Pájaros and Yalahau spring, and a chance to explore the village and beach. (US$305 pp, plus US$6–25 airport fees, minimum four people). If time is short, and money long, it's certainly a memorable way to visit.

GETTING AROUND

Holbox is very easy to get around on foot. Even the farthest hotels are no more than a half hour's walk from town, and it's very safe day or night. Though you can rent golf carts the only time you really need one is getting between the pier and your hotel with your bags. Golf carts serve as the island's taxis (some are even painted in yellow and black checkers). A ride from the pier into town is US$1 per person or US$2.50 to the hotels farther down the beach. There are always taxis parked around the plaza, or your hotel can call one.

Golf Cart Rental

It's hard to imagine really needing a golf cart, but if you find a reason there are numerous *rentadoras* (rental shops), including **Rentadora Glendy** (Av. Porfirio Díaz at Av. Morelos, tel. 984/875-2093, 7 A.M.–11 P.M.) and **Rentadora El Brother** (Av. Benito Juárez at Av. Igualdad, tel. 998/875-2018, 8 A.M.–10 P.M. daily). All charge about the same: US$8 per hour, US$30 for six hours, US$45 for 12 hours, and US$55 for 24 hours.

ISLA COZUMEL

All around Isla Cozumel, the Caribbean Sea glitters a hundred shades of blue. Beneath the waves, Cozumel's pristine coral reefs make for spectacular diving and snorkeling, the island's number one draw. San Miguel de Cozumel—usually just called Cozumel, since it's the only city on the island—is where the ferries from Playa del Carmen land. It's also where cruise ships, as many as 10 per day in the high season, arrive; it's then that the waterfront promenade becomes a human river, flowing slowly down a channel of jewelry stores, souvenir shops, and open-air restaurants.

Just a few blocks from the promenade, another Cozumel emerges, a small friendly community where old folks sit at their windows and dogs sleep in the streets. In spring, masses of orange *framboyán* (poinciana) flowers bloom on shade trees in the plaza, and festivals and religious celebrations are widely attended.

Cozumel's interior—including an important Maya ruin—and its eastern shore are yet another world, lacking even power lines and telephone cables. Heavy surf makes much of the eastern shore too dangerous for swimming, but you easily can spend a day beachcombing or relaxing on the unmanicured beaches and lunching at small restaurants overlooking the sea.

As Mexico's largest island, it shouldn't be surprising to discover that the island is so multifaceted. But it's hard not to marvel at how stark the differences are. Come for the diving and snorkeling, but leave time to experience a side of Cozumel you may not have expected.

© LIZA PRADO

HIGHLIGHTS

【 Museo de la Isla de Cozumel: Soak in the history and ecology of Mexico's largest island, a longtime Maya mecca and a bull's-eye for hurricanes (page 103).

【 Santa Rosa Wall: Sit back and enjoy the ride at one of the island's favorite dive sites, where a strong current whisks you past a stony wall teeming with sealife (page 106).

【 Palancar: Stretching a full three miles, this dive site has something for everyone, from snorkeler-friendly shallows to deep coral ravines (page 107).

【 San Gervasio: Thought to be dedicated to Ixchel, the goddess of fertility, this is Cozumel's best Maya ruin (page 107).

【 Parque Ecológico Punta Sur: Explore this popular national park, with a crocodile-infested lagoon, colorful coral reef, and even an ancient Maya lighthouse (page 116).

LOOK FOR **【** TO FIND RECOMMENDED SIGHTS, ACTIVITIES, DINING, AND LODGING.

PLANNING YOUR TIME

Don't let the cruise ship hubbub on Avenida Rafael Melgar turn you off from the town altogether. Besides the fact that most of the hotels, dive shops, banks, and other services are here, the town itself has much to offer, including a pleasant central plaza and a great museum. Budget a day or two to rent a car to explore the rest of the island, including the beach clubs, Maya ruins, family-friendly eco-parks, and the wild beaches and deserted coastline of Cozumel's eastern side.

HISTORY

Cozumel has been inhabited since 300 B.C. and was one of three major Maya pilgrimage sites in the region (the others were Chichén Itzá and Izamal in Yucatán state). The name is derived from the island's Maya name *Cuzamil* (Land of Swallows). The height of its occupation was A.D. 1250 to 1500, when Putún people (also known as the Chontol or Itzás, the same group who built Chichén Itzá's most famous structures) dominated the region as seafaring merchants. Capitan Don Juan de Grijalva "discovered" the island in 1518 and renamed it Isla de Santa Cruz, marking the beginning of the brutal dislocation of the native people by Spanish explorers and *conquistadores*. It eventually was overrun by British and Dutch pirates who used it as a base of operations. By the mid-1800s, however, the island was virtually uninhabited. The henequen, chicle, and coconut oil booms attracted a new wave of people to the Quintana Roo

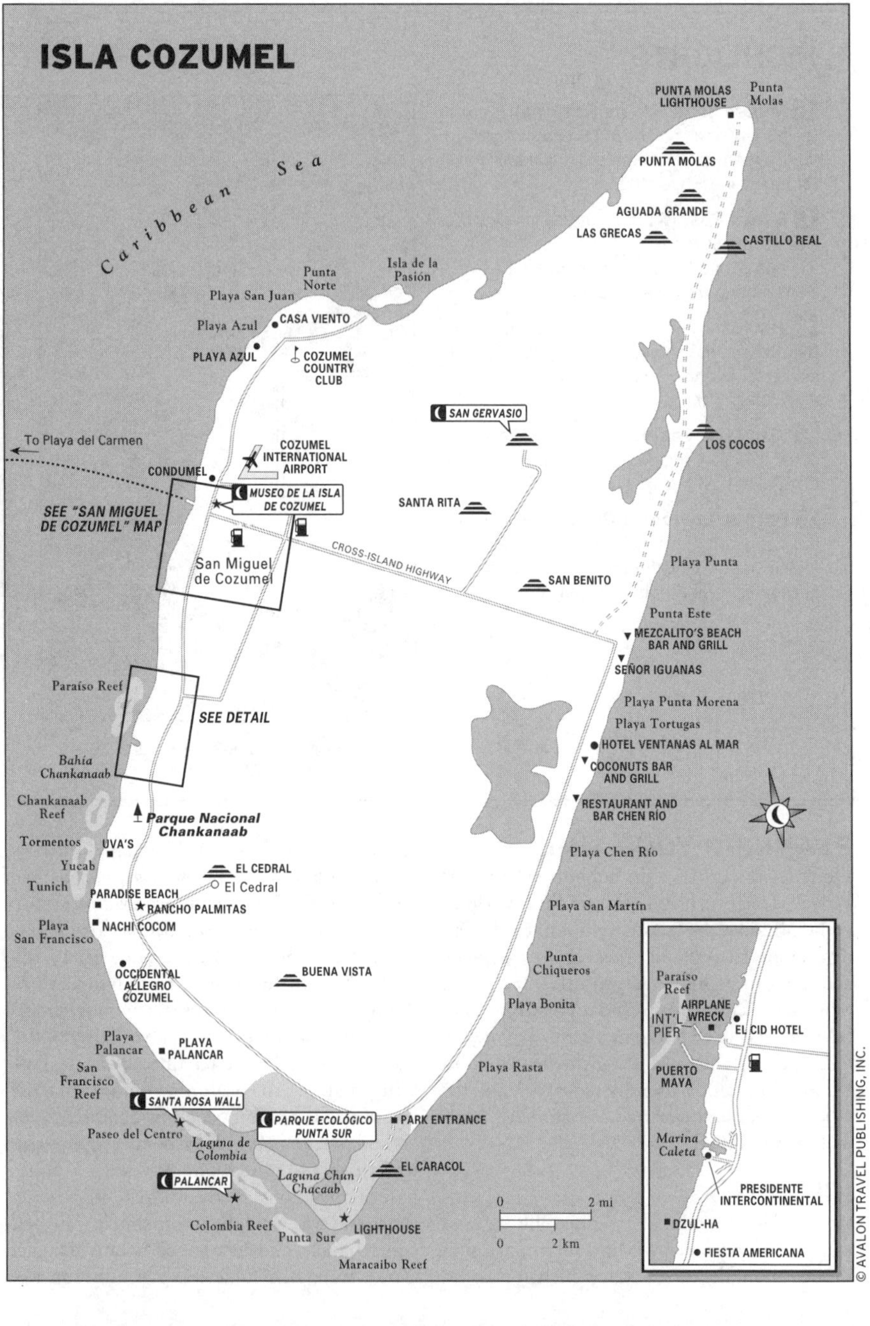

ISLA COZUMEL

ISLA COZUMEL

Caribbean Sea

PUNTA MOLAS LIGHTHOUSE   Punta Molas

PUNTA MOLAS

AGUADA GRANDE

LAS GRECAS   CASTILLO REAL

Punta Norte

Isla de la Pasión

Playa San Juan

Playa Azul   CASA VIENTO

PLAYA AZUL   COZUMEL COUNTRY CLUB

SAN GERVASIO

LOS COCOS

To Playa del Carmen

CONDUMEL

COZUMEL INTERNATIONAL AIRPORT

MUSEO DE LA ISLA DE COZUMEL

SANTA RITA

SEE "SAN MIGUEL DE COZUMEL" MAP

San Miguel de Cozumel

CROSS-ISLAND HIGHWAY

SAN BENITO

Playa Punta

Punta Este

MEZCALITO'S BEACH BAR AND GRILL

SEÑOR IGUANAS

Paraíso Reef

SEE DETAIL

Playa Punta Morena

Playa Tortugas

HOTEL VENTANAS AL MAR

Bahía Chankanaab

COCONUTS BAR AND GRILL

Chankanaab Reef

RESTAURANT AND BAR CHEN RÍO

Tormentos   **Parque Nacional Chankanaab**

UVA'S

Yucab

Tunich

EL CEDRAL

El Cedral

PARADISE BEACH   RANCHO PALMITAS

NACHI COCOM

Playa San Francisco

Playa Chen Río

Playa San Martín

BUENA VISTA

OCCIDENTAL ALLEGRO COZUMEL

Punta Chiqueros

Playa Bonita

Playa Palancar

San Francisco Reef

PLAYA PALANCAR

Playa Rasta

SANTA ROSA WALL

Paseo del Centro

PARQUE ECOLÓGICO PUNTA SUR   PARK ENTRANCE

Laguna de Colombia

PALANCAR

Laguna Chin Chacaab

EL CARACOL

Colombia Reef   Punta Sur   LIGHTHOUSE

Maracaibo Reef

0   2 mi

0   2 km

Paraíso Reef

AIRPLANE WRECK

INT'L PIER   EL CID HOTEL

PUERTO MAYA

Marina Caleta

PRESIDENTE INTERCONTINENTAL

DZUL-HA

FIESTA AMERICANA

© AVALON TRAVEL PUBLISHING, INC.

territory (it didn't become a state until 1974) and Cozumel slowly rebounded, this time with a mostly Mexican mestizo population. With the establishment of Cancún in the 1970s, and the "discovery" of Cozumel's reefs by Jacques Cousteau, Cozumel's future as a tourist and diving destination was set.

ORIENTATION

The town of San Miguel de Cozumel is located on the west side of the island. The main pas-

senger ferry lands here, across from the central plaza. Most streets are one-way in town; if you're driving, be aware that *avenidas* (avenues) run north–south and have the right-of-way over *calles* (streets), which run east–west. Once you leave town, there is a single road that circles the entire island.

Avenida Benito Juárez is one of the main streets in San Miguel de Cozumel, beginning at the central plaza, crossing town, and becoming the Cross-Island Highway.

SAN MIGUEL DE COZUMEL

SCALE NOT AVAILABLE

© AVALON TRAVEL PUBLISHING, INC.

HURRICANE WILMA

Hurricane Wilma was the worst hurricane of the worst storm season ever recorded in the Atlantic. There's a remarkable satellite image, which many shop owners in Isla Cozumel have tacked to their walls, of the huge spinning storm spread across the Caribbean, Isla Cozumel visible in its eye. Both Cozumel and Cancún received direct hits, and the storm took its time leaving: for nearly three days, the region was pummeled with severe rain, wind, and surf.

Wilma struck Mexico in late October 2005, having already rampaged through the Caribbean and headed for Florida. It was the 13th hurricane that year, the fourth to reach Category 5 – the weather service's strongest classification – and only the third Category 5 hurricane ever known to have developed in the month of October. At its peak, Wilma was the single most intense hurricane ever recorded in the Atlantic basin (by barometric pressure) and had wind speeds of 185 mph (296 kph). The weather service even retired the name Wilma, assuring the massive storm's place in history.

Tens of thousands of travelers and residents rode out the storm, despite urgent evacuation orders in the days just before it hit. News reports showed vacationers huddled in hotel ballrooms, even as windows shattered and waves crashed against 3rd-story balconies. In Mexico alone, Wilma killed eight people and caused US$7.5 billion in damages; in all, however, Wilma hit a half-dozen countries, caused 63 deaths, and totaled US$25 billion in damages.

Wilma hit Mexico's tourism industry just as hard, coming just before the all-important holiday season. After intense media coverage of the storm itself and of the travails of tourists trying to get home afterward, scant attention was paid to the region's recovery and cleanup, which was amazingly quick and complete. Many businesses reopened within days. But shaken tourists stayed away and the high season was a total wash. Anticipating this, a number of hotels jump-started long-planned renovations, in some cases quite extensive. Ironically, one of Wilma's long-term effects has been the *improvement* of overall hotel quality and star rating, especially in Cancún. And while the storm stripped some beaches bare – and sand had to be pumped in to refill them – other beaches turned out even wider and more accessible than ever, and remain so today.

Hurricane Wilma also underscored the remarkable camaraderie of locals and expatriates throughout the entire region. Almost to a person, residents describe emerging from their storm-lashed homes and businesses, picking up shovels and wheelbarrows, and working side-by-side with their neighbors to put their communities back together. It's this same resilience and spirit that has long made the Riviera Maya and Yucatán Peninsula a special place to visit, and will continue to do so, even as those famous satellite pictures of Wilma, still tacked to store walls, fade to yellow and curl around the edges.

The highway passes the turnoff to the San Gervasio ruins before intersecting with the coastal road. The coastal road follows Cozumel's eastern shore, which is dotted with a few beach clubs and restaurants. Rounding the southern tip, the road heads north along the west shore before becoming Avenida Rafael Melgar, and returning to the central plaza. Continuing north, the road passes turnoffs to the airport and a country club before turning to dirt and eventually dead-ending.

Sights

ISLA COZUMEL

THE CENTRAL PLAZA

In and around Cozumel's central plaza stand colonial and modern civic buildings, a boxy clock tower, and busts of the late Mexican president Benito Juárez and the general Andrés Quintana Roo. On Sunday evenings locals and tourists meet here. Families—sometimes three generations—gather around the white gazebo to hear Latin rhythms and tunes of the day played by local musicians. A few women still wear the lovely white *huipiles,* while men look crisp and cool in their traditional *guayaberas.* Children, dressed as miniatures of their parents, run, play, and chatter in front of the band. It's hard to say who does the best business—the balloon man or the cotton-candy vendor. In short, it's a pleasant place to spend an evening.

◖ MUSEO DE LA ISLA DE COZUMEL

The town's small but excellent museum (Av. Rafael Melgar at Calle 6, tel. 987/872-1434, 9 A.M.–5 P.M. Mon.–Sat., 9 A.M.–4 P.M. Sun., US$3) is on the waterfront in an old building that once housed a turn-of-the-20th-century hotel. Well-composed exhibits in English and Spanish describe the island's wildlife, coral reefs, and the fascinating, sometimes tortured history of human presence here, from the Maya pilgrims who came to worship the fertility goddess to present-day survivors of devastating hurricanes. Be sure to visit in the morning if you want to avoid the cruise ship crowds. The museum also has a small bookstore, a library, and a pleasant outdoor café overlooking the sea.

CORAL REEFS

Cozumel's coral reef—and the world-class diving and snorkeling it provides—is the main reason people come to the island. The reef was designated a national marine reserve more than two decades ago, and the waters have thrived under the park's rigorous protection and clean-up programs. Hurricane

© LIZA PRADO

Cozumel's central plaza is a hub of social activity.

ISLA COZUMEL

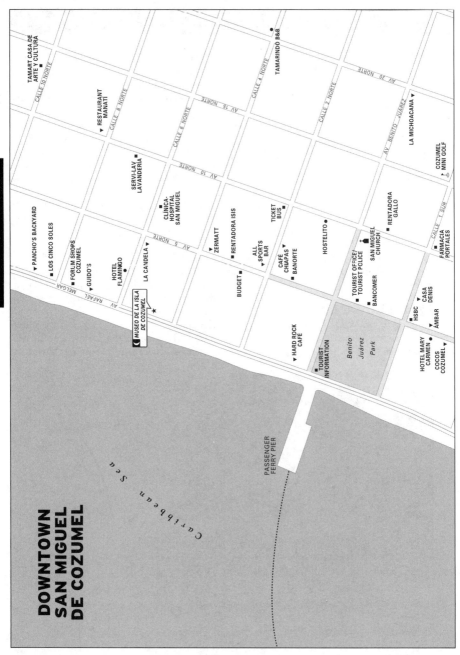

DOWNTOWN SAN MIGUEL DE COZUMEL

Caribbean Sea

TAMART CASA DE ARTE Y CULTURA

RESTAURANT MANATÍ

SERVI-LAV LAVANDERIA

PANCHO'S BACKYARD

LOS CINCO SOLES

FORUM SHOPS COZUMEL

GUIDO'S

HOTEL FLAMINGO

LA CANDELA

CLINICA-HOSPITAL SAN MIGUEL

ZERMATT

RENTADORA ISIS

ALL SPORTS BAR

CAFÉ CHIAPAS

BANORTE

BUDGET

TICKET BUS

HOSTELITO

RENTADORA GALLO

TOURIST OFFICE/ TOURIST POLICE

SAN MIGUEL CHURCH

BANCOMER

HSBC

CASA DENIS

AMBAR

FARMACIA PORTALES

LA MICHOACANA

COZUMEL MINI GOLF

MUSEO DE LA ISLA DE COZUMEL

HARD ROCK CAFÉ

TOURIST INFORMATION

Benito Juárez Park

HOTEL MARY CARMEN

COCOS COZUMEL

PASSENGER FERRY PIER

CALLE 10 NORTE
CALLE 8 NORTE
CALLE 6 NORTE
AV 20 NORTE
CALLE 4 NORTE
CALLE 2 NORTE
AV BENITO JUÁREZ
AV 15 NORTE
AV 10 NORTE
AV 5 NORTE
CALLE 1 SUR
AV RAFAEL MELGAR
TAMARINDO B&B

ISLA COZUMEL

SCALE NOT AVAILABLE

Mercado Público

AV PEDRO JOAQUIN COLDWELL

AV 25 SUR

CALLE ROSADO SALAS

CALLE 3 SUR

AV 20 SUR

HOTEL PEPITA

BLAU NET

DEEP BLUE

IMMIGRATION OFFICE

AMARANTO BUNGALOWS

SUITES COLONIAL

LAVANDERIA EXPRESS

PRIMA TRATTORIA

LA CHOZA

PANADERIA COZUMELEÑA

AV 15 SUR

PRO DIVE COZUMEL

CARIBBEAN DIVERS

ESPECIAS

VILLAS LAS ANCLAS

ISLAND COFFEE

EL CAPI NAVEGANTE

CALLE 5 SUR

PEPE'S GRILL

SUITES BAHIA

DIMI DIVERS

SABORES

WEB STATION

COFFEELINA

LE CHEF

AV 10 SUR

HYPERBARIC MEDICAL CENTER

VISTA DEL MAR

CALLE 7 SUR

MI CASA EN COZUMEL

CASA MEXICANA

CHA CHA CHA DIVE SHOP

FARMACIA DORI

AV 5 SUR

LA LOBSTERIA

CALLE 5 SUR

POST OFFICE

SEÑOR FROG'S

PUNTA LANGOSTA PIER

CARLOS'N CHARLIE'S

PUNTA LANGOSTA

CALLE 11 SUR

AV RAFAEL MELGAR

JEANNIE'S WAFFLES AND RAUL'S TACOS

NEPTUNO

1.5 TEQUILA LOUNGE

© AVALON TRAVEL PUBLISHING, INC.

Wilma took a major toll on the reef, snapping off coral and sponges with its powerful surge, and leaving other sections smothered under a thick layer of sand and debris. But hurricanes are nothing new to Cozumel or its coral, and reports of vast damage to the reef were greatly exaggerated. Cozumel's underwater treasure remains very much alive, supporting a plethora of creatures, its seascapes as stunning as ever. Dozens of dive and snorkeling sites encircle the island, and the 1,000-meter-deep (3,281-foot) channel between Cozumel and the mainland still provides spectacular drift and wall dives. Here is a list of some of the most popular dives, though by no means all of the worthwhile ones. (See *Sports and Recreation* for information on dive shops.)

Airplane Wreck

A 40-passenger Convair airliner lies on Cozumel's seabed, about 65 meters (195 feet) from the shore near the El Cid hotel. Sunk in 1977 for the Mexican movie production of *Survive II,* the plane has been broken into pieces and strewn about the site by years of storms. The site itself is relatively flat, though with parrot fish, damselfish, and a host of sea fans and small coral heads, there's plenty to see. With depth ranges from 3–15 meters (9–45 feet), this is a good site for snorkelers too.

Paraíso

Just south of the International Pier, and about 200 meters (656 feet) from shore, lies Paraíso, an impressive two-lane coral ridge. Medium-size coral—mostly brain and star—attract French and gray angelfish, squirrel fish, and sea cucumbers. This site is also popular for night dives because of its proximity to hotels, which means less time on the boat. Depth ranges from 11–15 meters (33–45 feet). Snorkeling is decent near the shore but be very careful of boat traffic.

Dzul-Ha

One of the best spots for snorkeling from shore, Dzul-Ha has small coral heads and sea fans that support a colorful array of fish like blue tangs, parrot fish, and queen angels. Steps lead into the ocean and concession stands rent snorkel gear (US$10) on the beach. Popular with tour groups. Depths range from 3–10 meters (10–30 feet).

Tormentos

About 60 coral heads can be seen at this site, each decorated with an assortment of sea fans, brain and whip corals, and sponges. Invertebrates like to hide out in the host of crevices—look for flamingo tongue shells, arrow crabs, and black crinoids. Lobster and nurse sharks like the scene too—keep your eyes peeled for them, especially at the north end of the site. Depth ranges from 10–20 meters (30–60 feet). Popular with photographers.

Yucab

A perfect drift dive, Yucab has archways, overhangs, and large coral heads—some as tall as 3 meters (10 feet)—that are alive with an incredible array of creatures: lobsters, banded coral shrimp, butterfly fish, and angelfish can almost always be found here. Video photographers typically have a field day. Depth ranges from 12–20 meters (36–60 feet).

Tunich

Tunich usually has a 1.5-knot current, which makes it an excellent high-velocity drift dive. The site itself has a white sand bottom with a gentle downward slope that ends in a drop-off. Along the way, the reef is dotted with basket sponges and intricately textured corals. Divers regularly encounter turtles, eagle rays, moray eels, bar jacks, and parrot fish. The depth ranges from 15–30 meters (45–90 feet).

◖ Santa Rosa Wall

With a sensational drop-off that begins at 22 meters (72.2 feet), this spectacular site is known for its tunnels, caves, and stony overhangs. Teeming with sealife, divers encounter translucent sponges, mammoth sea fans, file clams, blennies, fairy basslets, gray angelfish, and groupers. Strong currents make this a good drift dive, especially for experienced divers. Depth ranges from 10–30 meters (30–90 feet).

Paso del Cedral

A strip reef lined with small corals like disk and cactus, this site attracts large schools of fish like blue striped grunts and snapper—perfect for dramatic photographs. Southern stingrays often are seen gliding over the sandy areas just inside the reef. Depths range from 10–20 meters (30–60 feet).

☾ Palancar

This spectacular five-kilometer-long (3.1-mile) dive spot is actually made up of five different sites—Shallows, Garden, Horseshoe, Caves, and Deep. It is known for its series of enormous coral buttresses. Some drop off dramatically into winding ravines, deep canyons, and passageways; others have become archways and tunnels with formations 15 meters (49.2 feet) tall. The most popular site here is Palancar Horseshoe, which is made up of a horseshoe-shaped series of coral heads at the top of a drop-off. All the sites, however, are teeming with reef life. Palancar ranges in depth from 10–40 meters (30–120 feet).

Colombia

An enormous coral buttress, Colombia boasts tall coral pillars separated by passageways, channels, and ravines. Divers enjoy drifting past huge sponges, anemones, and swaying sea fans. Larger creatures—sea turtles, groupers, and spotted eagle rays—are commonly seen here. This drift dive is recommended for experienced divers. Depths range from 10–40 meters (30–120 feet).

Maracaibo

At the island's southern tip, Maracaibo is a deep buttress reef interspersed with tunnels, caves, and vertical walls. It is known for its immense coral formations as well as its large animals—sharks (blacktips, hammerheads, tigers, and bulls) and schools of manta and eagle rays. A deep-drift dive, this site is recommended for advanced divers only. Depths range from 30–40+ meters (90–120+ feet).

ARCHAEOLOGICAL ZONES

Isla Cozumel played a deeply significant role in the Maya world as an important port of trade and, more importantly, as one of three major destinations of religious pilgrimages (the others were Izamal and Chichén Itzá, both in Yucatán state). The island's primary site—known as San Gervasio today—was dedicated to Ixchel (Lady Rainbow), the Maya goddess of fertility (and of the Moon, childbirth, medicine, and weaving). Archaeologists believe that every Maya woman was expected, at least once in her life, to journey to Cozumel to make offerings to Ixchel for fertility—her own, and that of her family's fields. Cozumel's draw was powerful, as inscriptions there refer to places and events hundreds of miles away.

Twenty-four archaeological sites have been discovered, though only three are easily accessible, and only the largest—San Gervasio—can properly be called a tourist attraction. San Gervasio is certainly not as glorious as ruins found on the mainland, but well worth a visit all the same.

☾ San Gervasio

The area around San Gervasio (Cross-Island Hwy. Km. 7, www.cozumelparks.com, 7 A.M.–4 P.M. daily, US$5 Mon.–Sat., US$2 Sun.) was populated as early as A.D. 200, and remained so after the general Maya collapse (A.D. 800-900) and well into the Spanish conquest. In fact, archaeologists excavating the ruins found a crypt containing 50 skeletons along with numerous Spanish beads; the bodies are thought to be those of 16th-century Maya who died from diseases brought by the conquistadors.

Today's visitors will find a modest ruin, whose small square buildings, low to the ground with short doors, are typical of those found elsewhere on the island. This style, known as *oratorio,* almost certainly developed in response to climatic imperatives: Anything built here needed to withstand the hurricanes that have pummeled Cozumel for millennia.

© LIZA PRADO

San Gervasio is known for its small structures, well-preserved *sacbes* (stone causeways), and this archway, which leads to the site's central plaza.

(Sure enough, Hurricane Wilma did no major damage to San Gervasio's structures.)

San Gervasio has three building groups, connected by trails that follow the same ancient causeways used by the city's original inhabitants. Entering the site, you'll come first to a structure known as *Las Manitas* (Little Hands), so named for the red handprints still visible on one of its walls. This structure is thought to have been the home of one of San Gervasio's kings, and the inner temple was likely a personal sanctuary.

Bearing left, the trail leads to the Plaza Central, a large courtyard surrounded by low structures in various states of decay. This served as the seat of power in San Gervasio's latest era, from A.D. 1200 onward.

A 0.5 kilometer (0.3 mile) from there is the site's largest and most important structure: *Ka'na Nah,* (Tall House). Also dating to San Gervasio's later era, this was the temple of the goddess Ixchel, and in its hey-day would have been covered in stucco and painted red, blue, green and black.

Other structures on the site include a somewhat precarious looking arch that served as an entrance to the central plaza and *Nohoch Nah* (Big House), a boxy but serene temple at the edge of the city. With an interior alter, the temple might have been used by religious pilgrims to make an offering upon entering or leaving San Gervasio. It was originally covered in stucco and painted a multitude of colors.

Guides can be hired at the visitor's center for a fixed rate: US$17 for a one-hour tour in Spanish, English, French, or German. Prices are per group, which can include up to six people. Tips are customary and not included in the price.

El Cedral

South of town and just beyond Playa San Francisco, a paved turnoff leads to El Cedral (8 A.M.–5 P.M. daily, free), the oldest Maya structure on the island. Once the hub of Maya life on the island, it is the first Maya site that the Spaniards stumbled upon in 1518; allegedly, the first Catholic mass in Mexico was held here. Today, it is small and underwhelming though it still bears a few traces of the original paint and stucco. (Amazing, despite the passage of time—and its use as a jail in the 1800s—that these remnants are left). The ruin is located in the like-named village of El Cedral; tour operators often take visitors there to wander about and buy handicrafts.

El Caracol

Located inside Parque Ecológico Punta Sur, El Caracol is a small, conch-shaped structure that dates to A.D. 1200. It's believed to have been a lighthouse, where Mayas used smoke and flames to lead boats to safety. Small openings at the top of the structure also acted as whistles to alert Mayas to approaching tropical storms and hurricanes. The US$10 park admission includes access to the small site.

Castillo Real

Castillo Real is a partially excavated site with a temple, two chambers, and a lookout tower. It is believed to have been a Maya watchtower to protect against approaching enemies. It's located on the northeastern side of the island, on the sand road to Punta Molas. Unfortunately, at the time of research, it was prohibited to visit this part of the island because of a legal dispute (see *Northeastern Cozumel*).

BEACHES AND BEACH CLUBS

Cozumel isn't famous for its beaches, but it is not without a few beautiful stretches of sand. A series of beach clubs on the calmer west side are the best places to enjoy the sun and sand, but can get crowded. Beaches on the east side are windy and picturesque, and the surf can be fierce.

Western Cozumel

On the west side of the island with calm turquoise waters, a small beach, and lots of coconut trees, **Playa Palancar** (Km. 19.5, no phone, 9 A.M.–5 P.M. daily, minimum consumption US$10 pp) caters to visitors who just want to spend a quiet day lounging in a hammock or snorkeling in the nearby Palancar reef. A *palapa*-roofed restaurant serves classic Mexican seafood and a wide range of drinks (US$5–12). Trips to the reef leave as soon as there is a critical mass of people (snorkel US$30, 1.5 hours, scuba US$80/two tanks). Snorkel gear also can be rented (US$10) but with no reef within striking distance, there's not much point in spending your cash on it. The club is 750 meters (0.5 mile) down a dirt road from the central road; a taxi between here and town is US$20.

With over three kilometers (1.9 miles) of thick white sand and calm turquoise waters, **Playa San Francisco** is certainly one of Cozumel's most attractive beaches. Its beauty is compromised somewhat—to say nothing of the tranquility—by two huge busy beach clubs right in the heart of it: **Nachi-Cocom** (Carr. Costera Sur Km. 16.5, tel. 987/872-1811, www.cozumel nachicocom.net, 9 A.M.–5 P.M. daily) is the rowdier of the two, catering to party-minded cruise shippers who pay US$69 for lunch, unlimited drinks, and a whirlpool tub that's usually teeming with minimally clad visitors. **Paradise Beach** (Carr. Costera Sur Km. 14.5, tel. 987/871-9010, www.paradise-beach-cozumel .net, 9 A.M.–sunset Mon.–Sat., 11 A.M.–6 P.M. Sun.) is also lively, but more geared toward families and people hoping to spend the day catching up on backlogged *New Yorker* magazines. Both clubs have huge open-air restaurants serving lots of finger foods and seafood (US$8–14), snorkel trips (US$35 pp, two hours), and other water sports. The sand and sea are gorgeous all the same, and the din evaporates just a hundred meters down the beach.

Uva's (Carr. Costera Sur Km. 8.5, tel. 987/800-9806, 8 A.M.–5 P.M. Mon.–Sat., cover US$7) exudes cool understatement, with minimalist furnishings and mellow beats, plus a small clean pool and a pretty patch of beach. The club offers guided snorkel tours every hour (US$15 pp, 45 minutes) and you can keep the snorkel gear for the rest of the day for exploring on your own. Or take a "dry snorkeling" tour in a clear acrylic kayak (US$40 pp, 45 minutes). A taxi here from town costs US$10.

ISLA COZUMEL

Eastern Cozumel

On the east side of the island right where the Cross-Island Highway hits the Caribbean, you'll find a wild and windswept coastline dotted with beaches. Facing the open ocean, the surf here can be quite rough and only a few beaches are safe for swimming. The exception is when *nortes* (northern storm fronts) hit the island, and the west side turns choppy while the east side goes perfectly flat.

Right where the cross-island road hits the coast, two low-key restaurants sit alongside each other: **Mezcalito's Beach Bar and Grill** (tel. 987/872-1616, www.mezcalitos.com, 9 A.M.–6 P.M. daily) and **Señor Iguanas** (no phone, 8 A.M.–5 P.M. Mon.–Sat., 9 A.M.–5 P.M. Sun.). Both have similar menus (ceviche, fried fish, hamburgers, US$6–14), drinks (beer, margaritas, and tequila shots, US$2.50–5), and services (beachside chairs, hammocks, and *palapas*, free if you buy something from the restaurant). If you're feeling brave and have experience in rough waters, rent a boogie board from Señor Iguanas (US$3/two hours)—a lot of fun if you can handle the surf.

About six kilometers (3.7 miles) south is **Playa Tortugas,** a broad beautiful beach on the north side of the Ventanas al Mar hotel. Usually too rough for swimming, it's popular with surfers and is a good place to watch the wild and crashing waves.

A few steps away is **Coconuts Bar and Grill** (10:30 A.M.–sunset daily, US$5–13). Set on a magnificent bluff, tables and chairs are arranged so that patrons can enjoy the glorious views of the beach below and the Caribbean beyond. Meals are classic beach fare: nachos, ceviche, tacos—finger foods that go great with a cold beer. As long as you order something, you're free to hang out for as long as you'd like.

The best place to swim on the east side of the island is **Chen Río Beach** one kilometer (0.6 mile) south of Coconuts Bar and Grill fronting a wide protected bay and clear calm seas. It's popular with families, and lifeguards are usually on hand in case of any problems. Here you'll also find **Restaurant and Bar Chen Río**

(11 A.M.–6 P.M. daily, US$12–26), but the food is so expensive it's no wonder beachgoers bring a picnic.

Three kilometers farther south, **Playa Bonita** is another picturesque curve of sand with plenty of room to lay out a towel and soak in the sun. Heavy surf usually makes swimming here inadvisable, but provides for a dramatic scene. A small beach restaurant (10 A.M.–5 P.M. daily) serves hamburgers, fresh fish, and other standards.

Playa Rasta is the last beach you hit before turning west on the highway. It's mostly a rocky stretch of beach with a few sandy inlets and two restaurants blasting reggae at each other. It's not really the best place to spend the day, unless of course, you like rambling on rocks and have a craving for jerk chicken.

Northeastern Cozumel

Cozumel's northeastern coast has long been the "wild" part of the island. While paved roads run parallel to most of the island's shoreline, the northeast is reachable only by a rutted sand road extending 24.5 kilometers (15 miles) from the Cross-Island Highway up to Punta Molas, and passable only with a four-wheel drive vehicle. Now it's even harder to get there: Not only did Hurricane Wilma wash out large portions of the road, but the government environmental agency closed it entirely in January 2006, following an incident involving a foreign landowner. Evidently, the landowner was frustrated that the road hadn't been restored following the hurricane and decided to cut a new road—right through a protected mangrove swamp. A legal battle ensued, and no one seems in a hurry to re-open the area to visitors.

Presumably it *will* open eventually, and travelers will once again be able to explore this isolated and windswept part of the island. One way to visit is by joining an ATV tour, which are popular with cruise ship passengers (see *ATV Tours* in the *Sports and Recreation* section). More adventurous visitors can rent a jeep or even hike in, camping on the beach along the way. (If you drive in, be sure your four-wheel drive is engaged and that the insurance policy covers off-roading.) The first beaches you hit are nice beachcombing spots, and make for good places to pitch a tent. About 22 kilometers (14 miles) north, you'll pass the Maya site of **Castillo Real** and farther on is the **Punta Molas Lighthouse,** marking the northeastern-most tip of the island. Whether you come by Jeep or by foot, don't come alone or unprepared—there are absolutely no facilities, or even other people, out here. Take plenty of water and food, bug repellent, a flashlight, extra batteries, and a mosquito net if you plan to camp. Let someone know where you are going, and when you expect to return.

Entertainment and Events

DISCOTHEQUES AND BARS

The hottest spot in town when we were here, **1.5 Tequila Lounge** (Av. Rafael Melgar at Calle 11, tel. 987/872-4421, 9 P.M.–4 A.M. Mon.–Sat., US$4.75 cover) is an urban hipster lounge bar overlooking the Caribbean. It has comfy couches and chairs, outdoor decks, and cool fusion jazz playing in the background. Specialty shooters are the way to go, with an order of sashimi from the sushi bar as a chaser.

The urban chic **Ámbar** (Av. 5 between Calles 1 and Rosado Salas, tel. 987/869-1955, 11 A.M.–midnight Mon.–Thu., until 2 A.M. Fri.–Sat., and 5–11 P.M. Sun., no cover) is another go-to lounge on Friday and Saturday nights. Billowing white fabrics, dim lighting, modern white furniture, a martini bar, and a DJ spinning jazz, funk, and house make this a popular spot. An outdoor area with lounge chairs, umbrellas, and piped in (well, out) music is nice if you want to enjoy the ambience but still have a conversation. A small restaurant in front serves tapas and homemade pastas until 11 P.M. (US$8–14).

A classic Cozumeleño club, **Neptuno** (Av. Rafael Melgar at Calle 11, tel. 987/872-4374, 9 P.M.–4 A.M. Tues.–Sun.) is a good place to check out the local party scene. It has a large dance floor—check out the old-school lighting and disco ball—where revelers bump and grind to reggae, house, techno, and Latin beats. Things really get going after midnight.

If you're dying to catch the big game on a big screen (or at least a bunch of little ones), head to **All Sports Bar** (Calle 2 at Av. 5 Norte, tel. 987/869-2246, 10 A.M.–11 P.M. Mon.–Thurs., 10–3 A.M. Fri.–Sun.). With a full line-up of sports channels and plenty of TVs, you're sure to feel right at home.

For a spring break atmosphere all day—and all year—long, head to the Punta Langosta shopping center where **Carlos'n Charlie's** (tel. 987/869-1648, 10 A.M.–1:30 A.M. Mon.–Fri., 11 A.M.–1:30 A.M. Sat., 5 P.M.–1:30 A.M. Sun.), **Señor Frog's** (tel. 987/869-2246, 8 A.M.–midnight Mon.–Thurs., 8 A.M.–2 A.M. Fri.–Sat.), and **Hard Rock Café Bar & Gift Shop** (8 A.M.–midnight Mon.–Sat., 10 A.M.–6 P.M. Sun.), make driving beats, drink specials, and dancing on tables the norm.

FESTIVALS
Carnaval

Cozumel is one of the few places in Mexico where Carnaval is celebrated with vigor, though the island's one-night celebration is still pretty mellow compared to the weeks or months of partying that mark the holiday elsewhere in the Caribbean and in South America. Held in February, Carnaval in Cozumel centers around a parade of floats and dance troupes, all decked out in colorful dress, masks, and glitter. Entire families come out together to participate and watch. Spectators dance and cheer in the streets as the floats go by, and many join the moving dance party that follows the floats with the largest speakers. Eventually the parade ends up in the center of town, where more music, dancing, and partying continue late into the night.

Festival de El Cedral

Residents of the village of El Cedral celebrate

ISLA COZUMEL

Carnaval in Cozumel is celebrated with parades and dancing in the streets.

their namesake festival beginning around April 23 and culminating on May 3, the Day of the Holy Cross. Traditionally, the festival entails daily prayer sessions and ends with a dance called the *Baile de las cabezas de cochino* (Dance of the Pigs' Heads). The festival has morphed over the years into a somewhat more secular affair, with rodeos, dancing, music, and general revelry.

CALESA TOURS

Once a way for islanders to get around town, *calesas* (horse carriages) are now mainly used by tourists to see San Miguel. For US$25–30 you can hire a buggy to take you on a 30-minute tour of the town—from the waterfront to the interior. Look for the horses on Avenida Rafael Melgar by Calle 1.

CULTURAL AND MUSIC PERFORMANCES

Every Sunday evening, the city hosts an **open air concert** in the central plaza. Locals and expats come out to enjoy the show—put on

a clean T-shirt and your nicest flip-flops and you'll fit right in. Concerts typically begin at 7 P.M.

The **Alianza Francesa** (Blvd. Aeropuerto at Av. 20, 987/112-4826, 9 A.M.–1 P.M. and 4–9 P.M. Mon.–Fri., 9 A.M.–1 P.M. Sat.) is a worldwide educational and cultural center that offers a wide variety of French language classes and also sponsors cultural events for the community at large. The Alianza Francesa on Cozumel opened its doors in 2006. Although it was offering only language classes at the time we passed, the center was planning for events like film festivals, concerts, and other live performances. Worth a call to see what's on the schedule when you're in town.

CINEMA

Catch a relatively recent movie at **Cinépolis** (Av. Rafael Melgar between Calles 15 and 17, tel. 987/869-0799, US$4.25, US$2.75 before 3 P.M., US$2.50 all day Wed.) in the Chedraui supermarket complex.

Shopping

Shopping in Cozumel is aimed straight at cruise ship passengers—and its no wonder, they tend to spend a lot of money quickly. Avenida Rafael Melgar is where most of the action is, with a succession of marble-floored shops blasting air-conditioning to entice sweaty passersby in for a refreshing look around. Overpriced jewelry, T-shirt, and souvenir shops see the most buyer traffic, although, here and there are a few shops worth checking out.

For an impressive display of Mexican folk art, check out **Los Cinco Soles** (Av. Rafael Melgar at Calle 8, tel. 987/872-0132, www .loscincosoles.com, 8 A.M.–8 P.M. Mon.–Thurs., 8 A.M.–9 P.M. Fri.–Sat., 10 A.M.–4 P.M. Sun.). With room upon room of excellent examples of the country's artisanship—pre-Colombian replicas, *barro negro* pottery, colorful *rebosos* (shawls), and hand-carved furniture—it's definitely worth a stop, if even just to admire the art. There's a smaller satellite shop at the Punta Langosta mall.

Inspiración (5 Av. between Calles 3 and Rosado Salas, tel. 987/869-8293, www.inspiration cozumel.com, 10 A.M.–10 P.M. Mon.–Sat.) is a small gallery with a variety of quality Mexican artwork, from photos to jewelry to Maya replicas, all handpicked by the shop's friendly American owner.

Though a little pricey, **Pro Dive Cozumel** (Calle Rosado Salas at Av. 5, tel. 987/872-4123, prodivecozumel@prodigy.com.mx, www.pro divecozumel.com, 8 A.M.–10 P.M. Mon.–Sat., 9 A.M.–10 P.M. Sun.) has a great selection of snorkel and dive equipment—perfect if you've forgotten your mask or have lost a fin. For more options, try the **Cressi** retail shop kitty-corner to this one.

Punta Langosta (Av. Rafael Melgar between Calles 7 and 11, 9 A.M.–8 P.M. daily) is Cozumel's swankiest shopping center. An ultramodern open-air building, it's home to high-end clothing boutiques, air-conditioned jewelry stores, and even fancy ice cream shops.

A small shopping center on the north end of town, **Forum Shops Cozumel** (Av. Rafael Melgar at Calle 8, 8:30 A.M.–5:30 P.M. Mon.–Sat.) is nowhere near as nice as Punta Langosta, but it has a small collection of souvenir shops that are a bit more affordable.

© GARY CHANDLER

Cozumel's main plaza has numerous shops and restaurants.

ISLA COZUMEL

Sports and Recreation

SCUBA DIVING

Without a doubt, diving is the best reason to come to Cozumel. It should be no surprise then that Cozumel has a profusion of dive shops and operators—well more than 100 at last count. Rates are relatively uniform across the island: Expect to pay US$65–80 for a two-tank dive (plus US$10–20 for equipment rental, if you need it) and US$325–400 for a three- or four-day PADI open-water certification course. Most shops also conduct more advanced courses and offer discounts on multi-dive packages. Divers are also subject to a US$2 park entrance fee and a US$1 per day surcharge to support the *Servicios de Seguridad Sub-Acuática* (Underwater Safety Services) or SSS, which helps maintain Cozumel's hyperbaric chambers and marine ambulance.

Cozumel's diver safety record is good, and there are many more responsible, competent

a beach break between dives on Cozumel's tranquil western shores

outfits in town than those listed here. Consider this list your base, to be augmented by the recommendations of fellow divers, travelers, locals, and expats—whose judgment you trust, of course. Most important, go with a shop you feel comfortable with, not just the cheapest, the cheeriest, or the most convenient.

Dimi Divers (Calle 3 between Av. Rafael Melgar and 5 Av., tel. 987/872-2915, www.dimi scubatours.com) is a small, locally owned shop that offers very reasonable rates, and whose many repeat clients are testament to the high quality of service.

Scuba Gamma (Calle 5 at Av. 5 Sur, tel. 987/878-4257, www.scubagamma.net, 9 A.M.–7 P.M. daily) is a mom-and-pop shop (literally) run by an amiable French family. The shop is one of few with specialized training in teaching and guiding divers with disabilities.

ScubaTony (www.scubatony.com, tel. 987/ 869-8628, in U.S. 626-593-7122) is one of a growing number of scuba operations run without an actual storefront—lower overhead typically means lower prices. American Tony Anschutz leads all his own dives and courses and offers excellent service before, during, and after your trip.

Deep Blue (Calle Rosado Salas at Av. 10 Sur, tel. 987/872-5653, www.deepbluecozumel .com) is a long-standing shop with a reputation and track record that keep it busy even through the low season.

Liquid Blue (5 Av. between Calle Rosado Salas and Calle 3, 987/869-7794, www.liquid bluedivers.com) has somewhat higher rates than most shops, but it offers small groups and attentive, personalized service.

Careyitos Advanced Divers (Caleta harbor, near Hotel Presidente InterContinental, tel. 987/872-1578, U.S. tel. 218/963-7578, www.advanceddivers.com) caters to experienced divers, allowing up to 75 minutes bottom time and offering top-notch service.

Caribbean Divers (5 Ave. at Calle 3, tel. 987/872-1145, www.caribbendiverscozumel

© GARY CHANDLER

HOW TO CHOOSE A DIVE SHOP

There are over 100 dive shops on Isla Cozumel, and scores more at Isla Mujeres, Playa del Carmen, Cancún, Tulum, and elsewhere. Choosing just one – and then placing all your underwater faith into its hands – is not exactly easy.

Safety should be your number one concern in choosing a shop. Fortunately, the standards in Cozumel and the Riviera Maya are almost universally first-rate, and accidents are rare. But that's not a reason to be complacent. For example, don't dive with a shop that doesn't ask to see your certification card or logbook – if they didn't ask you, they probably didn't ask anyone, and an ill-trained diver is as dangerous to others as he is to himself.

Equipment is another crucial issue. You should ask to inspect the shop's equipment, and the dive shop should be quick to comply. Although few casual divers are trained to inspect gear, a good dive shop will appreciate your concern and be happy to put you at ease. If the staff is reluctant to show you the gear, either they aren't too proud of it or they don't see clients as equal partners in dive safety.

Of course, the most important equipment is not what's on the rack but what you actually use. Get to the shop early so you have time to **double-check your gear.** Old gear is not necessarily bad gear, but you should ask for a different BCD, wetsuit, or regulator if the one set out for you makes you uneasy. Learn how to check the O-ring (the small rubber ring that forms the seal between the tank and the regulator) and do so before every dive. Finally, open the tank and listen for any hissing between the regulator and the tank, and in the primary and backup mouthpieces. If you hear any, ask the dive master to check it and, if need be, change the regulator. Do all this before getting on the boat, so you can swap gear if necessary. Remember, *there are no stupid questions*.

Feeling comfortable and free to ask questions or raise concerns (of any sort at any time) is a crucial factor in safe diving. That's where a dive shop's **personality** comes in. Every dive shop has its own culture or style, and different divers will feel more comfortable in different shops. Spend some time talking to people at a couple of different dive shops before signing up. Try to meet the person who will be leading your particular dive – you may have to come in the afternoon when that day's trip returns. Chances are one of the shops or dive masters will "click" with you.

Finally, there are some specific questions you should ask about a shop's practices. Has their air been tested and certified? Do they carry radios and oxygen? Does the captain always stay with the boat? How many people will be going on your dive? How advanced are they? And how many dive masters or instructors will there be? How experienced are they?

And, of course, have fun!

.com) takes pride in its professional service and two 40-foot (12.2-meter) boats, which make surface intervals and getting to and from dive sites comfortable.

SNORKELING

If you don't have the time, money, or inclination to take up diving—and it's not for everyone—don't let that stop you from enjoying Cozumel's pristine coral reefs. In fact, many divers are also avid snorkelers, if for no other reason than plunking down US$100 a day for two 45-minute dives adds up really fast.

Many dive shops offer guided snorkeling tours, visiting 2–3 sites and spending a half-hour at each one (US$45–55 pp). Most often, snorkelers go out with a group of divers, and either snorkel in the same general location or go to a nearby site while the divers are underwater. While this can mean some extra downtime as divers get in and out of the water, you typically go to better, less crowded sites and have fewer people in your group. Be sure to agree beforehand on the number of sites you'll visit and for how long.

A number of shops sell snorkel tours from

DIVE INSURANCE

Although diving accidents are relatively rare on Cozumel, if you're planning on diving or snorkeling, consider purchasing secondary accident insurance through DAN (Divers Alert Network, toll-free U.S. tel. 800/446-2671, 24-hour emergency Mex. tel. 919/684-9111, accepts collect calls, www.diversalertnetwork .org), a nonprofit medical organization dedicated to the health and safety of snorkelers and recreational divers. Plans range from US$25 to US$70 per year and depending on the policy include medical and decompression coverage, lost equipment, airline and hotel costs, vacation cancellation insurance, accidental death and dismemberment benefits, as well as disability benefits. To be eligible for insurance, subscribers must become members of DAN, just US$29 per year.

booths on the central passenger pier. These trips tend to be less expensive (though with larger groups) and can be booked right as you debark from the ferry—handy if your time is short. **Cha Cha Cha Dive Shop** (Calle 7 between Avs. Rafael Melgar and 5 Sur, tel. 987/872-2331, www.chachachadiveshop.com, booth opens at 8 A.M.) offers 2–2.5-hour snorkeling trips on its glass-bottom boat for US$25 per person, including equipment. You'll snorkel for 30 minutes at each of three different sites. Its booth on the pier is easier to find than the actual shop, hidden down a narrow passage between souvenir stands and a tattoo parlor.

There are several terrific snorkeling spots right off the shore and not far from town where you don't need a guide at all; some of these are established snorkeling areas, others are recommended by locals. Cozumel's boat drivers are careful about steering clear of snorkelers, but even so do not swim too far from shore, look up and around frequently, and stay out of obvious boat lanes. If you plan to do a lot of snorkeling, especially outside of established snorkeling areas, consider bringing or buying

an inflatable personal buoy. Designed for snorkelers, they are brightly colored with a string you attach to your ankle or to a small anchor weight, alerting boat drivers of your presence. Also, be aware of the current, which typically runs south to north and can be quite strong.

KITEBOARDING

Kiteboarding has exploded in popularity around the world, eclipsing windsurfing among adrenaline seekers, in much the same way snowboarding has leapfrogged skiing. **Kite Cozumel** (tel. 987/103-6711, www.kitecozumel .com) is the kiting outfit of Cozumel-native Raul de Lille, a former Olympic-level windsurfer and now one of Mexico's top kiters and instructors. He doesn't come cheap: private lessons are US$125 an hour, and a three-day introductory course is US$900. For experienced kiters, de Lille offers clinics on kite control, tricks, and other specialties, plus adventuresome tours, like downwinding the entire island. Kite Cozumel operates out of the hotel Casa Viento, the island's only kiteboarding hotel and a short walk from the island's best kiting beach.

ECO- AND WATER PARKS
◖ Parque Ecológico Punta Sur

Parque Ecológico Punta Sur (Carr. Costera Sur Km. 27, tel. 987/872-0914, www.cozumel parks.com.mx, 9 A.M.–4 P.M. daily, US$10, children under 8 free) spans over 1,000 hectares (2,500 acres) of coastal dunes and mangroves at the island's southern tip. Declared a national reserve in 1996, it harbors dozens of animal species, including 30 types of seabirds and a vast array of sea creatures, reptiles, and amphibians (including some huge crocs). Just past the gate, a visitor center has displays about the history and ecology of the park, and a high platform overlooking Laguna Colombia, for spotting birds and crocodiles. A bit farther is a small Maya ruin known as *El Caracol,* believed to have been used for navigation and then the park's famous lighthouse and a small maritime museum. Private cars are not permitted beyond the lighthouse; a park truck ferries visitors to the beach area, where you can take a catamaran trip through the lagoon (US$3 pp, 40 minutes) or just spend time sunbathing, swimming, and snorkeling along the two kilometers (1.2 miles) of beautiful beaches. A small restaurant serves pricy food, and binoculars and snorkel gear can be rented at the visitor's center, if you don't have your own. Though this is a popular shore excursion for cruise shippers, it can still be rewarding for independent travelers.

Parque Nacional Chankanaab

Some 9 kilometers (5.6 mi.) south of town, Parque Chankanaab (Carr. Costera Sur Km. 14, tel. 987/872-9723, www.cozumelparks.com, 7 A.M.–5 P.M. daily, US$16 adult, US$8 children under 12) is a national park that doubles as a souped-up beach club. Visitors come to spend the day sunbathing, swimming in the ocean, and snorkeling. **Dolphin Discovery** (toll-free Mex. tel. 800/713-8862, www.dolphindiscovery .com, US$69–125 pp, 15–30 minutes) operates a popular dolphin and sea lion interaction program here. Reserve a spot as soon as you arrive, or better yet, book online. Park facilities include two thatch-roofed restaurants, a few gift shops, and a fully equipped dive shop. Popular with families, it is a good place to spend the day if you have little ones in tow.

SPORT FISHING

Cozumel boasts good deep-sea fishing year-round. It's one of few places anglers can go for the grand slam of billfishing: hooking into a blue marlin, a white marlin, a sailfish, and a swordfish all in a single day. It's also got plentiful tuna, barracuda, dorado, wahoo, grouper, snapper, and more. A **billfish tournament** is held every year in May, bringing fishing enthusiasts from all over—especially boaters from the United States who cross the Gulf of Mexico to take part in the popular event.

Albatross Fishing Charters (tel. 987/872-7904, in U.S. 888/333-4643, www.cozumel-fishing.net) charges US$400 for four hours, US$500 for six hours, and US$550 for eight hours. It has a fleet of five boats, with experienced captains and crew. Boats carry a maximum of six anglers. Trips include hotel pickup and drop-off, beer and soda, snacks, bait, and gear.

Other outfits include **Wahoo Tours** (www .wahootours.com, US$400/4hrs, US$545/8hrs, US$150 pp shared, up to six people) and **Go Fish** (book through www.cozumel insider.com, US$270/4hrs, US$320/6hrs, up to four people).

GOLF

Jack Nicklaus designed the beautiful par-72 championship course at **Cozumel Country Club** (tel. 987/872-9570, www.cozumelcountry club.com.mx, 6:30 A.M.–6 P.M. daily) located at the far end of the northern hotel zone. Green fees are US$149 until 1:30 P.M., when they drop to US$99. Carts are required, and included in the price; club rentals are US$29–50. In addition to the slightly rolling, moderately challenging course, the club has a driving range—the golf shop will loan you a club if you just want to hit some balls— putting and chipping areas, overnight bag storage, restaurant, retail shop, and available golf pro.

For something more laid-back, **Cozumel Mini Golf** (Calle 1 at Av. 15 Sur, tel. 987/872-6570, www.czmgolf.com, 10 A.M.–11 P.M. daily, US$7 adults, US$5 children under 11) features a fun and challenging 18-hole course set on a plot of 300 banana trees and a waterfall or two, just three blocks from the ferry. You'll get a walkie-talkie with your putter; use it to order dollar sodas and two-dollar beers and sangria, delivered to you right on the green. You can also pick out a CD (from a collection of 500) to be played over the course speakers. Watch for iguanas.

HORSEBACK RIDING

Located on the inland side of the highway across from Nachi Cocom beach club, **Rancho Palmitas** (Carr. Costera Sur Km. 16, tel. 987/878-7121) offers two horseback tours. A 2.5–3-hour tour (US$35 pp) includes stops at a cavern with a cenote, the archaeological site of El Cedral, and a few unexcavated Maya ruins. A shorter, 1.5-hour tour (US$25 pp) leads to the

ISLA COZUMEL

cavern only. Departures for either tour are at 8 A.M., 10 A.M., noon, 2 P.M., and 4 P.M. daily. A few additional ranches along this stretch of highway offer similar tours and prices.

ATV TOURS

For years, **Wild Tours** (tel. 987/872-5876 or toll-free Mex. tel. 800/202-4990, www.wild-tours.com) has offered ATV excursions along the island's undeveloped northeast shore, including visiting isolated Maya ruins and snorkeling at deserted beaches (US$80–90 pp, 4.5 hours). However, the tours were suspended in January 2006, when the government's environmental agency shut down the road after a private landowner damaged a large portion of protected mangrove forest there. The tours will presumably resume, though no one seems to know when—ask at your hotel. Wild Tours caters to cruise ship passengers, but trips are open to all. They leave from a staging area next to Mezcalito's restaurant on the east side of the island, where the Cross-Island Highway meets the coastal highway.

BODY WORK

Gym Club (Av. Benito Juárez between Calle 20 and Av. Pedro Joaquín Coldwell, tel. 987/872-7432, 6 A.M.–11 P.M. Mon.–Fri., 7 A.M.–6 P.M. Sat.) has free weights and weight machines in a smallish two-level exercise area. Use of the gym is US$5 a day or US$15 a week.

Though mainly geared toward children's dance instruction, **Tamart Casa de Arte y Cultura** (Calle 10 between Avs. 15 and 20 Norte, 987/869-8042, 8:30 A.M.–9 P.M. Mon.–Fri.) offers yoga and kickboxing classes for adults. Classes are typically offered two to three times per week and cost US$33–37 per month. Perfect if you're aching for a good workout and will be on Cozumel for more than a couple weeks.

Accommodations

Room prices can rise considerably during high season (mid-December–mid-April). Those listed here are high season (but not Christmas and New Year rates, which are even higher)—if you visit at another time rates may be 10–40 percent lower.

UNDER US$50

One block from the central plaza, **(Hostelito** (Av. 10 between Av. Benito Juárez and Calle 2 Norte, 987/869-8157, hostelitocozumelmx@gmail.com, US$11 dorm, US$10 dorm with a/c 4 guests minimum, US$35 s/d with a/c, US$50 studio with a/c) is an ultramodern hostel with a spacious coed dorm sporting 26 good beds and fans galore. Guests are provided with clean sheets, a huge locker, and continental breakfast; wireless Internet and cable TV are in the lobby. If you're traveling in a group, ask about the air-conditioned dorm with private bathroom, which is a steal at US$10 per head for four people. A spacious studio with a fully equipped kitchen is a great deal for couples or families planning an extended stay on the island. The only drawbacks here: not much natural light and no communal kitchen (though one was in the works).

(Hotel Pepita (Av. 15 Sur between Calles 1 and Rosado Salas, tel. 987/872-0098, US$35 s/d, extra person US$5) is a modest but well-located and surprisingly comfortable hotel—a good value for traveler 'tweens: post-hostel but pre-B&B. The friendly owners keep the rooms very clean and well maintained. All have air-conditioning, ceiling fan, cable TV, minifridge, and two double beds (albeit a bit saggy), and there's fresh coffee every morning in the long inner courtyard. Same rates year-round.

Half a block from the central plaza, **Hotel Mary Carmen** (5 Av. Sur between Calles 1 and Rosado Salas, tel. 987/872-0581, www.cozumelisla.com.mx, US$39 s/d with a/c) is a simple but unexpectedly pleasant hotel. Small-ish rooms have mosaic-tile headboards, good air-conditioners, and cable TV; bathrooms could stand to be remodeled but they're clean. Though not luxury, it's a good value for those on a limited budget. Ask for a room toward the back of the hotel, since some rooms get street noise.

US$50-100

Mi Casa en Cozumel (5 Ave. between Calles 7 and 9, tel. 987/872-6200, www.mi casaencozumel.com, US$55–90 s/d, US$170 suite) is perhaps Cozumel's first true boutique hotel, and surely its finest. Opened in 2006, the lofty structure is a study of curves and angles, the spiral staircase and curved interior walls counterbalancing the triangular patios and angled nooks occupied by whirlpool tubs. All units have king-size beds, sleek decor, and terraces with hammocks. The split-level suite has a full kitchen and a private hot tub. Free continental breakfast is served in a cozy cafeteria on the ground floor (where you can also get a wireless Internet signal).

Tamarindo Bed and Breakfast (Calle 4 between Avs. 20 and 25 Norte, tel. 987/872-6190, www.cozumel.net/bb/tamarind, US$44–47 s/d with fan, US$53 s/d with a/c, US$55 suite with a/c and kitchenette) is a pleasant bed-and-breakfast just a few blocks from the center of town, but comfortably removed from the hubbub. Owned by a friendly French expatriate who lives on-site, the hotel has seven units bordering a large, leafy garden. Each room is different from the other, from two boxy but comfortable hotel rooms to a whimsical *palapa* bungalow with boho flair. All have cable TV and wireless Internet. A good full breakfast is included in the rate (high season only; US$5 in low season) that is served on a sunny second-floor terrace. For those rooms without kitchenettes, there is a small communal kitchen. Rinse tanks and storage facilities also are provided for guests with dive gear.

Amaranto Bungalows (Calle 5 between Avs. 15 and 20 Sur, tel. 987/872-3219 or 987/103-1644, amarantocozumel@prodigy .net.mx, www.tamarindoamaranto.com, US$49 s/d, US$61 suite) offers seclusion and privacy, while still within easy walking distance from downtown. The three freestanding bungalows are fairly large and very clean, with modern bathrooms and attractive beachy decor. The two suites, however, are the Amaranto's shining stars. Occupying a three-story circular tower, both are spacious, with king-size beds, a separate sitting area, and nearly 360-degree windows. The lower suite has a high ceiling and more modern feel, while the upper unit looks up into the *palapa* roof, where a small lookout affords great town and ocean views. A large kitchen and dining room on the 1st floor has a TV and VCR and is open to all guests. Amaranto doesn't have a full-time attendant, so it's best to call ahead to let them know that you're coming.

Located on the main drag, **Vista del Mar** (Av. Rafael Melgar between Calles 5 and 7 Sur, tel. 987/872-0545, toll-free U.S. tel. 888/309-9988, www.hotelvistadelmar.com, US$83–94 with a/c) is a surprisingly charming hotel in the middle of a string of tacky souvenir shops. Rooms are classy and comfortable, with muted earth tones, beachy high-end decor, inlaid stone walls, and balconies (some with spectacular views of the Caribbean). All have cable TV, mini-fridges, safety deposit boxes, robes—even turndown service. There's also an outdoor mezzanine level with lounge chairs and a big Jacuzzi with a mosaic tile floor—a great space to hang out if it weren't for the rattling air-conditioners and the view of the souvenir shops.

Newly remodeled, the **Hotel Flamingo** (Calle 6 between Avs. Rafael Melgar and 5 Norte, tel. 987/872-1264 or toll-free U.S. tel. 800/806-1601, www.hotelflamingo.com, US$85 s/d with a/c, US$95 s/d superior with a/c, US$179 penthouse with a/c) offers three types of rooms: the standard are just that, basic hotel rooms with no views, air-conditioning, and cable TV; for US$10 more, superior units offer better beds and linens, mosaic tile bathrooms, and nice views—a good value; and for a big step up, the penthouse is a two-bedroom apartment with a fully equipped kitchen, a living room with ocean views, and one and a half bathrooms. All have wireless Internet; there's also a good restaurant/bar (7 A.M.–11 P.M. daily) on the ground floor. For a US$10–20 discount on accommodations, reserve online.

Suites Bahía (Calle 3 between Avs. Rafael Melgar and 5 Sur, tel. 987/872-9090 or toll-free Mex. tel. 800/227-2639, www.suites bahia.com, US$77–107 s/d with a/c) and **Suites Colonial** (Av. 5 Sur between Calles 1 and Rosado Salas, same tel., www.suitescolonial .com, US$77 s/d with a/c, US$79 suite with a/c) are sister hotels that rent unremarkable but functional rooms and studios, most with kitchenettes. The Colonial is on the pedestrian walkway downtown and feels newer, but the rooms at the Bahía (especially the ocean-view ones) are roomier and get more natural light. Neither hotel will win any awards for charm—both look as if they've been untouched since the early 1980s—but the rooms are clean and reasonably comfortable and a kitchen can definitely be nice for longer stays. Both include air-conditioning, cable TV, continental breakfast, and Internet service in the lobby.

OVER US$100

Villas Las Anclas (Av. 5 Sur between Calles 3 and 5, tel. 987/872-5476, www.las anclas.com, US$80–120 s/d with a/c) is a great option for those who want a little home away from home. Seven pleasantly decorated apartments each have air-conditioning, a fully equipped kitchen, a living room, and a loft master bedroom up a set of spiral stairs. Using the sofas as beds, the apartments can accommodate up to six people, making a good price even better. Apartments open onto a leafy, private garden. The friendly owner/operator is well informed of local dive shops, restaurants, and activities, and can help guests organize their stays.

In town, one of Cozumel's most modern hotels is **Casa Mexicana** (Av. Rafael Melgar between Calles 5 and 7, tel. 987/872-9090, U.S. tel. 877/228-6747, www.casamexicanacozumel .com, US$140–168 s/d with a/c) with its small infinity pool in its spacious lobby area and a view over the road to the big blue ocean beyond. The view is even better from the private

patio of the 20 oceanside rooms—notwithstanding the docked cruise ships and a large McDonald's sign. The other 70 rooms have views of the city or the soaring interior courtyard. The rooms are less inspired than the building itself, but are comfortable enough, with good beds, new air-conditioners, modern bathrooms, and large TVs. Rates include a full buffet breakfast in an impressive open-air dining room.

A long walk from town but worth every step, **Casa Colonial** (Av. 35 between Calles 8 and 10, tel. 987/872-6102, toll-free U.S., Canada, Europe 866/437-1320, www.cozumelrental villas.com, seven nights for US$1,036, villa with a/c) has four Mexican-style villas, each with two bedrooms. All are two stories with two-and-a-half bathrooms, a living room, a dining room, a fully equipped kitchen—even a washer and dryer and wireless Internet. It's like being home with the added bonus of daily maid service. All villas face a well-tended garden courtyard with a large pool and Jacuzzi. Dive rinse tanks also are available.

A leafy courtyard and gurgling fountain greet you at the **Hacienda San Miguel** (Calle 10 between Avs. Rafael Melgar and 5 Norte, tel. 987/872-1986, U.S. tel. 866/712-6387, www.haciendasanmiguel.com, US$100 studios with a/c, US$113–165 suites with a/c), a colonial-style hotel on the edge of town. Rooms need some sprucing up—a paint job and a little extra scrubbing in the showers would do wonders—but they're comfortable enough with air-conditioning, cable TV, and fully equipped kitchenettes. The two-story junior suites are the best units in the place with a comfortable living room and a balcony with nice views of the courtyard. Continental breakfast included in the rate.

OUTSIDE OF TOWN

Aptly named the House of Wind, **Casa Viento** (Country Club Estates, tel. 987/878-4537, www.casaviento.com, US$95–106) bills itself as a "guest house and kite camp" and caters almost exclusively to kiteboarders. Just minutes from some of the island's best kiteboarding spots, it is also home of Kite Cozumel, a kiting school and tour operator run by top Mexican kiteboarder Raul de Lille. Opposite the country club, Casa Viento has four charming detached rooms, and two in the main house where the kitchen and living room are located. A suite, complete with cupola, has terrific ocean views. A clean midsize pool completes the package. The place is almost too delightful—don't these kiters have a rep to keep?

Under US$150

The only hotel on the east side of the island, **Hotel Ventanas al Mar** (south end of Playa Tortugas, tel. 987/876-7687, www.ventanas almar.biz, US$89 s/d, US$169–189 d suite, includes full breakfast) has 12 large rooms and two suites, all with high ceilings and private patios or decks with marvelous ocean views. The interiors lack the detailing and upkeep you'd expect at this price, but are not uncomfortable, and suit the hotel's isolated feel. All have kitchenettes with microwave ovens and dishes; some have mini-fridges. Split-level suites can comfortably sleep four. There's no a/c, as the hotel runs almost entirely on wind and solar power. (Power lines have yet to reach the island's east side; the hotel was just installing a generator, but only for limited use.) Fortunately, the constant sea breeze keeps rooms cool. There's a good restaurant next door, but you'll probably want a car, as the east side has no ATM, grocery stores, or other services; the hotel does offer limited shuttle service, but only in the high season. Or you can embrace the isolation: Many guests spend a week or more without going to town at all. Playa Tortugas is a scenic windswept beach that's good for surfing—and has nesting turtles May to November—but it is often too rough for swimming or snorkeling.

US$150-200

An easy 15-minute walk north of town is **Condumel** (tel. 987/872-0892, www.aqua safari.com, US$159 apartment with a/c), an old school but well-kempt condominium complex on the main road. The 10 one-bedroom apart-

ments are spacious and have air-conditioning, a king-size bed, a sofa bed, marble bathroom, and a fully equipped kitchen—the refrigerator even comes stocked with regularly priced food items so that you don't have to go shopping right away. Oversized sliding-glass doors offer awesome views of the ocean, sunsets, and incoming airplanes. The coast here is iron shore, so it's rocky, but a small, semi-protected cove with steps and a ladder is perfect for swimming and snorkeling; there's even a diving board that screams cannonball. A small sandy area with lounge chairs also has been set up for guests who need a daily beach fix. Dive packages available.

Like many all-inclusives, the **Occidental Allegro Cozumel** (Carretera Sur Km. 16.5, tel. 987/872-9770, toll-free U.S. tel. 800/858-2258, www.allegroresorts.com, US$237 s with a/c, US$171 pp d with a/c) has a fantastic beach and pool area but rather unremarkable rooms and restaurants. The wide beach has powdery white sand dotted with beach chairs and umbrellas. On one side is a water-sports kiosk, where you can check out anything from snorkel gear (free) to small sailboats (extra charge). Two pools set end to end form a long corridor from the ocean toward the main building. Along the sides are two-story, *palapa*-roofed bungalows with four units apiece. Rooms are on the small side, and are showing their age—new furnishings would go a long way. The sister hotel **Occidental Grand Cozumel** (US$292 s with a/c, US$212 pp d with a/c), a five-star all-inclusive, is next door. The accommodations and installations are fancier there, but the beach is actually better at the Allegro. Daytime and nighttime activities include aerobics, cocktail parties, and theme nights.

Over US$200

After a year-long overhaul, the ◖ **Presidente InterContinental Cozumel Resort Spa** (Carretera Sur Km. 6.5, tel. 987/872-9500, toll-free U.S. tel. 888/424-6835, www.intercontinental .com, US$370–570) may well be the best hotel-resort in Cozumel. It features spacious, classy rooms with details like flat screen TVs, stereos, turndown service, and bathrobes. While the views can either be garden or ocean, all roads lead to one of the best hotel beaches on the island—thick white sand and calm, turquoise waters with excellent access for snorkelers and shore divers. A well-regarded dive shop, two lighted tennis courts, three restaurants, and a full-service spa round out an already relaxing stay.

As the name suggests, the **Fiesta Americana Cozumel Dive Resort** (Carretera Sur Km. 7.5, tel. 987/872-9600, U.S. tel. 800/343-7821, www.fiestamericana.com, $150–300 s/d with a/c) caters to divers, most of whom come on package tours arranged from the United States or Canada. Recently refurbished, rooms are comfortable and attractive with terraces and excellent ocean views. The beach is constructed on iron shore with barriers to hold in the imported sand—not exactly what you expect when you think "Caribbean beach" but

nice enough if you just want to take in the sun. There's also a well-regarded, if pricey, dive shop on-site. Continental breakfast included.

North of town and near the country club, **Playa Azul** (Zona Hotelera Norte Km. 4, tel. 987/869-5160, www.playa-azul.com, US$240–320) caters mostly to golfers, but it has packages for divers and honeymooners as well. Even if you don't golf much, you may as well get in a round or two if you stay here—guests pay no green fees. Medium-size rooms have modern furnishings and large bathrooms; most have a terrace with chairs and excellent ocean views. Top-floor rooms have a little cupola on the bedroom, a nice touch. The pool is clean and attractive, but the beach (already small) can get crowded with day guests visiting the hotel's beach club. That said, the overall atmosphere here is calm and quiet, removed from the noise and activity downtown.

Food

Cozumel isn't known as a culinary hotspot, but you do have plenty of options. Like any island it has terrific seafood (though many people are surprised to learn that much of the catch actually comes from around Isla Mujeres because the waters around Cozumel are protected areas). And the island's popularity with Americans, especially hungry Texan divers, means you'll never want for a steak, plate of pasta, fajitas, or a big breakfast. And the island's tight-knit community of European expats, especially French, keep numerous cafés, bistros, and international eateries in business.

MEXICAN

Popular among locals, **(Sabores** (Av. 5 between Calles 3 and 5, noon–4 P.M. Mon.–Fri., US$4–11) is a family-run restaurant operated out of a bright yellow house. A wide variety of traditional Mexican dishes are served as *comidas corridas* with soup, main dish, and fruit drink running US$4–8. Clients can choose between eating in the converted living room or under

the shade trees in the backyard. Check out the dry erase board for the daily offerings.

The breezy *palapa*-roofed **(La Candela** (Av. 5 at Calle 6 Norte, 987/878-4471, 8 A.M.–6 P.M. Mon.–Sat., US$2.50–5) is a favorite among locals and expats. Every day, a line-up of Mexican and traditional Yucatecan dishes are offered in a cafeteria-style setting. Check out what's steaming behind the glass window cases, find a seat, then place your order with your waiter. Lunch specials typically include soup or pasta, a main dish, and a drink.

Serving customers since 1945, **Casa Denis** (Calle 1 between Avs. 5 and 10 Sur, tel. 987/872-0067, 7 A.M.–11 P.M. Mon.–Sat., 6–11 P.M. Sun., US$4–15) is a yellow clapboard house just steps from the central plaza. With wood tables set up on the porch and along the pedestrian walkway, it makes a great spot for people-watching that's made even better with a cold beer and fresh fish empanadas.

Located deep in one of Cozumel's residential neighborhoods, **El Moro** (Av. 75 Bis. Norte between Calles 2 and 4, tel. 872-3029, 1–11 P.M. Fri.–Wed., US$7–18) isn't a fancy place but it has won the loyal following of many expatriates. You'll find just about any Mexican specialty here—from *enchiladas suizas* to chicken *mole*—and big portions to boot. Unfortunately, prices are a bit inflated, especially considering the surroundings.

Mexican-food lovers pack **La Choza** (Av. 10 at Calle Rosado Salas, tel. 987/872-0958, 7 A.M.–10:30 P.M., US$6–19), a simple restaurant with high *palapa* roof that fills with the rich smells and sounds of traditional Mexican and Tex-Mex cuisine: almost everything on the menu involves some sort of sizzling meat. Always crowded with loyal aficionados, locals and visitors alike. Service is fast and friendly.

The setting at **Pancho's Backyard** (Av. Rafael Melgar 27 between Avs. 8 and 10 Norte, tel. 987/872-2141, 10 A.M.–11 P.M. Mon.–Sat., 5–11 P.M. Sun., US$10–20) is Mexico epitomized—gurgling fountains, colonial-style decor, and marimba music. Add creative haute cuisine such as *chiles rellenos* (peppers stuffed with bananas and walnut) and *camarones a la naranja* (orange shrimp flambéed in tequila) and you'll leave wanting to return. Popular with cruise ship travelers, the restaurant is big enough that it never feels crowded.

SEAFOOD

The nautical-themed **(El Capi Navegante** (Av. 10 Sur between Calles 3 and 5, tel. 987/872-1730, noon–10 P.M. daily, US$10–30) is a favorite on the island because it serves some of the freshest seafood around. For a treat, try the *Parrillada Capi Navegante*—a delectable dish of grilled fish, shrimp, octopus, conch, and squid—you won't be disappointed.

The Caribbean chic **La Lobstería** (Av. 5 Sur at Calle 7, tel. 987/100-2510, noon–11 P.M. Mon.–Sat US$5–15) is a good place to get a creative seafood dish such as fish sautéed in orange, garlic, and cumin (US$8), smoked marlin salad (US$4.50), and coconut shrimp (US$11.50). As the name suggests, lobster is a big seller as well but the smallish sizes don't quite merit the largish price tag. The outdoor patio, right on the corner, is nice on a warm evening.

ITALIAN

Specializing in northern Italian dishes, **Prima Trattoria** (Calle Rosado Salas at Av. 5, tel. 987/872-4242, 4:30–11 P.M. daily, US$7–23) serves handmade pastas and great salads in a charming rooftop garden.

With a shady courtyard and a seemingly endless list of sauces, **(Guido's** (Av. Rafael Melgar between Calles 6 and 8, tel. 987/872-0946, 11 A.M.–11 P.M. Mon.–Sat., US$8–17) is perfect if you're in the mood for a special pasta dish or brick-oven pizza. Add a glass of sangria and a warm breeze and you've got the makings for a classic Cozumeleño night out. Popular with expatriates and locals alike.

OTHER SPECIALTIES

Set in one of the oldest clapboard houses on the island, the artsy **(Restaurant Manatí** (Av. 10 Norte at Calle 8, tel. 987/869-8568, noon–11 P.M. Mon.–Sat., US$5–11) is a breezy place to get a creative meal. While not exclusively vegetarian, the menu veers in that direction (think spinach and cheese pasta, mixed vegetables in mango sauce, curry shrimp). The filling *comida corrida* also is one of the best deals in town: choice of soup and main dish as well as all-you-can-drink fruit juices for US$4.75. Be sure to save room for the homemade desserts—the lemon pie is a taste bud's delight. There's live music on Thursday and Saturday nights, starting at 9:30 P.M.

For a tasty change of pace, head to **Especias** (Calle 3 Sur near Av. 5 Sur, tel. 987/876-1558, 6:30–11:30 P.M. daily, US$5–10), a small restaurant serving world food—Argentinean, Jamaican, Thai, Indian, and more. The zucchini stuffed with cheese and tomatoes and the *chistorro* (rolled thin sausage) are especially good ways to start your meal.

If you're craving a big American breakfast, head straight to **Cocos Cozumel** (Av. 5 Sur between Calles Rosado Salas and 1, 987/872-0241, 6 A.M.–noon Tues.–Sun., US$3–6). After you've tried the Grand Slam, a serious meal with eggs, ham, hash browns, and coffee, it'll be tough to get your breakfast fix anywhere else. Just a block from the central plaza, this diner is popular among travelers and locals alike. Closed September and October.

Pepe's Grill (Av. Rafael Melgar between Calles Rosado Salas and 3, tel. 987/872-0213, 10 A.M.–11 P.M. Mon.–Sat., 5–11 P.M. Sun., US$12–24) has long been popular for its good food and sunset views over the Caribbean. It's definitely old school, harkening back to the mid-1980s in its nautical style and synthesizer jam sessions, but if you're in the mood for prime rib or a big salad, this is the place to come.

An old-time favorite, **Jeannie's Waffles and Raul's Tacos** (Av. Rafael Melgar near Calle 11, 6 A.M.–11 P.M. daily, US$6–10) serves made-to-order waffles in every shape, way, and form—they even replace tortillas as the base for traditional *huevos rancheros*. Other breakfast options include eggs, hash browns, and homemade bread. Portions are hearty so come hungry or be prepared to leave some for Mr. Manners. As the name suggests, the restaurant also serves decent tacos for lunch and dinner.

The world's smallest **Hard Rock Café** (Av. Rafael Melgar between Calles 1 and 3, tel. 987/872-5271, 10 A.M.–1 A.M. Sun.–Wed., until 2 A.M. Thu.–Sat., US$6–18) has views of the Caribbean during the day and live music starting at 10 P.M. Thursday to Saturday night. Food is typical Hard Rock fare—burgers, potato skins, etc.—and a boutique near the entrance sells T-shirts and rock 'n' roll memorabilia.

CAFÉS AND BISTROS

With a tree growing in the middle of the main dining area, regular art exhibits on the walls, and Arabic tunes playing in the background, **◖ Coffeelia** (Calle 5 between Avs. 5 Sur and Rafael Melgar, tel. 987/872-7402, 7:30 A.M.–11 P.M. Mon.–Sat., 8A.M.–1 P.M. Sun., US$4–6.50) is a pleasing, bohemian place. The food, too, is a pleasure—light and varied with a dozen egg dishes, 18 crepe combos, and a small army of sandwiches and salads. A great place to kick back with a café au lait and catch up on postcards.

Owned and operated by a friendly French couple, **Crepería La Delicia** (Av. Felipe Ángeles near Calle 5 Sur, 5 –11 P.M. Sun.–Fri.,

US$3.50–6) is a breezy little place, serving more than 20 different crepes—delicious and filling for a meal, a dessert, or both. Three-item baguettes and omelets also are offered. Located deep in a residential neighborhood, it's worth the drive or long walk.

Restaurante del Museo (Av. Rafael Melgar and Calle 6, tel. 987/872-0838, 7 A.M.–2 P.M. daily, US$4–7) is a little outdoor café on the roof of the Museo Cozumel. Great for lunch after a morning at the museum or simply for a drink to watch the boats cruise past. Get there early on Sundays, when locals line up for the restaurant's famous *sopa de pancita* (cow's stomach soup)—an acquired, kind of furry taste.

A tiny bistro on a quiet corner, **Le Chef** (Av. 5 at Calle 5 Sur, 987/878-4391, 11 A.M.–4 P.M. and 6–10:30 P.M. Tues.– Sat., 6–10:30 P.M. Mon., US$5–20) serves up gourmet kosher meals and sandwiches, fancy cheese plates, fine steaks, and big salads. Service is molasses slow, but the ambiance makes up for it—a glass of wine often makes the time pass a little faster.

Across the street, the sterile-looking **Island Coffee** (Av. 5 near Calle 5 Sur, 987/872-1000, 7 A.M.–11 P.M. Mon.–Sat., 9 A.M.–2 P.M. Sun., US$2–5) doesn't have the charm its neighbor does but offers a fantastic array of coffee drinks, sandwich combos, and freshly made desserts. Great for an early morning caffeine kick or a mid-afternoon meal, the fact that it's open late and on Sundays makes it doubly special.

If you notice the aroma of roasting beans, follow your nose to **Café Chiapas** (Calle 2 between Avs. 5 and 10 Norte, tel. 987/869-2042, 8 A.M.–9 P.M. Mon.–Sat.). With just one stool and a countertop, this place sells some of the best coffee around—just take it to go.

SWEETS

Hands down, the best place to go for traditional Mexican baked goods is **◖ Zermatt** (Av. 5 Norte at Calle 4, tel. 987/872-1384, 7 A.M.–8:30 P.M. Mon.–Sat., 7 A.M.– 6 P.M. Sun.). Be sure to get a little something for the street dogs who like to sniff around outside—otherwise they'll follow you (and your bag of treats) back to your hotel.

If the bread is still baking at Zermatt, head to **Panadería Cozumeleña** (Av. 10 Sur at Calle 3, 7 A.M.–10 P.M. Mon.–Sat., 7 A.M.–9 P.M. Sun.) for a good sampling of Mexican breads and pastries.

For a cool treat, head to **La Michoacana** (Av. Juárez at Av. 20 Sur, 8:30 A.M.–11 P.M. daily), where there's always a changing variety of homemade *aguas* (fruit drinks), *nieves* (ice cream), and *paletas* (popsicles).

GROCERIES

If you are cooking for yourself, **Chedraui** (Av. Rafael Melgar between Calles 15 and 17, 7 A.M.–10 P.M. daily) is the largest supermarket on the island. For a traditional market experience—fresh produce and sides of beef hanging from hooks—head to the ***mercado público*** (Av. 25 between Calles 1 and Rosado Salas, 7 A.M.–3 P.M. daily).

Information and Services

TOURIST INFORMATION

The city tourist office has three **information booths** (8 A.M.–7 P.M. Mon.–Sat., 9 A.M.–2 P.M. Sun.) on the island—in the central plaza, at the International Pier, and at Puerta Maya pier. These booths are distinguishable from tour operators' kiosks by the staffers' uniforms—khaki pants and Hawaiian shirts with the tourism office logo—and the fact that they don't push area trips. English is spoken at all locations.

If the booths are packed or you simply prefer going to an office, the actual **tourist office** (Plaza del Sol, 2nd Fl., Av. 5 between Av. Juárez and Calle 1, tel. 987/869-0212, www.cozumel .gob.mx, 9 A.M.–7 P.M. Mon.–Fri.) is located in the central plaza.

Get a copy of the ***Free Blue Guide to Cozumel*** (tel. 987/872-1451, freeblueguide@ hotmail.com) for a good map and listings for a range of services, from restaurants to dive shops. Look for the booklet as you get off the ferry.

HOSPITALS

The **Hyperbaric Medical Center** (Calle 5 between Avs. Rafael Melgar and 5 Sur, tel. 987/872-1430, cozumel@sssnetwork.com, 8 A.M.–11 P.M. daily, on-call 24 hours) specializes in diver-related medical treatment though non-diving ailments also are treated. English spoken.

Clínica-Hospital San Miguel (Calle 6 between Avs. 5 and 10 Norte, tel. 987/872-0103, 24 hours daily) offers both general and diver-related medical services.

Centro Médico de Cozumel (CMC, Calle 1 between Avs. 45 and 55 Sur, tel. 987/872-9400, www.centromedicodecozumel.com .mx, 24 hours daily) accepts many foreign insurance plans though prices are higher here than elsewhere.

PHARMACIES

Farmacia Portales (Calle 1 at Av. 10 Sur, tel. 987/872-1448, 7:30 A.M.–10:30 P.M. Mon.–Sat., 8:30 A.M.–9:30 P.M. Sun.) has a complete range of medication, plus sunscreen, film, and snacks.

Farmacia Dori (Calle 7 Sur near Av. Rafael Melgar; tel. 987/872-5519, 7 A.M.–11 P.M. Mon.–Sat., 8 A.M.–10 P.M. Sun.) has this and two other locations in town; delivery available.

POLICE

The **tourist police** (Plaza del Sol, 2nd Fl., Av. 5 between Av. Juárez and Calle 1, no phone, 24 hours daily) is located in the central plaza, next to the city tourist office.

The police (Palacio Municipal, Calle 13 between Avs. 5 and Rafael Melgar, tel. 987/872-0092, 24 hours daily) also can be reached toll-free at 066.

MONEY

Accessing your money is not difficult in Cozumel, especially near the central plaza. **HSBC** (Av. 5 Sur at Calle 1, 8 A.M.–7 P.M. Mon.–Sat.), **Bancomer** (Av. 5 Sur between Av. Juárez and Calle 1, 8:30 A.M.–4 P.M. Mon.–Fri.), and **Banorte** (Av. 5 Norte between Av. Juárez and Calle 2, 9 A.M.–6 P.M. Mon.–Fri., 10 A.M.–2 P.M. Sat.) exchange travelers checks and have ATMs.

INTERNET AND TELEPHONE

For emailing, **Blau Net** (Calle Rosado Salas between Avs. 10 and 15, tel. 987/872-6275, 9 A.M.–10 P.M. Mon.–Sat., US$1/hr., US$5 to burn photos onto CD) is a quiet and reliable place. Calls to the United States and Canada cost US$0.37 per minute.

Web Station (Av. 5 Sur between Calles 3 and 5, tel. 987/872-3911, 10 A.M.–11 P.M. Mon.–Sat, 10 A.M.–10 P.M. Sun.) offers fast Internet service on flat-screen computers (US$1/hr.), international telephone service (US$0.37/minute to most countries), and best of all, wicked air-conditioning.

POST OFFICE

The post office (Av. Rafael Melgar at Calle 7, 9 A.M.–5 P.M. Mon.–Fri., 9 A.M.–1 P.M. Sat.) is next to Punta Langosta shopping center.

IMMIGRATION

The immigration office (Av. 15 Sur at Calle 5, tel. 987/872-3110) is open 9 A.M.–1 P.M. Monday–Friday only. There's an office at the airport as well (tel. 987/872-5604, 7 A.M.–9 P.M. daily).

LAUNDERETTE

Servi-Lav Lavandería (Av. 10 Norte between Calles 6 and 8, tel. 987/872-3951, 8 A.M.–8 P.M. Mon.–Sat., US$1/kg (2.2 lbs)) typically provides next-day service; if you drop off your clothes first thing in the morning though, you'll have a shot at same-day service at no additional cost.

Lavandería Express (Calle Rosado Salas between Avs. 5 and 10, tel. 987/872-2932, 8 A.M.–9 P.M. Mon.–Sat., 8:30 A.M.–4:30 P.M. Sun.) offers full service (two hours, US$7 for up to eight kg/17.6 lbs) but will also let you wash your own clothes for US$2 a load to wash, US$1.25 every 10 minutes to dry.

Getting There and Around

GETTING THERE
Air

Cozumel International Airport (CZM, 987/872-0485) is approximately three kilometers (2 miles) from downtown. The airport has an ATM in the departures area, and AmEx currency exchange at arrivals, and a few magazine stands and duty-free shops. Taxis to or from the airport are US$10; shared vans are US$4.25 per person.

Bus

Although there are no long-distance buses on Cozumel (it is a pretty small island, after all), tickets for buses departing Playa del Carmen are sold at **Ticket Bus** (Calle 2 at Av. 10 Sur, tel. 987/869-2553, 6 A.M.–2 P.M. and 2:30–9 P.M. daily) at no extra cost.

Ferry

Ferries to Playa del Carmen (US$10 each way, 30 minutes) leave from the passenger ferry pier across from the central plaza. Two companies—**UltraMar** (Av. Rosado Salas at Av. 45, tel. 987/869-3223) and **Mexico Water Jets** (Calle 6 Norte between Av. 20 and 25, tel. 987/872-1578)—operate the boats; the service and fares are identical, though UltraMar's boats are somewhat newer. Between the two companies, at least one ferry leaves Cozumel every hour on the hour from 5 A.M. to 11 P.M. daily.

UltraMar has built a second ferry pier in Playa del Carmen at the end of Avenida Constituyentes, 10 blocks north of Playa's existing pier on the south end of town. When service begins there—it hadn't yet as we went to

© LIZA PRADO

The passenger ferries from Playa del Carmen arrive in front of Cozumel's central plaza.

ISLA COZUMEL

press—be sure to ask in Cozumel where your ferry is headed. If you're catching a bus straight from the ferry, the new pier will be more convenient to Terminal Alterna (long-distance service), while the main pier is just steps from Terminal Turística (for local service, including to Cancún and Tulum).

GETTING AROUND

In town, you can easily walk anywhere you like. However, the powerful taxi union has succeeded in quashing any and all efforts to start public bus service out of town and around the island. It is a shame, really, since it would be so easy and convenient to have a fleet of buses making loops around the island, or even just up and down the western shore. Until that changes (don't hold your breath), you'll need a car, moped, or bike to explore the rest of the island.

Bicycle

A bike can be handy for getting to beach clubs and snorkel sites outside of town. Traffic on Avenida Rafael Melgar can be heavy south of town, but once clear of that, the roadway is relatively unhurried. Both **Rentadora Isis** and **Rentadora Gallo** (see *Car and Moped Rental*) rent bicycles for around US$10 a day, as well as snorkel gear (US$10/day).

Taxi

Taxis (tel. 987/872-0236 or tel. 987/872-0041) are everywhere—you can easily flag one down on Avenida Rafael Melgar, near the main passenger pier, and around the plaza. Cabs have set prices—US$1.50–2 around town, and US$3.50 to the airport from the central plaza for instance. To and from hotels and beach clubs out of town, however, the rates jump significantly, to US$7–20. As always, before getting into a taxi, be sure to agree upon the price.

Car and Moped Rental

Renting a car is a nice way to get out of downtown and see the rest of the island. It is virtually impossible to get lost, and you can visit all the main spots in a day or two.

FLYING TO COZUMEL

The following airlines service Cozumel International Airport (CZM):

- **AeroCozumel** (airport tel. 987/872-0468)

- **Aeroméxico** (airport tel. 987/872-3454, toll-free Mex. tel. 800/021-4010, www.aeromexico.com)

- **American Airlines** (toll-free Mex. tel. 800/904-6000, www.aa.com)

- **Click Mexicana** (airport tel. 987/872-3456, toll-free Mex. tel. 800/112-5425, www.clickmx.com)

- **Continental** (airport tel. 987/872-0847, toll-free Mex. tel. 800/900-5000, www.continental.com)

- **Delta** (toll-free Mex. tel. 800/123-4710, www.delta.com)

- **Mexicana** (airport tel. 987/872-2945, toll-free Mex. tel. 800/502-2000, www.mexicana.com)

- **United Airlines** (toll-free Mex. tel. 800/003-0777, www.united.com)

- **US Airways** (toll-free Mex. tel. 800/428-4322, www.usairways.com)

If you do decide to rent some wheels, go to the agency yourself—do not allow one of the friendly guys at the pier to lead you there. They are *comisionistas,* freelancers who earn hefty commissions for bringing tourists to particular shops, which then pass the cost on to you. Shop owners go along begrudgingly; if they decline the "service," the same freelancers will actively steer future tourists away from the shop, saying it's closed, burned down, fresh out of cars—you get the idea.

Excluding commissions, rental cars in Cozumel start at US$40–50 a day for a VW bug or other small car, including insurance and taxes. Mopeds rent for around US$20 a day. Be aware that scooters account for the majority of accidents here, as speed bumps, potholes, and windy conditions can upend even experienced drivers. Also remember that unpaved roads are not covered by most rental car insurance plans.

Rentadora Isis (Av. 5 Norte between Calles 2 and 4, tel. 987/872-3367, rentadoraisis@prodigy.net.mx, 8 A.M.–6:30 P.M. Mon.–Sat., 8 A.M.–6 P.M. Sun.) consistently has the island's best rates, and friendly service to boot. **Rentadora Gallo** (Av. 10 Sur between Calle 1 and Av. Benito Juárez, tel. 987/869-2444, 8 A.M.–7 P.M. daily) is also eager to please. **Budget** (Av. 5 Norte between Calles 2 and 4, tel. 987/872-0903, www.budgetcancun.com, 7 A.M.–7:30 P.M. daily) is one of a handful of international companies on the island. **Hertz** and **Avis** have booths at the airport.

Cozumel has three **PEMEX** gas stations (7 A.M.–midnight daily). Two are in town on Avenida Benito Juárez (at Avs. Pedro Joaquin Coldwell and 75) and the third is four kilometers (2.5 miles) south of town on the Carretera Costera Sur across from Puerta Maya, the main cruise ship pier.

THE RIVIERA MAYA

Cancún may be the name everyone recognizes, but for many visitors, the best of Mexico's Caribbean coast belongs to the Riviera Maya. Defined as the 131-kilometer (79-mile) stretch of coastline between Cancún and Tulum, the Riviera Maya has no shortage of marquee attractions: the world's longest underground river, the world's second-longest coral reef, beautiful beaches packed with sun-worshippers, ancient Maya ruins, gourmet restaurants, hipster lounge bars, and beach-side discotheques. With so much to see and do, the main trouble here may be fitting it all in. Then again, when you're on vacation in a place as beautiful as the Riviera Maya, doing nothing may well be the highlight of your trip!

PLANNING YOUR TIME

You'll probably want to pick a home base (or two) for your time here, and make day trips from there. Playa del Carmen is the area's only real city, with all the expected urban amenities, including nightlife. (It's also the gateway to Isla Cozumel.) Puerto Morelos and Akumal are smaller, and have numerous hotels and restaurants, but less hubbub. For even more isolation, the Riviera Maya has some secret getaways, like Xpu-Há, Punta Bete, and Tankah Tres. Day trips along the coast are easiest done in a rental car, though frequent public shuttles make getting up and down the coast fast and cheap. If you've got a week or more, consider spending half your time in the northern section—around Playa, for example—and then move farther south, to enjoy Akumal, Tankah Tres, and even Tulum.

© LIZA PRADO

HIGHLIGHTS

◖ **Puerto Morelos's Coral Reef:** Skip the tourist-trap snorkeling trips in Cancún and Playa del Carmen and go snorkeling where the reef is still healthy, the water uncrowded, and the price unbeatable (page 132).

◖ **Playa del Carmen's Quinta Avenida:** Ever growing yet wonderfully walkable, Playa's 5th Avenue has block after block of tempting restaurants, hipster boutiques, and lively bars (page 139).

◖ **Playa del Carmen's Beaches and Beach Clubs:** Chairs for rent, waiter service, and cool tunes make Playa's beaches – already among the Riviera Maya's most beautiful – some of the most enjoyable as well (page 142).

◖ **Xcaret Eco-Park:** Though not for everyone, the Riviera Maya's elaborate eco-parks are a hit with parents looking for a safe, active, friendly place to take the kids (page 147).

◖ **Laguna Yal-Ku:** A long elbow of water, where fresh and sea water mingle, and colorful fish live amid a jumble of underwater rocks and channels, makes this Akumal-area lagoon a favorite among snorkelers (page 167).

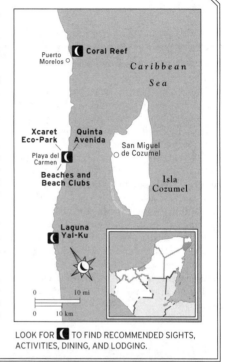

LOOK FOR ◖ TO FIND RECOMMENDED SIGHTS, ACTIVITIES, DINING, AND LODGING.

Puerto Morelos

Somehow little Puerto Morelos has escaped the mega-development that has swept up and down the Maya Riviera, and literally transformed its closest neighbors, Cancún and Playa del Carmen. Though Puerto Morelos can fill up with foreign tourists in the high season—and more and more condos and resorts are being built—it is still at heart a tranquil fishing town where kids and dogs romp in the streets, and life revolves around the central plaza. The beach isn't great, but Puerto Morelos has long been considered one of the best snorkeling spots on the coast. Local residents fought tirelessly (and successfully) to have the reef designated a national

reserve, and a town cooperative and local dive shops run well-recommended snorkeling and diving trips there. Puerto Morelos also is gaining popularity as a destination for yoga and meditation groups—no surprise given its serene atmosphere—and a growing number of hotels and resorts cater to that market. Be aware that the low season here is *very* low and many businesses close in May, September, and/or October.

SIGHTS
Beach

The beach here is disappointing—rocky in many places and strewn with seaweed that has

QUEEN CONCH

Tasty, easy to catch, and beautifully packaged – the Queen Conch (pronounced CONK) is a commercial angler's dream. Every part is sold: meat is exported to the United States and shells are bought as souvenirs by tourists. An easy way to make money – yes – but it's disappearing. Smaller conchs are being sold and anglers are being forced to go farther afield to make a profit.

It takes three to five years for this sea snail to grow from larva to market size. It also takes about that long for planktonic conch larvae, carried into fished-out areas by the currents, to replenish themselves. What's worse, the conch is easy to catch – large (up to 39 cm/15.4 in) and heavy (about three kg/6.6 lbs), the mollusk moves slowly and lives in shallow, crystalline water where it's easy to spot.

Biologists are working with various governments to impose restrictions on the fishing of Queen Conch, including closed seasons, minimum size, limits on the total numbers taken, and banning export.

Along with these proposed legal restrictions, science is lending a hand. Several mariculture centers, including one in Puerto Morelos, are experimenting with the Queen Conch. Raised in a protected environment, these creatures are released when they're large enough to survive in the wild. Unfortunately, this isn't always successful. One in 10 survives, as conch have to contend not only with humans but also with its other predators: lobsters, crabs, sharks, turtles, and rays.

The Queen Conch is not on the endangered species list yet but, by curbing our consumption – refusing to order it or to eat at establishments that serve it – we can help to save this creature.

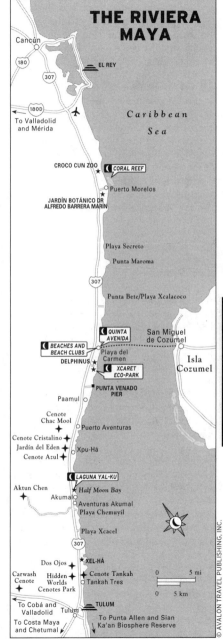

THE RIVIERA MAYA

washed ashore. The best spot is at the Ojo de Agua hotel, where even a small purchase at the restaurant lets you use the beach chairs, umbrellas, and the pool. You can arrange snorkel and ATV tours here, as well.

◖ Coral Reef

Puerto Morelos's most spectacular attraction is snorkeling on the reef. Directly in front of the village, around 500 meters (0.3 mile) offshore, the reef here takes on gargantuan dimensions—up to 30 meters (99 feet) wide. Winding passages and large caverns alive with fish and sea flora make for great exploring. And since it's a marine reserve and fishing and motor traffic is limited, the reef is more pristine here than almost any place along the Riviera. (See *Snorkeling* for information on guided tours of the reef.)

The Plaza

The little plaza has restaurants and shops on three sides, and the ocean on the fourth. On Sundays, a small *tianguis* (flea market) is held here, and you can have fun browsing through someone else's old treasures. Otherwise, expect it to be quiet and unoccupied, save for a few people chatting on shaded benches.

Tropical Petting Zoo

A charming little tropical zoo, **Croco Cun Zoo** (tel. 998/850-3719, www.crococunzoo.com, 9 A.M.–6 P.M. daily, US$17 adults, US$11 children age 6–12, under 6 free) is located five kilometers (3.1 miles) north of the Puerto Morelos turnoff. Ninety-minute guided tours, offered in English or Spanish, bring visitors up close and personal to all sorts of local creatures—if you're up for it, you can feed spider monkeys on your shoulder, walk through a crocodile enclosure, and hold boas, iguanas, and baby crocs. Don't forget your camera. Well-managed and reasonably affordable—compare this to swimming with the dolphins!—Croco Cun is a sure hit for youngsters and adults alike.

Botanical Garden

A half kilometer (one-third mile) south of the

© AVALON TRAVEL PUBLISHING, INC.

Puerto Morelos turnoff is the **Jardín Botánico Dr. Alfredo Barrera Marín** (tel. 983/835-0440, 8 A.M.–4 P.M. daily, US$7), a peaceful botanical garden, study center, and tree nursery spread over 60 hectares (150 acres). Two kilometers (1.2 miles) of trails wind beneath a canopy of trees and past many of the peninsula's plants and flowers; each with its name labeled in English, Spanish, and Latin. Habitats vary from semi-evergreen tropical forest to mangrove swamp. Look for the epiphyte area, with a variety of orchids, tillandsias, and bromeliads. As you wander around you'll also find a re-creation of a Maya *chiclero* camp (showing how chicle was harvested to be used in chewing gum), a few ruins from the Postclassic period, and a contemporary Maya hut illustrating day-to-day life—from cooking facilities to hammocks. Wear long sleeves, pants, and closed shoes, and definitely bring bug repellent—the mosquitoes can be fierce, especially in the late afternoon and after it rains.

SHOPPING

The artisans' market of **Hunab Kú** (1.5 blocks south of the plaza, 9 A.M.–8 P.M. daily) may be your best bet for finding nice handicrafts. Here, you'll find a bunch of stands with colorful blankets, ceramics, hammocks, masks, jipi hats, shell art…pretty much anything you'll see sold up and down the coast.

The best English-language bookstore on the peninsula, **Alma Libre Bookstore** (central plaza, tel. 998/871-0713, www.almalibre books.com, 10 A.M.–3 P.M. and 6–9 P.M. Tues.–Sat., 4–9 P.M. Sun.) has a whopping 20,000 titles, ranging from "beach trash to Plato," in the words of the friendly Canadian couple who own and operate the store. Maya culture, Mexican cooking, learning Spanish, bird-watching, snorkeling guides, classics, philosophy, mysteries, fiction, nonfiction, and not just in English but Spanish, French, German, Dutch, Italian, Norwegian, and more—your taste in books would have to be extremely narrow to not find something you like here. Books are both new and used, and trade-ins (two for one) are possible; the store also has a

YUCATECAN HAMMOCKS

Yucatecan *hamacas* (hammocks) have the reputation of being the best in the world. Many locals prefer sleeping in them to mattresses. Cool and easy to store, they make great traveling beds and wonderful souvenirs. Here are a few tips for buying one:

Material: Nylon, cotton, or a blend of the two are the materials used to make hammocks. Nylon is more resilient but cotton is often more comfortable. Try a few out to see if you have a preference. If you're ambivalent, consider how much you plan to use it and which thread serves your needs best. Beware of vendors selling hammocks supposedly made of henequen; outside of miniature ones that hold fruit, they don't exist. (Even if they did, they would be incredibly itchy.)

Size: Hammocks typically come in *individual* (twin), *matrimonial* (queen), and *familiar* (king). While twins may be snug for a person taller than five feet, queen-size hammocks are roomy enough for most people. To judge whether a hammock will be long enough for you, hold one end of the body (the woven section) to the top of your head and let it drop; the other end of the body should touch the floor for you to be comfortable. A little extra material is optimal.

Loops: Check the end strings, which are called *brazos* (arms). At least 100-150 triple loops are in a good *matrimonial* hammock.

Shop Around: Finally, be sure to look at several hammocks before buying one. Feel the thread, check out the different sizes, count the *brazos*, and decide which patterns and color schemes you like best – vendors will always stretch out the hammock if asked. You'll soon hone in on one that best fits your needs, style, and budget.

wide selection of guidebooks and maps. Usually closed June to mid-October.

SPORTS AND RECREATION
Snorkeling
Puerto Morelos is justly famous for its snorkeling, with a protected stretch of coral reef running very near shore. A **local cooperative** (8 A.M.–3 P.M. Mon.–Sat.) offers excellent and affordable tours, visiting two spots on the reef for 45 minutes apiece, and using boats with sunshades. Prices are fixed: US$25 per person, including equipment, park fees, and a bottle of water. Boats leave every 30 minutes from the municipal pier; if there are fewer than three people, you have to wait up to 30 minutes (but no more) for additional passengers to come. Sign up at the cooperative's kiosk at the northeast corner of the plaza; late morning is the best time to go, as the sun is high but the afternoon winds haven't started.

The **dive shops** in town also offer snorkeling tours for US$25 pp for a two-hour trip visiting two different sites. Prices include snorkel gear, but you should ask whether the park fee is additional.

Caution: *Do not swim to the reef* from anywhere along the beach. Although it's close enough for strong swimmers to reach, boats use the channel between the reef and the shore, and tourists have been struck and killed in the past.

Scuba Diving
Divers have two shops to choose from in town, both offering one- and two-tank dives, night and specialty dives, cenote dives, and a range of certification courses. Reservations are strongly recommended in the high season.

Next to Posada el Moro, **Dive Puerto Morelos** (Av. Javier Rojo Gómez 14, tel. 998/206-9084, www.divepuertomorelos.com, 8 A.M.–6 P.M. Mon.–Sat., 8 A.M.–noon Sun.) offers reef diving (US$50 one tank, US$70 two tanks), cenote diving (US$85 one tank, US$125 two tanks), open water certification (US$325) and other courses, plus fishing, snorkeling and multi-dive packages. Rates include park fees and complete gear, except wetsuit.

Scuba Gecko (Hotel Ojo de Agua, tel. 998/871-0198, www.scubagecko.com, 9 A.M.–noon and 4–8 P.M. Tues.–Sat.) is part of Wet Set Adventures, a longtime dive and tour operator. Dives are US$45 for one tank, US$60 for two, and US$350 for open-water certification.

Sport Fishing
Both dive shops in Puerto Morelos also offer fishing trips beyond the reef. Scuba Gecko guarantees you will catch fish on its tour or the trip is free. Trolling trips (US$55/hr or US$175/day for two anglers) reel in wahoo, mackerel, bonito, and barracuda year-round, plus marlin and sailfish in the late spring and summer. Bottom-fishing tours (same prices) regularly bring home grouper, snapper, and other tasty fish—the crew will even prepare the fish for your hotel restaurant to cook. Dive Puerto Morelos offers tours on a local *panga* (US$250 for four hours, four people) or a modern fishing boat with cabin (US$450, four hours, 4–8 people).

ATV Tours
Puerto Morelos Adventure (Hotel Ojo de Agua, tel. 998/884-2314, www.puertomorelos adventure.com, 8 A.M.–7 P.M. daily) offers a four-hour ATV tour (US$58pp double, US$68 single) that weaves through sand dunes and coastal forest with stops at two cenotes to cool off. One cenote has a zip line for a bit of a rush. A bilingual guide and light lunch at Ojo de Agua hotel are included.

ACCOMMODATIONS
Under US$50
On a quiet street two blocks from the beach, **Hotel Eden** (Av. Andrés Quintana Roo No. 788, tel. 998/871-0450, US$31 s/d with fan) may not be the paradise its name suggests, but makes a good budget option all the same. Decor and flair are in short supply—not to mention TVs—but the spacious studios do have ceiling fans, clean hot-water bathrooms, and small kitchenettes. The kitchens aren't furnished (strangely) but the friendly proprietors usually have some extra pots and pans to loan you.

A half a block from the central plaza **Posada El Moro** (Av. Javier Rojo Gómez, tel. 998/871-0159, www.posadaelmoro.com, US$50 with fan, US$55 with a/c, US$75 suite with kitchenette) is one of Puerto Morelos's most charming hotels, and a great deal to boot. Operated by a friendly, English-speaking family, the hotel has 10 brightly painted units with polished cement floors, cable TV, wireless Internet (US$1.50/hr), and a pleasant little pool in a grassy courtyard in back. Continental breakfast is included.

In front of the Caribbean, **Amar Inn** (Av. Javier Rojo Gómez at Av. Lázaro Cárdenas, tel. 998/871-0026, amar_inn@hotmail.com, US$45–65 s/d with fan, US$75 suite) is a hurricane-battered inn run by the Aguilar family. The nine rooms vary from cramped garden cabañas with lofts, to spacious suites with amazing ocean views. All are reasonably clean and come with fans and refrigerators. Breakfast also is included.

The wine-red **Club Marviya** (Av. Rojo Gómez s/n, three blocks north of the central plaza, tel. 998/871-0049, in Canada 450/492-9094, www.marviya.com; US$95 Dec.–Apr., US$45 May–Nov.) is a laid-back Quebecois and Mexican-run hotel with six rooms and a communal kitchen, just a few steps from the beach. The rooms, all on the 2nd floor of a converted mansion, have firm beds, ceramic floors, and terrific views (and cool sea breezes) from small terraces. Breakfast is included, served in the covered downstairs corridor patio, where the owners and guests often hang out over beers at night. Bikes and beach gear can be rented or borrowed, and nine studio apartments were in the works when we passed by.

US$50-100

Formerly known as Rancho Libertad, **Rancho Sak Ol** (1 km/0.6 mi south of the central plaza, tel. 998/871-0181, www.ranchosakol.com, US$85 s/d with fan or a/c, US$120 jr. suite with fan and 2 night minimum) is a *palapa* hideaway on a broad beach south of town. Rooms have hanging beds and individual patios with hammocks. Downstairs rooms have air-conditioning, upstairs rooms have cross-breezes. A large buffet breakfast is included, and guests can use the community kitchen, located beachside. The beach here is decent, if not spectacular, marred somewhat by the cargo ferry on one side and a huge new condominium complex on the other. But there's enough breathing room so as not to spoil Rancho Sak Ol's relaxing, hideaway feel. Adults only, except during the low season when children over the age of 10 are welcome. Use of snorkel equipment and bicycles is also included in the rate.

One block south of the plaza, **Hacienda Morelos** (Av. Rafael Melgar, tel. 998/871-0448, www.haciendamorelos.com, US$70 s, US$100 d) took a beating in Hurricane Wilma, but has bounced back, completely renovated. Large airy rooms have simple but attractive decor, and the ocean views make up for the bathrooms, which someone hit with a 1970s stick. A concrete sunbathing patio with a small pool separates the hotel from the beach, and there's a good restaurant on-site.

Hotel Ojo de Aqua (Av. Javier Rojo Gómez, two blocks north of plaza, tel. 998/871-0027, www.ojo-de-agua.com, US$56–75 s/d) offers 36 basic rooms overlooking a pretty beach. Rooms come with cable TV and air-conditioning; standards feel a bit cramped, deluxes are bigger, and studios have a refrigerator, stove, and sink. All are clean and comfortable, though lacking in character—the flowered bedspreads and tile floors are classic hotel room. Families will appreciate the protected pool area, and on-site dive shop and tour operator, which rents snorkel gear and kayaks, and organizes ATV and snorkel tours.

Over US$100

A block from the beach, **Villas Shanti** (Av. Niños Héroes s/n, tel. 998/871-0040, www.villasshanti.com, US$123 d with a/c) offers eight one-bedroom units, each with a modern bathroom, fully equipped kitchenette, and private patio; all face a sunny courtyard that has a clover-shaped pool and a large *palapa* strung with hammocks. A spacious two-bedroom villa with full kitchen, living room, and dining room also is available for four to six guests, starting at around US$2,000 a week. Yoga workshops and retreats are regularly held here—classes are in a bright indoor studio or a large *palapa* in the garden. Check the website for more information.

Although somewhat overpriced, **Ceiba Del Mar** (1.5 km/0.9 mi north of town, tel. 998/872-8060, www.ceibadelmar.com, US$437 s/d with a/c, US$493–840 suite with a/c, US$1008 suite with a/c and whirlpool, US$1,120 penthouse) offers a high-end resort experience in a laid-back town—something hard to come by. Located in eight three-story stucco buildings, the units are elegantly appointed and have the modern amenities you'd expect like flat-screen TVs with DVD, CD players, and minibars. Continental breakfast is included and is served in your room through a butler box—you won't even have to throw on your robe to open the door. The resort also boasts two glorious pools, a full-service spa, two restaurants, a dive shop, and tennis courts with night-lights.

FOOD
Who knows how it happened, but unassuming Puerto Morelos has an amazingly rich collection of restaurants and eateries, from cheerful holes-in-the-wall to international cuisine rivaling anything in Cancún or Playa del Carmen.

International
⟪ John Gray's Kitchen (Av. Niños Héroes, half block north of plaza, tel. 998/871-0665, 6–10 P.M. Mon.–Sat., US$10–25) is a reincarnation of the now-closed but famously good Johnny Cairo Restaurant. It is without question the finest restaurant in Puerto Morelos (as was its predecessor), featuring an inventive menu that changes every other day. Specials include various fine cuts of beef and pasta prepared with almonds and chorizo. Occupying a boxy building two blocks from the plaza, the dining room is elegant and understated and the service is excellent. Cash only.

Giving Mr. Gray a run for his culinary money is **⟪ Hola Asia** (central plaza, tel. 998/871-0679, 3–11 P.M. Mon.–Sat., 1–10 P.M. Sun., closed Tues., US$5–12) a small, popular restaurant serving a terrific pan-Asian menu of mostly Thai and Chinese inspiration. The simple one-room dining area can get crammed with diners, many who've come from Cancún or Playa del Carmen to eat here. For sweet and sour try General Tso's Chicken, for spicy go with Indian Yellow Curry. Closed in September.

The Argentinean and Uruguayan owners of **Los Gauchos** (Calle Tulum, tel. 998/871-0475, 4 P.M.–10 P.M. weekdays except Tues., 1 P.M.–10 P.M. weekends, US$1–5) serve homemade pizza and pasta, but don't leave without trying the *empanadas:* a classic Argentinean snack made of puffy, crispy fried dough filled with cheese or other goodies. At just US$1.25 apiece, a plate of five or six and a couple of sodas makes a great, cheap meal for two. Take them to go or eat at one of a few small tables on the sidewalk.

Everything you see at **Baraka** (Av. Rafael Melgar; 1 P.M.–10 P.M. Tue.–Sun., US$8–25)—the soaring *palapa,* the gorgeous wood floors, the sun-splashed patio—is in its second incarnation: the restaurant opened just days before Hurricane Wilma hit, destroying everything but the bathroom; check out the photo album while you're waiting for your meals. Lucky for everyone, it reopened and serves tasty Spanish-Mediterranean dishes, from *paella valenciana* to fresh sardines, accompanied by a full bar and friendly service.

A newcomer to the restaurant scene, **Tuna** (Av. Javier Rojo Gómez No. 801, tel. 998/206-9193, 8:30 A.M.–9:30 P.M. Tue.–Fri., 8:30 A.M.–11 P.M. Sat.–Sun., US$3–15) serves simple, tasty meals in a mellow, hip atmosphere. The menu sticks to Riviera Maya standards, like achiote chicken and garlic shrimp, but with a certain European flair: the French salad comes with chaya, pears, and blue cheese. Eat in the sleek dining area, then take a drink to one of the beach chairs and umbrellas. Saturday and Sunday evenings feature live music. By the way, *tuna* is the red fruit of the nopal cactus; *atún* is the fish you may have been expecting to see on the menu.

The Quebecois owners of **L'Oazis** (7:30 A.M.–10 P.M. Tue.–Sun.) serve mostly grilled dishes in their small, cheerful eatery. The menu includes tacos, burgers, NY steak, plus specialties like zucchini and eggplant with tzaziki sauce.

Mexican and Seafood

El Pirata (central plaza, tel. 998/871-0489, 8 A.M.–11 P.M. Mon.–Thurs., until 2 A.M. Fri.–Sun., US$5–15) has a good location on the central plaza just up from the pier where you take snorkeling tours. Choose from a large selection of hamburgers, fish burgers, *tortas,* tacos, and full entrées such as roast chicken or grilled beef, all served in a simple open-air dining area just off the street. Like many businesses here, El Pirata cuts back its hours in the low season, closing Mondays and the entire month of May.

C Doña Triny's (8 A.M.–1 A.M. daily; US$1–4) The bright orange and mural-bedecked exterior of this tiny restaurant on the northwest corner of the plaza make it impossible to miss. Come here for a friendly low-key ambiance and Mexican and Yucatecan standards, like quesadillas, huaraches, tacos, salbutes, and chile rellenos, all at great prices.

Los Pelícanos (central plaza, tel. 998/871-0014, 8 A.M.–10:30 P.M. daily, US$5–16) has a wraparound patio overlooking the plaza and the ocean—perfect for an afternoon beer or margarita. Food here can be a bit uneven, but with so many anglers it's hard to go wrong with shrimp, octopus, or fish, all served fresh in a half-dozen different ways.

Bakery and Sandwiches

A Puerto Morelos institution, **C Mama's Bakery** (Av. Rojo Gómez, one block north of plaza, tel. 044-998/845-6810, 7:30 A.M.–4 P.M. Tues.–Sat., 8:30 A.M.–1 P.M. Sun., US$3–5.50) is run by a friendly expat and baker extraordinaire—don't leave town without trying the sticky buns or carrot cake. Mama's is also a great place to come for fresh, healthy meals, like pancakes or breakfast burritos in the morning and smoothies and sandwiches on homemade bread for lunch. Typically closed Labor Day to November 1.

Groceries

The supermarket (north side of the central plaza, 6 A.M.–10 P.M. daily) has a fairly large selection of canned foods, pastas, snacks, and drinks, and has a small produce section near the back.

INFORMATION AND SERVICES

Although this town sees a fair number of tourists, the services remain somewhat sparse.

Hospitals

Dr. Carlos Taboada Olvera (tel. 044-998/894-0832, 8 A.M.–9 P.M. Mon.–Sat.) heads a small clinic in a new commercial building a block west of the plaza, and comes well-recommended by expats living in town. For major medical issues, use the hospitals in Cancún or Playa del Carmen.

Money

There is no bank in Puerto Morelos. However, you can get cash from the HSBC ATM, which is just outside the supermarket on the plaza's north side.

Internet and Telephone

Next door to Dive Puerto Morelos, **PixanNET** (Av. Javier Rojo Gómez, tel. 998/206-9275, 9 A.M.–4 P.M. and 6 P.M.–10 P.M. Mon.–Sat.) has arguably the fastest connection in town, charging US$2 per hour. You can also download and burn your digital photos to a CD here for around US$2. Calls to the United States and Canada are US$0.30 a minute.

Papelería Computips (tel. 998/871-0361, 8 A.M.–10 P.M. Mon.–Sat., 2–10 P.M. Sun.) is located just off the southwest corner of the central plaza, and charges US$2 per hour for Internet.

Launderette

A block south of the plaza, the aptly named **La Lavandería** (Av. Javier Rojo Gómez s/n, no phone, 8 A.M.–8 P.M. Mon.–Fri. and 9 A.M.–5 P.M. Sat.) charges US$1.25 per kilogram (2.2 pounds) to wash, dry, and fold your dirty duds. Minimum three kilograms (6.5 pounds). The same distance north of the plaza, **Lavandería Las Vivas** (8 A.M.–9 P.M. Mon.–Sat., 10 A.M.–4 P.M. Sun.) charges US$1 per pound, or US$1.50 per pound for two-hour service.

GETTING THERE
Bus
Buses pass the Puerto Morelos turnoff on Highway 307, but do not enter town. The northbound stop is right at the turnoff, while the southbound stop is across the street and a block south (tel. 998/871-0759). For Cancún (US$1.50, 30 minutes) and Playa del Carmen (US$1–1.50, 20 minutes), second-class buses and *combis* (shared vans) pass every 10 minutes 6 A.M.–1 A.M. daily, and less frequently throughout the night. Some go as far as Tulum (US$3.50–5.25, 1.5 hours), but you should double-check before getting on. Buses to the **Cancún airport** (US$3, 25 minutes) pass every hour 8:30 A.M.–6:45 P.M. daily.

The only long-distance service from here is to Mérida (US$19.50, four hours), with daily departures at 9 A.M., 4 P.M., and 6 P.M. For all others (and many more to Mérida) go to Cancún or Playa del Carmen.

Ferry
The port here no longer offers car ferry service to islands. To get your car to Cozumel, head to Punta Venado, just south of Xcaret ecopark. For Isla Mujeres, head to Punta Sam, north of Cancún.

GETTING AROUND
Unless you're staying at Ceiba del Mar, Maya Echo, or Rancho Sak Ol, you'll have little need for a car. The town is compact—you can walk it from end to end in about 20 minutes—and the beach runs the length of it and beyond.

Taxis
Taxis line up day and night at the taxi stand on the northwest corner of the plaza. Prices are fixed and prominently displayed on a signboard at the taxi stand. A ride to the highway costs around US$2.

Punta Bete and Playa Xcalacoco

The turnoff to Punta Bete and Playa Xcalacoco is easy to miss from the highway—there's no sign and only a big "Cristal" water plant to mark the entrance. The access road is no more promising, unpaved and often waterlogged, winding through abandoned fields and past various construction projects. The reward for perseverance is a handful of hotels—from modest bungalows to one of the Yucatán's most exclusive resorts—and a mellow beach scene where locals and travelers alike lose themselves in the swaying palms and gentle blue waves. The beach is just okay (the sand is coarse and the shoreline rocky in places), but the snorkeling is reasonably good; you'll see more people beachcombing and reading books

than playing beach volleyball or frolicking in the waves, and that seems to suit everyone just fine.

ACCOMMODATIONS
Hotel Kai-kaana (tel. 984/877-4000, www .kaikaana.com.mx, US$123) offers the comfort of a full-size hotel on this isolated stretch of beach, including a large pool, plenty of poolside lounge space, and a well-maintained beach area with *palapas* and hammocks. Rooms have one or two beds, cable TV, air-conditioning (though not mini-splits), and private balconies angled to provide everyone with a partial sea view. Breakfast is included in the rate, the restaurant serves up decent lunch and dinner. The staff is professional and affable.

Just steps from the beach **Bungalows Coco's** (tel. 998/874-7056, marsihel@hotmail.com, US$42 d queen, US$56 d king) has five *palapa*-roof bungalows squeezed onto a small, lush garden plot. The cabañas are charmingly decorated and have spotless bathrooms and private patios with hammocks to while away the day. There's a heart-shaped pool next to the open-air dining area and bar, and the beach is just 30 meters (100 feet) away. Reserve in advance so someone will be waiting for you when you arrive.

FOOD

Bungalows Coco's (see *Accommodations*, 7 A.M.–10 P.M., US$4–18) has a small outdoor bar and restaurant, serving dishes you don't often see in these parts, like fish and chips, blackened rib eye, and banana flambé.

GETTING THERE AND AROUND

From the highway, follow the access road two kilometers (1.2 miles) until it forks at the Ikal del Mar resort. Bear left to reach the hotels and beach.

Taxis

There is no taxi stand in this tiny community. Ikal del Mar offers free daily van service to Playa del Carmen; otherwise your hotel can call you a taxi from Playa del Carmen or Puerto Morelos. A ride to the airport will cost you US$30, to Playa del Carmen around US$7.

Playa del Carmen

Not all that many years ago, your stroll through Playa del Carmen would have been escorted by children, dogs, little black pigs, and incredibly ugly turkeys; you might even have seen the milkman delivering milk from large cans strapped to his donkey's back. No more. With its population increasing nearly 20 percent annually, Playa del Carmen is the fastest-growing city in Quintana Roo. It is a full-blown tourist destination, no question about it.

Playa is not Cancún, however. For one thing, it is still much smaller and has almost none of the glitzy high-rises and all-night dance clubs. And unlike Cancún, Playa attracts mostly Europeans, and even has a nascent Italian quarter. Playacar, a planned community south of town, does have many high-end resorts but is also largely residential and does not have the "strip" atmosphere that Cancún's Zona Hotelera does. And while the southern section of Playa del Carmen—the area around the pier and local bus terminal—can be kitschy and intrusive, the northern section has a more low-key atmosphere with some excellent restaurants, cool bars, and offbeat shops. A handful of huge condo and resort projects in the northern section may intrude on this pocket of funky charm, or push it farther north, but hopefully not destroy it.

Playa del Carmen has some pretty beaches (if you know where to go) and good snorkeling, diving, Maya ruins, cenotes, golf, and more are all nearby. It is a convenient base from which to explore and sample everything the Riviera Maya has to offer.

SIGHTS
⊂ Quinta Avenida

Playa's main pedestrian and commercial drag is Quinta Avenida, or 5th Avenue, which stretches almost 20 blocks from the ferry dock northward. Pronounced KEEN-ta av-en-EE-da, you may see it written as 5 Avenida or 5a Avenida, which is akin to "5th" in English but refers to the same street. The first several blocks, especially around the ferry dock, are typical tourist traps, with souvenir shops and chain restaurants. Around Calle 10 or Calle 12, the atmosphere turns mellower, with bistros, jazz bars, and funky clothing stores. You'll

THE RIVIERA MAYA

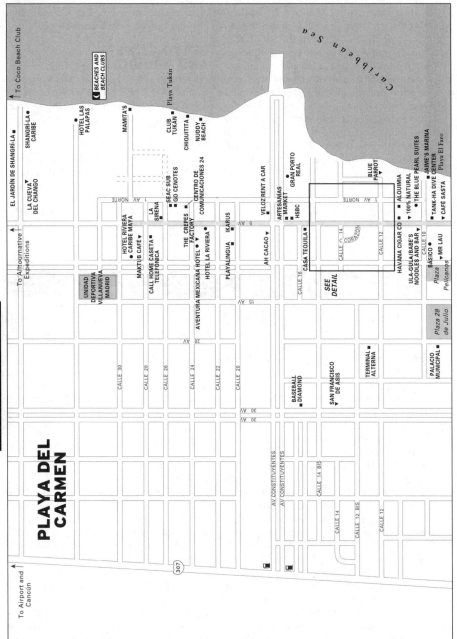

PLAYA DEL CARMEN

To Airport and Cancún

307

Caribbean Sea

To Coco Beach Club

BEACHES AND BEACH CLUBS

EL JARDIN DE SHANGRI-LA ■
SHANGRI-LA CARIBE ●
LA CUEVA DEL CHANGO ▼
HOTEL LAS PALAPAS ■
MAMITA'S ■
Playa Tukán
CLUB TUKAN ■
CHIQUITITA ■
NUDDY BEACH ■

To Alltournative Expeditions

UNIDAD DEPORTIVA VILLANUEVA MADRID

HOTEL RIVIERA CARIBE MAYA ▼
MAKTUB CAFÉ ●
CALL HOME CASETA TELEFÓNICA ■
AVENTURA MEXICANA HOTEL ●
THE CREPES FACTORY ●
HOTEL LA RIVIERA ▼
PLAYALINGUA ■
IKARUS ■
LA SIRENA ■

SEAC SUB ■
GO CENOTES ●
CENTRO DE COMUNICACIONES 24 ■

AV NORTE
5 AV
15 AV
20 AV
30 AV
30 AV

AH CACAO ▼
CASA TEQUILA ■
VELOZ RENT A CAR ■
ARTESANÍAS MARKET ■
HSBC ■
GRAN PORTO REAL ■

SEE DETAIL

CALLE 16
CALLE 14
C. CORAZON
CALLE 12
CALLE 10

BLUE PARROT ■
ALQUIMIA ■
100% NATURAL ●
THE BLUE PEARL SUITES ●
JAIME'S MARINA
Playa El Faro
TANK-HA DIVE CENTER ●
CAFÉ SASTA ▼
1 AV NORTE

HAVANA CIGAR CO ■
ULA-GULA/BABE'S NOODLES AND BAR ▼
BÁSICO ●
MR LAU ▼
Plaza Pelicanos

PALACIO MUNICIPAL ■
TERMINAL ALTERNA ■
Plaza 28 de Julio

BASEBALL DIAMOND
SAN FRANCISCO DE ASIS ▼

AV CONSTITUYENTES
AV CONSTITUYENTES

CALLE 30
CALLE 28
CALLE 26
CALLE 24
CALLE 22
CALLE 20
CALLE 14 BIS
CALLE 14
CALLE 12 BIS
CALLE 12

THE RIVIERA MAYA

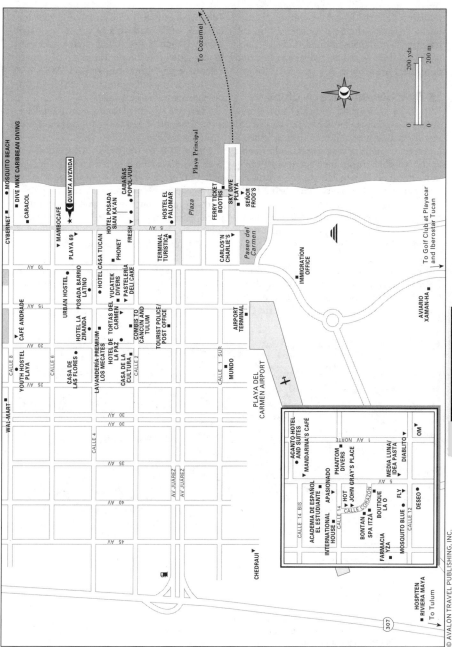

THE RIVIERA MAYA

© AVALON TRAVEL PUBLISHING, INC.

probably walk the length of Quinta Avenida once or twice—the best beaches are in the northern part, the bus terminal and ferry dock in the southern—and everyone seems to find his or her favorite part.

Beaches and Beach Clubs

With thick white sand and mild surf, **Playa Tukán** (entrance at 1 Av. Norte at Calle 26) is still the best beach in town. But it is being squeezed by condo developments, and its status as an accessible, truly public beach is definitely in peril. All beaches in Mexico are technically public, but resorts (like the ones being built) typically "claim" the stretch in front of them by setting up row after row of private chairs. The result is less and less space for non-guests, including locals, to lay out a towel for a day in the sun.

Several beach clubs on Playa Tukán rent chairs and umbrellas and have bar and restaurant service, along with small swimming pools, showers, and lockers for day guests. **Club**

Tukán and **Chiquitita** are mellow and good for families, while **Mamita's** (9 A.M.–6 P.M.) and **Nuddy Beach** (8 A.M.–6 P.M.) draw a younger, hipper set with techno music and beach beds. Prices are fairly uniform, around US$2–4 a day for chairs and umbrellas, US$8–15 for beach beds and large *palapas*.

There are also small tour operators on Playa Tukán that offer snorkeling tours, Hobie Cat trips, kayaks, and more.

Playa El Faro (between Calles 8 and 10) is an excellent beach just steps from the action on Quinta Avenida. Named for the large lighthouse *(faro)* at one end, there's still plenty of room to lay out your towel, unlike other stretches that have been snatched by encroaching hotels. Jaime's Marina (see *Snorkeling*), a well-recommended snorkel and sailing outfit, is located here.

Coco Beach Club is just a short distance north of Shangri La Caribe. It has good food, beach umbrellas, and sun beds, plus changing rooms and showers. The snorkeling here is the

© LIZA PRADO

Playa del Carmen's town beach is a popular spot, not only because it's beautiful but also because it's close to everything.

best in the Playa area; you can rent gear here if you don't have your own.

Bird Sanctuary

A short distance inside the Playacar entrance off 10 Avenida, **Aviario Xaman-Ha** (Av. Xaman Ha, tel. 044-984/106-8766, 9 A.M.– 5 P.M. daily, US$14 adults, free under 12) has more than 60 species of tropical birds, including toucans, flamingos, cormorants, and various types of parrots, all native to southeastern Mexico. The birds are divided by habitat and held in a variety of enclosures along a winding path—most people take a little less than an hour to see them all. Bring bug repellent, especially if you visit in the late afternoon or after it rains.

ENTERTAINMENT AND EVENTS

Playa del Carmen doesn't have the wild-and-crazy nightclubs that Cancún does, nor would many of the people who visit regularly want it to, but Playa does boast a great bar and lounge scene. You'll find plenty of lively spots along 5 Avenida any night of the week, but Playa's newest and hippest nightlife conflagration is happening at and around the corner of 1 Avenida and Calle 12, especially on weekends. The Blue Parrot, an oldy but goody, has been joined by a handful of newer bars, and you can dance from one to the next well into the wee hours.

Bars and Discotheques

One of Playa's classic hot spots, the **Blue Parrot** (Calle 12 at the beach, tel. 984/206-3350, www.blueparrot.com, 7:30 A.M.–4 A.M. daily, US$6–10 cover after 10 P.M.) is still going strong with a crowd most nights. Sand floors, swing bar seats, a candlelit *palapa* lounge, and a small dance floor all create the party feel that have kept customers streaming in for years. DJs play everything from retro to techno; be sure to check out the fire dancers—most nights shows start at 11 P.M. Service can be a bit brusque but seems to improve as your bikini (or Speedo) shrinks.

With retro tables and armchairs, and low beats and even lower lights, **Diablito** (1 Av. at Calle 12, tel. 984/803-3695, 1 P.M.–3 A.M.) is certainly the most stylish of the bars and clubs in this up-and-coming area. Order anything under the sun from the bar, and munch on unlikely Mexican-Japanese fusion snacks and meals. Quite pricey, but oozing cool.

Across the street, **Om** (Calle 12 near 1 Av., 984/879-4784, www.omplaya.com) is another popular spot, throwing rowdy parties and serving up cocktails made from fresh tropical fruit hanging at the bar.

Also nearby is the very cool and upscale **Fly** (5 Av. at Calle 12, tel. 984/803-1350, 1 P.M.– 2 A.M. daily), which tries hard to be a New York hangout on the streets of Playa del Carmen. Lots of outdoor seating makes for prime people watching as you sip your martini. Service can be a bit uppity but then again, that's kind of the point.

Kitty-corner, DJs spin urban beats at **Deseo** (5 Av. at Calle 12, tel. 984/879-3620, www .hoteldeseo.com), a sleek minimalist lounge bar that attracts local and foreign hipsters most nights of the week. Part of a like-named hotel, the rooftop lounge is the centerpiece of the place; a candlelit stone stairway leads to a pool surrounded by queen-size cushions and billowing curtains.

One of Playa's only gay bars, **Playa 69** (5 Av. between Calles 4 and 6, tel. 984/876-9466, 9 P.M.–3 A.M.) is hopping on weekends, when tequila shots are almost mandatory. Popular with locals, the entrance is kind of hard to spot— look for it on the west side of 5 Avenida.

The beach club **Nuddy Beach** (Playa Tukán) turns into a lounge bar Thursday–Saturday nights (7 P.M.–3 A.M., no cover) with mellow, modern music and a cool attitude so thick you can cut it. On Thursdays women drink for free, and Saturday's "Sunset Party" features two-for-one champagne and wine.

The restaurant/bar **Apasionado** (5 Av. at Calle 14, tel.984/803-1101, 4 P.M.–midnight daily) features live Latin jazz on Friday and Saturday nights in its breezy, second-floor dining area that overlooks 5 Avenida. The music starts around 8 P.M.

The place to go for salsa dancing, **Mambocafé** (Calle 6 between Avs. 5 and 10, 984/803-2656, www.mambocafe.com.mx, 10 P.M.–4 A.M. Tue.–Sun., cover free–US$14) features live Latin bands every night. A packed party atmosphere rules with balloons, foam, and lots of sweating bodies moving to Latin rhythms. On Tuesdays there's no cover and on Wednesday women drink for free 10 P.M.–midnight.

And of course you can always find a party at **Señor Frog's** (Ferry pier, 10 A.M.–1 A.M. daily) and **Carlos'n Charlie's** (Plaza del Carmen, southern end of 5 Av., 984/803-3498, 10 A.M.–1 A.M. daily), both near the Cozumel ferry pier. These Mexican beach-town fixtures are famous for their yard-long drinks, dancing on the tables, and non-stop parties. Drink specials and special events are the norm. They also serve overpriced but familiar dishes, including barbecued ribs and hamburgers.

Cinema and Arcade

Cines Hollywood (Plaza Pelícanos, 2nd Fl., 15 Av. between Calles 8 and 10, tel. 984/803-1417, US$4.25 Thurs.–Tues., US$2.75 Wed) has three screens showing fairly recent Hollywood movies. The first show starts around 5 P.M.

Next to the movie theater, **Recórcholis** (Plaza Pelícanos, 2nd Fl., 15 Av. between Calles 8 and 10, tel. 984/803-1419, 2–11 P.M. Mon.–Fri., 11 A.M.–11 P.M. Sat.–Sun.) is a decent arcade—a perfect place to kill time before a movie.

SHOPPING

One of the most popular destinations on the Riviera Maya, Playa del Carmen offers some of the best shopping around and 5 Avenida is where it's at. You'll find everything from high-end clothing, Cuban cigars, specialty tequila, spectacular *artesanía,* jewelry, T-shirt, and postcard stands. You name it, Playa del Carmen probably has it.

Artesanía

La Sirena (5 Av. at Calle 26, tel. 984/803-3422, 8 A.M.–9 P.M. daily) is a boutique selling exceptional art from around Mexico. Italian shop owner Patrizia personally selects the beauties that she sells in her charming shop—whimsical skeleton art, colonial statuettes of La Virgen de Guadalupe, tin-framed mirrors, funky portraits, bright shawls—you're sure to find something you can't resist.

Caracol (5 Av. between Calles 6 and 8, tel. 984/803-1504, 9:30 A.M.–10:30 P.M. daily) is a pricey boutique selling beautiful and unique Mexican textiles. It makes a great stop, even if just to admire the spectacular fabrics—clothing, tablecloths, bedding, and decorative art—that the German owner handpicks herself on buying trips throughout southern Mexico.

A popular place, **La Calaca** (5 Av. between Calles 12 and 14, tel. 984/873-0174, 8 A.M.–12:30 A.M. daily) is jam-packed with Mexican masks, colorful *alebrijes* (fantastical wooden creatures), and quirky skeleton art. The quality is just all right but the variety is impressive. For collection pieces, check out its branch in Paseo del Carmen.

Bookstores

The best bookshop in the region is in nearby Puerto Morelos, and a stop there can be part of nice day trip from Playa. In town, **Alquimia** (1 Av. Between Calles 10 and 12, tel. 984/803-1575, 7 A.M.–midnight Mon.–Sat.) is a hip café plucked out of San Francisco, with baguettes and cappuccinos, and a small bank of used books for sale or trade (two-for-one).

For a larger selection, **Mundo** (Calle 1 Sur between 20 and 25 Av., tel. 984/879-3004, www.pequemundo.com.mx, 9 A.M.–8 P.M. Mon.–Fri., 10 A.M.–6 P.M. Sat.) has several cases of English-language titles, new and used. Mysteries, romances, and other beach-reads abound, but a close look turns up some good novels and nonfiction books. Prices run US$2–12, and the shop will buy the book back for 50 percent, cash or trade. You'll also find a small selection of regional maps.

Bontan (Calle Corazón near Calle 14, tel. 984/803-3733, 10 A.M.–10 P.M. daily) sells artsy Mexican specialty books—perfect if you're looking for a coffee table book to take home. A handful of guidebooks and regional maps also are for sale near the front of the shop.

Other Specialty Items

The local **Seac Sub** shop (1 Av. Norte between Calles 24 and 26, tel. 984/803-1192, 8 A.M.–9 P.M. Mon.–Sat.) has a large selection of masks, snorkels, fins, wetsuits, and other equipment, most decently priced. The shop has mostly Seac Sub products, of course, but carries other brands as well.

For a decent selection of specialty tequilas, check out **Casa Tequila** (5 Av. near Calle 14 Bus., 9 A.M.–midnight daily), where in addition to fine tequila, you'll find a nice variety of silver jewelry. A small sister store also is at 5 Avenida at Calle 16.

For the best in cigars, stop by **Havana Cigar Co.** (5 Av. between Calles 10 and 12, tel. 984/803-1047, 9 A.M.–11:30 P.M. daily). Cuban and Mexican *puros* are sold individually (US$5–10) or by the box (US$55–450).

For funky, bohemian-style beachwear, head to **Boutique La O** (Calle Corazón at 5 Av., tel. 984/803-3171, 9:30 A.M.–10:30 P.M. daily) where you'll find tie-dyed dresses, flowing linen pants, and cool cotton tops. Very comfortable and very Playa.

Shopping Centers

At the southern end of 5 Avenida, **Paseo del Carmen** (10 A.M.–10 P.M. daily) is a shady outdoor shopping center with high-end clothing boutiques, jewelry stores, art galleries, and restaurants. With a series of modern fountains, it makes for a pleasant place to window-shop—or enjoy an upscale lunch—after a day at the beach.

Plaza Pelícanos (10 Av. between Calles 8 and 10, 10 A.M.–10 P.M. daily) has a handful of low-end shoe and clothing stores plus a mediocre food court. The main—scratch that—the *only* reasons to come here are for the ATM, public bathrooms, arcade, and movie theater.

For trinkets to take home, check out the **outdoor market** at the corner of 5 Avenida and Constituyentes (8 A.M.–10 P.M. daily). You'll find everything from Maya pyramid key chains to silver jewelry.

SPORTS AND RECREATION
Scuba Diving

Playa del Carmen has decent offshore diving, and relatively easy access to Cozumel and inland cenotes. It's a logical base if you want a taste of all three, plus the convenience of being near the airport and in town. However, if diving is the main reason you came, consider basing yourself on Cozumel itself, or closer to the cenotes, such as at Akumal or Tulum. This will save you the time, money, and effort of going back and forth.

Prices in Playa del Carmen are reasonable, and fairly uniform from shop to shop. (See the *How to Choose a Dive Shop* sidebar in the *Isla Cozumel* chapter.) Two-tank reef dives are always a better deal than one; in fact, Cozumel and cenote trips are only offered as two-tankers. Reef dives cost around US$65–75 for two tanks, while Cozumel trips and cenote trips are around US$105–120. Only one shop (Tank-Ha) sends a dive boat directly to Cozumel from Playa; with the rest, you take the ferry (US$20 round- trip, not included in dive price) and board your dive boat there. Be sure to ask if lunch is included, as well as marine park fees (for Cozumel) and entrance fees (for cenotes). Same goes for gear—it's usually included, but can be pricey if not. Multi-dive packages are available at most shops, and earn you a 10–15 percent overall savings. Most shops also offer the full range of courses, from Discover Scuba and open-water certifications to nitrox and full cave diving courses.

Tank-Ha Dive Center (5 Av. between Calles 8 and 10, tel. 984/873-0302, www.tankha .com, 8 A.M.–10 P.M. daily) is one of the longest-operating shops in Playa, and the only one that takes divers to Cozumel by private boat instead of the ferry.

Dive Mike Caribbean Diving (Calle 8 between 5 Av. and the beach, tel. 984/803-1228, www.divemike.com, 8 A.M.–10 P.M. daily) is a very friendly, professional, reasonably priced shop. Check out its excellent and informative website for additional info and pictures.

Phantom Divers (1 Av. Norte at Calles 14,

tel. 984/879-3988, www.phantomdivers.com, 8 A.M.–7 P.M. daily) is one of a handful of locally owned dive shops, offering friendly, casual service. No credit cards accepted.

Yucatek Divers (15 Av. between Calles 2 and 4, tel. 984/803-2836, www.yucatekdivers.com, 7:30 A.M.–6 P.M. daily) uses an area hotel's pool for beginner certification training and most fun dives are led by instructors.

Go Cenotes (1 Av. Norte between Calles 24 and 26, tel. 984/876-2629, www.gocenotes .com, 8 A.M.–8 P.M. daily) specializes in cave and cavern trips and courses for divers of all levels. Groups are always small (1–4 people) and the shop works hard to be sure you dive different cenotes every time.

Snorkeling

In Playa itself, you should take a tour since the snorkeling off the beach isn't too rewarding. The cenotes south of Playa also make for good, unique snorkeling.

Most of Playa's dive shops offer guided snorkeling tours to excellent sites. Ocean trips cost US$30–40, while cenote trips are US$50–60, all gear included. Be sure to ask how many people will be on the trip, how long the trip will last, and how many reefs you'll be visiting (for ocean trips). For cenote trips, we strongly recommend a wetsuit, even if it means renting one for a few extra bucks. The water is quite chilly, there's no sun, and you'll be better protected against cuts and scrapes.

Jaime's Marina (Playa El Faro, end of Calle 10, tel. 984/130-2034, www.jaimes marina.bravehost.com, 9 A.M.–5 P.M. daily) is just a kiosk on the beach, but it offers friendly service and good snorkeling tours, among a number of water activities. Snorkel trips (US$30, two hours) include an hour of snorkeling and sailing to and from the reef in a Hobie Cat. If you come before 10:30 A.M., a 1.5-hour trip is just US$19 per person. Or you can rent a kayak and snorkel gear and create your own tour (US$15 single, US$20 double, three hours). Ask about a small anchor so your kayak doesn't float away, and about lockers and dry bags for your stuff.

Wind Sports

Kiteboarding, sailboarding, and sailing have grown in popularity along the Caribbean, a trickle-down effect from the world-famous wind belt on the Gulf Coast northwest of here. You can catch at least some breeze almost any time of the year, but the strongest, most consistent winds blow November–March.

Ikarus (5 Avenida and Calle 20, tel. 984/803-3490) is a retail shop that also arranges classes in kiteboarding. Beginning classes are often conducted at nearby Puerto Morelos, where the beaches are much less crowded. Private classes are US$75 an hour, while groups are US$45–55 an hour per person (maximum three to a group). The shop recommends 3–6 hours of instruction to learn the basics. Retail and rental gear is also available. A sister store is two blocks south at 5 Avenida and Calle 16.

Jaime's Marina offers friendly **sailing classes and rentals** from its kiosk on Playa El Faro. A four-hour beginner's class is just US$110 for up to four people. Rent a three-person Hobie Cat for US$25–35 an hour (depending on how long you stay out), or a five-seater for US$35–65 an hour, with or without a guide. Jaime's also has lockers and dry bags for your gear.

Fat Cat (tel. 984/876-3316, www.fatcatsail .com) is a spacious custom-designed catamaran used for day-long excursions (US$89/49 adult/child) that include sailing to secluded Xaac Cove, with a nice beach, good snorkeling, and a small Maya ruin nearby. You can also try "boom netting," in which you are pulled through the water behind the boat on a thick boom net.

Swimming with Dolphins

With tanks set up in the ocean, **Delphinus** (Hwy. 307 between Playa del Carmen and Paamul, toll-free Mex. tel. 800/335-3461, www.delphinus.com.mx, US$149) is a park all about swimming with dolphins in an environment that tries to replicate the "living conditions of pods in the wild." While being forced to work with humans in a closed-in pen isn't exactly wild, this park is as good as it gets for performing dolphins. For visitors, it's one of the most rewarding dolphin programs in the region. For US$149, participants are permitted to interact with a dolphin pod for 50 minutes; standard tricks are performed while visitors are in the water—a series of jumps, a foot push, and a dolphin kiss—along with extras like snuba-ing and just plain swimming with the pod. An additional 40 minutes is dedicated to touring the facility and listening to a lecture on dolphins. Admission includes a locker, towel, wetsuit, goggles, and round-trip transportation from many of the hotels on the Riviera Maya. There's a 10 percent discount if you book online.

◆ Xcaret Eco-Park

Popular for good reason, Xcaret (Hwy. 307 between Playa del Carmen and Paamul, toll-free Mex. tel. 800/292-2738, www.xcaret.com .mx, 8:30 A.M.–9 P.M. daily, US$58/29 adult/child, US$82/41 adult/child including buffet, US$104–110 adult including buffet and transportation, US$53–55 child including buffet and transportation) is a mega eco-park offering water activities like snorkeling in underground rivers and swimming with dolphins; up-close animal viewing areas including jaguar and puma islands, a butterfly pavilion, and an aquarium; and spectacular shows, like a Maya ballgame, regional dance, and music performances. Beyond this, the park also is dedicated to protecting the region's flora and fauna; there are scarlet macaw- and turtle-breeding areas, a section dedicated to the endemic stingerless bee, and an orchid greenhouse—all with educational exhibits for visitors. If you're into organized activities or you're traveling with kids, this definitely is a worthwhile stop.

Ecotours

Alltournative Expeditions (5 Av. between Calles 38 and 40, tel. 984/803-9999, www .alltournative.com) offers fun daily tours that include activities such as kayaking, rappelling, zip lines, off-road bicycling, caving, and snorkeling, plus (depending on the tour you choose)

visits to a small Maya village and Cobá archaeological zone. The agency has three principal tours to choose from (half or full day; US$94–104 pp adults and US$84–94 pp children under 12) and guides who speak English, Italian, French, German, Dutch, and Spanish.

Sport Fishing

Playa de Carmen has excellent sport and bottom fishing, with plentiful wahoo, *dorado,* mackerel, snapper, barracuda, and—especially April–June—sailfish and marlin. On average, trips for 1–5 people last 4–5 hours and cost US$200, including tackle and drinks. Most dive shops listed in the *Diving* section offer tours, as does Jaime's Marina (see *Snorkeling*).

Golf

The **Golf Club at Playacar** (Paseo Xaman-Há opposite Hotel Viva Azteca, tel. 998/881-6088 www.palaceresorts.com, 6 A.M.–6 P.M. daily) is a challenging, 7,144-yard championship course designed by Robert Van Hagge and located in Playacar, the upscale hotel and residential development south of Playa del Carmen proper. Green fees are US$190/90 adult/under 17 or US$130 after 2 P.M., including cart, snacks, and drinks; free hotel pickup for full-price rounds. Extra riders pay US$35/55 in low/high season and club and shoe rentals are US$30–50. Reserve at least a day in advance November–January.

Skydiving and Scenic Flights

Its gleaming white beaches and brilliant blue and turquoise seas make the Riviera Maya a spectacular place for skydiving. If you're up for it, **Sky Dive Playa** (Plaza Marina, tel. 984/873-0192, www.skydive.com.mx, 9 A.M.–6 P.M.) has been throwing travelers out of planes at 10,000 feet since 1996. You cover 4,500 feet in about 45 seconds, followed by a 6–7-minute parachute to a soft landing on the beach. Tandem dives (you and an instructor; US$200) are offered every hour—reserve 1–2 days in advance in summer and high season.

If you enjoy the view but prefer to stay buckled in, **Alas Sky Tour** (tel. 984/803-3718,

THE RIVIERA MAYA

9 A.M.–4 P.M.) offers scenic flights in a modern ultralight aircraft. Flights last about 20–25 minutes and cost US$99. Sunset flights are gorgeous but can be bouncy; for a smoother flight, go in the morning. Each plane fits only one passenger (plus the pilot), but a couple can go up together in separate planes with radio communication.

Aerosaab (Playa del Carmen airport, tel. 984/873-0804, www.aerosaab.com) offers scenic full-day tours to Isla Holbox, a charming, little-developed island at the northeastern tip of the Yucatán Peninsula (see *Isla Holbox* in the *Cancún* chapter). The trip includes flying up the coast in a small Cessna airplane, touring the island's mangrove-fringed lagoons by boat, and exploring the beach and the tiny village there (US$305 pp, plus US$6–25 airport fees, minimum four people).

Body Work

Playa's swankiest gym is **Area Body Zone** (Paseo del Carmen shopping center, south end of 10 Av., tel. 984/803-4049, www.areabody zone.com, 6 A.M.–11 P.M. Mon.–Thu., 6 A.M.–10 P.M. Fri., 7 A.M.–5 P.M. Sat.–Sun.) with the latest exercise machines, a spacious free-weight and weight-machine areas, and regular sessions of aerobics, spinning, Pilates, and yoga. Day visits cost US$15, a 10-visit package US$55, and a month's membership US$110.

Across the street from the Shangri La Caríbe resort, **El Jardín de Shangri-la** (Calle 38 at Calle Flamingo, tel. 984/113-6151, 7:30 A.M.–9 P.M. Mon.–Fri., 8 A.M.–9 P.M. Sat.) is an undeveloped jungle lot reserved for, among others, yoga instruction, tai chi classes, and spiritual growth seminars. Instruction is mostly held under a huge *palapa* in the middle of the grounds but students are free to wander (and practice) on the lush property. Regular yoga, tai chi, capoeira, and meditation classes are offered weekly; classes cost US$7.50 per session, US$33 for a 10 pack, and US$47 per month (unlimited classes). Walk-ins welcome.

The well-tended **Unidad Deportiva Villanueva Madrid** (Av. 10 near Calle 30, 6 A.M.–10:30 P.M. daily) is Playa del Carmen's public sporting facility with a gym, tennis and basketball courts, track, and soccer field. All have night lighting and are open to the public at no charge; BYO equipment.

Treat yourself to an afternoon of pampering at **Spa Itzá** (Calle Corazón at 5 Av., tel. 984/803-2588, www.spaitza.com, 10 A.M.–9 P.M. daily), a full-service spa in the heart of Playa. Massage therapies (US$35–85), Maya healing baths (US$45), body treatments (US$45–75), and facials (US$45–85) are among the rejuvenating services offered.

Spanish Classes

Playa del Carmen is becoming a popular place to study Spanish, with several schools, plenty of options for cultural and historical excursions, and of course good nightlife and a great beach.

Solexico (35 Av. between Calles 6 and 6-Bis, tel. 984/873-0755, www.solexico.com) is a highly recommended school with a reputation for professionalism. Classes are offered in group (no more than five people) or individual settings, and for 15, 25, or 40 hours per week (US$159–564/wk). Students can stay with local families or at the school's 10-room student residence (US$25–35/night, including one or two meals), or arrange for hotel and condo rentals. Ask about volunteer opportunities.

Playalingua del Caribe (Calle 20 between 5 Av. and 10 Av., tel. 984/873-3876, www.playa lingua.com, 8 A.M.–8 P.M. daily) has a spacious learning center, with a leafy garden and small private pool. On-site rooms (small, clean, and air-conditioned) mean you can roll out of bed and be conjugating verbs in a matter of minutes. Most classes meet 10 or 20 hours a week, and the hourly cost is roughly US$9–25 per person, depending if you choose group, two-person, or private instruction. In addition to the rooms at the center (US$145–245 pp/week), students can also stay with a local family (US$150/week including half-board) or in a private apartment (US$50–100/day). One-time materials and inscription fees are about US$110; weekend excursions and extras classes, from salsa dancing to Mexican cooking, are also available.

International House (Calle 14 Norte between 5 Av. and 10 Av., tel. 984/803-3388, www.ihrivieramaya.com, 7:30 A.M.–9 P.M. Mon.–Fri., 7:30 A.M.–noon Sat.) occupies a pretty and peaceful colonial home, with a large classroom, garden, bar, and restaurant on-site. All instructors are university graduates with training in teaching Spanish as a foreign language. Intensive group classes (US$200/week) include four hours of class per day and can be joined on any Monday; classes typically have 3–4 students, and a maximum of eight. Private and two-person classes (US$29–35/hour) and packages including diving or Mexican cooking classes are also available. Age 16-plus only for group classes; all materials and inscription fees included. Family stays are US$175–US$200 a week, while a variety of furnished apartments and student rooms, with or without meals, run US$140–500 a week.

Academia de Idiomas El Estudiante (Restaurant Xlapak, 5 Av. between Calles 14 and 14-bis, tel. 044-984/876-0616, info@playaspanishschool.com, 8:30 A.M.–10 P.M. daily) is more low-key and backpacker-oriented, with a single open-air patio where classes are conducted over small wooden tables. Group classes (US$8/hr., 2–4 people only) meet four hours every weekday morning; private classes (US$15/hr.) can be conducted any time, including weekends. A one-time US$35 inscription fee covers books, copies, and other materials. The school helps organize outings, including trips to Cobá and Mérida, cooking and salsa classes, volleyball games, snorkeling tours, and more. Students can stay with a family (US$130/week, including breakfast) or in a shared apartment with a small kitchen and sometimes a pool (US$130/week d).

Art and Performance Classes

If you are staying for more than just a couple of weeks, consider taking a class or two at the **Casa de la Cultura** (Calle 2 at 20 Av., tel. 984/873-2654, 9 A.M.–10 P.M. Mon.–Sat.). Regional dance, guitar, painting, and singing are regularly offered.

ACCOMMODATIONS

Playa del Carmen has a huge selection and variety of accommodations, from youth hostels to swanky resorts to condos and long-term rentals. Most all-inclusives are located in Playacar, just south of town.

Under US$25

◖ Youth Hostel Playa (Calle 8´s/n at 25 Av., tel. 984/803-3277, US$10.25 dorm, US$28 d with shared bath) is Playa del Carmen's best hostel, despite being somewhat removed from downtown and the beach. The dorm rooms are narrow but clean, and have thick comfortable mattresses, individual fans, and free lockers. The simple private rooms are kept very clean, although light sleepers may be bothered by street noise. A well-equipped kitchen has plenty of space to work your culinary magic and a good cubby system to prevent groceries from disappearing. Best of all is the hostel's enormous common area, perfect for eating, playing cards, reading, watching TV, or whatever. Coffee and water are provided, but not breakfast. For better or worse, Playa's new Walmart is across the street.

Urban Hostel (10 Av. between Calles 4 and 6, tel. 984/803-3378, US$10 dorm, US$17.50–22 s/d with shared bath) has a welcoming entrance but the charm dries up somewhere in the narrow tunnel-like hallway that leads to the dorms and common area. Even a recent renovation didn't manage to improve the grubby, claustrophobic feeling here. Easy access to the bus terminal, free bike rental, and the cheapest rates in town (by a hair) are reason enough for some to stay, but there are better budget options to be had. This hostel is no longer affiliated with Urban Hostel in Isla Mujeres, but it remains to be seen who gets to keep the name.

Hostel El Palomar (5 Av. between Av. Juárez and Calle 2, tel. 984/873-0144, US$11 dorm, US$35 s, US$42 d) has giant dorm rooms crammed with row upon row of double bunks, and three smallish private rooms with a clean, shared bathroom and a terrace with hammocks and view of the ocean. The problem is there's no common area, save the rooftop

© LIZA PRADO

High-end resorts are popping up along Playa's gorgeous beachfront.

terrace with an open-air kitchen. The hostel is right across from the bus terminal; Internet access, continental breakfast, and large lockers are included.

US$25-50

Hotel Casa Tucan (Calle 4 between 10 and 15 Avs., tel. 984/873-0283, www.casatucan.de, US$38 s/d, US$50 studio) offers a labyrinth of basic rooms in a social environment. There are rustic cabañas with reasonably clean bathrooms, no-frill hotel rooms with fans, and small studios with even smaller kitchenettes. All of the units have fantastic murals, which spruce up the place quite a bit. There's also what is likely the deepest pool around—4.8 meters (15.7 ft.). (It's so deep, in fact, that it's used by dive shops for open-water certification training.) It's surrounded by lounge chairs and hammocks, perfect for whiling away an afternoon.

Near the bus station and with private access to a nice stretch of beach, **Cabañas Popol-Vuh** (Calle 2 near 5 Av., tel. 984/803-2149, pdcpopol_vuh@hotmail.com, US$20 s/d cabañas with shared bath, US$30 s/d cabaña with private bath, US$54 s/d with private bath and a/c) is a decent budget option. As you walk through the gate, you'll take in the site at a glance: nine cozy cabañas and four hotel rooms that face a small sand lot. The cabañas are simple wood-paneled structures but they're comfortable, have good screens, and strong fans. Those with private bathrooms also have small private porches. Those with shared bathrooms should wear flip-flops in the shower—they need a serious scrub down. The hotel rooms definitely are a major step up: tile floors, cable TV, minisplit air-conditioning, and a private bathroom. In this town, these units are a steal—and go fast! Call ahead to reserve.

One of the first hotels in Playa, **Hotel Posada Sian Ka'an** (Calle 2 near 5 Av., tel. 984/873-0202, www.labnah.com, US$38–48 s/d with fan) doesn't looks like it has been remodeled in over three decades. Rooms are functional and clean but a coat of paint, updated bathrooms, and a few new beds would be nice. That said, the location and the price almost can't be beat. Sitting just half a block from both 5 Avenida and the Caribbean doesn't get much better around here. Most rooms also have balconies or terraces—some with partial views of the ocean, the rest overlooking the garden. Continental breakfast included in the rates.

A simple two-story motel, **Hotel La Paz** (Av. 20 between Calles 2 and 4, tel. 984/873-0467, www.hotel-la-paz.com, US$48–58 s/d with a/c) has 20 rooms with tile floors, hot-water bathrooms, and air-conditioning. Rooms open onto a lush courtyard with swaying palm trees, a well-tended garden, and a gazebo—a remarkably appealing place that makes you almost forget how no-frills the rooms are.

US$50-100

On a peaceful section of 5 Avenida, the inviting ◖ **Hotel La Riviera** (5 Av. between Calles 22 and 24, tel. 984/873-3240, www .hotel-lariviera.com, US$65–75 s/d with a/c) has simple, recently renovated rooms. All have sponge-painted walls, tile bathrooms, cable TV, and quiet air-conditioners. Rooms in front also have balconies that overlook 5 Avenida—a great people-watching spot. Wireless Internet is accessible to all guests. Continental breakfast also is included if you book online.

◖ **Casa de las Flores** (20 Av. Between Calles 4 and 6; tel. 984/873-2898, www.hotel casadelasflores.com, US$65–75 s, US$90 d) offers a slice of charm at very reasonable prices. The cheerful hacienda-esque exterior gives way to a leafy courtyard and garden, with a small stone-paved pool and rooms arranged on two levels in back. Americans will appreciate the air-conditioning, Europeans the bidet, and no one can complain about the whitewashed walls, simple but classy decor, and friendly service. Higher-priced rooms have better light or small terraces.

Recently remodeled, **Hotel Riviera Caribe Maya** (10 Av. at Calle 30, tel. 984/873-1193, www.hotelrivieramaya.com, US$89–101 s/d with a/c, US$135–146 suite with a/c) offers bright rooms with hand-carved Mexican furnishings and modern amenities like cable TV,

in-room phone, and mini-fridge. Most look out onto the hotel's inviting pool, which is tucked into a pleasant courtyard. Internet access and continental breakfast are included in the rate.

If you can overlook the uppity service, the **Posada Barrio Latino** (Calle 4 between 10 and 15 Avs., tel. 984/873-2384, www.posadabarriolatino.com, US$60–62 s/d with fan, US$72 s/d with a/c) offers 16 charming rooms with details like mosaic tile bathrooms, stone-inlayed floors, and private balconies. Continental breakfast is included in the rate and is served in a leafy courtyard with a *palapa*-roofed lounge—a good place to write postcards or play cards too. Bicycles available free of charge.

Hotel La Ziranda (Calle 4 between 15 and 20 Avs., tel. 984/873-3933, www.hotel laziranda.com, US$60 s/d with fan, US$70 s/d with a/c) offers 16 sparse rooms—all with private balconies or terraces—that are spread out between two modern buildings. Rooms are spacious, spotless, and have nice tile bathrooms. While all are well-kempt, ask for a room on the 2nd floor—they have high ceilings and the best cross breezes. Look for the *palapa*-roofed lobby as you come down the street—it's unmistakable. Lots of ambivalent cats lounge about too.

US$100-150

Two hotels in one, **Aventura Mexicana Hotel** (Calle 24 between 5 and 10 Avs., tel. 984/873-1876, toll-free U.S. tel. 800/455-3417, www .hoteltierramaya.com, US$129–169 s/d with a/c, US$179–209 suite with a/c) is split into a family side and an adult-only side. Good idea but not-so-good execution—the adult-only side is significantly nicer. Boutiquey units have muted colors, elegant furnishings, and high-end amenities that open onto a nicely manicured garden with a "quiet" pool. In contrast, the family rooms are overly basic—tile floors, simple ironwork, and wood furnishings with a nondescript pool in the center—a classic mid-range room. If you have kids, your money is best spent elsewhere. Continental breakfast included in all the rates.

THE RIVIERA MAYA

Over US$150

Just half a block from the beach, ◖ **Acanto Hotel and Suites** (Calle 16 near 5 Av., tel. 984/873-1252, toll-free U.S. tel. 866/655-8819, www.acantohotels.com, US$185 one-bedroom condo with a/c) is a charming little hotel on a shady street. This quiet hotel offers seven South Asian–inspired condominiums—dark woods, luxurious fabrics, Asian art—each with one bedroom, a fully equipped kitchen, a living-dining room, and a patio. A small swimming pool with a large Buddha to one side sits in the middle of the complex. There's also a sundeck for guests who want to take in the sun without leaving the premises.

The ultramodern **Mosquito Blue** (5 Av. between Calles 12 and 14, tel. 984/873-1335, www.mosquitoblue.com, US$208–236 s/d with a/c, US$265–405 suite with a/c) boasts lush interior courtyards with two amoeba-shaped pools, an impressive *palapa*-roofed lounge with comfy couches and striking modern art throughout. Rooms, though somewhat cramped, are beautifully appointed and have the most modern in amenities: digital safes, wireless Internet, plush bathrobes, minibar, and cable TV. It has a similarly luxurious sister hotel, the aptly named **Mosquito Beach** (Calle 8 at the beach, tel. 984/873-0001, US$230–291 s/d with a/c, US$445 suite with a/c), located on a nice stretch of beach in the heart of town. During high season weekends, both hotels raise their rates by 25 percent. Guests over age 16 only.

For extended stays, ◖ **The Blue Pearl Suites** (Av. 1 between Calles 10 and 12, tel. 984/803-2379, www.thebluepearl.com.mx, US$143–172 one-bedroom condo with a/c, US$229 two-bedroom condo with a/c, minimum seven nights) offers super-stylish, comfortable, and eco-friendly apartments that sleep between two and eight people. All have fully equipped kitchens (with recycling and composting bins) and a private terrace or garden with hammocks and outdoor tub. Rooms have gorgeous original art but otherwise minimalist decor, plus wireless Internet and daily cleaning (even your dishes!). The hotel doesn't have beach club passes, but Playa El Faro—one of two good public beaches in town—is around the corner and there's a small pool and lounge area on the roof. Noise from nearby bars and clubs may be a problem for light sleepers, however.

Sitting on one of the best beaches in Playa, ◖ **Hotel Las Palapas** (Calle 34 between 5 Av. and the beach, tel. 984/873-4260, www.laspalapas.com, US$160–214 s with a/c, US$186–250 d with a/c) offers 75 thatch-roofed bungalows that open onto either a lush garden brimming with native flora or onto a white sand beach with breathtaking views. The peaceful units have comfortable beds, ample patios with hammocks, and radio access to an exceptional staff. No televisions or phones here. A stone-lined path leads guests to an inviting freshwater pool, a clubhouse, a full-service spa, a dive shop, and—of course—beach chairs and umbrellas on the Caribbean. Be sure to climb the tall lookout platform for a spectacular bird's-eye view of Playa del Carmen. Rates include a full buffet breakfast.

A sleek, urban-chic hotel, **Deseo** (5 Av. at Calle 12, tel. 984/879-3620, www.hoteldeseo.com, US$188–211 s/d with a/c, US$267 suite with a/c) boasts rooms that look as if they belong in a modern art museum. Think bananas, flip-flops, and a bikini top hanging from the walls. Add minimalist furnishings, including a low-lying bed, streamlined fixtures, and photo-shoot lamps. Now, pump in some tunes—techno or modern bossa nova—and you've got your room. Outside your door, is the hotel's bar/lounge/pool area with queen-size cushions serving as beach chairs, and flowing white curtains strung high above. Very cool. Unless, of course, you want to sleep—music from the lounge blasts until 2 A.M. every night. The hotel even provides earplugs. Use 'em or join the party. Continental breakfast included.

Just a block away, Deseo's hip younger sister, **Básico** (5 Av. at Calle 10, tel. 984/879-4448, www.hotelbasico.com, US$188–211 s/d with a/c, US$267 suite with a/c) has high-end rooms with an industrial-warehouse style. Staffers say the inspiration comes from the oil tankers that ply the Gulf of Mexico. Needless to say, despite the stark, cement look, the rooms are ultra luxurious—plush beds, fine linens, flat screen TVs, even a Polaroid camera to capture a particular, er, moment with your partner. A retro Mexican seafood restaurant/bar/lounge is on the top floor with a glorious view of the Caribbean. Like Deseo, it's ultra cool and ultra loud: techno will keep you up—or keep you dancing—late into the night.

About 10 minutes from the hubbub on Avenida 5 but at the peak of the action on the beach, **Shangri-La Caríbe** (Calle 38 near 5 Av., tel. 984/873-0611, toll-free U.S. and Canada tel. 888/896-0690, www.shangrilacaribe .net, US$175–325 s with a/c, US$200–325 d with a/c) is the epitome of a Caribbean resort. Over 100 *palapa*-roofed bungalows are connected by sand paths that lead to the resort's facilities: two swimming pools, three restaurants, two bars, an Internet center, and a dive shop. Bungalows are beginning to show their age but are comfortable nonetheless with private balcony or terrace. It's definitely a party place but no worries—if you're looking to catch up on your romance novels, a quiet spot is never far away. Full breakfast and dinner are included in the rate.

All-Inclusive Resorts
Most of Playa del Carmen's all-inclusives are in Playacar, an upscale hotel and residential development south of town. But a slew of condo and resort projects are slated for north Playa proper, especially on Avenida Constituyentes, until now the "quiet" part of town.

Gran Porto Real (Av. Constituyentes 1, at 1 Av. Norte, tel. 984/873-4000, www.real resorts.com.mx, US$175–275 pp) is a family-oriented resort, so honeymooners may want to look elsewhere. The rooms and pool are nice, but the beach is disappointing—very small and used by a constant stream of anglers to haul up their boats. You may spot some huge fish being unloaded, but all in all we'd rather have the extra beach space. Another problem is the hotel's habit of overbooking the junior suites, especially in high season, and switching guests to inferior rooms.

Iberostar Tucan (Av. Xaman-Ha, tel. 984/877-2000, www.iberostar.com, US$252–310 s, US$222–280 pp d) has a spacious lobby-entryway and wide attractive beach with palm trees, beach chairs, and mild surf. Between the two is a broad patch of healthy, well-maintained coastal forest, where you can spot monkeys, parrots, and other native creatures in the treetops. After so many sterile and manicured resorts, this is a welcome change of scenery. The pool is huge, and near the beach. Rooms occupy large buildings along the property's edges, and are clean and comfortable, though plain. Junior suites have sea views.

Rental Properties
Playacar has scores of houses for rent of all different sizes and styles. Prices vary considerably, but expect to pay a premium for ocean views and during peak seasons. A number of property-management companies rent houses, including **Playacar Vacation Rentals** (Calle 10 s/n, two blocks south of Av. Juárez near the Playacar entrance, tel. 984/873-0418, www.playacarvacation rentals.com) and **Vacation Rentals** (tel. 984/ 873-2952, www.playabeachrentals.com).

FOOD
Playa del Carmen has scores of restaurants and eateries offering a variety of culinary delights. Walk a block or two down Quinta Avenida and you're sure to spot something that you like.

Mexican
La Cueva del Chango (Calle 38 at 5 Av.; 8 A.M.–11 P.M. Mon.–Sat., 8 A.M.–2 P.M. Sun., US$4–12) means "Cave of the Monkey" but the restaurant is neither dim nor primitive: The covered dining area has light-hearted decor (and a back patio is ensconced in leafy vegetation) while the menu features crepes, empanadas, and innovative items like eggs with poleta and chaya. Well north of town, it's often packed with Playa's upper crust, though the prices make it accessible to all.

La Palapa Hemingway (5 Av. between Calles 12 and 14, tel. 984/803-0003, 8 A.M.–midnight daily) has a good all-you-can-eat

Mexican lunch buffet for under US$10. The menu has a varied selection of Mexican and Maya favorites, including chicken mole, *chile en nogada,* and Yucatecan grilled fish, and there are a full bar and wine list. Sit inside for the air-conditioning or outside for the pleasant tile-covered tables right on the avenue.

An old-school Mexican coffee shop, **Café Andrade** (Calle 8 near 20 Av., tel. 998/846-8257, 7 A.M.–11 P.M. daily, US$2–5) serves up mean breakfast and dinner plates with tacos, *chilaquiles, mole,* enchiladas…you name it, they'll whip it up. It's so typical, in fact, that you're likely only to see locals—during the week, businessmen puffing away at cigarettes, on weekends, families out for a bite.

For regional *tortas* (sandwiches), check out **Tortas del Carmen** (15 Av. between Calles 2 and 4, 984/129-7157, 8:30 A.M.–9 P.M. daily, US$2–4), serving massive sesame rolls piled high with refried beans, cabbage, avocado, *quesillo* (a soft cheese), tomatoes, and your choice of meat. Try the *Del Carmen,* with pulled pork and chicken fried steak, to fill up after a day at the beach. Outdoor seating only.

Other Specialties

◖ **John Gray's Place** (Calle Corazón near Calle 14, 984/803-3689, 6– 10 P.M. Mon.–Sat., US$10–20) is a sister restaurant to the original John Gray's Kitchen in Puerto Morelos, widely considered one of the best restaurants on the Riviera Maya. The new kid lives up to expectations, expertly fusing gourmet American cuisine with flavors from around the world. The menu changes daily, but expect dishes like asparagus soup or soy marinated tuna for starters, and entrées of roasted duck with tequila, chipotle and honey, or pork loin with Roquefort crust. Credit cards not accepted, so you may want to stop at the ATM before dinner. Don't worry, it's worth it.

◖ **Maktub Caffé** (5 Av. between Calles 28 and 30, 7 A.M.–1 A.M. daily, US$6–15) The first inklings of Arabic culture came to Mexico with the Spanish colonizers, whose food and architecture were deeply influenced by the Moors. Then came a wave of Palestinian and Lebanese

immigrants who settled here in the 18th and 19th centuries. (Mexican actress Salma Hayek is of Lebanese descent, in fact.) So it's no surprise to find restaurants like this one, serving excellent tabbouleh, hummus, falafel, and more, and hookahs and flavored tobacco to relax by. It's on a hip, bustling block, with restaurants and bars on both sides and across the street.

Friendly and unassuming, **Ula-Gula** (5 Av. at Calle 10, 2nd Fl., tel. 984/879-3727, 5:30 P.M.–11:30 daily, US$9–25) serves outstanding international gourmet dinners in an appealing second-floor dining area overlooking the street corner. Argentinean owned and operated, the pasta and meat dishes are excellent as expected, but seafood is the real standout here: Start off with Kubik tuna with wasabi and soy sauce, then dig into the fish of the day, prepared one of several fashions, from parsley gorgonzola sauce to smoked tomato broth. For dessert, the chocolate fondant—a small chocolate cake filled with rich chocolate syrup and accompanied by ice cream—is divine.

Although occasionally missing the mark, old-timer **Babe's Noodles and Bar** (Calle 10 between 5 Av. and 10 Av., tel. 984/804-1998, noon–11 P.M. Mon.–Sat., 5–11 P.M. Sun., US$6–14) still serves up delicious Thai and Asian-fusion meals in a hip, bistro setting. Dishes come in half and full orders. Don't miss a chance at ordering the *limonmenta,* an awesome lime-mint slushie. It's not a huge place so you may have to wait for a table during high season, or if you prefer, head to its sister restaurant down the street (5 Avenida between Calles 28 and 30, 2–11 P.M. Mon.–Sat.). Cash only.

Another Puerto Morelos import holding its own in Playa del Carmen, **Mr. Lau** (10 Av. between Calles 8 and 10, tel. 984/873-2020, 2 P.M.–11 P.M. daily, US$8–15) is an offshoot of the wildly popular Hola Asia restaurant just up Highway 307. The pan-Asian menu is the same, including Japanese-style tempura, Indian yellow curry, and the ever-popular General Tso's chicken—breaded chicken in sweet and spicy sauce, all terrific. A sushi bar is planned for the courtyard in back—stay tuned.

Mandarina's Café (5 Av. at Calle 14 bis,

tel. 984/803-1249, 11 A.M.–1 A.M. daily, US$12–25) oozes cool, with low pulsing music, candles, and gleaming white tablecloths set in a semi-covered patio dining area. The sign says "pizza and champagne," both of which come in a number of varieties. The menu also has a long list of crepes, from egg and mushroom to asparagus and cheese, plus gnocchi, lasagna, and other pastas. Right on the avenue, this is also a great spot for people watching. Frequent two-for-one drink specials.

100% Natural (5 Av. between Calles 10 and 12, tel. 984/873-2242, 7 A.M.–11 P.M. daily, US$5–11) serves mostly vegetarian dishes and a large selection of fresh fruit blends. Service can be a bit inattentive here, but the food is fresh and well prepared. Tables are scattered through a leafy garden area and covered patio.

Cafés and Bakeries

Chocolate lovers will melt over **Ah Cacao** (5 Av. at Constituyentes, tel. 984/803-5748, www.ah cacao.com, 7:30 A.M.–midnight daily, US$1.50–4), a chocolate café where every item on the menu—from coffees to cakes—is homemade from the sweetest of beans. Try a spicy Mayan Hot Chocolate for a true tasty treat (US$3).

You'll smell ◖ **Hot** (Calle Corazón at Calle 14, 7 A.M.–10 P.M. daily, US$2–8) from a block away—a café that makes freshly baked breads and pastries all day. Most people end up staying for more than just a brownie though—a full menu of sandwiches prepared on whole-wheat or sunflower-seed bread are almost impossible to resist. The shady outdoor eating area is a great place to enjoy a leisurely breakfast too.

The charming, old-world ◖ **Café Sasta** (5 Av. between Calles 8 and 10, 7 A.M.–11 P.M. daily, US$1.50–4.50) offers a tempting display of muffins, scones, cupcakes—even cheese-cake—to go along with the full coffee menu. Seating is available indoors and outdoors.

Pastelería Deli Cake (15 Av. between Calles 2 and 4, 8 A.M.–10 P.M. daily, US$0.25–2) is a classic Mexican bakery selling typical baked goods—*cuernos* (croissants), *donas* (doughnuts),

galletas (cookies), and a case full of cakes. Not fancy by any means, but cheap and good.

The Crepes Factory (Calle 24 at 5 Av., no phone, 8:30 A.M.–11:30 P.M. daily, US$3.50–6) is a simple café that serves great smoothies and tasty crepes—you can oversee the production of both if you sit griddle-side at one of the counter stools, or have them delivered to tables set up on the sidewalk.

Groceries

Wal-Mart (Calle 8 between Avs. 20 and 25, 7 A.M.–midnight daily) has arrived in Playa, opening a huge superstore behind city hall, with everything from clothes, shoes, and snorkel gear to groceries, prepared food, and a full pharmacy.

INFORMATION
Tourist Information

Playa del Carmen has no reliable tourist information office, but does have a few free tourist magazines that are worth picking up, especially if you are here for more than a couple of days. *Sac-Be* and *Playa Maya News* are monthly magazines printed on newsprint and oriented toward the expat community. For tourists, they both usually offer a handful of useful articles, listings, and events calendars (and a dose of not-so-useful drivel, as well). *Dive 'n' Sports* (aka D'N'S) has good maps of Playa, Puerto Morelos, Cozumel, Tulum, and Akumal, plus hotel and restaurant listings and short articles about kiteboarding, skydiving, and other activities. *Que Pasa? Playa Pocket Guide* is a small booklet with a somewhat confusing map but a good selection of ads and coupons, all organized into a convenient directory.

Hospitals

Hospiten Riviera Maya (main highway, tel. 984/803-1002, www.hospiten.com, 24 hours) is a private hospital offering modern, high-quality medical service at reasonable rates. Many of the doctors have U.S. training and speak English, and are accustomed to treating foreign visitors and expats.

PLAYA DEL CARMEN BUS SCHEDULES

TERMINAL TURÍSTICA (5 Av. and Av. Juárez, 984/873-0109 ext. 2501 or 01-800-702-8000) is located near the ferry dock and has frequent service north to Cancún and south to Tulum, and most locations in between. Long-distance buses use the Terminal Alterna.

Most Tulum-bound buses stop at the turnoffs for destinations along the way, including **Xcaret** (US$1, 10min.), **Paamul** (US$1, 15 min.), **Puerto Aventuras** (US$1, 20 min.), **Xpu-Há** (US$1.50, 25 min.), **Akumal** (US$2, 30 min.), **Xel-Ha** (US$3, 30 min.), and **Hidden Worlds** and **Dos Ojos** (both US$3, 40 min.).

Most Chetumal buses stop at **Carrillo Puerto** (US$8, 2 hrs), and **Bacalar** (US$11, 5 hrs).

Most Cancún buses stop at **Puerto Morelos** (US$1.50, 20 min.) but *not* the airport or Cancún hotel zone.

DESTINATION	PRICE	DURATION	SCHEDULE
Cancún	US$3.25	1 hr	every 10 min., 5:45 A.M.-midnight
Cancun Int'l Airport	US$7.50	1 hr	hourly 7 A.M.-6 P.M.
Chetumal (2nd Class)	US$12.25	6 hrs	every 1-2 hrs 5:15 A.M.-5:15 P.M., plus 11:15 P.M. (making all stops)
Tulum	US$2	1 hr	hourly 5:15 A.M.-11:15 P.M.
Xcaret (main entrance)	US$3	15 min.	9 A.M., 9:40 A.M., 10:20 A.M., 11:20 A.M.

*Denotes deluxe service; there are many more deluxe departures from Cancún.

For emergency ambulance service, call 065 from any public phone.

Pharmacies

Farmacia Yza (tel. 984/873-2727) has two 24-hour pharmacies—one on 10 Avenida between Calles 12 and 14, and the other on 30 Avenida between Calles 4 and 6. Order at least US$10 of medicine or snacks (it's also a mini-mart) and they'll deliver to your hotel.

Police

The tourist police (tel. 984/877-3340, or 060 from any pay phone) have an office on Avenida Juárez and 15 Avenida, and informational kiosks along 5 Avenida, theoretically operating 24 hours a day.

SERVICES
Money

Banks and free-standing ATMs are scattered around town. To access your money or exchange foreign cash try **Banamex** (Calle 12 at 10 Av., 9 A.M.–4 P.M. Mon.–Fri., 10 A.M.–2 P.M. Sat.) or **Banorte** (Plaza Pelícanos, 10 Av. between Calles 8 and 10, 9 A.M.–6 P.M. Mon.–Fri., 10 A.M.–2 P.M. Sat.).

Internet and Telephone

Call Home Caseta Telefónica (5 Av. at Calle 28; 8 A.M.–11 P.M.) makes checking email cool and comfortable, with air-conditioning and solid armchairs. Internet is US$1.50 an hour and phone calls are just US$0.20 a minute to

TERMINAL ALTERNA (Calle 20 between Calles 12 and 12-Bis, tel. 984/803-0944, toll-free 01-800/702-8000) departures include:

DESTINATION	PRICE	DURATION	SCHEDULE
Campeche	US$30	8 hrs	10:20 A.M.
Chetumal	US$16	5 hrs	every 1-2 hrs 6:15 A.M.-11:55 P.M.
Chichén Itzá	US$15	4 hrs	8 A.M.
Cobá	US$5.50	1.5 hrs	8 A.M.
Mérida	US$24-30	5.5 hrs	every 1-2hrs 6:30 A.M.-6:30 P.M., plus midnight and 12:30 A.M.
Mexico City	US$92	24 hrs	five departures 7:30 A.M.-9:15 P.M.
Palenque	US$41	12 hrs	Take San Cristóbal bus
San Cristóbal (Chiapas)	US$51	19 hrs	3:30 P.M., 5 P.M., 7 P.M.*, and 9:40 P.M.
Valladolid	US$12.50	2.5 hrs	8 A.M., 10:20 A.M., 11:30 A.M., 6:30 P.M., and 12:30 A.M.
Villahermosa	US$45	12 hrs	nine departures 12:15 P.M.-12:30 A.M., plus 7:30 A.M.
Xpujil	US$22	5.5 hrs	7:30 A.M., 12:15 P.M., 3:15 P.M., 6:15 P.M., and 12:40 A.M.

THE RIVIERA MAYA

the United States and Canada or US$0.40 to Europe.

Centro de Comunicaciones 24 (Calle 24 between 5 Av. and 1 Av. Norte, tel. 984/803-5778, Internet US$2.25/hr.) is often filled with clouds of cigarette smoke, but is open 24 hours and offers cut-rate international calling on Saturday and between midnight and 7 A.M.

Closer to the center, **Cybernet** (Calle 8 be-tween 5 Av. and the beach, tel. 984/873-3476, 8:30 A.M.–11:30 P.M. daily) has a fast Internet connection for US$1.50 per hour, and international calling from US$0.50 a minute.

Phonet Centro de Comunicaciones (10 Av. between Calles 2 and 4, 8 A.M.–11 P.M. daily) is a quiet place to check email (US$1.50/hr) and to make calls (US$0.42/min to U.S. and Canada, and US$0.75/min to Europe).

Post Office

The post office (9 A.M.–4 P.M. Mon.–Fri., 9 A.M.–noon P.M. Sat.) is next to the tourist police office at the corner of Avenida Juárez and 15 Avenida. Postcards and small letters cost US$1 to send to the United States, US$1.35 to Europe.

Immigration

Avoid using Playa del Carmen's immigration office (Plaza Antigua mall, 2nd Fl., Calle 10, tel. 998/881-3560, 9 A.M.–1 P.M. Mon.–Fri.), as the one in Cancún is much faster and friendlier. A simple tourist visa extension, or *prórroga*, can take a week or more in Playa and involves considerable documentation. In Cancún, the same process is simpler and takes as little as two hours.

Travel Agencies

Mayaluum Travel Agency (10 Av. at Calle 2, tel. 984/873-2961, www.mayaluum.com, 9:30 A.M.–2 P.M. and 3:30–7:30 P.M. Mon.–Fri., 9:30 A.M.–2 P.M. Sat.) handles plane tickets, package tours, and other travel arrangements.

Launderette

A convenient place to get your threads washed is **Lavendería Premium Los Mecates** (Calle 4 near 20 Av., 8:30 A.M.–8 P.M. Mon.–Fri., 8:30 A.M.–1 P.M. Sat.–Sun., US$1/kilogram). Same day service if you drop your clothes off early.

GETTING THERE
Bus

Playa del Carmen has two bus stations. **Terminal Turística** (aka Terminal Riviera, 5 Av. and Av. Juárez) is in the center of town and has frequent second-class service to destinations along the coast, including Cancún, Tulum, and everything in between. The **Terminal Alterna** (Calle 20 between Calles 12 and 12-bis) has first-class and deluxe service to interior destinations such as Mérida, Campeche, and beyond. There is some overlap, and you can buy tickets for any destination at either station, so always double-check

where your bus departs from when you buy a ticket.

Combis

Combis (public vans) are an easy way to get up and down the Riviera Maya. In Playa, northbound *combis* line up on Calle 2 near 20 Avenida, leaving every 15 minutes, 24 hours a day. The final destination is Cancún's main bus terminal (US$2.75, 50 minutes), but you can be dropped off anywhere along the highway, including Puerto Morelos (US$2, 20 minutes). *Combis* do not enter Cancún's hotel zone, but you can catch a bus there from outside the terminal. South from Playa del Carmen, *combis* leave from the same corner every 15 minutes, 5 A.M.–10 P.M. They go as far as the Tulum's bus station (US$2.50, 50 minutes), passing the turnoffs for Xpu-Ha (US$1.50, 20 minutes), Akumal (US$2, 25 minutes), Hidden Worlds (US$2.50, 40 minutes) and Tulum Ruins (US$2.50, 45 minutes) among others. To return, you can flag down *combis* anywhere along the highway.

Air

Playa del Carmen's airport does not receive regular commercial flights, though charters are available to and from locations around the peninsula and even Belize and Guatemala.

Car

If you are driving to Playa del Carmen look for the two main access roads to the beach—Avenida Constituyentes on the north end of town and Avenida Benito Juárez on the south. Playacar has its own entrance from the highway, but can also be reached by turning south on Calle 10 off Avenida Juárez.

Ferries to Isla Cozumel

Passenger ferries to Cozumel (US$10 each way, 30 minutes) leave from the pier at the end of Calle 1 Sur. **UltraMar** and **Mexico Water Jets** alternate departures and charge the same amount, though UltraMar's boats are newer. Their ticket booths are side-by-side at the foot of the pier, with the time of the next departure displayed prominently. The ticket seller will probably try to sell you a round-trip ticket, but it makes more sense, and costs the same, to buy a *sencilla* (one-way ticket) and wait to see which ferry has the next departure when you're ready to return. Between the two companies, there are ferries every 60–90 minutes 6 A.M.–10 P.M. daily.

South of Playa is **Punta Venado dock** (tel. 987/872-0916, www.maritimachankanaab.es.mw). Once used by the Calica Company to ship limestone products to the United States, today it is home to the only car ferry to and from Isla Cozumel. Ferries depart Punta Venado at 5 A.M., 7 A.M., 11 A.M., 5 P.M., and 9 P.M. Mon.–Sat. From Cozumel, the ferry leaves at 4 A.M., 9 A.M., 1 P.M., and 6 P.M. daily except Sunday. The trip takes about 1.5 hours and costs US$40 for a car including driver, and US$2.60 for each additional passenger. Arrive at least an hour in advance to get a spot.

GETTING AROUND

Playa del Carmen is a walking town, although the steady northward expansion is challenging that description. The commercial part of 5 Avenida now stretches 20 blocks and keeps getting longer. Cabs and bicycle taxis are a good option, especially if you have luggage. Parking in Playa in the high season can be a challenge, especially south of Avenida Constituyentes. Many hotels have secure parking, otherwise there are parking lots around town, including on Calle 2 at 10 Avenida (8 A.M.–10 P.M. daily, US$1/hour or US$8.50/day).

Taxi

Taxis around town cost US$1.50–5, or a bit more if you use a taxi stand or have your hotel summon one. All taxi drivers carry a *tarifario*—an official fare schedule—which you can ask to see if you think you're getting taken for a ride, so to speak. Prices do change every year or two, so ask at your hotel what the current rate is, and always be sure to agree on the fare with the driver before setting off.

Triciclos (bike-taxis) line up on Avenida Juárez alongside the Terminal Turística. The ride costs about the same as one in a taxi but makes an interesting alternative.

Car Rental

Playa has myriad car rental agencies and prices can vary considerably. Prices are highest at the major agencies, like Hertz, National, Avis and Executive, but they often have great deals online. At local agencies, like **Veloz Rent a Car** (Av. Constituyentes 111 between 5 Av. and 1 Av. Norte, tel. 984/803-2323, 8 A.M.–1 P.M. and 5 A.M.–8 P.M. daily) and **Zipp Rent-A-Car** (10 Av. between Calles 2 and 4, 998/873-0696, www.zipp.com.mx, 8 A.M.–6 P.M. daily) you may be able to negotiate lower rates, especially during low season and for rentals of a week or more. Expect to pay US$45–60 a day for a car, with taxes and insurance included.

THE RIVIERA MAYA

Paamul

What started out as an unassuming trailer park on a beautiful stretch of beach has now become a seaside community all its own. Located about 20 kilometers (12.4 miles) south of Playa del Carmen, Paamul has everything from RVs with elaborate wood and *palapa* structures over them to hotel rooms, a restaurant, and even a dive shop.

BEACH

Paamul stretches over a wide curving beach. It's clean and classically pretty with white sand and turquoise water—perfect for swimming and exploring. Watch your step on the south end of the beach, as its waters harbor prickly sea urchin—consider wearing water shoes.

SNORKELING AND SCUBA DIVING

The full-service **Scuba-Mex** (tel. 984/875-1066, toll-free U.S. tel. 888/871-6255, www.scuba mex.com, 8 A.M.–5 P.M. daily) offers one- and two-tank dive trips to open water sites and cenotes (US$29–80). A variety of packages and dive courses also are available at competitive rates. And if you're just interested in snorkeling off the beach, the shop rents snorkel gear for US$6 per day.

ACCOMODATIONS

Offering a little bit of everything, **Cabañas Paa Mul** (Carretera Cancún-Chetumal Km. 85, tel. 984/875-1051, www.paamul.com, US$10 pp tent, US$25 trailer spot, US$111 s/d cabañas, US$145 s/d with a/c) appeals to travelers of all budgets. Best of all are the modern hotel rooms, which were built in 2006. All are boutiquey in style, with muted colors, luxurious linens, gleaming bathtubs, mini-split air-conditioners, and gorgeous ocean views from private terraces. Next best are, surprisingly, the tent and trailer spaces.

Paamul's beach is a good place to spend the day.

© LIZA PRADO

Although set up in the main parking lot, all boast electricity, running water, and clean shared hot-water bathrooms—these are just steps from the Caribbean. Dead last—and with good reason—are the cabañas. Constructed in 2000, they look as if they've been through decades of wear and tear: wood floors with holes, cement walls with paint thrown on, and granny-style decor. Priced at over US$100, you're better off in a tent space.

FOOD

Open-air, modern, and with a great view of the Caribbean, the **Reefs of Paamul Restaurant and Bar** (8 A.M.–9 P.M. daily, US$5–15) serves up classic Mexican dishes along with a vari-ety of international meals. There's something for everyone, which makes it easy to eat most of your meals here. (Good thing, since it's the only restaurant in Paamul).

For groceries, the very mini **Mini Super Paa Mul** (7 A.M.–7 P.M. Mon.–Sat., 8 A.M.–2 P.M. Sun.) sells basic food stuff. Look for it on the highway turnoff to Paamul.

INFORMATION AND SERVICES

There are no health, banking, Internet, or postal services in Paamul. The closest town—and one of the best places in the region—for a full range of services is Playa del Carmen, 20 kilometers (12.4 miles) north.

Puerto Aventuras

Puerto Aventuras is an odd conglomeration of condos, summer homes, and hotels, organized around a large marina, including a swim-with-dolphins area. It's more than a resort, but not really a town. Whatever you call it, Puerto Aventuras's huge signs and gated entrance are impossible to miss, located a few minutes north of Akumal on Highway 307.

SIGHTS
Museo Sub-Acuatico CEDAM

Short for the Conservation, Ecology, Diving, and Archaeology Museum, CEDAM (Bldg. F, 9 A.M.–1 P.M., 2:30–5:30 P.M. Mon.–Sat., donation requested) is a very worthwhile mu-seum, displaying a wide variety of items: Maya offerings that were dredged from the penin-sula's cenotes; artifacts recovered from nearby colonial shipwrecks; early diving equipment; and photos of open-water and cenote explora-tions, some from the halcyon days of diving when *jeans* were the preferred get-up.

SPORTS AND RECREATION
Snorkeling and Scuba Diving

Some 25 dive sites lie within a 10-minute boat ride from the marina, each boasting the same rich coral, abundant sealife, and interesting fea-tures, like pillars and swim-throughs, found up and down the coast. **Aquanauts** (tel. 984/873-5041, www.aquanauts-online.com, 8:30 A.M.–5:30 P.M. daily) is a safe, full-service shop that has many repeat guests. Divers can count on per-sonal details (such as storing dry gear) and guest-first practices (such as staying under as long as your air permits, not just the standard 45 min-utes). The shop offers the full range of dives and courses, including reef dives (US$40/one tank, US$75/two tanks), cenotes dives (US$90/one tank, US$150/two tanks) and open-water cer-tification (US$415 private, US$385 pp group). Multi-dive packages are available; equipment rental is included in courses but not fun dives (US$15/one tank, US$20/two tanks). The shop also offers a 2.5-hour snorkel tour (US$40, in-cluding equipment, snacks, and drinks, four peo-ple minimum) visiting two different reefs and has a good selection of new equipment for sale. Reservations recommended in high season.

Swimming with Dolphins

Dolphin Discovery (Marina, tel. 984/873-5078, in U.S. 800/417-1736, www.dolphin discovery.com, 8 A.M.–5 P.M. daily) offers several

THE RIVIERA MAYA

CEDAM AND THE RIVIERA MAYA

In 1948, a small group of Mexican divers – active frogmen during World War II – created a nonprofit organization called Club de Exploración y Deporte Acuáticos de México (Exploration and Aquatic Sports Club of Mexico, or CEDAM). Their mission was to promote ocean conservation and educate others about its treasures and resources.

In 1958, the group set about salvaging the *Mantanceros*, a Spanish galleon that foundered offshore in 1741. It got permission to set up camp on present-day Akumal, then just a deserted beach owned by a man named Don Argimiro Arguelles. Argimiro leased CEDAM a workboat for their project, and even offered his services as captain.

It was this relationship that sealed Akumal's – and arguably, the Riviera Maya's – destiny. During a relaxed evening around the campfire, Don Argimiro sold Pablo Bush, the head of CEDAM, the bay of Akumal and thousands of acres of coconut palms north and south of it. For the next 12 years, CEDAM continued its work in the rustic and beautiful place – replacing their tents with sturdy *palapa* huts, and still using the creaky *SS Co-*

zumel to carry divers to sites up and down the coast.

It wasn't long before the idea of promoting tourism on Mexico's forgotten Caribbean coast arose. In 1968, the group – which had changed the words behind its initials to Conservation, Ecology, Diving, Archaeology, and Museums – donated 5,000 acres of land to the government, as well as the Cove of Xel-há, to create a national park. The aim was to open the isolated area to tourists, and in so doing, create jobs for local residents. CEDAM also provided housing, food, electricity, running water, a school for the children, and a first-aid station with a trained nurse.

Still based in Akumal, CEDAM has grown into an important international scientific and conservation organization. The group plays an active part in the archaeological exploration of cenotes, among other things, and hosts regular symposiums and seminars. A small but worthwhile museum in Puerto Aventuras – Museo Sub-Acuático CEDAM (Building F, 9 A.M.-2 P.M. and 3:30-6 P.M. Monday-Saturday) – displays some of the incredible items that the group has recovered in the region's waters.

dolphin-encounter activities, ranging in price and the amount and type of interaction you have. For the most contact, the Royal Swim program (US$139; 30 minutes' orientation, 30 minutes in water) includes two dolphins per group of eight people, with a chance to do a "dorsal tow," "footpush," and "kiss," plus some open swim time. The Swim Adventure (US$99) and Dolphin Encounter (US$79) have somewhat less direct contact. The center also has manatee and sea lion programs that can be taken in combo with dolphins. Programs start at 9 A.M., 11 A.M., 1 P.M., and 3 P.M. daily; free shuttle service is available to and from Playa del Carmen.

Golf and Tennis

Puerto Aventuras Club de Golf (across from Bldg. B, tel. 984/873-5109, 7:30 A.M.-5:30 P.M. daily, last tee time 3 P.M.) offers a nine-hole,

par-36 golf course right in town. The course, designed in 1991 by Tom Leman, is flat but has two par fives over a total 2,961 yards (3,255 championship). Green fees are US$80, including cart; after 1 P.M., they're US$65 with a cart, US$57 with a pull cart. Rates include a golf cart and are US$75 per person before 3 P.M. and US$55 per person afterward. Two tennis courts are also available for US$20 an hour. Golf club rentals cost US$24, tennis racquets run US$5.

Sport Fishing

Capt. Rick's Sportfishing Center (past Omni Puerto Aventuras hotel, tel. 984/873-5195 or toll-free Mex. tel. 800/719-6439, www.fish yucatan.com, office 8 A.M.–7 P.M. daily) offers customized fishing trips for groups and individuals. Trolling is the most popular, going for

© LIZA PRADO

Swimming with dolphins is one of the most popular activities along the Riviera Maya.

dorado, tuna, barracuda, sailfish, and even marlin. Bottom/drift fishing is also fun and targets "dinner fish" such as grouper, snapper, and yellowtail. You can also arrange time for visiting a deserted beach or Maya ruin, snorkeling on the reef, or just cruising by upscale homes and hotels. Choose between a 23-foot boat (two passengers maximum, US$250/450 half/full day), a 31- or 35-footer (eight passengers maximum, US$375/650 half/full day), or a 38-footer (10 passengers maximum, US450/800 half/full day). Shared trips are US$90 per person for half day and US$180 for full day. Full-day trips leave at 9 A.M. and return at 5 P.M.; half-day trips are 9 A.M.–1 P.M. and 1:30–5:30 P.M. Prices include equipment, bait, soft drinks, and water; full-day trips also include lunch. There's good fishing year-round, but April–July are best for hooking into a billfish.

Parasailing
Riviera Maya Parasail Adventures (past Omni Puerto Aventuras hotel, tel. 984/873-5623, www.snubamexico.com, office 8 A.M.–6 P.M. daily) offers single and tandem parasail trips (US$65 single, US$55 pp tandem, 9 A.M., 10 A.M., and 11 A.M.) several times daily. The flights last 10–12 minutes (although the whole excursion takes about an hour) and you reach up to 250 feet in the air. Others can accompany you on the boat for US$20 per person. The agency caters to cruise ships, so advance reservations are a good idea.

ACCOMMODATIONS
The main road bumps right into the **Omni Puerto Aventuras** (tel. 984/875-1950, www .omnihotels.com, US$308–342, includes breakfast), a small upscale hotel with the marina on one side and a fine, palm-shaded beach on the other. All 30 rooms have tile floors, one or two beds, colorful regional decor, and first-class amenities such as wireless Internet access. All rooms have private patios with hot tubs; those with an ocean view cost more. Large discounts in the low season.

Casa del Agua (Punta Matzoma 21, tel. 984/873-5184, www.casadelagua .com, US$350 d, US$1,400 house) is a beacon of class and charm amid the plastic commercialism of Puerto Aventuras. At the far southern end of town, the hotel's four spacious suites—the bathrooms alone are bigger than some hotel rooms—all have king-size beds, air-conditioning and fan, and come with a hearty breakfast, served on a common patio overlooking the bay. There is a small sunny pool and the beach is quiet and private, although rather steeply sloped. Guests are free to borrow kayaks and snorkeling gear, as well as the hotel's wireless Internet signal. Casa del Agua caters to honeymooners and small yoga and meditation groups, so children are allowed only if you rent the entire building; otherwise 12 and older only. Service is superb. Three-night minimum stay for individual rooms, seven-night minimum when renting the house.

For info on long-term rentals or even buying a place, try **Paradise Beach Sales and Rentals** (next to Café-C@fé coffee shop, tel. 984/873-5029, www.puertaaventurasrentals .com, 7 A.M.–7 P.M. Mon.–Sat.).

FOOD

It is easy to find a place to eat in Puerto Aventuras: Stroll around the marina for a few minutes and you'll run into every restaurant in town. The variety is slim, however—most menus have a similar selection of Americanized Mexican food, pastas, and grilled meats.

Café Olé International (Bldg. A, tel. 984/873-5125, 8 A.M.–10 P.M. daily, US$5–25) has something for everyone, and every price range. It's best known for its filet mignon and homemade desserts.

If you're in the mood for a big salad or a pizza—thin, regular, or deep dish—try **Richard's Quarterdeck Steakhouse and Pizza** (Bldg. A, tel. 984/873-5086, 11 A.M.–10 P.M. daily, US$6–32). Opened in 1994 by a Chicago native, food here is especially good if you're missing flavors from home.

If you've gone fishing, bring your catch to **Gringo Dave's** (Bldg. C, 7 A.M.–11 P.M. daily, US$6–31). For just US$5 per person, the chef will prepare your fish any way you want it and will even throw in rice, veggies, and a side of guacamole. The restaurant also hosts karaoke

Thursday and Sunday evenings, and has a direct view of one of the large dolphin enclosures.

Super Akumal (across from Omni Puerto Aventuras hotel, 8 A.M.–8 P.M. daily) is the local market and has a little of everything, including water, chips, sunscreen, toiletries, and so on.

INFORMATION AND SERVICES
Pharmacies

There is one local pharmacy, **First Aid Pharmacy** (Bldg. A, tel. 984/873-5305 or 984/206-6087, 9 A.M.–9 P.M. daily, or call by telephone 24 hours).

Money

Puerto Aventuras doesn't have an actual bank yet, but there's a **Banamex ATM** next to Capt. Rick's fishing shop and a **Santander ATM** near the entrance of Museo CEDAM. Both are accessible 24 hours.

Internet and Telephone

Café-C@fé (tel. 984/873-5728, www.cafe cafe-pa.com, 8 A.M.–6 P.M. Mon.–Sat low season, until 8 P.M. daily high season) has super-fast cable and wireless Internet for US$0.10 per minute, or at much better rates in prepaid plans of five hours (US$12) or 10 hours (US$18). You can also make **international calls** here for US$0.40 to the United States and Canada, US$0.80 to the rest of the world.

Azul Tequila Internet Bar (tel. 984/873-5673, 9 A.M.–11 P.M. daily) serves drinks along with Internet access (US$0.10/min or US$5/hr) and CD burning (US$3.50, plus US$1.50 for disc).

Post Office

The post office (10 A.M.–3 P.M. Mon., Wed., and Fri.) is in a large kiosk a short distance from the golf club entrance.

Launderette

Opposite the post office, the friendly owner of **Fresh Bubbles** (8:30 A.M.–8 P.M. Mon.–Sat.) will wash, dry, and fold clothes for US$1.50 a kilogram (2.2 pounds) the same day, or US$3 a kilogram (6.6 pounds) for two-hour express service, both with a minimum of two kilograms (4.5 pounds). Ironing is US$1–1.50 per piece; local pickup and drop-off can be arranged.

GETTING THERE AND AROUND

By public transportation take a *combi* from Cancún, Playa del Carmen, or Tulum

(US$2). Let the driver know where you're going and he'll drop you off on the side of the highway. From there, it's 500 meters (0.3 mile) into town. Arriving by car, there's a large control gate but no one who looks like a tourist is stopped.

In Puerto Aventuras, you can walk just about everywhere, as virtually all shops and services are centered around the marina.

Xpu-Há

A sleepy beachside community, Xpu-Há is made up of a sprinkling of hotels, a couple of restaurants, and a bunch of travelers just kicking back. On a spectacularly wide beach, it's definitely a known stop on the Riviera but it's managed to maintain a hideaway feel. Great for a couple of days (or weeks!) to catch up on that novel you've been meaning to read.

SPORTS AND RECREATION
Snorkeling

Besides the ocean, several privately operated cenotes on the inland side of Highway 307 north of Xpu-Há make for good snorkeling and swimming. They can get crowded with local families on weekends.

Cristalino Azul (Hwy. 307, 2 km/1.2 mi north of Xpu-Há, 8 A.M.–7 P.M. daily) charges US$3 for an adult, US$1.50 for a child, no rental gear. Much of this half-moon shaped cenote is shallow and covered in algae, but one section extends under a deep overhanging rock ceiling.

Jardín del Eden (Hwy. 307, 1.75 km/1 mi north of Xpu-Há, 7 A.M.–5 P.M. Sun.–Fri.) charges US$3.25 for an adult, US$2 for a child, mask and snorkel are US$3, life vest is US$3. Formerly known as Ponderosa Cenote, this is a much larger cenote than most—like a small lake—and can get busy with snorkelers, swimmers, and divers. A 6-meter (20-foot) cliff is fun to jump off.

At **Cenote Azul** (9 A.M.–6 P.M. daily, US$5 adult, US$3 child, mask and snorkel US$3, life vest US$3) a few large pools and a section of

overhanging rock are the highlights here, and walkways along the edges facilitate getting in and out. Still, it's not clear why this one is the most expensive of the Xpu-Há area cenotes.

Scuba Diving

Bahía Divers (tel. 044-984/127-3872, www.bahiadivers.com), operates out of a small hut a short distance down the beach from La Playa. It offers the full gamut of fun dives, courses,

THE RIVIERA MAYA

© LIZA PRADO

With a view like this, it's no wonder travelers come back so often.

and snorkeling and fishing trips, with the advantage of small groups and personal service. Reefs dives run US$35 for one tank, US$65 for two, US$120 for four; gear is US$15 per day. Two-tank cenote dives are US$100, plus US$20 for gear. Snorkeling trips cost US$35–75 per person, depending where you go—reef, cenote, lagoon, or a combination of the three.

Beach Activities

La Playa Xpu-Há (entrance at Carr. Cancún-Tulum Km. 93, tel. 984/106-0024) is a bustling club that offers a slew of classic beach activities, including parasailing, fishing, banana boats, snorkeling, and kayaking, all at standard prices.

For just lounging on the beach, you'll find a much quieter scene at the **Hotel-Villas del Caribe,** which has free beach chairs and umbrellas if you order from the restaurant.

Not exactly a beach activity, **Duck Putt** (8:30 A.M.–2 P.M. and 5 P.M.–7 P.M. weekdays., 8:30 A.M.–6 P.M. weekends, closed Tue.) is nevertheless Xpu-Há's very own 18-hole miniature golf course. It lacks the crazy creatures and moving obstacles that are half the fun back home, but it's a nice walk down the beach and only costs US$4 for adults, US$3 for kids. It's also the nearest place to check Internet, though service is spotty at best.

Body Work

Hotel-Villas del Caribe offers twice-weekly **yoga classes** (US$9/session) and **Sunday sunrise meditation** (free); all levels welcome.

ACCOMMODATIONS
Under US$50

South of the Copacabana resort, **Xpu-Há Bonanza** (entrance at Carr. Cancún-Tulum Km. 93, tel. 984/116-4733, US$4.50 pp camping, US$40 s/d with fan) offers eight spacious rooms with clean cold-water bathrooms and space for two beds and two hammocks. The units are rather dark, but the quiet beach and bargain prices are reasonable consolation. Travelers with tents can set up in the sand under a palm tree, and have access to cleanish shared bathrooms.

US$50-100

Down a tiny sand road next to the Copacabana resort, ◖ **Hotel-Villas del Caribe** (Xpu-Há X-4, tel. 984/873-2194, www.xpuhahotel.com, US$55–90 s/d with fan) is an oceanfront hotel with clean and comfortable rooms, most with terraces and/or hammocks. Rooms are repainted frequently in cheerful colors, and have simple, tasteful decor; the ocean breezes more than make up for the lack of air-conditioning. Rates vary according to the size and view: large or larger and garden or ocean. All that, plus a laid-back atmosphere and a fantastic restaurant make this an especially comfortable place to wind down for a few days.

FOOD

Wiggle your toes in the sand as you wait for your meal at **Café del Mar** (Hotel-Villas del Caribe, tel. 984/873-2194, 8 A.M.–9 P.M. Tues.–Sun., US$6–15). Right on the beach, this is an excellent open-air restaurant that offers an international menu made with the freshest of ingredients, and a full bar.

INFORMATION AND SERVICES

The only thing that qualifies under this heading is the unpredictable Internet service at **Duck Putt.** If you're lucky enough to find the shop open and the signal working, access is US$2 per hour. For everything else—cash machine, pharmacy, laundry, etc.—head to Akumal or Playa del Carmen.

GETTING THERE AND AROUND

The road to Hotel-Villas del Caribe is called "X-4" and runs along the north side of the Copacabana resort. It's poorly marked, but the Copacabana is easy to spot and most *combi* drivers know where to drop you. From the highway, it's about 500 meters (0.3 mile) to the beach and hotel. Xpu-Há Bonanza and La Playa Xpu-Há have a separate entrance, somewhat better marked and located a few hundred meters south of the Copacabana.

Akumal

Unreachable by land until the 1960s, Akumal (literally, Place of the Turtle) is a low-key, upscale community that has developed on two bays: Akumal and Half Moon. It's a quiet place with sand roads and dozens of condominiums and rental homes. The beach in town is decent—if you can handle the boats parked on the sand—and the one around Half Moon Bay is calm though rocky in places. What draws people here is a spectacular barrier reef, which protects Akumal's bays from the open sea and makes for ideal swimming and great snorkeling.

A short distance south of Akumal proper is Aventuras Akumal, another small bayside development. It doesn't have the townlike activity of Akumal (mostly private vacation homes, no restaurants) but two good condo-hotels and a truly gorgeous beach make this a tempting alternative. Aventuras Akumal has a separate access road from the highway, and walking there along the beach takes about 45 minutes.

SIGHTS
Beaches

Akumal Bay—the one right in front of town—has a long, slow-curving shoreline, with soft sand shaded by palm trees. The water is beautiful but a bit rocky underfoot, and you should be aware of boat traffic when swimming or snorkeling. Half Moon Bay can also be nice for swimming and snorkeling, but the shoreline is rocky in many parts; where there is beach, it is mostly narrow and covered with sea plants that have washed ashore.

◖ Laguna Yal-Ku

At the mouth of an elbow-shaped lagoon at the north end of Akumal, an endless upwelling of underground river water collides with the tireless flow of seawater—the result is a great place to snorkel, teeming with fish and plants adapted to this unique hybrid environment. Once a secret snorkeler's getaway, Laguna

© LIZA PRADO

At Half Moon Bay, top-notch diving and snorkeling is right outside your door.

THE RIVIERA MAYA

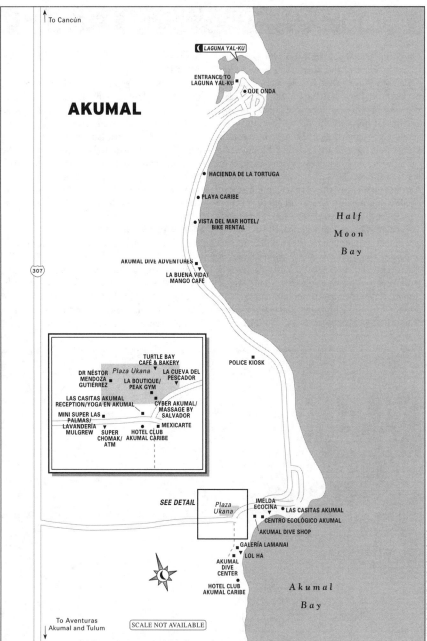

To Cancún

LAGUNA YAL-KU

AKUMAL

ENTRANCE TO
LAGUNA YAL-KU

QUE ONDA

HACIENDA DE LA TORTUGA

PLAYA CARIBE

VISTA DEL MAR HOTEL/
BIKE RENTAL

*Half
Moon
Bay*

307

AKUMAL DIVE ADVENTURES

LA BUENA VIDA/
MANGO CAFÉ

POLICE KIOSK

TURTLE BAY
CAFÉ & BAKERY

DR NÉSTOR   *Plaza Ukana*   LA CUEVA DEL
MENDOZA   PESCADOR
GUTIÉRREZ   LA BOUTIQUE/
             PEAK GYM

LAS CASITAS AKUMAL
RECEPTION/YOGA EN AKUMAL   CYBER AKUMAL/
                                 MASSAGE BY
MINI SUPER LAS   SALVADOR
PALMAS/
LAVANDERÍA   MEXICARTE
MULGREW   SUPER   HOTEL CLUB
           CHOMAK/ AKUMAL CARIBE
           ATM

SEE DETAIL   *Plaza
                  Ukana*   IMELDA
                                ECOCINA   LAS CASITAS AKUMAL
                                           CENTRO ECOLÓGICO AKUMAL
                                           AKUMAL DIVE SHOP

GALERÍA LAMANAI

LOL HA
AKUMAL
DIVE
CENTER

HOTEL CLUB
AKUMAL CARIBE

*Akumal

Bay*

To Aventuras
Akumal and Tulum

SCALE NOT AVAILABLE

© AVALON TRAVEL PUBLISHING, INC.

Yal-Ku (8 A.M.–5:30 P.M. daily, US$7 adult, US$4.25 child; US$14 snorkel gear; US$2 locker) now has a parking lot and a spot in every guidebook—come before 10 A.M., after 3 P.M., or anytime on Sunday for the least traffic. You can snorkel in the lagoons broad mouth, or up the narrow channel to its source. If possible, use a T-shirt or wetsuit instead of sunscreen—even the biodegradable kind can collect on plants and coral.

Akumal Ecological Center

Next to Akumal Dive Shop, the **Centro Ecológico Akumal** (CEA, tel. 984/875-9095, www.ceakumal.org, 9 A.M.–6 P.M. Mon.–Fri. 9 A.M.–1 P.M. Sat.) is a nonprofit founded in 1993 to monitor the health of Akumal's ecosystems, particularly related to coral and sea turtles. During turtle nesting season—May to July—you can join CEA volunteers on nighttime "turtle walks," covering about two kilometers (1.25 miles) of beach, looking for new nests and helping move eggs to protected hatcheries. From August to October, hatchlings are released back into the sea, which visitors can assist as well. Stop by the center for more details and to sign up; the activities are free but a US$5–10 donation is appreciated. The center also has free displays and frequent evening lectures on ocean ecology (in high season).

CEA also operates long-term volunteer projects on reef monitoring, sea turtles monitoring, and environmental education projects. Volunteers stay in the center's comfortable dorms, with kitchen and Internet access; minimum age is 21 and some fees are required. See website for details.

Aktun Chen

Maya for "Cave with an underground river," Aktun Chen (Carr. Cancún-Tulum Km. 107, tel. 998/892-0662, www.aktunchen. com, 9 A.M.–5 P.M. daily, last tour 4:30 P.M., US$24 adults, US$13 children under 11) is indeed that, and more. The cave itself has a breathtaking array of stalactites and stalagmites, and a 12-meter/40-foot-deep cenote filled with crystalline water at the end; light-

ing and a pathway make it accessible to all. Tours also include a brief nature walk (the park has almost 1,000 acres of protected forest) and a stop at the small zoo, where spider monkeys manage to charm everyone. Tours are offered in English and Spanish, and last about 75 minutes. Most hotels offer trips here that include transportation; otherwise, look for the turnoff just across from Aventuras Akumal, and continue three kilometers (1.9 miles) to the entrance. Mosquito repellent and a bottle of water are recommended.

SHOPPING

On the beach near Akumal Dive Center, **Galería Lamanai** (tel. 984/875-9055, 9 A.M.– 9 P.M. daily) was undergoing a major renovation at the time of research, but is sure to reopen with its consistently good selection of Mexican crafts and folk art.

La Boutique (Plaza Ukana, tel. 984/875-9208, 9 A.M.–5 P.M. Mon.–Sat., until 7 P.M. in high season) is the best of a cluster of three shops in the plaza area.

Mexicarte (9 A.M.–9 P.M. daily) is the small, bright pink shop just inside the arches on your right. The owner hand-selects the best folk art from around the region and country—prices are high, but so is the quality and artisanship.

SPORTS AND RECREATION
Scuba Diving

Some of the area's first scuba divers waded into the waves right here at Akumal Bay, and the area has been special to the sport ever since. While not as spectacular as other areas along the Riviera Maya, Akumal's diving is easy and fun, with a mellow current and few profiles that go below 20 meters (66 feet). The reef is predominantly boulder coral, which isn't as picturesque as other types, but still it teems with tropical fish and plant life. Visibility is decent by Caribbean standards—great by everyone else's—averaging 10–30 meters (33–99 feet).

Founded more than 30 years ago, **Akumal Dive Shop** (tel. 984/875-9032, www.akumal .com, 8 A.M.–6 P.M. daily) was the first dive shop in the Riviera Maya, long before anyone called it that. Still right on the beach, the shop offers fun dives and various certification courses in both open water and cave/cavern diving. Divers can take one- or two-tank reef dives (US$45/60), cavern or cenote dives (US$65/120), or buy packages of 4 or 10 dives for US$120/250. Fun dives do not include equipment rental (US$25/day, US$110/week). Open-water certification courses take 3–4 days and cost US$420, equipment and materials included.

Down the beach a short distance, **Akumal Dive Center** (tel. 984/875-9025, www.akumaldivecenter.com, 8 A.M.–5 P.M. daily) has operated in Akumal almost as long and offers the same dives and courses at comparable prices.

On Half Moon Bay, **Akumal Dive Adventures** (next to La Buena Vida restaurant, tel. 984/875-9157, toll-free U.S. tel. 877/425-8625, www.akumaldiveadventures.com, 8 A.M.–5 P.M. daily) offers similarly priced diving and courses, as well as a package of three nights' lodging and four reef dives for US$270 per person double occupancy, US$360 per person single occupancy, with an option to extend your stay or swap reef dives for night or cenote dives at an extra cost. Rooms are at the affiliated Vista del Mar hotel.

On a calm bay with a healthy reef, Aventuras Akumal has good diving (and snorkeling) right at your doorstep. **Aquatech Villas DeRosa** (tel. 984/875-9020, U.S. tel. 866/619-9050, www.cenotes.com) is a full-service dive shop operated at the Villas DeRosa hotel, offering a complete range of dives and courses, but specializing in cenote and cave diving. Reef dives run US$40 for one tank, US$60 for two; cenote dives are US$65 one tank, US$120 for two; open-water certification is US$350; and a cavern diving specialty course US$650 private, US$440 per person in groups. Equipment is included in courses, but not fun dives (US$35 per day for a full set). Multi-dive packages, night dives, and even fishing are also available.

Snorkeling

Laguna Yal-Ku (see *Sights*) is a favorite among many snorkelers for its large area, calm water, and unique mix of fresh- and saltwater ecosystems. Look for several modern sculptures standing somewhat incongruously along the lagoon's edges.

The northern end of **Akumal Bay** also makes for fine snorkeling and you can wade in right from the beach. It's a great little nook of fairly shallow water, where tropical fish dart about a labyrinth of rocks, boulder coral, and plant life. Fishing boats do not pass through here (another reason it's good for snorkeling), but you should be careful not to drift out of the area and into boat channels. Many snorkelers make their way toward the large buoy at the edge of the bay, not realizing it marks a channel that boats use to get through the reef. Be smart and steer clear. Half Moon Bay has some good shore snorkeling as well.

You can **rent snorkel gear** at any of Akumal's dive shops for around US$10 a day or US$50 a week. Rentals at Yal-Ku cost US$14 and can only be used on-site. The dive shops also offer **guided snorkel tours,** which vary from 1–3 hours, depending on the number of sites you visit, and cost US$10–40 per person, including gear.

Sailing

Akumal Dive Shop offers a popular Robinson Crusoe cruise: a five-hour excursion on a catamaran sailboat, with stops for fishing and snorkeling (US$65 including lunch and equipment). Or try the two-hour Sunset Cruise, which doesn't include fishing and snorkeling, but offers beautiful evening views of the bay.

Sport Fishing

All three dive shops offer fishing tours for US$90–120 per boat (US$30–50/hr. extra, 1–4 passengers) including equipment and beverages. Fishing is excellent year-round, but the best months for trolling are April–June when sailfish and marlin are most numerous and active.

Body Work

In a breezy upstairs studio in the archway to town, **Yoga en Akumal** (tel. 984/875-9114, www.yoga-in-akumal.com) offers hatha, hatha flow, and anusana classes, for all experience levels. Sessions are 90 minutes and cost US$15 per class, US$75 for a two-week pass, or US$125 for a month.

Peak Gym (Plaza Ukana, 1st Fl., tel. 984/ 875-9208, 8 A.M.–7 P.M. Mon.–Sat.) has a small air-conditioned exercise space that's crammed with free weights and machines. Stationary bikes are the only cardio option—no Stairmaster or elliptical, unfortunately. Day passes cost US$10, 3-day passes US$27, weekly rates rise to US$46, and the monthly membership is US$60.

For a breezy outdoor massage, try **Massage by Salvador** (Plaza Ukana, 2nd Fl., no phone, Mon.–Sat., US$65/hour). Salvador speaks English and has two weeks' worth of sign-up sheets outside his door; just stop by and sign up for an appointment.

ACCOMMODATIONS

Akumal's hotel prices tend to run in the high range. There are numerous condos and villas for rent around the bend at Half Moon Bay, and south of town in Aventuras Akumal; at the right time and shared among several people, these can turn out to be reasonably affordable. Backpackers might snag a dorm room at CEA, but it's no sure thing.

In Town

Centro Ecológico Akumal (see *Sights*) has several large comfortable dorms—most even have air-conditioning—and a well-stocked communal kitchen. CEA's volunteers have priority for the rooms, and they are usually full, but if not they're available to walk-ins for US$15 a night. A long shot, but definitely worth asking.

Hotel Club Akumal Caribe (reception in the arches at the entrance to town, tel. 915/584-3552, U.S. 800/351-1622, Canada tel. 800/343-1440, www.hotelakumalcaribe.com, US$123 s/d bungalow with a/c, US$156 s/d room with a/c) was the first hotel in Akumal, when it was used by members of a local diving and conservation club. The bungalows sorely need a remodel, but are roomy and affordable—popular with families. The ocean-

front hotels are much more appealing, with whitewashed walls, air-conditioning, refrigerator, and private balcony; some have kitchenettes. The main complaint here is the beds, some of which are rock hard. In front, there is a well-kempt swimming pool and beyond that, a palm-tree-laden beach. A good restaurant, pizzeria, private beach area, and a full-service dive shop also are on-site.

On the eastern end of the beach in town, **Las Casitas Akumal** (tel. 984/875-9071, toll-free U.S./Can. tel. 800/525-8625, www .lascasitasakumal.com) has 18 airy, furnished condominiums with two bedrooms, two baths, living room, fully equipped kitchen, and private patio. Some have two floors and space for six people; all have ocean views and direct access to a semiprivate section of the beach. High season rates range US$210–385 per night; holidays are more while rates drop significantly in May, September, and October. Reservations must be made for a minimum of seven nights and begin on a Saturday.

Half Moon Bay

Spacious one-, two-, and three- bedroom condominiums greet you at the 🌀 **Vista del Mar** (tel. 984/875-9060, toll-free U.S. tel. 888/425-8625; www.akumalinfo.com, US$101–123 s/d with a/c, US$207–224 one bedroom condo with a/c, US$207–247 two bedroom condo with a/c, US$325 three bedroom condo with a/c). Located about halfway around the bay, the 15 units have glorious oceanfront views from their long balconies or porches. All have huge fully equipped kitchens, living rooms with flat-screen TVs, dining rooms, and master bedrooms with king-size beds. Mexican decor like *talavera* tiles, bright hand-woven bedspreads, and tapestries lend the place even more charm. Sixteen oceanfront hotel rooms also are on-site; small but comfortable, they're a good alternative for those on a tighter budget. All accommodations share a well-tended beach with lounge chairs and *palapa* shades.

Along Half Moon Bay's dirt road, **Hacienda de la Tortuga** (tel. 984/875-9068, www.hacienda tortuga.com) offers spacious one-bedroom

(US$150) and two-bedroom (US$200) condos, all with huge windows overlooking the Caribbean. Although each is uniquely decorated, all units have a living room, fully equipped kitchen, (at least one) full bathroom, king-size beds, and air-conditioning in the bedrooms. A nice pool and the classy Mexican restaurant, **La Lunita,** only add to the relaxed feel of the place.

Nearby **Playa Caribe** (tel. 984/875-9137, www.amc-akumal.com, US$230 one-bedroom condo with a/c, US$275 two-bedroom condo with a/c) offers a similar deal: 12 one- and two-bedroom condos with fully-equipped kitchens and spectacular ocean views, each decorated differently from the other. There also is a well-tended pool that sits overlooking the beach. The main difference here is that the units have central air-conditioning in each room and satellite TV. That, and there's no on-site restaurant.

At the north end of Akumal and just a block from Yal-Ku Lagoon, **❮ Que Onda** (Caleta Yal-Ku, tel. 984/875-9101, www.queonda akumal.com, US$79 s/d, US$146–168 suite) has seven rooms, each lovingly decorated with tile floors, beautiful fabrics, and unique works of art, and two suites, including a split-level unit with wood floors and terrific views of the Caribbean and Yal-Ku. All face a verdant garden and a pool in the middle of the property. None have air-conditioning; the first-floor units can get a bit stuffy—the fans help—while upstairs rooms have terraces and sea breezes. Use of bicycles and snorkel gear are included in the rates—a big plus—and guests get 50 percent off admission to Laguna Yal-Ku. The Italian restaurant here can get busy.

Aventuras Akumal

Villas DeRosa (tel. 984/875-9020, U.S. tel. 866/619-9050, www.cenotes.com, US$79 s/d, US$150 one bedroom, US$207 two bedroom, US$263 three bedroom) offers hotel rooms with garden views, and one-, two-, and three-bedroom condominiums with ocean views and private balconies. The spacious accommodations have air-conditioning, cable TV, wireless Internet, stereos, and fully equipped kitchens

(in the condos). The bedrooms can feel a bit dark, but you're literally steps from a beautiful beach and the blue Caribbean water. The resort boasts a full-service dive shop, with a special emphasis on cenote diving; dive/accommodation packages available. Prices vary significantly depending on the season; call ahead.

Smaller and cozier than the DeRosa, **❮ Villa Las Brisas** (tel. 984/875-9263, www.lasbrisas akumal.icimx.com, US$90 s/d, US$101 studio, US$151 one-bedroom condo, US$213 two-bedroom condo) has just three units (two of which can be combined to make the two-bedroom condo), all spacious, spotless, and meticulously furnished, down to a stocked spice rack in the kitchen. Opened in 1998, the condos have large terraces with hammocks and stunning views; the smaller units have balconies that overlook a tidy garden. With comfortable beds, modern Mexican-style furnishings, and room to stretch out in, it's easy to feel at home here. Families are very welcome. Beach chairs and umbrellas are free, snorkel gear can be rented (US$5 per day), and there's a simple mini-mart at the entrance (8 A.M.–4 P.M. Mon–Sat.).

Rental Properties

The great majority of rooms for rent in Akumal are in privately owned homes along Half Moon Bay. For information and online listings, contact **Caribbean Fantasy** (U.S. tel. 800/523-6618, www.caribbfan.com), **Akumal Villas** (U.S. tel. 678/528-1775, www.akumalvillas.com), or **Loco Gringo** (www.locogringo.com). For retail and some rentals, stop by the office of **Akumal Real Estate** (entrance to town, tel. 984/875-9064, www.akumalrealestate.com, 9 A.M.–7 P.M. Mon.–Fri. and 9 A.M.–3 P.M. Sat.).

FOOD
In Town

Maya for "water lily," **❮ Lol Ha** (on the beach, tel. 984/875-9013, 7:30–11 A.M. and 6:30–10 P.M. daily, closed Oct.–mid-Nov., US$12–30) is Akumal's finest restaurant, easily living up to the class its name suggests. The beautiful wood and stucco dining room is topped with a high *palapa* roof and opens onto a pleasant veranda for outdoor dining. Expect excellent seafood and Mexican and American specialties, including prime USDA steaks, sushi-grade ahi tuna, and flambé specials prepared tableside. At breakfast, a basket of homemade sweet rolls comes immediately when you sit down, and the orange juice is freshly squeezed. The restaurant hosts Mexican folk dance performances on Mondays, flamenco on Wednesday, and jazz on Friday—a US$3 per person cover is added to the bill. For something especially romantic, ask about arranging a private dinner on the beach. Reservations strongly recommended, especially if you want to be on the veranda or by the window (though the views are nice throughout).

Next door to the mother restaurant, and nearly as big, **Snack Bar Lol Ha** (11:30 A.M.– 8 P.M. daily, US$8–13) serves the best hamburgers on the beach, and tasty *tacos de cochinita,* a fusion of Maya flavor and Mexican packaging. Three 32-inch TVs always have a sporting event on, whether Monday Night Football, March Madness, or the Kentucky Derby. Hundreds of people turn out for the annual Academy Awards and Super Bowl parties (proceeds of which go to local community groups). Kids will love the adjacent game room, with air hockey and Foosball.

For a fresh, healthy meal, try **Imelda Ecococina** (no phone, 8 A.M.–3 P.M. daily, US$3–6) next to Centro Ecológico Akumal. Breakfast options include eggs, omelets, pancakes, French toast, and more. For lunch, the *comida corrida* comes with a choice of main plate and a side dish or two. On Mondays and Thursdays the restaurant hosts a popular Maya buffet (US$20; 7 P.M.) followed by *cumbia* tunes and dancing.

In Plaza Ukana, **⟨ Turtle Bay Café & Bakery** (tel. 984/875-9138, 7 A.M.–3 P.M. daily, 6–9 P.M. Wed.–Sat., US$5–18) offers scrumptious creations such as grilled portabella mushroom burgers, achiote chicken, and summer burritos. For breakfast, think French toast, eggs Benedict, fruit plate with yogurt and granola. Enjoy your meal surrounded by palm trees, either in the outdoor *palapa*-roofed dining room or on the porch of the main building.

For fresh seafood, check out **La Cueva del Pescador** (Plaza Ukana, tel. 984/875-9205, noon–10 P.M.daily, US$5–25). Sink your teeth into fish kabobs, shrimp prepared nine different ways (e.g., grilled, à la tequila, with curry salsa, and so on), and lobster—all caught the day that you order it. The bar is an especially popular stop on weekends.

For groceries, the best prices are across from the Akumal turnoff on Highway 307 in **Super Express Mar Caribe** (7 A.M.–11 P.M. daily); look for the store about 100 meters (328 feet) west of the highway. Otherwise, just outside the arch, **Super Chomak** and **Mini Super Las Palmas** (both 7 A.M.–9 P.M. daily) charge an arm and a leg for canned and dried food, soups and pastas, fresh and packaged meat, and other basics like sunscreen, booze, and film. The former has a larger selection, the latter is slightly cheaper. Both also sell fresh fruit and veggies, but you may find a better selection at the **farmers market** held Wednesdays and Saturdays in Plaza Ukana.

Half Moon Bay

A fantastic flying serpent skeleton greets you at the beachfront **La Buena Vida** (tel. 984/875-9061, 10 A.M.–11 P.M.daily, US$6–26) where clients enjoy the varied menu—from hamburgers to shrimp ceviche—under *palapa*-shaded tables. If you've already had lunch, consider just stopping in for a drink at the…er, swing bar, where swings line the sand-floored bar. Try the specialty—La Buena Vida—a smooth combo of Baileys, Kahlua, rum, coconut cream, and Grand Marnier; happy hour typically runs from 5–7 P.M. Next door, its sister restaurant, the brightly painted **Mango Café** (6 A.M.–noon daily) serves up a good variety of breakfasts on the beach. Look for both restaurants just before the Vista del Mar condominiums.

Right on the Caribbean, **La Lunita** (Hacienda de la Tortuga, tel. 984/875-9068, 5–10 P.M. Mon.–Sat., US$8–23) is a classy, intimate bistro serving gourmet Mexican and Maya specialties. Seafood is king here, though there are plenty of options for vegetarians and serious meat eaters. With only a handful of tables, La Lunita is a perfect place for a romantic dinner—just be sure to make reservations. Located on the ground floor of the Hacienda de la Tortuga.

If you're in the mood for Italian, try the open-air restaurant at the hotel **Que Onda** (4–10 P.M. daily except Tue., US$7–18). The homemade linguine comes with a wide choice of sauces, from gorgonzola to curry shrimp. The lasagna is famously tasty, though a bit pricey. For dessert, try the chocolate mousse.

INFORMATION AND SERVICES
Tourist Information
Akumal doesn't have an official tourist office, but it's a small town and you can probably find what you're looking for by asking the first person you see. If that fails, the folks at Centro Ecológico Akumal are friendly, well informed, and most speak English.

Hospitals
For an English-speaking physician, call or stop by the offices of general practitioner **Dr. Néstor Mendoza Gutiérrez** (Plaza Ukana, tel. 984/875-4051, 8 A.M.–4 P.M. Mon.–Sat., after-hours emergencies 044-984/806-4616). For major medical matters, head to Playa del Carmen.

Police
The police can be reached by calling 060 from any public phone.

Money
There is an ATM in Super Chomak grocery store, just outside the arch.

Internet and Telephone
Cyber Akumal (Plaza Ukana, tel. 984/875-9313, 7 A.M.–1 P.M. daily) is just past the arches as you enter town. Internet is fast, but runs a hefty US$0.10 a minute. From 9 P.M. to closing, it's US$6 for as much time as you like. Telephone calls to the United States and Can-

ada run US$0.55 a minute, or US$0.30 a minute after 9 P.M.

For much more reasonable Internet rates, head to the other side of Highway 307. Directly across from the turnoff to Akumal is a small community where a no-name **Internet café** (7 A.M.–9 P.M. daily) charges US$1.75 per hour. Look for it on the town's main road, about 150 meters (492 feet) from the highway.

Post Office
The post office (9:30 A.M.–3 P.M. Tues. and Thurs. only) is inside the Centro Ecológico Akumal, in the center of town.

Launderette
Next to the Mini Super Las Palmas, **Lavandería Mulgrew** (7 A.M.–1 P.M. and 5–7 P.M. Mon.–Sat.) charges US$1.60 a kilogram (2.2 pounds) and will provide same-day service if you drop off your load before 8 A.M.; two-kilogram (4.4-pound) minimum.

GETTING THERE AND AROUND
Having a car or bike will make getting to and around Akumal much easier. Vans and second-class buses stop at the Akumal turnoff, but it's a one kilometer (0.6 mile) walk into town. Likewise, you can manage the center area by foot, but walking to and from Half Moon Bay can be long, hot, and dusty. Many guests rent a car for their entire stay—which let's you take day trips as well—while the condo-hotel **Vista del Mar** (Half Moon Bay, tel. 984/875-9060) rents decent bikes for US$1 per hour, US$6 per day, and US$30 per week.

Taxis gather near the Super Chomak grocery store at the entrance of town, just outside of the arches. A ride from town to Laguna Yal-Ku costs US$2.50.

For Aventuras Akumal, the access road is south of the main Akumal entrance, and it's about 500 meters (0.3 mile) into the community. Look for the sign to Hotel Villas DeRosa, as the community itself isn't well signed.

Tankah Tres

Tucked innocuously between Tulum and Akumal, Tankah Tres sees only a fraction of the tourist traffic that its better-known neighbors do. But that's just the way visitors to this little stretch of coastline prefer it, enjoying excellent snorkeling, diving, and pretty (if not spectacular) beaches, with a sense of isolation that's hard to find in these parts. The area has three small bays, and the scattered hotels, villas, and private homes along their shores were once connected (together and to the highway) by a U-shaped access road. But new development cut the U right in half; the southern entrance is still marked Tankah Tres, while the northern entrance has a sign for Oscar y Lalo restaurant and *Bahías de Punta Soliman*. You have to return to the highway to get from one side to the other.

SIGHTS

The three bays that make up Tankah Tres have fine snorkeling, diving, and kayaking. Add to that a pleasant beach and relatively few tourists,

and this becomes one of the better places on the Riviera Maya to spend a relaxing beach day.

Playa Tankah

Casa Cenote hotel fronts a pretty little beach, which non-guests are free to use if you order something at the restaurant.

Cenote Tankah

Across from Casa Cenote hotel, its namesake Cenote Tankah (no admission) forms a large lagoon perfect for snorkeling. The cenote's winding channels have crystal-clear water and a tangle of rocks, trees, and freshwater plants along their edges and bottoms. Look for schools of tiny fish near the surface, and some bigger ones farther down.

SCUBA DIVING AND SNORKELING

Run by a young American and based at the Tankah Inn, **Lucky Fish Diving** (tel. 044-984/129-6774, www.luckyfishdiving.com,

© LIZA PRADO
Small inlets and a healthy reef make snorkeling off of Playa Tankah a highlight of any trip.

8:30 A.M.–6 P.M. and 9 A.M.–4 P.M. Sun.) is a small friendly shop offering personalized dive trips and instruction. Dive sites here get substantially less traffic than at nearby Akumal, but offer the same spectacular coral and sealife: "Mountains of the Moon" is a favorite, with huge coral mounds rising from 12 meters (40 feet) nearly to the surface. And no dive site is more than 10 minutes away by boat. Reef dives cost US$40 for one tank, US$75 for two, while cenote dives are US$60 for one tank and US$100 for two; all equipment and entrance fees are included. The shop also rents snorkel gear for US$7.50 a day, but it can be hard to find the best sections of reef; you'll have more fun on a guided trip (US$20 pp, 2.5 hours), hitting three different spots.

The restaurant **Oscar y Lalo** also rents snorkel gear (US$4.75/day) and kayaks (US$7.50/hour) and sometimes arranges snorkel and kayaking tours into the lagoon that extends behind the property.

ACCOMMODATIONS

The northern entrance to Tankah Tres extends almost to the beach before forking; to the left is **Oscar y Lalo** (tel. 984/804-4189) a restaurant and campsite on an isolated palm tree–lined beach. Here, you can set up a tent among the coconut trees for US$5 per person and feel, if only for a night or two, that you are on a idyllic deserted island (that happens to have a bathroom with running water, of course). When the restaurant closes at 8 P.M., the place is yours, starry night and all. Be sure to bring mosquito nets in the rainy season.

Five spacious rooms with murals of Maya temples make up the ◖ **Tankah Inn** (southern entrance, 1.1 km/0.6 mi from the turnoff, U.S. tel. 918/582-3743, www.tankah.com, US$124 s/d with a/c). Right on the beach, each room has tile floors, a private terrace, and ocean views; all come equipped with five-gallon jugs of water and remote-controlled air-conditioning. A breezy common room has sweeping views of the Caribbean—comfy chairs and tables, a stereo, lots of board games, and an honor bar make this a popular area to hang out though the beach, with its lounge chairs and hammocks, is a tempting alternative. A full breakfast is included as is wireless Internet and the use of sea kayaks. There's also a dive shop on the premises. A perfect place to hole up for a few days or more.

Casa Cenote (southern entrance, 1.5 km/0.9 mi from the turnoff, tel. 998/874-5170, www.casacenote.com, US$150 s/d) was for many years the only life on this stretch of beach; more hotels have popped up, but this remains a favorite of old-timers and newcomers alike. All seven rooms have a/c, one or two large beds, wireless Internet and a stucco relief of Maya gods in each. A glass door opens onto a small patio with fine ocean views. The hotel built a new pool after Hurricane Wilma, and Cenote Tankah is just across the street. The hotel does its part for the earth by collecting rainwater and using natural wastewater processing. Breakfast is included.

Blue Sky Hotel (southern entrance, 1.7 km/1 mi from the turnoff, tel. 984/801-4004, www.blueskymexico.com, toll-free U.S. and Canada tel. 877/792-9237, US$168 s/d with a/c, US$213–258 suite with a/c) offers six breezy units with views of the Caribbean. All are modern and are decorated with Mexican flair—mostly high-end handicrafts with lots of recessed lighting. A nice pool opens onto the beach where there are plenty of toys—kayaks, boogie boards, and snorkel gear—for guests to use. Continental breakfast is included in the rate and served at the hotel's excellent *palapa* restaurant.

FOOD

Near the northern entrance to town, **Oscar y Lalo** (tel. 984/804-4189, 10 A.M.–8 P.M. daily, US$7–32) is an oceanside restaurant that serves excellent fresh seafood. All dishes come with fried banana, french fries, beans, and rice. Main dishes are definitely pricey—4–6 person specials run US$20–30 per person—but the view and the monster portions more than make up for it.

The restaurant at **Casa Cenote** (southern entrance, 2 km/1.25 mi from the turnoff, tel. 998/874-5170, www.casacenote.com, 8 A.M.–

9 p.m. daily, US$5–15) has a breezy patio dining area just steps from the sea's edge. You can order beach food such as quesadillas or a guacamole plate, or something heftier—the seafood is always tasty and fresh. Every Sunday at noon, the hotel hosts an awesome Texas-style barbecue, which is popular with locals and expats up and down the Riviera Maya. All settle in for an afternoon spent over heaping plates of great food and boisterous conversation. The regular menu includes fajitas, grilled fish, burgers, nachos, and more.

Worth treating yourself, the 【 **Blue Sky** (Blue Sky Hotel, southern entrance, 1.7 km/ 1 mi from the turnoff, tel. 984/801-4004, 8–10 a.m., noon–4 p.m., and 4–10 p.m. daily, US$5–24) offers delicious Italian and Mexican specialties. Dishes are prepared to order and the presentation is beautiful—try the grilled

calamari with vegetables, a simple meal that you'll remember long after you've gone home. With only a handful of tables, this is a perfect place for an intimate dinner. Just be sure to call for a reservation or arrive early.

INFORMATION AND SERVICES

There are no formal services here because it's not really a formal town. Head to Tulum for ATMs, medical services, Internet, groceries, and so on.

GETTING THERE AND AROUND

Arriving by car is definitely the best option—look for the Oscar y Lalo or Tankah Tres signs, depending on which part you want to go to. By bus, get off at either turnoff and start walking.

THE RIVIERA MAYA

TULUM AND SOUTHERN QUINTANA ROO

Set on a bluff overlooking the turquoise waters of the Caribbean Sea are the small but impressive ruins of Tulum. They represent a bridge between the bustling Riviera Maya and the state's decidedly less-traveled southern coast. Tulum is justly famous for its spectacular string of beaches and bohemian chic cabañas, but southern Quintana Roo holds even more: the pristine Sian Ka'an Biosphere Reserve; miles of deserted coastline; quiet fishing villages; rustic beaches; and eco-friendly B&Bs along the Costa Maya; the Caribbean-like colors of Laguna Bacalar; and Chetumal, the busy state capital and gateway to Belize. Take a few days (or weeks) to explore the region. You may find that Tulum and Southern Quintana Roo are just what you've been searching for:

untouched seascape, tropical wildlife, and an easy Caribbean dream that seems to exist just for you.

PLANNING YOUR TIME

Tulum is the first stop, of course, and for many people their main destination in this area. If you can tear yourself from the beach, the Sian Ka'an Reserve makes a great day or overnight trip. Farther south, you'll probably want a rental car as bus service is significantly less frequent. The seaside towns of Mahahual and Xcalak are great places to spend three or more days snorkeling, kayaking, and catching up on summer reading. Laguna Bacalar is worth a day or two, time enough to take a boat trip on the Caribbean-like water, swim in Cenote Azul, and visit the surprisingly good

© LIZA PRADO

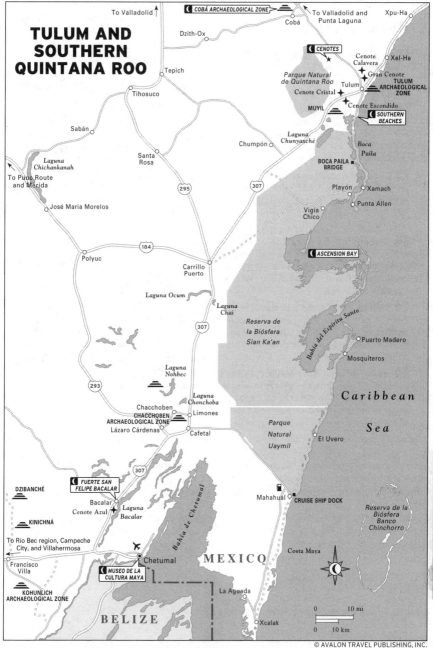

TULUM AND SOUTHERN QUINTANA ROO

To Valladolid

COBÁ ARCHAEOLOGICAL ZONE

Cobá

To Valladolid and Punta Laguna

Xpu-Ha

Dzith-Ox

CENOTES

Cenote Calavera

Xel-Ha

Tepich

Parque Natural de Quintana Roo

Tulum

Gran Cenote

TULUM ARCHAEOLOGICAL ZONE

Tihosuco

Cenote Cristal

MUYIL

Cenote Escondido

SOUTHERN BEACHES

Sabán

Laguna Chunyaxché

Chumpón

Boca Paila

Laguna Chichankanah

Santa Rosa

BOCA PAILA BRIDGE

To Puuc Route and Mérida

José Maria Morelos

Playón

Xamach

295

307

Vigía Chico

Punta Allen

184

Polyuc

Carrillo Puerto

ASCENSION BAY

Laguna Ocum

Laguna Chai

307

Reserva de la Biósfera Sian Ka'an

Bahía del Espíritu Santo

Puerto Madero

Mosquiteros

293

Laguna Nohbec

Laguna Chonchoba

C a r i b b e a n

Chacchoben

Limones

CHACCHOBEN ARCHAEOLOGICAL ZONE

Lázaro Cárdenas

Cafetal

S e a

Parque Natural Uaymil

El Uvero

307

DZIBANCHÉ

FUERTE SAN FELIPE BACALAR

Mahahual

CRUISE SHIP DOCK

Reserva de la Biósfera Banco Chinchorro

KINICHNÁ

Bacalar

Cenote Azul

Laguna Bacalar

Bahía de Chetumal

To Río Bec region, Campeche City, and Villahermosa

Francisco Villa

Chetumal

M E X I C O

Costa Maya

MUSEO DE LA CULTURA MAYA

KOHUNLICH ARCHAEOLOGICAL ZONE

La Aguada

0   10 mi

0   10 km

B E L I Z E

Xcalac

© AVALON TRAVEL PUBLISHING, INC.

TULUM AND QUINTANA ROO

HIGHLIGHTS

⊂ Tulum's Southern Beaches: Beaches like these – the white sand, the azure water, and the softly bending palms – are the reason you came to the Caribbean in the first place (page 185).

⊂ Cenotes near Tulum: Explore an unforgettable realm of crystal-clear water and eerily beautiful stalagmites and stalactites in the world's longest underground river system (page 186).

⊂ Cobá Archaeological Zone: Less than an hour from Tulum, Cobá boasts the peninsula's second-highest pyramid and is surrounded by a forest teeming with birds instead of tourists (page 199).

⊂ Ascension Bay: A huge untouched expanse of calm ocean flats and tangled mangrove forests make this a world-class destination for birders, anglers, and everyday travelers (page 203).

⊂ Fuerte San Felipe Bacalar: The museum in this star-shaped fort has excellent exhibits on piracy and the Caste War, plus it overlooks a lagoon the Maya called "Lake of Seven Colors" (page 220).

⊂ Museo de la Cultura Maya: Chetumal's phenomenal museum mirrors Maya cosmology with three levels of excellent exhibits on the religion, astronomy, writing, artwork, and daily life of ancient Mayas (page 224).

LOOK FOR ⊂ TO FIND RECOMMENDED SIGHTS, ACTIVITIES, DINING, AND LODGING.

piracy museum in town. Chetumal can be a logical stopover for those headed west toward the Río Bec region or crossing into Belize. But as a destination, Chetumal is far down the totem pole, and wouldn't rank at all but for the superb Maya museum there.

Tulum

Tulum has long captured the imagination of independent, beach-loving travelers. Maya ruins overlooking turquoise seas and picturesque cabañas set on deserted beaches were (and still are) the ideal anti-Cancún. Tulum has definitely grown and changed, but travelers of all sorts can still enjoy its remarkable natural beauty and isolated charm.

DECIPHERING THE GLYPHS

Mayanist and scholar Michael D. Coe's *Breaking the Maya Code* (Thames and Hudson, 1992) is a fascinating account of the decipherment of Maya writing.

For many years, scholars could not agree whether Maya writing contained anything more than numbers and dates. Many thought the text was not "real writing" as it did not appear to reproduce spoken language. Even those who believed the writing to be more meaningful despaired at ever reading it.

In 1952, Russian scholar Yuri Valentinovich Knorosov jump-started Maya scholarship by showing that Maya writing did in fact convey spoken words. Using a rough alphabet recorded by Fray Diego de Landa (the 16th-century bishop who, ironically, is best known for having destroyed numerous Maya texts), Knorosov showed that ancient texts contain common Yucatec words such as *cutz* (turkey) and *tzul* (dog). Interestingly, Knorosov conducted his research from reproductions only, having never held a Maya artifact or visited an ancient temple. When he did finally visit Tikal in 1990, Coe writes, Knorosov wasn't very impressed.

By the mid-1980s decipherment picked up speed. One of many standouts from that era is David Stuart, the son of Maya experts, who went to Cobá with his parents at age eight and passed the time copying glyphs and learning Yucatec words from local playmates. In high school he served as chief epigrapher on a groundbreaking exploration in Belize, and at age 18 he received a US$128,000 MacArthur Fellowship to, as he told Michael Coe, "play around with the glyphs" full-time.

Researchers now know that Maya writing is like most other hieroglyphic systems. What appears at first to be a single glyph can have up to four parts, and the same word can be expressed in pictorial, phonetic, or hybrid form. Depending on context, one symbol can have either a pictorial or phonetic role; likewise, a particular sound can be represented in more than one way. The word cacao is spelled phonetically as "ca-ca-u" but is written with a picture of a fish (*ca*) and a comblike symbol (also *ca*, according to Landa) and followed by -u. One of David Stuart's great insights was that for all its complexity, much of Maya glyphic writing is "just repetitive."

But how do we know what the symbols are meant to sound like in the first place? Some come from the Landa alphabet, others are suggested by the pictures that accompany many texts, still others from patterns derived by linguistic analyses of contemporary Maya languages. In some cases, it is simply a hunch that, after applying it to a number of texts, turns out to be right. If this seems like somewhat shaky scientific ground, it is – but not without a means of being proved. The cacao decipherment was confirmed when the same glyph was found on a jar with chocolate residue still inside.

Hundreds of glyphs have been deciphered and most of the known Maya texts can be reliably translated. The effort has lent invaluable insight into Maya civilization, especially dynastic successions and religious beliefs. Some archaeologists lament, not entirely without reason, that high-profile glyphic studies have diverted attention from research into the lives of ordinary ancient Maya people. Without question, there is much to be learned on that front. But it is hard not to marvel at how one of the world's great ancient civilizations is revealed in the whorls and creases of fading stone pictures.

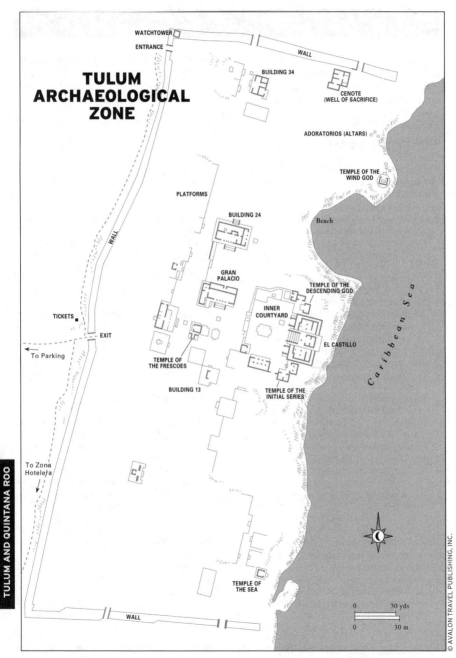

WATCHTOWER

ENTRANCE

WALL

TULUM ARCHAEOLOGICAL ZONE

BUILDING 34

CENOTE
(WELL OF SACRIFICE)

ADORATORIOS (ALTARS)

TEMPLE OF THE
WIND GOD

PLATFORMS

BUILDING 24

Beach

GRAN
PALACIO

TEMPLE OF THE
DESCENDING GOD

INNER
COURTYARD

TICKETS

EXIT

To Parking

TEMPLE OF
THE FRESCOES

EL CASTILLO

Caribbean Sea

BUILDING 13

TEMPLE OF THE
INITIAL SERIES

To Zona
Hotelera

TEMPLE OF
THE SEA

WALL

0   30 yds

0   30 m

© AVALON TRAVEL PUBLISHING, INC.

Tulum has three distinct parts. The Tulum ruins are the popular Maya temples. Tulum Pueblo (literally, Tulum Town) is south and inland from the ruins. And the Zona Hotelera (Hotel Zone) hugs the coast from the ruins to the entrance to the Sian Ka'an Biosphere Reserve.

The Zona Hotelera used to be a haven for backpackers and bohemians, with simple cabañas facing beautiful untouched beaches. The beaches are still beautiful, but the prices have long since gone through the *palapa* roof, catering more to urban escapists and upscale yoga groups. It's still a lovely place to stay, no matter who you are, just not as cheap as it used to be.

Tulum Pueblo used to be quite dumpy, but now has many small cafés, cool restaurants, and more and better hotels, as travelers who are priced out of the Zona Hotelera choose to stay there and go to the beach by day. A beachside cabaña will always be the most appealing place to stay, of course, but staying in town is no longer the huge step down that it was.

TULUM ARCHAEOLOGICAL ZONE

Perched on a cliff 12 meters (40 feet) above the turquoise Caribbean waters, Tulum (8 A.M.–5 P.M. daily, US$4.25) is justly the subject of thousands of postcards and is one of Mexico's best-known archaeological sites. While the structures themselves lack the grandeur of ruins in the interior, they are still interesting and well worth a visit.

The most important advice regarding Tulum is **get there early.** Thousands of package tourists arrive daily by bus from resorts in Cancún and Playa del Carmen; it used to be that the crush didn't begin until 11 A.M., but it creeps earlier and earlier every year. Still, if you're there right at 8 A.M., you'll have a good hour before the hoards descend; there is sometimes a lull 1:30 P.M.–2:30 P.M. as well. Consider wearing your swimsuit and bringing a towel—this may be the only Maya ruin with a great little beach right inside the archaeological zone.

History

Tulum was part of a series of Maya forts, watch-towers, and ports established along the coast as far south as Chetumal and north past Cancún. Its original Maya name was Zama (Sunrise) but was changed to Tulum (Wall), almost certainly in reference to the thick stone barrier that encloses the city's 60 main structures. Measuring 380 by 165 meters (1,247 by 541 feet), it's the largest fortified Maya site on the Quintana Roo coast, although small compared to most archaeological zones.

Tulum's enviable patch of seashore was settled as early as 300 B.C., but it remained little more than a village for most of its existence, overshadowed by the Maya city of Tankah, a few kilometers to the north. However, Tulum experienced a boom around A.D. 1200, during which time most of its main structures were built. These exhibit strong influences from the reigning power of that time, Mayapán. Around A.D. 1440, the influence of central Mexican civilizations grew, as it did across the Yucatán Peninsula. Strangely, the structures built during that time were of rather shoddy construction, so Tulum's temples are much more decayed than structures at other sites, built hundreds of years prior.

The Spanish got their first view of the then brightly colored fortress when Juan de Grijalva's expedition sailed past the Quintana Roo coast in 1518. This was also the Spaniards' first encounter with the indigenous people of the new continent, and according to ships' logs, the image was awe-inspiring. One notable entry describes "a village so large, that Seville would not have appeared larger or better." The city remained an important port well into the conquest, but was abandoned when European diseases decimated its population.

Visiting the Ruins

The Tulum ruins are made up of mostly small, ornate structures with stuccoed gargoyle faces carved onto their corners. By far the site's most impressive structure is **El Castillo** (The Castle), a large pyramid standing on the edge of a 12-meter (39-foot) limestone cliff overlooking the sea. The building was constructed in three different phases. A wide staircase leads to a two-chamber temple at the top; visitors are

TULUM AND QUINTANA ROO

© LIZA PRADO

A spectacular setting, Tulum ruins has a nice little beach – perfect for cooling off after exploring the site.

no longer allowed to climb this stairway, but the view from the hill on which the Castillo stands encompasses the sea, the surrounding jungle (with an occasional stone ruin poking through the tight brush), and scattered clearings where small farms are sprouting.

In the **Temple of the Frescoes,** looking through a metal grate you'll see a fresco that still bears a trace of color from the ancient artist. Archaeologically, this is the most interesting building on the site. The original parts of the building were constructed around 1450 during the late Postclassic period, and as is the case with so many Maya structures, it was added to over the years.

Across the compound, the small off-kilter **Temple of the Descending God** has a *palapa*-cover to protect a carving of an upside-down winged creature on the main lintel. The name is purely descriptive. Some archaeologists believe the carving depicts the God of the Setting Sun, while others say it represents the bee; in pre-Hispanic times, honey was revered and valued almost as much as maize.

Practicalities

Tulum's massive parking lot and strip mall–like visitors center ought to clue you in to the number of tourists that pass through here every day. (Did we mention to get here early?) You'll find a small museum and bookshop amid innumerable souvenir shops, fast food restaurants, and ATM machines that give U.S. dollars instead of pesos. Don't let the scene here turn you off to all Maya ruins—even Chichén Itzá is less commercialized, and most sites are not at all.

The site entrance and ticket booth are about one kilometer (0.6 mile) from the visitors center; if you don't feel like walking, a **trolley** ferries guests there and back for US$2 per person (kids under 10 ride free). Professional bilingual guides can be hired at the entrance for around US$33.

Getting There

Tulum ruins are seven kilometers (4.5 miles) south of Akumal on Highway 307. Arriving by bus or *combi,* be sure to ask the driver to let you off at *las ruínas* as opposed to the town, which is

© LIZA PRADO

Tulum's southern beaches are classic Caribbean – powdery sand and turquoise waters that are seemingly endless.

another 1.5 kilometers (one mile) south. To return, vans may be waiting near the site exit; otherwise flag a bus or van down on the highway. They pass frequently well after the ruins have closed. If you're driving, parking is US$2.50.

OTHER SIGHTS
Northern Beaches

The area north of the turnoff has two easy-to-reach beach areas that are ideal for people staying in town, at least for now: Most of this beautiful stretch of sand—right up to the ruins, in fact—was bought by the developers of The Tides, a huge condominium complex in Playa del Carmen. Plans to build condos had to be scrapped, thankfully, because of environmental laws against high-density development here. But it may be inevitable that this area sees the construction of high-end bungalows, which will be delightful for guests but will make getting to the beach as an ordinary traveler more and more tricky.

Nuddy Beach Club (tel. 984/130-0285, between La Vita Bella restaurant and Mar Caribe,

8 A.M.–6 P.M. daily, restaurant noon–6 P.M., beach bar 8 P.M.–2 A.M. Thu.–Sat.) occupies a wide beautiful stretch of sand known as Playa Paraíso. Once little more than a bar and some hammocks, the beach club has morphed into a bustling expanse of lounge chairs and umbrellas (for rent US$2–6/day), with waiters weaving between them, and a full-service water sport center offering snorkeling, diving, kiteboarding, and more. Busy but still wonderfully relaxing.

Travelers looking for less of a scene have migrated one beach north to the area known by the nearby bungalows, **Mar Caribe.** Broad and unspoiled, this is the place to come to lay out your towel or sheet on the white sand, which you share with a picturesque array of moored fishing boats. This is where backpacker shuttles operated by The Weary Traveler and Hostel Tulum come.

◖ Southern Beaches

Tulum's very best beaches—thick white sand, turquoise blue water, no one around—are toward the southern end of the hotel zone. Not

TULUM AND QUINTANA ROO

surprisingly, the most exclusive hotels are in the same area, and access to the beach can be difficult if you're not staying at one of them. That said, just south of the Zona Hotelera's mini-village there is a rocky public beach, the end of which marks the beginning of the southern beaches; from here just walk down the shore until you find a spot that fits your fancy—hotels are allowed to restrict use of their chairs and umbrellas, but the beach itself is public.

▶ Cenotes

Hidden Worlds Cenotes Park (Hwy. 307 between Tulum and Akumal, tel. 984/877-8535, www.hiddenworlds.com, 9 A.M.–5 P.M. daily) is an excellent place for first-timers to experience underground snorkeling or diving. Although sometimes crowded, Hidden Worlds earns its popularity by offering excellent tours and professional service. Snorkeling tours (US$40 pp for 2.5 hours, US$25 pp for 1.5

hours, gear included; 9 A.M., 11 A.M., 1 P.M., 2 P.M., and 3 P.M. daily, maximum 10 people/group) visit two different cenotes. You will explore huge caverns, see light beams penetrate distant pools, and (if you want) swim through channels with just a head's worth of airspace. One- and two-tank cavern dives (US$50 one tank, US$90 two tank, gear rental US$5–15, four divers maximum, 9 A.M., 11 A.M., 1 P.M. daily) also visit two cenotes and follow guidelines set by cave explorers. Exploration is ongoing—ask about Dreamgate, a stunning cavern opened to divers in September 2003. Hidden Worlds offers free hotel pickup if you're staying in or between Puerto Aventuras and Tulum. It's recommended to reserve at least a day in advance.

Just north, **Dos Ojos** (tel. 984/877-8535, 8 A.M.–5 P.M. daily) also offers guided snorkeling and dive trips. Like Hidden Worlds, it offers daily snorkeling tours (US$28 pp),

CENOTES: THEN AND NOW

One of the Yucatán Peninsula's most intriguing features is its cenotes, large freshwater sinkholes. Cenotes owe their formation to the massive meteorite that hit the Yucatán Peninsula 65 million years ago, near present-day Mérida. The impact shattered the peninsula's thick limestone cap like a stone hitting a car windshield. Over millions of years, rainwater seeped into the cracks, forming what is today the world's largest underground river system. Cenotes are former caverns whose roofs collapsed. (Cave-ins are extremely rare today, however.) Cenotes can be hundreds of meters deep and are usually filled with fresh water (occasional seawater intrusion in some cenotes forms haloclines – a bizarre and interesting sight).

Cenotes were sacred to the Mayas, who relied on them for water. They also were seen as apertures to the underworld, and sacrificial victims were sometimes thrown into their eerie depths, along with finely worked stone and clay items. Archaeologists have learned a great deal about early Maya rituals by dredging cenotes near archaeological sites.

Still revered by many Mayas, the peninsula's cenotes have attracted other worshippers: snorkelers and scuba divers. The unbelievably clear water – 100-meter (328-foot) visibility in places – attracts many underwater enthusiasts. But the real joy of snorkeling or diving here comes from the amazing stalactite and stalagmite formations. Formed in the ice age when water levels were extremely low, they were submerged in water as the climate warmed. Today, you can snorkel and dive past beautiful formations that you would walk around in a dry cave.

Divers with open-water certification can dive in the cenotes. Though "full-cave" diving requires advanced training, most cenote tours are actually "cavern" dives, meaning you are always within 40 meters (130 feet) of an air pocket. It's a good idea to take some open-water dives before your first cenote tour – buoyancy control is especially important in cenotes, and you'll be contending with different weights and finning technique.

with on-site guides leading visitors through this massive and spectacular cave system. *Dos Ojos* (Two Eyes) is a reference to the twin caverns that you can explore here. You can also snorkel independently for a small admission fee (US$7.50).

Other favorite cenotes include **Car Wash, Kolimba/Kin-Ha, Cenote Grande,** and **Calavera Cenote** (all west of Tulum on the road to Cobá); **Casa Cenote** (at Tankah Tres); **Cenote Azul** and **Cristalina** (Hwy. 307 across from Xpu-Há); and **Chaac Mol** (Hwy. 307, two km/1.2 mi north of Xpu-Há). All can be visited on a tour or by yourself, and most have snorkel gear for rent (US$6). Most are on private or *ejido* (collective) land and charge admission fees, usually US$5–8 for snorkelers and US$10 for divers. If you take a tour, ask if admission fees are included in the rate. Most cenotes are open 8 A.M.–5 P.M. daily.

Tours of Sian Ka'an Biosphere Reserve

CESiaK (Hwy. 307 just south of the Tulum ruins turnoff, tel. 984/871-2499, www.cesiak .org, 9 A.M.–2 P.M. and 4–8 P.M. daily) is a nonprofit environmental organization that offers several excellent trips into the rich Sian Ka'an Biosphere Reserve. The most popular is an all-day excursion (US$68 pp) that begins with a short introduction to the reserve and guided walk along the coastal dunes, followed by a motor boat tour of the lagoon complex and its many habitats and ecosystems (plus a remote Maya ruin), and then floating down a canal in the mangroves and snorkeling in one of the many cenotes. A sunset bird-watching tour (US$70 pp) starts in the afternoon and includes visiting (by motor boat) known nesting areas, including the aptly named Bird Island. A bird-watching tour by kayak is also available (US$45) or you can rent kayaks (US$20 single, US$30 double, three hours) and explore the lagoon yourself. Don't worry—a guide will give you tips on where to go, and how to get back! Fishing, mountain biking, and archaeological tours can also be arranged; most tours include hotel pickup,

lunch, and a bilingual guide. CESiaK also has well-recommended lodging just inside the reserve.

Sian Ka'an Ecoturismo (Av. Tulum between Calles Beta and Osiris, tel. 984/871-2363, 10 A.M.–7 P.M. Mon.–Sat.) also offers similar tours at similar prices—in fact, the two agencies used to be one. But whereas CESiaK typically enters from the Tulum-Boca Paila road, the canal tour here starts with a visit to Muyil archaeological site, south of Tulum on Highway 307, and enters the reserve from that side.

For more information on Sian Ka'an or if you want to spend more than just a few hours there, check out the *Sian Ka'an Biosphere Reserve* section later in this chapter.

SHOPPING

Mixik Artesanía Mexicana (Av. Tulum between Calles Alfa and Jupiter, tel. 984/871-2136, 9 A.M.–9 P.M. Mon.–Sat.) has a large selection of quality folk art, from green copper suns to carved wooden angels and masks, plus T-shirts, jewelry, cards, and more. There's a sister shop in the Zona Hotelera by the same name. Also in the hotel zone and near Mixik's sister store, **Joyería Studio** (Hotel Posada del Sol, tel. 984/876-6206, 8 A.M.–10 P.M. daily) sells good handmade *artesanía,* especially jewelry, from a small shop at the hotel entrance.

SPORTS AND RECREATION
Scuba Diving

The reef here is superb, but Tulum's diving claim-to-fame are the slew of freshwater cenotes and caves, all within easy reach. Divers with open-water certification can make "cavern" dives, defined as no more than 30 feet deep or 130 feet from an air pocket. (Full-cave diving requires advanced training and certification.) If you haven't dived in a while, definitely take several open-water dives before your first cenote trip, as buoyancy control is especially important in cavern environments.

Prices for cenote dives are fairly uniform among the various shops, around US$70–80 for one tank, US$120–140 for two tanks, including equipment, transportation, and entrance fees. Tulum's shops also offer multi-dive packages and cavern, intro to cave, and full-cave certification courses; they also offer snorkeling and reef diving, of course. As always, choose a shop and guide you feel comfortable with, not necessarily the least expensive one. (See *How to Choose a Dive Shop* sidebar in the *Isla Cozumel* chapter.)

The easiest introduction to cenotes is at **Hidden Worlds Cenote Park,** which runs excellent daily cavern diving (and snorkeling) trips on a private cenote system right at its shop, located a short distance north of Tulum.

Cenote Dive Center (Av. Tulum at Calle Osiris, tel. 984/871-2232, www.cenotedive .com, 8:30 A.M.–8 P.M. daily, low season closed Sun.) is affiliated with the Abyss Dive Center located by the turnoff to the Tulum ruins.

Aptly named after the Maya underworld, **Xibalba Dive Center** (Av. Tulum between Av. Satelite and the road to Zona Hotelera/Boca Paila, tel. 984/807-4579, www.xibalbadivecenter .com, 9 A.M.–7 P.M. daily) has a good reputation for safety and professionalism.

In Tulum's hotel zone, **Mexi-Divers** (Zama Hotel, 998/185-9656, mexidiverstulum@ hotmail.com, 8:30 A.M.–5 P.M. daily) in the mini-village area or **Dive Ollin** (984/876-4385, 9 A.M.–6 P.M. daily) at Playa Paraíso are both reliable operators.

Other recommended cenote-diving shops include **Aquatech** (tel. 984/875-9020, www .cenotes.com) in Aventuras Akumal and **Lucky Fish Divers** (tel. 044-984/129-6774, www .luckyfishdiving.com) in Tankah Tres, both a short distance north of Tulum.

Snorkeling
Like divers, snorkelers have an embarrassment of riches in Tulum, with great reef snorkeling and easy access to the eerie beauty of the area's many cenotes. Dive shops listed here offer snorkel trips of both sorts; reef trips cost around US$20 for a 2.5-hour trip, while cenote trips run US$30–45. Hidden Worlds is again the easiest introduction to cenotes, offering guided snorkeling tours offered several times daily.

To **rent snorkel gear** ask at any of the dive shops in town or along the beach. In the Zona Hotelera, a kiosk in front of Cabañas Punta Piedra (mini-village area, 7:30 A.M.–6:30 P.M. daily) rents snorkel gear for US$5 a day, and also offers tours.

Kiteboarding
Extreme Control (Playa Paraíso, 984/745-4555, www.extremecontrol.net, 8 A.M.–sunset daily) is based at the water sport center at Playa Paraíso and Nuddy Beach Club. Tulum's only kiteboarding outfit—for now, anyway—is run by an American-Italian couple and offers courses and rentals for all experience levels. A private full introductory class of four hours costs US$220, plus US$70 an hour for additional lessons; group classes are somewhat less. Multiday packages, including lodging at the shop's studio apartments, are a great deal if you're serious about learning and practicing the sport. Diving and specialty courses also available.

Eco-Parks
Snorkel in the ocean, snuba in a lagoon, float down a river, or swim with dolphins at **Xel-Há** (Hwy. 307, 9 km/5.6 mi north of Tulum, tel. 998/883-3293, www.xel-ha.com, 8:30 A.M.–6 P.M. daily, US$39/27 adult/child, US$59/41 adult/child including snorkel gear, meals, and beverages, US$74–88 adult including transportation, US$52–82 including transportation child). Promoted as a water lovers and marine life paradise, children and beginner snorkelers will probably list this as a highlight of their trip; others may find the waters overrun with tourists and underpopulated by fish and other sea creatures. Dolphin interaction program costs extra.

Cycling
Along with renting well-maintained bicycles, **Iguana Bike Shop** (Av. Satélite near Calle Andromeda, tel. 984/119-0836, 9 A.M.–7 P.M. Mon.–Sat.) offers mountain bike tours to snorkeling sites in various cenotes and beaches as well as turtle nesting grounds on Xcacel

beach. Prices vary depending on the tour, which typically last four hours and are limited to six cyclists.

Body Work

A holistic spa set over the beach at Copal hotel, **Maya Spa Wellness Center** (Carr. Tulum-Punta Allen Km. 5, tel. 984/871-2750, www.maya-spa.com, 8 A.M.–8 P.M. daily) offers a variety of massages (US$73–100 60 minutes, US$109–165 90 minutes), body wraps (US$79–165), and spiritual treatments like Reiki and Maya crystal therapy (US$36–73). Yoga instruction also is offered. For a full listing of offerings, check the website.

Located at the Ana y José hotel, **Om...Spa** (Carr. Tulum-Punta Allen Km. 7, tel. 998/887-5470, www.anayjose.com, 10 A.M.–6 P.M. daily) is a full-service spa set in a beachfront, ultra chic setting. Choose from a menu of massages (US$75–95) and body treatments (US$60–85); if you want a treat, ask about the Yumka Chocolate Spa (US$150, 120 minutes), which includes a chocolate body mask and a chocolate foaming bath. Just don't drink the water.

ACCOMMODATIONS

Chances are you've come to Tulum to stay in one of the famous beachside bungalow-type hotels. There are many to choose from, each slightly different, but most sharing a laid-back atmosphere and terrific beaches. However, the area has no power lines or fresh water wells, and some travelers are surprised by just how rustic some lodgings are. Even top-end hotels may have very limited nighttime lighting—or none at all, providing candles instead—and virtually all use salt water in the showers and sinks. (Air-conditioning is available in only a couple places.) At the same time, many hotels use generators to power their restaurants and reception area. Always ask for a room away from the generator but be ready to pay for it. Nothing is a bigger kill-joy than a giant diesel motor pounding outside your window, especially since the whole point of coming here is for the peace and quiet.

The Zona Hotelera has a short "northern section" (north of the turnoff to Tulum

© LIZA PRADO

Grab a book and a hammock and you're set to go in Tulum.

Pueblo) and a longer "southern section" (south of there). Addresses are designated by kilometer number, but there are no kilometer markers, so the point is moot unless you set your odometer. Both sections of the road are now paved, but you should drive slowly as there are several blind curves.

Hotels in town have improved steadily over the years, as prices on the beach make it harder for even mid-range travelers to stay there. With the beach a short cab or bike ride away, and prices for food, Internet, laundry so much lower than in the Zona Hotelera, it's not a bad option.

Under US$25
IN TOWN

Weary Traveler Hostel (Av. Tulum between Calles Jupiter and Calle Acuario, tel. 984/871-2390, www.wearytravelerhostel.com, US$11 dorm, US$28 d) is Tulum's longtime backpacker gathering spot. It operates on a largely do-it-yourself basis: breakfast is whatever you feel like making from the eggs, bread, pancake

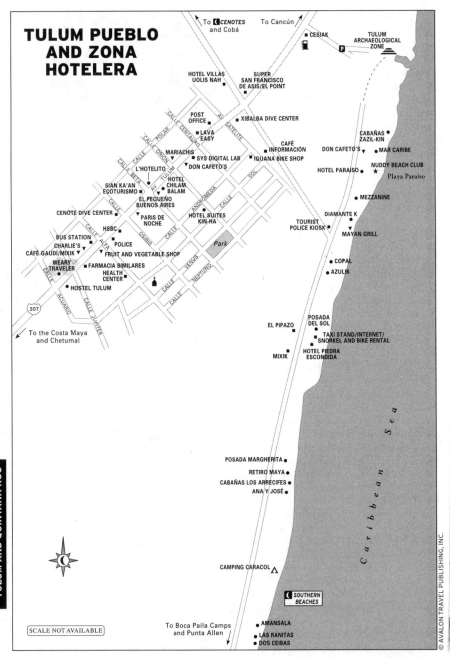

TULUM PUEBLO AND ZONA HOTELERA

To **CENOTES** and Cobá

To Cancún

CESIAK

TULUM ARCHAEOLOGICAL ZONE

HOTEL VILLAS UOLIS NAH

SUPER SAN FRANCISCO DE ASÍS/EL POINT

POST OFFICE

XIBALBA DIVE CENTER

LAVA EASY

CAFÉ INFORMACIÓN

CABAÑAS ZAZIL-KIN

DON CAFETO'S

MAR CARIBE

MARIACHIS

SYS DIGITAL LAB

IGUANA BIKE SHOP

L'HOTELITO

DON CAFETO'S

HOTEL PARAÍSO

NUDDY BEACH CLUB

Playa Paraíso

SIAN KA'AN ECOTURISMO

HOTEL CHILAM BALAM

EL PEQUEÑO BUENOS AIRES

MEZZANINE

CENOTE DIVE CENTER

PARIS DE NOCHE

HOTEL SUITES KIN-HA

DIAMANTE K

TOURIST POLICE KIOSK

MAYAN GRILL

HSBC

BUS STATION

CHARLIE'S

POLICE

CAFÉ GAUDÍ/MIXIK

FRUIT AND VEGETABLE SHOP

Park

COPAL

AZULIK

WEARY TRAVELER

FARMACIA SIMILARES

HEALTH CENTER

HOSTEL TULUM

307

To the Costa Maya and Chetumal

EL PIPAZO

POSADA DEL SOL

TAXI STAND/INTERNET/ SNORKEL AND BIKE RENTAL

MIXIK

HOTEL PIEDRA ESCONDIDA

POSADA MARGHERITA

RETIRO MAYA

CABAÑAS LOS ARRECIFES

ANA Y JOSÉ

Caribbean Sea

CAMPING CARACOL

SOUTHERN BEACHES

To Boca Paila Camps and Punta Allen

AMANSALA

LAS RANITAS

DOS CEIBAS

SCALE NOT AVAILABLE

© AVALON TRAVEL PUBLISHING, INC.

TULUM AND QUINTANA ROO

batter, etc. Ditto for the nightly barbecue (US$5 pp), which brings guests together over a hot grill and sizzling meat. There's a common kitchen, free salsa lessons, and free twice-daily shuttle service to and from the beach. The hostel also provides large safety deposit boxes and luggage storage if you've got a late bus. The big drawback here are the rooms, which are dim, grubby, and in serious need of renovation. Each dorm—which can be converted to a private—has just four bunks, a fan, and small unappealing bathroom. Fortunately, the hostel's environs and the allure of the beach mean you probably won't be spending much time inside anyway.

Across the street, **Hostel Tulum** (Calle Jupiter 20, tel. 984/871-2089, tulumhostel@ hotmail.com, US$10 dorm, US$18.50 d shared bath, US$28 t with private bath) is for backpackers happy to forgo the scene at Weary Traveler in exchange for newer, cleaner dorms, including one for women only. Thick mattresses and bright linens are a plus, though the bathrooms could use a scrubbing and the "private" rooms have thin walls that don't reach the ceiling. Lockers, continental breakfast, use of a small communal kitchen, and once-daily shuttle to the beach are all included.

IN ZONA HOTELERA

The rustic **Mar Caribe** (between Nuddy Beach Club and Tulum ruins, no phone, US$2.75 pp camping, US$10 s/d cabaña BYO hammock, US$14 s/d cabaña with bed) occupies a broad, windswept beach with a handful of fishing boats tied ashore and views of the Tulum ruins. There are plenty of spots to set up a tent and a handful of extremely basic cabañas with sand floors, hammock hooks or saggy beds, and sand blowing through the gaps in the walls. All share three grubby bathrooms—definitely wear your flip-flops when you use them. Not very pleasant, Mar Caribe nonetheless is cheap and on a beautiful beach.

US$25-50

IN TOWN

Although the rooms at **Hotel Chilam Balam** (Av. Tulum between Calles Beta and Orion, tel.

984/871-2042, US$33–37 s/d with a/c) are showing their age, they're spacious and very clean. All have air-conditioning, flat-screen TVs, sponge-painted walls, and bright bedspreads. Many rooms open onto an interior hallway—if you like natural sunlight, ask for one facing the street.

L'Hotelito (Av. Tulum between Calles Beta and Orion, no tel., hotelito@viaggiland .it, US$33 s/d with fan, US$37 s/d with a/c) has 10 worn rooms that open onto wide corridors. Rooms are made more cheerful by colorful walls and Mexican *artesanía,* but there's no hiding the fact that the bathrooms need scrubbing and many of the beds are saggy. At least it's cheap and well-located. And if you like *palapa* roofs, the fan units on the 2nd floor have them.

Villa Matisse (Av. Satelite 19, tel. 984/871-2636, shuvinito@yahoo.com, US$40) has six simple comfortable rooms, a pleasant garden and reading area (with book exchange), and a community kitchen. The rooms are spotless, and the grounds and common areas equally well maintained; the multilingual owner sets out coffee and small snacks in the morning, and often supplies rooms with fresh flowers. No air-conditioning, but rooms have fans and good cross-ventilation. Use of the hotel's bikes are included in the rate.

IN ZONA HOTELERA

Diamante K (north of intersection, tel. 984/ 876-2115, www.diamantek.com, US$42 s/d with shared bathrooms, US$100–223 suite) is a classic Tulum cabaña hotel and a good mid-range option. Although there are a handful of suites, most of the units are simple wood bungalows with *palapa* roofs, concrete floors, and hanging beds; all share decent bathrooms. The shore here is a jagged rocky shelf, and the hotel has various nooks and crannies with cushions, chairs, or hammocks where guests can watch the waves crash ashore. For swimming or sandcastles, there's a tiny private beach or, better yet, follow a path that leads a few hundred meters north to a broad unkempt beach. Other than the litter, which is avoidable, it's all part of the rustic, unpolished charm of the place. The hotel also has a bohemian chic restaurant and bar.

Behind an enormous sand dune, **Cabañas Los Arrecifes** (Carr. Tulum-Punta Allen Km. 7, tel. 984/879-7307, www.losarrecifestulum.com, US$30 s/d with shared bathroom, US$50 s/d bungalow with shared bathroom, US$100–150 s/d with private bathroom) offers a range of accommodations on an ample palm-tree-laden property. The beachfront bungalows are basic—sand floors and a bed—but the view can't be beat; and the modern hotel rooms are clean and comfortable though charmless. The remaining rooms are at the back of the property; be sure you're not stuck in there—these rooms are effectively cement boxes, dark and gnarly.

More than an eatery, **Mayan Grill** (north of intersection, tel. 984/116-3292, marel-merida@yahoo.com.mx, US$24–42 s/d with shared bathroom) has six basic cabañas that are squeezed into a *tiny* beachfront lot. All have cement floors, decent beds, and mosquito netting on the windows. A generator is run until 10 P.M. nightly—if you can, try to get a cabaña as far from it as possible.

US$50-100
IN TOWN

Arguably the best place in town, **◖ Hotel Villas Uolis Nah** (Carr. Tulum-Cobá Km. 0.2, tel. 984/745-2898, www.uolis nah.com, US$65 studio with kitchen, US$75 studio with kitchen and a/c) also is about the only place that has fully equipped kitchens in each guest room. Set in a leafy garden, units are simple, clean, and comfortable with little touches like mosaic tile bathrooms and *palapa*-shaded terraces with hammocks. With Super San Francisco just steps away, it's also no problem to get groceries if you don't have a car. Affiliated with the kiteboarding school Extreme Control, guests receive discounts on courses too.

Set in a leafy tropical garden, **Hotel Suites Kin-Ha** (Calle Orión near Calle Andromeda, tel. 984/871-2321, www.hotelkinha.com, US$55 s/d with fan, US$70 s/d with a/c) offers 10 colorful rooms with thick mattresses, tile floors, and mosaic tile accents. Each has a small *palapa*-shaded patio—perfect for writing post-

cards. The hotel also has a sister hotel on the beach **Playa Kin-Ha** (Carr. Tulum-Punta Allen Km. 5.5, US$110 s/d, US$130 suite); guests of the Kin-Ha in town are welcome to enjoy the beach amenities there. Transportation between the two is even included in the rate.

IN ZONA HOTELERA

Posada del Sol (mini-village, tel. 984/876-6206, www.laposadadelsol.com, US$75–150) has seven attractive rooms—three on the ocean side of the road, four on the other—all with private bath, fan, and most with terrace and hammock. The hotel has an artesanía shop in the reception area, so it's no surprise the rooms also have an artsy feel, from driftwood beams to Mexican rugs. Stay here if you prefer to spend a little less and have a little more atmosphere—in this cluster of hotels are also a few restaurants, Internet access, a market and some stores, plus money exchange, taxi post, and a place to rent bikes.

Hotel Paraíso (Playa Paraíso, north of the intersection, tel. 984/130-0285, US$83 d, US$91 t) offers 10 small artful rooms, a beautiful beach, and Maya ruins within walking distance, which all make this a comfortable and reliable choice. The decor is simple but pleasing: blue walls, modern porcelain sinks, cement floors inlaid with stone. There's a water-sports center on the beach, and a bar and restaurant (though Don Cafeto's, nearby, is better and cheaper). On the downside, the hotel is definitely secondary to the beach club, so service can be slow; guests can use the beach chairs, you pay for the beach beds like everyone else. While not the classic Tulum locale—it's a hotel, not bungalows, and the beach can get busy with day-trippers—but a comfy room, 24-hour electricity, and easy access to food, beach, and activities may be just the amount of "experience" you're after.

Neither too rustic nor too chichi, **Dos Ceibas** (Carr. Tulum-Punta Allen Km. 10, tel. 984/877-6024, www.dosceibas.com, US$50–133) offers comfortable affordable bungalows on a beautiful stretch of beach. Units have polished cement floors, brightly painted walls, and firm beds with mosquito nets hanging from the *palapa* roof. Like many hotels here, the shower and sink use salt water. All but the two breezy oceanfront rooms have fans, though the power is turned off during daylight hours. The eight units range from a 2nd-floor honeymooner just steps from the beach, to a bargain bungalow with a detached bathroom (and near enough the road to hear passing cars). Children are welcome and service is consistently superb. The restaurant, though overpriced, serves tasty meals in a shady, sand-floor dining area. At night, a profusion of candles set in niches along the back wall light up the restaurant area, while more glow in paper bags, marking the path to the beach.

Posada Lamar (Carr. Tulum-Punta Allen Km. 4.5, tel. 984/876-6206, www.posada lamar.com, US$100–150) has eight comfortable and beautifully decorated bungalows. The painted cement floors with inlaid tile and stones, the salvaged-wood detailing, even the exposed water pipes, all lend an appealingly artistic flair. Managed by an amiable Mexican couple, service is friendly but definitely hands-off; come here for a real getaway, not to be pampered. Bungalows have fans, but the electricity is on only from 6–11 P.M.; oceanfront rooms have the best sea breeze, and may be worth the higher rate in the summer. The beach here is stunning, and the hotel has a well-maintained beach area with chairs, beds, and *palapas*. Posada Lamar is a sister hotel to Posada del Sol, a kilometer away in the mini-village area.

Over US$100

IN ZONA HOTELERA

While Tulum has many beach bungalows with a touch of class, **Mezzanine** (1.5 km/1 mi north of intersection, tel. 998/112-2840, www.mezzanine.com .mx, US$250 d) is a high-class boutique hotel that happens to be on the beach. Seven rooms (four with ocean view) exude modern design, from unexpected color combinations to chic dark-wood furnishings. The pool here is more decorative than functional, and beach beds aren't on the beach at all, but on a platform overlooking it. (A path leads down to the sand, if you must.) The restaurant serves outstanding Thai-fusion dishes and a full bar stirs up mixed drinks to hip beats.

Beachy and hip, **❰ Posada Margherita** (Carr. Tulum-Punta Allen Km. 4.5, tel. 984/100-3780, www.posadamargherita.com, US$120–180 s/d) boasts just eight rooms on its oceanfront property. Each is decorated differently but all have stone-inlaid showers, private porches, and art from around the world. All are located just feet from a nice stretch of beach and an open-air lounge. Posada Margherita also is run on solar energy, which means 24 hours of silent electricity—a luxury in this part of the Riviera. Don't miss eating dinner at the hotel restaurant, as it's one of the best in Tulum.

Known as the "Bikini Boot Camp," **Amansala** (north of Las Ranitas, tel. 984/100-0805, www.amansala.com, US$111–263 s/d, six nights all-inclusive US$2,777 s, US$1,959 pp d) is a chic resort that caters to people who are looking to buff up in the sun. Located on a stunning white sand beach, the 14 eclectic rooms are set in two-story *palapas* with wood floors that are beautifully appointed with stone-inlaid walls, paper lanterns, and fine linens. All-inclusive packages include yoga and Pilates instruction on the beach, outdoor cardio and strength workouts, low-calorie meals, and body treatments. Biking and kayaking excursions are included as is a tour of the Tulum archaeological site. Popular with women, though everyone is welcome. And unlike the army, no one is forced to do push-ups.

Perfect for a romantic getaway, **Azulik** (Carr. Tulum-Punta Allen Km. 5.1, toll-free U.S. and Canada tel. 877/532-6737, www.ecotulum .com, US$325–350) has 15 spacious villas set on high rocky bluffs overlooking the Caribbean. The *palapa* villas are luxurious, soothing, and private—with floor-to-ceiling windows, a large deck with lounge chairs, two tubs each (a dugout tree indoors, a mosaic tile one outdoors), and hanging king-size beds. There's no electricity—the moon and candles rule at night—and access paths lead to a nude beach below (like the beach, the hotel is nude friendly). The two end units lend a bit more privacy, while three others are on the beach itself. Waiters come by in the morning to take your breakfast order (not included in rate), and deliver it for you to eat on your patio, a perfect way to start the day. Adults only.

Ana y José (Carr. Tulum-Punta Allen Km. 7, just south of Cabañas Los Arrecifes, tel. 998/892-0910, www.anayjose.com, US$202–320) stands out as one of the few hotels on the beach to offer 24-hour air-conditioning and a swimming pool. It sports a gorgeous beach, full spa, restaurant, car rental agency, and concierge, and hosts numerous weddings. The standard rooms are pleasant but with a cookie-cutter style that's odd for a resort of this caliber. The suites are a cut above, with king-size beds, living rooms, ocean views, and chic decor...which they ought to be for the even higher price they fetch. In fact, rates (for rooms and meals alike) are the main complaint here, being inflated even by Tulum's standards. Still, for those who require air-conditioning and a pool and other comforts, there's no real competition.

An upscale eco-resort, **Las Ranitas** (Carr. Tulum-Punta Allen Km. 9, tel. 984/877-8554, www.lasranitas.com, US$120–250 s/d, US$300–420 suite) boasts one of the most spectacular beaches in Tulum—expansive white sand, huge palm trees, and a mellow turquoise sea. Rooms themselves are set in bungalows that are surrounded by lush vegetation; each is ample and airy with a private terrace or balcony. The decor is a little tacky—think ceramic frogs—but the rooms are comfortable and very private. Stone-inlaid walkways lead guests to an inviting pool, a paddle tennis court, and the welcoming main house, where there's a lounge, reading room, and good restaurant.

FOOD

Most of the hotels and beach clubs in the Zona Hotelera have restaurants, which are usually rather pricey, but handy for the days you don't feel like going anywhere. If you can drag yourself from the beach, a few eateries in town and in the hotel zone definitely stand out from the crowd.

Mexican

Charlie's (Av. Tulum between Calles Alfa and Jupiter, tel. 984/871-2573, 7:30 A.M.–11 P.M.

Tues.–Sun., US$5–12) is one of Tulum's most popular restaurants, with a large airy dining area under a high *palapa* roof. The menu has classic Mexican dishes, such as *chiles rellenos,* enchiladas, tacos, and even a vegetarian plate or two. The restaurant hosts live music on Saturday nights during the year-end high season.

As popular as Charlie's is, locals and visitors looking for truly home-style cooking head to ◖ **Don Cafeto's** (Av. Tulum between Calles Centauro and Orion, tel. 984/871-2207, 7 A.M.–11 P.M. daily, US$5–9) for fresh seafood and grilled meat platters, Mexican staples like mole and enchiladas, and ceviche plates that are meals unto themselves. On a hot day, try a tall cold *superlimonada* or a *chayagra,* an uplifting blend of pineapple juice, lime juice, cucumber, and chaya (similar to spinach). On the beach, try the like-named **sister restaurant** (8 A.M.–10:30 P.M. daily) at Mar Caribe cabañas.

Open late every night, **Mariachis** (Av. Tulum at Calle Orion, tel. 984/871-2972, 9 A.M.–3 A.M. daily, US$4–20) is good for a midnight plate of tacos or just to throw back a couple of beers. Grilled seafood is the specialty—the *parrillada del mar* comes with thick grouper fillets, octopus, and shrimp—a meal big enough for two.

In the Zona Hotelera, the restaurant at **Cabañas Zahra** (mini-village, 7 A.M.–11 P.M. daily, US$6–16) offers reliable Mexican fare with a good number of vegetarian options—not surprising considering the number of health-conscious travelers in Tulum. A good place to have breakfast before you head out for a day on the beach.

Other Specialties

One of the best restaurants in Tulum is at ◖ **Posada Margherita** (Carr. Tulum-Punta Allen Km. 4.5, tel. 984/100-3780, 7:30–10:30 A.M., noon–9 P.M. Mon. –Sat., US$6–18). Serving gourmet Italian meals, dishes are prepared with the freshest of ingredients, including organic products and homemade pastas and breads. A huge tree-trunk plate of appetizers also is brought to each table (think olives, roasted red peppers, and artichoke hearts)—almost a meal in and of itself. Beyond the extraordinary food, the beachside setting—a chic sand-floored restaurant with billowing white fabrics and candles—leave you wanting to come back.

❿ El Pequeño Buenos Aires (Av. Tulum between Calles Orion and Beta, tel. 984/871-2708, 10 A.M.–11 P.M. Mon.–Sat., US$5–17) serves excellent cuts of beef, plus an array of crepes and even a few vegetarian dishes—not exactly a norm for Argentinean grills! The *parrillada Argentina* comes piled with different cuts and sausages—a perfect sampler if you can't decide exactly what you want. For lunch on a budget, try the *menu ejecutivo*—the special of the day plus a drink for US$4–5.50.

Fusion Thai is the specialty at **Mezzanine** (8 A.M.–10 P.M. daily, US$10–25), Tulum's newest, chicest hotel on the beach. Curries—red, green, or pineapple—and fried Thai tofu in peanut sauce are among the dishes served in a fashionable dining area or shaded outdoor patio, both with fine sea views. Full bar and cool music make this a nice place to linger.

Pizzería Il Basilico (Av. Tulum at Calle Beta, tel. 984/876-2632, 11 A.M.–11 P.M. daily except Tues.) is a reliable Italian restaurant specializing in pizza from its *forno a legna* (wood-burning oven).

Cafés

❿ Café Gaudí (Av. Tulum between Calles Alfa and Jupiter, no phone, 7 A.M.–10 P.M. daily, US$3–6) is a small café-restaurant serving light fresh fare. Breakfast options are named after works by the Catalan architect and namesake, like Sagrada Familia and Park Güell, and include fruit and yogurt, or eggs any way you like; the authentic Spanish tortilla and salami or roasted vegetable sandwiches make a good lunch.

On the inland side of the Zona Hotelera road, **Casa Banana** (Carr. Tulum-Punta Allen Km. 8.5, 7:30–11 A.M. and 6–9 P.M. Wed.–Mon., US$5–7) offers a good variety of breakfast dishes, sandwiches, and other light fare. Set under a high *palapa* and surrounded by the jungle, it makes a great place to linger over your iced coffee while you catch up on postcards.

Groceries

Tulum has a great local **fruit and vegetable shop** (6 A.M.–9 P.M. daily) on Avenida Tulum at Calle Alfa.

For basics and them some, head to the **Super San Francisco de Asis** (Av. Tulum at the turnoff to the Zona Hotelera, 7 A.M.–10 P.M. daily).

The Zona Hotelera's largest market, **El Pipazo** (mini-village, 9 A.M.–9 P.M. daily) is attached to Nohoch Tunich hotel; it has one room filled with essentials such as snack food, canned food, water, liquor, and sunscreen.

INFORMATION
Hospitals

Tulum's modest clinic is known as **SESA** (Calle Andrómeda between Calles Jupiter and Alfa, tel. 984/871-2050, 24 hours). For serious medical matters, go to Playa del Carmen or Cancún.

Pharmacies

Farmacia Similares (Av. Tulum at Calle Jupiter Sur, tel. 984/871-2736) is open 8 A.M.–10 P.M. Monday–Saturday, and until 9 P.M. Sunday. A doctor is available for simple consultations 5 P.M.–9 P.M. Monday–Saturday.

Police

The police station is in the city hall on Avenida Tulum and Calle Alfa, next to the HSBC bank. Dial 066 from any public phone for emergency assistance.

SERVICES
Money

HSBC (Av. Tulum at Calle Alfa next to city hall, 8 A.M.–7 P.M. Mon.–Sat.) has a reliable ATM machine and will change foreign cash and AmEx travelers checks 10 A.M.–5 P.M. Monday–Saturday.

An **exchange booth** (9 A.M.–9 P.M. daily) in the Zona Hotelera will change euros, U.S. dollars, and AmEx travelers checks.

TULUM BUS SCHEDULES

Departures from the **main bus terminal** (Av. Tulum between Calles Alfa and Jupiter, tel. 984/871-2122) include:

DESTINATION	PRICE	DURATION	SCHEDULE
Cancún (1st class)	US$6	2 hrs	12 times daily 7:15 A.M.–10 P.M.)
Cancún (2nd class)	US$5	2.5 hrs	16 times daily 6:25 A.M.–10:15 P.M.
Chetumal	US$13	3.5 hrs	six times daily 8:20 A.M.–4:25 P.M., plus 10 P.M.
Chichén Itzá	US$8.50	2.5 hrs	9 A.M. and 2:30 P.M.
Cobá	US$2.75	1 hr	7:30 A.M., 9 A.M., 10 A.M., 11 A.M., 5 P.M. and 6 P.M.
Carrillo Puerto	US$5	1 hr	8:20 A.M., 11:45 A.M., 12:50 P.M., 4:25 P.M. and 10 P.M.
Mérida	US$15.25	4 hrs	1:25 A.M., 12:25 P.M., and 2:30 P.M., and 7:40 P.M.
San Cristóbal, Chiapas	US$48.50	15 hrs	4:40 P.M. and 6:10 P.M.
Valladolid	US$4.50	2 hrs	1:25 A.M., 9 A.M., 12:25 P.M., and 2:30 P.M., and 7:40 P.M.
Xpujil	US$18.50	5 hrs	8:40 A.M., 1:25 P.M., 4:40 P.M. and 4:45 P.M.

Internet and Telephone

In town, **Sys Digital Lab** (Av. Tulum near Calle Centauro, 8:30 A.M.–11:30 P.M. Mon.–Sat., 10 A.M.–4 P.M. Sun.) charges US$1.50 an hour for Internet, US$0.37 a minute for calls to the United States, and US$0.46 a minute to Europe.

Next to the grocery store at the turnoff to Cobá, **El Point** (tel. 984/871-2715, 8 A.M.–11 P.M. Mon.–Fri., 9 A.M.–9 P.M. Sat.–Sun.) has modern computers and a fast connection for US$2.25 a minute.

In the Zona Hotelera, **Cabañas Zahra** (7 A.M.–11 P.M. daily) has Internet access for US$3 per hour. Two coin-operated public phones are just outside the front door of **El Pipazo** market.

Post Office

The easy-to-miss post office is located on the north end of Avenida Tulum between Avenida Satelite and Calle Centauro (9 A.M.–4 P.M. Mon.–Fri.).

Launderette

Lava Easy (Av. Tulum between Av. Satelite and Calle Centauro, 8 A.M.–8:30 P.M. Mon.–Sat.) charges US$1.50 per kilogram (2.2 pounds), with a three-kilogram (6.6-pound) minimum; two-hour rush service costs US$2.50 per kilogram, with a one-kilogram (2.2-pound) minimum.

Storage

The main bus terminal (open 24 hours) has luggage storage for US$0.50–0.75 an hour depending on the size of the bag.

GETTING THERE
Bus

Tulum's main bus terminal is at the south end of town, a block up from The Weary Traveler hostel. (If you're returning for the first time in a while, you're not losing your marbles: The terminal used to be on the other side of the street.)

White vans known as *combis* also go to Cobá (and all the spots in between), albeit less frequently. Catch them at the intersection of Highway 307 and the Cobá/Boca Paila road (US$2, one hour).

Combis

By now you probably know about *combis,* white collective vans that zip between Tulum and Playa del Carmen (US$2.50, 50 min) all day, every day. They leave more frequently than buses, and are handier for intermediate stops, like Hidden Worlds, Dos Ojos, Akumal, and Xpu-Ha. Flag them down anywhere on Avenida Tulum or Highway 307.

Car

Highway 307 passes right through the middle of Tulum Pueblo. Whether heading south from Cancún or Playa del Carmen, or north from Chetumal and Carrillo Puerto, you can't miss it.

GETTING AROUND
Bicycle

A high-end bike shop, **Iguana Bike Shop** (Av. Satélite near Calle Andromeda, tel. 984/119-0836, hugo_bike@hotmail.com, 9 A.M.–7 P.M. Mon.–Sat.) rents beach cruisers (US$4.75/24 hours) and mountain bicycles (US$10–14/24 hours) in excellent condition. Rates included a helmet, front and back lights, lock, basket, as well as life and accident insurance. English spoken.

Car

Tulum Pueblo is very walkable, but if you're staying in the Zona Hotelera—or plan to go there during your stay—a car will come in very handy. It's three kilometers (2 miles) just to the coast, and significantly farther to many of the hotels and best beaches.

Taxi

Taxis are plentiful and fares run about US$2 in town and US$3–8 to get to the Zona Hotelera (depending where exactly you're going). In the Zona Hotelera, there is a taxi stand at the mini-village area; rates are roughly the same, within the Zona Hotelera or back into Tulum Pueblo. From either area, a ride to Tulum ruins costs about US$3, and US$55 to the Cancún airport.

Cobá

The Maya ruins of Cobá (7:30 A.M.–5 P.M. daily, US$3) make an excellent complement—or even alternative—to the beautiful but vastly overcrowded ruins at Tulum. Cobá doesn't have Tulum's stunning Caribbean view and beach, but it's surrounded by lakes and thick forest, making it a great place to see birds, butterflies, and tropical flora. In fact, some people come here more for the bird-watching than the ruins. Which is not to say the ruins are unimpressive. To the contrary, Cobá boasts the second-tallest pyramid on the peninsula—and this one you can climb!—and other intriguing, if badly decayed, structures and temples.

The Cobá ruins are 42 kilometers (26 miles) of well-paved but speed bump–infested

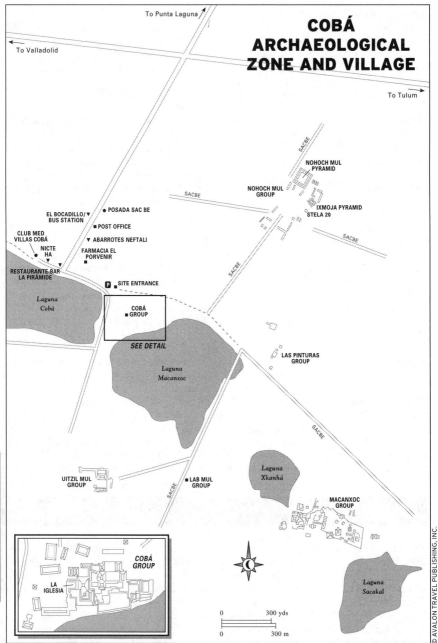

COBÁ ARCHAEOLOGICAL ZONE AND VILLAGE

To Punta Laguna

To Valladolid

To Tulum

SACBE

NOHOCH MUL PYRAMID

NOHOCH MUL GROUP

SACBE

IXMOJA PYRAMID STELA 20

EL BOCADILLO/ BUS STATION

● POSADA SAC BE

■ POST OFFICE

CLUB MED VILLAS COBÁ

▼ ABARROTES NEFTALI

NICTE HA

FARMACIA EL PORVENIR

RESTAURANTE BAR LA PIRÁMIDE

SACBE

SACBE

P ■ SITE ENTRANCE

Laguna Cobá

COBÁ GROUP

LAS PINTURAS GROUP

SEE DETAIL

Laguna Macanxoc

SACBE

Laguna Xkanhá

UITZIL MUL GROUP

■ LAB MUL GROUP

MACANXOC GROUP

COBÁ GROUP

LA IGLESIA

Laguna Sacakal

0   300 yds
0   300 m

© AVALON TRAVEL PUBLISHING, INC.

road from Tulum to Cobá—drive slow and pray you'll still have your muffler when you get there.

Just five minutes on foot from the Cobá ruins, a **village** by the same name offers a few dining and lodging options.

◖ COBÁ ARCHAEOLOGICAL ZONE

Cobá is especially notable for the complex system of *sacbeob,* or raised stone causeways, that connected it to other cities, near and far. Dozens of such roads crisscross the Yucatán Peninsula, but Cobá has more than any other city, underscoring its status as a commercial, political, and military hub. One road extends in an almost perfectly straight line from the base of Cobá's principal pyramid to the town of Yaxuna, more than 100 kilometers (62 miles) away. No small feat considering it was 1–2 meters (3.3–6.6 feet) high and about 4.5 meters (15 feet) wide, and covered in thick white mortar. (The term *sacbeob*—whose singular form is *sacbé*—means "white road.") In Cobá, some roads were even bigger—10 meters across (32.8 feet)—and archaeologists have uncovered a massive stone cylinder believed to have been used to flatten the broad roadbeds.

HISTORY

The Yucatán Peninsula has virtually no rivers, lakes, or other aboveground water. The same was true in ancient times, so a collection of small lakes, teeming with fish and fowl, some 40 kilometers (25 miles) from the coast would have been no small wonder. And it was no accident that a great city would rise up around this fortuitous geographic feature. Cobá was settled as early as 300 B.C. and over the next 500 years became an important center of trade, especially with the Petén region in present-day Guatemala. Petén influence is obvious in Cobá's temples, which resemble the high steep structures constructed in cities like Tikal. Cobá reached its zenith A.D. 600–800, when it controlled most of the northeastern portion of the peninsula. By then Cobá had a population of more than 40,000, making it among the largest urban centers in the northern lowlands; archaeologists have mapped more than 6,000 structures pertaining to the city, spread over some 50 square kilometers (31 square miles). Cobá fought a protracted war against the Itzá at Chichén Itzá, and was beaten decisively in the middle of the 9th century. A widespread Maya collapse—of which the fall of Cobá was not the cause, though perhaps an early warning sign—occurred over the next century. Cobá was briefly re-inhabited in the 13th or 14th century, and a few structures added, but was again abandoned to the forest by the time of the Spanish conquest.

La Iglesia

The first group of ruins you come to after entering the site is known as the Cobá Group. La Iglesia (The Church) is the group's primary structure; in fact, at 22.5 meters (74 feet) it's the second-highest pyramid at the site. Rising steeply from a low platform, the structure clearly follows the style of Tikal and other Petén cities, and could hardly be more different than the long palaces and elaborate facades common in the nearby Puuc and Chenes regions. Visitors are no longer allowed to climb the Iglesia pyramid, due to the poor state of its stairs. Next to Iglesia pyramid is a ball court that's been nicely restored—perhaps too nicely, in fact, as the reproduction scoring rings stand out like sore thumbs against the original weathered stones.

Nohoch Mul

Leaving the Cobá Group, the path skirts the edge of Laguna Macanxoc for about 500 meters (0.3 mile). Along the way you'll pass the Xaibé, or "Crossroads" temple, so-called because it marked the intersection of several *sacbeob.* For the same reason, archaeologists believe it may have served as a watchtower, though it's peculiar shape suggests a more important, but as-yet-unknown, function. Bearing left when the path forks, its another kilometer (0.6 mile) to the Nohoch Mul Group. The namesake pyramid, Nohoch Mul (aka Ixmoja) rises 42 meters (139 feet) above the forest floor, the equivalent of 12 stories. It was long touted as the highest structure in the Yucatán, until the main pyramid at Calakmul in Campeche was found to be higher—and by a good 12 meters (38.4 feet). The view from the top of Nohoch Mul is impressive—a broad flat expanse draped in thick forest. A small temple at the top bears a fairly well-preserved carving of the Descending God, and a rope running down the stairs makes going up and down easier.

Las Pinturas Group

At the intersection is the **Grupo de las Pinturas** (Paintings Group), a collection of five platforms encircling the plaza. Their name comes from paintings that once lined the walls; minute traces of the images, in layers of red and blue, are still visible in the largest structure, but you can't really get close enough to see them. The temples here, among the last to be constructed in Cobá, are well preserved, and picturesque with green moss growing up the gray limestone walls.

Macanxoc Group

Back on the main path, and taking the second fork this time, walk about a kilometer (0.6 mile) to the Macanxoc Group. Numerous stelae have been found here, indicating it was a place of great ceremonial significance. The most famous of these monuments is Stela 1, aka the Macanxoc Stela. It depicts a scene from the Maya creation myth—"the hearth stone appears"—along with a Long Count date referring to a cycle ending with the equivalent of 41.9 billion, billion, billion years in the future. It is the most distant Long Count date known to have been conceived and recorded by the ancient Maya.

Flora and Fauna

The name Cobá (Water Stirred by the Wind) is surely a reference to the group of shallow lagoons here (Cobá, Macanxoc, Xkanha, and Sacakal). The archaeological site and the surrounding wetlands and forest are rich with birdlife—herons, egrets, motmot, parrots, and the occasional toucan are not uncommon. Ar-

rive early to see the most birds—at the very least you'll get an earful of their varied songs and cries. Later, as the temperature climbs, you'll start to see myriad colorful butterflies, including the large, deep-blue *morphidae* and the bright yellow-orange barred sulphur.

If you look on the ground, you'll almost certainly see long lines of leaf-cutter ants. One column carries freshly cut leaves to the burrow, and the other marches in the opposite direction, empty-jawed, returning for more. The vegetation decays in their nests, and the fungus that grows on the compost is an important staple of the ants' diet—a few scientists even claim this makes leaf-cutter ants the world's second species of agriculturists. Only particular types of leaves will do, and the columns can be up to a kilometer (0.6 mile) long.

Practicalities

It takes several kilometers of walking to see the whole site, or you can rent a bike or hire a bicycle taxi near the entrance. Whether you walk or ride, don't forget a water bottle, comfortable shoes, bug repellent, sunscreen, and a hat. Watch for signs and stay on the designated trails. Guide service is available—prices are not fixed, but typically are US$35 per group (two hours, up to six people).

OTHER SIGHTS

About 17 kilometers (10.6 miles) north of Cobá, **Punta Laguna** (6 A.M.–6 P.M. daily, US$4) is a forested area where spider and howler monkeys can be spotted and heard. The largest number of monkeys can be seen in the early morning and at dusk; there also are several small unexcavated Maya ruins along the path. While the admission fee grants access to the forest trails, your best chance of spotting monkeys is by hiring one of the guides near the entrance (US$26 per group, 10 people maximum); guides typically speak basic English. Whether you hire a guide or not, be sure to wear good walking shoes and bring plenty of bug repellant. Traveling by car, look for the cutoff road from Cobá toward Nuevo Xcan—that'll lead you straight to the entrance.

In Cobá village, the main activity is watching **alligators being fed** off of the pier near the ruins. Local kids usually charge US$1 per person for the show.

ACCOMMODATIONS

There aren't many hotel options in this tiny town—three to be exact and only two worth considering. Be sure to call ahead to reserve a room; no worries if all the rooms are booked—Tulum, with its surplus of hotels, is just 40 minutes away.

The modest **Posada Sac Be** (Calle Principal s/n, tel. 984/206-7067, US$23.25 d with fan, US$32.50 d with a/c) has spotless rooms with one or two beds, television, and a small desk. All have private bathrooms and nice yellow tile floors. If no one is around to show you a room, go two doors down to the no-name *artesanía* shop that doubles as the post office. Someone inside will be able to assist you. Very friendly service.

Club Med Villas Cobá (facing Laguna Cobá, tel. 984/206-7000, scottsdale.mexicores@clubmed.com, www.clubmed.com, US$81 s/d with a/c, US$135 suite with a/c) is one of three identical Club Med mini-resorts at Maya archaeological sites (the others are at Chichén Itzá and Uxmal). Boxy but attractive rooms surround a courtyard with a well-tended pool. The hotel also has a restaurant that serves good, somewhat overpriced meals, a reading room with a good selection of books on the Maya, and a tennis court. The hotel faces Laguna Cobá—a pretty view but be sure not to jump in since crocodiles make it unsafe for swimmers.

FOOD

With a large raised patio overlooking the lagoon, **Restaurante-Bar La Pirámide** (Calle Principal at Laguna Cobá, tel. 984/858-1450, 7:30 A.M.–9 P.M. daily, US$5–12) is a nice place for lunch après-ruins or beer and snacks in the evening. The restaurant receives a number of tour groups, and it often has a buffet set up (US$9.50); otherwise, the menu has grilled fish, chicken, and meat dishes as well as typical Mexican fare.

A few doors down and just before the entrance to Club Med Villa Cobá, **Nicte Ha** (facing Laguna Cobá, tel. 984/206-7025, 8 A.M.–7 P.M. daily, US$1.50–4) is a small place serving tacos, enchiladas, and various pork dishes. The name Nicte Ha (Flower of the Water) may refer to the eyes of a hungry resident crocodile the restaurant owner feeds occasionally—raw chicken is his favorite, apparently.

The restaurant at **Club Med Villas Cobá** (tel. 984/206-7000, 7:30 A.M.–10 P.M. daily, US$4.50–12) is comfortable and has the best selection of dishes in town, including pasta, seafood, and Yucatecan dishes. The prices are a bit high; depending mostly on your mood, eating here is a worthwhile splurge or an unnecessary expense.

Across the street from a peach-colored church, **Abarrotes Neftali** (Calle Principal s/n, 7 A.M.–11 P.M. daily) is a mini-mart that sells canned goods, bread, and some fresh produce.

INFORMATION AND SERVICES

Cobá has neither an official tourist office nor a health clinic. There also are no banks or ATMs—the nearest banking and medical services are in Tulum and Valladolid.

Pharmacies: Facing the lagoon, **Farmacia El Porvenir** (Calle Principal s/n, 9 A.M.–1 P.M. and 2 A.M.–9 P.M. Mon.–Sat.) is a small shop selling basic medicines, toiletries, and film.

Police: Impossible to miss, the police station is halfway down the main drag, before you hit the lagoon.

GETTING THERE AND AROUND

You can easily walk to any of the listed hotels, restaurants, and services in town; the archaeological site is just a five-minute walk down the main road along the lagoon.

Bus: A tiny bus station operates out of El Bocadillo restaurant (Calle Principal s/n). There's only one first-class bus, which departs Cobá at 3:30 P.M. for Tulum (US$2.75, one hour), Playa del Carmen (US$6, 2.5 hours), and Cancún (US$9.50, 3.5 hours). Second-class buses also serve those destinations, as well as Valladolid and Chichén Itzá, though departures are limited.

Car: Getting to Cobá is easiest by car. The roads are smooth and fast, if a bit narrow in places, cutting though pretty farmland and small towns; watch for *topes* (speed bumps).

Just outside of Cobá is a large roundabout—head south a few hundred meters to town and the ruins; west via Chemex to get to Valladolid, Chichén Itzá, and Mérida; north for Punta Laguna and Cancún; or east to Tulum. For Playa del Carmen, go via Tulum.

Sian Ka'an Biosphere Reserve

Sian Ka'an is Maya for "where the sky is born," and it's not hard to see how the original inhabitants arrived at such a poetic name. The unkempt beaches, blue-green sea, bird-filled wetlands and islets, and humble accommodations are manna for bird-watchers, artists, snorkelers, and kayakers. But most of the visitors come here for the fishing—Sian Ka'an is one of the best fly-fishing spots in the world, especially for the "big three" catches: bonefish, tarpon, and permit.

The reserve was created in 1986, designated a UNESCO World Heritage Site in 1987, and expanded in 1994. It now encompasses around 1.3 million acres of coastal and mangrove forests, wetlands, and some 113 kilometers (70 miles) of pristine coral reefs just offshore. A huge variety of flora and fauna thrive in the reserve, including four species of mangrove, many medicinal plants, and about 300 species of birds, including toucans, parrots, frigate birds, herons, and egrets. Monkeys, foxes, crocodiles, and boa constrictors also populate the reserve, and are spotted by locals and visitors with some regularity. Manatees and jaguars are the reserve's largest animals, but also the most reclusive: You need sharp eyes and a great deal of luck to spot either one. More than 20 Maya ruins have been found in the reserve, though most are unexcavated.

A long spit of land extends south from Tulum, separating the ocean from a tangle of lagoons, mangroves, and channels. At the far end is tiny **Punta Allen** (pop. 400, also known as Rojo Gómez), where around 100 families survive by lobster fishing and (increasingly)

tourism—not surprisingly, many of the local young men have become uncannily sharp fly-fishing guides.

Spending a few days in Sian Ka'an is the best way to really appreciate its beauty and pace. Hotels and tour operators there can arrange fishing, bird-watching, and other tours, all with experienced local guides. But if time is short, a number of tour operators in Tulum offer day trips into the reserve as well.

SIGHTS
Muyil Archaeological Zone

The most accessible Maya site within the Sian Ka'an reserve is Muyil (Hwy. 307, 25 km/15.5 mi south of Tulum, 8 A.M.–5 P.M. daily, US$2.50), on the western edge of the park. Also known as Chunyaxche, it is one of the oldest archaeological sites in the Maya world, dating back to 300 B.C. and occupied continuously through the Conquest.

Resting on the edge of a limestone shelf near Laguna Muyil (aka Laguna Chunyaxche), the site is believed to have been an ancient Maya seaport. Only a small portion of the city has been excavated, however, so it makes for a relatively quick visit. There are six main structures ranging from two-meter-high (6.6-foot) platforms to the impressive **Castillo** (Castle). At 17 meters (51 feet), it is one of the tallest structures on the peninsula's Caribbean coast. The Castillo is topped with a unique solid round masonry turret from which the waters of the Caribbean Sea can be seen. Unfortunately, climbing it is prohibited.

A *sacbé* (raised stone road) runs about a

© LIZA PRADO

A small site, Muyil has a handful of excavated structures.

half kilometer (a third of a mile) from the center of the site to the edge of the lagoon. Part of this *sacbé* is on private property, however, so if you want to walk to the lagoon from the ruins there is an additional—and hefty—charge of US$3.75 per person. Along the way, there is a lookout tower, which adds some bang to your buck.

Boat tours on the lagoon also are offered for US$25 per group; a pleasant way to enjoy the water, you'll also get a view of several otherwise inaccessible ruins along the edge of the water. Visitors can either walk to the lagoon on the *sacbé* mentioned here or can drive there for free. Follow the signs on Highway 307, just south of the entrance to the archaeological site.

◖ Ascension Bay

Ascension Bay covers about 20 square kilometers (12.4 square miles) and its shallow flats and tangled mangrove islands teem with bonefish, tarpon, and huge permit—some of the biggest ever caught, in fact. It is a fly fisher's

dream come true, and it has been attracting anglers from around the world since the mid-1980s. And not just guys in waders—the spin fishing is fantastic, too, and the offshore reef yields plenty of grouper, barracuda, *dorado,* tuna, sailfish, and marlin.

SPORTS AND RECREATION
Sport Fishing

Ascension Bay has world-class fishing. All of the hotels listed in this section arrange tours, and most specialize in it, using their own boats and guides.

Bird-Watching and Ecotours

Sian Ka'an is also an excellent place for bird-watching. Trips to Bird Island and other spots afford a look at various species of water birds—in the winter, male frigates show off their big red balloonlike breasts. Tours often combine bird-watching with time snorkeling and walking around one or more bay islands. Hotels in Punta Allen and along the coastal road can arrange tours, as do outfits in Tulum.

ACCOMMODATIONS

Punta Allen is the only real town on the peninsula and has the most options for lodging, food, tours, and other services. A smattering of lodges and private homes are on the long unpaved road to Punta Allen; the nearest to Tulum, Boca Paila Camps, just four well-maintained kilometers (2.5 miles) from the entrance of the reserve, is also perhaps the best. Past Boca Paila—an inlet between the ocean and the lagoon, spanned by a bridge—you'll see a lot of deserted coastline and not much else until reaching Punta Allen.

Road to Punta Allen

◖ **Boca Paila Camps** (four km/2.5 mi south of the entrance to the reserve, tel. 984/871-2499, www.cesiak.org, US$73–95, including continental breakfast) is perfect for eco-minded travelers looking for an outdoorsy experience with the comforts of a Caribbean vacation. Spacious "tent cabins"—heavy-duty

© LIZA PRADO

Sian Ka'an Biosphere Reserve has miles of little-visited beaches.

canvas tents set on platforms—are surprisingly comfortable, with real beds, quality linens, and tasteful decor, including hand-painted headboards. Cabins are spread well apart, and have private terraces with views of the Caribbean or lagoon. Shared bathrooms are spotless and have rainwater showers, modern compost toilets, and 24-hour lighting. The cabins themselves don't have electricity, but guests are provided with candles and battery-powered lamps. The main building, completely solar- and wind-powered, houses a good restaurant too. Operated by CESiaK, an environmental foundation that offers excellent kayak and bird-watching tours, it also rents bikes and kayaks to guests so that they can explore the lagoon on their own.

Eight kilometers (five miles) before Punta Allen, **Rancho Sol Caribe** (fanny@cancun .net, www.locogringocom/siankaan/sol-caribe .html, US$107 s/d, US$162/135 s/d per person all-inclusive) has four comfortable cabañas, each with two double beds, private hot-water bathroom, patio with hammocks

and chairs, and 24-hour electricity. The hotel owners organize sport- and fly-fishing trips, departing from a private pier on the lagoon. Fishing trips can be combined with lodging and meal packages—email for rates and availability. Snorkeling, bird-watching, and other boat tours also can be arranged. Transfer to and from Cancún International Airport is included for all-inclusive guests staying seven-plus nights.

Also north of town is **Ascension Bay Beach Club** (toll-free U.S. tel. 866/787-9676, www .letitbeinn.com, three nights/two days fishing US$2,395 s, US$1,100 pp d; seven nights/six days fishing US$3,595 s, US$2,400 pp d). It has just three oceanfront *palapa* cabañas, each with two beds, private hot-water bathroom, tile floors, and a porch with chairs and hammocks. With a maximum of just six guests at any one time, the hosts give friendly and personalized service. Everything here is geared toward anglers, down to rod racks in the cabins and beers and fly-tying in the main cabin. Fishing trips begin at 7:30 A.M. and don't return until 4:30 P.M., with a pre-packed lunch and a cooler full of drinks onboard. Visits typically run Friday-to-Friday, including airport pickup at the Cancún Airport; shorter stays begin and end on Saturdays.

Punta Allen

One of the original fishing lodges in town, **Cuzan Guesthouse** (tel. 983/834-0358, www .flyfishmx.com, US$30–90 s/d, four nights/ three days fishing US$1,358 s, US$1,289 pp d; seven nights/six days fishing US$2,158 s, US$2,089 pp d) still has a loyal following despite the ever-growing pool of competitors. Basic *palapa*-roofed wood cabañas have private bathrooms, porches with hammocks, and ocean views. The hotel also boasts one of the best restaurants in town. Beyond fishing trips, Cuzan Guesthouse also can arrange birdwatching, snorkeling, and kayaking tours.

About 100 meters (328 feet) from the beach **Posada Sirena** (tel. 984/877-8521, www.casa sirena.com, US$30–50 s/d) offers large, simple "Robinson Crusoe-style" bungalows. Each sleeps up to eight people and have private bathrooms and fully equipped kitchens. All-day flyfishing trips run US$140 per person or US$190 for solo anglers. Half- and full-day tours of the bay, including snorkeling and bird-watching also can be arranged.

On the coastal road just past Punta Allen, **Serenidad Shardon** (tel. 984/876-1827, www .shardon.com, US$10 dorm, US$80–90 s/d with kitchen, US$100 large room maximum eight guests, US$150 two-bedroom apartment) offers a variety of accommodations for all sorts of budgets; rooms vary from dorms with shared bathrooms to private cabañas with fully equipped kitchens. Right on the beach, Serenidad Shardon makes a good place to just kick back and relax. If you want a little more action, the owners are also happy to arrange area tours.

FOOD

Punta Allen isn't a foodie's village but it does have a handful of eateries in town, all specializing in fresh seafood. A few mini-marts and a bakery round things out a bit, especially if you're planning on staying more than a couple days. Most of the hotels also offer meal plans.

Restaurants

Cuzan Guest House's (8 A.M.–9 P.M. daily, US$5–15) sand-floor restaurant may be the best in town. Beyond mouthwatering seafood dishes (the ceviche is a must), the menu has a good variety of Mexican and Yucatecan cuisine—all cooked with fresh herbs and spices.

With a beautiful view of the Caribbean, **Muelle Viejo** (near the main pier, 11 A.M.– 10 P.M. Mon.–Sat.) is an excellent choice for seafood and enjoying a breezy evening with a beer.

Chary's, near the central plaza, is a locals' joint with good, cheap eats.

Worth the drive back toward Tulum, the restaurant at **Boca Paila Camps** (8 A.M.–9 P.M. daily, US$5–15) serves an unexpectedly creative menu, including cilantro fish fillet and nopal (cactus) salad. Tables are set up on the rooftop patio—come for lunch or an early dinner for stunning views of the lagoon to the west and the Caribbean to the east.

Groceries

Tienda Socorro (one block south of the central plaza) is one of a few mini-marts that sells basic food stuff and snacks.

INFORMATION AND SERVICES

Don't expect much in the way of services in Sian Ka'an—if there is something you can't do without, definitely bring it with you. There are **no banking services** and none of the hotels or tour operators accept credit cards. Punta Allen does have a modest **medical clinic** and **pharmacy.** A few local entrepreneurs buy **gas** in Tulum and sell it for a small premium, and most hotels offer laundry service.

GETTING THERE

Many of the hotels include airport pickup/ drop-off, which is convenient and helps avoid paying for a week's car rental when you plan on fishing all day. That said, a car is useful if you'd like to do some exploring on your own.

Bus

The only public transportation to Punta Allen is from Carrillo Puerto, via the village of Playón. Shuttles to Playón (US$10, two hours, 9:30 A.M. and 3 P.M.) leave Carrillo Puerto twice daily from a stop kitty-corner to the market area; look for a "Playón" sign in front of a hair salon). From there you take a water taxi across the lagoon to Punta Allen (US$2 pp, 10 minutes, 6 A.M.–10 P.M. daily). On the return trip, shuttles leave Playón at 5 A.M. for Tulum, and 6:30 A.M. and 3:30 P.M. to Carrillo Puerto.

Car

There are two good ways to enter the reserve. The first entrance is about eight kilometers (five miles) south of the Tulum ruins on the Zona Hotelera/Boca Paila road. From the control kiosk—where you pay a US$2 park fee—it's almost 60 kilometers (37 miles) of unpaved and sometimes rutted road to Punta Allen. The drive is no piece of cake, with sections of deep mud and others of deep sand. A four-wheel drive is best, but an ordinary car can make it as long at it hasn't rained in the last 2–3 days. If you get stuck, you may have to wait several hours before another vehicle passes. Leave early, and fill up on gas before leaving Tulum.

The other entrance is from the west, off Highway 307 between Tulum and Carrillo Puerto. From Tulum, go south of Highway 307 for 24 kilometers (14.4 miles) to the Playón/Punta Allen turnoff—it's a tiny road and tiny sign, so keep your eyes peeled. (The turnoff is about two km/1.25 mi past a much more visible road and sign to the right for Chaccoben.) This is also a rough and sometimes muddy road but it's much shorter than the northern route. You weave through tangled wetlands to the port of Playón. From there, ferries take passengers across the bay to Punta Allen. You'll have to leave your car; someone in Playón usually watches vehicles, and theft isn't common, but don't tempt fate by leaving anything valuable in plain view.

Carrillo Puerto

Highway 307 from Tulum to Chetumal passes through Carrillo Puerto, a small city that holds little of interest to most travelers except to fill up on gas. Historically, however, it played a central role in the formation of Quintana Roo and the entire peninsula.

HISTORY

The town of Noj Kaj Santa Cruz (present-day Carrillo Puerto) was the center of a pivotal movement during the Caste War. As the Mayas lost ground in the war, two indigenous leaders enlisted a ventriloquist to introduce—or invent, to some—the *Cruz Parlante* (Talking Cross) in Noj Kaj Santa Cruz. The cross "spoke" to the battle-weary population, urging them to continue fighting, even issuing tactical orders and predicting victory in the long, bitter conflict. Thousands joined the sect of the cross, calling themselves Cruzob (People of the Holy Cross, a conflation of Spanish *cruz* or "cross" and the Maya pluralization -*ob,* in this case, "people of"). Some accounts portray the talking cross as little more than political theater for a simpleminded audience, but it seems likely that many or most of the Cruzob understood the ruse behind the Talking Cross and saw it as a form of channeling or simply much-needed motivation. Whatever the case, it reinvigorated the Maya soldiers, and Noj Kaj Santa Cruz remained the last redoubt of organized indigenous resistance, finally submitting to federal troops in 1901. Today, the Talking Cross itself is housed in a small sanctuary in town.

The town's name was changed in 1934 in honor of a former governor of Quintana Roo,

THE CASTE WAR

On July 18, 1847, a military commander in Valladolid learned of an armed plot to overthrow the government that was being planned by two indigenous men – Don Miguel Antonio Ay and Cecilio Chí. Ay was arrested and executed. Chí managed to escape punishment and on July 30, 1847, led a small band of armed men into the town of Tepich. Several officials and Euro-Mexican families were killed. The military responded with overwhelming force, burning villages, poisoning wells, and killing scores of people, including many women, children, and elderly. The massacre galvanized indigenous people across the peninsula, sparking what came to be called the Caste War.

Supplied with arms and ammunition from Britain, the indigenous troops tore through colonial cities, killing and even enslaving terrified non-Mayas. Valladolid was evacuated in 1848 and was left abandoned for nearly a year. By 1849, the peninsula's indigenous people, drawing on centuries of misery and abuse, were close to expelling the colonial elite. However, as they were preparing their final assaults on Mérida and Campeche City, the rains came early, forcing the Maya soldiers to choose between victory and famine. The men returned to their fields to plant corn.

Mexican troops immediately took advantage of the lull, and the Mayas never regained the upper hand. For the next 13 years, captured indigenous soldiers (and increasingly *any* indigenous person) were sold to slave brokers and shipped to Cuba. Many Mayas eventually fled into the forests and jungles of southern Quintana Roo. The fighting was rekindled when a wooden cross in the town of Noj Kaj Santa Cruz (today, Carrillo Puerto) was said to be channeling the voice of God, urging the Mayas to keep fighting. The war ended, however, when troops took control of Noj Kaj Santa Cruz in 1901. An official surrender was signed in 1936.

much revered by indigenous and working-class people for his progressive reforms, for which he was ultimately assassinated.

SIGHTS

The **Santuario de la Cruz Parlante** (Calle 69 at Calle 60, irregular hours) is a sacred place where the Talking Cross and two smaller ones are housed in a small wooden church. Shoes and hats must be removed before entering. Ask permission before snapping any photographs.

Like many places of worship in the region, Carrillo Puerto's main church, the **Iglesia de Balam Nah** (central plaza) was built by slaves, but they weren't Maya or African. During the Caste War, indigenous troops captured Spaniards and white Mexicans, some of whom they enslaved and forced to work.

Despite outward appearances, Maya nationalism is still very much alive and aware of the sometimes invasive effects of mass tourism. Check out the beautifully painted **mural** in the central plaza that reads: *La zona Maya no es un museo etnográfico, es un pueblo en marcha* (The Maya region is not an ethnographic museum, it is a people marching forward).

ACCOMMODATIONS

Owned and operated by one of the founding families of the city, **Hotel Esquivel** (Calle 63 between Calles 66 and 68, tel. 983/834-0344, esquivelhotel@quintanaroo.com, US$23–28 s/d, US$30–35 s/d with A/C, US$46 s/d with a/c and kitchenette) offers 37 rooms in four buildings, each with private bathroom and cable TV. The main building has by far the best rooms—gleaming tile floors, simple furnishings, decent beds, and some with small balconies overlooking a pleasant park. The property across the street—once the family home called La Casona—is pretty sad. Dilapidated and dark, they're clean enough to be acceptable in a pinch.

FOOD

La Casona (5:30 P.M.–midnight daily, US$5–10) opens right onto the central plaza

TULUM AND QUINTANA ROO

CARRILLO PUERTO BUS SCHEDULES

DESTINATION	PRICE	DURATION	SCHEDULE
Bacalar	US$5	1.5-2 hrs	take any Chetumal bus
Cancún	US$9-US$12*	3.5-4 hrs	30-60 min. 12:30 A.M.-9:30 P.M.
Chetumal	US$6-8*	2-2.5 hrs	every 30-90 min. 5:45 A.M.-11:15 P.M.
Mahahual	US$5.50	2 hrs	3 A.M. and 10:30 A.M.
Mérida	US$11-13*	5-6 hrs	13 departures 12:30 A.M.-7:15 P.M.
Ticul	US$9	4 hrs	take any Mérida bus
Tulum	US$4.50	1 hr	take any Cancún bus
Valladolid	US$6	2 hrs	9 A.M.-4:30 P.M.
Xpujil	US$15	5 hrs	6:15 P.M.

*Denotes first class service; not available for all departures.

and offers excellent Mexican fare at reasonable prices. Although it's not obvious, this is actually part of the Hotel Esquivel—you can reach the restaurant from the plaza or from the other side by going through the hotel.

El Faisán y el Venado (Av. Benito Juárez at Calle 67, tel. 983/834-0043, 6 A.M.–10 P.M. daily, US$5–7) is Carrillo Puerto's best-known restaurant, as much for its location and longevity than for any particular noteworthiness of its food. The menu is mostly reliable Yucatecan standards, including 8–10 variations each of fish, chicken, and beef, plus soup and other sides.

INFORMATION
Tourist Information
Although the tourist office (Av. Benito Juárez at Av. Santiago, 9 A.M.–4 P.M. Mon.–Fri.) is relatively helpful, the city's official website, **www .fcarrillopuerto.com.mx**, is an especially good source of information, if you can get it to load.

Hospitals
The Hospital General (Calle 51 between Av. Benito Juárez and Calle 68, tel. 983/834-0092) is open 24 hours daily.

Pharmacies
Farmacia Similares (Av. Benito Juárez at Av. Lázaro Cárdenas, tel. 983/834-1407) is open 8 A.M.–10:30 P.M. Monday–Saturday and 9 A.M.–10:30 P.M. on Sunday.

Police
The police department (central plaza, 983/834-0369, 24 hours daily) is located in the *Palacio Municipal* (city hall).

SERVICES
Money
Next to the Pemex station, **HSBC** (Av. Benito Juárez at Calle 69, 8 A.M.–7 P.M. Mon.–Sat.) has one 24-hour ATM.

Internet
Facing the central plaza, **Balam 'Nah Internet** (tel. 983/834-1026, 7 A.M.–1 A.M. Mon.–Fri., 8 A.M.–1 A.M. Sat.–Sun.) charges US$0.75 an hour for Internet access.

Post Office
The post office (Calle 69 between Calles 64 and 66) is open 9 A.M.–4 P.M. weekdays.

GETTING THERE
Bus
Carrillo Puerto's main bus terminal (tel. 983/834-0815) is just off the central plaza, with new service to Mahahual, and long-standing routes to Cancún, Chetumal, Mérida, and elsewhere.

Car
Fill your gas tank in Carrillo Puerto, especially if you're headed to Mahahual, Xcalak, Xpujil, or Ticul. There are other roadside gas stations ahead (and in Chetumal), but they get less and less reliable—having either no gas or no electricity to pump it—just as the stretches of empty highway grow longer and longer.

La Costa Maya

The coastline south of Tulum loops and weaves like the tangled branches of the mangrove trees that blanket much of it. It is a mosaic of savannas, marshes, lagoons, scattered islands, and three huge bays: Bahía de la Asensión, Bahía del Espiritu Santo, and Bahía de Chetumal. Where it's not covered by mangroves, the shore has sandy beaches and dunes, and just below the turquoise sea is one of the least impacted sections of the great Mesoamerican Coral Reef. Dozens of Maya sites have been located here, but few excavated, and much remains unknown about pre-Hispanic life here. During the conquest, the snarled coastal forest proved an effective sanctuary for indigenous rebels and refugees fleeing Spanish control, not to mention a haven for pirates, British logwood cutters, and Belizean anglers.

In the 1990s, Quintana Roo officials launched an effort to develop the state's southern coast, which was still extremely isolated despite the breakneck development taking place in and around Cancún. (It has always been a famous fly-fishing area, however.) The first order of business was to construct a huge cruise ship port, which they did in the tiny fishing village of Mahahual. They also needed a catchy name: Riviera Maya was already taken, so this area was dubbed the Costa Maya. The moniker applies to the coastal areas south of Tulum, es-pecially the Sian Ka'an Biosphere Reserve; the towns of Mahahual and Xcalak; Laguna Bacalar; and Chetumal, the state capital and by far the largest city in the area. Few locals use it.

Okay, it's hard not to be cynical when cruise ships lumber into this remote stretch of the Caribbean, and their passengers belly about Mahahual, beer bottles in hand. Then again, it's doubtful the area would have paved roads, power lines, or telephone service if not for the cruise ships. Driving the rutted coastal road to Xcalak—an even smaller town south of Mahahual—took a half-day or more; today, a two-lane paved road has cut the trip to under an hour. The state government has vowed to control development by limiting hotel size and density; monitoring construction methods; and protecting the mangroves and coral reef. Small eco-friendly B&Bs have thrived, not surprisingly, and more and more independent travelers are drawn to the Costa Maya for its quiet isolation and pristine natural beauty.

MAHAHUAL
Mahahual is a place of two faces—cruise ship days, when the town's one road is packed with day-trippers looking to buy T-shirts and throw back a beer or two; and non-cruise ship days, when Mahahual is sleepy and laid-back and

TULUM AND QUINTANA ROO

TULUM AND QUINTANA ROO

© LIZA PRADO

On cruise ship days, Mahahual's beaches are jam-packed.

the narrow, seaweed-strewn beaches are free to walk for miles. Whether you stay here a night or a week, you're likely to see both. It's a good thing. You can be in a major party zone one day, and the next be the only snorkeler in town—all without changing hotels. If what you seek are long quiet days every day, definitely stay outside of town. You'll see a few ATVers flying by now and again but that's as much partying as you'll see.

Orientation

Mahahual is pretty easy to manage. Most of its hotels and services are located on the sand road that runs through town and south along the coast. One inland street runs parallel to this coastal road, you'll find a supermarket and the police station on it. Just northwest of town, the tiny residential community of Nuevo Mahahual (aka Las Casitas) has a good supermarket, a few decent restaurants, and a launderette. To get there, head west on the paved road that leads out of town and turn north at the Nuevo Mahahual sign.

Sports and Recreation

Scuba Diving: Mahahual has terrific diving on the coral reef just off shore, with dozens of sites a short boat ride away. It's also one of two jumping-off points for trips to Chinchorro Bank, the largest coral atoll in the Northern Hemisphere. The other departure point is Xcalak, south of Mahahual.

Don't be deterred by the slew of cruise shippers who crowd into **Dreamtime Dive Resort** (Av. Mahahual Km. 2.5, 983/834-5823, www.dreamtimediving.com) almost every day—the shop is an indy operation at heart, and sends its students and "regular" guests on separate boats in groups of six divers or less. On non-cruise ship days, instructors may take small groups to unchartered portions of the reef for exploratory trips. Fun dives cost US$40 for one tank, US$75 for two, and US$25 a day for rental equipment. Snorkel trips run US$35 per person, including equipment. Open-water, advanced, and other courses are also available.

Bucanero del Caribe (Tequila Beach pier, tel. 983/120-5306, www.bucanerodiving.com,

9 A.M.–4 P.M. daily) is run by Arturo García, a friendly English-speaking native of Mexico City. He offers great rates on local dives (US$65 two tanks, including gear), plus trips to Chinchorro and other distant sites. Tequila Beach is a beach club just outside of Mahahual proper, catering to cruise shippers, though García's trips can be personalized for indy travelers.

Blue Ocean Safari (Av. Mahahual Km 1.6, 983/834-5742, www.blueoceansafari.com) operates in affiliation with the Luna de Plata hotel and offers fun dives and courses for similar prices. Ask for Phil or Julie, or at Luna de Plata.

Snorkeling: You can rent snorkel gear for around US$10 a day from a number of kiosks that pop up on cruise ship days and swim or kayak out to the reef. However, you'll see more on a guided tour—not every spot on the reef is worth snorkeling—and have extra safety and convenience.

Mahahual's dive shops all offer snorkel trips for around US$35 per person. Or contact Joaquín Corrales Solís, aka **Huacho** (Av. Mahahual Km. 9, brumars@hotmail.com), a friendly, English-speaking former diver who leads custom snorkeling tours, also for US$35 per person. Most trips last four-plus hours, and guests can set the agenda, whether it's maximum snorkeling time or a more laid-back outing including lunch and sunbathing on an isolated beach. Huacho typically stops by hotels to talk to new arrivals, or you (or your hotel) can contact him ahead of time to arrange a trip.

Kiteboarding: Kiteboarding has taken off as one of the hottest new wind sports in the world; with optimal winds between January–April, Mahahual is a good place to learn or practice. You can rent kiteboarding equipment or take lessons from Luca Sancinelli, an experienced kiteboarder and Italian expatriate who runs the gelateria and kiteboarding school, **Kite Zone** (Av. Mahahual, 983/130-7898, luca4685@virgilio.it). Five classes (10 hours, equipment included) run US$200 per person and are limited to two students. Equipment rental costs US$40 per hour, with an additional security deposit of US$100.

Community Service: Global Vision International (www.gvi.co.uk, 984/116-4208) operates a popular volunteer-for-pay program in Mahahual, in partnership with Amigos de Sian Ka'an, a local nonprofit. GVI "expeditions," as they are called, typically last 5–10 weeks and require open-water diver certification. The Mahahual center (Av. Mahahual s/n) has a dorm for around 12 volunteers, plus cold-water bathrooms and a community kitchen. Fees are not cheap: US$2,500 for five weeks, US$4,450 for 10 weeks, including room board and equipment, but not airfare. Advance registration is required, as the center is not designed to handle walk-ins. GVI has programs in Tulum and Sian Ka'an Biosphere as well.

Shopping

Mahahual is no shopper's heaven—pretty much all you'll see are folding tables laden with knickknacky souvenirs that are set up on the main drag. The one exception—and a pricey one—is **El Ziricote** (Av. Mahahual, just south of Kite Zone, 9 A.M.–5:30 P.M. Mon.–Fri., 9 A.M.–noon Sat.), which has mostly high-end handicrafts from the states of Chiapas and Michoacán. It's definitely worth at least a peek to check out the beauties that are created in other parts of the country.

Accommodations
UNDER US$25

Recently renovated, [**Las Cabañas del Doctor** (Av. Mahahual between Calles 2 and 4, tel. 983/832-2102, primomm@hotmail.com, US$4.75 pp camping, US$24 s/d with bathroom, US$33 s/d with shared bathroom) offers spotless *palapa*-roofed bungalows across from the town beach. All have cement walls, tile floors, and fans. Campers (BYO gear) set up on grassy areas on the lot and share cold-water bathrooms with the guests in bungalows. An excellent value.

US$25-50

Another excellent value, [**Kohunbeach Cabañas** (Carr. Antigua Km. 7, no phone, www.kohunbeach.o-f.com, US$37 s/d) offers three

TULUM AND QUINTANA ROO

© LIZA PRADO

Kayaking is a favorite water activity.

TULUM AND QUINTANA ROO

spacious and modern cabañas that have comfortable queen beds with beautifully hand-carved headboards, picture windows with views of the Caribbean, and mosaic tile bathrooms. Each is spotless and solar powered. Continental breakfast is included in the rate and is served under a huge *palapa*. Kayaks also are available for guest use. If you make online reservations, be sure to email well in advance—the owner doesn't check email daily.

Xiq'ita Kabah-Nah (Carr. Antigua Km. 8, tel. 983/700-5917, www.kabahna.com, US$35 s/d with shared bath, US$40 s/d with private bath) has five simple *palapa* cabañas, each with two beds, concrete floors, and good mosquito nets. Three have clean, brightly painted private bathrooms; the others share a bathroom that could use a scrubbing. Bring a good book as you'll surely while away an afternoon or two in the beachside hammocks. The beach here isn't fantastic—few in this area are—but the seaweed and driftwood manage to complement the hotel's rustic, laid-back atmosphere. There's also a simple boho-style restaurant that offers light meals.

US$50-100

One of Mahahual's finest hotels, **Balamkú** (Av. Mahahual Km. 5.7, tel. 983/839-5332, www.balamku.com, US$75 s/d including breakfast) combines comfort and style with ecological awareness, and at a great price to boot. Rooms occupy a series of circular two-story buildings and are spacious, clean and artfully decorated with Mexican and Guatemalan *artesanía*. The friendly Canadian owners have eschewed diesel generators and septic tanks for solar panels, wind turbines, and a nonpolluting wastewater system—ask for a short tour of the green technology used here. A full breakfast is included, and guests have free use of the hotel's wireless Internet, kayaks, and library, with plenty of books, board games, and music. Yoga classes, snorkeling tours, and other outings are described in a binder at reception, and can be arranged by the hotel.

A peaceful spot along the coast, **Maya Luna** (Av. Mahahual Km. 5.6, tel. 983/836-0905, www.hotelmayaluna.com, US$65/75 s/d) offers four modern bungalows, all with

24-hour solar/wind power, rainwater showers, and *palapa*-shaded porches. Each has a fantastic mural depicting a different regional scene—Banco Chinchorro and a set of ruins in the jungle, for instance. Best of all, each unit has a private rooftop terrace with glorious views of the Caribbean in front, and the jungle in back; lounge chairs and hammocks make it an easy place to while away a few hours with a good book and a drink. A hearty and healthy breakfast also is included in the rate. An excellent value.

One of the only hotels offering rooms with fully equipped kitchens, **Margarita del Sol** (Av. Mahahual Km. 7, www.margaritadelsol .com, US$95 studio) is a perfect option if you want to save a bit and cook on the road. The units themselves are spacious and very modern in style; each has an eating area, a private porch or terrace with an ocean view, and features like wireless Internet and DVD players (there's a decent library of DVDs). Use of kayaks and snorkel gear also is included.

Dreamtime Dive Resort (US$65 d) has eight free-standing wooden cabañas—six with two beds and two with king-size beds—surrounding a palm-shaded sandy lot; all have a ceiling fan, a painted stucco interior, and a private front patio. Breakfast is included, served in the lodgelike main building, which also has wireless Internet (BYO laptop). There's an okay beach in front, and a better one a short walk away. Most guests here are divers, or learning to dive, but not exclusively so. Guests of the resort receive a 10 percent discount on all trips, including snorkeling.

A friendly Italian couple runs **Luna de Plata** (Av. Mahahual Km. 2, tel. 983/834-5741, www.lunadeplata.info, US$40–80 d), a popular place with a restaurant in front and seven hotel rooms in back. All have plain but tasteful decor, like ruddy ceramic floors and painted *talavera* sinks, and simple boxy furniture, including firm wood-frame beds. Hot water, ceiling fan, and wireless Internet cover the basic creature comforts. Town is a pleasant walk away, while a patch of beach and a dive shop in front give you plenty of reason to stay nearby.

Right in the middle of town, **La Posada de Los 40 Cañones** (tel. 983/834-5803, www .los40canones.com, US$70 standard, US$80 superior, US$160 suite) has fared better than its namesake, the best-known shipwreck off Chinchorro Bank. Smallish standard rooms have comfy beds, modern baths, and a clean, bright feel. Superior rooms and two huge suites have more artful decor—the hanging beds are very Tulumesque—and extras like king-size beds, jet baths, and (for one) a big private patio. All have mini-split air-conditioners, but only numbers 2 and 8 have full sea views—get 'em if you can. The rooms form a horseshoe around an attractive entrance and patio area. The hotel also has an Internet café, a recommended restaurant, and a beach area with chairs and full bar across the street.

At three stories high, **Arrecifes** (Av. Mahahual Km. 2.5, tel. 983/834-5956, arrecifes-costamaya@prodigy.net.mx, US$80 d, US$100 d with ocean view) is a veritable skyscraper in low-lying Mahahual. Its gleaming white exterior gives way to 10 plain but very clean and comfortable rooms, all with two double beds, wireless Internet, and mini-split air-conditioners (6 P.M.–8 A.M. only), but no TV. The manager, a former dive instructor, can arrange snorkel and fishing trips; if he's not at reception, check one of the stools at the beach bar (also part of the hotel) across the street.

OVER US$100

About 21 kilometers (12.5 miles) north of Mahahual, **Mayan Beach Garden Inn** (no tel., www.mayanbeachgarden.com, US$103 s/d, US$146 suite) has five spacious cabañas with 24-hour solar power. Simple but pleasing, each has whitewashed walls, and Mexican-style decor, and thick mattresses. All also have gorgeous ocean views from private porches. A hearty breakfast is included in the rate, as is use of the kayaks. All-inclusive meal packages are available and, if you don't want to venture far, a must (the nearest restaurant is in Mahahual). In the high season, there's a three-night minimum.

Food

Just outside of town, **Luna de Plata** (Av. Mahahual Km. 2, tel. 983/834-5741, 11:30 A.M.–3:30 P.M. and 6 P.M.–midnight daily, US$4–15) serves tasty and well-prepared Italian dishes, from a slice of good, crispy pizza to fresh-made pasta with shrimp or lobster. There are a few international variations as well, such as veggie curry pasta, and a full bar. The Italian owners also operate the **Blue Iguana** (8 A.M.–6 P.M. daily, US$3–5), right across the street and a great spot for breakfast.

Toward the southern end of town, but still very much in the thick of things, little **Casa del Mar** (7 A.M.–9 P.M. daily, US$3–6) serves sandwiches, waffles, beer-batter shrimp tacos (the specialty), and other cheap eats perfect for the beach. A cook shack on the inland side of the road has a handful of tables, or you can eat in the restaurant's small beach area. Beer and cocktails also served.

In Nuevo Mahahual, **Aroma** (Av. Paseo del Puerto, 7 A.M.–noon and 5 P.M.–midnight, Sun.–Fri., US$4–13) is a cool corner bistro, open to the street on two sides, with plastic tables and chairs before a open kitchen. An international menu offers respite from standard Mexican fare: gazpacho, mousaka, beef medallions in soy balsamic sauce. Worth the trip.

Around the corner from Aroma, **Restaurante Monserat** (Paseo Chac Choben at Av. Paseo del Puerto, 7 A.M.–9 P.M. daily, US$4–10) serves up Mahahual's best tacos and other authentic Mexican dishes, in a large no-frills, family-friendly dining area. Service can be abrupt, but it's all part of the experience.

The restaurant at **◖ La Posada de Los 40 Cañones** (center of town, 7:30–10:30 A.M., 12:30–2:30 P.M., 7–9 P.M. Mon.–Sat., 7:30 A.M.–11 P.M. Sun., US$5–15) serves breakfasts of various international extractions: the Italian is bread and Nutella, the Mexican is eggs any way you like, the American is pancakes and bacon. For lunch or dinner, choose among items like fajitas, grilled fish, and homemade pasta, which comes with your choice of sauce, from olive oil and garlic to shrimp and lobster sauce.

Eat on the shaded patio for entertaining people watching.

◖ Travel In' (Carr. Antigua Km. 6, 8 A.M.–12:30 P.M. and 5 P.M.–11 P.M. Mon.–Sat., US$4–15) is a great little restaurant a few kilometers down the coastal road. Pita bread is baked fresh daily and makes for great sandwiches—hamburger, fish, BLT, etc.—as well as a curious but tasty "pita pizza." The curry is popular here, and daily seafood specials vary according to the day's catch and what's available in town. Well worth the walk (or ride) down the coast.

For groceries, the best mini-mart is **Los Hermanos Martín** (Paseo Chac Choben, 8 A.M.–11 P.M. daily) in Nuevo Mahahual. If you just need the basics, try **Chepemart** (6:30 A.M.–9 P.M. daily), which is located on the sand road that runs parallel to Avenida Mahahual.

Information and Services

Cruise ships have brought considerable modernization to this once-isolated fishing village, but tourist services are still somewhat limited, including no bank, ATM, or post office.

Hospitals: The **Centro de Salud** (8 A.M.–2:30 P.M. daily, after 5 P.M. emergencies only) is located two blocks from the beach, on the road to the elementary school.

Pharmacies: Farmacia del Caribe (9 A.M.–9 P.M. Mon.–Fri., until 5 P.M. Sat.) is on Avenida Paseo del Puerto in Nuevo Mahahual, three blocks from the turnoff on the left.

Police: The police department (toll-free tel. 066, 24 hours daily) is located on the sand road that runs parallel to the main drag in town.

Internet and Telephone: Check email and make international phone calls at **Mobius Playa Internet** (tel. 983/834-5973, 9 A.M.–9 P.M. Mon.–Sat.) inside La Posada de Los 40 Cañones. Internet is US$3 an hour, and calls to the United States and Europe are US$0.30–0.60 a minute. A number of restaurants and beach bars (in addition to hotels) offer free wireless Internet to customers; just look for laptops and the bottles of *Leones* beer.

Launderette: Lavandería Lavahual

(8 A.M.–2 P.M. and 5 P.M.–8 P.M. Mon.–Sat., and 8 A.M.–2 P.M. Sat.) is kitty-corner from Aroma restaurant, at the entrance to Nuevo Mahahual. Wash, dry, and fold is US$1.50 per kilogram (2.2 pounds) with a three kilogram (6.6 pound) minimum.

Getting There and Around

Just south of the grubby roadside town of Limones, a good paved road with signs to Mahahual breaks off Highway 307 and cuts through 58 kilometers (36 miles) of coastal forest and wetlands tangled with mangroves. It's a scenic stretch, whether in car or on a bus, along which you should see egrets, herons, and other water birds.

Bus: Mahahual's ADO "terminal" is a modest affair—an open-air lot near the entrance of town—but daily first-class service makes coming and going a breeze. Buses to Cancún (US$15.50, 5.5 hours) leave at 8:30 A.M. Monday–Saturday, 12:30 P.M. Sunday, and 5:30 P.M. daily, stopping at the major towns in between. To Chetumal (US$6.50, 2.5 hours) buses depart at 7:30 A.M., 1 P.M., and 6:30 P.M. daily, plus 10:30 A.M. and 3 P.M. on Sunday. The ticket booth is open a short time before and after scheduled departures only.

Taxi: Cabs abound in this town, especially on cruise ship days. In general, rates run US$1 per kilometer (1.6 miles).

Car: There is a **PEMEX** gas station (24 hours daily) on the main road to Mahahual, just east of the turnoff to Xcalak. It runs out of gas occasionally, so definitely fill your tank in Carrillo Puerto or Chetumal on your way here.

Mahahual proper is very walkable—in fact, town leaders are trying to have the beach-front road converted to a pedestrian walkway, and divert cars down the back street. However, if you're staying outside of town, you'll definitely need some wheels, whether car, scooter, bike, or taxi to get around.

XCALAK

The tiny fishing village of Xcalak lies just a short distance from the channel that marks the Mexico-Belize border, and a blessed long ways

Still relatively untouched, Xcalak's beaches and small eco-hotels make a perfect getaway.

© LIZA PRADO

TULUM AND QUINTANA ROO

from anything else. The town started out as a military outpost, and didn't get its first real hotel until Costa de Coco opened in 1988 (and still going strong, by the way). Villagers had to wait until another decade to get a paved road; before that, the only way in or out of town was by boat or via 55 kilometers (34 miles) of rutted beach tracks. Electrical lines were installed in 2004 but only in the village proper, so many outlying areas (including most of the better hotels) still rely on solar, wind, and generators. The town has no bank, no public phones, and no gas station. That is to say: Perfect!

The area doesn't have much beach but makes up for it with world-class fly-fishing, great snorkeling and diving, and a healthy coral reef and lagoon. A growing contingent of expats, mostly American and Canadian, have built homes, some for personal use, others for rent, others as small hotels. Large-scale tourism may be inevitable but still seems a long way off, and Xcalak remains a small and wonderfully laid-back place, perfect for those looking for some honest-to-goodness isolation.

Sports and Recreation

Scuba Diving and Snorkeling: The Xcalak Reef National Park (Parque Nacional Arrecifes de Xcalak) was established at the end of 2003, affording protection to the coastal ecosystem as well as Xcalak's nascent tourist economy. The park spans nearly 18,000 hectares (44,479 acres), from the Belize border well north of town, and includes the reef—and everything else down to 100 meters (328 feet)—as well as the shoreline and numerous inland lagoons. A US$4 a day fee technically applies to all divers and snorkelers (and kayakers and anglers); dive shops typically add it to their rates, while most hotels have a stack of wristband-permits to sell to guests snorkeling right from shore. The somewhat steep fee, uneven enforcement, and bonehead features like using paper wristbands that disintegrate in water have stirred some grumbling and scattered noncompliance by locals and hoteliers alike. With luck (and time) the problems will be resolved and everyone will contribute

a fair share. For the time being, ask at your hotel for the latest.

The main coral reef lies just 90–180 meters (100–200) yards from shore and the water is less than 1.5 meters (five feet) deep almost the whole way out. Many snorkelers prefer the coral heads even closer to shore, which have plenty to see and less swell than the main reef. The shallow waters keep boat traffic to a minimum and anglers are good about steering clear of snorkelers (you should still stay alert at all times, however).

Divers and snorkelers can also explore the reef at around 20 official sites and many more unofficial ones. Most are a short distance from town, and shops typically return to port between tanks. "La Poza" is one of the more unique dives, drifting through a trench where hundreds, sometimes thousands, of tarpon congregate, varying in size from one-meter (three-foot) "juveniles" to two-meter (seven-foot) behemoths.

And, of course, there is **Banco de Chinchorro** (Chinchorro Bank), which is by some measurements the largest coral atoll in the Northern Hemisphere and a paradise for divers and snorkelers alike. About 48 kilometers (30 miles) northeast from Xcalak, Chinchorro is a marine reserve and is known for its spectacular coral formations, massive sponges, and abundant sealife. Scores of ships have foundered on the shallow reefs through the years, but (contrary to innumerable misreports) the wrecks cannot be dived. Not only are they protected as historical sites, most are on the eastern side of the atoll where the surf and currents are too strong for recreational diving. The famous "40 Cannons" wreck, in about three meters (10 feet) of water on the atoll's northwest side, is a good for snorkeling but not diving, and there are nowhere near 40 cannons there, thanks to looters. There are small government and fishermen's huts on one of the three cays, but tourists are not permitted to stay the night.

To get to Chinchorro, it's a 1.5–2-hour boat ride, which can be pretty punishing depending on conditions. You typically set out around

7:30 or 8 A.M., dive three tanks, have lunch onboard, and return to port around 4:30 or 5 P.M. Dive shops usually require at least four divers (or eight snorkelers) and may not go for days at a time if the weather is bad.

XTC Dive Center (north end of town, across bridge, www.xtcdivecenter.com, 9 A.M.–5 P.M. daily) is a full-service dive shop that specializes in trips to Chinchorro Bank; its acronym officially stands for "Xcalak to Chinchorro," though the ecstasy-inducing dives here certainly figured into the name. Trips to Chinchorro are US$160 per person for three tanks or US$100 per person for snorkelers, including lunch and drinks. Closer to home, reef dives cost US$45 for one tank, US$65 for two, and US$85 for three; equipment is an extra US$15 a day if you need it. Snorkel tours run US$25–50 per person depending on how long and far you go; five-hour trips include jaunts into the lagoon and Bird Island, which can be fascinating, especially in January and February when the birds are most plentiful. A 10 percent tax applies to most rates. **Costa de Cocos** also offers diving, as does **Casa Carolina** though for its own guests only. Prices at all three shops are comparable.

Sport Fishing: Xcalak also has world-class sport fishing, with huge saltwater and brackish flats where hooking into the grand slam of fly-fishing—tarpon, bonefish, and permit—is by no means impossible. Add a snook and you've got a super slam. Oceanside, tarpon and barracuda abound, in addition to grouper, snapper, and others. **Costa de Cocos** is the area's only true fishing resort, with highly experienced guides and numerous magazine write-ups, including *Fly Rod & Reel* and *Gray's Sporting Journal*. Options range from half-day outings (US$175, including gear and guide) to 2–7-night packages including lodging, meals, open bar, and of course nonstop fishing (US$1,020–3,820). All the dive shops also arrange guided fishing tours.

Accommodations

Xcalak's most appealing accommodations are on the beach road heading north out of town. Few places accept credit cards on-site, but many have payment systems on their websites.

UNDER US$50

Right at the entrance of town, **Cabañas Tío Bon** (983/836-6954, US$23) are very basic but reasonably clean and the cheapest digs in town. Three pink-painted wooden cabins right alongside the owners' home—you share a front gate—have tiny private bathrooms, fan, and 24-hour electricity. A queen bed and a hammock mean up to three people can squeeze into each cabin. Plywood interior and lack of hot water will prevent any confusion between Uncle Bon's and the Westin.

US$50-100

Four cheerful units with fully equipped kitchenettes make **Casa Carolina** (2.5 km/1.6 mi north of town, no tel., www.casacarolina.net, US$95 s/d) a fine choice. Add perfect ocean views from the private balconies, free use of kayaks and bicycles, and a wide beach with palm trees, and you've got the formula for a relaxing beach vacation. Owner Bob Villier is an experienced NAUI dive instructor trainer and offers personalized certification classes plus diving and snorkeling trips. Continental breakfast, including divine homemade muffins, is included.

Hotel Tierra Maya (2.1 km/1.3 mi north of town, toll-free U.S. tel. 800/216-1902, www.tierramaya.net, US$90–101 s/d) is a pleasant hotel on a well-tended stretch of beach. Its six rooms are ample and decorated with simple furnishings, Mexican tile accents, and bright blankets. All have private terraces and balconies with views of the Caribbean. Continental breakfast is included in the rate and is served in the hotel's excellent beachfront restaurant. All-inclusive fly-fishing packages also are available.

Xcalak's first hotel and only true fishing and diving lodge, **Costa de Cocos** (3 km/2 mi north of town, tel. 983/839-8537, www.costadecocos.com, US$73 s, 84 d) eschews fluff and formality for a laid-back sportsman's atmosphere that's perfectly suited to its clientele. Individual wood-paneled cabañas are clean and comfortable, with tile floors and hot water, and surround a well-kept sandy lot. Travelers looking for "cute" or "charming" won't find it here—certainly not like at neighboring B&Bs—and that seems to be just how the staff and guests prefer it. The restaurant is open late, serving up pizza, steak, beer, and all manner of tall tales—though with fishing as good as it is, many just happen to be true.

OVER US$100

It's hard not to feel at home at ❨ **Sin Duda** (eight km/five mi north of town, www.sinduda villas.com, US$84 d, US$112 studio, US$125 apartment), one of Xcalak's best-loved hotels. The three standard rooms, one studio, and two two-bedroom apartments are all charmers: beautifully furnished, whimsically decorated, most with breathtaking views of the turquoise Caribbean Sea. Two roof decks offer an even better angle: uninterrupted 360-degree views of the jungle, lagoon, and sea. On arrival, owners Margo and Robert (and their four corgis) show you around the delightful villa, tell you where to find the self-serve snorkel gear, kayaks, and bicycles, and even point out the best coral heads to snorkel to. Evening time brings cocktail hour, when guests can join the hosts for a "margo-rita" in the cozy lounge that doubles as a common kitchen and library. A home away from home, without a doubt.

Run by friendly Minnesota retirees, **Sand-Wood Villas** (7.9 km/4.9 mi north of town, tel. 983/839-5428, www.sandwood.com, US$122 d, 145 t) has three apartments, each with two bedrooms, two small bathrooms, a full kitchen—from gas stoves to juicers—and gorgeous sea views. The decor veers from plain to old-fashioned and back again, but the units themselves are comfortable and roomy. Snorkel gear, kayaks, and canoes are available for exploring the reef or the lagoon, and bikes for getting in and out of town. The owners here also manage **Coral Garden Inn** (www.coralgardeninn. com, US$675–800/wk) which has two spacious two-bedroom apartments with kitchens about one kilometer (0.5 mile) farther north.

A hotel where "all you need is your smile," **Playa Sonrisa** (6.9 km/4.3 mi north of town, tel. 983/114-9895, www.playasonrisa.com, US$112 s/d, US$146 s/d with a/c) is a cloth-ing-optional resort on a palm-tree-laden beach. Rooms are divided between beachfront units and garden view cabins. The beachfront units are comfortable and clean—the stand alone bungalows are the nicest—but lack charm. The garden view cabins are worn and depressing and not worth the US$112 price tag. What you pay for here is the freedom to enjoy the Caribbean in the buff without being ogled or disrespecting local mores. Couples and nudist families only. Continental breakfast, kayaks, and snorkel gear included in the rate.

Food

❨ **Xcalak Caribe** (noon–8 P.M. Wed.–Fri., 11–5 P.M. Sat.–Sun., US$6–12) serves seaside standards like shrimp quesadillas and garlic grilled fish, plus an ever-changing selection of specials. Restaurant options are slim in Xcalak, but the large tasty dishes, friendly service, and casual atmosphere would make this a popular watering hole anywhere. Look for the yellow *palapa*-roofed building just south of the lighthouse, facing the beach.

Xcalak's hoteliers heap praise onto the ❨ **Leaky Palapa Restaurant** (no phone, 11:30 A.M.–9 P.M. Sat.–Mon., US$4–16) like Cuban guys scooping sugar into their coffee. A small bohemian *palapa*-roofed restaurant run by two Canadian expats, the menu varies according to the day's catch and what the food truck brings but is invariably delicious. A must for any stay here. Open November–May only.

The restaurant at **Costa de Cocos** (7 A.M.–10 P.M. daily, US$5–18) serves solid familiar fare, like burgers, steak, grilled fish, and pizza. Not particularly outstanding, but the kitchen is open daily, no reservations required, and the full bar and casual atmosphere make this a reliable choice.

The Maya Grill (Tierra Maya Hotel, 2.1 km/1.3 mi north of town, toll-free U.S. tel. 800/216-1902, 6:30 A.M.–1:30 P.M. and 5–9 P.M. daily, US$5–17) is a beachside hotel restaurant offering fresh ingredients in its Mexican-inspired meals. Seafood is the focus but chicken and meat dishes edge their way onto the menu too. Dinners are pricey but hearty, including an appetizer, soup, and dessert.

If you are cooking for yourself, a **grocery truck** passes through town and down the coastal road on Tuesdays, Fridays, and Sundays every week. It comes stocked with eggs, yogurt, grains, basic produce, fresh meats, and canned food. You can also buy a broom or two. In town, try the no-name **mini-mart** (one and a half blocks south of the elementary school, 9 A.M.–9 P.M. daily), which sells basic canned and dried foods along with a good variety of chips.

Information and Services

Xcalak has no bank, ATM, or currency exchange office, and only a few places take credit cards. Plan accordingly!

Hospitals: There's a basic health clinic (8 A.M.–noon and 2–6 P.M. Mon.–Fri.) near the entrance of town.

Internet and Telephone: There was no reliable Internet café when we passed through, though many hotel owners will let you use their computers in a pinch. To place an international or domestic call, head to **Telecomm/ Telégrafos** (near The Leaky Palapa, 9 A.M.–3 P.M. Mon.–Fri.).

Getting There and Around

Bus service is somewhat erratic in Xcalak. Theoretically, buses leave every day at 5 A.M. and 2:30 P.M., though departures are sometimes delayed or cancelled without notice. From Xcalak, buses pass Mahahual (including a portion of the coastal road south of town), then continue to Limones and Chetumal. If you're arriving, your hotel may send a car to pick you up; otherwise a taxi from town is about US$1 per kilometer (0.6 mile).

Most travelers come in a rental car, which certainly simplifies life here. The closest gas station is on the main road to Mahahual, near the turnoff for Xcalak. However, it occasionally runs out of gas, so you should fill up on Highway 307 as well—Carrillo Puerto is a good spot. In a pinch, a few Xcalak families sell marked-up gas from barrels in their front yards; ask your hotel owner for help locating them.

CHACCHOBEN ARCHAEOLOGICAL ZONE

Chacchoben (8 A.M.–5 P.M. daily, US$3, free on Sundays) got its name from archaeologists, who, after uncovering no inscription indicating what the city's original residents called it, named it after the Maya village to whom the land pertained. The exact meaning of the name is lost, even to local villagers, though the accepted translation is "Place of Red Corn." The area may have been settled as early as 1000 B.C., and most of the building activity probably took place A.D. 200–700, the Classic period.

Visiting the Ruins

Entering the site, a short path leads first to Temple 24, a squat pyramid that is the primary structure of a small enclosed area called Plaza B. Across that plaza—and the larger Plaza Central beyond it—is a massive raised platform with the site's largest pyramid, Temple 1, atop it. Also on the platform, two smaller structures, dubbed Las Vasijas and Los Gemelos, were likely used for ceremonial functions. The site has some well-preserved stucco and paint and for that reason none of the pyramids can be climbed. Though it can get crowded on cruise-ship days, Chacchoben has an appealingly remote feel, nestled in the forest with towering mahogany and banyan trees.

Practicalities

Turismo Chacchoben (www.chacchoben ruins.com) is a small friendly tour operation run by David Villagómez and Ivan Cohuo, both born and raised in Chacchoben village, and extremely knowledgeable about the ruins and Maya history, culture, and belief systems. Tours are of the ruins alone (US$43 pp, 3–4 hours) or in combination with a visit to the guides' home village (US$70 pp, six hours); all tours are offered in Spanish, English, or Italian, and include air-conditioned transport from Mahahual, entrance fees, and drinks. The tours are geared for the cruise ship crowd (as they must) but are limited to 14 people and are warmly recommended by hotel owners to independent travelers as well.

Laguna Bacalar

Almost 50 kilometers (31 miles) long, Laguna Bacalar is the second-largest lake in Mexico and certainly among the most beautiful. Well, it's not technically a lake: A series of waterways do eventually lead to the ocean, making Bacalar a lagoon; but it is fed by natural springs and the water on the western shore, where the hotels and town are, is 100 percent *agua dulce* (fresh water).

The Maya name for the lagoon translates as "Lake of Seven Colors." It is an apt description, as you will see on any sunny day. The lagoon's sandy bottom and crystalline water turn shallow areas a brilliant turquoise, which fades to deep blue in the center. If you didn't know better, you'd think it was the Caribbean.

ORIENTATION

The hub of the Laguna Bacalar region is the town of Bacalar. Located on the west side of the lake, it won't win any prizes for charm but it does have a terrific museum, one of the best hotels around, a handful of good restaurants, and of course, gorgeous views of the lagoon. A handful of hotels are sprinkled a few kilometers on either side of town and the enormous Cenote Azul is just south of it.

SIGHTS
◖ Fuerte San Felipe Bacalar

The 17th-century Fuerte San Felipe Bacalar (central plaza, Av. 3 at Calle 20, 9 A.M.–7 P.M. Tues.–Thurs. and Sun., 9 A.M.–8 P.M. Fri.–Sat., US$4.75) was built by the Spanish for protection against the pirates and Mayas that regularly raided the area. In fact, attacks proved so frequent—and successful—that the fort was destroyed in 1858 during the Caste War. Today, the star-shaped stone edifice has been restored to its former glory: drawbridge,

A beautifully restored fort, Fuerte San Felipe Bacalar has one of the best museums in the region.

© LIZA PRADO

cannons, moat, and all. The fort also houses the excellent **Museo de la Piratería,** a state-of-the-art museum with exhibits on the history of the area with a focus on the pirates who regularly attacked these shores.

Cenote Azul

As good or better than the Laguna Bacalar for swimming, Cenote Azul (Carretera Chetumal-Bacalar Km. 15, tel. 983/834-2038, 8 A.M.–8 P.M. daily, free) is said to be the widest cenote in Mexico, measuring 185 meters (607 feet) across and 61 meters (200 feet) deep. Filled with crystalline blue water, short ladders make getting into the water easy. A rope stretches clear across, so even less-conditioned swimmers can make it to the far side. A large, breezy restaurant (US$6–16) has smallish portions of unremarkable seafood, but the pretty waterside tables are perfect for fries and a beer. Located two kilometers (1.25 miles) south of town.

ENTERTAINMENT AND EVENTS
Fiesta de San Joaquín

Every July, the town of Bacalar celebrates San Joaquín, its patron saint. For nine consecutive days, different neighborhoods host festive celebrations, each trying to outdo the other for the year's best party. Visitors are welcome and should definitely join the fun—expect plenty of food, music, dancing, and performances of all sorts. Cockfights also are popular, and a three-day hydroplane race usually follows the festivities in early August.

SPORTS AND RECREATION
Ecotours

A friendly German couple founded **Active Nature** (Villas Ecotucan, tel. 983/834-2516, www.activenaturebacalar.com) in 2006 after fate and car trouble cut short their planned tour of the Americas and left them in lovely Laguna Bacalar. Tour options include kayaking through mangrove channels to hidden lagoons and freshwater beaches, sunset and moonlight canoe rides, biking to a Great Curassow breeding reserve and research center,

and morning bird-watching walks. Prices range from US$10–40 per person, including gear and often lunch and water; children under 10 are free, under 14 half-off. Tours begin at Villas Ecotucán and guests there get a 10 percent discount. A portion of proceeds is donated to the Great Curassow center.

Swimming and Boating

In town, on the waterfront, the **Club de Vela Bacalar** (Av. Costera at Calle 20, tel. 983/834-2478, 9 A.M.–6 P.M. daily) rents sea kayaks for US$7 an hour single or US$9.50 an hour double. The pier here is one of the best places to swim in town; a wooden footbridge leads water babies from land to a swimming dock, where the water is crystal clear and deep.

Other good swimming spots include those at Rancho Encantado and Hotel Laguna; plan on ordering something from the hotel restaurant to be able to use the waterfront.

ACCOMMODATIONS
In Town

Located in the heart of town, [**Casita Carolina** (Av. Costera between Calles 16 and 18, tel. 983/834-2334, www.casitacarolina .com, US$23–42 s/d with shared kitchen, US$37–US$42 s/d, US$51 s/d cabaña with kitchen) is one of the area's most charming and convenient accommodations. Three of the six units occupy a converted family home and share a common living room and kitchen. The other units—a cabaña apartment, a cozy casita, and a *palapa* bungalow—face a large grassy garden that runs to the lakeshore. The rooms vary in size and decor, but all have private bath, fan, and a homey feel. American host and owner Carolyn Niemeyer Weiss lives on-site and loves to visit with guests; she also hosts a weeklong artist's retreat in February.

Hotelito Paraíso (Av. Costera at Calle 14, tel. 983/834-2787, US$37 s/d with fan, US$47 s/d with a/c) has six aging units surrounding a large grassy area that runs right to the lakeshore. There's a generally downtrodden feel about the place, however, with cavernous rooms, nonfunctioning kitchens, and rather saggy beds. Newer units are better, in a pinch.

Outside of Town

Located on approximately 40 hectares (98.8 acres) of mostly undeveloped land, **Villas Ecotucán** (Carr. Chetumal-Cancún Km. 26.5, tel. 983/834-2516, www.villasecotucan .info, US$5/tent camping, US$50 s/d cabañas including breakfast) is a perfect place to enjoy the outdoors. There are plenty of activities for everyone—jungle walks, swimming, kayaking, badminton as well as excellent bird-watching and lake tours. Accommodations consist of just five *palapa*-roofed cabañas. Each is spacious and simple with a separate sitting area and checkerboard floors. Camping is permitted near the lake on a broad expanse of grass. A family-orientated place, rates include two adults and two kids.

If you can get used to the persistent hum of traffic from nearby Highway 307, **Rancho Encantado** (two km/1.25 mi north of town, tel. 983/101-3358, U.S. tel. 505/894-7074, www .encantado.com, US$160–190 s/d, US$245 suite) is a good option. A New-Agey hotel on a lush lakeside property, it has 12 spacious casitas featuring Mexican tile floors, good beds, and small porches that overlook either the garden or the lagoon. The prettiest spot here, however, is a pier that leads to a shady dock strung with hammocks—it's perfect for swimming and relaxing. There's also a small kiosk built over the lake where guests receive massages and body treatments; a Jacuzzi is nearby. Rates include buffet breakfast and dinner.

Built on a bluff overlooking the lagoon, **Hotel Laguna Bacalar** (Blvd. Costero 479, tel. 983/834-2206, www.hotellagunabacalar .com, US$51 s/d with fan, US$64 s/d with a/c) has spacious rooms, most with a balcony and an impressive view of the lake. The decor is seriously tacky and worn—seashells and animal prints figure prominently—but the rooms are clean. Stairs zigzag down to the water, where a pier, ladder, and a diving board make swimming fun and easy. Otherwise, there's a small pool (filled only during high season) near the

rooms. The hotel **restaurant** (7:30 A.M.–9 P.M. daily, US$4–15) serves basic, predictable meals. From the highway, look for the large sign and white and aqua structure on the south side of town.

FOOD
Restaurants

El Carboncito (central plaza, Av. 5 near Calle 20, 5–11:30 P.M. Wed.–Mon., US$2.50–5.50) is a popular *puesto* (outdoor food stand with tables) that serves up grilled favorites like hot dogs, hamburgers, and tacos.

For a laid-back, indoor eatery, **Señor Café** (central plaza, Av 5. at Calle 22, tel. 983/834-2852, 7 A.M.–11 P.M. daily, US$3.50–5.50) offers Mexican favorites like tacos and enchiladas along with sandwiches and egg dishes. Service is excruciatingly slow but the wait is worth it.

For a more formal option, try **La Cosa Nostra** (central plaza, Calle 22 between Avs. 3 and 5, 1–11 P.M. Wed.–Mon., US$5–7), a pleasant little restaurant serving up a variety of salads, baguettes, and pasta dishes.

The lagoon-front **Club de Vela Bacalar** (Av. Costera at Calle 20, tel. 983/834-2478, 9 A.M.–6 P.M. daily, US$8–15) serves seafood and regional food in its open-air restaurant. The prices are somewhat inflated for what you get but the view and the variety are welcome.

Groceries

On the central plaza, **Dunosusa** (Calle 22 between Avs. 3 and 5, 7:30 A.M.–9 P.M. Mon.–Sat., 8:30 A.M.–8 P.M. Sun.) is a surprisingly well-stocked supermarket.

INFORMATION AND SERVICES
Tourist Information

Bacalar does not have a tourist information office yet but www.bacalarmosaico.com is a bilingual website offering useful information on the area's sights, activities, and businesses.

Hospitals

The **Centro de Salud** (Av. 3 between Calles 22 and 24, tel. 983/834-2756, 24 hours daily) is located a block from the central plaza, across from the post office.

Pharmacies

Farmacia San Joaquín (Av. 7 between Calles 20 and 22, 8 A.M.–3 P.M., 6–9 P.M. daily) is just a couple blocks north of the central plaza.

Police

The police station (Calle 20 near Av. 3, 24 hours daily) is just east of the central plaza, across the street from the Fuerte San Felipe Bacalar.

Money

There is no bank in town but there is a **Banorte** ATM on the west side of the central plaza. If you need any other money services or the ATM has run out of cash, the closest bank is in Chetumal.

Internet and Telephone

The most convenient place to email is the **Nave de Papel** (central plaza, Av. 5 between Calles 20 and 22, 2–10 P.M. daily, US$0.75 per hour).

For telephone calls, your best bet is to use the public phones on the central plaza; Ladatel telephone cards can be purchased at the supermarket and at most corner stores.

Post Office

The post office (Av. 3 near Calle 24, 9 A.M.–3 P.M. Mon.–Fri.) is just east of the Fuerte San Felipe Bacalar.

Launderette

Lavandería Lolita (Av. 7 between Calles 24 and 26, tel. 983/834-2069, 9 A.M.–10 P.M. daily) offers same-day service for US$1 per kilogram (2.2 pounds). Pickup and delivery available.

GETTING THERE
Bus

Just one block south of the central plaza, Bacalar's modest bus terminal (Av. 5 near Calle 18, tel. 983/834-2517) has mostly *de paso* (mid-route) service, which means you have to wait for the bus to arrive before buying your ticket, space permitting. Arriving from the north, be sure get off in front of the church; because of the one-way streets, the bus doesn't stop at the station itself. Leaving, first-class ADO buses to

BACALAR BUS SCHEDULES

DESTINATION	PRICE	DURATION	SCHEDULE
Cancún	US$14-17*	6 hrs	every 1-2 hrs, 5:30 A.M.-7:15 P.M., plus 10:45 P.M., and 12:45 A.M.
Chetumal	US$1.75	45 min.	every 30-60 min. 5:30 A.M.-11:15 P.M.
Carrillo Puerto	US$5	2.5 hrs	take Cancún bus
Mahahual	US$5	2 hrs	3-4 times daily
Playa del Carmen	US$11-14*	5 hrs	take Cancún bus
Tulum	US$8.50-9*	4 hrs	take Cancún bus

*Denotes first-class; not available for every departure.

TULUM AND QUINTANA ROO

Cancún (US$18, 5.5 hours) pass at 9:15 A.M. and 3:15 P.M. daily, while second-class Mayab buses (US$15, 6 hours) pass every 1–2 hours 5:30 A.M.–12:45 A.M. Buses to Chetumal pass at roughly the same frequency, but most people catch a *taxi colectivo* or *combi* (US$1.25–1.75, every 30 minutes) in front of Iglesia San Joaquín on Avenida 7, one block up from the lake. You can also flag down Chetumal-bound buses along the highway, if your hotel is closer to there than the terminal.

GETTING AROUND

You can easily walk to all the sites of interest in Bacalar, with the exception of Cenote Azul. A taxi there from town costs US$1–2; you can usually find one around the central plaza or on Avenida 7.

Chetumal

Chetumal is the capital of Quintana Roo and the gateway to Central America. Not the prettiest of towns, most guidebook-toting travelers just pass through, on their way to or from Belize or southern Campeche. However, Chetumal's modern Maya museum is one of the best you'll find, and well worth a visit. In fact, many tour groups stop here just to visit the museum. And if you're dying to see the Guatemalan ruins of Tikal, a shuttle from Chetumal can get you there in eight hours (cutting through Belize), and back again just as fast. The beautiful Laguna Bacalar, north of town, and intriguing Kohunlich and Dzibanché ruins, west of town, make for easy day trips (sans border crossings) too.

SIGHTS
⊂ Museo de la Cultura Maya

One of the best museums in the Yucatán, Museo de la Cultura Maya (Av. de los Héroes at Calle Cristóbal Colón, tel. 983/832-6838, 9 A.M.–7 P.M. Tues.–Thurs. and Sun., 9 A.M.–8 P.M. Fri.–Sat., US$4.75) extends over three levels—the upper represents the world of gods, the middle the world of humans, and the lower *Xibalba,* the underworld. Each floor has impressive, well-designed exhibits describing Maya spiritual beliefs, agricultural practices, astronomy and counting, and more, all in English and Spanish. The exposition area past the ticket booth usually has good temporary art shows too.

On your way into the museum, check out the **Monumento al Mestizo,** a striking sculpture symbolizing the joining of the Spanish shipwrecked sailor Gonzalo Guerrero and a Maya woman—the birth of the mestizos.

Museo de la Ciudad

The city museum (Calle Héroes de Chapultepec between Avs. Juárez and de los Héroes, tel. 983/832-1350, 9 A.M.–7 P.M. Tues.–Sun., US$1) is a small, well-organized museum describing the political, economic, and cultural history of Chetumal; it spans the period from its founding in 1898 to its naming as capital of Quintana Roo in 1915, to present day. There's a small art exhibit at the end too. Signage in Spanish only.

Kohunlich's intricate Temple of the Masks is worth a day trip from Chetumal.

© LIZA PRADO

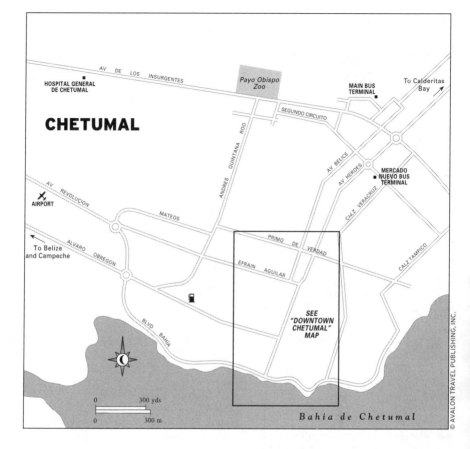

© AVALON TRAVEL PUBLISHING, INC.

Boulevard Bahía

This breezy bayside promenade lacks beaches but makes for a fine bay front stroll. Along it you'll find cafés, sculptures, monuments, a lighthouse, and, hopefully, a cooling breeze. The backstreets harbor pastel-colored, clapboard buildings with a classic Caribbean look.

Kohunlich Archaeological Zone

The archaeological site of Kohunlich is outside Chetumal. Neither as grand as Calakmul nor as glorious as Uxmal, it is still worth a trip if only to visit the compelling **Temple of the Masks.** Dedicated to the Maya sun god, this stone pyramid features haunting stucco masks with star-incised eyes, mustaches, and nose plugs. Standing two meters (6.6 feet) tall, these masks are rarities, to say the least. Be sure to wander through the jungle site; you'll be rewarded with more than 200 structures, stelae, and uncovered mounds that date to late Preclassic (A.D. 100–200) through the Classic (A.D. 600–900) periods. Open 8 A.M.–5 P.M. daily, US$3.

Dzibanché and Kinichná Archaeological Zones

If you want to explore a couple of semi-excavated sites, consider heading to Dzibanché and it's smaller neighbor, Kinichná. Located two kilometers (1.2 miles) apart, they date to

TULUM AND QUINTANA ROO

TULUM AND QUINTANA ROO

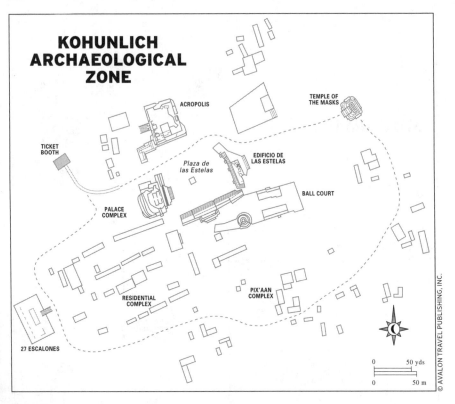

© AVALON TRAVEL PUBLISHING, INC.

A.D. 300–800 and are thought to have been part of a Maya city extending 40 square kilometers (25 square miles). Although Dzibanché is known for the extraordinary wood lintels found there, the main reason visitors come is to wander among the ruins' towering structures, most waiting to be uncovered. Both are open from 8 A.M.–5 P.M. daily; admission is US$3 and good for both archaeological zones.

ENTERTAINMENT AND EVENTS

Every Sunday at 6 P.M., locals gather at the **Plaza la Bandera** (Av. de los Héroes at waterfront) to enjoy city-sponsored events, typically performances by the municipal band or local musicians and singers. The events are free and family-friendly, with vendors selling drinks and street food.

SHOPPING

There is a fine **bookstore and gift shop** (tel. 983/832-2270, 9 A.M.–7 P.M. Tue.–Sat., 9 A.M.–2 P.M. Sun.) near the entrance of Museo de la Cultura Maya, carrying a small selection of maps, posters, T-shirts, and Spanish-language books and magazines.

Across from the museum, **Mercado Ignacio Manuel Altamirano** (Efraín Aguilar between Avs. Belice and de los Héroes, 8 A.M.–4 P.M. daily) sells everyday items geared at locals, from clothing to kitchenware. For travelers, it's a good place to buy a pair of flip-flops or a travel clock, if the need arises.

The **Corozal Duty Free Zone** is an area

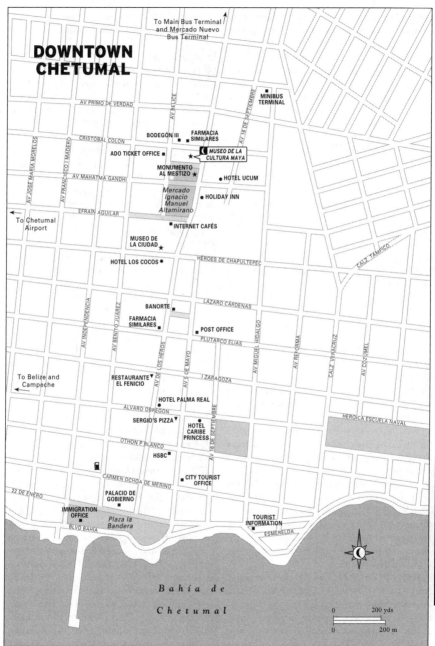

DOWNTOWN CHETUMAL

To Main Bus Terminal
and Mercado Nuevo
Bus Terminal

MINIBUS TERMINAL

AV PRIMO DE VERDAD

AV BELICE

AV 16 DE SEPTIEMBRE

CRISTÓBAL COLÓN

BODEGÓN III

FARMACIA SIMILARES

ADO TICKET OFFICE

MUSEO DE LA CULTURA MAYA

MONUMENTO AL MESTIZO ★

AV JOSÉ MARÍA MORELOS

AV FRANCISCO I MADERO

AV MAHATMA GANDHI

HOTEL UCUM

Mercado Ignacio Manuel Altamirano

HOLIDAY INN

EFRAÍN AGUILAR

← To Chetumal Airport

INTERNET CAFÉS

MUSEO DE LA CIUDAD ★

HOTEL LOS COCOS ●

HÉROES DE CHAPULTEPEC

CALZ TAMPICO

LÁZARO CÁRDENAS

AV INDEPENDENCIA

AV BENITO JUÁREZ

BANORTE

FARMACIA SIMILARES

POST OFFICE

PLUTARCO ELÍAS

AV MIGUEL HIDALGO

AV REFORMA

CALZ VERACRUZ

AV COZUMEL

To Belize and Campeche ←

RESTAURANTE EL FENICIO

AV DE LOS HÉROS

AV 5 DE MAYO

I ZARAGOZA

HOTEL PALMA REAL

ÁLVARO OBREGÓN

SERGIO'S PIZZA ▼

HOTEL CARIBE PRINCESS

OTHON P BLANCO

HSBC

HEROICA ESCUELA NAVAL

AV 16 DE SEPTIEMBRE

CARMEN OCHOA DE MERINO

CITY TOURIST OFFICE

22 DE ENERO

PALACIO DE GOBIERNO

IMMIGRATION OFFICE

Plaza la Bandera

TOURIST INFORMATION

BLVD BAHÍA

ESMERELDA

Bahía de Chetumal

| 0 | 200 yds |
| 0 | 200 m |

© AVALON TRAVEL PUBLISHING, INC.

TULUM AND QUINTANA ROO

jam-packed with stores selling products from around the world. Located in Belize, visitors can enter and leave the area without paying taxes on their purchases, mostly household and personal items. Lots of people complain of second-rate quality, but it's worth a visit if you're in the region for more than a couple weeks and want to stock up on specialty foods or liquor.

ACCOMMODATIONS

Although Chetumal is by no means a resort town, its status as the state capital and its location on the Belize border make it a busy town. Arrive as early in the day as possible to have your choice of hotel rooms. Better yet, call ahead for a reservation.

Under US$50

The basic but very clean **Hotel Ucum** (Av. Mahatma Gandhi between Avs. 5 de Mayo and 16 de Septiembre, tel. 983/832-0711, US$18.50 s/d with fan, US$22 s/d with fan and cable TV, US$32.50 s/d with a/c and cable TV) is the best budget option in town. Just one block from the Museo de la Cultura Maya, rooms are decent size, beds are comfortable, and there's a great pool with a separate wading area for small children. The parking lot also is secure. Ask for a room on the top floor for the best breeze.

With tile floors, wood furniture, and flower bedspreads, rooms at the **Hotel Caribe Princess** (Av. Alvaro Obregón between Avs. 5 de Mayo and 16 de Septiembre, tel. 983/832-0900, caribe_princess@hotmail.com, US$36 s with a/c, US$43 d with a/c) are a good value. They're on the small side, but all have air-conditioning, cable TV, and complimentary coffee in the morning. Ask for a room facing the interior of the building—the avenue in front is a busy one.

Hotel Palma Real (Av. Alvaro Obregón at Av. de los Héroes, tel. 983/833-0964, htldene gocios@yahoo.com.mx, US$34–39 s/d with a/c) is another bright spot on the hotel scene. Rooms are spacious, clean, and have appealing decor. Some also have balconies that face the

main drag—a somewhat loud but interesting bird's-eye view of the hubbub downtown.

US$50-100

(Hotel Los Cocos (Av. de los Héroes at Calle Héroes de Chapultepec, tel. 983/835-0430, toll-free Mex. tel. 800/719-5840, www.hotelloscocos.com.mx, US$70 s/d standard, US$83 s/d premiere, US$95 s/d villas) is a stylish surprise in this small town. Renovated rooms—premiere and villas only—are absolutely worth the price: sleek furniture, gleaming tile floors, and the newest in amenities. Older rooms—standards—are overpriced: outdated white furniture, bathrooms that are begging for new tiles, and air-conditioning units that could use a tune-up. Regardless where guests stay, however, all have access to the lush garden and inviting pool area. There's also a good open-air restaurant on-site.

If Los Cocos is full, try the **Holiday Inn** (Av. de los Héroes near Av. Mahatma Gandhi, tel. 983/835-0400, toll-free U.S. tel. 888/465-4329, www.holiday-inn.com/chetumalmex, US$95). Rooms are comfortable and utilitarian with air-conditioning, cable TV, in-room telephone, and Internet access. The hotel also boasts perks like a pool, Jacuzzi, gym, and business center.

Outside of Chetumal

On the road to Kohunlich is the luxurious **(Explorean Kohunlich** (tel. 555/201-8350, toll-free Mex. 800/366-6666, U.S. 877/397-5672, www.theexplorean.com, US$231 s, 360 d, includes meals, open bar, and one excursion/day). This Fiesta Americana all-inclusive resort boasts 40 deluxe suites set in 30 hectares (74 acres) of jungle property. Each has gleaming stone floors, high *palapa* ceilings, elegant furnishings, and private stone-walled yards for sunbathing. Breakfast is served in a private outdoor living room or—if you prefer—in the indoor sitting area. At the main building, a fine restaurant serves delicious regional fare (7:30–10:30 A.M., 1:30–4 P.M., 7:30–10:30 P.M. daily, US$10–20, open to nonguests), a full-service spa is at the ready, and a sleek lap pool overlooks the jungle below (you can even see the ruins at Kohunlich from here). One excursion per day—including rappelling in the jungles of Campeche, kayaking through a crocodile reserve, or mountain biking through forgotten forests—also is included in the rate. Add in all your meals, drinks, and taxes and this is great deal on a great place.

FOOD

⟨ Restaurante El Fenicio (Av. de los Héroes at Calle Zaragoza, tel. 983/832-0026, 24 hours daily, US$4–10) is our favorite restaurant in Chetumal, not only because it's open late but also because of its tasty, reliable meals. Be sure to try the "make your own taco" dish, a platter stacked with chicken, chorizo, beef, and melted cheese, and served with tortillas and all the fixings.

Set in a dark wood, dimly lit, faux–Tiffany lamp dining room, **Sergio's Pizza** (Av. 5 de Mayo at Av. Alvaro Obregón, tel. 983/832-0491, 7 A.M.–midnight daily, US$4–16) serves much more than pizza—the extensive menu covers the gamut of Italian and Mexican dishes—from meat lasagna to *molletes rancheros*. Meals are tasty and service is excellent. Popular with families.

Bodegón III (Calle Cristóbal Colon between Avs. Belice and de los Héroes, 5 A.M.–9 P.M. Mon.–Sat., 5 A.M.–3 P.M. Sun.) is a large grocery store with a decent selection of canned and dry foods and a huge display of fruits and veggies in front. Nos. I and II are nearby.

INFORMATION
Tourist Information

Near the waterfront, the city tourist office (Av. 5 de Mayo at Carmen Ochoa de Merino, 983/835-0500, 9 A.M.–4 P.M. Mon.–Fri.) has a decent selection of brochures and maps. It also maintains a kiosk on the waterfront at Avenida Hidalgo.

Hospitals

About two kilometers (1.2 miles) from the center of town, **Hospital General de Chetumal** (Avs. Andrés Quintana Roo at Juan José Isior-

dia, tel. 983/832-8194, 24 hours daily) is the city's main hospital.

Pharmacies

Farmacia Similares (Av. de los Héroes at Calle Plutarco Elias, 8 A.M.–9 P.M. Mon.–Sat., 8 A.M.– 8 P.M. Sun.) also has a sister store behind the Maya museum (Calle Cristóbal Colón between Avs. Belice and de los Héroes) that is open 24 hours daily.

SERVICES
Money

HSBC (Othon P. Blanco between Av. 5 de Mayo and Av. de los Héroes, 8 A.M.–7 P.M. Mon.–Sat.) and **Banorte** (Av. de los Héroes between Lázaro Cárdenas and Plutarco Elias, 9 A.M.–4 P.M. Mon.–Fri.) both have ATMs. There also is an ATM at the bus station.

Internet and Telephone

A string of Internet cafés are conveniently lined up across from the **Mercado Ignacio Manuel Altamirano** (Efraín Aguilar between Avs. Belice and de los Héroes). Charging around US$1 an hour, most are open 7 A.M.–2 A.M. Monday–Saturday and 8 A.M.–midnight on Sunday. Many also have cheap international telephone service.

Post Office

The post office (Av. Plutarco Elias Calles between Avs. 5 de Mayo and 16 de Septiembre, 8 A.M.–6 P.M. Mon.–Fri., 9 A.M.–1 P.M. Sat.) is just a block from the main drag.

Immigration

The immigration office (Calzada del Centenario 582, tel. 983/832-6353) is open 9 A.M.– 1 P.M. Monday–Friday.

For information on the Belizean and Guatemalan consulates, see the *Foreign Consulates* sidebar in the *Essentials* chapter.

Storage

Conveniently located in the bus station, **Revistas and Novedades Laudy** stores bags for US$0.50 per hour.

CHETUMAL BUS SCHEDULES

Departures from Chetumal's **main bus terminal** (Av. Insurgentes at Av. de los Héroes, tel. 983/832-5110, ext. 2404) include:

DESTINATION	PRICE	DURATION	SCHEDULE
Campeche	US$23	7 hrs	noon
Cancún	US$17-20*	5.5-7 hrs	every 30 min. 8:30 A.M.-5 P.M., plus 6:30 A.M. and every 1-2 hrs 6 P.M.-midnight.
Flores, Guatemala	US$16 plus border fees	7-8 hrs	6 A.M.
Mahahual	US$7.50	3 hrs	5 A.M., 2:30 P.M., 7:30 P.M.
Mérida	US$22	6 hrs	7:30 A.M., 1:30 P.M., 5 P.M., and 11:30 P.M.
Palenque	US$27	7 hrs	7:55 P.M., 9:25 P.M., and 11:25 P.M.
Xpujil	US$5-7	1.5-2 hrs	every 1-2 hrs 11:30 A.M.-11:45 P.M.

*Denotes first class service; not available for all departures.

Buses to **Bacalar** (US$1.50, 20 min.) leave from a **minibus terminal** (Av. Primo de Verdad at Av. Miguel Hidalgo, no phone) every hour 9 A.M.-6 P.M.

Buses for **Corozal** (US$1.50, one hour), **Orangewalk** (US$4, two hours), and **Belize City** (US$7, three hours) leave the **Mercado Nuevo** (Av. de los Héroes and Circuito Segundo, no phone) six times daily 5 A.M.-4:45 P.M. Some pass the main ADO terminal en route.

Buses to the **Zona Libre** (US$1, 30 min.) leave every 15 min. 6:30 A.M.-8 P.M.

GETTING THERE

Air

The small **Chetumal Airport** (CTM, tel. 983/832-0898) receives only a few flights each day. Airlines serving it include: **Aviacsa** (toll-free Mex. tel. 800/006-2200, www .aviacsa.com), **Click Mexicana** (toll-free Mex. tel. 800/112-5425, www.clickmx.com), and **Mexicana** (toll-free Mex. tel. 800/502-2000, www.mexicana.com).

Bus

Most first- and second-class buses leave from the main bus terminal (Av. Insurgentes at Av. de los Héroes, tel. 983/832-5110, ext. 2404). You can buy tickets there or at a ticket office (Avs. Belice and Cristóbal Colón, tel. 983/832-0639) just west of the Maya museum. Two other terminals—the Minibus terminal (Av. Primo de Verdad at Av. Miguel Hidalgo, no phone) and Mercado Nuevo (Av. de los Héroes and Circuito Segundo, no phone)—have service to Bacalar, the Zona Libre, and to Belize.

Car

The highways in this area have improved immensely in recent years. The roads from Chetumal to Mahahual, Tulum, and Xpujil have transformed from isolated adventure roads to modern highways with very few potholes.

GETTING AROUND

Chetumal is a relatively large city, but the parts most travelers will be interested in are all within easy walking distance—mostly along Avenida de los Héroes. The exception is the main bus terminal and Mercado Nuevo (where you catch buses to Belize), both of which are 10–12 grubby blocks from the center. A cab to either terminal, or anywhere around town, costs US$1.50.

There is no public transportation to either archaeological zone. Highway 186, however, leads to both turnoffs. The bumpy turnoff to **Dzibanché** is about 50 kilometers (31 miles) east of Chetumal and runs north for 24 kilometers (14.9 miles) before hitting the site. The turnoff to **Kohunlich** is three kilometers (1.9 miles) farther west on Highway 186; it's another 8.5 kilometers (5.3 miles) south on a paved road to the site.

TULUM AND QUINTANA ROO

THE STATE OF YUCATÁN

If culture were money, Yucatán would be the richest guy on the block. And in a way, it already is. Yucatán is home to a stunning array of cultural treasures: ancient Maya ruins and contemporary indigenous villages; sprawling haciendas and gorgeous colonial cities; modern museums and a worldly population. Add to that the state's natural riches, including the world's largest colony of the world's largest (and pinkest) flamingos, and geologic idiosyncrasies like cenotes and a vast network of caves. There is something here for every sort of traveler and whether you have a week or a month, you'll leave feeling like you've won the lottery.

PLANNING YOUR TIME

You can sample a little of everything in Yucatán in five days, but you won't be sorry to have a week or more. Budget at least two days for Mérida itself, and at least another two to visit the ruins—one for the Puuc Route and another to visit Chichén Itzá and its surroundings. If you love ruins, budget three or four days—that way you won't feel rushed to get through them. Finally, leave a day for an outdoorsy trip, like visiting the flamingos in Celestún or Río Lagartos, or swimming in cenotes.

Mérida is well known as one of Mexico's hottest cities, with high humidity and average temperatures of 37°C (97°F) from April to July. The same months are blessed with almost daily rain showers, which provide cooling relief, and most travelers adapt quickly to the climate. However, families and older travelers should take special care.

© LIZA PRADO

HIGHLIGHTS

 **Museo Regional de Antropología e Historia:** It's no surprise that a state brimming with ancient ruins would have an anthropology museum as outstanding as this one, with fascinating displays on Maya art, astronomy, architecture, and more (page 239).

 **Museo MACAY:** History is palpable in Mérida, but that doesn't mean it's stuck in the past – the city's modern art museum has a terrific collection of paintings and sculptures by local and international artists (page 239).

 **Domingo en Mérida:** Sunday is the day Mérida celebrates itself. Locals and tourists alike throng to the main plaza to munch on street food, watch dance performances, and share in the joy of simply being there (page 240).

 **Uxmal Archaeological Zone:** Soaring structures and graceful design make Uxmal one of the most beautiful of all Maya ruins (page 263).

 **Cenotes de Cuzamá:** Ride a horse-drawn trolley through abandoned henequen fields and then climb down through a crack in the earth to swim in the cool, iridescent waters of ancient cenotes (page 284).

 **Flamingo Tours:** The world's largest and pinkest flamingos congregate in the mangrove-fringed estuaries at Celestún (page 287) and Río Lagartos (page 323), where boat tours bring you up close to these most peculiar of birds.

 **Convento de San Antonio de Padua:** Both beautiful and troubling, Izamal's stately yellow convent was built on top of a sacred Maya temple – some of the pilfered stones are still visible in the church walls (page 300).

 **Chichén Itzá Archaeological Zone:** The Yucatán's most well-known ancient ruins also is the most heavily visited. Arrive early to enjoy the site's awesome scale and superlative design, including the largest ball court in the Maya world (page 304).

LOOK FOR  TO FIND RECOMMENDED SIGHTS, ACTIVITIES, DINING, AND LODGING.

THE STATE OF YUCATÁN

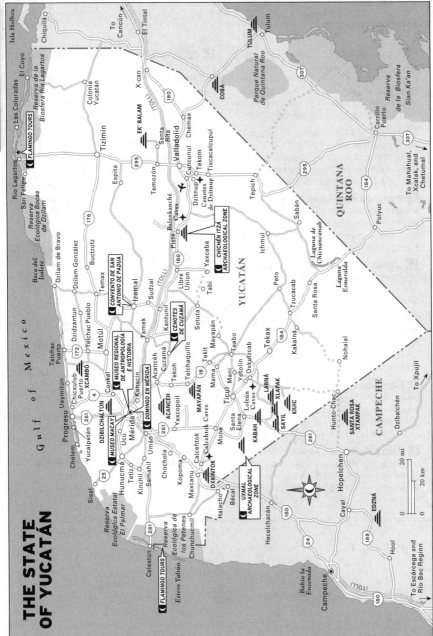

THE STATE OF YUCATÁN

© AVALON TRAVEL PUBLISHING, INC.

Mérida

Mérida bursts with art and culture, in a way unrivaled by any other city on the Yucatán Peninsula (and few in the whole country). The city's rich artistic and architectural heritage can be enjoyed in its museums, monuments, churches, colonial mansions, and beautiful government buildings, while tree-lined parks and plazas offer a peek into ordinary Mexican life. But it's the city's commitment to music and dance that really sets it apart, with city-sponsored performances and concerts held every day and weekly street parties that feature live bands and performers—all this, all year long, and all for free. Pull out your dancing shoes and grab hold of your camera, you're sure to need both even if you just stay a night.

ORIENTATION

Mérida is laid out in a neat grid pattern of one-way numbered streets. The even-numbered streets run north to south, the odd east to west.

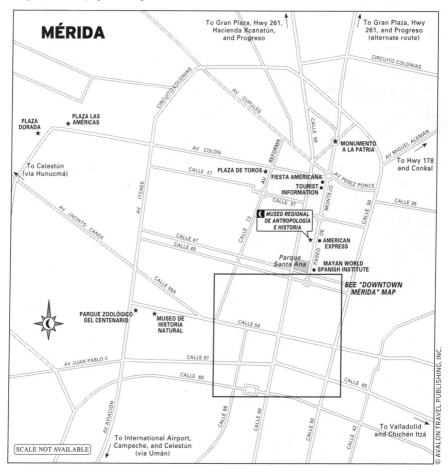

MÉRIDA

SCALE NOT AVAILABLE

© AVALON TRAVEL PUBLISHING, INC.

The central plaza is the center of town and you can easily walk to most downtown attractions, shops, and marketplaces. Buses provide frequent service in and around the city and outlying areas, and cabs are plentiful.

SIGHTS
Plaza de la Independencia

Surrounded by aristocratic colonial buildings, the large green central plaza is an oasis in the middle of this busy town. This is a city where people stroll the streets after dark and feel safe and comfortable. Men in woven panama hats and guayaberas gather in the morning; women in colorful *huipiles* sit in the shade or tend small sidewalk stands, and white, S-shaped chairs are quaint reminders of former courtship rituals.

La Catedral de San Ildefonso

The most prominent building on the plaza is the cathedral. Built with stones taken from Maya structures, it was completed in 1598 making it one of the oldest buildings on the continent. The architecture reflects the combination of Moorish and Renaissance styles that were prevalent in Spain at the time. Inside, immense stone columns hold up a beautiful latticed stone ceiling, and a huge wood Christ stands behind the altar in place of more elaborate altarpieces seen in other churches. Overall, the exterior and interior are stark in comparison to some of the ornately adorned churches in other parts of Mexico—this is partly owing to the traditional austerity of Franciscan design, and partly to damage and looting that took place during the Caste War and the 1910 revolution.

On the left side of the cathedral, a small but elaborately decorated iron and glass chapel houses a revered image of Jesus called **El Cristo de las Ampollas** (The Christ of the Blisters). Carved from a tree in Ichmul that had been engulfed in flames but remained undamaged, the wooden statue reportedly went through another fire in Ichmul's church that destroyed the church but only left blisterlike welts on the statue. A religious festival is held in honor of El Cristo de las Ampollas every September,

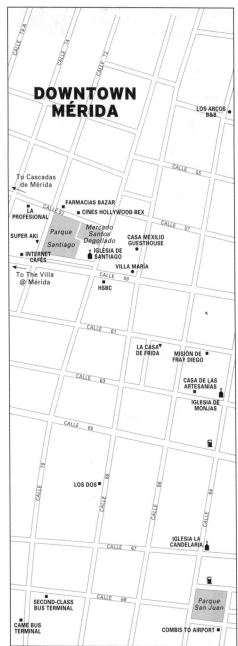

DOWNTOWN MÉRIDA

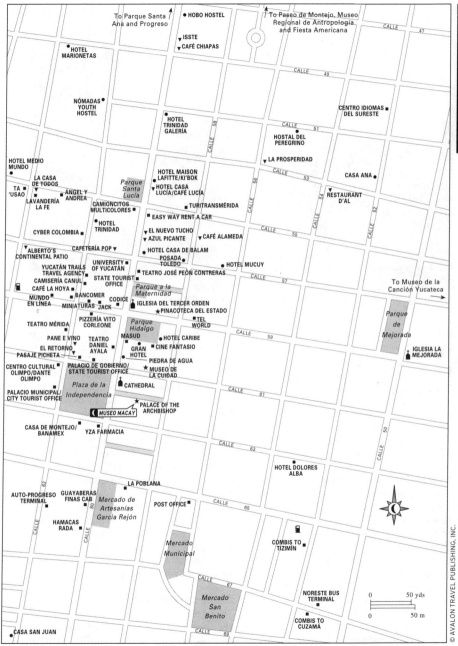

© AVALON TRAVEL PUBLISHING, INC.

© GARY CHANDLER

A leafy, comfortable place, Mérida's central plaza is a popular spot for locals and travelers alike.

though on Sundays you'll see the devout come to see the statue and to say a brief prayer.

Palace of the Archbishop

Next to the cathedral, this sprawling building was originally the residence of the archbishop. It became the local military post after the revolution, and eventually—after being remodeled— was transformed into the **Museo MACAY,** Mérida's museum of contemporary art.

Los Palacios Gobernales

On the northeast corner of the Plaza de la Independencia is the **Palacio de Gobierno** (8 A.M.–10 P.M. daily), the seat of government offices for the state of Yucatán. Inside and in the upper galleries there are several abstract paintings by the famous Mérida-born artist Fernando Castro Pacheco. Created between 1971 and 1974, these works depict the history of the region—from the time of the ancient Maya to modern-day Mexico. Restoration of these works was completed in 2004 under the supervision of Pacheco himself by four professional restoration artists from the Centro de Restauración de Bellas Artes in Mexico City.

On the west side of the Plaza de la Independencia is the **Palacio Municipal.** This architectural beauty dates from 1543 and serves as Mérida's city hall. The building was renovated in the mid-1800s.

One of the most outstanding structures in Mérida sits on Paseo de Montejo: the **Palacio Cantón** (Paseo de Montejo at Calle 43). Designed by the same architect who built the Teatro Peón Contreras, this impressive rococo-facade building was built between 1909–1911 for Francisco Cantón Rosado, a former governor of Yucatán. It served as the official state residence between 1948–1960 and in 1977 became the city's **Museo Regional de Antropología.**

Casa de Montejo

Facing the southern edge of the central plaza is the Casa de Montejo, once the home of Francisco de Montejo "El Mozo" (The Younger).

SIGN LANGUAGE

As you navigate through the numbered streets of Mérida, you'll soon begin noticing whimsical street signs – carved pictures of animals, household items, and people – adorning street corners. These signs pay homage to Mérida's past when, because of the high illiteracy rate, the city government hung painted wooden signs of familiar figures so that every inhabitant could find an address. Typically, these signs directly related to establishments or sights nearby: a pair of nuns to signal a convent, a violin to indicate an instrument maker, a bull to direct people to the *Plaza de Toros* (bull ring). Look around, and you'll not only get a flavor of where things were in Mérida's past, but also where they still might be today.

The building was constructed in 1549 by Maya slaves. Note the carvings of Spaniards standing at attention with their feet firmly planted on the heads of the Mayas—a lasting reminder of Spanish tyranny. Until the mid-1800s, 13 generations of Montejos lived in the house. Afterward, it changed hands several times until to it was sold to Banamex in 1980. Today, the bank takes up the entire structure; the enormous interior courtyard can be seen during banking hours (9 A.M.–4 P.M. Mon.–Fri., 10 A.M.–2 P.M. Sat.).

◀ Museo Regional de Antropología e Historia

Mérida's **Museum of Anthropology and History** (Palacio Cantón, Paseo de Montejo at Calle 43, tel. 999/923-0557, 8 A.M.–8 P.M. Tues.–Sat., 8 A.M.–2 P.M. Sun., US$3) houses the finest collections of Maya artifacts in the Yucatán Peninsula. Only the national anthropology museum in Mexico City is better, and it irks many Yucatecans that the best pieces often get whisked off to the capital. There's no shortage of wow-power in Mérida, however: the museum's collection ranges from ornately painted ceramic jars to massive funerary urns,

from delicate jewelry and ritual items made of jade, obsidian, and sea shells to imposing stone monoliths covered in hieroglyphics. There are detailed descriptions of the Maya calendar, and advancements in astronomy, architecture, and agriculture, all in Spanish and English. The museum includes exhibits and artifacts from across the peninsula, from Pre-Classic to present-day eras, making this a great complement to a tour of the Yucatán's archaeological sites.

◀ Museo MACAY

Museo MACAY (Pasaje Revolución between Calles 58 and 60, tel. 999/928-3258, www .macay.org, 10 A.M.–6 P.M. Wed.–Mon., free) is a first class modern art museum, boasting an impressive collection of Yucatecan modern art, including paintings by Gabriel Ramírez Aznar, Fernando García Ponce, and Fernando Castro Pacheco (who painted the arresting murals in the Palacio de Gobierno). The museum occupies a beautiful 16th century building next to the Cathedral; in fact, it was originally part of the Cathedral, but the two were separated in 1916. The annex was used as a cultural center, then for government offices, before the MACAY opened here in 1993. The passageway between the museum and cathedral serves to display rotating sculpture exhibits. The museum also oversees the terrific large-scale installations seen along Paseo Montejo.

Other Museums

The **Museo de la Cuidad** (Calle 58 at Calle 61, tel. 999/923-6869, 8 A.M.–8 P.M. Tues.– Fri. and 8 A.M.–2 P.M. Sat. and Sun., free) is a history museum focused on the development of Mérida. Housed in a former colonial church, the exhibits include Maya artifacts, antique weapons and maps, photographs, and various scale models. Signage is in both Spanish and English and staff members happily answer questions.

The **Museo de la Canción Yucateca** (Calle 57 at Calle 48, tel. 999/923-7224, 9 A.M.–5 P.M. Tues.–Sun., US$1.50, free Sun.) describes the development of Yucatecan music and its artists. Divided into five areas, the first provides a historical overview of the region's music, from its beginnings in the late 1800s to present day. The remaining exhibit halls pay homage to Yucatán's most famous composers, singers, and musicians and contain portraits, instruments, and some personal belongings. Signage, unfortunately, is only in Spanish. The museum also hosts a free concert once a month; the featured music is dedicated to Yucatecan musicians born in that month.

Pinacoteca del Estado Juan Gamboa Guzmán (Calle 59 between Calles 58 and 60, tel. 999/924-5233, 8 A.M.–8 P.M. Tues.–Sat. and 8 A.M.–2 P.M. Sun., US$2.25) is located in an annex to an abandoned Jesuit church, El Jésus. Known today as *Tercera Orden,* it houses mostly religious works of art from the colonial period though it also has a handful of paintings by the famous Yucatecan artist Juan Gamboa Guzmán and bronze statutes by Enrique Gottidiener, an influential Mexican artist who lived and died in Mérida. The building itself is beautiful to wander in, and if you're lucky, you'll be able to sneak a peek into the dilapidated church itself.

Despite being inaugurated in 1987, the **Museo de Historia Natural** (Calle 59 between Calles 84 and 84-A, tel. 999/924-0994, 9 A.M.–4 P.M. Tues.–Sun., US$0.50, free Sun.) looks as if its exhibits were mounted in the early 1970s and haven't been touched since. Nevertheless, the museum does a decent job of explaining the basics of the solar system and the development of Earth. Signage, unfortunately, is in Spanish only.

Conkal, a small town a few minutes northeast of Mérida, is home to the religious art museum, **Museo de Arte Sacro en Yucatán** (behind the church in the central plaza, tel. 999/912-4198, 10 A.M.–5 P.M. Tues.–Sat., 10 A.M.–2 P.M. Sun., free). Opened in 2001, this museum is housed in a beautifully renovated ex-convent and while its permanent collection of sacred art is far from impressive, it often has excellent visiting exhibits. Call or check with the tourist office in Mérida before you head out.

ENTERTAINMENT AND EVENTS

As one of Mexico's colonial shining stars, Mérida is the region's cultural supernova. With free nightly performances, four theaters, four cinemas, art galleries, a planetarium, and a bullring, there is absolutely something for everyone. For up-to-date information on monthly events, there are several free tourism magazines and brochures that are incredibly helpful. Among the best are *Yucatán Today, Explore Yucatán, Cartelera Divertimento,* and the city tourism office's *Programa Mensual de Actividades Culturales.*

◖ Domingo en Mérida

Sunday is a wonderful day in Mérida. Everyone puts on their Sunday best and comes to the city center, where the streets are closed to traffic. *Artesanía* vendors set up stalls, and pushcarts do a lively business selling *tortas* (sandwiches), *elote* (corn on the cob), drinks, and sweets. Be sure to catch one of the many free performances throughout the day. The most popular is folkloric dancing presented in front of the Palacio Municipal, often featuring the city's remarkably skilled youth dance troupe. A new addition to the Sunday lineup is the "Bici-Ruta," a five-kilometer route, including a section of Paseo de Montejo, where cars are restricted to make room for bicycling; it's popular with local families, but visitors can easily rent bikes and join in.

Music and Dance

Music is heard all over Mérida, and dancing is a way of life. Informal and free concerts and other entertainment are regularly presented for Mérida's residents and visitors at parks and plazas throughout the city. Every Saturday night, Calle 60 is closed from the central plaza past Parque Santa Lucía, restaurants bring out tables and chairs, and live bands play salsa and merengue, encouraging dancing in the streets. Sunday features traditional music and dance performances in the center. In fact, all of the regularly scheduled events throughout the week involve music and dancing in some way, whether to watch or to join in.

MÉRIDA'S WEEKLY CULTURAL EVENTS

SUNDAY (DOMINGO EN MÉRIDA)

- **Plaza Independencia:** handicrafts market and outdoor food stands (10 A.M.–6 P.M.)

- **Palacio Municipal:** regional dance performances (1 and 3 P.M.)

- **Parque Santa Lucía:** antiques bazaar (mornings) and live regional music (11 A.M.)

- **Parque Hidalgo:** comedy acts and live marimba music (11:30 A.M.)

- **Bici-Ruta:** five kilometers (three miles) of streets in the historical center are open to bicyclists and pedestrians only (8 A.M.–12:30 P.M.). Bicycles can be rented in front of the Palacio Municipal (US$1-2 per hour).

MONDAY

- **Palacio Municipal:** regional dance performance (9 P.M.)

TUESDAY

- **Parque Santiago:** live big-band music and dancing (8:30 P.M.)

- **Centro Cultural de Mérida Olimpo:** classical guitar and ballad performance (8:30 P.M.)

WEDNESDAY

- **Teatro José Peón Contreras** ballet folklórico performance (US$5, 9 P.M.)

- **Centro Cultural de Mérida Olimpo:** live theater or music performance (9 P.M.)

- **Museo de la Canción Yucateca:** regional music concert held on the last Wednesday of every month (9 P.M.)

THURSDAY

- **Parque Santa Lucía:** regional dance, music, and spoken-word performances (9 P.M.)

FRIDAY

- **Universidad de Yucatán:** live regional music performance (9 P.M.)

SATURDAY

- **Paseo de Montejo at Calle 47:** Noche Mexicana – food stalls, handicrafts booths, live music, and dance performances (8 P.M.–midnight

- **Calle 60 (between Plaza Independencia and Calle 53):** En El Corazón de Mérida – the street closes for live bands, dancing, and outdoor eating (9 P.M.–2 A.M.)

Theater

Built during Mérida's boom in the early 1900s, **Teatro José Peón Contreras** (Calle 60 at Calle 57, tel. 999/923-7354, 9 A.M.–9 P.M. Tues.–Sat., 9 A.M.–3 P.M. Sun.) is a beautiful, mammoth building: The main staircase is made of Carrara marble and various murals and paintings adorn the walls and ceiling. Today, the theater hosts mostly music concerts and *ballet folklórico* performances. For a listing of events, stop by the box office or check at the tourist information center, at the corner of the theater building. When there aren't rehearsals, you also can take a look around the theater for free from 9 A.M.–6 P.M.

Teatro Mérida (Calle 62 between Calles 59 and 61, tel. 999/924-9990, 10 A.M.–9 P.M. Tues.–Sun.) is an art-deco venue housing a main theater and two smaller ones. It's an artsy place with top-notch programming year-round—productions vary from modern dance programs to international film festivals.

Renovated in 2006, **Teatro Daniel Ayala** (Calle 60 between Calles 59 and 61, tel. 999/924-0277, 9 A.M.–9 P.M. Tues.–Sun.) is a cavernous theater that is used mainly for dramatic performances.

Cultural Centers

Centro Cultural de Mérida Olimpo (Calle 61 at Calle 62, tel. 999/942-0000, ext. 477,

10 A.M.–10 P.M. Tues.–Sun.) is a cultural center housed in an award-winning modern space. There are exhibition halls, a research library, a planetarium, and theaters where films are screened and concerts are held. The programming is chock-full each month—check the bulletin board at the entrance for listings. One concert that never fails is the *Noche de Trova*, which takes place every Tuesday at 8:30 P.M. and is free.

Festivals

Since 2001, the city of Mérida has hosted the **Annual Yucatán Bird Festival Toh** (www.yucatanbirds.org.mx) in late November/early December. For a weekend, birders from around the world gather to attend conferences, see exhibits, and observe (or at least get a glimpse of) the 442 bird species registered in the state (543 species are registered in the entire peninsula). It's a well-attended conference and one that welcomes amateurs and experts alike. It's a great way to see the state and to learn about its myriad birds.

Mérida also plays host to the international modern dance festival **Festival Oc' Ohtic.** Professional dancers from all over the world come to perform, often creating such a buzz that there are enormous lines to see the shows. The festival typically takes place during the first two weeks in December—if you're in town, be sure to catch at least one performance. With affordable ticket prices—around US$5—it's hard to resist.

The month-long **Festival Internacional de las Artes** is held every January to commemorate the founding of the city of Mérida. Started in 2005, the festival brings hundreds of artists from around the world to share their works of art, dance, music, drama, film, and literature with the community. Events and workshops are held in Mérida's historic buildings and parks. For a list of scheduled events, ask at one of the tourist offices.

Lounge Bars and Discotheques

An open-air hipster lounge, **El Cielo** (Paseo de Montejo at Calle 15, tel. 999/944-5127, 8 P.M.–2 A.M. Tues.–Sun.) is a great place to start a balmy night. All-white decor with mellow tunes set the mood perfectly. The place where beautiful people come to see and be seen.

La Casa de Todos (aka Peña, Calle 64 at Calle 55, 9 P.M.–2 A.M. most days) Reggae, rock, and *trova* figure prominently in this small bar known for its live music and leftist leanings. Drinks and light fare served; opening hours and cover charge vary with the act.

Live Caribbean rhythms get people spinning at **Mambocafé** (Plaza Las Américas mall, 999/987-7533, 9 P.M.–2:30 A.M. Wed.–Sat.). Yes, it's in a mall; and yes, it's a chain but that doesn't stop it from being one of the hottest dance spots in town. Especially fun—and crowded—after 11:30 P.M. No cover on Wednesdays, open bar Thursday (US$14 men, US$6.50 women), US$5.50 cover Friday and Saturday.

Azul Picante (Calle 60 between Calles 55 and 57, 9 P.M.–3 A.M. Wed.–Sat., US$4) is another Latin music dance spot where live salsa and merengue bands keep the crowd moving. On Saturdays, bands often play outdoors—you're sure to see people spinning on Calle 60—experts and novices alike.

Tequila Boom (Paseo de Montejo at Av. Campestre, 9 P.M.–3 A.M. Wed.–Sat., US$5) is a classic discotheque with a DJ spinning everything from Mexican rock to retro funk. Popular with 20-somethings.

Salones Familiares

A classic Meridian experience, the *salon familiar* is a place where locals head for regional food, drink, and entertainment at reasonable prices. Performances typically include live music, comedy acts, and *ballet folklórico*. It's a place where everyone is welcome and a party atmosphere rules. On weekends and during vacation periods, you'll see lots of families inside. The most popular *salones* downtown are: **La Prosperidad** (Calle 53 at Calle 56, 11:30 A.M.–8 P.M. daily, US$4–7)—a big, noisy, friendly place with a stage. Performances run daily 2 P.M.–7:30 P.M. While you enjoy the entertainment, try the Yucatecan *botanas* (appetizers) or one of the huge entrées, most of which are pork- or chicken-based; and **El Nuevo Tucho** (Calle 60 between Calles 55 and 57, tel. 999/928-2858, 11:30 A.M.–9:30 P.M. daily, US$5–10) with special performances from 4:30–7 P.M., and live music the rest of the night. While it's a good introduction to regional food and entertainment, don't expect much conversation at this place—the speakers blast away any possibility of interaction. In fact, pointing at the menu might be easier than trying to shout your order.

City Tours

Bus tours of the city are a good way to get your bearings straight, and to get a sense of which places in Mérida you'd like to return to spend extra time (and which not). There are two bus operators that give city tours; though different, both provide a good lay of the land.

As the name suggests, **Camioncitos Multicolores** (Calle 55 at Calle 60, tel. 999/927-6119, US$7 adult, US$4 child) are multicolored open-air buses used for two-hour guided driving tours of the city, with explanations in English and in Spanish. The route includes drive-bys of the historical center and outlying neighborhoods. Tours leave at 10 A.M., 1 P.M., 4 P.M., and 7 P.M. Monday–Saturday, and 1 P.M. and 4 P.M. Sunday. Look for the multicolored bus in front of Parque Santa Lucía on Calle 55. Reservations are not necessary.

Turibus Circuito Turístico (Hotel Fiesta Americana, Calle 56 at Av. Colón, tel. 999/920-7636, www.turibus.com.mx, 9 A.M.–9 P.M. daily, US$10 adult, US$5 children under 12) operates a fleet of apple red double-decker buses that have all-day "hop-on hop-off" service along a preset route; the stops include Fiesta Americana Hotel/Zona Hotelera, the central plaza, Museum of Anthropology, Itzimná church and park, Gran Plaza mall, Monumento a la Bandera, and Parque Las Americas. Buses pass any given stop approximately every 45 minutes. Multilingual recorded explanations of various historical buildings and points of interest also are played along the way.

© LIZA PRADO

Calesas (horse-drawn buggies) are always on call for a city tour.

Mérida's narrow streets were originally designed for *calesas* (horse-drawn buggies) and you can still ride one through the historical center where mansions with carved facades, stone gargoyles, and wrought-iron fences still stand (although some much better than others). Sunday is the best day to hire a *calesa* as many streets are closed to vehicular traffic and the rest are relatively quiet; other days, you'll have to share the streets with the exhaust from passing cars. The easiest places to hire a *calesa* is either at the Plaza de la Independencia or in front of the Hotel Fiesta Americana (Paseo de Montejo at Av. Colón). Drivers are typically at both sites 8 A.M.–midnight daily. Tours last between 30–90 minutes and range from US$25–35. Definitely agree upon a price before sitting down for the ride.

The **city tourist office** (central plaza, Calle 62 between Calles 61 and 63, tel. 999/942-0000 ext. 801119) offers a free walking tour Monday–Saturday at 9:30 A.M. in English and Spanish. The tour lasts 1.5 hours and focuses on the buildings around the Plaza de la Independencia. To sign up, just go to the tourism office at 9:15 A.M. on the morning you'd like to join the group.

Regional Tours

There is a *lot* to see and do around Mérida: Maya ruins, colonial churches, cenotes, caves, bird-watching, mountain biking, snorkeling, and repelling, and more. Guided tours are a practical way—and in a few cases, the only way—to see and do it all. But don't feel bound by set trips—small tour companies often customize outings to fit travelers' particular interests and stamina.

Tour prices vary widely, from US$40 day trips to week-long tours that cost over 1,000 bucks. Be sure to ask about extra costs, like admission to the ruins, and whether trips include guide service or simply transportation. Popular package tours include must-sees like Chichén Itzá, Uxmal, Celestún, and cenote tours. Private tours may cover the same places, or venture into less visited ones, and often focus on specific themes, like Maya culture, or birds and wildlife.

Ecoturismo Yucatán (Calle 3 between Calles 32-A and 34, Col. Pensiones, tel. 999/920-2772, www.ecoyuc.com.mx) offers excellent outdoors tours, including to Calcetok caves, Celestún, and biking to nearby cenotes, haciendas and archaeological sites. The agency is also known for customized 7–15-day tours that range as far as Campeche's Río Bec region and Akumal on the Caribbean coast.

Iluminado Tours (tel. 999/900-1414, www.iluminado-tours.com) specializes in multi-day tours that combine visits to places like Ek' Balam and Izamal with an emphasis on Maya spirituality and personal enlightenment. Popular tours include the "Mayan Wisdom" and "Ixchel Mayan Goddess" programs. Run by a Canadian expat in association with local experts, including a former director of Chichén Itzá. Longer tours must be booked well in advance, while day trips can be arranged with less notice.

Yucatán Backroads Tours (Calle 53 between Calles 66 and 68, tel. 999/924-0117, www.yucatanbackroads.com) is operated by seventh-generation Meridiano Ivan R. de Leon. His all-day "Yucatán Insider" takes you to villages, cenotes, working haciendas, and small Maya ruins, using the region's numerous and fascinating back roads. Friendly and extremely knowledgeable, de Leon can tailor tours to your interests, and does not combine parties, so you are sure to get the trip you want with the people you want.

Yucatán Trails (Calle 62 between Calles 57 and 59, tel. 999/928-2582, yucatantrails@hotmail.com, 9 A.M.–6:30 P.M. Mon.–Fri., 9 A.M.–1 P.M. Sat.) is a reliable agency offering all the most popular package trips, including cenote tours, Uxmal and Kabah, and Chichén Itzá. Groups are relatively small, and most trips include a multilingual guide.

Nómadas Travel (Calle 62 at Calle 51, tel. 999/924-5223, www.nomadastravel.com) is the travel agency run out of Nómadas Youth Hostel. Guests of the hostel get discounts, but trips are open to anyone who's interested, like birdwatching in Celestún and snorkeling in cenotes.

Turitransmérida Calle 55 between Calles 58 and 60, tel. 999/924-1199, www.turitrans merida.com.mx, 8 A.M.–1 P.M. and 4–7 P.M. Mon.–Fri., 8 A.M.–1 P.M. Sat.) may be Mérida's largest tour operators, with a fleet of buses and various excursions offered daily. The quality of tours isn't bad, but groups can be up to 40 people in high season.

Bullfights

If you're interested in what makes bullfighting so popular in Mexico, catch a *corrida* (literally, a running) at the **Plaza de Toros** (Calle 72 at Calle 33). Unless you want to work on your tan, opt for the premium *sombra* (shade) seats—the extra charge is worth every bead of sweat you save. Tickets are available at the bullring's box office the day of the event or from a table that's set up in front of the Olimpo— they cost between US$3.50–35 depending on the caliber of the bullfighter. Look around the Plaza de la Independencia for posters advertising the next *corrida* or ask at the tourist office for more information.

For Kids

Parque Zoológico del Centenario (Av. Itzaes at Calle 59, 999/928-5815, 8 A.M.–5 P.M. Tues.–Sun., free) is the city zoo and a popular spot for families, especially on weekends. The park has kiddy rides, playgrounds, and an overwhelming number of concession stands. The zoo has a decent selection of animals but the cramped quarters can be upsetting. The aquarium, with its extensive goldfish wing, is skippable. On Sundays, magicians, clowns, puppets, and theater groups come out in full force to entertain children and their parents.

Ángel y Andrea (Calle 55 between Calles 62 and 64, tel. 999/923-0705, 3–7 P.M.) is the puppet theatre company formed by master puppeteer Wilbert Herrera. Shows are ostensibly for children (and in Spanish only), but plenty of adults attend, and emerge equally delighted. The season runs September–January, during which performances are held on Sundays at 11 A.M. and 5 P.M.; tickets are US$4.

Cinema

In Parque Hidalgo, **Cine Fantasio** (Calle 59 at Calle 60, tel. 999/942-1414, US$3.25 Fri.–Sun., US$2.50 Mon.–Thurs.) is the most centrally located of Merida's movie theaters.

Cines Hollywood Rex (Calle 57 between Calles 70 and 72, tel. 999/928-5980, US$2) shows U.S. and Mexican films on its two screens.

For a megaplex, head to either of the two shopping malls: Gran Plaza houses **Hollywood Cinema** (tel. 999/942-1429, US$3 before 3 P.M., US$4.25 before 6 P.M., US$4.75 after 6 P.M., US$2.75 Wednesday) and **Hollywood Cinema Platinum VIP** (same tel., US$7.50, US$4.25 Wednesday), with its comfy seats, extensive menu, and waiters. A little closer to the center of town, Plaza América has the popular **Cinepolis** (tel. 999/987-6003, US$3 before 3 P.M., US$4.25 before 6 P.M., US$4.75 after 6 P.M., US$2.75 Wednesday) inside its doors.

Just up the street from the Plaza de la Independencia, **Teatro Mérida** (Calle 62 between Calles 59 and 61, tel. 999/924-9990, 10 A.M.–9 P.M. Tues.–Sun.) occasionally shows alternative art films and hosts international film festivals.

SHOPPING

If there is any place in the Yucatán Peninsula where you are certain to find something that you absolutely cannot resist, it's Mérida. From small family-run stores to rambling *artesanía* markets, Mérida attracts the treasures of the region: hammocks, *guayaberas, huipiles,* handcrafted toys, ceramic figurines, *jipi* hats, and Maya replicas. Explore the markets and peek into sidewalk stores, and you're sure to find the beauties that are made in this part of the world.

Markets

The **Mercado Lucas de Galvez** (Calle 67 between Calles 56 and 58, 8 A.M.– 8 P.M. daily)—better known as the **Mercado Municipal**—is a block-wide, two-story building bustling with vendors of all sorts. It's an experience all its own, and one worth taking a camera to. The 1st floor—with its myriad colors and layers of scents—is where the main action is: rows of neatly stacked fruits and vegetables, flowers of all sorts, beef and pork parts (you're sure to see heads, hooves, and stomachs), mounds of herbs and spices, incense and religious icons, children's toys, rows of women's shoes, stand upon stand of gold jewelry—just about anything you're looking for (and aren't) is here. The 2nd floor is quieter and focused on *artesanía: guayaberas,* hand-woven hammocks, sandals, and *huipiles* from the Yucatán plus folk art from other parts of the country. And if you get hungry and aren't a stickler about hygiene (it's on the edge, to say the least), there are dozens of restaurants serving cheap local fare on both floors. In early 2005, the city opened the huge new market building **Mercado San Benito** (Calle 54 between Calles 67 and 69, 10:30 A.M.–8 P.M. Mon.–Fri.) behind the Mercado Municipal. The plan was to move all the vendors from the old building to the new one, and create a park where the old market stood. To date, however, there appears to be little movement by vendors or the city. For the foreseeable future, both buildings are open and functioning as market areas.

Near the Mercado Municipal, the **Artesanías Bazar García Rejón** (Calle 60 at Calle 65, 9 A.M.–8 P.M. daily) is a market devoted entirely to local arts and crafts. There's a good selection of sandals, clothing, hammocks, and other regional items. Remember to bargain—most items have been marked up in anticipation of the custom.

A boho **open-air market** (Calle 60 between Calles 57 and 59, sunset–11 P.M. daily) is often set up in the evenings alongside Parque Maternidad. Handmade jewelry, batik, feather art, and clothing from Chiapas are the top sellers.

Each Sunday, an **Antique and Artesanía Bazaar** is held at Parque Santa Lucía as part of the weekly city-sponsored Domingo en Mérida. Booths wind through the park and are packed with all sorts of tchotchkes, local crafts, and tempting *antojitos.* Live Yucatecan music also is played throughout the day and chairs are set up so that you can take it all in.

Artesanía Shops

Codice (Calle 59 near Calle 60, tel. 999/924-1779, 9 A.M.–10 P.M. daily) is one of the best Mexican folk art boutiques in downtown Mérida. The works are high end and unique plus the prices are relatively affordable. If you're looking for a special gift or just want a beautiful piece of *artesanía* for yourself, definitely stop here.

Casa de las Artesanías del Estado de Yucatán (Calle 63 between Calles 64 and 66, tel. 999/928-6676, 9 A.M.–8 P.M. Mon.–Sat., 9 A.M.–2 P.M. Sun.) is a state-owned arts and crafts shop run out of a converted convent. Some of the items are worthwhile, especially the clothing and woodwork, but a great deal of kitsch has crept into this once superb shop. Definitely have a look around, but head to the register once you hit the coconut monkeys.

The quirky **Miniaturas** (Calle 59 between Calles 60 and 62, tel. 11 A.M.–9 P.M. Mon.–Sat.) is devoted to selling a wide variety of *tiny* arts and crafts from every state in Mexico. Be sure to check out the whimsical papier-mâché skeletons.

Yucatán is renowned for producing some of the best hammocks in Mexico. And they're just about everywhere you look in Mérida in varying colors, lengths, and materials. If you want a sure thing, head to the mom-and-pop shop **La Poblana** (Calle 65 between Calles 58 and 60, tel. 999/928-6093, 8 A.M.–6:30 P.M. Mon.–Fri., 8 A.M.–5 P.M. Sat.), or **Hamacas Rada** (Calle 60 between Calles 65 and 67, tel. 999/924-1208, www .cmerida.com/rada, 9:30 A.M.–6 P.M. Mon.–Fri., 9:30 A.M.–2:30 P.M. Sat.), a wholesaler of cotton hammocks. Look for the latter just inside the entrance to a parking garage, in a 3rd-floor warehouse.

Traditional Clothing Boutiques

Although you'll be able to find traditional clothing in the markets, there are several stores with excellent selections—better quality but pricier—in downtown Mérida.

If you're on the search for the perfect *huipil* or *terno* (traditional women's dresses), try the following: **Casa de las Artesanías del Estado**

TRADITIONAL CLOTHING

Mérida is known as the *Ciudad Blanca,* or the "White City," in part because of the all-white outfits men and women commonly wore in the colonial era, and well into the 20th century. Even today, Meridianos tend toward traditional cuts and styles, even as the fabrics and designs have become more colorful. Two articles of clothing in particular – the *huipil* for women and the *guayabera* for men – come from previous eras but are still in wide use today.

* A *huipil* is a beautiful type of dress first worn by Maya women at the insistence of hacienda *patrones.* The squared neck and hem are edged with brightly colored embroidery, and a lace-finished petticoat peeks out at the bottom. The similar, long *terno* is more elaborate than the *huipil* and is worn at parties and celebrations. Both are practical and cool and are now used by Yucatecan women of all classes. Prices vary considerably (US$10–550) depending upon the type of fabric (cotton, linen, or synthetic) and whether they have been hand-embroidered or machine-made.

* *Guayaberas* – button-down shirts with piping and hip pockets – are traditionally white, cotton, and short-sleeved, but you now find them in pastel tones, in linen, polyester, or silk, and sometimes even long-sleeved. They are a staple of menswear in the Yucatán, and harken back to the time – not so long ago, really – when a combination of poor roads and frequent boat traffic meant Mérida had closer ties with Cuba and even Europe than it did with the rest of Mexico.

There are many shops in Mérida to buy *huipiles* and *guayaberas.*

---

de Yucatán, Masud (Parque Hidalgo, Calle 60 between Calles 59 and 61, tel. 999/923-8132, 9 A.M.–noon, 5–8:30 P.M. Mon.–Fri., and 9 A.M.–5 P.M. Sat.), and **Camisería Canul** (Calle 62 between Calles 57 and 59, tel. 999/923-0158, guayaber@sureste.com, 8:30 A.M.–8 P.M. Mon.–Sat., 10 A.M.–1 P.M. Sun.).

If a fine *guayabera* (traditional men's shirt) is what you're looking for, head to: **Fábrica Jack** (Calle 59 between Calles 60 and 62, 10 A.M.–9 P.M. Mon.–Sat., 10 A.M.–3 P.M. Sun.) and **Canul Jr.** (Calle 59 between Calles 60 and 62, tel. 999/923-1811, 9 A.M.–8 P.M. Mon.–Sat., 10 A.M.–1 P.M. Sun.). If you want a custom-made *guayabera* (who doesn't want a red silk shirt with lightning bolts stitched in?), one can be made in about a week for off-the-rack prices. Ask a salesperson for details at any of the shops listed above.

Traditional panama or *jipi* (HE-pee) hats— ones that can be folded and stuffed in a pocket without harming it—also can be found at **Fábrica Jack** or **Casa de las Artesanías del Estado de Yucatán.** Not cheap, *finos* (the most supple) can run as high as US$80.

Bookstores

Next to the Palacio Municipal, **Dante Olimpo** (Calle 61 near Calle 62, tel. 999/928-2611, 8 A.M.–10:30 P.M. daily) has an excellent selection of reading material and CDs in English. It has one sister store downtown: **Dante 59** (Calle 59 between Calles 60 and 62, tel. 999/928-3674, 8 A.M.–9:30 P.M. Mon.–Sat., 10 A.M.–6 P.M. Sun.).

The small **Librería Juan García Ponce** (Calle 60 near Calle 61, tel. 999/930-9485, 9 A.M.–9 P.M. daily) is another option for English-language reading materials; there's an especially good variety of regional travel guides, literature on the Maya, and children's books.

Colloquial for "It's Used," **Ta 'Usao** (Calle 64 at Calle 55, tel. 999/928-1059, 9 A.M.–1:30 P.M. and 3:30–7 P.M. Mon.–Fri., 9 A.M.–2 P.M. Sat.) has a small collection of used English-language books amid a collection of bulky used furniture.

The **Mérida English Library** (Calle 53 between Calles 66 and 68, tel. 999/924-8401, www.meridaenglishlibrary.com, 9 A.M.–1 P.M. Mon.–Fri., 6:30–9 P.M. Mon., 4–7 P.M. Tues.

and Thurs., 10 A.M.–1 P.M. Sat.) has a huge selection of English-language books. It is mostly set up for long-term visitors—only registered members can check out books—but tourists can read books in the library's quiet reading area, buy books from the for-sale rack, and join weekly programs and get-togethers. Those include monthly socials, English-Spanish conversation exchanges, AA meetings (in English), children's story hour, and House and Garden tours—call or email for the current schedules. There is also an excellent bulletin board with postings of tours, short- and long-term housing, and items for sale.

Shopping Centers and Malls

Facing the plaza and next to the Palacio de Gobierno, the **Pasaje Picheta** (Calle 61 between Calles 60 and 62, 8 A.M.–midnight daily) is a small shopping center with a few boutiques selling trendy items, a couple of overpriced Internet cafés, and a handful of fast-food eateries. The food court in the center is a good place to rest if it's raining outdoors and the small art gallery on the mezzanine has interesting and changing expositions. There is also a public bathroom on the 2nd floor (US$0.25).

Gran Plaza (Calle 50 Diagonal 460, tel. 999/944-7658, 10 A.M.–9:30 P.M. daily) is the city's largest and fanciest mall with dozens of upper-end stores and two movie theaters mostly showing recent American films.

Plaza America (Calle 56-A at Av. Colón, tel. 999/920-2196, 10 A.M.–9:30 P.M. daily) is a standard mall with a J. C. Penney, lots of ATMs, and a Cinepolis movie theater.

SPORTS AND RECREATION
Golf

Just a 20-minute drive north of Mérida is the **Club de Golf La Ceiba** (Carr. Mérida-Progreso Km. 14.5, tel. 999/922-0053, 6:30 A.M.–6 P.M. daily). At the far end of an upscale, gated community, the 18-hole, par-72 golf course is open to the public and costs US$95 per round. Equipment rentals available.

Spanish Classes

The **Centro Idiomas del Sureste** (CIS, Calle 52 between Calles 49 and 51, tel. 999/923-0954, www.cisyucatan.com.mx) is a great place to perfect your Spanish while living with a local family. All levels of Spanish are taught with class size varying from one to six students; courses last at least one week. Students also can get intensive language training that's geared to their area of interest—CIS is a favorite with Spanish teachers as well as Maya scholars because of this. Classes are held at three locations: the downtown historical district and residential areas north and west of downtown.

Located in the historic center, **Instituto Benjamin Franklin de Yucatán** (Calle 57 No. 474-A, tel. 999/928-0097, www.benjamin franklin.com.mx) offers Spanish grammar and conversation courses that last anywhere from one week to a year. An entrance exam is given to all students to determine their language ability. Mexican history courses also are offered as well as area field trips. Home stays also can be arranged.

Mayan World Spanish Institute (Calle 47 at Paseo de Montejo, tel. 999/927-7813, www.mayanworldsi.com) also offers all level of instruction, though courses are more regimented—each lasts four weeks, with at least 20 hours of instruction per week and have set start dates. Some courses include field trips and dance lessons. Housing, including home stays, also can be arranged.

Cooking Classes

A great way to spend a day in Mérida is learning about Yucatecan cuisine at **Los Dos** (Calle 68 between Calles 65 and 67, tel. 999/928-1116, www.los-dos.com) cooking school. American David Sterling, a Manhattan transplant and accomplished chef, conducts fun and informative classes at his gorgeously refurbished colonial home. The popular "Taste of Yucatán" course (US$75 pp, minimum four people, 8:30 A.M.–4 P.M.) starts at Los Dos with pastries and coffee and a short introduction to Maya and modern Yucatecan cuisine. Then it's off to the market with David to buy fresh vegetables, fish, meat, *chiles,* cilantro, corn dough for tortilla chips or tamales—anything and everything you'll need. Back at the kitchen you don a Los Dos denim apron (yours to keep) and prepare a midday snack of tacos and homemade salsa. After a short break, the real cooking begins; depending on what you found at the market, it may include *cochinita pibil, pollo pibil, tamales, panuchos,* or other Yucatecan classics. The class ends with a grand, white-tablecloth dinner featuring your creations, plus complimentary wine and beer. Friends can join you for drinks and dinner for US$35 per person. Private classes and three-day workshops are also available. Reserve by email at least 48 hours in advance—and preferably more—as the schedule fills up fast.

ACCOMMODATIONS

Accommodations suited to all tastes and budgets are in Mérida, from backpacker hostels to small boutique inns to high-rise hotels.

Under US$25

(**Nómadas Youth Hostel** (Calle 62 at Calle 51, tel. 999/924-5223, www.nomadas-travel.com, US$6 pp camping, US$7–8 dorm, US$17.50 d with shared bath, US$22 d with private bath) is an excellent hostel six blocks north of the plaza. Dorms are clean and comfortable, especially the spacious women-only room. All bunks have an individual light, fan, and locker, and the bathrooms are spotless. Private rooms are medium-size and have fans—no air-conditioning. Bread, fruit, and coffee are available every morning, and guests can use the fully equipped kitchen (also very clean) at any time. The hostel offers free salsa classes and organizes trips to nearby sights for less than you'll find elsewhere. All in all, a great place for backpackers.

Set in a renovated colonial mansion, **Hobo Hostel** (Calle 60 between Calles 47 and 49, tel. 999/928-0880, www.hotelhobo.com.mx, US$5.60 dorm) offers mixed and single-sex dorms in spacious rooms, some with gorgeous tile floors. Bunk beds have thick mattresses and each guest gets sheets, a pillow, and a large metal locker to store his or her stuff. The bathrooms are gleaming and huge with rows of hot-water showers and plenty of toilets—no

waiting in line here. There's no kitchen, unfortunately, but guests can store perishables in a communal fridge.

(**Hotel Mucuy** (Calle 57 between Calles 56 and 58, tel. 999/928-5193, US$18.50 s with fan, US$20.50 d with fan, US$23 s with a/c, US$25 d with a/c) is one of the best deals in town. A motel-like building behind a colonial facade, rooms open onto a sunny courtyard with a tile pool that is fed by a splashing cascade. The units are small but spotless with hot-water bathrooms; most have twin beds with flower bedspreads and slated windows. The owner, Doña Ofelia, is a true delight and has earned many repeat guests since the hotel opened in 1974.

US$25-50

A excellent deal in this range is the **Hotel Dolores Alba Mérida** (Calle 63 between Calles 52 and 54, tel. 999/928-5650, www.dolores alba.com, US$42 s/d, US$46.50 t, US$51 q). Rooms are spotless, with tile floors, firm beds, and a small table and chairs; those on the middle and upper floors get more sunlight. All have air-conditioning, cable TV, and phone. In the courtyard, lounge chairs surround a genuinely inviting outdoor swimming pool. The hotel's only drawback is its location—3.5 blocks east of the plaza through a busy market area. Free parking and very friendly service.

Kind of a mixed bag, **Posada Toledo** (Calle 58 at Calle 57, tel. 999/923-1690, hptoledo@ prodigy.net.mx, US$46.50–50 s/d with a/c) offers clean but dark rooms in a rambling old mansion. The oldest of the lot have five-meter (16.4-foot) high ceilings and beautiful tile floors but aging furnishings; the newer ones look like they were remodeled in the early 1980s and are somewhat charmless but have better bathrooms. The common spaces—long, open-air corridors with comfy chairs, a formal dining room with soft lighting and old portraits, and a verdant courtyard in the middle— make the experience unique. All in all, the rate is a bit high for the rooms but still, the Toledo is a classic old-school Mexican hotel, the sort that you remember fondly.

Hotel Trinidad Galería (Calle 60 at Calle 51, tel. 999/923-2463, www.hotelestrinidad .com, US$28 s/d, US$37 s/d with a/c, US$42–51 suite with a/c) is a quirky meld of budget hotel and modern art gallery; paintings, sculptures, and carvings crowd the lobby and every bit of wall and floorspace. It also has an eclectic café and a pleasant swimming pool. Rooms, however, leave a lot to be desired: old mattresses, awful lighting, musty...There's just so far hipster common areas will stretch. The only rooms worth your pesos are the suites, with fine art, mini-split air-conditioning, and cable TV. Rooms are somewhat better at the Galería's sister hotel, **Hotel Trinidad** (Calle 62 at Calle 55, tel. 999/924-2033, www.hotelestrinidad.com, US$20.50 s/d with shared bathroom, US$30 s/d, US$37–42 s/d with a/c), which also has a common kitchen, wireless Internet, and large-screen TV.

US$50-100

Just north of Parque Santa Lucía, **[** **Hotel Maison Lafitte** (Calle 60 between Calles 53 and 55, tel. 999/923-9159 or toll-free U.S./Canada tel. 800/538-6802, www.maison lafitte.com.mx, US$70 s with a/c, US$75 d with a/c) is a classy hotel that's more intimate than a high-rise but less homey than a bed-and-breakfast. The 30 rooms are modern and comfortable, if a bit small; hyrdromassage showers, wireless Internet, and minibars are standard. Ground-floor rooms get some foot traffic in front—if you don't mind the climb, ask for an upstairs unit, where you'll have a view of the hotel's leafy courtyard and the lovely tiled pool. A guitar trio plays soothing Mexican music in the lobby and restaurant Thursday–Saturday evenings as well as Saturday–Sunday mornings—a perfect start to a day or evening. An extensive breakfast buffet also is included in the rate.

Facing Parque Hidalgo, the **Gran Hotel** (Calle 60 at Calle 59, tel. 999/924-7730, www .granhoteldemerida.com.mx, US$57 s with a/c, US$61 d with a/c, US$88–107 suite with a/c) is a classic Victorian building, with Corinthian columns, beautiful tile floors, and

a soaring atrium surrounded by several airy corridors set with armchairs and low tables. Opened in 1901 and restored in the 1980s, it's worth peeking into even if you don't stay. If you do stay, you'll find elegant, (mostly) spacious rooms with *tiny* bathrooms, all with ironwork headboards and heavy wood furnishings. Be sure to look at a few rooms before deciding: some have no windows and others have industrial carpeting—both features that are painfully out of place.

Hotel Caribe (Calle 59 at Calle 60, tel. 999/924-9022, U.S./Canada tel. 888/822-6431, www.hotelcaribe.com.mx, US$52–59 s with a/c, US$56–64 d with a/c, US$90 suite with a/c) is ideally located on Parque Hidalgo, just one block from the central plaza with dramatic views of the cathedral from the rooftop swimming pool. Rooms on the lower floors are colonial in style—bright yellow walls, high ceilings, and tile floors—but are somewhat musty and showing their age. Top-floor units are remodeled and sport modern decor, small bathrooms, and low ceilings—they're reminiscent of a souped-up Super 8 Motel but have direct access to the pool. All units open onto wide tiled corridors with archways that overlook a leafy courtyard. A huge plus—and rare treat—is that guests can enjoy complimentary rounds of golf at the Club de Golf La Ceiba.

US$100-150

The charming **[** **Hotel Casa del Balam** (Calle 60 at Calle 57, tel. 999/924-8844, www .hotelcasadelbalam.com, US$120 s/d with a/c, US$150–190 suite with a/c) occupies a 15th-century building—the lounge and courtyard area used to be where the horse-drawn carriages would pull in and park. Floors have been added, but the large, clean rooms maintain the building's colonial character, with wrought-iron fixtures, heavy, dark-wood furniture, and checkerboard floors. Of course, modern touches such as new bathrooms, central air-conditioning, satellite TV, comfortable beds, and double-paned glass let you enjoy colonial times without actually living in them. Five honeymoon suites and three master suites occupy original rooms and have antique decor. Diners can eat in the shady courtyard bistro, with a splashing fountain and lush tropical plants. A small pool in back is a nice plus.

Misión de Fray Diego (Calle 61 between Calles 64 and 66, tel. 999/924-1111, in US and Canada 866/639-2933, www.lamisionde fraydiego.com, US$108 s/d standard, US$119 s/d special, US$126 s/d junior suite, US$136 s/d master suite) is a former monastery converted into a classy colonial hotel—you'll find some fine religious art here. Standard rooms lack some detailing, making specials, with their five-meter (16.4-foot) ceilings and attractive woodwork, worth the extra price. The hotel has two courtyards—the first has an attractive garden and fountain and the next a small clean pool and deck chairs. A quiet restaurant serves good Spanish food, especially paella. This is a sister hotel to Hotel Caribe, and guests enjoy free green fees at the Club de Golf La Ceiba.

Located just steps from the central plaza, **Piedra de Agua** (Calle 60 between Calles 59 and 61, tel. 999/924-2300, www.piedradeagua .com, US$103 s with a/c, US$135 d with a/c, US$146–200 suite with a/c) is one of Mérida's boutique hotels. Rooms are modern and elegantly sparse with deep beds and fine linens. Unless you opt for one of the suites, they're also a bit cramped—there's barely enough space to walk around the room, much less set you bags down. All open onto a sunny, three-story interior courtyard, the 1st floor of which doubles as the hotel restaurant. A chic outdoor lounge and pool area is a plus.

Over US$150

Across from Santa Lucía park, **Hotel Casa Lucía** (Calle 60 between Calles 53 and 55, tel. 999/928-0740, www.casalucia.com.mx, US$141–158 s/d with a/c, US$199 suite with a/c) is an elegant hotel built in the shell of a 19th-century mansion. Rooms are spacious and sumptuous with deep beds, thick curtains, and marble bathrooms; Persian rugs and antique furnishings are nice touches. The large interior courtyard has a well-kempt pool and *palapa* lounge—a fine place to cool off after

a day of sightseeing. Continental breakfast is included in the rate.

Serene and understated, **Villa María** (Calle 59 at Calle 68, tel. 999/923-3357, www.villa mariamerida.com, US$140 s/d with a/c, US$164–187 suite with a/c) has 11 comfortable rooms in a renovated colonial mansion. Many are two stories, with a loft for the bedroom and a small sitting room below. All have canopy beds, tile floors—some beautifully patterned, others simply white—and original artwork on display. Units open onto a sunny atrium with Moorish arches and a small fountain; it doubles as the hotel restaurant, which is highly recommended for its French cuisine.

The **Fiesta Americana** (Calle 56-A at Av. Colón, tel. 999/942-1111, www.fiestamericana .com, US$135–165 s/d with a/c, 240–708 suite with a/c) is Mérida's top luxury chain hotel. Rooms are modern and well appointed, though some at the standard and executive levels had surprisingly saggy beds—you may want to check your room before committing to it. Governor and presidential suites are huge and luxurious with private terraces and sweeping city views. Though the pool area is marred by noisy air-conditioners, the common areas are gorgeous, with a soaring lobby, luxurious spa area, and upscale shopping center below. ADO also offers first-class and deluxe long-distance bus service, including to Cancún, directly from the hotel.

Small Inns and Bed-and-Breakfasts

Mérida has a profusion of charming little inns and bed-and-breakfasts, and staying in one is a highlight for many visitors. Virtually all are restored *casonas* (large colonial homes) whose resurrection has been a labor of love for an expatriate couple. The inns vary from faithful replicas of colonial residences to miniature museums full of folk and modern art, but all are very comfortable and classy. Most listed here have fewer than 10 rooms, so it's best to call ahead or reserve online.

UNDER US$50

Six blocks from the central plaza, **[** **Hostal**

del Peregrino (Calle 51 between Calles 54 and 56, tel. 999/924-5491, www.hostaldel peregrino.com, US$16 dorm, US$37 s/d, US$45 s/d with a/c) occupies a refurbished colonial home with gorgeous original tile floors. It offers two types of rooms: spacious fan-cooled dorms, most with single beds (not bunks), lockers, and spotless bathrooms; and comfortable private rooms with ironwork furnishings, patchwork quilts, and private bathrooms. A well-equipped kitchen is available to all guests, and best of all, there's a rooftop terrace with nice views and an even nicer breeze. Continental breakfast included.

Located 10 blocks from the central plaza, **Casa Ana** (Calle 52 between Calles 51 and 53, tel. 999/924-0005, www.casaana.com, US$35–45 s/d, US$45–55 s/d with a/c) is good if you want a smaller place and don't mind the walk. The rooms are large and airy with simple, colorful decor. All face an interior garden with a small stone-floored pool and an outdoor *palapa* lounge. Four are in a building at the back of the property; they have pre-fab bathrooms, with plastic walls on runners that open at the top—a bit less private than some may be accustomed to. The best room is the only one in the main building, with homier decor and a "regular" bathroom (i.e., four full walls and a door). Continental breakfast is included in the rate.

Casa San Juan (Calle 62 between Calles 69 and 71, tel. 999/923-6823 or tel. 999/986-2937, www.casasanjuan.com, US$35 s/d with fan, US$45 s/d with a/c, US$55 suite, two-night minimum stay, free continental breakfast) occupies an antiquated town house built in 1850. The location isn't ideal—far from the center and a little dodgy at night—but for budget travelers it's better than a hostel without the expense of most B&Bs. Rooms have comfy beds and impressive five-meter (16.4-foot) ceilings; numbers 2 and 5 are the only ones with fully enclosed bathrooms. Suites have fridge, microwave, and face the tranquil, pretty garden. Be sure taxi drivers don't confuse this with *Hotel* San Juan, near Parque Santa Lucía. Reservations required.

US$50-100

One of Mérida's most charming B&Bs, **Hotel Marionetas** (Calle 49 between Calles 62 and 64, tel. 999/928-3377, www.hotel marionetas.com, US$85 s/d with a/c) gets its name from the building's former tenant—a well-known puppet theater company. The eight spacious rooms are each slightly different, from the color of the walls to the design of the tile floors. Decor is attractive but uncluttered, making the most of select items—an ornate wood-framed mirror in one room, a wrought-iron vanity in another. There's a sunny inner courtyard, small pool, and a covered dining area where a full fresh breakfast (included in the price) is served. The cheerful owners and staff provide excellent service.

Another excellent option is **Hotel MedioMundo** (Calle 55 between Calles 64 and 66, tel. 999/924-5472, www.hotelmedio mundo.com, US$60 s/d with fan, US$75–80 with a/c), a hacienda-style guesthouse just a few blocks away. Within high blue-painted walls are a courtyard with fountain and a small inviting pool area, where a great South American–style breakfast is served. (One of the owners is Uruguayan.) The decor is intentionally spare—for maximum relaxation—and all 12 rooms have deep beds, large spotless bathrooms, and beautiful tile floors from the original construction. The friendly owners can arrange various outings, including alternative ones like exploring natural medicine and Maya shamanism.

The award-winning **Casa Mexilio Guesthouse** (Calle 68 between Calles 57 and 59, tel. 999/928-2505, U.S./Canada tel. 800/210-4341, www.casamexilio.com, US$50–95 s/d, penthouse US$120, all include continental breakfast) occupies a gorgeous colonial *casona* a block from Parque Santiago. Nine rooms are tucked into the home's many nooks and crannies; the plant-filled courtyard has a small clear pool, connected by stairways and short bridges to the 2nd-floor dining room and quiet rooftop bar. Rooms vary from cozy fan-cooled units to the penthouse, with air-conditioning, king-size bed, and large private terrace; all have spotless tile bathrooms and comfortable beds. The hotel is literally brimming with high-quality artwork from Mexico and around the world. Service can be hands-off to the point of brusqueness, more like a European inn than a typical B&B. Online reservations required.

Virtually every inch of wall space at **Los Arcos Bed & Breakfast** (Calle 66 between Calles 49 and 53, tel. 999/928 0214, www .losarcosmerida.com, US$75 s, US$95 d, US$15 extra person) is filled with artwork, some from Mexico, some from Africa, some painted by the owners themselves. Add potted houseplants, a small swimming pool, and a troop of tiny dogs, and you've got this unique, eclectic guesthouse. The rooms—there are only two—are comfy, with high ceilings, canopy beds, big bathrooms, and CD players. There's wireless Internet throughout, but no parking (street parking is plentiful, however). Big breakfast included.

Designed to drown out the city sounds, **Cascadas de Mérida** (Calle 57 between Calles 74-A and 76, tel. 999/923-8484, www.cascadas demerida.com, US$75 s with a/c, US$87 d with a/c) is surrounded by stone walls with water cascading down them. Guests hear the faint sound of gurgling water instead of city buses careening down the streets. Best of all, each shower—designed with walls of thick glass—looks onto a private waterfall (no worries about being seen lathering up, the walls are close to one another). The rooms themselves are comfortable and classy with exposed stone walls, sky lights, Mexican furnishings, and bright Guatemalan bedspreads. All have cable TV, wireless Internet, and mini-split air-conditioning. They open onto a sunny courtyard with a large pool, hammocks, and lots of leafy plants. A full breakfast is included.

OVER US$100

The Villa @ Mérida (Calle 59 between Calles 80 and 82, tel. 999/928-8466, in the U.S. 888/737-2124, www.thevillasgroup.com, US$265–290, including breakfast and airport pickup and drop-off) is a gorgeous seven-room boutique hotel, one of Mérida's finest. The deep red exterior gives way to high-ceilinged rooms, with deep beds and elegant dark wood furniture. The sumptuous grounds include beautifully-tiled corridors, a palm-shaded garden, and mid-size swimming pool, plus terrific modern artwork throughout. But as the mantra goes, "Location, location, location." The hotel is on a very busy street, four blocks from Parque Santiago and 10 blocks from the center of town. Taxis are plentiful enough, but it's hard not to feel isolated here.

FOOD

Mérida has a rich selection of restaurants, from great hole-in-the-wall pizza joints to award-winning restaurants. Yucatecan as well as Mexican food predominates, but you'll also find good alternatives around town.

Yucatecan

For delicious local eats in a locals environment, head to █ **Restaurant D'AI** (Calle 54 at Calle 53, tel. 999/923-7012, 9:30 A.M.–9 P.M. Mon.–Fri., 9:30 A.M.–5:30 P.M. Sat., US$2–5). A small, off-the-beaten-track restaurant that will undoubtedly leave you satisfied. Daily *comida corrida* specials are especially good deals—for US$3–4, you'll get a big entrée with a bunch of sides and a drink. You'll leave wishing you had a fridge for leftovers.

Pórtico Del Peregrino (Calle 57 between Calles 60 and 62, tel. 999/928-6163, noon–midnight daily, US$5–14) is an intimate and upscale restaurant offering excellent Yucatecan dishes in a vine-covered patio or two air-conditioned dining rooms. Be sure to try the house specialties—*sopa de lima* (lime soup), *pollo pibil* (chicken with Maya spices wrapped in banana leaves), and *berenjenas al horno* (slices of eggplant layered and baked with chicken and cheese). Reservations recommended for outdoor evening dining.

Café La Habana (Calle 59 at Calle 62, open 24 hours daily, US$3–10) is a classic greasy spoon diner with a Yucatecan twist: Legions of waiters in crisp white shirts and dark bow ties serve strong and hot coffee along with local and Cuban fare. The *chilaquiles con huevo* (fried corn tortillas in tomato sauce and cheese with a fried egg on top) is excellent. The large smoking section—with its clouds of cigarette and cigar smoke—is always bustling; nonsmokers are segregated to the far end of the room with a handful of air-conditioners.

Mexican

(La Casa de Frida (Calle 61 at Calle 66, tel. 999/928-2311, 6–11 P.M. Mon.–Sat., US$5–11) is an eclectic restaurant with bright pink walls and loads of Mexican art hung throughout the place. The menu is rife with delicious meals that are beautifully presented. Be sure to try the *crepas huitlacoche* (crepes stuffed with corn fungus—a delicacy, really!) or the *flan de berenjena* (eggplant flan) for a tasty spin on traditional Mexican fare. Seating is either in a softly lit courtyard or a colorful interior room.

With funky 1970s decor and a retro mural on the back wall, **Cafetería Pop** (Calle 57 between Calles 60 and 62, tel. 999/928-6163, 7 A.M.–midnight Mon.–Sat., 8 A.M.–midnight Sun., US$3–7) seems like a total hipster diner but, in fact, has just maintained its look since it opened three decades ago. Friendly waiters serve simple Mexican food in this all-welcoming place—you'll find everything from guayabera-clad locals arguing over politics to five-year-old tourists munching on cornflakes. Breakfast specials are particularly good.

Italian

Arguably the best pizzeria in Mérida, **(Pizzería Vito Corleone** (Calle 59 between 60 and 62, tel. 999/923-6846, 11 A.M.–11 P.M. daily, US$2.50–7.50) is not much to look at: a true hole-in-the-wall with tables crammed into two floors and a handful of fans furiously blowing hot air around. The slices are worth every bead of sweat though: The thin-crust pizza comes smothered in cheese and red sauce and loaded with toppings of your choice. Made in four sizes, a medium is enough for two hungry travelers. Come with an appetite, order a couple of cold beers, and remember to wear a tank top. Delivery available.

Café Lucía (Calle 60 between Calles 53 and 55, tel. 999/928-0740, 7 A.M.–midnight daily, US$6–20) is an upscale restaurant featuring light Italian dishes in a space beautifully decorated with fine art—much of it for sale. On Thursday evenings, the restaurant sets up tables across the street in the Parque Santa Lucía so that diners can enjoy the weekly *serenata* over a fine meal or dessert.

Facing Teatro Mérida, **Pane e Vino** (Calle 62 between Calles 59 and 61, tel. 999/928-6228, 6 P.M.–midnight Tues.–Sun., US$6–12) is a simple but nice restaurant with thick wood tables, whitewashed walls, and art posters hung about. The food is reliable—mostly pasta dishes with a variety of classic Italian sauces. If you want more than just an entrée, order an appetizer or dessert—the side dishes tend to be skimpy.

Middle Eastern

Alberto's Continental Patio (Calle 64 at Calle 57, tel. 999/928-5367, 1–11 P.M. Mon.–Sat., 6–11 P.M. Sun., US$11–24) is a superb choice if you're looking for a change of pace. Specializing in Lebanese dishes, it is set in an 18th-century *casona* that is said to have been built with stones from Maya ruins. Diners can choose between eating at a candlelit table in a vine-covered patio or in a softly lit dining room decorated with antiques. The prices are a bit high considering the menu—tabbouleh, grilled kabobs, and cabbage rolls feature prominently—but the food is tasty and the service top-notch.

(Café Alameda (Calle 58 between Calles 55 and 57, tel. 999/928-3635, 7 A.M.–5:30 P.M. daily, US$2–5) is a simple restaurant—think plastic tables and fluorescent lights—serving inexpensive Lebanese cuisine. Popular with locals and expatriates, the menu is varied and the food outright delicious. If you can't decide on just one entrée, consider ordering a few side dishes to make a meal. Don't miss the *baba ghanoush* (grilled eggplant spread)—it's one of the best we've ever had.

Other Specialties

Half an hour from Mérida and well worth the trip is the **(Casa de Piedra** (Carr.

Mérida-Progreso Km. 12, tel. 999/941-0213, 8–11:30 A.M. daily, 1:30–11 P.M. Mon.–Sat., and 1–6 P.M. Sun., US$10–25). An award-winning restaurant located in the luxury hotel Hacienda Xcanatún, the menu offers an exquisite fusion of French, Caribbean, and Yucatecan (Frebbecan?) dishes. Diners enjoy their meals in an elegant dining room with five-star service. An excellent choice, especially if you're craving something a little different.

With tables overlooking Calle 60, **Ki'bok** (Calle 60 between Calles 53 and 55, tel. 999/928-5511, 6 P.M.–1 A.M. Tues.–Thurs. and Sun., 6 P.M.–2 A.M. Fri.–Sat., US$5–10) offers an eclectic menu with dishes varying from traditional Yucatecan, Italian, and Greek specialties to fresh pastries and coffee drinks. Portions are a good size and the service is attentive.

At Misión de Fray Diego hotel, **Restaurante El Convento** (Calle 61 between Calles 64 and 66, 7 A.M.–11 P.M. daily, US$3–14) specializes in Spanish food, including Spanish tortillas for breakfast and paella for dinner. The dining area is a cozy, wood-and-glass dining room opening on the hotel's pretty central courtyard.

La Nao de China (Calle 31 between Calles 22 and 24, tel. 999/927-9997, noon–11 P.M. daily, US$5–10) is a decent place to head for Chinese food. Particularly popular are the mixed buffet (1–5 P.M. Mon.–Thurs., US$7) and the all-Chinese buffet (1–6 P.M. Fri.–Sun.) Or order standard Chinese dishes à la carte at any time.

Trotter's (Calle 31 between Calles 34 and 36, tel. 999/927-2320, 1 P.M.–2 A.M. Mon.–Sat. and 1–6 P.M. Sun., US$12–30) is Act Three of an ever-changing performance by father-and-son Wayne and Paul Trotter; they also founded Pancho's, a tacky downtown tourist trap serving Mexican food, and La Trotto, a well-liked Miami-style Italian restaurant. Wildly popular since its opening in 2005, Trotter's serves excellent seafood and pasta, but the steak is to die for: generous cuts of choice imported beef are perfectly prepared, and accompanied by potatoes or veggie medleys. Creative salads and appetizers may prove irresistible—eating here is a hefty splurge, but a worthy one.

The swanky **Néctar Food & Wine** (Av. 1 No. 412, Col. Diaz Ordaz, tel. 999/938-0858; 7:30 P.M.–2 A.M. Wed.–Mon., US$19–37) serves delicious gourmet fusion dishes—most with a Yucatecan flair—in a sleek dining room. Choose one of the creative delicacies and treat yourself to a glass of wine from the extensive international wine list. Popular with Mérida's upper crust, especially for a late-night meal.

Cafés and Sweets

Café La Hoya (Calle 62 between Calles 57 and 59, 9 A.M.–midnight Mon.–Sat., US$3–8) is a hip coffeehouse with a sunny front area and two rooms in back where college kids gather around high round tables to talk, laugh, and smoke. Breakfast options include eggs and waffles; for lunch and later try a salami, chicken, or veggie panino. A stack of games, books, and magazines are available if you like to linger.

Café Chiapas (Calle 60 at Calle 49, tel. 999/928-2864, 9 A.M.–8 P.M. Mon.–Sat.) is a tiny place offering fantastic coffee drinks made from Chiapanecan beans. Order a cold cappuccino to go or enjoy a flavored coffee at one of the three tables. Ground coffee and beans are also sold in pretty boxes for US$7.75–10.25 per kilogram (2.2 pounds).

El Retorno (Calle 62 between Calles 59 and 61, tel. 999/928-5634, 6 A.M.–9 P.M. daily) is one of the city's best bakeries with one shop half a block from the Plaza de la Independencia and several others throughout the city. Here you'll find cookies, cakes, and breads of all tastes and shapes.

Groceries

Facing Parque Santiago, **Super Aki** (Calle 72 at Calle 59, 6:30 A.M.–9 P.M. daily) is a full grocery store offering canned goods, produce, fresh meats, and dairy products, and more.

Just south of Parque Santa Ana, **ISSTE** (Calle 60 between Calles 47 and 49, 8 A.M.–9 P.M. Mon.–Sat., 9 A.M.–7 P.M. Sun.) is a state-run supermarket with a warehouselike atmosphere.

The **Mercado Municipal** (Calle 67 between Calles 56 and 58, 8 A.M.–8 P.M. daily) is a rambling, two-story market offering every fruit, vegetable, and meat sold in the region. Upstairs, there also are about a dozen cheap eateries—not the cleanest but the bustling shoppers and yelling vendors are definitely an experience; *comidas corridas* (two-course meals with a drink) cost between US$1.50–3 but you can also order tacos, tamales, ceviche, and *tortas* for around US$1 each.

For fresh fruit, vegetables, and meats without the hustle and bustle of the larger Mercado Municipal, head to the **Mercado Santos Degollado** (Calle 57 between Calles 70 and 72, 6 A.M.– 2 P.M. daily). On Parque Santiago, this market gives you a taste of how the locals shop with its myriad of fruit and vegetable stands, *tortillerías,* shoe repair shops, and flower sellers. Stay for a meal—the handful of small restaurants are known citywide for their excellent seafood tacos and *tortas*. Prices run US$1–3 for a full meal.

INFORMATION
Tourist Information
When you get to Mérida, pick up a copy of *Yucatán Today* or *Explore Yucatán,* two of the most helpful tourist magazines anywhere in Mexico. Published monthly and distributed free at hotels, shops, and tourist offices, the magazines have maps, suggested itineraries, short articles, and lists of upcoming events. While focusing on Mérida, both also cover Progreso, the Puuc Route, Izamal, Chichén Itzá, and Valladolid. The hotel and restaurant listings are not comprehensive but they're fine complements to this and other guidebooks.

The city and state tourism boards— **Información Turística del Ayuntamiento** and **Departamento de Turismo del Estado de Yucatán,** respectively—maintain a total of five tourist offices in Mérida. At any one of them, you'll find a wide selection of maps, brochures, and usually someone who speaks English.

In general, we've found the staff at the city offices much more helpful for specific questions and any information not found in the brochures. The most convenient city tourist office is in the Palacio Municipal (central plaza, Calle 62 between Calles 61 and 63, tel. 999/942-0000 ext. 801119, www.merida.gob .mx, 8 A.M.–8 P.M. Mon.–Sat., 8 A.M.–2 P.M. Sun.). There are two other locations—a sidewalk kiosk (Paseo de Montejo at Av. Colón, 8 A.M.–8 P.M. daily) and a booth in the arrivals *(llegadas)* area of the CAME first-class bus terminal (Calle 70 between Calles 69 and 71, roughly 8 A.M.–2 P.M. Mon.–Fri.).

The state tourist offices are two blocks apart: one is next to the Teatro José Peón Contreras (Calle 60 between Calles 55 and 57, tel. 999/923-7354, 9 A.M.–9 P.M. Tues.–Sat., 9 A.M.–3 P.M. Sun.), the other is just inside the front doors of the Palacio de Gobierno (central plaza, Calle 61 at Calle 60, tel. 999/930-3101, 8 A.M.–9 P.M. Mon.–Sat., 8 A.M.–8 P.M. Sun.).

Hospitals
Clínica Mérida (Av. Itzáes 242, Col. García Ginerés, tel. 999/920-0411, www.clinica demerida.com.mx) is a state-of-the-art hospital with 24-hour emergency service.

Centro Médico de las Américas (CMA, Calle 54 near Calle 33, tel. 999/927-3199, www.cmasureste.com.mx, 24 hours daily) also is a good option.

Pharmacies
On the Plaza de la Independencia, **Yza Farmacia** (Calle 63 between Calles 60 and 62, tel. 999/926-6666, 24 hours daily) is an excellent choice—not only is it a fully stocked pharmacy but it also makes deliveries.

Facing Parque Santiago, **Farmacias Bazar** (Calle 57 between Calles 70 and 72, tel. 999/928-5454, 8 A.M.– 9 P.M. Mon.–Fri., 8 A.M.– 8:30 P.M. Sat., 8 A.M.– 2 P.M. Sun.) also offers delivery service.

Police
The police station (Calle 61 between Calles 52 and 54, tel. 999/925-2034) is open 24 hours daily.

SERVICES
Money
You'll have no problem accessing your money in Mérida. Virtually every bank in town—

and there are a lot of them—has a 24-hour ATM that happily accepts foreign debit cards. Many convenience stores also have cash machines. Most banks exchange AmEx travelers checks and U.S. dollars, most accept euros, and a few will change other currencies. You can also try changing cash at a *casa de cambio* (currency exchange office), or at the front desk of an upscale hotel, but the rates at either are rarely good.

Most of the banks and ATMs are on or near the Plaza de la Independencia and along Calle 59. Among many others are: **Banamex** (Casa de Montejo, Calle 63 between Calles 60 and 62, 9 A.M.–4 P.M. Mon.–Fri., 10 A.M.–2 P.M.Sat.); **HSBC** (Calle 59 between Calles 68 and 70, 8 A.M.–7 P.M. Mon.–Sat.); and **Bancomer** (Calle 59 at Calle 62, 8:30 A.M.–4 P.M. Mon.–Fri.).

American Express (Paseo de Montejo between Calles 43 and 45, tel. 999/942-8200, 9 A.M.–6 P.M. Mon.–Fri., 9 A.M.–1 P.M. Sat.) is located across from the Anthropology Museum.

Internet and Telephone

Internet cafés are in almost every block surrounding Plaza de la Independencia, and the list here is by no means exhaustive.

Mundo En Línea (Calle 59 between Calles 62 and 64, tel. 999/928-7936, 9 A.M.–11 P.M. daily) is a very professional place with air-conditioning, good computers, and a fast connection. Standard rates are US$1 per hour; on Wednesdays, it's US$1.50 for two hours and US$1.25 for 1.5 hours on Sunday. Other services include CD-burning (US$16/disc) and international telephone calls (US$0.25 to the United States and Canada, US$0.35 to Europe).

Cyber Colombia (Calle 62 between Calles 57 and 59, 8:15 A.M.–11 P.M. Mon.–)Sat., 11 A.M.–11 P.M. Sun) charges US$1 per hour, but has a midday "happy hour" (10 A.M.–2 P.M.) when it's only US$0.80 per hour. Offers inexpensive international calling, as well.

On Calle 59, a half-block past Parque Santiago, several **side-by-side Internet cafés** all charge around US$1 an hour and are open all day Monday to Saturday, and Sunday afternoons.

As the name suggests, **Tel World** (Calle 59 near Calle 58, tel. 999/928-6856, 8 A.M.–9 P.M. Mon.–Sat., 10 A.M.–5 P.M. Sun.) offers telephone service within Mexico (US$0.18/minute), the United States and Canada (US$0.19–0.37/minute), and Europe (US$0.28–0.55/minute). Internet service also is available (US$0.85 per hour).

Post Office

The post office (Calle 65 at Calle 56, 8 A.M.–4:30 P.M. Mon.–Fri., 9 A.M.–1 P.M. Sat.) is in front of the Mercado Municipal.

Immigration

The immigration office (Av. Colón at Calle 8, Col. García Ginerés, tel. 999/925-4553, 9 A.M.–1 P.M. Mon.–Fri.) is four long blocks west of the Fiesta Americana. Visa extensions typically can be approved the same day if you arrive early.

Consulates

Many European countries have closed their Mérida consulates and moved services to their offices in Cancún. A number of countries still maintain honorary consulates, often in private homes or offices; services vary from emergency-only assistance to basic passport and visa matters. Call ahead to see if the consulate can help you or if you're better off going to Cancún. (See the *Foreign Consulates* sidebar in the *Essentials* chapter for more information.)

Travel Agencies

Carmen Travel Service (Pasaje Picheta, next to Palacio de Gobierno, Calle 61 between Calles 60 and 62, tel. 999/928-3060, www.carmentravel.com, 9 A.M.–7:30 P.M. Mon.–Fri., 9 A.M.–2 P.M. Sat.) sells ADO, ADO-GL, and UNO bus tickets, so you don't have to go all the way to the terminal to reserve a seat.

Yucatán Trails (Calle 62 between Calles 57 and 59, tel. 999/928-2582, yucatantrails@hotmail.com, 9 A.M.–6:30 P.M. Mon.–Fri., 9 A.M.–1 P.M. Sat.) can handle national and international plane tickets, plus hotel and package reservations.

Nómadas Travel (Calle 62 at Calle 51, tel. 999/924-5223, www.nomadastravel.com) sells international student and hostelling cards and has good rates on international plane tickets.

Launderette

Centrally situated, **Lavandería La Fe** (Calle 64 at Calle 55, tel. 999/924-4531, 8 A.M.–6 P.M. Mon.–Fri., 8 A.M.–3 P.M. Sat.) charges US$3.75 for the first three kilograms (6.6 pounds), and US$2 for each additional kilogram (2.2 pounds). Same-day service is typical if you drop off your clothes in the morning. Pickup and delivery service can be arranged for a small extra fee.

Half a block from Parque Santiago, **La Profesional** (Calle 57 between Calles 72 and 74, tel. 999/924-8712, 9 A.M.–7 P.M. Mon.–Fri., 9 A.M.–2 P.M. Sat.) is a friendly place offering same-day service for US$2.50 for three kilograms (6.6 pounds) and US$1 for each additional kilogram (2.2 pounds). Sneakers and daypacks also can be washed separately for US$1.50 apiece.

Storage

Store your bags at **Guarda Plus** (across from CAME bus terminal, Calle 70 between Calles 69 and 71, 6 A.M.–9:30 P.M. daily) for US$0.40–$1/hour per bag, depending on the size. There is no daily rate.

GETTING THERE
Air

Mérida's **Crescencio Rejón International Airport** (MID, Avenida de Itzaes/Highway 180, 999/946-1530) is located seven kilometers (4.2 miles) southwest of the town center. The airport has several car rental agencies, and a 24-hour ATM.

Taxis charge a fixed US$10 from the airport to town, while the return costs approximately US$8—agree on a price beforehand. There is no airport bus, per se, but vans marked "UMAN" leave every 10 minutes from Parque San Juan (Calle 69 between

FLYING TO MÉRIDA

The following airlines service Mérida's **Crescencio Rejón International Airport** (MID):

- **Aerocalifornia** (Fiesta Americana, Calle 56-A at Av. Colón, tel. 999/920-3855, airport tel. 999/946-1682, toll-free Mex. tel. 800/237-6225, www.aerocalifornia.com)

- **Aeroméxico** (Fiesta Americana, Calle 56-A at Av. Colón, tel. 999/920-1260, airport tel. 999/237-1740, toll-free Mex. tel. 800/021-4000, www.aeromexico.com)

- **American Airlines** (airport tel. 999/925-5967, toll-free Mex. tel. 800/904-6000, www.aa.com)

- **Aviacsa** (Fiesta Americana, Calle 56-A at Av. Colón, tel. 999/925-6890, airport tel. 999/946-1850, toll-free Mex. tel. 800/006-2200, www.aviacsa.com)

- **Click Mexicana** (Paseo de Montejo between Calles 43 and 45, tel. 999/924-6633, airport tel. 999/946-1332, toll-free Mex. tel. 800/502-2000, www.clickmx.com)

- **Continental Airlines** (Paseo de Montejo 427, tel. 999/926-3100, airport tel. 999/946-1888, toll-free Mex. tel. 800/900-5000, www.continental.com)

- **Delta Airlines** (airport tel. 999/920-7626, toll-free Mex. tel. 800/123-4710, www.delta.com)

- **Magnicharters** (Calle 21 between Calles 22 and 24, tel. 999/926-1616, airport tel. 999/946-2122, www.magnicharters.com.mx)

- **Mexicana** (Paseo de Montejo between Calles 43 and 45, tel. 999/924-6633, airport tel. 999/946-1332, toll-free Mex. tel. 800/502-2000, www.mexicana.com)

Calles 62 and 64) and pass the airport entrance road (US$0.50, 25 minutes). Be sure to ask the driver to let you off at *el aeropuerto;* it's a 500-meter (0.3-mile) walk from the stop to the terminal. From the airport, you can walk to Avenida de Itzaes and catch an UMAN van to Parque San Juan—there is a bus stop just to your right when you reach the main road. Or wait for a "79-Aviación" bus (US$0.30, 30 minutes) in front of the Budget office just outside the terminal—they pass less frequently (every 15–20 minutes) but you don't have to walk so far. Bus No. 79 goes to Parque San Juan as well, passing the first- and second-class bus terminals along the way. Note the UMAN vans don't have much room for luggage—if you are loaded down, consider springing for a cab.

Bus

Mérida has four bus stations. The first-class station is known by the acronym **CAME** (KAH-may, Calle 70 between Calles 69 and 71, tel. 999/924-8391, toll-free Mex. tel. 800/702-8000) and has ADO, ADO-GL, OCC, and UNO service. Most of your bus travel, especially long-distance, will be from here.

Around the corner, the **second-class bus terminal** (Calle 69 between Calles 68 and 70, tel. 999/923-2287, Clase Europea tel. 999/924-4275) serves many of the same destinations as are offered at CAME, but the added comfort and safety of a first-class bus are definitely worth the few extra pesos. Note that the all-day Puuc Route Tour bus leaves from here as do buses to Chiquilá, where you catch the ferry to Isla Holbox.

Terminal Noreste (Calle 67 between Calles 50 and 52, Noreste tel. 999/924-6355, Oriente tel. 999/928-6230, Lineas Unidas tel. 999/924-7865) is the base for regional bus lines. Most tourists using this terminal are headed to Río Lagartos to see the flamingos, or to Cuzamá to visit the cenotes; other destinations include Mayapán and Izamal.

Terminal Auto-Progreso (Calle 60 between Calles 65 and 67) primarily serves Progreso (US$1, 50 minutes), with departures every 10–20 minutes 5 A.M.–10 P.M. If you're headed to the ruins at Dzibilchaltún, you can take a Sacnité bus from this terminal, or else get on a Progreso bus and ask the driver to drop you off at the turnoff. From there it is about a kilometer (0.6 mile) to the site.

Car

Good highways approach Mérida from all directions. Be prepared for one-way streets and avoid arriving on Sunday—a large area in the

DRIVING DISTANCES FROM DOWNTOWN MÉRIDA

LOCATION	DISTANCE
Airport	7 km (4 mi)
Campeche	196 km (122 mi)
Cancún	320 km (199 mi)
Celestún	86km (52 mi)
Chichén Itzá	120 km (75 mi)
Cobá	232 km (145 mi)
Dzibilchaltún	23 km (14 mi)
Ek' Balam	179 km (111 mi)
Izamal	72 km (44 mi)
Palenque	555 km (346 mi)
Progreso	33 km (20 mi)
Río Lagartos	263 km (165 mi)
Ticul	84 km (50 mi)
Tulum	274 km (171 mi)
Uxmal	80 km (50 mi)
Valladolid	160 km (100 mi)

MÉRIDA BUS SCHEDULES

The first-class bus station **CAME** (Calle 70 No. 555 between Calles 69 and 71, tel. 999/924-8391, toll-free Mex. tel. 800/702-8000) serves most major destinations, including:

DESTINATION	PRICE	DURATION	SCHEDULE
Campeche	US$10.75	2.5 hrs	every 30-60 min., 6 A.M.-11:45 P.M.
Cancún	US$20.50-23*	4 hrs	every 30-90 min., 5:30 A.M.-midnight
Chetumal	US$22	5.5 hrs	7:30 A.M., 1 P.M., 6 P.M., and 11 P.M.
Chichén Itzá	US$7.50	1.75 hrs	6:30 A.M., 9:15 A.M., and 12:40 P.M., or take 2nd class bus
Mexico City	US$89-104*	19-21 hrs	six departures daily 10 A.M.-9:15 P.M.
Palenque	US$24	7.5-8 hrs	8:30 A.M., 7:15 P.M., 10 P.M., and 11:30 P.M.
Playa del Carmen	US$24-28.50*	5-5.5 hrs	hourly 6:40 A.M.-3:40 P.M., plus 10:40 P.M. and midnight
San Cristóbal (Chiapas)	US$40-50	13-14 hrs	7:15 P.M. and 7 P.M.*
Tulum	US$18	4 hrs	6:30 A.M., 10:45 A.M., and 12:45 P.M.
Valladolid	US$10	2 hrs	eleven departures daily 5:30 A.M.-6:05 P.M.
Villahermosa	US$34.25	9 hrs	13 departures daily 7:15 A.M.-11 P.M., most after 7 P.M.

*Denotes deluxe service; not available on all departures.

The **SECOND-CLASS BUS TERMINAL** (Calle 69 between Calles 68 and 70, tel. 999/923-2287 or 999/924-4275) serves nearer destinations, including:

DESTINATION	PRICE	DURATION	SCHEDULE
Chichén Itzá/Pisté	US$5	2.5 hrs	every 30–60 min., 6 A.M.–7 P.M. and 10 P.M.–midnight
Chiquilá	US$13.25	5.5 hrs	11:30 P.M.; or connect via Tizimín (Terminal Noreste)
Puuc Route	US$12	7–8 hrs (round-trip)	8 A.M.
Santa Elena	US$4	1.75 hrs	6 A.M., 9 A.M., 10:40 A.M., noon, 2:30 P.M., 5 P.M., and 6 P.M., or connect via Ticul
Ticul	US$4	1.5 hrs	hourly 4 A.M.–midnight
Uxmal	US$3.25	1.25 hrs	every 1–2 hrs 6 A.M.–6 P.M.
Valladolid	US$7	3 hrs	every 30–60 min., 6 A.M.–7 P.M. and 10 P.M.–midnight

TERMINAL NORESTE (Calle 67 between Calles 50 and 52) has several small bus lines serving destinations, including:

Celestún	US$4	2.25 hrs	hourly 5 A.M.–8:30 P.M., except 7 A.M.
Chiquilá	US$11	6 hrs	10:30 A.M.
Cuzamá *(combi)*	US$1.25	1 hr	every 30 min., 5:30 A.M.–8 P.M.; vans queue up on Calle 67 in front of terminal
Izamal	US$3	1.5 hrs	hourly 4:45 A.M.–9 P.M.
Mayapán Ruínas	US$1.25	1.25 hrs	hourly 5:30 A.M.–8 P.M.
Río Lagartos & San Felipe	US$10	3.5 hrs	5:30 P.M.
Tizimín	US$9	2.5 hrs	6:45 A.M., 9 A.M., noon, 2 P.M., 4:30 P.M., 5:30 P.M. and 8 P.M.; be sure to take 1st class bus.

center of town is closed to vehicles. If you don't know the city, it can be a real headache to drive to your hotel, since many are downtown. The *periférico* is a wide, freshly paved traffic loop that circumscribes the city, making it possible to bypass the congested downtown streets if you're headed from Chichén Itzá to Celestún, for example.

Highway 180D is an eight-lane toll highway (*carretera cuota*) that runs from Mérida to Cancún. It begins 16 kilometers (10 miles) east of Mérida at Kantunil; from Mérida take Highway 180 toward Valladolid. Tolls are pricey—US$5.85 to Chichén Itzá, US$28 to Cancún. The toll road is in great condition, with rest stops, gas stations, and clearly marked exits; it's also nearly empty since most bus and trucking companies choose to take the *libre* (free road), which runs parallel to the highway. Although the *libre* is slower and teeming with speed bumps, it takes drivers through small villages and past fields of henequen and corn—sights worth seeing if you're not in a rush.

GETTING AROUND

The best way to see Mérida is on foot. Granted, some of the sidewalks are narrow, and the traffic can be thick, but the city is a pleasure to wander. Look up for street names, which are usually found at the intersection on the building corners, high up.

Bus

The most useful city buses are the ones that go between downtown and points along Paseo de Montejo. Downtown, catch an "Itzmna" bus on Calle 59, between Calles 56 and 58. You can catch the same bus all along Paseo de Montejo, including right in front of the U.S. Consulate.

Taxi

Cabs generally are found at taxi stands in most neighborhoods parks. If it's late, any hotel, café, or disco will call one for you. Some taxis are metered, but most aren't, so establish your fare in advance. Taxi fares are higher than in other cities, averaging US$1.50–5 around

a typical street corner in Mérida

© LIZA PRADO

town. Bargaining still helps. A cab to the airport is US$8–10.

Car Rental

Mérida has a number of car-rental agencies. Rates fluctuate with the season and according to competition, but start at US$30–40 a day for a basic car, including tax and insurance.

Most international companies have offices at the Fiesta Americana hotel, including **Hertz** (tel.999/925-7595), **Avis** (tel. 999/925-2525), **Executive** (tel. 999/920-3732), and **Europcar** (tel. 999/925-3548). Always check online for the best rates.

Recommended local agencies include: **Easy Way Rent a Car** (Calle 60 between Calles 55 and 57, 999/930-9500, from U.S. or Canada 877/846-3279, www.easyway rentacar-yucatan.com, 6 A.M.–11 P.M. daily), **Business Car Rental** (Calle 60 between Calles 45 and 47, tel. 999/928-8828, www .businesscar.com.mx, 8 A.M.–8 P.M. Mon.–Fri., 8 A.M.–2 P.M. Sun.), and **Mexico Rent-A-Car** (tel. 999/923-3637, 8 A.M.–12:30 P.M. and 6–8 P.M. Mon.–Sat., 8–10 A.M. Sun.), which is on the pedestrian walkway by Teatro José Peón Contreras, between Calles 58 and 60.

The Puuc Route and Around

You can easily spend a day or two in this region south of Mérida, with its rich concentration of Maya ruins, caves, and small appealing towns. The Puuc ruins are the main attraction of course, from the stunning size and accomplishment of Uxmal to the fantastic artistry of smaller sites like Labná and Kabah. The Loltún caves are a great introduction to the Yucatán's vast underground world, and a tour of nearby Hacienda Tabi reveals the splendor (and pervasive inequality) of the state's colonial era.

Getting There

Bus: An ATS bus headed for the Puuc Route leaves Mérida's second-class bus terminal every day at 8 A.M., spends a half hour at Kabah, Sayil, Labná, and Xlapak, and two hours at Uxmal, before returning to Mérida around 4 P.M. (US$12, entry fees are not included). There are also ordinary buses to Uxmal, as well as the nearby towns of Ticul and Santa Elena; see *Mérida Bus Schedule* for details.

Returning to Mérida, you can catch the ATS bus when it leaves Uxmal (around 2:30 P.M.), even if you didn't take it down. Or flag down a second-class bus on the highway; they pass the Uxmal turnoff at roughly noon–1 P.M., 2:30–3:30 P.M., 4:30–5:30 P.M., and 7:30–8:30 P.M.

Car: If you're driving, Highway 261 leads to the Puuc Route. From Mérida, the drive to Uxmal takes about one hour; from Campeche allow two hours.

◖ UXMAL ARCHAEOLOGICAL ZONE

Uxmal's massive scale, elegant structures, and intricate decoration make it one of the most memorable Maya ruins in the Yucatán, and a perennial favorite for casual visitors and Maya-buffs alike. It was the greatest of the Maya cities in the Puuc region, and contains some of the best—and best-preserved—examples of Puuc-style architecture. And though Uxmal is located just 80 kilometers (50 miles) from Mérida, it doesn't get the crush of visitors that sites like Chichén Itzá and Tulum do, making a visit here all the more enjoyable.

History

Some believe Uxmal was founded by Mayas from Guatemala's Petén region in the 6th century. Others contend it dates back even further, perhaps to the Preclassic period. Unlike most of northern Yucatán, the Puuc region has good soils, allowing for greater population density than other areas. Uxmal emerged as the dominant city-state between A.D. 850 and 900,

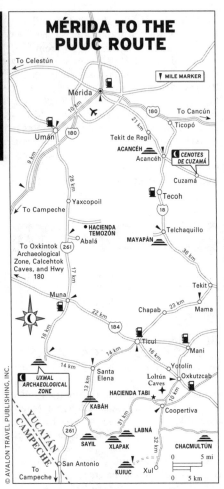

MÉRIDA TO THE PUUC ROUTE

To Celestún

▼ MILE MARKER

Mérida

10 km

To Cancún
180

21 km

Ticopó

Umán   180

Tekit de Regil

ACANCÉH

Acancéh   ☾ CENOTES DE CUZAMÁ

28 km

Cuzamá

To Campeche   Yaxcopoil   Tecoh
18

■ HACIENDA TEMOZÓN   Telchaquillo

Abalá   MAYAPÁN

To Oxkintok (261)
Archaeological
Zone, Calcehtok
Caves, and Hwy
180   36 km

17 km   Tekit

Muna   22 km   Chapab   23 km   Mama

184

16 km   Ticul   16 km

14 km   Mani

14 km   Santa   Yotolín
Elena   Loltún   Oxkutzcab
☾ UXMAL   Caves
ARCHAEOLOGICAL
ZONE   HACIENDA TABI ★

13 km   KABÁH   Coopertiva

YUCATÁN
CAMPECHE   261   31 km   LABNÁ

SAYIL   XLAPAK   32 km   CHACMULTÚN

0   5 mi

San Antonio   KUIUC   Xul   0   5 km

To
Campeche

© AVALON TRAVEL PUBLISHING, INC.

---

based in the nearby town of Mani spuriously claimed to be descended from Uxmal's rulers and occupied the ruins. All that said, however, relatively few stelae have been found at Uxmal, so less is known about the ruling dynasties here than at other major sites.

The Maya word *Uxmal* (oosh-MAHL) means "Thrice Built." The name notwithstanding, it is believed that Uxmal was built five times, each time over top of the last. Puuc architecture is one of the major achievements of Mesoamerica, whose hallmarks include unadorned lower levels, heavily decorated upper friezes, boot-shaped vault stones, thin squares of limestone veneer, and rows of pseudo-columns. The constant threat of drought also inspired the Mayas to adorn their structures with hundreds of stone masks and carvings representing the rain god, Chac, easily identified by his prominent hooked nose. Unlike most Maya centers in Yucatán, Uxmal was not built around a cenote, since there are none in this arid part of the peninsula. Rainwater was collected in *aguadas* (natural holes in the ground) as well as in man-made *chultunes* (cisterns) built into the ground, sometimes right inside a house or under a patio.

Pyramid of the Magician

Passing through the visitors center, and up a slow-sloping pathway, the first structure you reach is Uxmal's tallest and among its most distinctive. The Pyramid of the Magician stands 38 meters (125 feet) high, and has a distinctive elliptical base, rather than the square or rectangular base of most pyramids. The softly curved edges combined with its impressive height and girth lend the temple a striking elegance. You will approach the Pyramid of the Magician from the back, but the other (west) side is by far the most ornate. There, a staircase rises at an imposing 60-degree angle, lined by the hooked-nose masks representing Chac, the rain god. Three-quarters of the way up, a huge "Monster Mouth" facade—borrowed from Chenes-style construction from present-day Campeche—surrounds a temple door. At the top is a two-story

---

when the Pyramid of the Magician, the Great Pyramid, and the Nunnery were built, and is believed to have been the hub of a district of about 160 square kilometers (100 square miles) encompassing many sites, including the lesser sites in the area: Kabah, Sayil, Labná, and Xlapak. However, in the mid-10th century, Uxmal was abruptly abandoned, probably after being defeated by armies from Chichén Itzá and as part of a pan-Maya collapse around that time. During the Postclassic era, the Xiu clan

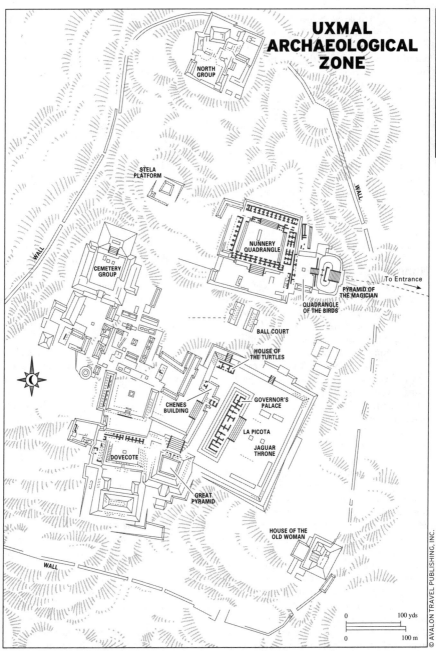

UXMAL
ARCHAEOLOGICAL
ZONE

NORTH
GROUP

WALL

STELA
PLATFORM

NUNNERY
QUADRANGLE

WALL

CEMETERY
GROUP

To Entrance

PYRAMID OF
THE MAGICIAN

QUADRANGLE
OF THE BIRDS

BALL COURT

HOUSE OF
THE TURTLES

CHENES
BUILDING

GOVERNOR'S
PALACE

LA PICOTA

JAGUAR
THRONE

DOVECOTE

GREAT
PYRAMID

HOUSE OF THE
OLD WOMAN

WALL

0   100 yds

0   100 m

© AVALON TRAVEL PUBLISHING, INC.

rectangular temple, with crosshatch panels beside the doors. You'll have to take our word for it, though, as tourists are no longer allowed to climb the pyramid, nor those at many other ruins. The restrictions are to prevent undue erosion, as well as accidents (of which there have been many, including a fatal tumble by a tourist at Chichén Itzá in 2005).

Before leaving, take note of the small but attractive plaza on the House of the Magician's west wide. It's known as the **Quadrangle of the Birds,** so named for the birds carved into the upper frieze of the small building opposite the house of the Magician. And there are more than just birds, but also Puuc-style decorative columns, faux thatching (or bird feathers?), and crescent-moon edging, all in remarkably good condition.

Nunnery Quadrangle

The Nunnery Quadrangle is the huge courtyard directly west of the House of the Magician. Covering an area of 60 by 45 meters (197 by 148 feet), the (almost) square is bounded on each side by long buildings. The buildings contain numerous small rooms, and reminded the first Spanish explorers of nunneries in Spain, hence the name. The buildings evidently were built in a single concentrated effort at the end of the 9th century, shortly before the city collapse.

The combination of a plain lower level topped by an ornate frieze—a staple of Puuc architecture—can be seen in all four buildings of the Nunnery Quadrangle. The West building has the most ornate frieze. Notice the stacked Chac masks at either end and, working toward the center, geometric spirals that represent clouds (the Maya glyph for cloud has a similar design). Interspersed are panels with lattice patterns, also typical of Puuc design. (Here they are especially fine, embedded with flowers.) The niche over the center door contains the figure of the God of the Underworld (God N, to archaeologists) with the body of a turtle, sitting under a canopy of feathers. The designers of Uxmal were obsessed with the male phallus, and figure at the ends of the facade are disrobed, with rather prodigious members that appear scarred or tattooed—yikes! (A large phallus also stood in the center of the Nunnery Quadrangle, but it has since disappeared.) Finally, notice the two long, feathered snakes that weave (and interweave) the length of the frieze. From the mouth of one emerges a human face, a way of emphasizing the divine origin of Uxmal's leaders.

The North building is the largest and highest of the four, affording great views of the entire site from its broad platform. The frieze contains exquisite Chac masks, with finely curved incisor teeth and distinct upper and lower eyelids.

To many observers, the East building is the most refined in its design and execution. Simple latticework is broken by triangular forms over the doors. On closer look, you can see the forms are in fact an inverted stack of two-headed feathered serpents. Above them are shields depicting owls, which the Maya associated with warfare and sacrifice.

The South building has a vaulted arch, giving access to and from the quadrangle. High on its sloped walls, look for red handprints, left from the original construction. Notice, too, the carvings of thatched huts, or *na,* over each of the door. In fact, you can see such images in numerous temples in this region, and beyond. The precise meaning of the huts is unclear—they may have represented the newborn universe, as in some Maya creation myths—but like the handprints in the archway, they lend a powerful humanism to these ancient ruins, not least because the very same *na* remains a fixture of Maya communities today.

Governor's Place

An archway leads out of the Nunnery Quadrangle across a grassy esplanade and past Uxmal's modest Ball Court. Bearing left, you'll climb a large platform to the Governor's Palace. At the top of the steps, pause a moment to appreciate the scope of this complex, considered by some to be the height of Puuc architecture. The platform you just climbed is artificial—it was built by hand out of piled stone, and measures a mind-boggling 187 meters (613.5 feet) long, 170 meters (558 feet) wide, and 8–10 meters (26.3–33 feet) high. On top of it are a number of structures, the most notable being the Governor's Palace, which measures 98 meters (321.5 feet) long and 12 meters 40 feet) wide (and it's built on still another 7-meter/23-foot high platform). The upper frieze has lattice patterns, feathered serpents, and over 100 Chac masks; in all, it took some 15,000 individual stone pieces to create it. Over the center door was the face—now gone—of a god, probably Lord Chac, surrounded by feather headdress, featuring Chac masks. Two arrow-shaped corbel arches originally allowed passage from one side to the pother, but were later plugged, perhaps to create more rooms or to stabilize the structure. The high-vaulted interior rooms are musty and unpleasant, but do walk around the north end, where, at the corners, near the ground, some excellent carved pieces can be examined close-up.

On the small platform in front of the palace, a throne in the shape of a two-headed jaguar was uncovered by John Stephens in 1841, and remains today. Such thrones were a common symbol of Maya authority—a similar one was found in Palenque and a single-headed one deep inside El Castillo at Chichén Itzá. Stephens tried to take the artifact with him but, lucky for us, found it "too heavy to carry away." He evidently never thought to look beneath it—there, archaeologists found a cache of nearly a thousand extremely fine jade, obsidian, and ceramic items.

Also on this platform is the **House of the Turtles,** a simple but elegant structure measuring 11- by 30-meters (36- by 100-feet). The lower half is very plain, but the upper part is decorated with a frieze of columns, topped by a cornice adorned by a series of turtles. The Maya associated turtles and other wetland creatures with rain and fertility, and this structure, like so much else in Uxmal, was probably used for ceremonies to bring rain. Inside is a sunny courtyard, and from the north side is a fine view of the ball court,

with the Nunnery Quadrangle and the Pyramid of the Magician beyond.

The Great Pyramid

Behind the Governor's Palace is the Great Pyramid, a more typical Maya pyramid, standing 30 meters (100 feet) on a series of terraces. You can see that it predates the Governor's Palace, as the latter's platform partially overlaps the pyramid's northeast corner. At the top—you can still climb this one—a small temple contains an impressively large, but partially buried, Chac mask. The temple's exterior is adorned with latticework and, most notably, panels depicting macaws.

Dovecote

Beside the Great Pyramid, excavation continues on a part of Uxmal known as the Dovecote. The name derives from the patchwork of niches in the roofcomb of the complex's most prominent feature, a high wall separating two of the three large plazas identified here. In addition to its ornate roofcomb, the wall contains a beautiful vaulted arch, and several vaulted rooms on its lower level. Its facade once had large figures molded from stucco; they've long since been destroyed or removed, but several protruding stone struts remain. The struts would have supported the fragile stucco figures, and are, in a modest way, an insight into these silent structures, and the people who built them. The ruins did not spring ready-made from the ground, but were built by regular people, who faced the same challenges modern designers do, like: How do we keep all these decorations from falling off?

Light Show

Every evening a sound and light show is presented at the ruins overlooking the awe-inspiring Nunnery Quadrangle. Different structures are lit up as an accompaniment to the Maya lore that is played over loudspeakers and headsets. The narration is a little corny and sometimes unintelligible but if you've never seen one of these shows, it's worth checking out. Simply being at the archaeological site at night with the ancient stone structures looming around you and the occasional flash of lightning in the distance, is undeniably impressive. You can't help but cast your mind back to ancient times, to imagine living in this mysterious city on a warm dark night gazing at the stars, the same ones we see today.

Practicalities

The ruins and museum are open 8 A.M.–5 P.M. daily; the sound and light show takes place at 7 P.M. in the winter (October–April) and at 8 P.M. in the summer (May–September). General admission to the ruins and sound and light show is US$9 for adults; children under 13 enter free. (Unfortunately, there are no reduced or refunded tickets if you don't plan on going to the sound and light show, or if it's cancelled because of rain or other reasons.) Tickets for the show are US$3, plus US$2.50 for headphones with the translation from Spanish. It's possible to go to the sound and light show the night before you visit the ruins for the single general admission price, but you must inform the ticket-seller before buying a ticket. You will buy part of the general admission ticket for US$5—not the US$3 show-only ticket—and then pay the remaining US$4 the next day. Don't lose your ticket from the show, as you must show it the next morning. Parking is US$1 per car; use of a video camera is US$3.

Guides to the ruins charge fixed prices and can be hired right at the entrance. Tours last around 90 minutes and cost US$37 in Spanish or US$42 for English, Italian, French, or German.

In addition to the museum and gift shop, the visitor/entrance center has an ATM, snack bar, postal drop box, and an excellent Dante bookstore.

Accommodations

A handful of large upper-end hotels (each with a restaurant) are clustered at and near the entrance of Uxmal. Smaller and more affordable lodging and food can be had in the nearby towns of Santa Elena, Ticul, and Oxkutzcab.

If you've seen the Club Med in Cobá or Chichén Itzá, then walking into **Club Med Villas Uxmal** (tel. 997/974-6020, scottsdale.mexicores@clubmed.com, www.clubmed.com, US$ US$81 s/d with a/c, US$135 suite with a/c) will be like dejá vu. Actually, it *is* dejá vu; these Club Meds are replicas of one another. Constructed around a tropical courtyard with a pool, the resort has boxy but attractive rooms with beds set on concrete platforms—kind of like a Maya bedroom. A reading room with a complete library on the history and culture of the Maya, a billiards table, and tennis court add to an already restful stay. Just steps from the ruins, the location is almost unbeatable. Look for it past The Lodge at Uxmal.

The original residence of the first archaeologists to excavate Uxmal, **Hacienda Uxmal** (Carr. Mérida-Campeche Km. 78, tel. 997/976-2012, www.mayaland.com, US$190–240 s/d with a/c) is now a colonial hotel offering 80 charming rooms. Units are decorated in a Yucatecan style with striking tile floors, marble bathrooms, heavy carved furniture, and ironwork beds (though the mattresses could stand to be replaced); more expensive rooms have private Jacuzzis. The lush grounds also include a pool, tennis court, and nice jogging trails. A spacious dining room offers reliable but unremarkable meals. You can often get a substantially better price calling the hotel directly, rather than booking through the corporate website.

Just 30 meters (98 feet) from the entrance to Uxmal, **The Lodge at Uxmal** (tel. 997/976-2010, toll-free U.S. tel. 800/235-4079, uxmal1@sureste.com, www.mayaland.com, US$374–445 s/d with a/c) is the nicest of the hotels in this area. Surrounded by lovely gardens with two inviting pools, the 40 bungalow rooms are modern, ample, and have comfortable beds. Most rooms have whirlpool tubs, intricately carved doors, and gaudy stained-glass windows as well. Definitely not worth the rate—at about US$400 per night you'd expect a boutique hotel with personalized service, a spa, and at least breakfast included (no go on all counts)—still, it is a relaxing spot. If the location appeals but the price doesn't, consider heading to the Club Med, a few steps up the road.

Food

Set in a lovely Mexican-style dining room as well as under a *palapa* by the pool, the restaurant at **Club Med Villas Uxmal** (Carr. Mérida-Campeche Km. 76, tel. 997/974-6020, 7:30 A.M.–10 P.M., US$5–18) offers a decent international menu. Service is good and the ambiance is typically mellow. A good place to relax after a day at the ruins.

Conveniently situated just outside of Uxmal's entrance is the restaurant at **The Lodge at Uxmal** (tel. 997/976-2010, 7 A.M.–10 P.M., US$5–20). Although it's often busy with tour groups, it's a good place to stop for a variety of food—from Mexican specialties to pastas and sandwiches. If you're really hungry, opt for the Yucatecan buffet, which is offered for all meals (US$10). Live music often is performed at peak hours too.

KABAH ARCHAEOLOGICAL ZONE

Kabah ruins (8 A.M.–5 P.M., US$3) are located 22 kilometers (14 miles) southeast of Uxmal, on the other side of the small town of Santa Elena. Kabah's major temples were constructed in A.D. 850–900, though the area was probably first settled as far back as 300 B.C.– A.D. 250. The site spans many square kilometers, though only the ceremonial center has been cleared and restored, and no major archaeological excavation has been conducted here. The highway cuts right through the ancient city, so there are ruins on either side. The main points of interest are on the east side of the road, where the ticket booth is.

Codz Poop

From the entrance, walk parallel to the road to the southernmost structure. A short but very steep staircase leads to a raised platform and to Codz Poop, Kabah's most ornate building and one of the most arresting structures on the Puuc Route. Dedicated to the rain god, Chac,

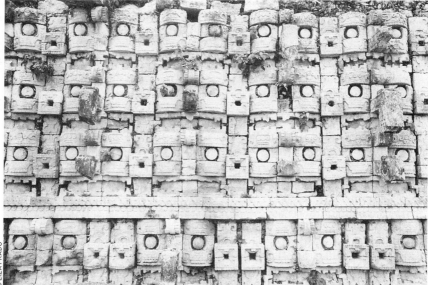

© LIZA PRADO

Keep on counting: the facade of Codz Poop has hundreds of Chac masks.

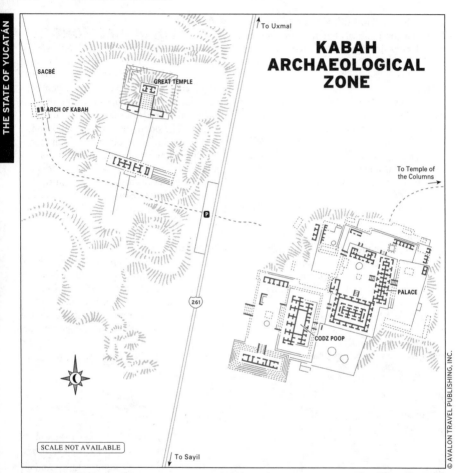

KABAH ARCHAEOLOGICAL ZONE

To Uxmal

SACBÉ

GREAT TEMPLE

ARCH OF KABAH

To Temple of the Columns

P

PALACE

261

CODZ POOP

SCALE NOT AVAILABLE

To Sayil

© AVALON TRAVEL PUBLISHING, INC.

and measuring nearly 45 meters (147.6 feet) long and 6 meters (19.7 feet) high, the temple's entire west facade is covered in some 250 Chac masks, with the typical googly-eyes and long hooked nose. Even the steps into the doorways are modified Chac noses. Looking close, you can see how each mask is made of the same set of pieces, and can imagine a Maya manufacturing line, with carvers churning out scores of eyelids, pupils, teeth, etc., and others assembling the masks on the temple.

The rear side of Cotz Poop is nearly as impressive, with huge stucco figures set against a latticework frieze. Be sure to peek at the side panels of the main door, where impressive bas-reliefs depict battle scenes.

Palacio and Temple of the Columns

A path from Codz Poop leads to the raised platform where the Palacio (Palace) stands. A broken set of stairs leads to the top, though climbing it is not allowed. The Palacio displays more typical Puuc architecture, with ornate friezes atop unadorned lower facades.

Around the northern edge of the Palacio, a

path leads through the trees to the mildly interesting Temple of the Columns. The name says it all, as the facade is covered in attached decorative columns. Two *choltunes* used to collect and store water flank the path just as you reach the temple—be careful not to tumble in!

Arch of Kabah and Great Pyramid
On the other side of the road (and through the parking area), a path leads 200 meters to the impressive Arch of Kabah. The six-meter (19.7-foot) high arch dates to A.D. 670–770 and marked one end of a grand *sacbé*, or raised stone-paved road, that extended 30 kilometers (18.6 miles) from Kabah to Uxmal, and is still traceable today. The first 15 kilometers (9.3 miles), from Kabah to the settlement of Nohpat, the road runs perfectly straight, before veering slightly to reach Uxmal. North of the path leading to the arch is the Great Pyramid, the largest structure in Kabah. Yet to be excavated and off-limits to climbing, it remains for now an impressively huge mound covered in grass and trees.

SAYIL ARCHAEOLOGICAL ZONE
Sayil (8 A.M.–5 P.M., US$3) is even more spread out than Kabah, but the long leafy paths between monuments is part of the pleasure of visiting this site. Archaeologists believe the area was settled as early as the 2nd or 3rd century A.D., though virtually all of its major structures were built in a short period between the end of the 8th century and middle of the 10th. Sayil's population most likely peaked at around 10,000 people, with another 7,000 living in outlying areas.

Sayil is located just seven kilometers (4.4 miles) from Kabah; coming from Kabah on Highway 261, look for the well-marked left-hand turnoff.

Great Palace
The path from the parking and ticket area leads past several deeply decayed stele to the Great Palace, also called the *Palacio Norte*. As the on-site plaque makes clear, the structure contains

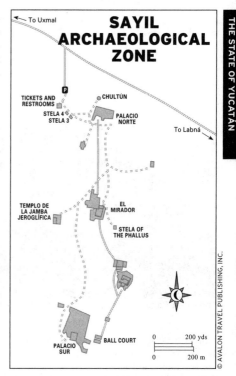

more than 90 rooms, and may have housed up to 350 people; the west side is better preserved than the east. Although the palace appears to be three stories, in fact each level is supported by a core of piled stone, as opposed to the story below it—just another example of how Maya architects were accomplished illusionists. Visitors aren't allowed to climb to the upper levels, but you can still appreciate the craftsmanship of the palace's 2nd-floor frieze;. Most notable are curious "Diving Gods" over the doorways, their upturned legs easily discerned. Tulum and Cobá have similar figures, which may represent the God of Maize (God E, to archaeologists). The corners have imposing Chac masks and decorative columns help unify the nearly 60-meter (197-foot) building.

El Mirador
A path leads south from the palace to El Mirador,

© LIZA PRADO

The Great Palace at Sayil Archaeological Zone has over 90 rooms.

a small temple whose name means "lookout." Built atop a crumbling pyramid, the structure has five rooms and a high-reaching roof comb. Though substantially collapsed, the structure is still impressive for its height and complexity of its comb.

The path continues another 50 meters (164 feet) past El Mirador to the Stela of the Phallus, or "Yum Keep." Kabah's spiritual leaders, like those of Uxmal and other cities, were obsessed with the male phallus. Here, a rather poorly executed stone panel depicts an ancient Dirk Diggler, his face and hands still partly visible, and an enormous penis hanging to his knees.

Other Temples

Sayil's remaining temples aren't terribly impressive as such, but the walk there, with sunlight filtering through the foliage overhead, is rewarding. A path forks off the main one between the Palacio and El Mirador. First, the Temple of the Hieroglyphic Jambs is not nearly as its name might suggest. The structure is lit-erally buried in the forest floor, with only the roof and a small portion of the carved door-ways visible. The path continues 500 meters (0.3 mile) to the much-decayed *Palacio Sur,* with columns, broken Chac masks and other figures discernable on the southern frieze. Beside the complex is Sayil's ball court, also in significant disrepair.

XLAPAK ARCHAEOLOGICAL ZONE

Xlapak (8 A.M.–5 P.M., free admission) is the smallest and most skippable of the Puuc ruins; indeed many tours don't stop here. That said, its single restored building has ornate facades on both sides, including some very well-preserved Chac masks.

LABNÁ ARCHAEOLOGICAL ZONE

Labná (8 A.M.–5 P.M., free admission) is for many people the best of the four smaller Puuc ruins. At least 60 *chultunes* (underground cis-terns) have been found in the Labná area, suggesting a population of about 3,000 residents at its peak, around A.D. 750–1000.

El Palacio

Labná's impressive main palace is the first structure you come to after passing through the ticket area. As the plaque there explains, the structure underwent at least 12 different constructions, and has 67 rooms distributed over two main levels and seven patios. It stretches 135 meters (443 feet) and stands on an even larger artificial platform. The west end (left, as you face it) probably housed Labná's ruling family, while the east side contained *metates* (stones used for grinding corn) and was therefore most likely used by their servants.

Take time to appreciate the palace's fantastic frieze. Many familiar elements have been embellished here: the noses and eyes of the Chac masks are turned upward as if peering into the sky, and the latticework is more complex than simple x-patterns seen elsewhere. On one corner, right of the central stairs, a human face can be seen emerging from the mouth of a feathered snake. It seems to have been a late modification: notice how the hooked nose of the prior mask was turned around to make room for the snake's gaping mouth. Some argue the presence of the plumed snake—shown here "giving birth" to the man emerging from its mouth—suggests strong influence from Central Mexico, where the Quetzalcoatl (aka Kukulcán), the feathered snake, was widely worshipped.

Arch of Labná

From the Palacio, a *sacbé* (raised road) leads across a plaza of high flowing grass to the south side of the site to its most famous structure, the Arch of Labná. It's an exquisitely constructed portal vault, with a smooth elliptical ceiling, forming a spacious 3- by 6-meter (10- by 20-foot) passageway—one of the largest and finest arches ever built by the Maya. In its heyday, the arch most likely served as an elegant passageway between residential and administrative structures reserved for Labná's elite. Both sides are decorated, one with deep-relief spirals and checkerboard patterns (associated

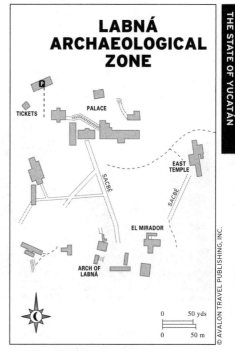

LABNÁ ARCHAEOLOGICAL ZONE

P

TICKETS

PALACE

EAST TEMPLE

SACBÉ

SACBÉ

EL MIRADOR

ARCH OF LABNÁ

0   50 yds

0   50 m

© AVALON TRAVEL PUBLISHING, INC.

with clouds and rain) and the other with two *na*, or thatched Maya huts. The doors of the huts were used as niches, probably to display important figures, and red and blue paint is still visible there. Remarkably, only the arch's stairs and the roofcomb required significant restoration. The rest has stood, as is, for over 1,000 years.

El Mirador

Opposite the arch, a squat temple sits at the peak of a high, steep pile of rocks. Atop the temple, an impressive roofcomb soars even higher. This is El Mirador, the building which explorer John Lloyd Stephens called "the most curious and extraordinary structure" he'd seen in his travels through the Maya world. Stone struts suggest the roof comb was once adorned with a complex array of stucco figures, including a huge statue over the center door. Stephens reported only "scattered arms and legs" remained at his

© LIZA PRADO

The Arch of Labná marked the dividing point between residential and administrative structures.

visit, more than a century and a half ago; today only the legs of a single figure remain.

LOLTÚN CAVES

Seven kilometers (4.3 miles) southwest of Oxkutzcab, the Loltún *grutas* are the largest known caves in Yucatán. This vast underground network served ancient people as a source of water and pottery clay—ceramics and carved reliefs dating from 1600 B.C. have been discovered here. It eventually developed into an important pilgrimage and ceremonial space for Mayas (caves typically represented fertility and the entrance to *xibalbá,* the underworld). Researchers working in Loltún also uncovered bones belonging to mastodons and other extinct mammals that date to 9000 B.C. While some argue that early hunters dragged these animals to the caves, it has yet to be proven. Instead, stone tools dating to 5000–3000 B.C. mark the earliest sign of humans in Loltún.

Visiting the Caves

A route through caverns has been wired for lights, which are turned on and off by the guide as groups move through. Loltún means Stone Flower in Maya and you'll see many carvings of small flowers. One of the more intriguing sights are dozens of handprints on the cavern walls, either in silhouette or negative outline, whose meaning remains a mystery. Early Mayas also placed stone cisterns *(chultunes)* under the dripping stalactites to catch "virgin water," important in ceremonies honoring Chac, the rain god. But the most important archaeological find here is the relief dubbed "The Warrior," which is carved on a rock face just outside the Nahkab entrance to Loltún. Strangely, it appears to follow the Izapan style of Kaminaljuyú, the enormous Preclassic city near Guatemala City. Toward the end of the hour-long tour you come to an opening in the roof of an enormous two-story-high cavern. The sun pours into the room, creating dust-flecked shafts of golden light. The gnarled trunk of a towering tree grows from the floor of the cave, reaching hundreds of feet up through the sunny opening, and flocks of birds twitter and flit in and around the green leafy vines that dangle freely into the immense chamber from above.

Practicalities

Wear decent walking shoes in the caves. For the most part it's an easy two-kilometer (1.25-mile) walk; however, it's dark and damp, and in a few places the paths between chambers are steep, rocky, and slippery.

For safety reasons, you may enter the caves only at set times with a guide. Tours begin daily at 9:30 A.M., 11 A.M., 12:30 P.M., 2 P.M., 3 P.M., and 4 P.M., and last about an hour. Admission is US$4.75 (children under 13 are free), but none of that goes to the guides—budget an-

other US$2–5 per person for tip. Tours are given in English or Spanish—let the ticket-seller know which language you prefer so you are paired with the right guide.

There is a small restaurant across the street from the caves, with friendly service, basic meals, and nice cold beer.

HACIENDA TABI

Seven kilometers (4.3 miles) northwest of the Loltún caves, Hacienda Tabi (8 A.M.–4 P.M. daily, US$1) makes an interesting side trip if you enjoy poking around old haciendas and have some extra time. The soaring 2,044-square-meter (22,000-square-foot) main structure has 24 rooms and faces a

---

HACIENDAS TURNED HOTELS

After lying abandoned for decades or even centuries, the Yucatán Peninsula's old henequen haciendas are returning to – and surpassing – their former colonial glory. Many have been restored as unique and super-deluxe hotels, making great use of the thick walls, high ceilings, and lush grounds. Rates aren't low-end, but the setting and service are unforgettable. Near Mérida, a few of the best include:

Once a sisal-producing hacienda, **La Hacienda Xcanatún** (Carr. Mérida-Progreso Km. 12, tel. 999/941-0213, www.xcanatun.com, US$311 s/d with a/c, US$342-378 suite) boasts 18 beautifully restored suites set in winding tropical gardens. Rooms have Lebanese-style floors, hand-carved furnishings, Mexican and Far Eastern antiques, and original oil paintings. Most also enjoy private sitting areas and whirlpool tubs. A full-service spa, two pools, and a gourmet restaurant only add to the tranquility.

A gem of a hotel, **Hacienda Temozón** (Off Hwy. 261, tel. 999/923-8089, www.thehaciendas .com, US$377 s/d with a/c, US$475-730 suite) has 28 elegant rooms and suites. Each has 5-7 meter (16.4-23 feet) ceilings, gleaming tile floors, luxurious amenities, and modern furnishings. Outside, the manicured grounds feature a spectacular stone pool, walking trails,

tennis courts, and stables. The original machinery used to process henequen also marks the entrance to its full-service spa.

Temozón's little sister, **Hacienda Santa Rosa** (Off Hwy. 180, tel. 999/910-4852, www .thehaciendas.com, US$377 s/d with a/c, US$475-730 suite) is an equally classy option though less splendid on all counts: 11 similarly decorated rooms, beautifully maintained but smallish grounds, a nice pool with shade trees, and an outdoor spa. The main attraction here is the privacy and personalized service that you receive from the moment you book your reservation. There definitely aren't the bells and whistles that you'll find at other haciendas, but you'll enjoy a restful and ultra-comfortable stay.

A 400-year-old estate, **Hacienda San Pedro Nohpat** (Off Hwy. 180, tel. 999/988-0542, www .haciendaholidays.com, US$85-125 s/d with a/c, US$150 suite) offers seven spacious rooms, each tastefully decorated with wrought-iron furnishings and subtle colors. All have modern amenities like mini-split air-conditioners, cable TV, and mini-fridges. The grounds are well-kept and include a sparkling pool, Jacuzzi, and comfy indoor and outdoor lounges. Continental breakfast is included in the rate too. Best of all, it's just a mile from Mérida!

huge grassy area, with a windmill, stables, rum distillery, and sugar mill running along the edges. In front, through the trees, there's also a massive, beautifully decaying chapel and two stout chimneys. Tabi was founded in 1750 and operated for nearly 200 years—at its height, Tabi encompassed 14,000 hectares (35,000 acres) and is unique for cultivating sugar rather than henequen. The hacienda finally closed in 1948, and was declared a protected area in 1997. A team of researchers sponsored by the Cultural Foundation of Yucatán in Mérida have been studying the hacienda since 1996—with so much attention paid to the Yucatán's ancient ruins, relatively little is known about life on the colonial-era haciendas, despite the fact that poor working conditions there helped spark the Caste War and later the Mexican Revolution. Hacienda Tabi is the first and only hacienda in the Yucatán to be excavated using archaeological methodology. There is a small museum onsite, and you may be able to get a guided tour from the guard/docent. To get here, follow the signs from Loltún caves; the last half kilometer (third of a mile) is dirt.

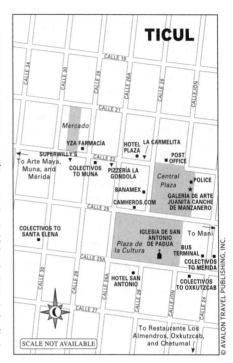

TICUL

Northeast of Santa Elena, the pleasant town of Ticul is an agricultural zone and a pottery and shoemaking center. Like Santa Elena, Ticul is a good place to base yourself if you think you'll want more than one day along the Puuc Route. You'll avoid the long drive back to Mérida after the first day of ruins and get an earlier start the next day.

Sights

Ticul's elaborate, high-domed 18th-century **main church** (Calle 25A between Calles 24 and 26) has a beautiful stained-glass window over an arched doorway framed by simple columns. Other than those flourishes, the structure possesses the pleasant unadorned austerity typical of so many Franciscan churches in this region. Next to it is a Franciscan monastery built 200 years earlier. Both are on the central plaza—impossible to miss.

The **Galería de Arte Juanita Canche de Manzanero** (central plaza, 9 A.M.–1 P.M. and 7–9 P.M. Mon.–Fri., and 4–9 P.M. Sat.–Sun.) is a modest gallery, with photos, paintings, and occasional exhibitions and performances. It is named for the mother of famed Mexican crooner Armando Manzanero, who wrote and performed hundreds of songs, including *Somos novios* and *Voy a apagar la luz*. Manzanero was born in Mérida, but his mother is a native of Ticul.

Shopping

The hills and riverbeds around Ticul have great clay, and the town has long been famous for its pottery. By far, the most highly regarded studio here is **Arte Maya** (Calle 23 between Calles 46 and 46-A, tel. 997/972-1669, 8 A.M.–8 P.M. Mon.–Fri.) on the highway toward Muna. The studio was founded by the late Wilbert González and now operates as

© LIZA PRADO

the elegant church in the small town of Ticul

an art school, women's cooperative, and pottery store. The shop specializes in high-quality reproductions of classic Maya art, using laboriously prepared clay and all-natural "paint" made from local soils and minerals. The artists typically model their work from photographs of pieces found during excavations—the finished products are by no means cheap, but they are remarkable in their faithfulness to the originals. In fact, the shop holds a license from INAH—the government body that oversees all things Maya—to make such exact copies, and all pieces bear a special mark to distinguish them from actual artifacts. Short tours (in Spanish) are given on request, and if someone is working you are usually free to watch. The shop is most active between November and April.

Accommodations

Facing the central plaza, **Hotel Plaza** (Calle 23 between Calles 26 and 26-A, tel. 997/972-0484, www.hotelplazayucatan.com, US$30 s, US$35.50 d) is a good choice with spotless, simple, tile-floor rooms that open onto an interior courtyard. Beds are decent and have bright bedspreads that liven up the somewhat characterless rooms. All units have air-conditioning, cable TV, and in-room telephone. Plus, there's private parking.

Across from the main church, **Hotel San Antonio** (Calle 25-A between Calles 26 and 26-A, tel. 997/972-1893, www.hotelsan-antonio.com, US$22 s with a/c, US$27–30 d with a/c) offers bright rooms with balconies, cable TV, in-room phones, and aging air-conditioners (definitely check the decibel level of the air-conditioning before you settle into a room). Units above the entrance to the hotel have king-size beds and good views of the central plaza. Off-street parking is available and there's a good, inexpensive restaurant on-site too.

Food

Near the southern entrance to town, **Restaurante Los Almendros** (Calle 24 s/n; 997/972-0021; 10 A.M.–9 P.M. daily, US$5–12) is a Ticul institution and one of the best *típico* eateries in town. The restaurant claims this is where *poc chuc*, a very popular meat dish served all over the Yucatán Peninsula, was invented. True or not, the food here, mostly Maya-influenced, is excellent.

Facing the central plaza, **La Carmelita** (Calle 23 at Calle 26, tel. 997/972-0515, 9:30 A.M.–6:30 P.M. daily, US$2–8) is a mom-and-pop restaurant serving good, no-frills Yucatecan dishes to a loyal clientele. The fish plates and shrimp cocktails are particularly popular and with good reason—they're fresh and tasty, a rarity this far from the coast. Look for the tinted windows.

Pizzería La Gondola (Calle 23 at Calle 26-A, tel. 997/972-0112, 8 A.M.–1 P.M. and 5–11 P.M. daily, US$4–10) may have somewhat reluctant service, but the pizza and pasta dishes are well prepared and make a nice culinary alternative to Mexican food, if you need it.

Super Willy's (Calle 23 between Calles 28 and 30, 7:30 A.M.–9:30 P.M. daily) is a large supermarket with produce, canned food, munchies, and more. Across the street, the small town **mercado** (6 A.M.–2 P.M. daily) has fresh fruits, vegetables, and small lunch stands dishes, plus clothes, shoes, and other doodads.

Information and Services

For a 24-hour pharmacy, head to the reliable and well-stocked **YZA Farmacía** (Calle 23 at Calle 28, tel. 997/972-1080).

The **police station** (central plaza, tel. 997/972-0210) is staffed 24 hours every day.

On the central plaza, **Banamex** (Calle 26 between Calles 23 and 24, 9 A.M.–4 P.M. Mon.–Fri.) exchanges travelers checks and cash until 3 P.M. Around the corner, **HSBC** (Calle 23 between Calles 24 and 26, 8 A.M.–7 P.M. Mon.–Sat.) exchanges money until 6 P.M. Both have 24-hour ATMs.

The **post office** (Calle 23 at Calle 26, 8 A.M.–2 P.M. Mon.–Fri.) is on the central plaza, at the entrance to the Palacio Municipal.

Camheros.com (Calle 26 near Calle 23, 9 A.M.–11 P.M. Mon.–Sat., 9 A.M.–2 P.M. and 5–11pm Sun., US$0.95/hr.) is a reliable and breezy Internet café above an ice cream shop.

Getting There

Ticul has a small bus terminal (tel. 997/972-0162) and large *colectivo* terminal, almost across the street from each other on Calle 24 behind the church and central plaza. A number of smaller terminals have *colectivo* service to nearby towns.

The *colectivo* terminal has the fastest and cheapest service to Mérida (US$3, 1 hour, 4 A.M.–7:30 P.M.). Vans leave whenever full (usually every half hour); buy a ticket at the counter, where you also select a numbered seat assignment.

The bus terminal also has service to Mérida (US$3.50, 1.5 hours, every 30–60 minutes 5 A.M.–11 P.M., as well as to Campeche (US$7, 3 hours, 7 P.M. only), Carrillo Puerto (US$9, 4 hours, every 1–2 hours 4:30 A.M.–11:30 P.M.), and Chetumal (US$14, 6 hours, 4 A.M., 8:30 A.M., 1 P.M., 6:30 P.M., and 12:30 P.M.). For Cancún, it's faster to go to Mérida and catch a direct bus from there.

Colectivos to nearby villages use separate terminals, including to Santa Elena (US$0.80, 20 minutes, board on Calle 30 between Calle 25 and 25-A), Muna (US$1, 15 minutes, board on Calle 23 between Calles 26-A and 28), and Oxkutzcab (US$1, 30 minutes, board on Calle 25-A between Calles 24 and 26). Colectivos leave whenever they fill up, typically every 30–60 minutes and roughly 7 A.M.–8 P.M.

You can also get from town to town quite affordably by taxi, and that is recommended at night when *colectivo* service is reduced or nil. A taxi from Ticul to Santa Elena, for example, costs US$7.50.

SANTA ELENA

This peaceful community lies smack-dab in the middle of the Puuc Route, just 16 kilometers (9.9 miles) east of Uxmal and seven kilometers (4.3 miles) north of Kabah, the first of the smaller sites. It's a pleasant and convenient base for exploring the entire region, with two fine lodging options, a couple good restaurants, and an impressive church.

Sights

Long before reaching Santa Elena, you can

see its imposing **Iglesia de San Mateo** rising like a misplaced airplane hangar from a distant hilltop. (Some say it was built atop a Maya ruin—not at all uncommon—but you can see from the town's central plaza that it's simply a rocky hill.) A huge pinkish stone box standing 35 meters (115 feet) high, 50 meters (165 feet) long, and 20 meters (66 feet) wide, the church has almost no exterior adornment. The cavernous nave is also austere, with thick white walls and wood pews. The exceptions are the ornate wooden altar and large wooden *retablos* (hand-carved religious scenes depicted in ornate boxes) along the walls. Be sure to ask the church attendant (he's usually hanging out in the nave) to let you up to the roof, reached via a rickety spiral staircase. Near the top is the organ platform (sans organ) with a dizzying view down into the nave from a wooden patio and narrow corridors along the sides. The roof affords an awesome vista of the surrounding countryside.

A small **museum** alongside the church (8 A.M.–7 P.M. daily, US$1) has detailed and somewhat disturbing displays of the mummified remains of four children who died in the 1800s and were buried in the church floor (a common practice), and uncovered during renovations in 1980. Twelve bodies were discovered; five were reburied, three were taken by authorities and never returned, and four displayed in glass cases here. The tiny corpses may have been children of German transplants brought during the French occupation that died (or were killed) during the Caste War. The museum also has a replica Maya tomb under glass in the floor of the same room. (Notice a theme?) It shows a skeleton and common burial items, like a stone axe and ceramic dishes, thought to be needed in the next world. Photos, a painted Maya doorway, and a few pre-Hispanic and colonial items round out the displays.

Accommodations and Food

Set in a tropical garden, **The Flycatcher Inn** (southern end of town, off Hwy. 261, no phone, www.flycatcherinn.com, US$37–55.50 s/d with fan, US$55.50–65 with a/c, extra person US$9.50) is a tranquil bed-and-breakfast occupying what was once a water-purification facility. There is nothing industrial about the place, though: the three spotless rooms, one suite, and new stand-alone cottage all have large windows, handmade ironwork furniture, and sunny patios. The owners, Kristine Ellingson and Santiago Domínguez, are incredibly versed in the region's sights and history. A large and healthy breakfast is included in the rate, during which Kristine doles out advice and info to guests preparing their day's itinerary. The property encompasses another 10 hectares of lush forest behind the hotel, and a loop trail makes for a pleasant 40-minute walk, especially in the morning or the afternoon when the birds are out. Reservations recommended.

A kilometer south of town, **Sacbe Bungalows** (Hwy. 261 Km. 127, tel. 997/978-5158 or 985/858-1281, www.sacbebungalows.com.mx, US$21.50–27) offers eight simple, comfortable cement-block bungalows, all with private bath, sturdy mosquito screens, and porches. The grounds are lush and well maintained, with labels on the fruit trees, and their produce on your breakfast plate (US$4.75 pp). Owned by a friendly French-Mexican couple, Sacbe no longer offers camping or trailer hookups, but continues to be a reliable and affordable fixture on the Puuc Route.

On the main road to the ruins, the *palapa*-roofed **Restaurant El Chac-Mool** (Calle 18 No. 211-B, tel. 997/971-0191, 8 A.M.–9 P.M. daily, US$3.75–7.50) serves basic Yucatecan specialties, sandwiches, and a smattering of vegetarian options. The food is unremarkable—sometimes reheated, sometimes freshly made—but it's reliable. Service is sluggish so best save this place for a post-ruins visit.

The Pickled Onion Restaurant (999/923-0708, 11 A.M.–9 P.M. daily, US$4–10) is a labor of love by the English-Canadian expat who runs it. Here you can munch on wings, shepherd's pie, onion soup and other old-country fav's at outdoor tables with wonderful afternoon light. The restaurant also prepares box lunches to take ruin-hopping—a great idea, as there are so few places to eat along the Puuc

Route. The restaurant is the yellow building set up off the road, halfway between the Flycatcher and Sacbe Bungalows.

Information and Services

There is almost nothing in the way of traveler services in this town; it's still very much a small Yucatecan village despite the popularity of the area. Count yourself lucky, then, if **Ciberspace@.com** (tel. 997/978-5045, 10 A.M.–1 P.M. and 3–9:30 P.M. Mon.–Fri. and 10 A.M.–9 P.M. Sat.–Sun.) is actually open and has working computers and Web access. Internet is US$1.25 an hour, and international calling is available. Look for it at the bottom of the paved road (not the stairs) leading to the church.

The nearest ATMs are at Uxmal ruins and Ticul, and the nearest gas stations are in Ticul and Muna.

Getting There and Around

Like almost everywhere on the Puuc Route, Santa Elena is easiest to reach and negotiate if you have a car. That said, many people do visit by bus and do just fine. Second-class buses between Campeche and Mérida pass in both directions on Highway 261, a block from Flycatcher Inn and right in front of Bungalows Sacbe.

Leaving Santa Elena, the bus to Campeche (US$7, 3 hours) passes at around 7:30 A.M., 10:30 A.M., noon, 1:30 P.M., 4:30 P.M., 6:30 P.M. and 7:30 P.M. For Mérida (US$4, 1.5 hours), the same bus passes at around 6:30 A.M., 7:30 A.M., 8 A.M., noon, 2:30 P.M., 4:30 P.M., and 7:30 P.M.

To see the ruins, you can catch the ATS Puuc Route bus from Mérida as is passes through Santa Elena, at around 9:15 A.M. every morning. It stops for 25–30 minutes at each of the four smaller Puuc ruins, before returning to Uxmal, passing back through Santa Elena. You can get off then, or continue to Uxmal and catch a Campeche-bound bus back to Santa Elena later in the afternoon.

OXKUTZCAB

Oxkutzcab is conveniently located near the Loltún caves, Hacienda Tabi, and the Puuc Route. It's a small village that is surrounded by extremely fertile land—it is known as the orange capital of the Yucatán Peninsula, and a huge citrus processing plant nearby employs many area residents. As you approach town,

FRAY DIEGO DE LANDA

Just north of Oxkutzcab, the town of Mani has a quiet, peaceful atmosphere that belies a wrenching history. It was here, in 1562, that Fray Diego de Landa conducted his infamous *auto-da-fé*, in which he burned an untold number of irreplaceable Maya codices, pottery, and other records because he deemed them works of the devil. He accused numerous Maya religious leaders and laypeople of idolatry, and ordered them tortured, publicly humiliated, and imprisoned. The act was outrageous, even by Spanish colonial standards, and Landa was shipped back to Spain to face the Council of the Indies, the colonial authority. He was eventually absolved – a panel of inspectors found he had broken no laws – but during the ordeal Landa evidently came to regret his act.

Confined to a convent awaiting judgment, he set about writing down all he could remember about the Maya.

It was no minor document: Landa spoke Maya fluently, and had lived, traveled, and preached in the Yucatán for 13 years before his expulsion. In all, Landa spent close to a decade completing *An Account of the Things of Yucatán*. He eventually returned to Mérida, where he died in 1579, and the work was forgotten until being rediscovered in 1863. Among other things, the manuscript contains a crude alphabet, which proved invaluable to the modern-day decoding of the Maya hieroglyphics. Ironically, it was the very man who destroyed so much of the Maya's written history, who provided the key for future researchers to unlock what remained.

be sure to look for the orange groves alongside the high healthy fields of corn, banana, and coconut palms farms.

Sights

Oxkutzcab's **central plaza** is bordered by a large Franciscan church, the **Templo y Ex-Convento de San Francisco** and an attractive arched building, which holds municipal offices. The plaza itself has concrete benches, a gazebo, and a painted plaster statue of a woman carrying a load of oranges on her head.

Leonardo Paz is an accomplished painter and muralist and an Ozkutzcab native son. He painted the long, beautiful **mural** above the market and several smaller works around town. In the plaza, look on the backside of the gazebo to see paintings depicting the War of the Castes and the infamous *auto-da-fé*, when in 1562 Franciscan priest Fray Diego de Landa burned scores of irreplaceable Maya codices and sculptures.

Facing the town church, **Mercado 20 de Noviembre** (6 A.M.–4 P.M. daily) is worth wandering into. Paz's colorful mural mirrors the scene just below it, with indigenous women sitting in front of huge piles of fruit and packing boxes stacked in every free space. Most memorable is the incredible assortment of citrus fruits, including oranges, limes, grapefruit, gaudy pink *pitayas,* and tiny yellow *nanzim.*

Entertainment and Events

Oxkutzcab's two-week **Orange Festival** is celebrated in late October or early November and is renowned throughout Yucatán. Definitely stop by if you are in the area, and be sure to make a hotel reservation if you want to stay overnight during the festivities.

Accommodations and Food

On the road that leads toward Loltún Caves, **Hotel Puuc** (Calle 55 at Calle 44, tel. 997/975-0103, hotelpuuc@hotmail .com, US$20.50 s with a/c, US$25 d with a/c) offers 24 rooms, most spacious but all

clean with mini-split air-conditioners and cable TV. There's plenty of parking and a good mom-and-pop restaurant on-site. The friendly owners also know a lot about area ruins, churches, and caves—be sure to ask for advice if you need it.

At the Hotel Puuc, **Restaurante Labná** (Calle 55 at Calle 44, tel. 997/975-0103, 7 A.M.–4 P.M. daily, US$2–6) serves regional food in a simple, brightly decorated dining area. Menu items include Yucatecan-style chicken and pork plus Mexican standards such as quesadillas and grilled beef.

There also are a few simple eateries on the town's central plaza.

Information and Services

Banamex (central plaza, 9 A.M.–4 P.M. Mon.–Fri.) has an ATM and exchanges cash and travelers checks.

Check your email at **InterCafé** (Calle 52 at Calle 51, no phone, 8 A.M.–9 P.M. Mon.–Sat., 9:30 A.M.–4:30 P.M. Sun., US$1.25/hr.).

Across from InterCafé is **Farmacia María del Carmen** (Calle 51 at Calle 52, tel. 997/975-2793, 8 A.M.–midnight Mon.–Sat., 8 A.M.–2 P.M. Sun.).

Getting There

Oxkutzcab's **main bus terminal** (tel. 997/975-0308, Calle 51 at Calle 56) has service on Mayab and ATS bus lines. Both are second-class, but ATS service is slightly faster and more expensive. Destinations include:

Chetumal, US$13, five hours, 1 A.M., 4:20 A.M., 9 A.M., 10:45 A.M., 1:20 P.M., and 7 P.M.

Carrillo Puerto, US$8, 4 hours, 5 A.M., 6 A.M., 6:30 A.M., 7:30 A.M., 8 A.M., 10 A.M., 11:30 A.M., 4 P.M., 6 P.M., 10 P.M., and midnight.

Mérida, US$4, 2 hours, every 30–60 minutes 5:30 A.M.–8:30 P.M., stopping in Uman, Muna, and Ticul.

You can also catch *colectivos* to Tecax (US$0.75, 25 minutes) every 30–45 minutes 6:30 A.M.–7 P.M., until 5 P.M. only Sunday, from outside the terminal; and to Ticul

(US$0.75, 30 minutes) every 10–15 minutes 6 A.M.–8:30 P.M. daily from the corner of Calles 51 and 54.

To get to Loltún Caves, flag down a *combi* outside Hotel Puuc.

NORTHWEST OF THE PUUC ROUTE
Yaxcopoil

Just off Highway 261 between Mérida and Uxmal, **Hacienda Yaxcopoil** (Hwy. 261, 33 km/20.5 mi south of Mérida, tel. 999/910-4469, www.yaxcopoil.com, 8 A.M.–6 P.M. Mon.–Sat., Sun. 9 A.M.–1 P.M., US$4.75, children free) was one of dozens of huge henequen (a type of cactus, sometimes referred to as sisal) estates that dotted the Yucatán Peninsula. Built in the 17th century, Yaxcopoil (yawsh-ko-po-EEL) grew to encompass 11,000 hectares (27,181 acres), reaching its zenith during World War I, when rope made from the thorny, fibrous henequen plant was in great demand. A visit to the hacienda today leaves much to be desired—guide service or written descriptions for starters—but you can stroll through the grand old rooms, where antique furniture, old photos, and original tile floors give a sense of the life the *patrones* (landowners) enjoyed. Don't leave without visiting the machine room out back, which you may have to ask to be unlocked. There, huge machinery once used to extract fiber from the henequen leaves and bind it into bales still stands. The high brick chimney is from the days of steam power (notice the narrow tubes running underfoot) while the massive diesel engine was added in 1913 and used until the hacienda stopped production in 1984. Admission to Yaxcopoil is a bit steep considering how little formal information there is, but if you speak any Spanish, definitely chat up whoever is there—many staffers either worked the hacienda, or their parents or grandparents did, and many have fascinating stories. The history of henequen production—the grandeur of the estates, the cruel exploitation of indigenous workers, the political and economic influence wielded by hacienda owners—is as fascinating as it is little understood.

Muna

This small town is home to many of the people who work at or around the Uxmal archaeological site. For travelers, there's not much reason to stop, and now that the highway loops around it, many people don't make it into town. But Muna does have a 17th-century Franciscan church that's notable for its facade, which is adorned with lacy belfries that glow a mellow gold in the late afternoon. People are friendly and the shady plaza has a number of fruit stands. This also is a good place to fill your gas tank or, if you don't have a rental, to pick up the ATS Puuc Route bus from Mérida.

There was no bank or ATM in Muna at the time of research. The **PEMEX** gas station is on the central plaza.

There is no bus station in Muna, so buses stop at the northwest corner of the plaza, near the church. There is usually a bus representative hanging around selling tickets. Buses to Mérida (US$2, one hour) leave frequently 5:30 A.M.–midnight. Buses to Uxmal (US$1, 25 minutes) leave every 1–2 hours 7 A.M.–7 P.M.; the ATS Puuc Route bus from Mérida arrives here around 8:45–9 A.M. daily.

Oxkintok Archaeological Zone

Oxkintok (8 A.M.–6 P.M. daily, US$3) doesn't have the wow factor of better-known ruins, but it's a beautiful, well-maintained site that can make an extra day on the Puuc Route rewarding. The site is big and varied, with pyramids, plazas, and palaces scattered amid high grass and trees. Best of all, you'll probably have it completely to yourself. The ruins sit in a fertile plain at the edge of the hilly Puuc region and may have been connected to Uxmal by a limestone *sacbé*. Oxkintok has attracted a fair amount of attention in the past few years, as archaeologists uncover an urban center at least three square miles. Tombs have been found in a number of the structures, though many of the artifacts were lost to looters. To reach Oxkintok, follow the signs eastbound from Highway 180. Consider combining a visit here with a tour of the Calcehtok caves.

THE STATE OF YUCATÁN

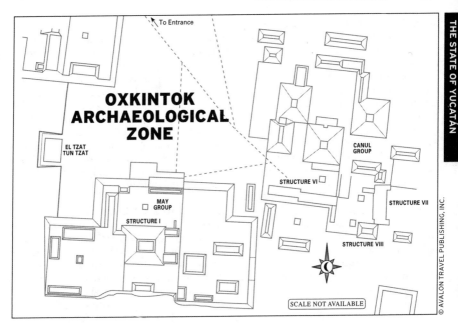

To Entrance

OXKINTOK ARCHAEOLOGICAL ZONE

EL TZAT TUN TZAT

CANUL GROUP

STRUCTURE VI

STRUCTURE VII

MAY GROUP

STRUCTURE I

STRUCTURE VIII

SCALE NOT AVAILABLE

© AVALON TRAVEL PUBLISHING, INC.

Calcehtok Caves

These may be the most adventure-oriented of the *grutas* (caves) along the Puuc Route. Up to four kilometers (2.5 miles) of the cave can be visited, during which you squeeze through narrow gaps, teeter along slippery pathways, and crawl and clamber through muddy passageways. Along the way are huge chambers filled with stalactites and stalagmites, and tiny rooms where archaeologists have found human bones and other remains of pre-Hispanic Maya ceremonies. Calcehtok's caves are definitely less commercialized than others—you don't need any technical experience, but be prepared to get dirty.

To get here, follow the signs on Highway 184 until you reach a turnoff that leads to a small parking lot. A guide should be waiting up the short path. (If not, it means he is with other people and you can either wait or come back later. *Never* enter this or any cave without a guide.) There are several tours available, depending how far and deep into the cave you want to go. Prices vary accordingly, but

it works out to roughly US$14 an hour for up to three people, with tours ranging from two to five hours. Before going in, agree with the guide how long the tour will last and how far into the cave you will get. If you have a flashlight, bring it as a backup. Do not wear flipflops—tennis shoes or boots are best, although Tevas should be fine.

NORTHEAST OF THE PUUC ROUTE

Located along or just off Highway 18, these sights are easily reached by car and make for interesting stops between Mérida and the Puuc Route.

Ruínas de Acancéh

The official **Acancéh ruins** (8 A.M.–5 P.M. daily, US$2) consist of two main parts: a large pyramid and secondary temple right in the center of the town of Acancéh, and a second somewhat smaller structure called El Palacio de Estucos (Palace of the Stuccos) a few blocks away. In reality, the majority of the remains of this ancient city are scattered throughout town; most are on private property—backyards, front yards, under houses, etc.—and it is either impossible or impractical to excavate them. Still archaeologists believe the area was settled as early as 300 B.C. but didn't reach its peak until A.D. 400–600. Curiously, Acancéh's structures show strong influences from Petén (northern Guatemala) as well as Teotihuacán in central Mexico, both quite distant.

Driving though town, the pyramid is impossible to miss, facing a large dirt lot (Acancéh's central plaza actually). A small kiosk at the corner is where you buy your ticket, and a guide may accompany you up the pyramid (no fee, but a small tip would be considerate). At the top, under a protective tin roof, are a series of large stucco masks; unfortunately the actual faces are missing or significantly deteriorated. They surely depict important gods, but archaeologists have been unable to identify most of them.

If you've got a car, the guide will likely lead you to the Palacio de los Estucos on his bike. A large, complex palace, it shows a blending of architectural styles, including, for example, both curved and squared corners. On the uppermost level is a long frieze of impressive stucco designs (hence the structure's name) in the shapes of birds, a ram, and man-jaguar, among others. Your guide will also likely point out the lintel of a particular doorway on the top level, which is made of a deeply grooved *metate,* used for grinding corn. Too worn down for its original purpose, it was reused in the construction here. Not only resourceful, it lends a certain human touch to the structure.

◖ Cenotes de Cuzamá

A tour of the cenotes at Chunkanan, better known as the Cenotes de Cuzamá (US$12 per trolley, up to 4 people), is one of our favorite non-archaeological outings from Mérida. When the henequen plantations were functioning, the harvest was stacked on small trolleys that were pulled by horses over long networks of lightweight rails. The residents of the small town of Cuzamá have put their trolleys back to

© GARY CHANDLER

Watch your step as you descend into the ground to enjoy a dip in one of Cuzamá's cenotes.

use, outfitting the carts to hold four passengers and offering horse-pulled tours to three beautiful cenotes along the rail line. The trip to the cenotes is half the fun—there is only one set of rails and there's an etiquette as to which driver has to pull over, which entails unloading the passengers and hoisting the cart off the tracks before the other trolley clatters past. With a few starts and stops, you make it to the cenotes. The first is the largest and easiest to get into, with concrete stairs leading to a cavernous pool. The second two are more challenging—in both you have to negotiate a slippery steel ladder from the cavern roof down to the water. Wear Tevas or sneakers. Once down, swimming in the crystalline water with sunbeams and tree roots angling down though the roof…well, it's simply sublime. The whole trip

takes about three hours with a half-hour stop at each cenote. *Tábanos* (horseflies) are the only annoyance, buzzing around the horse and cart. They have a nasty bite, so be careful not to let one land on you.

The entrance to the cenotes is 3.3 kilometers (2 miles) from the center of Cuzamá; if you've traveling by public transportation, take a *trici-clo* (bicycle taxi) from the center of town to the cenotes (US$1.85 each way). If you're driving, follow the signs through town.

Cenote Tza Ujun Kat

One kilometer (0.6 mile) west of Cuzamá in the town of Homun, lies the Cenote Tza Ujun Kat (9 A.M.–sunset daily, US$0.30). Visited mostly by locals, it's a large clear blue swimming hole that's accessible by a short cement

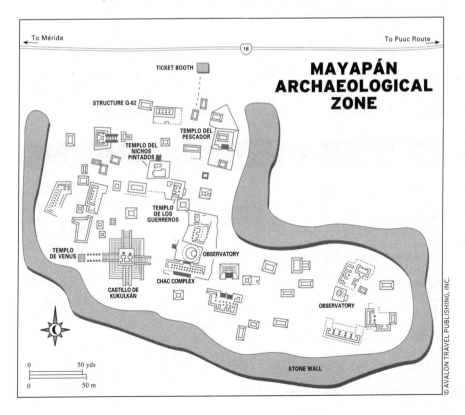

stairway. An opening in the cavern roof allows shafts of light to beam in during the late afternoon—an inspiring view and a great photo op to boot. This is a good alternative if you want to go to a cenote but don't have the time to take the tour in Cuzamá. Look for the **Restaurant Bar El Familiar** on the main road—the cenote is behind it.

Tecoh Caves

The Tecoh caves (10 A.M.–5 P.M. Mon.–Fri., 8 A.M.–5 P.M. Sat.–Sun., US$3) is something of a mixed bag: A 1.5-hour tour leads you past a dozen crystalline underground cenotes, but the walls and limestone formations are marred with the spray-painted messages of local kids and couples. The payoff is a 50-meter (164-foot) crawl to the last and largest cenote, which has beams of sunlight entering from two holes in the roof and makes for a refreshing swim.

Mayapán Archaeological Zone

Mayapán (8 A.M.–5 P.M. daily, US$2.25) is thought by some to have been one of the most important cities in the pre-Hispanic Maya world, although you'd never know from the trickle of visitors the site gets nowadays. May-

apán is not on any tour-group itinerary, and independent travelers tend to skip it going to or from the "main" Puuc sites farther south. While not as grand as Uxmal or Chichén Itzá, people who do stop are rarely disappointed. Mayapán is a compact, immaculately maintained site with two primary pyramids, an observatory, cenote, and excellent fresco paintings and stucco masks. It was founded around A.D. 1000 after the powerful Cocom dynasty left Chichén Itzá to establish the region's capital here. (Chichén Itzá was subsequently abandoned except as a place for religious worship and pilgrimages.) Mayapán dominated northern Yucatán almost until the mid-15th century, when it was abruptly abandoned, perhaps because of an internal revolt. The first indigenous people met by the Spanish newcomers still called themselves *maya uinic* (Maya men) in reference to their former capital, and it is from there that modern use of the word Maya emerged. Unfortunately, there are few explanatory plaques on-site.

Second-class buses from Mérida's Noreste terminal pass the ruins' entrance in both directions; just be sure you get on one for Mayapán ruins, not Mayapán town, which is in an entirely different area.

Celestún

Celestún is a small fishing village on the northwest shoulder of the Yucatán Peninsula; it sits on the mainland side of a 22-kilometer (13.7-mile) long inlet-estuary known as the Ría Celestún. The shallow super-salty waters are an ideal breeding and feeding area for *phoenicopterus ruber ruber,* the largest and pinkest of the five flamingo species. The peculiar pink birds—along with hundreds of other species of birds—are Celestún's primary attraction. It has helped to make this inlet one of Mexico's best bird-watching areas and is known by bird enthusiasts worldwide.

Though tourism is growing, Celestún's coastal waters teem with fish and octopus, and catching them is still the main industry

of locals here. The town has about 8,000 permanent residents but 10,000 fisherman ply the coast from here to Río Lagartos during octopus season (August–December). Celestún is also an important salt extraction area, producing 21,000 tons of salt every year. Salt production has been a vital industry since A.D. 600, and fishing goes back even further, of course.

If you're not a hard-core birder, a trip to the flamingo reserve is about the only reason to come to Celestún, and the town is just close enough to Mérida (96 km/59.7 mi) to make day trips possible. Numerous tour operators offer tours here from Mérida, or you can do it yourself relatively easily by bus—either way it's a pretty long day. If you have some time and a car, staying a night or even two lets you visit the reserve pressure-free and to check out some additional area tours.

FLAMINGO RESERVE

The **Reserva Ecológica de los Petenes** (Petenes State Ecological Reserve; the reserve's little-used official name) is one of just a few breeding areas in the northern hemisphere for the American flamingo; it is home to the species' largest colony—15,000–20,000 birds can gather here in the November–February mating season. Hundreds of other birds and waterfowl nest in the wetlands and mangrove forests—about 300 of the 509 identified bird species in the Yucatán Peninsula can be spied here. It's not unusual to see a blue heron or an anhinga perched on a tree stump with wings outstretched, drying in the sun.

One reason for the diversity of bird life is the diversity of habitat, which includes mangrove forests, coastal dunes, savannas, low deciduous forest, hummocks (small islands of mangroves in the wetlands), seashore, and of course the Celestún estuaries.

◖ Flamingo Tours

No matter how you do it, a standard flamingo tour unfolds in four parts: a visit to the "petrified" forest (a stand of ghostly, leafless trees killed by saltwater intrusion), then to the fla-

mingo feeding grounds, followed by a short ride through the mangroves, and then a stop at an *ojo de agua* (freshwater spring; literally, an "eye of water") to go swimming. Because the sites are relatively far apart—the petrified forest is at the mouth of the *ría* while the flamingos congregate near its top, around 15 kilometers (9.3 miles) away—you spend a good amount of time motoring from one place to the next. In a 2–2.5-hour trip, you'll spend 20–30 minutes observing the flamingos (and somewhat less at the other spots). It doesn't sound like much, but most people find it sufficient. If you want more time with the flamingos—especially if the flock is at its height—private guides are the most flexible. With either the state guide service or the fishermen's cooperative, you'll have to get everyone in the boat (and the guide) to agree to adjust the schedule.

The **Parador Turístico Cultur** is the rather inelegant name for the pier and visitor center where the state-sponsored guide service is based. It is two kilometers (1.25 miles) from Celestún, on the west side of the highway bridge spanning the *ría*. From there, you can book a complete tour (US$100, 2.5 hours) or a shortened tour that doesn't include the petrified forest (US$60, 1.5 hours); in either case, there's a US$2 per person park fee. The people at the ticket counter won't necessarily offer to put small groups together; the best way to join other travelers is

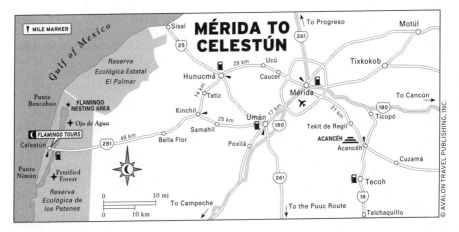

© AVALON TRAVEL PUBLISHING, INC.

© LIZA PRADO

Celestún hosts the largest American flamingo colony in the world.

to arrive around 10 A.M. (if you're coming from Mérida by bus, take the 8 A.M. departure) and ask around. Guide service is available in Spanish, English, and Italian.

The **fishermen's cooperative** has a stand on the beach, at the end of Calle 11. Trips from here are basically the same, though you have to motor along the coast first to the entrance of the estuary, and the tour starts with the petrified forest. It cannot be shortened, as tours from the bridge can. Tours cost US$85 for a private group (2.5 hours, up to seven people) or US$14 per person on a shared trip. If you end up waiting for more than an hour for a group to develop, captains often will take groups of 2–4 people for somewhat less.

Other Tours

Celestún Expeditions (in Mérida 999/924-8283, celexp@sureste.com) is operated by David Bacab, one of the region's best-known bird-specialists and a longtime guide for the Celestún area. Besides the standard flamingo tour (using the official services, with Bacab as an additional guide) you can also take an early morning "bird walk"; a "butterfly walk" for those interested in the region's numerous species of butterflies and moths; or a bike and kayak tour to the abandoned salt-producing village of Hacienda Real de Salinas and through the mangroves.

Also in Mérida, **Ecoturismo Yucatán** (Calle 3 between Calles 32-A and 34, Col. Pensiones, tel. 999/920-2772, www.ecoyuc .com.mx) is one of several agencies that offer ecological tours to the area, especially for those interested in birding.

ACCOMMODATIONS
Under US$50

In a bubblegum pink building, the **Hostal Ría Celestún** (Calle 12 at Calle 13, tel. 988/916-2170, US$5.50 dorm, US$14 s/d with shared bath) is the only hostel in town—too bad, because the pressure of competition might prod the management into a little better maintenance. As it is, rooms are cheap but in need of a good scrubbing. The communal kitchen is all right, and the common areas better still—you'll surely spend more time there than in your room. A spotty Internet terminal is US$2 an hour, and bikes can be rented for US$2 an hour or US$5 a day.

Half a block from the pier, **Hotel María del**

Carmen (Calle 12 between Calles 13 and 15, tel. 988/916-2170, US$18.50 s, US$23 s with a/c, US$23 d, US$29 d with a/c) is a small reliable hotel on a attractive stretch of beach. Each of the clean simple rooms has sturdy window screens, two double beds, and a balcony or terrace. Most also have ocean views. If your budget permits, the air-conditioned rooms are worth the extra five bucks.

Near the northern edge of town, **Ecohotel Flamingo Playa** (Calle 12 at Calle 5, tel. 988/916-2133, US$37–46.50 s/d) offers simple beachfront rooms with tile floors, air-conditioning, and cable TV. There's also a small but inviting pool that overlooks the ocean. All in all, a good deal.

US$50-100

Hotel Manglares (Calle 12 near Calle 5, tel. 988/916-2156, www.hotelmanglares.com, US$74 s/d, cabana US$150) is Celestún's best hotel, owned by the same two brothers who operate Restaurante La Palapa. All 24 double rooms have air-conditioning, satellite TV, and telephone, while four beachfront cabañas have the same, plus a small living room, king-size bed, and kitchenette. A small pool completes the package.

Over US$100

Ten kilometers (six miles) north of town, **Hotel Eco Paraíso Xixim** (Antigua Carretera a Sisal Km. 10, tel. 988/916-2100, www.ecoparaiso .com, US$152 s, US$178 d) boasts 15 oceanfront *palapa*-roofed bungalows that rest on 61 acres of land. Each unit has a sitting area, comfortable beds, and an ample patio with hammocks. A short walk reveals a modern pool, an immense shade *palapa,* and a tall lookout platform that affords views of the sea and coast. As the name suggests, it's an eco-friendly hotel: Solar energy is used, all water is recycled, and the land has been protected by building upon only 1.2 percent of it. There also are a handful of ecologically diverse trails for walking or biking. No question, it's a long way from city life but it's a perfect retreat with sun, white sand, and the emerald sea at your doorstep. Be sure

to ask about the educational tours. Rates include full breakfast; half-board available.

For longer stays, consider **Playa Maya Resorts** (Antigua Carretera a Sisal s/n, tel. 999/938-0839, www.playamaya.net, US$100–210 s/d, weekly and monthly rates available), a beachfront condominium complex with one to two bedroom units with fully equipped kitchenettes, simple wood furnishings, and private verandas. All face a wide expanse of beach along the Gulf of Mexico and are next to a large, well-kempt pool. There's also a decent restaurant on-site. Located seven kilometers (four miles) north of town. Rates include transportation to and from Mérida's airport.

FOOD

◖ **La Palapa** (Calle 12 between Calles 11 and 13, tel. 988/916-2063, 11 A.M.–6 P.M. daily, US$5–12) is easily the best and most reliable restaurant in Celestún, serving tasty seafood, plus various chicken and beef dishes beneath a soaring *palapa* roof. Whereas other restaurants in town have a somewhat liberal approach to appearance and cleanliness (we tracked down one restaurant owner chopping chicken in the kitchen with no shirt on), the service, facilities, and food prep at La Palapa are impeccable. Tour groups often eat here, but the dining area is large enough to give everyone space.

Restaurante Boya (Calle 12 at Calle 11, tel. 988/916-2129, 9 A.M.–7 P.M. daily, US$5–9) serves a standard seaside menu of fish fillet, shrimp, seafood soup, and more, plus cheap beer and a full bar. Eat in a somewhat dim indoor dining area or at shady tables set up in the sand on the beach.

Restaurante El Lobo (Calle 10 at Calle 13, no tel., 8 A.M.–noon, 6–11 P.M. daily, US$3–6) has great breakfast options, including Belgian waffles and yogurt with mixed fruit. For dinner, the pizza is decent and a welcome alternative if you are seafooded out.

The **mercado municipal** (central plaza, 7 A.M.–6 P.M. daily) has a decent selection of fruit, veggies, bread, and other foodstuff. There also are several cheap taco stands near the entrance.

INFORMATION AND SERVICES

There are no banks, ATMs, or currency exchange offices in Celestún, and few places accept credit cards. Be sure to take enough cash to cover your hotel, food, and excursions. There's also no post office, so save your postcards until you hit a bigger town.

Celestún's **Centro de Salud** (Calle 5 between Calles 8 and 10, tel. 988/916-2046, 8 A.M.–4 P.M. Mon.–Fri.) is a basic health clinic. While emergency service is provided, serious injuries should be treated in Mérida.

Farmacia Similares (central plaza, no tel., 9 A.M.–9 P.M. daily) has a modest selection of medications and toiletries.

The **police** (central plaza, tel. 988/916-2025) are stationed in the *palacio municipal* (city hall). Note that the phone number is the general number to city hall, so you may not get an answer after-hours or on weekends.

You can surf the Web at **Hostal Ría Celestún** (Calle 12 at Calle 13, US$2/hr.).

GETTING THERE
Bus

Buses to Celestún leave from Mérida's Noreste bus terminal every hour every day 5 A.M.–8:30 P.M. (except 7 A.M.). Assuming you're coming for the flamingo tours, the driver usually stops at the *parador* (staging area) before going the rest of the way into town. In Celestún, the small bus terminal (tel. 988/916-2067) is at the southeast corner of the central park, near the Celestún Expeditions office. There are buses to Mérida (US$4, two hours, hourly 5 A.M.–8 P.M.) as well as to many of the intermediate towns.

Car

From Mérida, there are two routes to Celestún: the southern route that goes through Umán, and the northern one that passes through Hunucma. Both routes lead to Kinchil, where Highway 281 leads directly to Celestún.

The southern route is more convenient, as long as you don't get lost in Umán (which is easy to do!). When entering Umán, you'll come to a broad three-way intersection, often packed with cars, *tricíclos* (three-wheeled bike taxis), pedestrians, and an overworked traffic cop. Be sure to bear right at this intersection, and keep your eyes peeled for signs to Celestún. If you end up missing the turn, just loop around the small village and start over again.

GETTING AROUND

You can walk just about anywhere in Celestún, although when it's hot you may prefer to take a *tricíclo;* a ride in town costs under a dollar. You can also take a *tricíclo* to the river port where flamingo trips start, about three kilometers (two miles) back down the highway.

Bicycling is another possibility, mostly to visit Hacienda Real de Salinas. You can rent bikes (or arrange bike tours) at Restaurante El Lobo, Hostal Ría Celestún, and Celestún Expeditions; the cost is around US$5 a day.

Dzibilchaltún

A quick 25-minute trip north of Mérida on Highway 261 brings you to the important but somewhat underwhelming archaeological site of Dzibilchaltún (dzee-beel-chawl-TOON) (Hwy. 261 Km. 15 turnoff, 8 A.M.–5 P.M. daily, US$5.50). Recognized as the oldest continuously used Maya ceremonial and administrative center on the peninsula, it was inhabited as early as 1000 B.C. through to the arrival of the Spanish. The intriguing **Temple of the Seven Dolls** is the only known Maya temple with windows, and its orientation suggests it was used for astronomical observations. The temple is named for a set of small clay figures that were found inside during excavation. The seven dolls and other artifacts are displayed in the site's exceptional **Museo del Pueblo Maya**

(8 A.M.–4 P.M. Tues.–Sun.), which focuses on the archaeology of Dzibilchatún as well as the area's cultural and economic development; signage is in Spanish and English. A 350-meter-long (1,148-foot) ecological path links the museum to the ruins. Along the way, trees and plants are labeled and small *palapa*-roofed billboards have information on local flora and fauna.

From **Terminal Auto-Progreso** (Calle 60 between Calles 65 and 67), buses to the town of Sacnité pass the Dzibilchatún entrance (US$0.70, 7:20 A.M., 9:30 A.M., 11:35 A.M., 1:30 A.M. and 3:40 P.M.); otherwise, take any Progreso-bound bus (departures every 10–20 minutes) which will drop you at the highway turnoff, about a kilometer (0.6 mile) from the ruins.

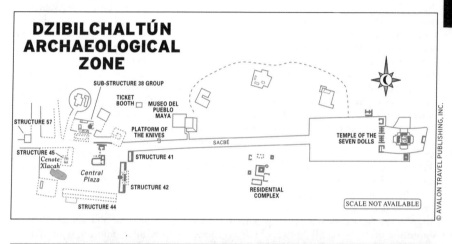

Progreso

On the Gulf of Mexico, Progreso is Mérida's closest access to the sea, an easy 33-kilometer (20.5-mile) drive on Highway 261. Meridianos flock here in summer to escape the intense heat and sticky humidity—as many as 150,000 during July and August weekends. The whole town comes to life; all the restaurants are open, usually quiet shops hustle, and the beaches are filled with families enjoying the surf and sea. Cruise ships also land here two to three times a week, disgorging several thousand passengers each. Many of those passengers take buses straight to Mérida and the Puuc Route, but Progreso has made a number of improvements to its waterfront in an attempt to entice cruise-shippers to stick around. One drawback the town can't do anything

about is the constant and sometimes powerful wind, which buffets the entire northern coast. In fact, Mexico has sent two windsurfers to the Olympics; they trained in nearby Chicxulub Puerto. You'll see little wind-sport activity directly in front of Progreso, however, as the long pier disrupts the airflow.

HISTORY

Progreso was founded in 1856, and during the halcyon days of the henequen industry, huge ships were a regular feature of the town waterfront and its then-amazing two-kilometer (1.25-mile) long wharf. (It's now about seven kilometers (4.3 miles) long.) Henequen entrepreneurs built mansions east of town; there are still mansions there, albeit more modern constructions befitting their current owners, mostly Canadians and Mérida's well-to-do.

SIGHTS
La Playa

Travelers arriving from the Caribbean side of the peninsula will find the Gulf coast rather underwhelming. The sand is coarser, and the water doesn't have the brilliant shades of blue that make the Quintana Roo coast justly famous. But the beach at Progreso is still fairly broad and clean and will do just fine, especially when the mercury rises inland. The water stays shallow a long way out and is relatively calm, although expect some chop during the stormy season (June–October) and know that the wind never really dies down. The beach is dotted with *palapa*-roofed sun shelters; across the street are a line of restaurants and cafés.

El Faro

Built between 1885 and 1891 on the site of an earlier lighthouse, today's 40-meter (131-foot) *faro* (lighthouse) was originally lit with kerosene. It was converted to electricity in 1923; a 1,000-watt light bulb and a backup generator ensure there's always light to lead sailors through the shallow Gulf waters into Progreso.

It's not officially open to tourists, but lighthouse buffs may be able to finagle a visit by asking for permission at the tourist office.

The Wharf

At the turn of the 20th century, Progreso's two-kilometer-long (1.25 mile) pier was the longest stone wharf in the world. It had to be—the Yucatán Peninsula sits on a long limestone shelf that drops ever so gradually into the Gulf, making this and most of its bays extremely shallow. In fact, some scientists conjecture that at one time Yucatán, Cuba, and Florida were all one long extension of land.

Despite the length of Progreso's pier, it sat in only six meters (19.7 feet) of water, which proved insufficient for larger container ships. The activity on the pier declined greatly after an alternative one was built in 1968 in the Yucalpetén harbor, six kilometers (3.7 miles) west of town. Progreso's pier continued to receive ships—mostly cruise ships and those that came to pick up exports such as honey, cement, fish, salt, and steel. In an effort to accommodate them and to attract more, the pier was extended and now stretches 4.3 kilometers (2.6 miles) into the Gulf. There's a fleet of trucks and buses to ferry cruise-

Progreso's pier is one of the longest in the world.

© LIZA PRADO

shippers and cargo back-and-forth. Tourists used to be able to walk or take a ride to the end of the pier, but that has been halted for security reasons.

Parque Nacional Arrecife Alacranes

Declared a marine park in June 1994, Parque Nacional Arrecife Alacranes is made up of five islands located 125 kilometers (78 miles) north of Progreso in the Gulf of Mexico. Covering nearly 300 square kilometers (186 square miles)—the islands themselves make up only a fraction of that figure—the reserve is a haven for a variety of marine birds, turtles, lobster, conch, shark, and other species that are at risk of extinction. There were no organized tours to the reserve at the time of our research—little tourist interest in combination with the high cost of gas make the trip from Progreso too expensive to be profitable for tour operators.

ENTERTAINMENT

Cines Hollywood (Plaza Del Mar, Calle 27 between Calles 76 and 78, tel. 969/934-4200, US$2.50) shows U.S. and Mexican films on its two screens.

SHOPPING

For Mexican folk art and crafts, drop in on the open-air *artesanía* **market** held in the plaza in front of the Casa de la Cultura (Calle 80 at Calle 25, 8 A.M.–5 P.M.) whenever there's a cruise ship in town, typically Monday, Tuesday, and/or Wednesday.

Plaza Del Mar (Calle 27 between Calles 76 and 78, 8 A.M.–10 P.M.) is a small shopping center with T-shirt shops, a few clothing boutiques, a food court, and a supermarket.

SPORTS AND RECREATION

You can rent Jet Skis, kayaks, and other gear from small kiosks on the beach, including in front of El Viejo y El Mar restaurant (Calle 19 at Calle 78). There, the equipment is available 10 A.M.–4:30 P.M. daily; ask in the restaurant if you don't find anyone on the beach.

ACCOMMODATIONS

Progreso has a growing but still limited selection of accommodations. Finding a room can be hard in July or August and on high-season weekends—be sure to make reservations.

Under US$50

Just a block from the beach, **Hotel Embajadores** (Calle 64 between Calles 21 and 23, tel. 969/935-5673, www.progreso hotel.com, US$23.25 s/d with fan, US$28 s/d with a/c, US$37 suite) offers basic but clean rooms with cable TV. There's a pleasant rooftop lounge plus guests receive a half and hour of free Internet access per day. Most of the staff is bilingual and offer lots of great information about the area. Children under 12 stay for free.

Near the center of town, **Hotel San Miguel** (Calle 78 between Calles 29 and 31, tel. 969/935-1357, US$21 s/d with fan, US$23.25 s/d with a/c) is a simple hotel offering rooms with private bathrooms, hot water, and cable TV.

US$50-100

Located in a renovated colonial home, **Hotel Yakunah** (Calle 21 between Calles 48 and 50, tel. 969/935-5600, www.hotelyakunah.com .mx, US$65 s/d with a/c, US$100 casita with a/c) offers spacious rooms with gorgeous *talavera* tile floors. A huge backyard surrounds a well-kept pool—a nice place to sun yourself or to catch up on that novel you've been meaning to read. Although it's across from the beach, it is a bit far from the action in town. Still, it makes for a comfortable stay. Continental breakfast included.

Condhotel Progreso (Calle 21 between Calles 66 and 68, tel. 969/935-5079, www.condhotelprogreso.com, US$35–41 s/d, US$50–64 one bedroom, US$74–79 two bedrooms) offers 23 apartments, all equipped with full kitchen, satellite TV, and air-conditioning as well as seven hotel rooms without the kitchen amenities. Some have balconies and ocean views—ask to look at a few before choosing. A small but clean pool at the entrance of the property is a bonus. Discounts available for weekly/monthly rentals.

Just four kilometers west of Progreso, **Sian-Ka'an** (Calle 17 s/n, tel. 969/935-4017, www.hotelsiankaan.com, US$50 s/d, US$65 q) is a quiet hideaway with nine rooms on a nice stretch of beach in the town of Yucalpetén. While all have fully equipped kitchenettes and cable TV, they vary greatly in style, view, and comfort; take a look at a few before choosing. Rooms closest to the ocean don't have air-conditioning, while those in back do—the price is the same for either. There's also a small clean pool that faces the ocean, where there are several *palapa* sun shades for guests. For eats, the hotel's glass-enclosed restaurant **Yikil-Ha** (8 A.M.–8 P.M. daily, US$4–14) is a reliable choice.

FOOD

Progreso's restaurants are typical of Mexican seaside resorts: if you like freshly caught fish you've come to the right place—it's hard to find much else.

Restaurants

Flamingos (Calle 19 at Calle 72, tel. 969/935-2122, 8 A.M.–midnight daily, US$6–12) serves big portions under a breezy *palapa* roof. Shrimp, fish fillets, and ceviche are the most popular, but you'll also find brochettes, meat and chicken dishes, and even a few Chinese options. Nice views of the beach and waterfront.

Next door, **Shark Restaurant** (Calle 19 at Calle 72, tel. 969/935-2116, 11 A.M.–7 P.M. daily, US$6–15) is a somewhat newer, hipper place, specializing in seafood *carpacho*—a version of carpaccio made from thinly sliced fish, octopus, or conch served in an olive oil, vinegar, and white wine sauce. The restaurant also has shrimp, chicken, beef, and pasta options as well.

Le Saint Bonnet and **El Viejo y El Mar** (Calle 19 at Calle 28, tel. 969/935-2299, 8 A.M.–11 P.M. Sun.–Thu., until 1 A.M. Fri.–Sat., US$5–15) are sister restaurants right next to each other

on the *malecón*. They keep the same hours (more or less) and share a menu of mostly international seafood: Try the three-person seafood platter or the *filete de mero empapelado*, fresh grouper baked in aluminum foil with shrimp. There are also pizza, pasta, and standard Mexican plates. Le Saint Bonnet has tablecloths and is a bit classier with live music Friday and Saturday nights, while El Viejo y el Mar caters to a slightly younger crowd with drink specials and DJ music Friday and Saturday nights. There also is a small swimming pool that guests of either place can use.

All the way at the east end of the waterfront, **Viña del Mar** (Calle 19 between Calles 60 and 62, tel. 969/934-4747, noon–8 P.M. daily, US$5–10) is worth the walk. The dining room is pretty plain, but the dishes are creative and tasty, such as the *filete viña*, prepared with a cilantro and *chaya* sauce, or the coconut shrimp made with fresh coconuts.

Lito's II (Calle 23 between Calles 72 and 74, tel. 969/934-4383, 1 P.M.–1 A.M. Tues.–Sun.) is a downtown offshoot of the original Lito's, a Progreso institution. The kitchen specializes in seafood, while the bar serves up a variety of beers and cocktails. Live music, often jazz, is featured Friday, Saturday, and Sunday nights.

Groceries

Mercado Municipal (Calle 80 between Calles 25 and 27, 7 A.M.–3 P.M. daily) is a place where locals shop for their daily needs: fruits, veggies, fresh meats, clothes, toiletries, and other personal items. There are a handful of eateries offering cheap meals and snacks too.

Super San Francisco de Asis (Calle 80 between Calles 29 and 31, 7 A.M.–9 P.M. daily) is a large modern supermarket across from HSBC bank.

INFORMATION
Tourist Information

The **tourist office** (Calle 80 at Calle 25, tel. 969/935-0104, 8 A.M.–8 P.M. Mon.–Fri. and 9 A.M.–1 P.M. Sun.) proffers friendly and capable assistance from its bustling office in the Casa de Cultura.

Hospitals

Centro Médico Americano (Calle 33 between Calles 80 and 82, tel. 969/935-0951) is the best hospital in Progreso, with a 24-hour emergency room.

Pharmacies

Farmacia Yza (Calle 78 at Calle 29, tel. 969/935-0684) is open 24-hours daily, and offers home delivery 8 A.M.–10 P.M. However, you may find better prices around the corner at **Farmacias Similares** (Calle 29 between Calles 78 and 80, tel. 969/934-4205, 7:30 A.M.–9:30 P.M. Mon.–Sat., 8:30 A.M.–5 P.M. Sun.).

Police

The police station is located on Calle 19 at Calle 66 (tel. 969/935-0026, 24 hours daily).

SERVICES
Money

A block apart, **Banamex** (Calle 80 between Calles 27 and 29, 9 A.M.–4 P.M. Mon.–Fri.) and **HSBC** (Calle 80 between Calles 29 and 31, 8 A.M.–7 P.M. Mon.–Sat.) have reliable ATMs and exchange cash and travelers checks.

Internet and Telephone

Consorcio Navarro Bolio (Calle 80 at Calle 29, tel. 969/935-3174, 8 A.M.–8 P.M. Mon.–Sat., 8 A.M.–2 P.M. Sun.) is lottery center that also happens to offer Internet and long-distance phone service (and laundry!). Check your email for US$1/hr, or call the United States and Canada for US$0.40 a minute, and Europe for US$0.60 a minute.

Post Office

The post office (Calle 31 between Calles 78 and 80, 8:30 A.M.–3 P.M. Mon.–Sat.) is located just east of Parque Independencia.

Launderette

Lavandería Caremi is at the back of Consorcio Navarro Bolio (Calle 80 at Calle 29, 8 A.M.–8 P.M. Mon.–Sat.) and charges US$1/kilo, with a three-kilogram minimum (6.6 pounds).

GETTING THERE
Bus

From Mérida, buses leave the Auto-Progreso terminal on Calle 62 between Calles 65 and 67 every 10–15 minutes 5 A.M.–10 P.M. daily (US$1.25, 45 minute). You'll be dropped off at the bus station in Progreso (Calle 29 between Calles 80 and 82, tel. 969/935-3024), a few blocks from the center of town and a short walk from the *malecón*. To return, buses leave the Progreso station for Mérida every 15 minutes 5:20 A.M.–10 P.M. daily.

Vans also make the round-trip from Mérida to Progreso, leaving Mérida from a small station at Calle 60 between Calles 65 and 67 every 15 minutes or so (when full). In Progreso, the same vans head back to Mérida from the corner of Calles 31 and 82.

Car

From downtown Mérida, drive north on either Paseo de Montejo or Calle 60. The two streets eventually merge and become Highway 261, which leads directly to Progreso.

GETTING AROUND
Bus

To head a few kilometers east or west of Progreso, go to the corner of Calles 82 and 29, where you'll find a small parking lot filled with *combis* (Volkswagen minivans) headed to destinations such as Chicxulub Puerto and Yucalpetén. *Combis* leave about every five minutes and cost US$0.25.

To get as far as Telchac Puerto, cross the street from the *combis* to a run-down bus stop with benches. Here at 7 A.M. and 2 P.M. you can catch a bus out (one hr.) for US$1.50.

Car

To go east or west of Progreso by car, head south from town on Highway 261 until you hit the turnoffs.

Golf Cart and Moped Rental

Rentadora Damson (Calle 19 at Calle 70, 8 A.M.–5 P.M. daily) and **Rentadora Big Banana** (Calle 19 between Calle 66 and 68, 11 A.M.–midnight daily) both rent golf carts and scooters for around US$10/day.

East of Progreso

CHICXULUB PUERTO

East of Progreso, the coastal road wanders behind a long string of summer houses for seven kilometers (4.3 miles) to the small fishing village of Chicxulub Puerto. The town is run-down, has few hotels, and the beach is always filled with boats—not too appealing for most travelers. However, the strong, steady wind and shallow, obstacle-free shoreline make for ideal sailing, windsurfing, and kiteboarding conditions, and wind-sport athletes come to Chicxulub from all over the world to play and train. The town is home base for two of Mexico's 2004 windsurfing Olympians.

Sights

You can't really *see* it, but Chicxulub is inside (and is the namesake of) a massive **crater** left by a meteorite that hit Earth 65 million years ago. Geologists and paleontologists believe the impact and its aftermath killed most of the world's dinosaur species and ushered in the age of mammals and eventually humans. Chicxulub Puerto may be barely a blip on most travelers' radar screens, but it is oddly compelling to find yourself at ground zero of arguably the most important and cataclysmic event of all time.

Sports and Recreation

The best—and perhaps only—reason to visit Chicxulub Puerto is for the wind sports. And for that, all roads lead to **Marina Silcer** (Antigua Carretera Progreso-Chicxulub km. 3.5, tel. 969/934-0491, www.marinasilcer.com, 10 A.M.–6 P.M. Tues.–Sun.). One-on-one instruction is available for all levels in windsurfing (US$167/eight 1.5-hr. sessions), sailing (US$232/four 1.5-hr. sessions for two people), and kiteboarding (US$350/six 1.5 hour sessions). You also can rent gear by two-hour increments and afterward use the marina's semi-Olympic-size swimming pool. There's a good seafood restaurant on-site too. To get here, turn left at the old gasoline station on the outskirts of town.

Food

On the main drag, **Los Barriles** (Calle 19 between Calles 16 and 18, tel. 969/934-0403, 11 A.M.–8 P.M. daily, US$5–10) is hard to miss with the entryway in the shape of two enormous barrels, hence the name. The main restaurant in town for almost a quarter century, Los Barriles serves good, reliable seafood dishes such as fish fillets, shrimp platters, and ceviche.

Information and Services

The **post office** is on Calle 21 between Calles 10 and 12. There were no banks or ATMs in Chicxulub Puerto when we came through, so it's best to take out cash in Progreso.

Getting There

By car, take Highway 261 north out of Mérida. As you approach Progreso, follow signs east to Chicxulub. By public transportation, go to the corner of Calles 82 and 29 in Progreso, where you'll find a small parking lot filled with *combis* (Volkswagen minivans) that leave about every five minutes and cost US$0.25.

UAYMITÚN RESERVE

Farther east, you'll pass the small town of Uaymitún (why-mih-TOON), which, in addition to a number of upscale summer houses and rental properties, is home to the **Mirador Ecoturístico Uaymitún** (Uaymitún Eco-touristic Viewpoint, Carretera Chicxulub-Telchac Puerto Km. 15, 8 A.M.–6 P.M. daily, open until 7 P.M. during summer, free). Well worth a stop, it's a high wooden platform overlooking a protected part of the extensive marshland that runs just inland along much of the Gulf coast. Thousands of flamingos come here to feed, and with binoculars you can get a decent look at these beautiful, peculiar birds in their natural habitat. If you're lucky, some may come closer to the platform. May to November has the highest flamingo population, but the *mirador* makes a good

© LIZA PRADO

Stretch your legs and check out the pink flamingos at Uaymitún Reserve.

stop at any time since you're sure to see other bird species as well. Binoculars are lent at the visitor's booth at no extra cost. Tip: Another spot to see flamingos is along the road to Xcambó ruins; the road cuts across the marshland and the birds are sometimes feeding quite close by.

XCAMBÓ

A few kilometers inland from Telchac Puerto, on the road to Tixkokob, are the none-too-exciting Maya ruins of Xcambó (Carretera Dzemul-Xcambó Km. 14, 8 A.M.–5 P.M. daily, free). Various low-lying structures without surface ornamentation surround two plazas. On a clear day, you can see the coast from the top of the highest point, Pyramid of the Cross. More than 600 skeletons were unearthed during excavations here, but there is no museum and the reconstruction was overzealous, leaving the ruins very artificial looking. The Catholic chapel on a small rise nearby was built from stones of the dismantled pyramids.

TELCHAC PUERTO

Continuing along the coast east from Chicxulub Puerto, the road parallels the sea for 75 kilometers (46.6 miles) to Dzilam de Bravo. Along the way are several small villages, all tuned in to life on the sea. The largest of these villages is Telchac Puerto, about 40 kilometers (25 miles) east of Progreso.

Accommodations

On the main road into town, **Libros y Sueños** (Calle 23 between Calles 30 and 32, tel. 991/917-4125, www.l-y-s.net, US$24 s, US$28–40 d) offers basic and clean rooms, all with ceiling fans, two blocks from the ocean. First floor rooms are little stuffy—ask for one upstairs to catch the evening breeze. The hotel also has an extensive **English-language bookstore** (hence the name) in case you're in need of something for the beach.

Across the street, **Hotel Principe Negro** (Calle 23 between Calles 30 and 32, US$25–35 s/d with fan, US$45 s/d with a/c) has clean rooms with cable TV and small refrigerators.

There also is an inviting pool if you tire of the ocean. Discounts are available during the low season and for extended stays.

Hotel Reef Yucatán (Carretera Progreso-Telchac Puerto Km. 32, tel. 999/941-9494, www.reefyucatan.com, US$101 pp s, US$83 pp d) is an all-inclusive resort just outside of Telchac Puerto. Rooms are absolutely charmless—picture white tile floors, a bed, a TV, dark brown furnishings, and not much more. The main restaurant also feels more like a school cafeteria than a resort with its plastic chairs, fluorescent lights, and lines of people. All that said, the beach is one of the finest on this coast—wide, clean, and overlooking the emerald ocean—and just about everything *is* included: meals, snacks, alcoholic and nonalcoholic drinks, nightly shows, tennis courts, and a gym. There are also two well-kept pools and a kids club. If you don't want to stay the night but do want some R&R on the beach, the Reef Club offers a **day pass** (US$47 men, US$42 women, US$26–28 children). The day pass is good 9 A.M.–3 P.M. and includes breakfast, lunch, open bar, and use of all the amenities.

Food

Restaurante Miramar (Calle 19 at Calle 99, no phone, 10 A.M.–6 P.M. daily, US$5–15) is a big, basic eatery with plastic tables, a *palapa* roof and a menu full of—what else?—seafood. *Pulpo en su tinta* (octopus cooked in its ink) is sure to be fresh, and the large ceviche platter could feed a hungry basketball team. The restaurant actually has a large, decent section of beach, which you are free to use if you order something.

Information and Services

There are no services here—withdraw cash, check Internet, and mail your postcards in Progreso.

Getting There

Having your own car is by far the easiest and surest way to see this lonely stretch of coast. From Mérida, take Highway 261 north toward the coast; as you approach Progreso, follow signs east (or right) to Telchac Puerto. Otherwise, buses theoretically leave Progreso at 7 A.M. and 2 P.M. daily and cost US$1.75 (one hour). Ask at the run-down bus stop at the corner of Calles 82 and 29.

Izamal

North of Highway 180 between Mérida and Chichén Itzá, Izamal is a fine old colonial city with a beautiful and famous convent, friendly residents, and a fascinating history. Most tourists arrive here on a tour bus, visit the convent and the city center for an hour or so, and then motor off again. But Izamal is a great place for independent travelers to stay a night or two, soaking in atmosphere and rich history of this classic Yucatecan town.

The first thing you notice about Izamal is the color: Virtually all the buildings and facades in Izamal are painted a rich mustard yellow, as is the convent. And Izamal has not one but two large tree-filled plazas—Parque la Estrella and Parque Dr. Crecencio Carrillo y Anacona (named after an Izamal-born dra-

matist)—which form the heart of the city. It is a very walkable city, and part of the pleasure of Izamal is simply wandering about its narrow streets, discovering picturesque facades, stone churches, artistic workshops and even Maya pyramids behind every other corner.

HISTORY

Pope John Paul II visited Izamal in August 1993, instantly transforming the city and cathedral into places of high Catholic importance. But it has been an important religious site since the time of the ancient Mayas—it was one of three major pilgrimage sites in pre-Colombian Yucatán, along with Chichén Itzá and San Gervasio on Isla Cozumel. Spanish priests and colonizers recognized the area's

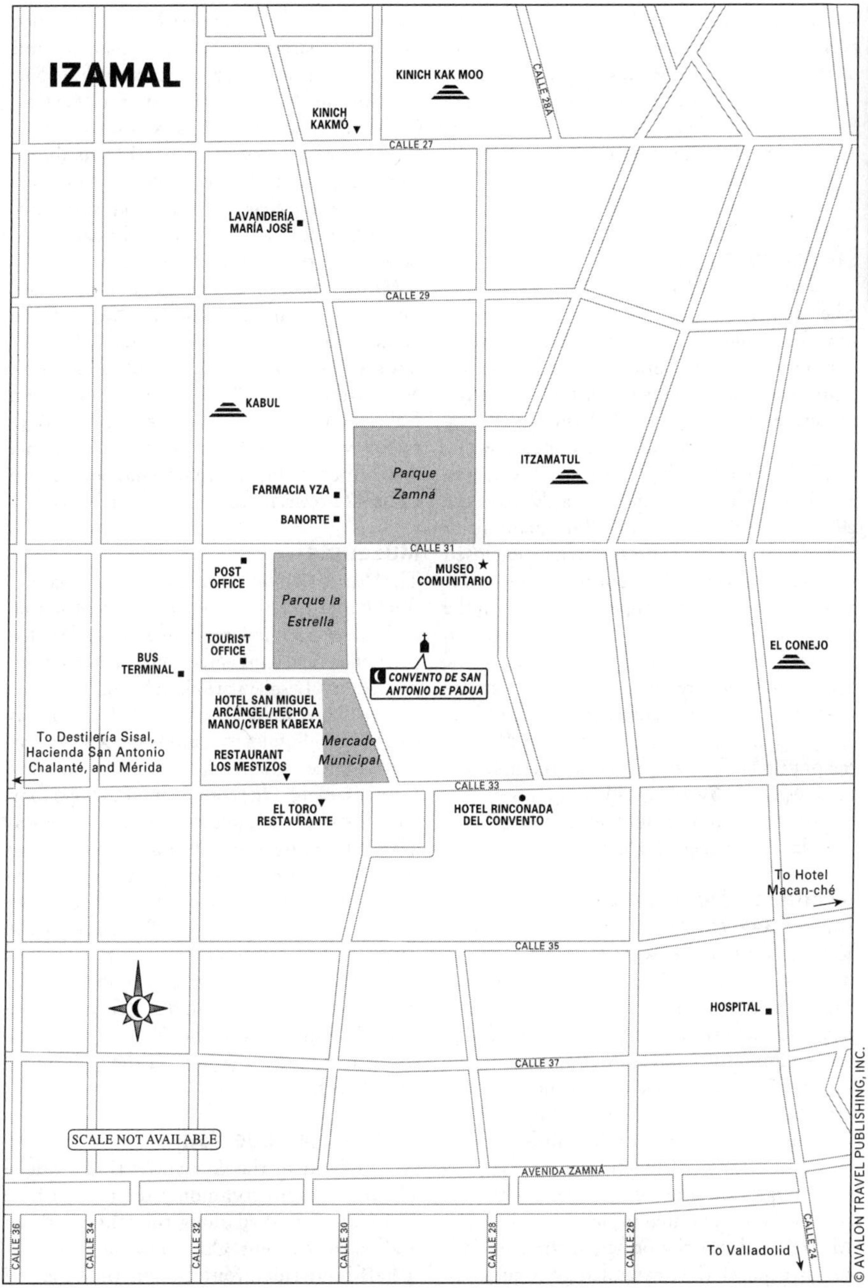

IZAMAL

KINICH KAK MOO

CALLE 28A

KINICH KAKMÓ

CALLE 27

LAVANDERÍA MARÍA JOSÉ

CALLE 29

KABUL

ITZAMATUL

Parque Zamná

FARMACIA YZA

BANORTE

CALLE 31

POST OFFICE

MUSEO COMUNITARIO

Parque la Estrella

TOURIST OFFICE

EL CONEJO

BUS TERMINAL

CONVENTO DE SAN ANTONIO DE PADUA

To Destilería Sisal, Hacienda San Antonio Chalanté, and Mérida

HOTEL SAN MIGUEL ARCÁNGEL/HECHO A MANO/CYBER KABEXA

Mercado Municipal

RESTAURANT LOS MESTIZOS

EL TORO RESTAURANTE

HOTEL RINCONADA DEL CONVENTO

CALLE 33

To Hotel Macan-ché

CALLE 35

HOSPITAL

CALLE 37

SCALE NOT AVAILABLE

AVENIDA ZAMNÁ

CALLE 36

CALLE 34

CALLE 32

CALLE 30

CALLE 28

CALLE 26

CALLE 24

To Valladolid

© AVALON TRAVEL PUBLISHING, INC.

importance and lost little time constructing a magnificent convent and church atop one of the largest existing Maya pyramids, even using the same stones as building materials. Fray Diego de Landa, who would later gain notoriety for burning dozens of Maya codices, oversaw the church.

SIGHTS
◖ Convento de San Antonio de Padua
The most imposing structure in this small town is the mustard-colored Convento de San Antonio de Padua (Parque la Estrella, 8 A.M.–9:30 P.M. daily). Completed in 1562 under the direction of Fray Diego de Landa, the convent was built upon what was once the immense Maya temple Pap-Hol-Chac. If you look closely, you'll even see some Maya glyphs in the church walls themselves. A 7,806-square-meter (25,610-square-foot) grassy atrium enclosed by 75 arches sits at the front of this beautiful complex. It's the largest open-air atrium in the Americas and, many say, the second-largest in the world (the largest is at Saint Peter's in the Vatican). There are also two small museums on-site—one commemorating Pope John Paul II's visit, another paying homage to Nuestra Señora de Izamal, the Yucatan's religious patronness (see *Museums*). There's a mildly interesting sound and light show at 8:30 P.M. Tuesday, Thursday, and Saturday.

Archaeological Zones
Kinich Kak Moo (also known as Kinich-Kakmó, Calle 27 between Calles 28 and 30, 8 A.M.–5 P.M. daily, free) is one of numerous Maya ruins right in Izamal proper. While the others are relatively modest, Kinich Kak Moo is a whopping 195 meters (640 feet) long, 173 meters (568 feet) wide, and 34 meters (111.5 feet) high, making it the largest pyramid in the state of Yucatán, and the third- to fifth-largest in Mexico, depending on how you define "large." Built around A.D. 400–600, the pyramid was dedicated to the sun god, or Fire Macaw, and was the principal structure of a massive plaza that extended over much of

present-day Izamal. Interestingly, it was once a deeply important site for Maya shamans and worshipers, just as Izamal's Convento de San Antonio de Padua has become for Mexican Catholics today. Kinich Kak Moo is not as fully restored as pyramids like El Castillo in Chichén Itzá, but it is still worth a climb, especially for the views of the city and surroundings. On a clear day, you can see Chichén Itzá, 50 kilometers (31 miles) to the east.

Other smaller pyramids can also be visited (or at least seen), including **Itzamatul** (Calle 26 at Calle 31, 8 A.M.–5 P.M., free) which affords a fine view of the city and Kinich Kak Moo. Others are **El Conejo** (Calle 24 between Calles 31 and 33) and **Kabul,** which on private property; access is restricted. You can catch a glimpse of it down a maintenance road on Calle 32 between Calles 29 and 31.

Museums
The **Museo Comunitario** (Calle 30, kitty corner from Banorte bank, 8 A.M.–1 P.M. and 4–6 P.M. daily, free) is a small museum with modest displays on Izamal's ancient, colonial, and modern-day history. Displays are all in Spanish.

The Convento de San Antonio de Padua has two small **religious museums** (10 A.M.–1 P.M. and 3–6 P.M. Mon.–Sat., 9 A.M.–4 P.M. Sun., US$0.50 each). One commemorates Pope John Paul II's 1993 visit to the convent; it's not terribly interesting—lots of photos and random facts—but an easy stop on your way to the museum created in honor of Nuestra Señora de Izamal. Considered the Patroness of the Yucatán, this statue of the Virgin Mary has supposedly performed several miracles. Religious followers from around the Yucatán often make pilgrimages to see her; you may see some of them climbing the steps of the convent on their knees.

Horse Carriage Tours
At any hour of the day, you'll find a queue of *calesas,* more commonly referred to here as *victorias,* parked along the long northern wall of the convent. Ostensibly for tourists—a half-hour ride around town runs around

US$4.65—these tiny, horse-pulled buggies do an active business carrying locals (often whole families) from place to place. It is one of relatively few cities in Mexico where this is the case.

Destilería Sisal Tour

About two kilometers (1.25 miles) from the center of town is the Destilería Sisal (end of Calle 42, tel. 999/925-9087, 8 A.M.–7 P.M. Mon.–Fri., free), where sisal, a variation of tequila made from the henequen, or sisal plant, is produced. Although henequen is closely related to the agave cactus and distilled in the same way, this new liquor cannot be called tequila owing to trademark restrictions of the sort France placed on sparkling wines produced outside the region of Champagne. ("Real" tequila is produced only in and around the town of Tequila in the western state of Jalisco and a few other locations.) Sisal looks and tastes very much like tequila—the main difference is that you won't find the rich, ultra-aged variations because the distillery only opened in September 2003. The plant offers brief tours, including an explanation of the distillery process and a small tasting. However, visits obviously aren't a priority here, and there isn't always someone available to show you around.

SHOPPING

Hecho a Mano (Parque 5 de Mayo, Calle 31 No. 308, tel. 988/954-0344, 11 A.M.7 P.M. daily) is a small folk-art boutique owned and operated by the collector-photographer team Hector Garza and Jeanne Hunt. The pieces and photos are beautiful and museum quality with prices that often match. If you're looking for a special gift or simply like window shopping, you're sure to enjoy a stop here.

There also are several **artisan workshops** where passersby can stop in, watch how a particular piece of folk art is made, and of course, buy something straight from the artist. Wandering around town you'll see signs for tin workers, hammock weavers, woodworkers, and jewelry makers. Most of the workshops are run out of people's homes so opening hours

are pretty casual—don't be shy about knocking if the shop appears closed—at worst, you'll be told when's a good time to come back.

Another good option is browsing the *artesanía* tables set up in Parque Zamná. Most days, vendors set up display tables in the park from 8 A.M.–3 P.M.

The nearby town of Kimbilá is known as the place to go for fine *guayaberas* and *huipiles* at wholesale prices—many of the shops in Mérida stock up there. **Exclusivas Addy** (Calle 20 No. 49, tel. 988/916-3016, 7 A.M.–9 P.M. daily) is one of a handful of mom-and-pop shops in the center of town—just follow the main road to the plaza. Both hand- and machine-stitched items are available. Prices aren't rock bottom, especially if you're only buying one, but the selection is excellent.

SPORTS AND RECREATION

You can go **horseback riding** at Hacienda San Antonio Chalanté, about 11 kilometers (6.8 miles) south of Izamal. Well-marked dirt roads and trails lead from the hacienda to abandoned churches, caves, and cenotes, where the guide can help you clamber down for a swim in the cool clear waters. Tours are US$7.50 an hour.

ACCOMMODATIONS

Housing is somewhat limited in Izamal, mainly because until recently few travelers stayed the night. Even today, most visitors arrive on large tour buses and stay just long enough to visit the convent and climb the pyramid at Kinich Kak Moo. Yet one of the Yucatán's most charming restored haciendas is a few miles away, and there are a couple of good options in town. There are rumors, too, that the famous Hernández family is buying property to build another luxury hacienda-like hotel here—true or not, there is no doubt that Izamal is rising fast as a tourist destination and accommodations of all sorts aren't far off.

Under US$50

Hotel Rinconada del Convento (Calle 33 No. 294, tel. 988/954-0151, www.hotelizamal.com, US$40 s with a/c, US$50–65 d with a/c) is a good value in a perfect location. Facing the convent, the Rinconada del Convento (literally, kitty corner from the convent), is a rambling remodeled home with eleven somewhat sterile but comfortable rooms. All have mini-split air-conditioning, tile floors, and heavy wood furnishings. The unexpected plus here are the common areas—a beautiful terraced garden, a manicured lawn with lounge chairs, a well-maintained lap pool, and a lovely tile-roofed patio overlooking it all. Continental breakfast is included in the rate and is served outdoors, of course.

The grounds at **Hotel Macan-ché** (Calle 22 between Calles 33 and 35, tel. 988/954-0287, www.macanche.com, US$22–26 s/d with fan, US$35–57 s/d with a/c) overflow with tropical plants and local fruit trees, while the bungalows are decorated according to individual themes—Santa Fe, Casa Maya, Catherwood. Most have patios and a hammock, perfect for whiling away a lazy afternoon. Ditto for the small pool, which has a natural stone bottom, like a cenote might have. Breakfast is included and served in a pleasant open-air dining area; dinner is available—and highly recommended—if arranged in advance.

US$50-100

Also in the heart of Izamal, **Hotel San Miguel Arcángel** (Calle 31-A between Calles 30 and 31-A, tel. 988/954-0109, www.sanmiguelhotel .com.mx, US$54–59 s/d with a/c) is a good alternative if you want to be in the center but Hotel Riconada is full. If you don't mind traffic noise in the morning, the large balcony rooms have terrific views of Parque La Estrella and the San Antonio de Padua convent. Rooms have high ceilings, tile floors, and of course those balconies, making them marginally better than at Hotel Rinconada, but the grounds, even with a Jacuzzi in back, aren't as good. Continental breakfast is included.

Outside of Town

About 11 kilometers (6.8 miles) south of Izamal is the charming 【 **Hacienda San Antonio Chalanté** (outskirts of the town of Sudzal,

tel. 999/132-7411, www.haciendachalante .com, US$35–50 s/d with fan, US$60–70 with a/c). Originally built as a Franciscan monastery and later transformed into a henequen farm, today this hacienda is a lovingly restored colonial-style bed-and-breakfast. Two manor houses hold nine uniquely named rooms, all have seven-meter (23-foot) ceilings, beautifully tiled bathrooms, and antique furnishings. The main house has a warmly decorated salon that begs you to stay late into the night, flipping through one of the archaeology books on one of the overstuffed couches. Fifteen horses also call the hacienda home—you'll be sure to see a few wandering untethered on the grounds. And if you enjoy riding, guided horseback tours of the backcountry are offered for US$7.50 an hour. A stone-floored swimming pool and a *temascal* (Maya sauna) also are on-site. Rates include a full—and very tasty—breakfast. A taxi here from Izamal is about US$5.

FOOD

Near the ruins, **Kinich Kakmó** (Calle 27 between 28 and 30, 10 A.M.–7 P.M. Sun.–Wed., until 10 P.M. Thu.–Sat. US$4–7) is a pleasant *palapa*-roofed restaurant that serves regional dishes, including a full meal of *poc-chuc* (marinated grilled pork), beans, salad, and tortillas for US$5. And if you've never seen tortillas being made, check out the tiny *palapa* in back, where two women often can be found sitting around a small fire, patting and cooking them into shape for your meal.

Next to the mercado, **Restaurant Los Mestizos** (Calle 33 near Calle 30, tel. 988/954-0289, 7 A.M.–11 P.M. daily, US$5–9) is jam-packed with heavy wood tables, streamers hanging from the ceiling, and Christmas lights flickering around the edges. But the party seems not to have materialized, and Los Mestizos is actually a rather quiet place for a cool drink and a plate of regional food.

Just half a block away, **El Toro Restaurante** (Calle 33 between Calles 30 and 32, tel. 988/967-3340, 8 A.M.–11 P.M. Tues.–Thurs., 8 A.M.–midnight Fri.–Sun., US$5–9) offers a similar menu—try the *salbutes, papadzules,* or quesadillas day or night.

Mercado Municipal (facing Parque la Estrella) is where you'll find fresh produce, dairy, and meats. Shops are open 6 A.M.–2 P.M. daily, and some stay open as late as 8 P.M. Mon–Sat. Behind the market, next to El Toro restaurant, **Super Willy's** supermarket is open 7 A.M.–10 P.M. daily.

A short drive or taxi ride from town, **◖ Hacienda San Antonio Chalanté** (outskirts of the town of Sudzal, tel. 999/132-7411, US$4–10) serves delicious home-style meals in a beautiful colonial-era setting. The resident chef serves Yucatecan specialties and international dishes that will leave you wanting to come back for more. Special meals—low cholesterol, low sodium, meatless—are prepared without a fuss; just be sure to let the staff know before you arrive. Reservations required.

INFORMATION
Tourist Information
The **tourist office** (Parque la Estrella, tel. 988/954-0692, 9 A.M.–6 P.M. Mon.–Sat.) is in the Palacio Municipal. There are plenty of brochures and maps; staffers often speak English too.

Hospitals
Izamal's public hospital (Calle 24 between Calles 35 and 37, tel. 988/954-0241) has a 24-hour emergency room. The telephone is answered only 8 A.M.–8 P.M.; after-hours, go directly to the clinic.

Pharmacies
Farmacia Yza (Calle 28 at Calle 31, tel. 988/954-0600) is the only pharmacy in town open 24 hours. It faces Parque Zamná, next to the bank.

Police
The tourist police in Izamal may be the friendliest in the Yucatán Peninsula, and sometimes flag down tourists simply to offer assistance (no tip expected). One or more officers are usually stationed at intersections around the center or ask at the tourist office in the Palacio Municipal.

SERVICES
Money
Banorte (Calle 28 at Calle 31, 9 A.M.–3 P.M. Mon.–Fri.) has a 24-hour ATM.

Internet and Telephone
Cyber Kabexa (Pasaje Comercial Hun Pic Tuc, 10 A.M.–10 P.M. daily, US$1/hr) is located in a small commercial walkway off Parque La Estrela, under the hotel San Miguel Arcángel.

Pay phones are oddly hard to find in Izamal. There is one affixed to a support column in the Mercado Municipal, on the south side of Parque la Estrella—there may be a line to use it.

Post Office
The post office (8 A.M.–3 P.M. Mon.–Fri.) is on Calle 31 at Calle 30-A, next to the Palacio del Gobierno.

Launderette
Lavandería María José (Calle 30 between Calles 27 and 29, tel. 988/954-0037, 8 A.M.–2 P.M. and 4–8 P.M. Mon.–Sat.) is close to the center of town and charges US$0.70 per kilogram (2.2 pounds), with a three-kilogram minimum (6.6pounds). Clothes are typically ready within 2–3 hours.

GETTING THERE
Bus
Izamal's bus terminal is one block west of the Palacio Municipal, at the end of Calle 31-A. There's only one first-class bus (to Cancún); the rest are second-class, on **Oriente** (tel. 988/954-0107) and **AutoCentro** (tel. 999/101-9167). Hours listed here are for both lines—ask at the terminal which bus is leaving at the hour you need.

- Cancún: US$11 first-class, 3.5 hours, 6 P.M. only; or US$9.50 second-class, five hours, every 60–90 minutes, 5–11:30 A.M.

and 2:30–7:30 P.M., plus 10:30 P.M. and 1:15 A.M.

- Mérida: US$3, 1.5 hours, every 30–45 minutes 5 A.M.–7:30 P.M.

- Tizimín: US$5.25, 2.5 hours, 7:30 A.M., 8:35 A.M., and 6:25 P.M. only.

- Valladolid: US$3.75, two hours, take any second-class Cancún bus.

- Kimiblá: US$0.60, 10 minutes, take any Mérida bus.

Car

From Mérida, the quickest route is on the Mérida-Cancún highway. Follow the signs for the *cuota* (toll road) until just past the turnoff to Kantunil at Km. 68. The exit for Izamal will be to the left and is very well marked, and comes before the toll plaza so you don't have to pay any tolls. (This is the same exit you'd take coming from Cancún.) Headed north, it's four kilometers (2.5 miles) to the small town of Xanaba and another four kilometers (2.5 miles) to Sudzal. Turn off here if you are going to Hacienda Chalanté (2.7 km/1.7 mi farther; follow the signs) or continue straight to reach Izamal proper.

You can also take a more scenic route to Izamal. From Mérida, follow Calle 65 out of town and across the Periférico. Using rural roads, you'll pass through the town of Tixcocob, and can make side jaunts to Aké ruins and Hacienda San José Cholul.

GETTING AROUND

Izamal is easy to navigate on foot: the bus terminal, major sights, and a handful of hotels and restaurants are all within easy walking distance. Of course, having a car will allow you to stay at Hacienda San Antonio Chalanté (or at least go there for a meal or a horseback tour) as well as visit the sisal distillery and the small town of Kimbilá, where you can buy good *huipiles* and *guayaberas* for less.

Car

As in so many towns throughout the peninsula, street signs here are inconsistent and one-way streets—of which there are many—are not always marked. (When they are, it is usually with a small black arrow with a red circle and line through it; note that many streets turn from two-way to one-way as you approach the center.) Fortunately, folks are fairly good-natured about foreigners who make wrong turns—if you are heading the wrong direction someone will likely call out *"sentido contrario!"* (wrong way!), which is your cue to make a U-turn.

Chichén Itzá and Pisté

Chichén Itzá is one of the finest archaeological sites in the northern part of the peninsula, and in all of Mesoamerica. It is also one of the most visited. Located just two hours from Cancún (and two from Mérida), the site is inundated by tour groups, many of them bikini-clad day-trippers on loan from the pool at their all-inclusive. That fact should not dissuade independent travelers from visiting—crowded or not, Chichén Itzá is a truly magnificent ruin and a must-see on any archaeology tour of the Yucatán. Just be sure to arrive early, and you can see the big stuff first and be exploring the outer areas by the time the tour buses roll in.

Pisté is a one-road town that is strangely underdeveloped considering it is just two kilometers (1.2 miles) from such an important and heavily visited site. The hotels and restaurants here are unremarkable and there's not much to do or see beyond the ruins.

◆ CHICHÉN ITZÁ ARCHAEOLOGICAL ZONE

Chichén Itzá is a monumental archaeological site, remarkable for both its size and scope. The

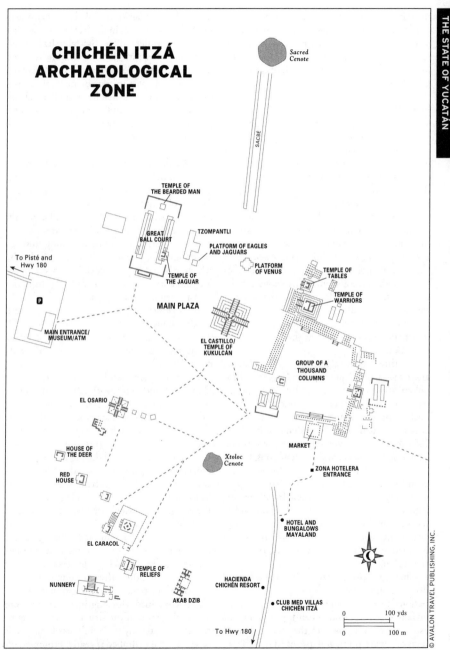

CHICHÉN ITZÁ ARCHAEOLOGICAL ZONE

Sacred Cenote

SACBÉ

TEMPLE OF THE BEARDED MAN

GREAT BALL COURT

TZOMPANTLI

PLATFORM OF EAGLES AND JAGUARS

TEMPLE OF THE JAGUAR

PLATFORM OF VENUS

TEMPLE OF TABLES

TEMPLE OF WARRIORS

To Pisté and Hwy 180

MAIN PLAZA

MAIN ENTRANCE/ MUSEUM/ATM

EL CASTILLO/ TEMPLE OF KUKULCÁN

GROUP OF A THOUSAND COLUMNS

EL OSARIO

HOUSE OF THE DEER

RED HOUSE

MARKET

Xtoloc Cenote

ZONA HOTELERA ENTRANCE

EL CARACOL

TEMPLE OF RELIEFS

NUNNERY

AKAB DZIB

HACIENDA CHICHÉN RESORT

HOTEL AND BUNGALOWS MAYALAND

CLUB MED VILLAS CHICHÉN ITZÁ

To Hwy 180

0   100 yds

0   100 m

© AVALON TRAVEL PUBLISHING, INC.

ruins include impressive palaces, temples, and altars, as well as the largest-known ball court in the Maya world. One of the most widely recognized (and heavily visited) ruins in the world, it was declared a World Heritage site by UNESCO in 1988.

History

What we call Chichén Itzá surely had another name when it was founded. The name means "Mouth of the Well of the Itzá" but the Itzá, an illiterate and semi-nomadic group of uncertain origin, didn't arrive here until the 12th century. Before the Itzá, the area was controlled—or at least greatly influenced—by Toltec migrants who arrived from central Mexico around A.D. 1000. Most of Chichén's most notable structures, including its famous four-sided pyramid, and images like the reclining *chac-mool*, bear a striking resemblance to structures and images found at Tula, the ancient Toltec capital, in the present state of Hidalgo. Before the Toltecs, the area was populated by Maya, evidenced by the Puuc- and Chenes-style design of the earliest structures here, such as the Nunnery and Casa Colorada.

The three major influences—Maya, Toltec, and Itzá—are indisputable, but the exact chronology and circumstances of those groups' interaction (or lack thereof) is one of the most hotly contested issues in Maya archaeology. Part of the difficulty in understanding Chichén Itzá more fully is that its occupants created very few stelae, and left few Long Count dates on their monuments. In this way Chichén Itzá is very different from virtually every other ancient city in the Yucatán. It's ironic, actually, that Chichén Itzá is the most widely recognized "Maya" ruin considering it was so deeply influenced by non-Maya cultures, and its history and architecture are so atypical of the region.

Chichén Itzá's influence ebbed and flowed over its many centuries of existence and occupation. It first peaked in the mid-9th century, or Late Classic period, when it eclipsed Cobá as the dominant power in the region. The effects of a widespread collapse of Maya cities to the south (like Calakmul, Tikal, and Palenque) reached Chichén Itza in the late 900's. The city rose again under Toltec and later Itzá influence, but went into its final decline after an internal dispute led to the rise of Mayapán, which would come to control much of the Yucatán peninsula. Chichén Itzá was all but abandoned by the early 1200s, though it remained an important pilgrimage site long after the arrival of the Spanish.

El Castillo/Temple of Kukulcán

The most dramatic structure in Chichén Itzá is El Castillo (the Castle), also known as the Temple of Kukulcán. At 24 meters (79 feet) it's the tallest structure on the site, and certainly the most recognizable. Dating to around A.D. 850, the Castillo was built according to strict astronomical guidelines. There are nine levels, which, divided by the central staircase, make for 18 platforms, the number of months in the Maya calendar. Each of the four sides has 91 steps; together with the platform on top, there are 365 steps, or one for each day of the year. There are 52 inset panels on each face, equal to the number of years in each cycle of the Calendar Round.

On the spring and autumn equinoxes (March 21 and September 22), the afternoon sun lights up a bright zigzag strip on the outside wall of the north staircase and the giant serpent heads at the base, giving the appearance of a serpent slithering down the steps. Chichén Itzá is mobbed during those periods, especially by spiritual-minded folks seeking communion with the ancient Mayas. The effect also occurs in the days just before and after the equinox, and there are many fewer people blocking the view.

Climbing the Castillo used to be a given for any visit to Chichén Itzá, and the views from its top level are breathtaking. However, an elderly tourist died in 2005, after tumbling from near the top of the pyramid to the ground. The accident, combined with longtime warnings from archaeologists that the structure was being irreparably eroded by the hundreds of thousands of visitors who climbed it yearly, prompted of-

© LIZA PRADO

Chichén Itzá's El Castillo is one of the most visited structures in the Maya world.

ficials to close it off. Pyramids at other sites have been restricted as well, and it's looking more and more like a permanent policy.

Deep inside the Castillo, and accessed by way of a steep, narrow staircase are several chambers. Inside one archaeologists discovered a red-painted, jade-studded figure of a jaguar.

Great Ball Court

Chichén Itzá's famous Great Ball Court is the largest ball court in Mesoamerica, by a wide margin. The playing field is 135 meters (443 feet) by 65 meters (213 feet), with two parallel walls eight meters high (26 feet), with scoring rings in impossibly high perches in the center. The players would've had to hit a 12-pound rubber ball through the rings using only their elbows, wrists, and hips. They wore heavy padding and the game likely lasted for hours. At the game's end, the captain of one team—or even the whole team—was apparently sacrificed, possibly by decapitation. There's disagreement about *which* team got the axe, however. Some say it was the losers—

otherwise the game's best players would constantly be wiped out. Some argue that it was the winners, and that being sacrificed would have been the ultimate honor. Of course, it's likely the game varied from city to city, and evolved over the many centuries it was played. Along the walls, reliefs depict the ball game and sacrifices.

On the outside of the ball court, the **Lower Temple of the Jaguars** has incredibly fine relief carvings depicting the Maya creation myth. An upper temple is off-limits to visitors, but is decorated with a variety of carvings and remnants of what were likely colorful murals.

The Platforms

As you make your way from the ball court to the Temple of Warriors, you'll pass the gruesome **Tzompantli** (Wall of Skulls). A low T-shaped platform, it is decorated on all sides with row upon row of carved skulls, most with eyes staring out of the large sockets. Among the skulls are images of warriors holding the heads of decapitated victims, skeletons intertwined with snakes, and eagles eating human hearts (a common image in Toltec design, further evidence of their presence here). It is presumed that ceremonies performed on this platform culminated in a sacrificial death for the victim, the head then left on display, perhaps with others already in place. It's estimated that the platform was built A.D. 1050–1200. Nearby, the **Platform of Venus** and **Platform of Eagles and Jaguars** are smaller square structures, each with low stairways on all four sides, and were likely used for ritual music and dancing.

Sacred Cenote

This natural well is 300 meters (984 feet) north of the main structures, along the remains of a *sacbé* (raised stone road) constructed during the Classic period. Almost 60 meters (197 feet) in diameter and 30 meters (98.4 feet) down to the surface of the water, it was a place for sacrifices, mostly to Chac, the God of Rain, who was believed to live in its depths. The remains of scores of victims, mostly children and young adults, were dredged from the cenote, as well as innumerable jade and stone artifacts. On the edge of the cenote is a ruined sweat bath, probably used for purification rituals before sacrificial ceremonies. The name Chichén Itzá (Mouth of the Well of the Itzá) is surely derived from this deeply sacred cenote, and it remained an important Maya pilgrimage site well into the Spanish conquest.

Temple of Warriors and Group of a Thousand Columns

The Temple of Warriors is where some of the distinctive, reclining *chac-mool* figures are found. However, its name comes from the rectangular monoliths in front, which are carved on all sides with images of warriors. (Some are also prisoners, their hands tied behind their backs.) This temple is also closed to entry, and it can be hard to appreciate the fading images from the rope perimeter. You can get a much closer look around back, on the temple's south side, where you can easily make out the figures' expressions and dress. There you can also check out the temple's impressive south-facing facade. A series of well-preserved human and animal figures adorn the lower portion, while above, human faces emerge from serpents' mouths, framed by eagle profiles, with masks of Chac, the hook-nosed God of Rain, on the corners.

The aptly named Group of a Thousand Columns is adjacent to the Temple of Warriors. Its perfectly aligned cylindrical columns likely held up a grand roof structure.

Across the plaza, the **Palacio de las Columnas Esculpidas** (Palace of Sculptured Columns) also has cylindrical columns, but with intricate carvings, suggesting this was the ceremonial center of this portion of the complex. Continuing through the trees, you'll reach **el Mercado** (the Market). The name is purely speculative, though it's easy to imagine a breezy bustling market here, protected from the sun under a wood and *palapa* roof built atop the structure's remarkably high columns.

Osario, Caracol, and the Nunnery

From the market, bear left (away from the Cas-

tillo, just visible through the trees) until you meet the path leading to the site's southern entrance. You'll pass the **Osario** (Ossuary) also known as the Tomb of the High Priest. Like a miniature version of Castillo, the pyramid at one time had four stairways on each side and a temple at the crest. From the top platform, a vertical passageway leads into a cave where seven tombs were discovered, along with numerous copper and jade artifacts indicating the deceased were of special importance (and hence the temple's name). Continuing on, you'll pass two more large structures, **Casa del Venado** (House of the Deer) and **Casa Colorada** (Red House).

But the highlight of this portion of Chichén Itza is **El Caracol** (The Shell), also known as the Observatory and perhaps the most graceful structure at Chichén Itzá. A two-tiered circular structure is set atop a broad rectangular platform, with window slits facing south and west, and another aligned according to the path of the moon during the spring equinoxes. Ancient astronomers used structures like this one to track celestial events and patterns—the orbits of the Moon and Venus, and the coming of solar and lunar eclipses, for example—with uncanny accuracy.

Beyond the Caracol is the **Nunnery,** so-named by Spanish explorers who thought it looked like convents back home. Judging from its size, location, and many rooms, the Nunnery was probably an administrative palace. Its exuberant facades show strong Chenes influence, another example of the blending of styles in Chichén Itzá.

Museum

In the visitor services area, Chichén Itzá's museum (8 A.M.–5 P.M. daily) is curiously small for a site as important and oft-visited as this one, but it's worth visiting nonetheless. An air-conditioned auditorium nearby shows films (circa 1971, apparently) on Chichén Itzá and other sites.

Light Show

The site puts on a nightly high-tech sound and light show at 7 P.M. (winter hours) and 8 P.M.

(summer hours). The fee to enter is included in the general admission, although if you'd like to see the show the night before you visit the ruins, you can pay for the light show portion of the ticket (US$4.50) in advance. Just be sure to let the salesperson know that you would like to buy a half ticket and save the stub so that you're not double-charged the next day. The show is presented in Spanish. For an additional US$2.25 you can rent earphones with translations in English, French, and German.

Practicalities

The grounds are open daily 8 A.M.–5 P.M. Admission is US$9 per person, plus US$3 to bring a video camera. The fee includes entrance to the ruins, plus the sound and light show, presented nightly at 7 P.M. in the winter (October–April) and at 8 P.M. in the summer (May–September); hold onto your ticket. There is no discount if you don't wish to go to the sound and light show, but there is a show-only price (US$3). You can go to show the night before you visit the ruins, but be sure to buy a US$5 partial entrance—not the US$3 show-only ticket—and keep your stub for credit the next morning. Just tell the ticket seller your plan, and he'll sell you the right ticket.

Guides can be hired at the entrance according to fixed and clearly marked prices: US$35 for a 1.5- or two-hour tour in Spanish, US$42 in English, French, Italian, or German. Prices are per group, which can include up to eight people. Tips are customary and not included in the price. The visitor center also has restrooms, ATM, luggage storage, a café, bookstore, gift shop, and information center.

OTHER SIGHTS
Balankanche Caves

Six kilometers (3.7 miles) east of Chichén Itzá, the **Grutas de Balankanche** (9 A.M.–5 P.M., US$4.65, children under 13 free) are a disappointment. The 1959 excavation of the caves by the National Geographic archaeologist Dr. E. Wyllys Andrews uncovered numerous artifacts and ceremonial sites giving researchers a better understanding of ancient Maya cosmology, especially related to the notion of *xibalbá* (the underworld). Nowadays, the caves are basically a tourist trap—a wide path meandering 500 meters (0.3 mile) down a tunnel with urns and other artifacts supposedly set up in their original locations. Wires and electric lights illuminate the path, but the recorded narration does nothing of the sort—you can hardly understand it, no matter what language it's in.

Entry times are fixed according to language: Spanish at 9 A.M., noon, 2 P.M., and 4 P.M.; English at 11 A.M., 1 P.M., and 3 P.M.; and French at 10 A.M. A minimum of six visitors are needed for the tour to depart.

Parque Ecoarqueológico Ik Kil

Three kilometers (1.9 miles) east of Pisté, the centerpiece of the Parque Ecoarqueológico Ik Kil (Carretera Mérida-Cancún Km. 122, tel. 985/858-1525, 8 A.M.–6 P.M. daily, US$5.50 adults, US$2.75 children) is the immense, perfectly round **Cenote Sagrado Azul** with a partial stone roof. Although real, the alterations to the cenote's natural state—supported walls, a set of stairs leading you in, a waterfall—make it feel pretty artificial. While not representative of the typical cenote experience, this is a good option if you are traveling with small children and need a spot to cool off. The cenote and on-site restaurant get packed with tour groups 12:30–2:30 P.M.; try visiting outside those times for a mellower visit. Better yet, stay at one of the on-site bungalows.

ACCOMMODATIONS

A handful of upscale hotels make up the small *Zona Hotelera* (Hotel Zone) on the east side of Chichén Itzá, complete with its own entrance to the ruins. Nearby, in the town of Pisté, there are a handful of budget and mid-range options. Be sure to reserve early during the spring and fall equinoxes.

Under US$25

At the eastern end of Pisté, **Pirámide Inn** (Calle 15 No. 30, tel. 985/851-0115, www .chichen.com, US$4 pp camping) has a grassy garden for camping and several open-air *palapas* with concrete floors where you can hang hammocks. Shared bathrooms are clean, and you can use the swimming pool. The hotel rents hammocks for another US$4 a night, if you need one.

Posada Olalde (Calle 6 s/n at Calles 17, tel. 985/851-0086, US$23.25 s/d, US$26 s/d bungalow) is the best budget option in town. Rooms are no frills but they are brightly painted, have a shared porch, and face a leafy courtyard. The hotel also has four bungalows, which sound nice (and cost more) but are inferior to the rooms, with saggy beds, bad light, and a dank feel about them. The posada is a little hard to find—coming from Mérida, turn right on a narrow dirt alley across from El Pollo Mexicano restaurant. From there it's two blocks down on the right.

Posada Flamboyanes (Calle 15 s/n, no phone, US$18.50 s/d with fan, US$21 with a/c) has only three small simple rooms, and the low price and welcoming pink exterior means they are often taken. Moreover, the caretaker is often running errands, leaving no one to attend the rooms. If you do manage to get one, it should be relatively clean and will open onto an airy covered corridor. Coming from Mérida, look for it on your right, just beyond the Hotel Chichén Itzá.

US$25-50

The ◖ **Hotel Dolores Alba Chichén** (Carretera Mérida-Cancún Km. 122, tel. 985/858-1555, www.doloresalba.com, US$42 s/d with a/c) is one of the best deals in the area especially given its choice location three kilometers (1.9 miles) east of the ruins, one kilometer (0.6 miles) from the Balankanche Caves, and across the street from the Parque Ecoarqueológico Ik Kil. Rooms are spotless and smallish, with good beds and simple tile work on the walls to spiff up the decor. The hotel has a pleasant outdoor restaurant (7 A.M.–10 P.M. daily, US$4–10) and two large swimming pools—the one in back has a mostly natural stone bottom, with holes and channels reminiscent of an ocean reef, which is perfect for kids with active imaginations. The hotel also provides free shuttle service to the ruins.

On the eastern end of Pisté, **Pirámide Inn** (Calle 15 No. 30, tel. 985/851-0115, www.chichen.com, US$4 pp camping, US$38 s/d) is a low sprawling hotel with large rooms that are clean though a bit dark. The decor is distinctly 1970s den, with some rooms sporting bubblegum paint jobs and lacquered brick walls. The air-conditioning units appear to be from the same era, and can be loud. On the upside, there's a pool in back, facing a pleasant garden, and a restaurant serving reliable breakfasts and dinners. The bus station is nearby, and the ruins are just a kilometer (0.6 miles) down the road.

US$50-100

Set in a lush, green forest ◖ **Parque Ecoarqueológico Ik Kil** (Carretera Mérida-Cancún Km. 122, tel. 985/858-1525, US$93 s/d with a/c) offers 12 modern and ultra-comfortable bungalows. All are spacious and have Jacuzzi tubs, comfortable beds, and pull-out sofas. Silent air-conditioning and a private porch make it all the better. Unlimited use of the popular cenote on-site is included too. A fantastic value, especially if traveling with kids.

Club Med Villas Chichén Itzá (Zona Hotelera, Carr. Mérida-Valladolid Km. 120, tel. 985/856-6000, scottsdale.mexicores@clubmed.com, www.clubmed.com, US$81 s/d with a/c, US$135 suite with a/c) is a pleasant two-story hotel with a mellow ambiance. Boxy, though nice, rooms are set around a lush courtyard with an inviting L-shaped pool in the center. A library/TV room with comfy couches and a variety of books—from romance novels to archaeology books—also faces the courtyard. A decent restaurant and a tennis court are on-site too.

US$100-150

In a former life, the **Hotel Chichén Itzá** (Calle 15 s/n, tel. 985/851-0022, US$74–111 s/d with a/c) was the Hotel Misión Chichén, before being bought and renovated by the hotel/tour conglomerate Mayaland. When we passed through it was in the midst of being remodeled (again) and acquired (again), this time by the Best Western chain hotel. Regardless of who owns it when you're in town, it is definitely the nicest hotel in Pisté proper. All rooms have simple Mexican decor, comfortable furnishings, and large modern bathrooms; the least expensive rooms face the street and can be noisy, while the top ones are larger and overlook the hotel's attractive garden and pool area. There's also a cavernous restaurant (7 A.M.–10 P.M. daily) that's often packed with tour groups.

Over US$150

Once the headquarters for the Carnegie Institute's Chichén Itzá expedition, the **Hacienda Chichén Resort** (Zona Hotelera, Carr. Mérida-Valladolid Km. 120, tel. 999/920-8407, toll-free U.S. tel. 877/631-4006, www.haciendachichen.com, US$160 s/d with a/c, US$170–225 suite) now is a tranquil hotel set in a lush tropical garden. A beautiful setting, most of the rooms are in the original cottages used by the archaeologists—very cool to stay where they once lived but not-so-cool to have to look at cinder block walls and to deal with the musty smell that pervades some of the older units. The decor is simple—tile floors, exposed beam ceilings, wood furnishings—but the rooms are quite comfortable. Be sure to wander the grounds with an eye for the narrow-gauge railroad tracks that were used to transport artifacts from Chichén Itzá and the original hacienda chapel. A pool, full-service spa (9 A.M.–2 P.M., 5–10 P.M. daily), and a fine dining room also are nice finds.

The **Hotel and Bungalows Mayaland** (Zona Hotelera, Carr. Mérida-Valladolid Km. 120, tel. 985/851-0100, www.mayaland.com, US$150–370 s/d) is literally at the entrance to Chichén Itzá—guests and non-guests alike must pass through the resort and by two of its gift shops to get to the ticket booth. The grounds are gorgeous: 100 acres of tamed tropical jungle filled with birds, plus three restaurants and four pools. Tour groups stop here for meals and shopping, and their sudden loud presence can be a turnoff for paying guests; however, you can avoid the crush by asking the reception desk what time the buses will arrive. Definitely take advantage of being so close to the ruins by getting there right at opening time. Rooms and bungalows are pleasant if somewhat dated, including stained-glass windows, hardwood furniture, and terraces. Suites have whirlpool tubs and, in some, a view of Chichén Itzá's Observatory. If you really want to splurge, ask about the Pavarotti Suite, a luxurious suite that was expressly built for the corpulent tenor when he sang in concert at Chichén Itzá. The restaurants here are pricey and so-so at best; better to take your appetite to Hacienda Chichén, a five-minute walk away.

FOOD

Eating options are pretty limited in Pisté but improve somewhat if you have a car and can get to and from the large hotels.

The newly remodeled █ **Restaurante Las Mestizas** (Calle 15 s/n, tel. 985/851-0069, 7:30 A.M.–10:30 P.M. daily, US$2.50–8) is without a doubt the best place to eat in Pisté, with an airy, colonial-style interior and tasty, good-sized portions. The food is classic Yucatecan fare, from *panuchos* to *pollo pibil*. Service is exceptional.

True to its name, **Restaurante y Pizzería Mr. Pizzas** (Calle 15 s/n, tel. 985/851-0079, 2–11 P.M. Tue.–Sun., US$6–11) serves mostly pizza, plus hamburgers and other items. The dining room is appealing—not fancy but clean—and the service is good.

Set in a 16th-century hacienda, the █ **Hacienda Chichén Resort's restaurant** (Zona Hotelera, tel. 999/920-8407, 7 A.M.–10 P.M. daily, US$10–16) is a relaxing place to eat after a long day at the ruins. The menu is varied—Yucatecan specialties, pastas, sandwiches, and on the occasional evening, a trio plays regional music.

Although often inundated by day-trippers from Club Med Cancún, the restaurant at the **Club Med Villas Chichén Itzá** (Zona Hotelera, Carr. Mérida-Valladolid Km. 120, tel. 985/856-6000, 7:30 A.M.–10 P.M. daily, US$6–16) is a good option. With an international menu, indoor and outdoor seating, and a lunch buffet, there's something for everyone.

If you can stand the tour groups, the lunch buffet at **Hotel and Bungalows Mayaland** (Zona Hotelera, Carr. Mérida-Valladolid Km. 120, tel. 985/851-0100, noon–3 P.M. daily, US$14.50) is a good choice. With its variety of hot and cold dishes, you definitely will find something to fill you up. Live music, ballet folklórico shows, and outdoor seating are nice touches.

For groceries, **Abarrotes Alba** (Calle 15 s/n, 50 m/164 ft east of the plaza, 6 A.M.–10 P.M. daily) has a decent selection of fresh fruit, canned goods, drinks, and toiletries.

INFORMATION AND SERVICES

There is no tourist office in Pisté; if you have questions about the region or the ruins, ask at the front desk of your hotel.

Hospitals

Clínica La Promesa (Calle 14 between Calle 13 and 15, tel. 985/851-0005, open 24 hours) is the only clinic in town. For anything serious, you're better off going to Valladolid.

Pharmacies

Farmacia Lidia (Calle 15 s/n, no phone, 7 A.M.–10 P.M. daily) is on the west end of town, 25 meters (82 feet) from Abarrotes Alba.

Police

The police have an office (but no phone) in the Palacio Municipal (City Hall), facing the church. An officer is on duty 24 hours a day.

Money

Pisté doesn't have a bank, but there are reliable ATMs in Chichén Itzá's visitor complex.

Internet and Telephone

Across from the bus terminal, **Tienda San Antonio** (tel. 985/851-0089, 9 A.M.–9 P.M. Mon.–Fri., 10 A.M.–9 P.M. Sat., 10 A.M.–6 P.M. Sun.) is a quiet shop with Internet service (US$1.50/hr) and international calling to the United States and Canada for US$0.50 a minute and to Europe for US$1 a minute.

A handful of small Internet shops near the central park charge the same and are open late, but cater to local kids and can be crowded and noisy.

Launderette

Lavandería Guadalupe (Calle 10 near Calle 13, 8 A.M.–6 P.M. Mon.–Sat.) charges US$0.90 per kilogram (2.2 pounds) to wash and dry clothes; same-day service if you drop your load off first thing in the morning. Located two blocks north of the main drag—turn north at the Posada Kari sign, east of Abarrotes Alba.

GETTING THERE AND AROUND

Buses from all directions converge on Chichén Itzá and Pisté; those from Mérida and Cancún often will drop off passengers at the main entrance to the ruins, which is about 1.5 kilometers (0.9 mile) west of town. If you are in Pisté, passing bus drivers may be willing to drop you at the entrance for around US$0.50, or just walk.

Bus

Most bus service here is on Oriente, ADO's second-class line, but there are a few first-class buses as well, and are worth the extra cost. Pisté's small bus terminal (tel. 985/851-0052, 7 A.M.–6 P.M. daily, cash only) is at the far east end of town, next to the Pirámide Inn. There is also a ticket office in the gift shop at the ruins (tel. 985/851-0377, 10 A.M.–5 P.M.). All buses stop at the terminal, and at the ruins if it's between 8 A.M. and 5:30 P.M. Departure times listed here are for the terminal—those from the ruins will be slightly earlier or later depending on the direction you're headed. The visitor center has **luggage storage,** which is handy if you plan to catch an onward bus after visiting the ruins.

To Mérida, first-class buses (US$7.50, two hours) leave Pisté at 2:10 P.M. and 5 P.M., plus 3:50 P.M. on Sat., while second-class buses (US$5, 2.5 hours) leave every 30–60 minutes 7 A.M.–5:30 P.M.

To Cancún, one daily first-class bus (US$10.50, 2.5 hours) leaves at 4:15 P.M. Second-class buses (US$8.50, 4.5 hours) depart every 30–60 minutes 8:30 A.M.–6:30 P.M.

To Valladolid, first-class buses (US$3.25, 45 minutes) depart at 8:10 A.M., 11:10 A.M., 2:20 P.M., and 4:15 P.M., while second-class service (US$2, one hour) is available every 30–60 minutes, 7:30 A.M.–4:30 P.M.

To Tulum, first-class buses (US$10, 2.5 hours) leave Pisté at 8:10 A.M., 2:20 P.M., and 4:15 P.M., and there's one second-class departure at 7:30 A.M. (US$6, three hours).

For Playa del Carmen, take the first-class Tulum bus at 2:20 P.M. or 4:15 P.M. (US$13.25, 3.5 hours) or the 7:30 A.M. second-class bus (US$7.50, five hours).

To Cobá town and archaeological site, take the second-class Tulum/Playa del Carmen bus (US$4.25, 2.5 hours). The first-class buses do not stop there.

Car

Chichén Itzá lies adjacent to Highway 180, 40 kilometers (25 miles) west of Valladolid, 120 kilometers (75 miles) east of Mérida, and 200 kilometers (124 miles) west of Cancún. An eight-lane highway known as the *cuota* (toll road) connects Cancún and Mérida; exit at Pisté. Tolls from Mérida are US$6, but a whopping US$28 from Cancún. You can save a little by getting off at the Valladolid exit (US$18) and taking the *libre* (free road) for the remaining 45 kilometers (27 miles). Or take the *libre* the whole way; it's slower but in good condition, passing through numerous villages and past simple farms. Watch for *topes* (speed bumps) around villages—in all, there are nearly 100 between Mérida and Cancún, and hitting one at anything faster than a crawl can jar you—and your rental—to the bones.

Air

Aeropuerto Internacional Chichén Itzá (tel. 985/851-0408) is 16 kilometers (9.9 miles) east of Pisté, between the towns of Xcalacot and Kaua. Inaugurated in April 2000, it is one of the most modern airports in the country, with an 1,800-meter (5,900-foot) runway capable of receiving 747 jets. Although initially receiving dozens of regular and charter flights, its license was suspended in 2001. Today it stands virtually empty, receiving only a smattering of charters, mostly from Cancún, Cozumel, and Chetumal.

Valladolid

Valladolid is gaining attention from tourists because of its colonial atmosphere and its central location: 30 minutes from the archaeological zones of Chichén Itzá and Ek' Balam, an hour from the ruins at Cobá and the flamingo reserve in Río Lagartos, and two hours from Mérida, Cancún, and Tulum. It's an easy bus or car ride to any of these destinations, restaurants and hotels are reasonably priced, and you have the advantage of staying in a colonial Mexican town. If you're en route to one of the regional sites or simply want to have a small-town experience, consider spending a night here—you're sure to be happily surprised.

HISTORY

The site of several Maya revolts against the Spanish, Valladolid was conquered in 1543 by Francisco de Montejo, cousin of the like-named Spaniard who founded Mérida. It was once the Maya city of Zací; Montejo brutalized its inhabitants and crushed their temples, building large churches and homes in their place. It is perhaps not surprising, then, that the Caste War started in Valladolid, and that the city played an important role in the beginning of the Mexican Revolution. Today, Valladolid is a charming colonial town with a rich history and strong Maya presence.

THE STATE OF YUCATÁN

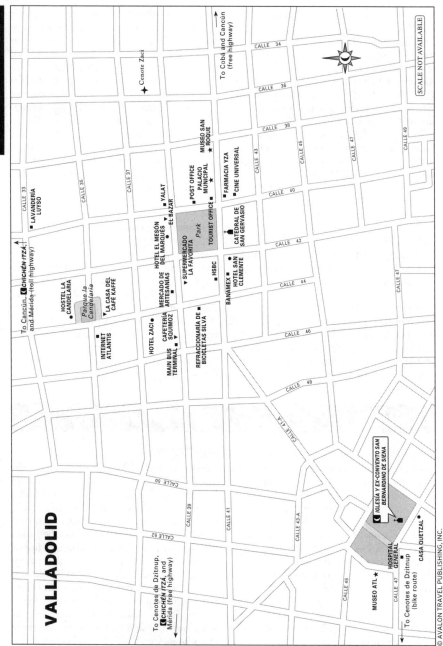

VALLADOLID

SCALE NOT AVAILABLE

To Cobá and Cancún (free highway)

CALLE 34

CALLE 36

CALLE 38

CALLE 43

CALLE 45

CALLE 47

CALLE 49

CALLE 40

CALLE 42

CALLE 44

CALLE 46

CALLE 48

+ Cenote Zaci

To Cancún, ◖CHICHÉN ITZÁ, and Mérida (toll highway)

CALLE 33

CALLE 36

CALLE 37

■ LAVANDERÍA LUYSO

HOSTEL LA CANDELARIA ●

Parque la Candelaria

▼ LA CASA DEL CAFÉ KAFFÉ

■ INTERNET ATLANTIS

HOTEL ZACI ●

■ CAFETERÍA SQUIMOZ

■ MAIN BUS TERMINAL

REFRACCIONARIA DE BICICLETAS SILVA ■

MERCADO DE ARTESANÍAS ■

HOTEL EL MESÓN DEL MARQUÉS ■

▼ SUPERMERCADO LA FAVORITA

HSBC ●

BANAMEX ●

HOTEL SAN CLEMENTE ■

▼ YALAT
■ EL BAZAR

▶ POST OFFICE

PALACIO MUNICIPAL ★

MUSEO SAN ROQUE ★

■ FARMACIA YZA

■ CINE UNIVERSAL

Park

TOURIST OFFICE ■

CATEDRAL DE SAN GERVASIO ■

CALLE 50

CALLE 39

CALLE 41

CALLE 52

CALLE 43-A

CALLE 41-A

To Cenotes de Dzitnup, ◖CHICHÉN ITZÁ, and Mérida (free highway)

MUSEO ATL ★

CALLE 45

CALLE 47

To Cenotes de Dzitnup (bike route)

◖ IGLESIA Y EX-CONVENTO SAN BERNARDINO DE SIENA

HOSPITAL GENERAL ■

CASA QUETZAL ●

© AVALON TRAVEL PUBLISHING, INC.

ORIENTATION

Valladolid is easy to get around. It's laid out in a grid pattern with even-numbered streets running north to south, odd-numbered streets running east to west. The central plaza at the center of the city, is bordered by Calles 39, 40, 41, and 42.

SIGHTS
Iglesia y Ex-Convento San Bernardino de Siena

In a well-kept colonial neighborhood several blocks southwest of the *parque central,* the Iglesia y Ex-convento San Bernardino de Siena (Calle 41-A, tel. 985/856-2160, 8 A.M.–noon and 5–7 P.M. Tue.–Sat., until noon Sun.) is one of Valladolid's most attractive structures. Built by Franciscan missionaries between 1552 and 1560, the church entrance is through a series of arches, and the facade, covered in a checkerboard-like stucco pattern, rises into a squat tower complete with turrets. Annexed to it, the ex-convent has rooms radiating from a center courtyard, which features, uniquely, a cenote. Called *Sis-Há* (Cold Water), the cenote helped the monks to be self-reliant. In 2004, an exploration of the cenote resulted in the discovery of 164 rifles and one canon—neither the age nor the nationality of the arms have been disclosed. Mass is held in the church at 7 P.M. Tuesday to Saturday, and at 7 A.M., 9 A.M., 11 A.M., 6 P.M., and 7 P.M. on Sunday. Special permission is required to visit the ex-convent; call ahead or ask in the church office.

Museo San Roque

A long high-ceilinged room—this used to be a church—the Museo San Roque (Calle 41 between Calles 38 and 40, 9 A.M.–8 P.M. daily, free) is a worthwhile stop, with fascinating displays on Valladolid's history, with a focus on the Caste War and the beginning of the Mexican Revolution. Interestingly, both conflicts, so important to Mexican history, grew out of incidents in and around Valladolid. Displays of local handicrafts also are notable. Signage, unfortunately, in Spanish only.

Palacio Municipal

On the 2nd floor of the city hall (7 A.M.–7 P.M. daily, free) is a large balcony overlooking the plaza, with four large paintings by local talent Manuel Lizama. The paintings depict events in Valladolid's history: pre-Hispanic communities, the city's founding, the Caste War, and the Mexican Revolution. Not spectacular, exactly, but something to see.

Cenote Zaci

Cenote Zaci (Calle 36 between Calles 37 and 39, 8 A.M.–7:30 P.M. daily, US$1.50, under 13 US$1) is in the middle of town and often pooh-poohed in comparison to the cenotes at Dzitnup. But it's a peaceful, attractive spot, especially if you have it to yourself. (You can scope out the scene before going in by looking over the wall halfway down Calle 37, around the corner from the entrance.) A dark natural pool lies in a huge cavern with a bank of trees on one side and a path looping down from the entrance. You may find leaves and pollen floating on the water's surface, but it's still refreshing. There's also a small—and sad—zoo and a simple eatery.

Cenotes de Dzitnup

Four kilometers (2.5 miles) west of Valladolid on Highway 180 is the small community of Dzitnup, home to two appealing underground cenotes. Both make for a unique and refreshing swim—in fact on warm days both can be somewhat crowded. At both cenotes, there are parking lots and many small *artesanía* stands at the entrance, and you'll be aggressively pursued by children offering to watch your car or sell you a postcard.

Although the two are across the street from each other, **Cenote X'keken** (8 A.M.–6 P.M. daily, US$2.50 adults, US$1.50 under 17, video cameras US$2.75) has been open longer and is better known; many postcards and travel guides show it as "Cenote Dzitnup." After a reasonably easy descent underground (in a few places you must bend over because of a low ceiling; there's a hanging rope to help), you'll come to a circular pond of clear, cool water. It's a pretty, albeit damp, place, with a high dome ceiling that has one small opening at the top letting in a ray of sun and dangling green vines. Often an errant bird can be seen swooping low over the water before heading to the sun and sky through the tiny opening. Stalactites and at least one large stalagmite adorn the ceiling and cenote floor.

At **Cenote Samula** (7 A.M.–5 P.M. daily, US$2.50 adults, US$1.50 under 17, video cameras US$2.75) tree roots dangle impressively from the ground-level roof all the way down to the water. Enter through a narrow tunnel, which opens onto a set of stairs that zigzag down to the water. Fearless kids jump from the first or even second switchback, into the clear turquoise water below.

Many people ride their bikes here—a bike path runs parallel to the highway, making it a pleasant trip. A cab to the cenotes runs about US$5.

ENTERTAINMENT AND EVENTS

Cine Universal (Calle 40 between Calles 41 and 43, tel. 985/856-2040, US$3.75) shows mostly Hollywood films on its two screens. Ticket prices cover the nightly double feature, which begin at 7 P.M. and 9 P.M. If you're only interested in seeing one movie, there are no discounts.

SHOPPING

Although you're likely to be followed around the shop by vigilant salespeople, **Yalat** (Calle 39 at Calle 40, tel. 985/856-1969, 9 A.M.–8 P.M. daily) is worth a stop if you're interested in purchasing high-end Mexican handicrafts and art. Definitely pricey—almost astronomical—the quality of the items sold is excellent.

Mercado de Artesanías (Calle 39 at Calle 44; 8 A.M.–8 P.M. Mon.–Sat., 8 A.M.–2 P.M. Sun.) has a decent variety of *guayaberas,* embroidered *huilpiles,* hammocks, and other popular handicrafts. The selection isn't very large—there are only about a dozen shops here—so be sure to bargain.

ACCOMMODATIONS

Valladolid offers a good selection of simple and mid-range hotels. All are convenient to the central plaza.

Under US$50

Hostel La Candelaria (Parque La Candelaria, Calle 35 between Calles 42 and 44, tel. 985/856-2267, candelaria_hostel@hotmail.com, www.hostellingmexico.com, US$8.25 dorm, US$19.50 s with shared bath, US$26 d with shared bath) offers clean though somewhat worn rooms—many beds needed to be replaced and a coat of paint would do wonders. Still, it's a good choice, given the outstanding common areas: an outdoor kitchen that is amazingly equipped with loads of kitchenware, spices, and even tea; a laundry area (hand wash only) with soap provided; a comfy indoor lounge decorated with Mexican art and instruments; and a lush garden with hammocks, tables, and chairs. There's lots of information about the region, plus a great book exchange. Continental breakfast is included in the rate as are sheets and private lockers.

With spotless rooms set along a grassy, flower-lined courtyard, **Hotel Zaci** (Calle 44 between Calles 37 and 39, tel. 985/856-2167, US$23 s, US$31.50, US$32.50 d with a/c, US$36 d with a/c) is a good option. Rooms are kept up nicely and have details such as stenciling on the walls and iron-work furnishings. The top-floor rooms are a bit cheaper—the decor and amenities are a bit dated—so if you're counting your pennies, ask for one of those. A small, clean pool is a nice plus.

Across from the cathedral, **Hotel San Clemente** (Calle 42 between Calles 41 and 43, tel. 985/856-2208, www.hotelsanclemente.com.mx, US$32 s/d with fan, US$37 s/d with a/c) has 64 rooms surrounding a pleasant courtyard and pool. The rooms are spacious and clean with simple decor. Some units have a musty smell, unfortunately; ask for one on the top floor, which have the benefit of a good breeze.

US$50-100

Originally a 16th-century home, **Hotel El Mesón del Marqués** (central plaza, Calle 39 between Calles 40 and 42, tel. 985/856-2073, www.mesondelmarques.com, US$53–65 s/d with a/c, US$99 junior suite with a/c) is a favorite among travelers—a traditionally Mexican hotel with lush courtyards, a gurgling fountain, arches upon arches, and personalized service. Rooms are divided into three categories: standard, superior, and junior suite. The first two are decorated similarly with heavy wood furniture, iron headboards, and brightly colored woven bedspreads—the difference is that the superior is bigger and more expensive. Junior suites are brand new rooms, with modern decor and amenities, and even more space than the others. All of the rooms lead to an egg-shaped pool in a verdant garden—a perfect place to relax after a day of sightseeing. Be sure to enjoy at least one meal at the hotel restaurant, considered one of the best in town.

Located just a half-block from pretty San Bernardino de Siena church, **Casa Quetzal** (Calle 51 No. 218, tel. 985/856-4796, www.casa-quetzal .com, US$55.50 s/d, including breakfast) is Valladolid's first true B&B. Five large high-ceilinged rooms surround a pretty garden and swimming pool, while a community kitchen and lovely reading room—with excellent Mexican artwork, especially from Oaxaca and Jalisco—lend a homey feel. The plain ceramic floors and somewhat flimsy furniture clash with the hacienda-esque style intended here, but it's a charming place nonetheless and a model that is sure to be replicated and refined in this increasingly popular colonial city. All rooms have air-conditioning and wireless Internet, and four additional suites were in the works. The hotel is a bit removed from the central plaza—which can be a good thing—but you can easily walk into town or catch a taxi (US$1).

FOOD

◖ La Casa del Café Kaffé (Parque La Candelaria, Calle 35 at Calle 44, tel. 985/856-2879, 9 A.M.–1 P.M., 6:30 P.M.–midnight daily, US$1.25–4.25) is a fantastic place to get breakfast or a late-night snack. Owned and run by a welcoming Chilean couple, the menu features empanadas, quesadillas, sandwiches, fruit shakes, and a nice variety of coffee drinks. If you don't see what you crave on the menu, be sure to ask for it—meals often are made to order. With

tables on the lovely Parque Candelaria, tasty food, and great service, you can't go wrong.

Located next to the bus station, **◖ Cafetería Squimoz** (Calle 39 near Calle 46, tel. 985/856-4156, 7 A.M.–9:30 P.M. Mon.–Sat., 8 A.M.–3 P.M. Sun., US$2.50–6) is well worth a stop even if you're not on your way out of town. Big breakfasts and sandwiches made to order are the specialties, though the coffee drinks and to-die-for milkshakes can't be overlooked. If you've got a sweet tooth, be sure to try the homemade flan.

On the central plaza, the restaurant at the **◖ Hotel El Mesón del Marqués** (Calle 39 between Calles 40 and 42, tel. 985/856-2073, 7 A.M.–10:30 P.M. daily, US$4–12) is considered the best eatery in town. The setting is classic Mexican—an interior courtyard with a colonial-style fountain and masses of fuchsia-colored bougainvillea draped over the balconies—and the menu is ambitiously Yucatecan and international. For breakfast try the scrambled eggs with *chaya* (a local green similar to spinach), for lunch, order the marinated chicken breast salad, and for dinner, start with the *sopa de lima* before moving on to the *poc chuc*. A fine experience any time of day.

El Bazar (central plaza, Calle 39 at Calle 40, 7 A.M.–11 P.M. daily, US$2.50–6) is a local food court, with a dozen or so inexpensive eateries, mostly selling pre-made Yucatecan specialties. Food is hit or miss—take a look at the offerings and decide which looks the freshest. Better yet, order something off the menu that hasn't been sitting around like scrambled eggs or salbutes. Avoid the rubbery tamales.

For groceries, **La Favorita** (Calle 39 between Calles 42 and 44; tel. 985/856-2036, 9 A.M.–3 P.M., 6–9:30 P.M. Mon.–Sat., 9 A.M.–3 P.M. Sun.) has a decent selection of fresh and canned foods.

INFORMATION
Tourist Information

Try your best at prying some useful information from Valladolid's tourist office (Palacio Municipal, Calle 40 at Calle 41, tel. 985/856-2063, ext. 115, 9 A.M.–9 P.M. Mon.–Fri., 9 A.M.–7 P.M.

Sat., 9 A.M.–1 P.M. Sun.). At the very least, you should be able to get a map or two.

Hospitals
For medical assistance, head to the **Hospital General** (Parque de Sisal, Calle 49 s/n, tel. 985/856-2883, 24 hours).

Pharmacies
Just off the central plaza, **Farmacia Yza** (Calle 41 near Calle 40, tel. 985/856-4018) is open 24 hours.

Police
The police (Parque Bacalar, Calle 41 s/n, 24 hours) can be reached at tel. 985/856-2100.

SERVICES
Money
Half a block from the central plaza, **HSBC**

VALLADOLID BUS SCHEDULES

Departures from Valladolid's **bus station** (Calle 39 at Calle 46, tel. 985/856-3448) include:

DESTINATION	PRICE	DURATION	SCHEDULE
Campeche	US$20	4 hrs	1:45 P.M.
Cancún	US$6.50-10*	3 hrs	every 30-60 min., 6 A.M.-10:30 P.M.
Chetumal	US$12	5 hrs	5:30 A.M., 7:30 A.M., and 2:30 P.M.
Chichén Itzá	US$2-3	45 min.	every 30-60 min., 7:15 A.M.-5:30 P.M.
Chiquilá	US$6	3 hrs	2:45 A.M.
Cobá	US$2	1 hr	9:30 A.M., 2:45 P.M., and 5:15 P.M.
Izamal	US$3.75	1.5 hrs	12:45 P.M. and 3:50 P.M.
Mérida	US$6.75-10.25*	3 hrs	every 30-60 min., 5 A.M.-10:30 P.M.
Playa del Carmen	US$7-13*	3 hrs	8:30 A.M., 9:30 A.M., 2:45 P.M., and 5:15 P.M., plus 6:30 A.M. (Mon., Tue., Sat. only)
Tizimín	US$1.75	1 hr	every 30-75 min., 5:30 A.M.-8 P.M.
Tulum	US$4-6.50*	2 hrs	eight departures daily 8:30 A.M.-5:20 P.M.

*Denotes first-class service; not available for all departures.

(Calle 41 between Calles 42 and 44, 8 A.M.–7 P.M. Mon.–Sat.) and **Banamex** (Calle 41 between Calles 42 and 44, 9 A.M.–4 P.M. Mon.–Fri.) both have ATMs.

Internet

Internet Atlantis (Calle 35 near Calle 44, 10 A.M.–11 P.M. daily) charges US$1 per hour.

Post Office

This tiny post office (central plaza, Calle 40 between Calles 39 and 41) is open 9 A.M.–3 P.M. Monday–Friday.

Launderette

The busy **Lavandería Luyso** (Calle 40 at Calle 33, tel. 985/856-3542, 8 A.M.–8 P.M. Mon.–Sat., 8 A.M.–2 P.M. Sun., US$0.75 per 1 kg/2.2 lbs) offers next-day service only.

GETTING THERE AND AROUND

Bus: Valladolid's bus station (Calle 39 at Calle 46, tel. 985/856-3448) is an easy walk from the central plaza, or if you have a lot of bags, a cheap taxi ride. With the exception of a few first-class departures, most of the service here is second-class.

Taxi: Taxis are relatively easy to flag down, especially around the central plaza. If you need to call one, try **Catedral** (tel. 985/856-2090).

Bicycle Rental: Rent bikes at **Refraccionaría de Bicicletas Silva** (Calle 44 between Calles 39 and 41, tel. 985/856-3667, 9 A.M.–8 P.M. daily) for US$0.65 an hour or US$3.75 a day.

Ek' Balam

Ek' Balam (8 A.M.–5 P.M., US$3) is a unique and fascinating site that has only recently been appreciated by researchers and tourists. Maya for "Black Jaguar," serious restoration didn't begin here until the mid-1990s. It was during that time that a remarkable and incredibly well-preserved stucco mural was uncovered partway up the site's largest pyramid. The discovery revealed a great deal about this commercially-important city, which thrived A.D. 700–1100, though much remains unknown. Although it's located just 30 kilometers (19 miles) north of Valladolid, and in close proximity to Cancún and Mérida, Ek' Balam has not attracted the bus loads of tourists that other sites have. That may change: already a huge parking lot has been completed, a new visitor center is underway, and there are plans to widen the access roads.

A **village** by the same name is two kilometers (1.2 miles) away and provides basic accommodations and food; for more options and other traveler services, head to Valladolid.

EK' BALAM ARCHAEOLOGICAL ZONE

Entering Ek' Balam, you'll pass through a low thick wall and an elegant corbeled arch. Walls are rare in Maya cities, and were most commonly used for defense, as in the cases of Becán and Tulum. Ek' Balam's low thick walls would not have slowed marauding rivals, however, and so they most likely served to enforce social divisions, with some areas off-limits (but not out of view!) to all but the elite. They may also have been decorative—the city possessed great aesthetic flair, as the arch at the entrance and the site's famous stucco frieze demonstrate.

Acrópolis and El Trono

The highlight of Ek' Balam is, without question, an artful and remarkably pristine stucco frieze known as El Trono (The Throne). It is located under a protective *palapa* roof, about two thirds the way up the Acrópolis, a massive pyramid at the north end of the site, and Ek' Balam's largest structure. (In fact, at 32 meters (105 feet) high and 158 meters (514.8 feet)

THE STATE OF YUCATÁN

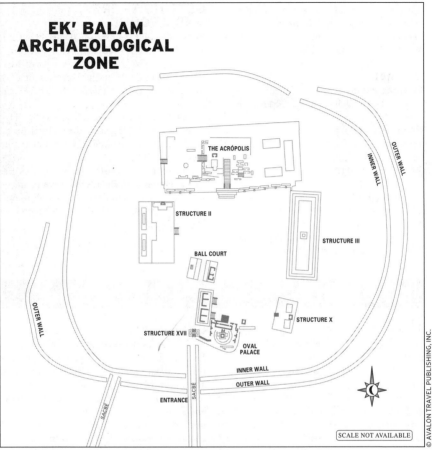

EK' BALAM ARCHAEOLOGICAL ZONE

THE ACRÓPOLIS

OUTER WALL

INNER WALL

STRUCTURE II

STRUCTURE III

BALL COURT

STRUCTURE X

OUTER WALL

STRUCTURE XVII

OVAL PALACE

INNER WALL

OUTER WALL

SACBE

SACBE

ENTRANCE

SACBE

SCALE NOT AVAILABLE

© AVALON TRAVEL PUBLISHING, INC.

wide, it is among the largest Maya pyramids ever built.) A steep stairway leads up the center of the pyramid, and a platform to the left of the stairs provides visitors a close-up view of El Trono.

About 85 percent of El Trono is the original stucco. Often structures like this would have been painted blue or red, but not so here. In fact, shortly after it was built, El Trono was sealed behind a stone wall 50–60 centimeters (19–24 inches) thick. It remained there untouched until the 1990s, when restoration workers accidentally dislodged one of the pro-

tective stones while removing a tree growing above it.

The tall, winged figures immediately catch your eye, as they appear so much like angels. In fact, they are high priests. Notice that one is deformed—his left arm is longer than the right, and has only four fingers. The Maya considered birth defects to be a sign of divinity, and the priest depicted here may have risen to his position precisely because of his deformation.

Directly over the door is a seated figure (unfortunately, the head is missing). This represents Ukit Kan Le'k Tok,' one of Ek' Balam's

© LIZA PRADO

The one-of-a-kind winged figures at Ek' Balam are worth a visit.

former rulers, described in inscriptions as the "king of kings," and the person for whom El Trono was built and dedicated. A tomb was discovered in the chamber behind the frieze that contained thousands of jade, gold, obsidian, and ceramic artifacts, left as offerings to this powerful leader. The small face at the king-figure's navel represents a rival whom he defeated in war.

Viewed as a whole, the frieze is unmistakably a Chenes-style "monster mouth": a huge stylized mask in which the doorway represents the gaping mouth of a high god. The pointed upper and lower teeth are easy to spot, as are the spiral eyes. Monster mouths are never mundane, but this one is especially elaborate: notice how two beautifully crafted figures straddle the lower eyelids, while hoisting the upper lids with their shoulders. At least five more figures, plus lattice patterns and other designs, adorn the rest of the mask.

Before heading down, climb the rest of the way to the top of the Acrópolis to take in the view. With the exception of the odd telephone and radio tower, and the site's large new visitor's center, the view of the broad flat Yucatecan landscape is probably not all that different than the one Maya priests and kings enjoyed from this very same vantage point, more than a thousand years ago.

South Plaza

Chances are you bee-lined straight from the entrance to the Acrópolis and the frieze—who can blame you? Descending the pyramid, you can see that Ek' Balam is a small site, with buildings somewhat crowded together. It has two plazas (north and south) with the ball court in the middle.

On the south side of the south plaza—opposite the Acropolis—stands **La Rodonda,** or the Oval Palace. A squat midsize structure, La Rodonda has an eclectic array of overlapping lines and curves, stairs and terraces. It underwent numerous iterations, as did virtually all Maya temples, but the result here was especially eclectic. Archaeologists suspect La Rodonda was used for astronomical observations, and the discovery of several richly adorned tombs suggest it had a ceremonial purpose as well.

Flanking La Redonda are **Las Gemelas** (The Twins), known as Structure 17. As the plaque indicates, these identical structures are perhaps the best example of Ek' Balam's particular architectural style. Having perfected the use of stucco, Ek' Balam's builders did not concern themselves with precise masonry, as the stones would be covered in a thick stucco cap. However, stucco proved much less resilient to erosion, and centuries later the structures here appear shabbier than even much older ones, like in the Río Bec region, where stucco was less common and stone blocks were more carefully cut and fitted.

Guides usually can be hired at the entrance to the ruins, or arranged via Genesis Ek' Balam.

ACCOMMODATIONS AND FOOD

In the Maya village near the ruins, **Genesis Ek' Balam** (tel. 985/101-0277, www.genesis retreat.com, US$50–62 d, family unit US$75– 100) has nine rooms and cabañas, set on a leafy enclosed property with a natural bio-filtered pool in the middle. Six units share a large clean bathroom, three have private bathrooms, one has air-conditioning, and all are different in style and decor. One of the favorites, the Birdhouse, has screen windows on all sides and a small balcony overlooking the pool and garden. A full breakfast is included, and lunch is open to non-guests as well (1– 3 P.M. only, US$8–12). The mostly-vegetarian dishes make ample use of *chaya,* a rich spinach-like plant used by the Maya since before the conquest (and still today), and grown

right in the Genesis garden. The hardworking Canadian owner offers tours of the village and local artisan workshops (US$7 pp, minimum 4 people) and can arrange guided excursions to the ruins, plus nearby cenotes, haciendas, and more. Be aware that a number of friendly pooches that lounge about the property—fine if you like dogs, but not everyone's thing.

Much more rustic accommodations are available at **Uh Najil Ek' Balam** (US$32.50 cabin), a community-run complex a short distance from Genesis Ek' Balam. Eleven wood bungalows have very basic furnishings; a few have private bath, others share equally basic common bathrooms and showers. The concept is great—a cooperative of more than 20 local people share in the camp's operation and profit—but the place could use a little better upkeep. Guests can use the kitchen here. The best feature may be the new **observation tower** (US$2.50) that affords a terrific view of the village and surroundings.

GETTING THERE AND AROUND

If you're driving from Valladolid, head north on Highway 295 toward Tizimín. After about 17 kilometers (10.6 miles), turn right (east) onto the well-marked turnoff toward Ek' Balam. From there, it's another 11 kilometers (6.8 miles) to a fork: One direction leads to the village and accommodations, the other to the archaeological site.

A taxi from Valladolid to the village costs US$15–20 for up to four people. If you're just visiting the ruins, you can negotiate for a driver to take you there and wait 1–2 hours and bring you back for around US$25.

Río Lagartos and San Felipe

A little more than 100 kilometers (62 miles) north of Valladolid, on the northernmost point of the Yucatán Peninsula, Río Lagartos is justly famous for the huge colonies of flamingos that nest and feed here.

Nearby San Felipe is a much more pleasant place to spend an afternoon or night, and it's still convenient to the tours from Río Lagartos. If you have a car, consider staying in San Felipe and driving into Río Lagartos for a flamingo tour.

RÍO LAGARTOS

Tens of thousands of pink and cerise *phoenicopterus ruber ruber* flamingos throng to the area's *ría* (saltwater lagoon), which winds several kilometers east of the town of Río Lagartos. In addition to the flamingos, bird-watchers will spot plover, white egret, heron, cormorant, hawks, and pelican.

Río Lagartos itself is an isolated, rather dumpy community that would not merit a visit were it not for the flamingo and bird-watching tours. The town was pummeled by Hurricane Isadora in 2002, and still seems to be recovering. There are numerous abandoned houses, and the main street wasn't paved until 2004. The population is a mix of longtime local families and itinerant workers from as far away as Chiapas and Veracruz who come to fish and work in the salt factory in nearby Las Coloradas; you'll see the factory's huge mounds of salt during the flamingo tour. (Salt has been harvested throughout the gulf coast since pre-Hispanic times.) The constant ebb and flow of semipermanent workers may explain why the town exudes so little community spirit.

C Flamingo Tours

While a group of flamingos remains in Río Lagartos year-round, you'll see the highest concentration April, June, and July. From November to March, the young are just beginning to color. At hatching, flamingos are mostly white,

and at three months the black feathers along their wings begin to grow.

The locals and government are both very protective of the flamingos. During the April–June brooding season, visitors are not allowed to approach the nesting area, as the skittish birds sometimes knock their eggs out of their nests (they lay only one per year). During this time, however, the feeding area can still be visited.

Río Lagartos Expeditions (Restaurante Isla Contoy, Calle 19 No. 134, tel. 986/862-0000, www.riolagartosexpeditions.com) is the most experienced and recommended tour operator. Be aware that freelancers will flag you down on the street entering town, offering tours, even saying Río Lagartos Expeditions has closed—don't believe them. Trips take 2–2.5 hours and cost US$56 for 1–6 people, plus a US$2 per person natural reserve fee. If you call ahead, guides will usually merge smaller groups to save you money. Tours are offered 6 A.M.–7 P.M. daily, and the earlier you go the better. Although you can see the flamingos all day, it takes almost 45 minutes to get to the flamingo sites and leaving early means seeing other water birds along the way. The water is also calmer in the morning. It is best to arrange your trip the day before; English- and Italian-speaking guides typically are available. Binoculars aren't absolutely necessary but nice to have; bring your own or ask to borrow a pair.

Accommodations

Hotel Villa de Pescadores (Calle 14 No. 93, tel. 986/862-0020, US$32.50 s with fan, US$37 d with fan, US$47 d with a/c) is the best option in town. Right on the waterfront, all nine rooms have spectacular views of the estuary and the Gulf of Mexico beyond. Each is clean and spacious and has a balcony or terrace to boot.

You get what you pay for at the **Posada Leyli** (Calle 14 at Calle 11, tel. 986/862-0106, US$18.50 s/d with shared bath, US$23.25 s/d with private bath), a very basic hotel with old

FLAMINGOS IN THE YUCATÁN

The wetlands along the Yucatán's northern coast are shallow and murky and bordered in many places by thick mangrove forests. The water content is unusually high in salt and other minerals – the ancient Mayas gathered salt here, and several salt factories still operate. A formidable habitat for most creatures, it's ideal for *phoenicopterus ruber ruber* – the American flamingo, the largest and pinkest of the world's five flamingo species. Nearly 30,000 of the peculiar birds nest here, feeding on algae and other tiny organisms that thrive in the salty water. Flamingos are actually born white, but they turn pink from the carotene in the algae that they eat.

For years, flamingos nested only near Río Lagartos, near the peninsula's northeastern tip. But in 1988, Hurricane Gilbert destroyed their nesting grounds – not to mention the town of Río Lagartos – and forced the birds to relocate. They are now found all along the north coast, including three major feeding and reproduction grounds: Río Lagartos, Celestún, and Uaymitún.

The best way to observe flamingos is on a sunrise boat tour. That's when the birds are most active, turning their heads upside down and dragging their beaks along the bottom of the shallow water to suck in the mud that contains their food. (In the morning, you should see dozens of other birds too, such as storks, herons, kingfishers, and eagles.) If you go in the spring, you may see the male flamingos performing their strange mating dance, craning their necks, clucking loudly, and generally strutting their stuff.

All three sites have flamingos year-round, but you'll see the highest numbers at Río Lagartos in the spring and summer and at Celestún in the winter. Uaymitún stays pretty uniform but has no boat tours – instead you observe the birds through binoculars from a raised platform. No matter when you go, make as little noise as possible and ask your guide to keep his distance. Flamingos are nervous and easily spooked into flying away en masse. While no doubt an impressive sight, this may cause the birds to abandon the site altogether.

---

beds, toilets without seats, one bare fluorescent bulb per room, and walls that are begging for a coat of paint. It'll do for a night though. Try to snag one with a balcony.

Posada Isla Contoy (tel. 986/862-0000, US$18.50 s/d with fan) is the name given to five small, very basic bungalows operated by Restaurante Isla Contoy and Río Lagartos Expeditions. Located next to the restaurant, all have private bathrooms and hot water.

Food
Restaurante Isla Contoy (end of Calle 19, tel. 986/862-0000, 8 A.M.–9 P.M. daily, US$4.50– 11) is a good spot to get breakfast after an early-morning tour although it's a decent option at any time. Breakfast specials mostly include eggs, beans, and coffee; for lunch or dinner the specialty is seafood, including *filete,* shrimp cocktail, and ceviche.

A simple eatery, **Los Negritos** (Calle 10 s/n, no phone, 9 A.M.–6 P.M. daily, US$4–10) serves good Mexican fare—the seafood is especially good. Located on the main road near the entrance of town.

Information and Services
There is no tourist office in Río Lagartos, though the folks at Restaurante Isla Contoy typically are very helpful. There also is no bank nor ATM, and no immediate plans for either. For medical attention, it's best to head to Valladolid.

Getting There and Around
Noreste has service from Río Lagartos from its terminal a few blocks from Restaurante Isla Contoy—ask for directions there as most of the streets here are not signed. Buses depart there for San Felipe (US$0.50, 15 minutes) and Tizimín (US$2, one hour, seven departures daily) and Mérida (US$10, 4.5 hours, four departures daily).

SAN FELIPE

While Río Lagartos is somewhat downtrodden, San Felipe has well-maintained streets and sidewalks, brightly painted houses, and a clean, attractive waterfront promenade. The hotels and restaurants are nicer, and the atmosphere much more agreeable.

Accommodations

Hotel Posada La Hacienda (Calle 12 between Calles 15 and 17, tel. 986/862-2048, US$23 s/d with fan, US$28 s/d with a/c, US$32.50 t with fan, US$37 t with a/c) is a charming hotel just four blocks from the oceanfront. Rooms are nicely decorated in a Mexican style: adobe-colored tile floors, heavy wood furniture, and *talavera* sinks. They also are very clean. With cable TV, they are a steal in this part of the state.

Right on the waterfront, **Hotel San Felipe** (Calle 9 between Calles 14 and 16, tel. 986/862-2027, sanfelipehotel@hotmail.com, US$34–43 s/d with fan, US$36–46 s/d with a/c) is a pleasant hotel with 18 rooms. Each room is slightly different, but all are clean and comfortable. Rooms with a view are especially nice, inside and out. If you **fly fish** and aren't going to make it to Sian Ka'an or Xcalak, this hotel arranges recommended tours (US$250, 1–2 people, eight hours, including guide, lunch, and water).

Food

The memorably named ⟨ **Restaurant El Popular Vaselina** (The Popular Grease Restaurant, Calles 9 at Calle 12, tel. 986/862-2083, 11 A.M.–7 P.M. daily, US$4–10) serves excellent, super-fresh seafood in a big, airy dining area. Try the ceviche—usually an appetizer, the servings here are big enough to make a meal, and then some. Fronting San Felipe's pleasant promenade, some of the tables have nice views and get a breeze off the water. Service is friendly and prompt.

The restaurant at **Hotel San Felipe** (Calle 9 between Calles 14 and 16, tel. 986/862-2027, 8 A.M.–9 P.M. daily, US$5–10) is another reliable choice, with longer hours.

Information and Services

San Felipe had no bank or ATM and no tourist office when we visited. A small **clinic** is on

© LIZA PRADO

Dozens of fishing boats dot San Felipe's port in the afternoon.

Calle 15 at Calle 10-A but was open 8 A.M.–1 P.M. and 5–8 P.M. Tuesday–Thursday only.

Getting There

The **Noreste** bus terminal is on the main street entering town. It is closed when there is no bus leaving or arriving. Most buses departing Río Lagartos stop here en route. There's infrequent direct service to Cancún and Mérida; otherwise connect in Tizimín (US$2, one hour, seven departures daily).

If you're driving, the cutoff to San Felipe is a few kilometers before entering Río Lagartos and well signed.

TIZIMÍN

A busy grubby town, there's no real reason to stop in Tizimín, unless you're switching buses or are staying the night on your way to or from Río Lagartos.

Accommodations and Food

Just a couple of blocks from the bus station is the **Hotel 49** (Calle 49 between Calles 46 and 48, tel. 986/863-2136, US$23 s/d with fan, US$32–42 s/d with a/c). The tile-floored rooms are surprisingly clean and well kept. Cable TV, free wireless Internet, and secure parking make it even better. A great option if you have to stay the night.

About two blocks from the cathedral, **Restaurant Candy** (Calle 52 between Calles 55 and 57, tel. 986/863-4058, 7 A.M.–4 P.M. daily, US$3–8) is a popular spot for regional fare.

Getting There

Bus: Tizimín takes its role as a transportation hub very seriously. There are two bus terminals and numerous *colectivo* stops, all with overlapping services. Fortunately, everything is close together so you don't have to lug bags back and forth across town.

The **Oriente/Mayab terminal** (tel. 986/863-2424, Calle 46 between Calles 45 and 47) has first-class and semi-direct service.

Cancún, US$8, 3.5 hours, 3:30 A.M., 5:15 A.M., 8:30 A.M., 2:30 P.M., 5:15 P.M.

Mérida, US$7, 3.5 hours, 5:30 A.M., 11 A.M., 4 P.M.

Valladolid, US$1.75, 1 hour, every 30–90 minutes 5:30 A.M.–7:30 P.M.

The **Noreste terminal** (tel. 986/863-2034, Calle 47 between Calles 46 and 48) is around the corner and has mostly second-class service.

Chiquilá, US$5, 2.5 hours, 4 A.M., 11 A.M., 1 P.M., and 2:15 P.M.

Río Lagartos & San Felipe, US$2, 1–1.5 hours, seven departures 6:30 A.M.–7:45 P.M.

You can also catch a *colectivo* to Río Lagartos (US$2, one hour) at the corner of Calles 47 and 48, departing daily at roughly 5 A.M., noon, and 4 P.M.

Car: If you're driving from Valladolid, be aware that the highway feeds onto the main street through town, and becomes one-way (the wrong way, in this case) a few blocks before the center. You have to jog one street up but the one-way sign is hard to spot, so look carefully.

THE STATE OF CAMPECHE

It's not easy having to compete for attention when your neighbors are powerhouses like Quintana Roo, Yucatán, and Chiapas. So it's no surprise Campeche is the least-visited state in the region, which means it's a great time to visit! Most travelers are surprised to find that Campeche City has a gorgeous city center, first-rate museums, and a nascent arts and music scene. (The lodging and restaurants are still a bit disappointing, but are definitely improving.) Even more startling are Campeche's fantastic Maya ruins: in the Río Bec region, a half-dozen ruins pack plenty of wow-factor, yet see only a fraction of the tourists that Uxmal, Chichén Itzá, and Palenque do. The United Nations named Campeche City a World Heritage site in 1999 and a visit here is a chance to partake in Campeche's slow emergence from the shadow of its better-known neighbors.

PLANNING YOUR TIME

You will probably want 2–3 days in Campeche City, to take in the city center as well as some of the outlying sights. Budget at least three days in the Río Bec area—a full day for Calakmul and Balamkú and 1–2 days for the ruins near the town of Xpujil.

Having a car will make your visit to Campeche much more rewarding. You can access Campeche City by bus, but service to and around the Río Bec region is much too infrequent to be practical. More and more travelers fly into Cancún and rent a car for a couple of weeks, making a large counterclockwise loop hitting Mérida, Campeche, the Río Bec region, Chetumal, Tulum, and back up to Cancún.

© GARY CHANDLER

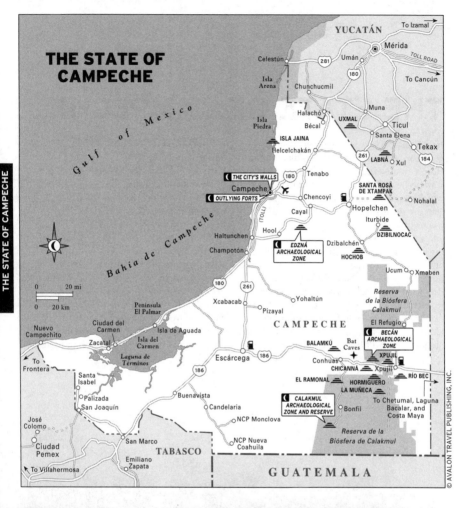

THE STATE OF CAMPECHE

THE STATE OF
CAMPECHE

Gulf of Mexico

Bahía de Campeche

© AVALON TRAVEL PUBLISHING, INC.

Campeche City

Campeche earned its United Nations World Heritage designation primarily for its network of city walls, bastions, and forts, and visiting them is high on travelers' lists; most have been meticulously restored and contain small but excellent museums. It's also worth just wandering around the central plaza and city center, where you'll find a number of historical churches and buildings worth peeking into, and can soak in the colorful facades and cobble-stoned streets along the way.

HISTORY

"Campeche" is a Spanish corruption of "Ah Kim Pech," the name of the Maya town that occupied the same spot. Ah Kim Pech was

HIGHLIGHTS

(The City's Walls: Built three centuries ago to ward off marauding pirates, Campeche's massive walls and bastions are now picturesque walkways and terrific museums (page 330).

(Outlying Forts: Jade masks and exquisite clay figurines are highlights at this fort-turned-museum, showcasing Campeche's rich archaeological sites. The view of the Gulf isn't too shabby either (page 331).

(Edzná Archaeological Zone: Survey your domain from the top of the magnificent Temple of Five Stories, just an hour from the up-and-coming city of Campeche (page 344).

(Calakmul Archaeological Zone and Reserve: A mega-ruin nestled deep in a forest reserve, Calakmul is home to toucans, howler monkeys, and the largest Maya pyramid ever (page 349).

(Becán Archaeological Zone: Palaces, pyramids, and passageways make this a perfect site for people who like to clamber around ruins. A recently discovered 1,500-year-old mask is an added bonus (page 357).

YUCATÁN

Gulf of Mexico

Outlying Forts

Campeche (— The City's Walls

(Edzná Archaeological Zone

0 50 mi

0 50 km

Becán Archaeological Zone (

CAMPECHE

Calakmul Archaeological Zone and Reserve (

TABASCO

GUATEMALA

LOOK FOR (TO FIND RECOMMENDED SIGHTS, ACTIVITIES, DINING, AND LODGING.

THE STATE OF CAMPECHE

an important indigenous commercial center, serving as a gateway between the Yucatán Peninsula and central Mexico. Spanish explorers first arrived here by ship in 1517; recognizing its strategic location, they immediately set out to control it themselves. The Maya were not pleased, and dealt the would-be conquerors one demoralizing defeat after another. In fact, the Maya kicked serious Spanish arse for the next 23 years; it wasn't until October 4, 1540, that Spanish soldiers led by Francisco de Montejo finally conquered Ah Kim Pech and founded the city of Campeche. Before long, the city was once again a major port and trade center, though for Spanish galleons instead of Maya canoes. Among other exports was *palo de Campeche*

(Campeche wood), a tropical wood used to make fabric dyes and highly valued in Europe and elsewhere.

The Spanish had their favor returned, however, in the form of marauding pirates. Many were supported by Spain's archenemies, England and France, and were attracted by the easy pickings at Campeche's ports and busy ship lanes. For nearly 200 years—until Campeche's defensive walls were finally completed—the people of Campeche endured nearly constant harassment and assault from ne'er-do-wells and scalawags. The city was destroyed on several occasions, including February 9, 1663, when pirates killed scores of men, women, and children in the worst massacre in the city's history. Another infamous

THE STATE OF CAMPECHE

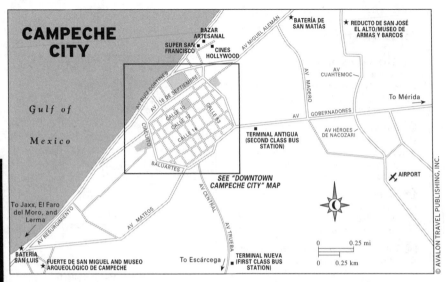

assault was led by Laurent Graff, also known as Lorencillo, who attacked Campeche with an army of 700 men on July 6, 1685. They didn't stop with just sacking the city, they also took dozens of prisoners and demanded the city leaders pay an exorbitant ransom. After two months of occupation, the city hadn't paid—it didn't have the money—so the pirates planned a mass execution. After the first round of killings, a city representative talked the pirates out of the plan, and even out of the city.

The ordeal prompted the Spanish crown to build fortifications, which would eventually bring relative peace and protection to Campeche. A wall was built around the city, eight meters (26 feet) high and three meters (10 feet) thick, of solid stone and mortar. There were four gates on each of the four sides; two of them—Puerta del Mar (Sea Gate) and Puerta de la Tierra (Land Gate)—are still used. Nine *baluartes* (bastions) were erected in strategic locations, in order to best defend the city from attacks of any kind. Part of the wall extended into the sea and was outfitted with a huge gate, which was opened to let merchants in, but could be quickly closed to the pirates in constant pursuit. Although isolated attacks continued until 1717, the walls served their purpose, bringing the reign of pirate terror to an end.

SIGHTS
◖ The City's Walls

Campeche's imposing walls, bastions, and forts lend a wonderful old-world ambience to the city. Most contain museums and exploring them is a great way to spend an afternoon, or whole day. Five of the seven bastions surrounding the city center can be visited (provided they aren't being renovated) as can two forts on the city's edges.

Just off the central park, **Baluarte Nuestra Señora de la Soledad** (Calle 8 at Calle 57, 8 A.M.–7 P.M. Tues.–Sun., US$2.25) is the largest of the city's bastions, and home to a small but very worthwhile museum. The **Museo de la Arquitectura Maya** has a superb collection of stelae and other artifacts from the Río Bec and Puuc regions, accompanied by modern displays and explanations in both Spanish and English. With just four rooms, it offers a primer on Maya writing, sculpture, and architectural styles without

THE STATE OF CAMPECHE

screen—be sure to get a front-row seat to be able to read them.

Near the waterfront, **Baluarte San Carlos** (Calle 8 between Calles 63 and 65, 8 A.M.–7:30 P.M. Tues.–Sun., US$2.50, free Sunday) houses yet another small museum, this one about the city's history. Explanations of Campeche's development are incredibly detailed and in Spanish only, but the exhibits include some antique weapons and suits of armor if your eyes start to glaze over. San Carlos was completed in the early 1600s, the first of the nine bastions to be built.

Built in the 1790s, **Baluarte San Pedro** (Calle 16 at Calle 51, 9 A.M.–9 P.M. daily, free) has had several incarnations—a stronghold, barracks, INAH research center, and arts and crafts market. Today, it houses a tiny museum highlighting Campeche's handicrafts. Exhibits include explanations on the origins and the processes of making various artesanía. Signage in Spanish only.

Baluarte Santiago (Calle 49-C at Calle 8, 8 A.M.–8 P.M. Mon.–Sat., 8 A.M.–2 P.M. Sun., free) was completed in 1704, nearly a century after the first. It was torn down in the early 1900s to make room for government offices, but was reconstructed at the same location in 1955. Today, this tiny fort houses the **Jardín Botánico Xmuch'haltun,** a small botanical garden that, at the time of research, was being redesigned.

◖ Outlying Forts

If you go to only one sight, make it **Fuerte de San Miguel and Museo Arqueológico de Campeche** (Av. Escencia s/n, 9 A.M.–7:30 P.M. Tues.–Sun., US$2.75), about 2.5 kilometers (1.6 miles) south of the center. Built in the 18th century, the fort sits atop a large hill and includes a moat, drawbridge, and a breathtaking view of the Gulf. The museum here is the real highlight though, housing a truly fantastic collection of Maya artifacts from around the state, including several pieces from the ruins at Isla Jaina, six spectacular jade funeral masks found at Calakmul, and urns decorated with tapirs, monkeys, and turtles from Río Bec. Signage is in Spanish and English; look for the

© LIZA PRADO

Campeche City was named a UNESCO World Heritage site in 1999.

being overwhelming. Outside the entrance are more stelae, and a ramp leading to the top of the wall.

Puerta de Tierra (end of Calle 59; 8 A.M.–8 P.M. daily, US$1) was one of two heavily fortified gates into the city. The entrance fee allows you onto the eight-meter (26-foot) walls, where a narrow causeway makes for a memorable stroll to **Baluarte San Juan** on one end and **Baluarte San Francisco** on the other. The latter has a small museum about pirates, which is included in admission.

The Puerta de Tierra is also where the **Espectáculo de Luz y Sonido** (Sound and Light Show; 8:30 P.M. daily in high season, Tues., Fri., and Sat. only in low season, US$3.75 adults, US$1 children), a 90-minute program that includes a brief film at Baluarte San Francisco and a live performance about Campeche's violent past featuring colored lights, blasting speakers, some firecrackers, and a sword fight or two atop the wall. Pretty cornball but can be fun for the kids. English and French subtitles are projected onto a tiny

THE STATE OF CAMPEC

Gulf of Mexico

AV AH KIM-PECH

Deportivo 20 de Noviembre

IMMIGRATION OFFICE
PALACIO FEDERAL

BALUARTE SANTIAGO/JARDÍN BOTÁNICO XMUCH'HALTUN

AV MIGUEL ALEMÁN

▼ LA PIGUA

El Malecón

HOTEL DEL MAR

TEATRO JUAN DE LA CABADA

■ POST OFFICE

TODO NATURAL ▼

CIRCUITO BALUARTES

HOTEL BALUARTES

AV RUIZ CORTINES

Plaza Patrimonio Mundial

CALLE 8

MANSION CARVAJAL

BALUARTE NUESTRA SEÑORA DE LA SOLEDAD/MUSEO DE LA ARQUITECTURA MAYA

LA GRAN ▼ MICHOACÁN

HOTEL PLAZA CAMPECHE

STATE TOURIST OFFICE

PUERTA DEL MAR

Central Principal

■ MUNICIPAL TOURIST OFFICE

CATEDRAL DE LA CONCEPCIÓN INMACULADA

PALACIO DE GOBIERNO

MONKEY HOSTEL/ CASA NO.6

MARGANZO ▼

■ HSBC

GALERÍA DE ARTE JOAQUIN ★ CLAUSELL

PALACIO LEGISLATIVO ★

NUEVA ESPAÑA PANADERÍA ▼

LA PARROQUIA ■

HOSTAL LA PARROQUIA

TEATRO DE LA CIUDAD FRANCISCO PAULA TORO

GARIBALDI ★

BANORTE

HOTEL REGIS

CHEF COLOR ▼

BALUARTE SAN CARLOS ★

HOTEL AMÉRICA ●

CAFÉ TULUM ▼

XTAMPAK TOURS

TUKULNA ▼

CALLE 51

HECHO EN MÉXICO

ARCHIVO GENERAL DEL ESTADO ■ DE CAMPECHE

HOSPITAL CAMPOS

CIBER & CHAT ●

NUTRIVIDA

INTERNET FÁCIL ■

LAVANDERÍA ■ LAVA KLIN

EX-TEMPLO DE SAN JOSÉ ★

INSTITUTO DE CULTURA DE CAMPECHE

HOTEL COLONIAL ■

BALUARTE SAN PEDRO ★

AV GOBERNADORES

SALA DE ARTE DOMINGO PÉREZ PIÑA

HOTEL LÓPEZ

CALLE 59

CALLE 51

To Terminal Antigua (Second Class Bus Station), International Airport, and Edzná

SIR FRANCIS DRAKE HOTEL ●

CALLE 14

MAYA CAMPECHE HOTEL ●

INAH ■

HOSTAL DEL PIRATA ●

CIRCUITO BALUARTES

CALLE 10-B

FARMACIA SIMILARES ■

BALUARTE SANTA ROSA ★

CALLE 63

CALLE 16

HACIENDA PUERTA CAMPECHE ●

BALUARTE SAN FRANCISCO ★

CALLE 18

PUERTA DE TIERRA ★

MERCADO PRINCIPAL

CIRCUITO BALUARTES

BALUARTE SAN JUAN ★

AV CENTRAL

BUSES TO EDZNÁ

To Terminal Nueva (First Class Bus Station)

DOWNTOWN CAMPECHE CITY

© AVALON TRAVEL PUBLISHING, INC.

SCALE NOT AVAILABLE

---

cardboard information sheets in each exhibit hall. If using public transportation, take a "Playa Bonita/Lerma" bus in front of the post office (US$0.35). The bus will drop you off at the turnoff to the fort, which is about another 500 meters (0.3 miles) up a steep hill.

Below the Fuerte de San Miguel is the **Batería de San Luis** (8 A.M.–6 P.M. daily, free), a small fortification that is empty save one exhibit on Captain Pedro Sáinz de Baranda y Borreiro, a native of Campeche and naval commander who in 1835 became the governor of Yucatán.

On the other side of town, the **Reducto de San José El Alto** (Av. Francisco Morazán s/n, 8 A.M.–8 P.M. Tues.–Sun., US$2) is a well-renovated fort complete with cannons, thick walls, and a spectacular view of the Gulf of Mexico. It also houses the small **Museo de Armas y Barcos,** a maritime and weaponry museum where you'll find model ships, 18th-century weapons, and a few other colonial-era artifacts. Explanations in Spanish only. You'll need a car or taxi to get there, and even so it's easy to get lost.

City Center

Bright pastel facades and cobblestone streets

© LIZA PRADO

The roof of Fuerte de San Miguel holds colonial-era cannons, while its ground floor has an excellent archaeological museum.

make Campeche's city center one of the most beautiful in the whole peninsula. Add to that its famous walls and bastions (and all those pirate tales) and it's no wonder the United Nations designated Campeche's walled center a World Heritage Site in 1999. The **central plaza** is a pleasant, shady spot to rest your feet, and a good place to begin and end a tour of the many sites. Better yet, on Saturdays and Sundays the streets around the central plaza are blocked to traffic and fill up with food carts and small vendors, and local families come out to chat and stroll about. In the evening, one or two *lotería* games start up—tourists are welcome—and the municipal band gives a classic oompah concert, blaring forth on trumpets, clarinets, tubas, and cymbals with the energy of a great orchestra.

On one side of the plaza is **Catedral de la Concepción Inmaculada** (Calle 55 between Calles 8 and 10), the city's cathedral and one of the oldest churches on the Yucatán Peninsula. Construction was ordered by Francisco de Montejo in 1540 and completed in 1760

(and you thought it took the contractor a long time to finish your deck). On another side, an arcaded passageway known as **Los Portales** provides an airy shaded corridor for a number of small shops and restaurants.

Built by the Jesuits in 1700, the **Ex-Templo de San José** (Calle 10 at Calle 63) is a beautiful structure, decorated with an impressive blue and yellow tile facade. The history of the building is as varied as that of the city of Campeche: It has gone from being a church to being the first lighthouse in Campeche (check out the spires) to library to warehouse to—today—an art museum.

The **Galería de Arte Joaquín Clausell** (Calle 12 between 51 and 53, tel. 981/811-3653, 9 A.M.–2 P.M. and 4–8 P.M. Mon.–Fri., 9 A.M.–2 P.M. Sat., free) and the **Sala de Arte Domingo Pérez Piña** (Calle 12 at Calle 65, no tel., 9 A.M.–1 P.M. and 5–8 P.M. Mon.–Sat., free) are small galleries featuring changing works of art by regional artists.

Peek into the **Archivo General del Estado de Campeche** (Calle 12 between Calles 57 and 59, tel. 981/816-0939, 8 A.M.–3 P.M. and 6–8 P.M. Mon.–Fri., free), the state archives building, to see its latest art or historical exhibit. Displayed on the 1st floor, the shows are usually compiled by INAH or ICC, the national and state history and cultural institutes, and can be quite good.

Like the Centro Cultural Casa No. 6, the **Mansión Carvajal** (Calle 10 between 51 and 53, tel. 981/816-7419, 8 A.M.–2:30 P.M. Mon.–Fri., free) is an old mansion that has been restored to its original beauty. Built at the beginning of the 1800s to be the home of the wealthy Carvajal family, by the late 1900s it had been converted twice—once into a hotel, later into a dance hall. Today, it houses the offices of DIF (the family services branch of the state government). Open to the public, it is well worth a quick visit: Check out the Moorish-style architecture, art nouveau staircase with Carrera marble steps, iron balustrade, and the black-and-white tile floors.

The modern concrete and glass building near the waterfront with the colorful mosaic is the **Palacio de Gobierno** (Calle 8 between Calles 61 and 63). The strange concrete building next to it—the one that looks like a UFO—is the **Palacio Legislativo,** the state legislature building.

ENTERTAINMENT AND EVENTS
Weekends in the Central Plaza

Every weekend, the city streets around the central plaza are closed for pedestrians only, restaurants place their tables outdoors, food and trinket vendors set up stalls, and bingo games get going in front of the Cathedral. Both evenings, the city hosts cultural events—typically, a concert or other live music performances—and people fill the park benches to enjoy the show. The weekend is a time when locals come out to enjoy the city, to meet with friends, or to spend time with their family. It's a perfect opportunity for travelers to stroll around the plaza and to get a sense of how Campechanos enjoy their city.

Theater

Built in 1833 and restored in 1990, the **Teatro de la Cuidad Francisco Paula Toro** (Calle 12 between Calles 51 and 53, 981/811-3653, US$5–20) is said to be the first theater in Mexico. It hosts dance, dramatic, and musical performances throughout the year. Open only when there is a scheduled event, stop by or call to see if there is anything showing while you're in town.

The **Teatro Juan de la Cabada** (Av. 16 de Septiembre at Calle 53) is the city's modern theater space; it offers a wide range of dramatic, dance, and musical programming. Like the Teatro de la Cuidad, the box office only is open when there is a scheduled performance.

Cultural and Arts Centers

Facing the park, and occupying a restored colonial-era home, **Centro Cultural Casa No. 6** (Calle 57 between Calles 8 and 10, tel. 981/816-1782, 9 A.M.–9 P.M. daily, free) hosts various cultural events in its sunny courtyard, including *trova* concerts and art exhibitions. Even if nothing's going on, you can pop in to visit the center's artsy gift shop and bookstore, and grab a sandwich and coffee at the small café (US$1–4). The information desk at the entrance is usually friendly, but be alert for the occasional pushy tour vendor.

The **Instituto de Cultura de Campeche** (Campeche Culture Institute, Calle 12 between Calles 59 and 61) also organizes numerous arts and cultural events throughout the year; check out the bulletin boards at the entrance or go around the corner to its small administrative offices (Calle 61 between Calles 12 and 14, tel. 981/811-3636, www.institutodecultura.gob.mx, 9 A.M.–9 P.M. Mon.–Fri.) for additional information.

City and Gulf Tours

Trolley tours around the city center, historic neighborhoods, and to the outlying forts are offered by **Trambia de la Ciudad** (9 A.M.–1 P.M. and 5–8 P.M. daily, US$8). Tours are typically led in English and Spanish and last 45 minutes. Trolleys leave from the central plaza on weekdays and from the Plaza Patrimonio Mundial (Calle 8 between Calles 55 and 53) on weekends.

Fun for kids, the **Barco Pirata Lorencillo** (tel. 981/816-1990, departures at noon and 6 P.M. daily, US$10 adults, US$5 children) is a 90-minute boat ride along Campeche's coast with a pirate show as the main event. Drinks and snacks are sold aboard. Catch the boat at the fishing pier in the village of Lerma, eight kilometers (5 miles) south of town.

Dancing Fountains

A very mini Vegas-style **water fountain show** (Calle 8 between Calles 55 and 53, 6–10 P.M. daily, 20 minutes) is presented in the Plaza Patrimonio Mundial every night. Buy a *paleta* from a local vendor, scout out a spot on a park bench, and watch as the water fountains "dance" to classical beats and multicolored lights.

Festivals

The **Festival Histórico de Campeche** is a huge cultural festival when musicians, dance troupes, and artists come to perform or exhibit their work in and around at the city. Most of the events take place in the central plaza, including the kickoff concert. Lasting the entire month of December, festivalgoers enjoy the added bonus of checking out local handicrafts as well as tasting Campeche's culinary treats, both sold at street-side stands.

Since 1996, the **Festival de Jazz** has been held in Campeche city during the entire month of December. Attracting musicians from all over the world, a different guest country and Mexican state are the focus of the programming. Call or stop by the state tourism office for detailed information on the scheduled events and concerts.

Bars and Discotheques

Campeche's bars and clubs are open Thursday–Saturday; other days, there's really not much going on. Cover is rarely more than US$5, and often free. Longtime favorites for locals and travelers alike include **JAXX** (Av. Resurgimiento,

near El Faro del Moro restaurant) and, believe it or not, **Lafitte's,** (Av. Ruiz Cortinez No. 51) the pirate-theme restaurant at the Hotel del Mar that turns into a nightclub. You can also do some dancing at **La Jungla** (behind Plaza Campeche hotel), which has two dance floors—one for techno, the other for salsa and *cumbia*. For a more mellow scene, head to **Rum** (Av. Ruíz Cortines) a new hipster bar on the inland side of the malecón, six blocks from the center.

Cinema and Billiards

Just outside the city walls, **Cines Hollywood** (Av. Ah-Kin-Pech s/n, tel. 981/816-1500, US$4, US$2.50 on Wed.) runs U.S. and Mexican films on its six screens. Look for it near the convention center.

If you're looking to shoot some pool—or some virtual bad guys—the cavernous **Diversiones del Centro** (Calle 55 between Calles 10 and 12, 8 A.M.–2 A.M.) has a bunch of video games and a pool hall (US$2/hour). Popular with local teens, mostly guys.

SHOPPING

Shopping in Campeche is a limited sport. Most shops are geared toward local needs, so you'll find lots of paper stores, teen clothing boutiques, and shoe shops. Those stores that are geared toward tourists often are kitschy, offering a smattering of T-shirts, ashtrays, and key chains. Campeche is a fast-growing town though—by the time you read this, there may be much more to check out.

Artesanía

Tukulná (Calle 10 between Calles 59 and 61, tel. 981/816-9088, www.tukulna.com, 9 A.M.–8 P.M. Mon.–Sat.) is a state-run shop that offers top-notch items that it buys directly from local artisans. Inside, you'll find every type of Campechano handicraft—from handmade clothing to rocking chairs. In the back, there's also a tacky re-creation of a Maya home as well as a *jipi* bat cave.

Selling artsy, eclectic handicrafts from around the country, **Hecho en México** (Calle 59 between Calles 10 and 12, tel. 981/816-4405,

10 A.M.–9 P.M. Mon.–Sat.) is a great place to stop to pick up a unique gift to take home.

The **Bazar Artesanal** (Centro Comercial Ah Kim Pech, 10 A.M.–10 P.M. daily) is an upscale handicraft market across from the Malecón. Artisans sell their work directly to customers here; though most of the items are of high quality, many are surprisingly costly—up to three times the norm. Worth a stop, at least to window-shop.

Bookstores

Librería Levante (Calle 12 between Calles 59 and 61, tel. 981/816-5473, 9 A.M.–3 P.M. and 5 P.M.–8 P.M. Mon.–Sat.) Next to the Campeche Cultural Institute, this bookstore carries a few English-language titles, including guides, books on the Maya, and children's books, plus maps and *artesanía*. There's another bookstore a couple doors down, if you don't find what you're looking for.

SPORTS AND RECREATION
El Malecón

Campeche's *malecón* (promenade) stretches for three kilometers (two miles) along the Gulf of Mexico, and has been rescued from years of neglect with the addition of monuments and benches. Morning and evenings are especially popular, when you'll share the pathway with dog-walkers and inline skaters, and couples out for a brisk stroll. You can join the walkers or, better yet, rent a bike in town for a couple hours. The adjacent avenue can get busy, and the piers used by fishing boats a bit odorous, but it's still a fun outing.

ACCOMMODATIONS

If Campeche has a downside, it's the quality and value of its lodging. The city center is perfect for spacious colonial hotels and charming little B&Bs, like you find in Mérida and San Cristóbal de las Casas. Unfortunately, in Campeche a hotel's bright exterior too often gives way to an unimaginative and poorly maintained interior. The lower-mid-range options are decidedly unreliable—if you're not

crashing at a hostel, consider splurging a bit to avoid being disappointed.

Under US$25

Monkey Hostel (Parque Principal, Calle 57 and Calle 10, tel. 981/811-6605, www.hostal campeche.com, US$7–7.50 dorm, US$15.50–17.50 s/d) has a great location overlooking the central park and is a good place to meet other backpackers. Rooms here are barebones: the dorms are fairly spacious, while private rooms are tiny white cubes—get a room with a balcony if you can. All are reasonably clean, and share well-maintained common bathrooms. The large common area is unkempt, but benefits mightily from large windows and park views. There's even better air and views from the rooftop deck—the hostel's highlight. Includes continental breakfast, full kitchen, Internet, laundry, and bikes for rent.

Hostal del Pirata (Calle 59 between Calles 14 and 16, tel. 981/811-1757, piratehostel@hotmail.com, US$7 dorm, US$18.50 d with shared bath, US$21 d with private bath) isn't as centrally located, but the common areas—a shady courtyard with tables, a TV room, and a rooftop kitchen and dining area—are classier and more appealing. The dorms and rooms are so-so: men's and women's dorms have beds with individual lights, fans, and lockers, but there's only one toilet and shower for 12 beds. Private rooms with shared bathrooms have saloon-style doors, which some may find, well, not too private, but they're still better than the cramped and stuffy rooms with their own bathrooms. Cool and eclectic, El Pirata doesn't have the scene that the Monkey does, which is good or bad depending on your taste. Includes continental breakfast, Internet, laundry service, and bike rentals.

Hostal La Parroquia (Calle 55 No. 8, tel. 981/816-2530, www.hostalparroquia.com, US$10 dorm, US$20 s, US$30 d) Campeche's newest hostel occupies a 17th-century mansion, complete with high ceilings and two small sunny courtyards. Internet, Ping-Pong, board games, and bike rental are all available in the lobby. The private rooms are tiny with springy beds, but the dorms are comfy enough, with sturdy bunks and individual lockers; the Cathedral room is the biggest and best. Continental breakfast is served at the sister restaurant next door, one of Campeche's most reliable. The community kitchen is disappointing though—basically a microwave and hotplate—but the biggest bummer is shared bathrooms, which are clean but smell awful thanks to poor plumbing.

Hotel Colonial (Calle 14 No. 122, tel. 981/816-2230, US$17 s, US$22 d, US$30 d with a/c) offers the cheapest private room in town, and if you get one with an actual window and actual natural light, you're stoked. But there are only a handful of those, and the place is so popular, especially with European tour groups, that you're more likely to get a moist interior room. All are clean and have hot water (and exposed plumbing), a few have air-conditioning, and there's a pleasant common area. The owner-operators are quirky, but in a good way.

US$25-50

A colonial-style hotel, the ◖ **Maya Campeche Hotel** (Calle 57 between Calles 14 and 16, tel. 981/816-8053, toll-free Mex. tel. 800/561-8730, www.mayacampechehotel.com.mx, US$35 s with a/c, US$41 d with a/c) offers simple but charming rooms in the heart of the city. All have high ceilings, stenciled walls, and ironwork furnishings. The rooms are a little small and dark but the overall ambiance combined with quiet air-conditioning, flat-screen TVs, and spotless bathrooms make all the difference. Wireless Internet available in the lobby.

Hotel López (Calle 12 between Calles 61 and 63, tel. 981/816-3344, hotellopez campeche.com, US$39 s/d, extra person US$4) gets points for renovating its rooms, something few hotels in Campeche bother to do. The rooms are pretty sterile, yes, but artwork and arch doorways go away once the lights are out, while clean linens and firm beds last all night long. All units have hot water, cable, and mini-split air-conditioning; there's wireless Internet in the lobby, and free parking. If you're after comfort and value, this is a fine choice.

Occupying a two-story colonial building, **Hotel Regis** (Calle 12 between Calles 55 and 57, tel. 981/816-3175, hotelregis@prodigy.net .mx, US$25 s with a/c, US$29 d with a/c) has seven rooms that vary from big to huge, with high ceilings, black-and-white tile floors, one or two double beds, and mini-split air-conditioning. The bathrooms are tiny and could use a scrubbing but overall, it's a good value.

Hotel América (Calle 10 between Calles 59 and 61, tel. 981/816-4588, www.hotelamerica campeche.com, US$39 s, US$45 d) occupies a pleasant old three-story mansion. There are better hotels in this price range, but if you do end up here ask for a room on the 2nd floor, whose breezy corridor is more welcoming than the dark hallway a floor above. Rooms 117 and 118 look onto a quiet interior courtyard, while rooms 101–103 are large, with street views (but also noise). Continental breakfast is included.

US$50-100

Many travelers end up staying at a slightly fancier hotel since the mid-range options in Campeche aren't stellar.

Sir Francis Drake Hotel (Calle 12 between 63 and 65, tel. 981/811-5626 or 800/433-7253, www.hotelfrancisdrake.com, US$55 s with a/c, US$64 d with a/c, US$73–US$84.50 suite) is a cozy, classy hotel at the southeastern edge of the center. All 24 rooms and suites have comfortable beds, marble bathrooms, and attractive wood furnishings; the suites have extras like desks and sitting rooms. Ask for a room with a balcony for better light and a view of the cobblestone street. Some rooms have Internet, but all guests can use the hotel's small computer center for free. There's no elevator, and the restaurant is humdrum, but those are small drawbacks to an otherwise terrific value. Friendly service, parking.

◖ **Hotel Plaza Campeche** (Calle 10 between Calle 51 and Circuito Baluartes, tel. 981/811-9900, toll-free Mex. tel. 800/007-5292, www.hotelplazacampeche.com, US$97 s/d with a/c, US$107–236 suite) has two buildings a block apart—one inside the city walls, the other just outside of them. Be sure you reserve the one inside the walls as it is newer, quieter, and much smaller, making the service more personalized. Rooms themselves are somewhat sterile but have good beds, mini-split air-conditioning, and boast little details like bathtubs, flat-screen TVs, and key cards. The hotel also has a sparkling mosaic tile pool in its interior courtyard. Be sure to reserve your room by telephone, as rates are often better as compared to the website.

The **Hotel del Mar** (Av. Ruiz Cortinez 51, tel. 981/811-9191, www.hoteldelmar.com.mx, US$84 d with city view, US$120 d with ocean view) was Campeche's top hotel before the Puerta Campeche opened, and is still a good choice for business travelers or tourists looking for first-class accommodations without the luxury/boutique price tag. All rooms have comfortable beds and modern furnishings; wireless Internet is available on the executive floor, dial-up only in the rest. If the view is important to you, rooms facing the Gulf have small balconies and are worth the cost—ask for the end units, nos. 221 and 222.

Hotel Baluartes (Av. 16 de Septiembre at Av. Ruiz Cortinez, tel. 981/816-3911, toll-free Mex. tel. 800/667-1444, www.baluartes.com.mx, US$76 s with a/c, US$88 d with a/c, US$132–160 suite) is a high-rise hotel fronting the *malecón*. It has comfortable rooms with air-conditioning and cable TV; all were in the process of being remodeled when we passed through—updated rooms are sleek and elegant with quality linens and heavy furnishings. Ask for one of the slightly larger oceanfront rooms; the views are superb and they cost the same as those facing the parking lot. Wireless Internet is available in the lobby, and there's also a pool and decent restaurant on-site.

Over US$100

The **⟨ Hacienda Puerta Campeche** (Calle 59 at Calle 18, tel. 981/816-7508, www.thehaciendas.com, US$377 s/d with a/c, US$475–658 suite) is easily the best hotel in town. Several adjoining colonial houses were gutted and transformed into an intimate 15-room hotel. The guest rooms are luxurious with the deep beds, high ceilings, large marble bathrooms, and artful decorations found at all Starwood resorts. But the swimming pool is the hotel's most memorable feature: It weaves through several enclosed rooms of the original houses, complete with doorways and brightly painted walls. The garden-side restaurant also is one of the best in town.

Outside of Town

Located 20 minutes from Campeche City on the road to Edzná, **Hacienda Uayamón** (Carretera a Edzná Km. 20, tel. 981/829-7527, www.thehaciendas.com, US$500 s/d with a/c, US$600 suite) is a sister hotel of Hacienda Puerta Campeche. The hacienda was built in 1700 and has 12 freestanding units, each with deluxe furnishing and amenities, including thick beds, large bathrooms, high ceilings, and private terrace. The grounds are gorgeous, and several unused buildings have been left in a state of semi-disrepair to create a more authentic ambience. The pool is ensconced within the two remaining walls of the once-elegant ballroom; the dining room's large picture window looks out over former henequen fields. The restaurant (7 A.M.–10 P.M. daily, US$10–30) specializes in seafood. Reservations required for non-guests.

FOOD

Campeche has a smattering of cozy cafés and classy Mexican and international restaurants, and more and more are opening as the city awakens to a more modern tourist market, both national and foreign.

Seafood

Considered one of the best eateries in town, **La Pigua** (Av. Miguel Alemán No. 179-A, tel. 981/811-3365, 1 P.M.–5:30 P.M. & 7:30–11 P.M. daily, US$7–15) is an upscale restaurant and popular lunchtime stop for professionals and couples. The food is pricey but excellent—coconut shrimp with apple chutney is the specialty—and the service is first-rate. Recent renovations did wonders for the A-frame dining area, which went from being dark and downcast to bright and stylish, despite a narrow layout and high stone walls on either side.

The (**Marganzo** (Calle 8 between Calles 57 and 59, tel. 981/811-3898, 7 A.M.–11 P.M. daily, US$4–15) screams tourist-trap—the male staff sport pirate outfits—but it can't be beat for tasty food, reasonable prices, and friendly service. Seafood is the specialty—*pampano relleno de mariscos* (white fish filled with seafood) is a favorite among regulars—but the chicken *pibil* and other meat dishes do not disappoint. Servings are large, and come with a table-full of appetizers.

Steps from the Monumento al Resurgimiento and just below Fuerte de San Miguel, **El Faro del Moro** (Av. Resurgimiento No. 120, tel. 981/816-1990, noon–7 P.M. daily) doesn't look like much from the outside but gets rave reviews from people who visit Campeche frequently. Tables are on a patio overlooking the Gulf—strangely enough, it's one of the few places in this seaside town where you can have a meal right on the water. Tortillas filled with cheese and shrimp are one of several favorites.

Mexican and Campechano

Open 24 hours a day, the diner-style (**La Parroquia** (Calle 55 between 10 and 12, tel. 981/816-2530, US$2.50–10) is always busy. You'll find good Campechano dishes, a handful of traditional Mexican meals, and a T.V. tuned to soap operas or a soccer game. The daily special (US$4.75) includes a main dish, beans and rice, dessert, and a large drink.

For home cooking, cafeteria style, check out **Chef Color** (Calle 12 at Calle 55, tel. 981/811-4455, 12:30–5:30 P.M. Mon.–Sat., US$2–3). A standard meal includes rice, beans, fried plantains, tortillas, and a choice of entrée. Good, cheap eats in the heart of town.

(**Takitos** (Av Ruíz Cortines, tel. 044-981/126-1849, 8 A.M.–2 P.M. Tues.–Thurs., until 4 P.M. Fri.–Sun., and 6 P.M.–2 A.M. daily except Mon., US$3–7) Yes, it's a chain, but the laid-back setting and surprisingly tasty food make this a go-to pit-stop if you're walking or biking along the malecón. Among the options here are motuleños for breakfast, ham baguette for lunch, and tacos of all sorts for dinner. The open-air dining area looks across the road to the Gulf, and service is friendly.

Garibaldi (Calle 8 at Calle 61, 11 A.M.–1 A.M. daily, US$4–10) has the mixed blessing of occupying the same space as the Miramar restaurant, a old-time Campeche institution that closed in 2006, once did. Tacos are the specialty here, including less-likely fillings like rib eye and *cochinita pibil*, accompanied by frequent beer and drink specials. The dining area is brighter and cleaner than the Miramar ever was, though it's hard to eat here without a twinge of nostalgia.

Other Specialties

The restaurant at the Hacienda Puerta Campeche, (**La Guardia** (Calle 59 at Calle 18, tel. 981/816-7508, 7 A.M.–11 P.M. daily, US$10–25) is Campeche's most upscale restaurant. Dark wood tables are set up in an attractive dining area that looks onto a lush garden courtyard. Gourmet regional cuisine—seafood figures prominently—is the focus of the menu although several international specialties are offered as well. Service is impeccable.

Don't be dissuaded by the lonely looking entrance—the artsy bohemian (**Café Tulum** (Calle 59 near Calle 10, no tel., 8 A.M.–9 P.M. Mon.–Sat., US$2.50–4) is a great little place to enjoy a meal. Light fare, smoothies, and coffee drinks are served in a bright interior courtyard. Take in the modern paintings and poster art while you linger over your meal. Before you leave, check out the flyers for cultural events going on around town.

Nutrivida (Calle 12 between Calles 57 and 59, 8 A.M.–2 P.M. and 5:30–8:30 P.M. Mon.–Fri., 8 A.M.–2 P.M. Sat., US$1.50–3) is a popular joint offering great soy-based meals, lots of veggie burgers, yogurt, and fruit dishes. Plans were afoot to convert this hole-in-the-wall into a full-fledged restaurant—prices may increase, but the owner says it'll stay vegetarian.

Sweets

La Nueva España Panadería y Pastelería (Calle 59 at Calle 10, 6:30 A.M.–9:30 P.M. daily) offers great egg breads and sweet breads.

Be there 11 A.M., 1 P.M., or 4 P.M. to get the goods hot and fresh.

Just north of the central plaza, **La Gran Michoacán** (Calle 8 between 53 and 55, 7:30 A.M.–10 P.M. daily, US$0.60–2.50), offers a good variety of refreshing treats—homemade popsicles, ice cream, and fruit juices.

Groceries

For the freshest fruits and vegetables, check out the *mercado principal* (Circuito Baluartes Este at Calle 57), which is open daily 5 A.M.–4 P.M.

A large supermarket, **Super San Francisco** (Calle 51 between Av. Adolfo Ruiz Cortínez and Av. Pedro Sainz de Baranda, 7 A.M.–10 P.M. daily) sells the usual foods and household items. It also has a small pharmacy just inside its doors.

INFORMATION
Tourist Information

Behind the Palacio Legislativo is the **state tourist office** (Plaza Moch-Couoh, Av. Ruiz Cortines between Calles 63 and 65, tel. 981/811-9229, www.campechetravel.com, 8 A.M.–9 P.M. Mon.–Fri., 9 A.M.–8 P.M. Sat.–Sun.). The knowledgeable staff shares detailed information about local and regional sites. The office also provides guides that lead private tours of the city (US$55, 4 hours). Ask about prices for personalized statewide trips. All tours must be booked in advance, preferably with one week's notice. English is spoken.

The **municipal tourist office** (central plaza, Calle 55 between Calles 8 and 10, tel. 981/811-3989, 9 A.M.–9 P.M. daily) has plenty of maps and brochures that often prove more helpful than the staffers.

Newspapers

The three main newspapers covering Campeche are *Tribuna de Campeche, Novedades Campeche,* and *El Sur de Campeche,* available at most newsstands in the capital and statewide.

Hospitals

Campeche City's main hospital is the **Hospital Dr. Manuel Campos** (Calle 49 at Calle 14, tel. 981/816-2409 or 816-1709, 24 hours daily).

Pharmacies

The pharmacy at **Hospital Dr. Manuel Campos** (Calle 49 at Calle 14, tel. 981/816-2409) is open 24 hours but you may get better prices at the bustling **Farmacia Similares** (Circuito Baluartes at Calle 55, tel. 981/816-3316, 8 A.M.–9 P.M. Mon.–Sat.,8 A.M.–8 P.M. Sun.).

In the city center, try **Farmacia Canto** (Calle 10 and Calle 59; 7 A.M.–10 P.M. Mon.–Sat., 8 A.M.–8 P.M. Sun.).

Police

You can reach the police by dialing 060 or 066 from any public phone.

SERVICES
Money

There are plenty of banks in the city center, including **Banorte** (Calle 57 at Calle 10, 9 A.M.–6 P.M. Mon.–Fri., currency exchange 9 A.M.–4 P.M. only), which is on the central plaza and has one ATM, and **HSBC** (Calle 10 between Calles 53 and 55, 8 A.M.–7 P.M. Mon.–Sat.), which has two ATMs.

Internet and Telephone

The best Internet place in town is **Internet Facil** (Calle 49 between Calles 14 and 16, 9 A.M.–11 P.M. daily, US$0.85/hr, US$1–2 CD-burning). Connections are fast, plus there's air-conditioning.

Ciber & Chat (Calle 59 at Calle 12, 9 A.M.–10 P.M. Mon.–Sat.) offers decent Internet connections for US$1.25 per hour. CD-burning costs US$1.75.

The cheapest place to make a phone call is on a public pay phone. If you prefer a call center, **Compufast** (Calle 10 between 65 and Circuito Baluartes, 8 A.M.–9 P.M. Mon.–Fri., 9 A.M.–2 P.M. Sat.) offers pricey telephone service to the United States and Canada (US$0.90/minute) as well as to the rest of the world (US$1/minute). Domestic calls cost US$0.35 per minute.

Post Office

The post office (Av. 16 de Septiembre at Calle 53, 8:30 A.M.–3:30 P.M. Mon.–Fri., 9 A.M.–1 P.M. Sat.) is in the Palacio Federal.

Immigration

The immigration office (Av. 16 de Septiembre at Calle 53, 1st Fl., tel. 981/816-0369, 9 A.M.–1:30 P.M. Mon.–Fri.) is located in the same building as the post office.

Travel Agencies and Tour Operators

Xtampak Tours (Calle 57 between Calles 10 and 12, tel. 981/811-6473, www.xtampak.com, 8:30 A.M.–3 P.M. and 5 P.M.–9 P.M., Mon.–Sat.) is the most-recommended agency in the center, and its flyers are ubiquitous in hotels and Internet café around town. It offers a pleasant trip to Edzná (US$14 pp transportation only, US$23pp including guide and admission, minimum two people) that takes about four hours, and a 14-hour marathon journey to Calakmul and Balamkú (US$51 pp transport only, US$70 pp with guide and admissions) that frankly makes no sense: despite leaving at the crack of dawn and returning after dark, you only get three hours at Calakmul and 45 minutes at Balamkú, too brief for either site. The agency also offers a two-day version that includes Becán, Chicanná, and Xpujil, but you're really better off renting a car and doing the trip on your own.

Part of a national chain, **Intermar Campeche** (Hotel Baluartes, Av. 16 de Septiembre between Calles 59 and 61, tel. 981/816-9006, 9 A.M.–9 P.M. Mon.–Fri., 9 A.M.–4 P.M. Sat., 10 A.M.–2 P.M. Sun.) arranges city and regional tours but specializes in national and international travel. Guests at select hotels receive discounts on tours; ask the concierge to see if yours is one of them.

Launderette

Lavandería Lava Klin (Calle 49 between Calles 14 and 16, 8 A.M.–6 P.M. Mon.–Fri., 8 A.M.–4 P.M. Sat., US$1.15 per 1 kg/2.2lbs) offers same-day service if you drop off your laundry first thing in the morning.

GETTING THERE

Campeche city is on the Gulf Coast, 190 kilometers (118 miles) southwest of Mérida, and is a natural stopover on your way to (or from) the states of Chiapas or Tabasco.

Air

Campeche's tiny airport, **Aeropuerto Internacional de Campeche Alberto Acuña Ongay** (CPE, Carr. Campeche-Chiná, tel. 981/816-5678) lies about two kilometers (1.25 miles) northeast of the city. There are no convenient bus routes to or from the airport. To get there, a taxi costs about US$8 and takes about 15 minutes; from the airport, taxis meet most flights and charge a bit more.

Aeroméxico (airport tel. 981/816-3109, toll-free Mex. tel. 800/021-4010, www.aeromexico.com) is the only airline regularly serving Campeche City.

Bus

Campeche has two bus terminals—the first-class ADO station, known as *la terminal nueva* (the new terminal) and the second-class station, known as *la terminal antigua* (the old terminal). There's also a stop for Autobuses Ejidales, which has service to Edzná archaeological site.

Car

Two good highways link Campeche and Mérida. Highway 180 is known as the *vía corta* (the short route) and goes north from Campeche through Hecelchakán, Bécal, and Umán, while Highway 261 is known as *vía larga* (the long route) because it veers east through Hopelchen and then north through Santa Elena and the Puuc region. Driving time is about the same (2–2.5 hours) their monikers notwithstanding. If you're driving to Uxmal and the Puuc region (and aren't planning to stop at Edzná), take Highway 180 to Hecelchacán and cut across to Highway 261. With fewer towns to pass through, you'll save about 45 minutes.

From Campeche south to Champotón, you can take Highway 180-Cuota (toll road) or

CAMPECHE BUS SCHEDULES

Campeche's **FIRST-CLASS BUS STATION** (tel. 981/811-9910, toll-free Mex. tel. 800/702-8000) is located on Avenida Central at Avenida Casa de Justicia, a bit too far to walk with bags, but just five minutes in a taxi. Many buses here are *de paso* (mid-route) which means they have limited space and may depart up to 15 minutes early or late. Tickets on *de paso* buses can only be booked same-day, so get to the terminal a half-hour early to be sure to snag a seat.

DESTINATION	PRICE	DURATION	SCHEDULE
Cancún	US$29	7 hrs	five departures 7:35 A.M.-11:55 P.M.
Chetumal	US$22	7 hrs	noon
Mérida	US$10-12	2.5 hrs	every 30-60 min. 1:35 A.M.-11:55 P.M.
Mexico City	US$80-95	18 hrs	seven departures 12:30 P.M.-11:40 P.M.
Palenque	US$19-20	6 hrs	12:30 A.M.*, 2 A.M.*, 11 A.M.*, 9:45 P.M.
San Cristóbal (Chiapas)	US$32-37	10-11 hrs	9:40 P.M. and 11:45 P.M.*
Villahermosa*	US$24-28	6 hrs	ten departures 9:40 A.M.-2:20 A.M.
Xpujil	US$16	4 hrs	noon

Highway 180-Libre (free road). The former is a wide, fast highway and costs US$4.75; the latter goes nearer the ocean (but not always right alongside it) and passes through several small towns with their ubiquitous speed bumps. At Champotón, you can continue on Highway 180 to Ciudad del Carmen and on to Tabasco state, or take Highway 261 farther south to Escárcega, where you turn right for Palenque and the highlands of Chiapas or left for Calakmul and eventually the Caribbean coast.

GETTING AROUND

Campeche's city center is small and very easy to navigate on foot, but unless you have a bike or rental car, you will need a taxi or local bus to get to and from the bus terminals, airport, and some of the outlying sights.

Bus

To get to the first-class bus station, take an "S.E.P./Av. Central" bus or minivan (US$0.30, every 15 minutes) from in front of the market on Calle 18 at Calle 53; the trip takes about 20 minutes. To get to the Fuerte de San Miguel and the Museo de Cultura Maya, take a "Lerma/Playa Bonita" bus (US$0.30, every 30 minutes) from Calle 55 (on the market side) or from the front of the post office on Avenida 16 de Septiembre (also known as Circuito Baluartes) at Calle 53; ask

Campeche's **SECOND-CLASS BUS STATION** (Av. Gobernadores at Calle Chile, tel. 981/816-3445) is several long noisy blocks beyond the city walls.

DESTINATION	PRICE	DURATION	SCHEDULE
Dzibalchén	US$5.25	3 hrs	hourly 6:45 A.M.–6:30 P.M.
Hopelchén	US$3.75	1.5 hrs	hourly 6 A.M.–5 P.M.
Santa Elena	US$7	3 hrs	6 A.M., 9:15 A.M., noon, 2:30 P.M., and 5 P.M.
Uxmal ruins	US$7.25	3.5 hrs	Use Santa Elena bus
Xpujil	US$12	6 hrs	5:15 A.M., 8:15 A.M., 6:30 P.M., and 10 P.M.

AUTOBUSES EJIDALES (Av. República, near the market) operates buses along the road to Edzná ruins. The last returning bus passes Edzná around 4 P.M.

Edzná ruins	US$2	60–90 min.	7 A.M., 11 A.M., noon, 1 P.M., 2:15 P.M., and 3 P.M.

*Deluxe service available on some departures.

the driver to let you off about four kilometers (2.5 miles) south of town, at *la subida San Miguel* (the climb to San Miguel). From there, it's a tough half-kilometer (one-third mile) climb to the fort.

Taxi

Cabs are relatively easy to flag down around town, and there are taxi stands next to the cathedral, near the market, and in front of both bus terminals. Your hotel also should be able to call one for you; if not, try **Radio Taxi Gaviotas** (981/815-3036) or **Frente Único de Trabajadores del Volante** (981/813-1113). Fares around town are US$2–2.50; a cab to the airport will run about US$8. If you call a cab or take one after 11 P.M., fares are raised by about US$1. Be sure to confirm the price before getting in.

Car Rental

Payless Car Rental (Hotel del Paseo, Calle 10 no. 252, tel. 981/816-4214, www.payless carrental.com, 9 A.M.–9 P.M. Mon.–Sat., 9 A.M.–2 P.M. Sun.) and **Maya Car Rental** (Hotel del Mar, Av. Ruiz Cortinez No. 51, tel. 981/816-0670, viasetur@yahoo.com.mx, 9 A.M.–9 P.M. Mon.–Sat., 9 A.M.–2 P.M. Sun.) cater to business travelers and have compact cars with air-conditioning starting at around US$60 a day.

THE STATE OF CAMPECHE

Bicycle Rental

Bikes can be a fun way to see the *malecón* and the outlying sights. Rent some wheels at **Monkey Hostel** (US$2 for two hours, US$0.50 additional hour) or at **Hotel del Mar** (US$2.50/hr or US$10/day). It's worth asking about a helmet, but don't count on getting one.

Archaeological Zones near Campeche City

☪ EDZNÁ ARCHAEOLOGICAL ZONE

The Edzná ruins (8 A.M.–5 P.M. daily, US$3) are the nearest major archaeological site from Campeche city, and make for an excellent day trip.

History

Nestled in a fertile valley between low mountains, the area is thought to have been settled by small farmers as early as 600 B.C., and its earliest lasting structures built around 300 B.C. It eventually grew into a large city and regional power, supporting a population in the tens of thousands. Edzná's regional influence is illustrated by the variety of architectural styles and influences found there, including Petén, Chenes and Río Bec styles, as well as some of the earliest-known examples of the Puuc architecture. Edzná also is notable for its network of water canals, measuring 22 kilometers (14 miles) in all, which helped control flooding, irrigate fields, and drain fields. Archaeologists have also found some 70 *chultunes* (underground reservoirs) used to collect and store water for Edzná's burgeoning population. Several scenes in Mel Gibson's 2006 release *Apocalypto* were filmed at Edzná, the actual temples serving as backdrop for models built by the crew.

Edzná entered its peak period around A.D.

Edzná's most imposing structure is the 31-meter (102-foot) Temple of Five Stories.

© LIZA PRADO

600, and prospered until around A.D. 900, when it went into a rapid decline, as did many other Maya cities at that time. But Edzná managed to avoid total collapse—probably thanks to its consistently rich agricultural resources—and remained an important population center as late as A.D. 1450, when it was finally abandoned. Early researchers postulated Edzná meant "House of Grimaces" and was a reference to a series of masks that decorated the comb of the Temple of Five Stories. Now archaeologists believe the name means "Home of the Itzáes," a reference to settlers who emigrated from central Mexico well after the Maya

collapse of the 9th and 10th centuries, and reoccupied many of the fallen cities. If so, the city's original name has been lost to history.

Gran Plaza

Coming from the entrance, a path deposits you on the northwest corner of the a huge grassy courtyard known as the **Gran Plaza.** To your left is the **Platform of the Knives,** on top of which are the much-decayed remains of several fine residences, most likely used by Edzná's elite. The platform's name comes from a small offering of flint knives found by archaeologists in one of the structures. To your right is

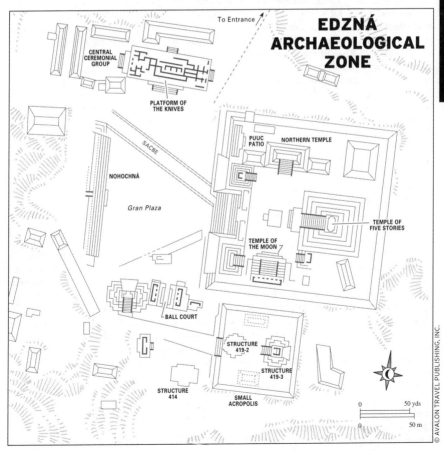

EDZNÁ ARCHAEOLOGICAL ZONE

CENTRAL CEREMONIAL GROUP

PLATFORM OF THE KNIVES

To Entrance

SACBE

NOHOCHNÁ

Gran Plaza

PUUC PATIO

NORTHERN TEMPLE

TEMPLE OF FIVE STORIES

TEMPLE OF THE MOON

BALL COURT

STRUCTURE 419-2

STRUCTURE 419-3

STRUCTURE 414

SMALL ACROPOLIS

0   50 yds

0   50 m

© AVALON TRAVEL PUBLISHING, INC.

THE STATE OF CAMPECHE

the narrow end of another platform, this one called **Nohoch-Ná** (Big House) and extending an impressive 125 meters (410 feet) along the Gran Plaza's western edge. Atop are bases for what were once four long halls, probably used for administrative functions like collecting tributes or mediating conflicts. High stairs run the entire length and most likely doubled as bleachers for events and ceremonies held in the Gran Plaza itself.

Gran Acropolis

On the east side of the Gran Plaza, a wide bank of stairs lead up to the Gran Acropolis, an artificial platform 160 meters (539 feet) wide and 7.5 meters (25 feet) high. It was the center of ceremonial life at Edzná, and contains the site's most significant structure, the 31-meter (102-foot) **Temple of Five Stories.** Visible above the vegetation from a great distance, the imposing pyramid can be climbed, with some difficulty, by way of the crumbling front stairway. From the top is a view of Edzná's arid but verdant surroundings; some of the brush-covered mounds are actually unexcavated structures. The temple underwent at least five distinct construction periods, each one adding to the last. The temple's first four levels were probably used by priests as living quarters; a shrine and altar are on the highest level, with a roof comb (a decorative element built to make the pyramid appear even higher) rising over that. At one time, this comb was covered with ornate stucco masks and carvings, and the rest of the building's stones were coated with smooth stucco and painted brilliant colors.

Flanking the Temple of Five Stories on the Gran Acropolis are several smaller structures, including the Northwest Temple, Southwest Temple, and the House of the Moon, with its steep stairs leading to vestiges of rooms on the top platform. Like the chambers in the main temple, rooms in and around the smaller structures also probably served as residences for priests.

Ball Court

Dividing the two areas is the Ball Court with a north–south pitch, and ramps and scoring rings (barely visible here) facing each other on the east and west sides. This orientation, common in Maya ball courts, emphasized the religious significance attached to the game, casting it as sunrise versus sunset, light versus dark, good versus evil. Royalty would have likely watched the game from rooms on top of the two ramps, while commoners would have crowded around the ends, if they were allowed to watch at all.

Small Acropolis

South of the Gran Plaza is the Small Acropolis, which includes some of Edzná's oldest structures, but also some of its newest. Archaeologists believe the Small Acropolis served as the ceremonial center until the Classic era, when it was overshadowed by the building of the Gran Acropolis and the Temple of Five Stories. Centuries later, after Edzná's sudden collapse and slow recovery, its new residents once again began construction projects in this area of the city. The **Temple of the Relief Stairways,** built in the Late-Classic or Early Postclassic era, is the largest such structure. It's name comes from the curious use of *stelae* (carved monoliths) left over from Edzná's glory days to build the new temple's staircase; this may have been a deliberate insult to the fallen kings, but a simpler explanation is that the newcomers were illiterate…and evidently short on stones.

At the south edge of the Small Acropolis, the **Temple of the Masks** contains Edzná's best-preserved stucco decorations. The carved stone masks at the temple's east and west ends represent the sun god's face in its dawn (young) and dusk (old) incarnations, respectively. The faces have scarifications on the cheeks, large ear ornaments, and teeth filed to a point—all characteristics of the Maya nobility. Traces of the original red paint remain.

Tours

Agencies in Campeche offer van service to Edzná, with or without a guide, which can be convenient if your time is short or you don't want to risk missing the bus home.

Getting There

If you're driving from Campeche, take Highway 180 east to Chencoyil, then go east on Highway 261 to Cayal, where you turn right and continue to the Edzná site. The 60-kilometer (37.3-mile) drive takes about one hour. Second-class service is available from Campeche. Ask the driver to drop you at the *desvío Edzná* (turnoff to Edzná); it's about 200 meters (656 feet) from there to the entrance. The last bus back to Campeche passes the turnoff at 3 or 4 P.M., but double-check with the driver on your way there.

SANTA ROSA DE XTAMPÁK ARCHAEOLOGICAL ZONE

Like many Maya cities in the Yucatán Peninsula, Santa Rosa Xtampák (8 A.M.–5 P.M. daily, US$2.50) reached its heyday around A.D. 600–850, and archaeologists believe that this old city was once the heart of the Chenes Empire. It had more than 60 *choltunes* (underground water reservoirs) suggesting a population of more than 10,000 people. It's main structure, the **Palacio** (Palace), is one of the most architecturally complex buildings in the Maya world, with three floors, 11 staircases, and dozens of rooms. The site has scores of structures, though only a half-dozen or so have been extricated from the thick trees and brush. Opposite the palace is a residential structure with a beautiful **monster-mouth entrance,** a classic feature of Chenes sites. Farther down the path, the huge **Cuartel** hulks, in semi-collapse, amid the trees.

John Stephens visited Xtampák in the mid-1800s, but major excavation didn't begin until the mid-1990s, and continues today. For that reason, much of the Palace is off-limits, as are other structures, but if you're there when workers are present, it's offers a unique opportunity to see the difficult and dirty process of real-life archaeology in action.

Getting There

Now for the bad news: Santa Rosa Xtampák lies 45 kilometers (28 miles) down a road that is practically more pothole than pavement. Count on 90 minutes each way, and that's just from the highway. If this is a stopover between Campeche and Mérida—or even Santa Elena or Ticul—start early and count on a long day; in fact, casual ruin-hoppers may not find the trip a good use of their time. Driving from Campeche, take Highway 261 past Hopelchén to a marked turnoff just north of town.

ISLA JAINA

About 96 kilometers (58 miles) north of Campeche city, the swampy offshore island of Jaina holds the largest-known Maya burial ground on the Yucatán Peninsula; more than 1,000 interments have been found inside the two imposing pyramids on the island: **Zacpol** and **Sayasol.** According to the archaeologist Sylvanus Morley, who discovered the impressive site in 1943, Jaina was used by the Maya elite—probably Puuc nobility—beginning in A.D. 652. Bodies were carried in long, colorful processions to this island and were interred

© LIZA PRADO

Excavation and rebuilding are ongoing at most archaeological sites; Santa Rosa de Xtampák is no exception.

THE STATE OF CAMPECHE

in burial jars in crouched positions, their skin often stained red—a symbol of eternal life—and bodies wrapped in either a straw mat or white cloth. Some were found with a jade stone in their mouths. Plates with food, jewelry, weapons, tools, and other precious items were placed on the heads of the dead to accompany them to the afterlife. Small figurines (4–10 inches tall) also were buried, resting on the deceased's folded arms. These finely crafted ceramic sculptures now are considered masterpieces of Mesoamerican art. They portray the buried in ritual costumes, like those of warriors and ball players, and are frozen in ritual positions, including as captives being tortured. These tiny sculptures also often doubled as rattles, with clay balls rolling around the hollow interiors. Interestingly, to build the pyramids and the other ceremonial structures on the island, the Mayas raised the low elevation of the island by building platforms made of *sascab* (limestone material) brought from the mainland in canoes. This material covered the brittle coral of the island.

Visiting the Island

Isla Jaina is not officially open to the public, but the National Institute of Anthropology and History (INAH) can issue special permission to those interested in visiting. Call or apply in person at INAH's Campeche office (Calle 59 between Calles 14 and 16; tel. 981/816-9111, 8 A.M.–5 P.M. Mon.–Fri.), which can process the paperwork in a single day, if you're lucky. The island is usually reached by boat, though there is a reportedly rickety bridge that allows vehicle access; ask at INAH or the Campeche **state tourist office** (Plaza Moch-Couoh, Av. Ruiz Cortines between Calles 63 and 65, tel. 981/811-9229, www.campechetravel.com, 8 A.M.–9 P.M. Mon.–Fri., 9 A.M.–8 P.M. Sat.–Sun.) for assistance in securing transportation and a knowledgeable guide.

HECELCHAKÁN

About 60 kilometers (37 miles) north of Campeche on Highway 180 toward Mérida, the small town of Hecelchakán has some fine sculptures and Jaina burial art at the **Museo Arqueológico del Camino Real.** The hours are supposedly 10 A.M.–1 P.M. and 4–7 P.M. Tuesday–Saturday, and 4–7 P.M. Sunday, but the place never seems to be open. Fortunately, a large part of the collection is displayed in a small garden along the street and is perfectly visible through the fence.

Río Bec Region

Campeche's Río Bec region is located in the southern part of the state, cut lengthwise by Highway 186. It's flanked by the tiny towns of Xpujil and Escárcega and filled with the remarkable—and remarkably untouristed—Río Bec archaeological sites. The earliest occupation of the Río Bec area occurred between 1000 and 300 B.C., though the height of construction was much later, between A.D. 550 and 830. At the end of the 9th century, however, Maya cities across the region suddenly collapsed, and their populations dispersed. By the time of the Spanish conquest, the once-glorious cities were almost completely abandoned. The Río Bec sites were rediscovered early in the 20th century by chicle tappers and are still being explored and excavated today. Indeed, this area has been the source of many of the most noteworthy archaeological discoveries of the last decades.

Today, you'll find the massive Calakmul ruins, the mother of Río Bec sites, and possibly the Maya world. It boasts the largest Maya pyramid, the most number of stelae of any Maya ruin, and possibly the greatest number of total structures (they are still being mapped and counted). If that weren't enough reason to visit, Calakmul is located deep in a nature reserve, and it's common to spot monkeys and tropical birds in the thick tree cover.

Farther along Highway 186, there are several smaller sites, and, while lacking the sheer size and scale of Calakmul, are no less compelling. Balamkú is near the turnoff to Calakmul; Chicanná, Becán, and Xpujil are closer to the village of Xpujil (the only town of any size in the area); and El Hormiguero is down a rough dirt road. Río Bec archaeological site is currently off-limits to independent visitors, but tours can be arranged.

Most share the distinctive Río Bec architectural style, with its meticulous stonework and high steeple-like towers. There's no doubt that this area is the next Puuc Route, but for now you can have stunning sites practically to yourself.

◖ CALAKMUL ARCHAEOLOGICAL ZONE AND RESERVE

An UNESCO World Heritage Site, Calakmul ruins (8 A.M.–5 P.M. daily, US$3) may be the remains of the largest city-state in Maya history, home to as many as 60,000 people—and thousands more under its sphere of influence—and the seat of immense military, cultural, and economic power. Calakmul boasts the largest Maya pyramid yet discovered, looming nearly 60 meters (200 feet) above the forest floor. A whopping 6,750 structures have been mapped and the thousands more remain covered in thick brush and forest. Nine jade funeral masks and some 120 stelae have been found here, more than at any other Maya site. Another measure of Calakmul's influence can be found in the stelae of other Maya cities, in which Calakmul appears more often than any other.

History

Calakmul was originally called Kaan (Kingdom of the Serpent Head). The Maya name Calakmul (Two Adjacent Mounds) was coined by a Maya-speaking botanist and explorer, who spotted the site's two most prominent pyramids from an airplane while surveying for chicle in 1931. However, the site went unexplored for over 50 years, even as archaeologists discovered numerous references in the

THE STATE OF CAMPECHE

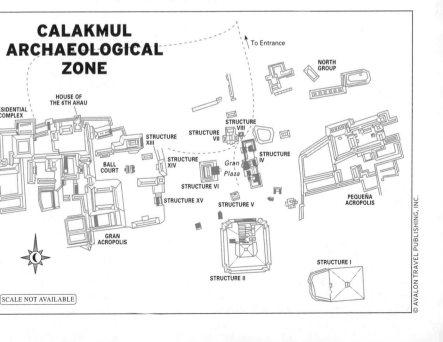

© AVALON TRAVEL PUBLISHING, INC.

TROPICAL MONKEYS

© LIZA PRADO

Arrive early or leave late to have the best chances of hearing – and seeing – howler monkeys in Calakmul.

The jungles of Mexico are home to three species of monkeys: spider, howler, and black howler. Intelligent and endearing, these creatures are prime targets for the pet trade. They have been so hunted, in fact, that today all three are in danger of extinction. Experts estimate that for every monkey sold, three die during transportation and distribution. In an effort to protect these creatures, the Mexican government has prohibited their capture or trade. As you wander through the ruins of Calakmul or Cobá, keep your ears perked and your eyes peeled. You're sure to see – or, at least, hear – a few tropical monkeys. A tip: Spider and howler monkeys are most active at sunrise and sundown; if possible, consider waking early or staying late to increase your chances of spotting a few. Other places to see these monkeys are the Punta Laguna reserve and Yaxchilán archaeological site.

inscriptions of Palenque, Tikal, and other cities to a powerful but as-yet-unknown kingdom. The first major excavation of Calakmul began in 1985, and the importance of the long-lost city quickly emerged.

Much remains unknown about Calakmul, however. It's clear that the city was enormous, with more than 6,000 structures spread over 70 square kilometers (27 square miles). Around 60,000 people lived here at the city's peak, possibly the largest Maya city ever. It was also a very old city, first settled in the 6th century B.C., with many of its major structures erected by A.D. 250. The size of Calakmul's structures is attributable, in part, to the Maya custom of adding new temples and layers over and atop existing structures to mark significant dates or political changes. Over the centuries, they added up to create some of the Maya world's largest pyramids.

Calakmul emerged as a major power in the Classic era; the greatest number of stelae found here are dated between A.D. 431 and 790. The city used its military and economic power to forge many strategic alliances (usually skewed to Calakmul's advantage), and waged fierce battle with those kingdoms with whom it couldn't come to terms. Calakmul attacked Palenque in A.D. 599 and 611, and then Tikal in 657, under the leadership of king "Yukom the Great." That ruler's son, known as Jaguar Paw, attacked Tikal again in 695, but was defeated, and his capture is glorified in inscriptions at Tikal. After that ignominious loss, Calakmul went into steady decline, a precursor to the widespread collapse of Classic Maya cities over the next two centuries.

Visiting the Ruins

Calakmul is deep in the Calakmul Biosphere Reserve, a dense protected forest teeming with animal life. Look for howler and spider monkeys, toucans, parrots, and other assorted birds and rodents as you wander the site, as well as on the winding 60-kilometer (37-mile) road from the highway to the entrance. The reserve is home to five of Mexico's six wildcat species, including jaguars and pumas, and every so often visitors are treated to a glimpse of one.

Everyone will tell you that in order to see wildlife, you need to visit Calakmul early in the morning. But think about it: even if you leave Xpujil at 5 A.M.—ouch—you don't get into the core of the reserve until 6:30 A.M., well past sunrise. (And how many creatures will you spot from your car, anyway?) Worse, you're dog-tired for the actual ruins, which are huge. We recommend you wake up at a reasonable hour, have a good breakfast, visit Balamkú on your way in (you'll be too tired on your way out), and get to Calakmul with enough time to be finishing up around 4 or 5 P.M. That's the time birds and monkeys return from feeding to hang out in the trees near the ruins, and you're liable to see just as many as in the morning. The exception is the big cats, which, yes, are most active just before dawn. Then again, we spotted a puma (our one-and-only) trot-

ting down the road at 5 P.M.! The fact is, spotting animals is mostly a matter of luck. Even if you don't see many (or any at all), the jungle is impressive, especially viewed from atop one of the pyramids. The ruins are just 35 kilometers (21.8 miles) from Guatemala, and on a clear day you can spot El Mirador ruins, just across the border.

From the entrance, a path leads about a kilometer (0.6 miles) through the forest before splitting into long, medium, and short routes. The long route loops past two smaller complexes, and begins in earnest in the Gran Acrópolis. The short route leads directly to the Gran Plaza, which has the largest and most impressive structures. (The following route was adapted from a self-guided tour prepared by Diane Lalonde of Río Bec Dreams hotel; see *Accommodations* in *Xpujil Town and Around.* For even more detail, Diane offers excellent guided tours of the Río Bec sites, including Calakmul.)

Gran Acrópolis

Following the "Ruta Larga" path, you'll pass a right-hand turnoff for the **Mural Group**, aka the **North Group**, which is currently being excavated. Inside the low, simple structures are panels of pristine murals, reportedly on par with the famous murals at Bonampák, Chiapas. The public isn't allowed in—and the entry is sealed with cement when workers aren't there—but the discovery bodes well for the excavation of the scores of similarly innocuous-looking temples in the future.

Continue on the path to another turnoff, this one to the **Residential Group,** aka **Casa del 6 Ahau,** an elegant complex of rooms most likely used by an extended family among Calakmul's elite. The rooms' walls have niches and holes, which were surely used to hold wooden doors, curtain rods, or beams supporting the thatched roof. Rooms vary in size, some facing a central patio, others reached by narrow corridors, and it's easy to imagine a nuanced domestic scene unfolding here, with royal leaders coming and going, and children playing in the patio watched by elder grandparents, sitting in their doorways. The kingly name "6 Ahau" was

THE MAYA COLLAPSE

Something went terribly wrong for the Mayas between the years A.D. 800 and A.D. 900. Hundreds of Classic Maya cities were abandoned, monarchies disappeared, and the population fell by the million, mainly by death and plummeting birth rates. The collapse was widespread but was most dramatic in the Southern Lowlands, a swath of tropical forest stretching from the Gulf of Mexico to Honduras and including once-glorious cities such as Palenque, Tikal, and Copán. (Archaeologists first suspected a collapse after noticing a sudden drop-off in inscriptions; it has been confirmed through excavations of peasant dwellings from before and after that period.)

There are many theories for the collapse, varying from climate change and epidemic diseases to foreign invasion and peasant revolt. In his carefully argued book *The Fall of the Ancient Maya* (Thames and Hudson, 2002), archaeologist and professor of anthropology at Pennsylvania State University David Webster suggests it was a series of events, not any single event, that led to the collapse. Webster argues that a population boom just before the collapse left agricultural lands depleted just as demand was at its highest. Maya farmers probably did not have large stores of corn and other food, as their farming methods – and especially the lack of draft animals – kept productivity relatively low. Even if they could generate large surpluses, storage was difficult in the lowlands' humid climate. And with so many rival states – whose populations were also increasing – there was little undepleted land to cultivate. When "too many farmers grew too many crops on too much of the landscape," as Webster puts it, the population would have suffered malnutrition, disease, lower birthrates, increased infighting, and it would have been especially vulnerable to a large-scale catastrophe such as drought or epidemic disease. Whatever blend of social stress existed – and they surely varied somewhat from kingdom to kingdom – it seems clear that in the 9th century ordinary Mayas finally lost all faith in their leaders who, after all, legitimized their rule by being able to please or appease the gods. When the elites abandoned their positions, large-scale collapse was not far behind.

inscribed on a vault here, though nothing more of that ruler is known.

The path leads over a small rise to the **Gran Acrópolis.** Structure XX will be on your right, with its small maze of rooms and columns. Continuing counterclockwise (keeping the structures to your right), you'll pass Structures XVI, XVII, and XV, all with huge deteriorating stelae at their bases. The next one, **Structure X,** has somewhat better-preserved stelae, including **Stela 75,** which purportedly marks the birth of Yukom the Great, Calukmul's most accomplished leader, in A.D. 600. The stairway of Structure X is crumbling, but an older stairway—preserved beneath the outer one, a consequence of the Maya habit of draping new structures upon existing ones—has been exposed and is easily climbed.

Continue across the acropolis's center through Calakmul's modest **Ball Court,** which was built from stones gathered from an older building that was destroyed. At the north end of the Ball Court is a remarkably well-preserved stela, depicting a ball player. An inscription on the stela suggests the Ball Court was constructed in A.D. 751.

At the north end of the Gran Acrópolis is **Structure XIII.** Impressive in its own right, Structure XIII is also notable for being one of the best places to get a photograph of Structure II (the big one). Getting to the top is a little tricky: Climb the stairs and go to the far left. There, you can clamber up the end of a broken wall, and then another, to reach the third level. Go back to the center and cut through one of the doorways, where a narrow ledge zigzags to the top.

Gran Plaza

Descending Structure XIII, bear left to **Structure XIV,** a rare "two-sided" temple with stairways on either side of the structure. It dates to the Late Classic era and has stelae marking the year of the temple's construction, A.D. 740. Climb up and over Structure XIV—or take the path around—and continue beneath the trees to the **Gran Plaza.** As in the Gran Acrópolis, make a counterclockwise loop through this large plaza, keeping the buildings to your right.

The first one you pass is **Structure VI,** a large pyramidlike temple with two reasonably well-preserved stelae at its summit; some of the original red paint is still visible. The structure's precise orientation suggests it was used for astronomical purposes, primarily observations of the sun; it is aligned with Structure IV, on the opposite side end of the plaza, allowing Maya astronomers to mark the yearly equinoxes and solstices.

Continuing on, you'll encounter **Structure V,** a small square temple surrounded by well-preserved stelae. Dates on the stele are from the 7th century, and the glyphs and images commemorate accomplishments of Yukom the Great and his father, Scroll-Serpent.

And then there's the big guy: **Structure II,** also known as the Great Pyramid. It forms the southern edge of the Gran Plaza, rising 53 meters (174 feet) over a hefty five-acre footprint. It's the largest Maya pyramid yet discovered, and the highest in the Yucatán peninsula. Unlike sites like Chichén Itzá, where the most impressive structures were built relatively late, Structure II dates to the very beginning of Calakmul's rise to power, in the Pre-Classic period. The huge stoic masks flanking the central staircase were covered by subsequent additions, and were discovered only recently. Structure II has proved a treasure trove of Maya artifacts: several exquisite jade funeral masks have been found in elaborate tombs housed in temples at the top of the structure (a total of nine such masks have been found in Calakmul, more than any other site, and are displayed in Campeche City). More recently, archaeologists discovered a perfectly preserved temple deep in Structure II's core (à la the Rosalila Temple in Copán, Honduras.) The temple is still being excavated, and is off-limits to the public, but in time visitors may be allowed to view this inner sanctum via a short tunnel about halfway up the main stairway. Climbing Structure II is a must for most visitors, though it's no easy task—use the right-hand staircase, as it's in the best condition.

Continuing around the Gran Plaza, **Structure IV** is the oldest building in the group, and one of the oldest in the city. Its core sections—others were added in later years—date to between 300 B.C. to A.D. 250. **Structure VII** completes the loop around the plaza; it was here that one of Calakmul's most recognizable jade masks was found. Climb Structure VII for one last look, over the treetops, of Structure II in all its glory. And if you're there in the late afternoon, you may spot a family of howler monkeys that gathers in the Gran Plaza's trees.

From the Gran Plaza, a path cuts between Structures IV and VII and back to the entrance and parking lot. For those who can't get enough, two more structures await your

THE STATE OF CAMPECHE

© LIZA PRADO

Structure II at Calakmul is the largest pyramid discovered in the Maya world.

exploration: **Structure I,** another huge pyramid, is visible from Structure II, though it remains almost completely ensconced in dark green vegetation. To get there, look for a path on the east side of Structure II. From Structure I, another path leads to the **Structure III,** a Petén style structure and the principle temple in the East Group, the oldest part of the city. Structure III is unique for apparently having never been altered; two jade masks were found in tombs here. From the East Group, a path leads back to the Grand Plaza.

Accommodations and Food

Inside the Reserva de la Biósfera de Calakmul there are two excellent lodging and eating options. They are on opposite ends of the budget spectrum, which makes staying inside the reserve and near the ruins possible for everyone.

Run by Servidores Turísticos de Calakmul, **C Camping Yaax 'che** (Carr. Calakmul Km. 6.5, tel. 983/871-6064, servidoresturisticos@ yahoo.com.mx, www.pormex.com/datos/ cam18.htm, US$4.65 pp camping, US$9.25–14 pp camping including all equipment) is one of the few honest-to-goodness campgrounds you'll find here or just about any place in Mexico. A short distance down the road to Calakmul, campsites are scattered in a pleasant wooded area, with clean toilets and showers, and a large fire pit. Rental equipment is quite nice, and the staff will set it up for you. There's also a simple eatery near the entrance, **Restaurant Oxté Tun** (6 A.M.–10 P.M. daily, US$3–5) that serves up good, basic meals; along one side of it, artesanía, honey, and natural remedies also are sold. The campground is run by a friendly Xpujil couple with incredible knowledge of, and passion for, the reserve. They offer **bicycle and walking tours** of the reserve and the ruins, which are highly recommended.

Just past the gate at the highway turnoff to Calakmul ruins, **C Hotel Puerta Calakmul** (Carr. Escárcega-Chetumal Km. 98.5, tel. 786/206-9492, www.puertacalakmul.com.mx, US$110 s/d) offers 15 deluxe cabins—and more are being built—in a large wooded plot. The cabins, spacious and spaced well apart, have comfortable beds with mosquito nets, painted cement floors with patterns made of inlaid stones, and large sitting rooms or outdoor terraces with hammocks and polished wood furniture. The restaurant has a high bank of windows and serves fresh breakfasts and pre-set three-course dinners. An on-site pool is a nice way to wash off a long day of ruin-going, but isn't always filled because of water shortages. The owner was considering remodeling and raising the rates significantly, so call ahead if this is near your upper limit.

If you are going to check out the other ruins along Highway 186, consider switching hotels and staying at one in or around Xpujil. And if you get stuck between Campeche City and Calakmul, a night in Escárcega is your only choice.

Getting There

Calakmul is a solid two hours' drive from Xpujil. From the turnoff on Highway 186, it's 60 kilometers (37 miles) down a paved but narrow and winding road to the archaeological zone. Drive carefully and be ready to pull over for other cars, animals, or (most likely) pheasants in the road. There's a US$4 per person toll to use this road.

BALAMKÚ ARCHAEOLOGICAL ZONE

For years archaeologists and the area's few tourists paid scant attention to little old Balamkú (8 A.M.–5 P.M. daily, US$3) preferring instead to focus on Calakmul, Becán, and the grander sites of this region. But in 1990 archaeologists uncovered an incredibly well-preserved 20-meter (65-foot) **stucco frieze** inside a ruined pyramid here, and Balamkú instantly became a must-see on the southern Campeche Maya route.

Balamkú (House of the Jaguar) shows signs of occupation as early as 300 B.C. It reached its peak in the Early Classic era (A.D. 300–600) before collapsing, along with so many other Maya cities, toward the end of the first millennium. The frieze was built around A.D. 550–650 and is located in one of three bases that make up **Structure I,** in the site's central group. The

© LIZA PRADO

Balamkú's famous stucco frieze was purposely buried inside of Structure I.

frieze had been deliberately covered, probably in the course of enlarging the pyramid. Relatively little has been excavated here, and there's not much to see beyond the frieze.

Balamkú's frieze depicts a rich scene of gods, animals, and men quite different from those appearing at surrounding sites. Some 20 meters (65 feet) long and in remarkably good condition, including a great deal of original color, the frieze has four frames. At the center of each is an animal—a toad and two crocodiles are discernable, the forth has decomposed. Toads and crocodiles (both amphibious) represented fertility to the Maya, especially in this arid region. Above the animal figures—in the case of the toad, emerging from its gaping upturned mouth—are kings, sitting cross-legged on jaguar-skin cushions and surrounded by lilies, another sign of fertility. The implication is that the king, too, is endowed with powers of rebirth and prosperity, and will deliver them to his subjects. The frames are separated by jaguars with reptile heads. Two are bound like prisoners, and were likely meant to evoke war,

ritual sacrifice, and the middle world between life and death.

The cardinal directions figure prominently in Maya mythology, and Maya artisans had to develop ways of portraying the four directions in two-dimensional forms. In Balamkú's frieze, the bottom of each frame has a mask portraying *cauac,* the snaggle-toothed Earth Monster. The end masks are in profile, and represent north and south. The center masks both face forward; however, the one beneath the toad is pictured with a serpent devouring a bird, a symbol for "west." Epigraphers, who decipher ancient writing, believe such devices would have been readily understood by most Maya observers, even illiterate commoners, and visitors from far-off cities and kingdoms.

The chamber where the frieze was found has been carefully reconstructed to protect the fragile stucco and preserve the appearance of the surrounding structure and plaza—from the outside you can hardly tell anything is there. It is accessible through a side door that is kept locked—ask at the entrance, or the attendant at the site, to open the door for a peek inside.

Getting There

Balamkú is located just off of Highway 186, about five kilometers (three miles) west of the turnoff to Calakmul.

CHICANNÁ ARCHAEOLOGICAL ZONE

The name **Chicanná** (House of the Serpent Mouth) (8 A.M.–5 P.M. daily, US$2.75) is a reference to the site's most impressive feature: huge stone jaws framing the doorway of the main palace. The ornate design, commonly called a "monster mouth," is a classic feature of Chenes-style architecture, and Chicanná's is one of the best around. But the site also contains elements of Río Bec architecture, another example of the mixing of styles common in this region.

Despite the ominous name, archaeologists believe Chicanná was a retreat used by the elite of Becán, which is just two kilometers

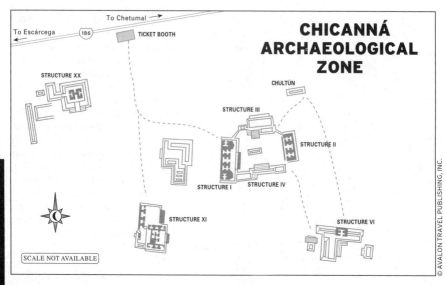

To Chetumal →
To Escárcega ← 186 TICKET BOOTH

CHICANNÁ ARCHAEOLOGICAL ZONE

STRUCTURE XX

CHULTÚN

STRUCTURE III

STRUCTURE II

STRUCTURE I   STRUCTURE IV

STRUCTURE XI

STRUCTURE VI

SCALE NOT AVAILABLE

© AVALON TRAVEL PUBLISHING, INC.

THE STATE OF CAMPECHE

(1.2 miles) west of here and connected by an ancient roadway. From the entrance, you'll first pass **Structure XX,** a small but exquisitely designed temple-residence. Its main doorway is framed by a monster mouth, and gives way to a foyer-type room and, farther in, a twin staircase leading to the upper level. The upper facade also has a monster mouth doorway, and to either side, columns of masks representing Chac, the hook-nosed god of rain. The elegance of this structure and others, plus details like the small rosettes on the 1st floor (with little human faces in the middle!) are a primary reason Chicanná is thought to have been a royal retreat.

Continuing along the path, you'll pass a turnoff to **Structure XI,** the oldest in the group, dating to A.D. 300, before reaching Chicanná's central complex. The first building you reach is **Structure I,** whose two tall, steeply pitched towers are typical of Río Bec style. Opposite is **Structure II,** with its spectacular monster mouth facade framing the doorway. The two spiral features above the door are the eyes, similar spirals to each side are the ears, and the teeth are quite obvious, above the door and protruding up

from the patio like a snake with a mean underbite. Left of the main entrance, a smaller door is topped with a stone decoration in the form of a *na,* the traditional thatched hut used by ancient Maya, and still common today. The exact meaning of the image here (and seen at Uxmal, Labná and other ruins) is unclear, though a thatched hut—with a three-stone hearth inside it—represents the beginning of the universe in some Maya creation myths.

Completing this central plaza are **Structures III and IV,** both multiroom buildings, while **Structure VI** stands a short distance southeast of the plaza. Look for a footpath between Structures II and IV.

If you visit Chicanná in the afternoon, you may spot families of keel-billed toucans and the similar-looking collared aracari. In the trees, keep an eye out for rodents and small mammals, including the gray fox.

Getting There

Chicanná is located 8.8 kilometers (5 miles) west of Xpujil on Highway 186. The site is just 500 meters (one-third mile) from the highway turnoff.

© LIZA PRADO

The "monster mouth" doorways in Chicanná are its most impressive feature.

◖ BECÁN ARCHAEOLOGICAL ZONE

West of Chicanná on Highway 186 is the turn-off to Becán (8 A.M.–5 P.M. daily, US$3). The largest of the Río Bec sites (save Calakmul, of course), Becán is a fascinating site, especially if you enjoy climbing and clambering around.

History

The area around Becán was settled as early as 600 B.C, but did not rise to greatness until more than 1,000 years later, in part, because it dwelled under the ever-present shadow of Calakmul. When Calakmul went into decline at the turn of the 8th century, Becán quickly emerged as one of the most important commercial and political centers of the Río Bec region. The sheer size of its pyramids and other structures suggest it commanded a labor force of many thousands.

The name Becán means "Ravine formed by water," no doubt a reference to the huge dry moat that forms a half-moon around the site. Measuring an impressive 15 meters (50 feet) wide and 4 meters (13 feet) deep, the moat was most likely used for defense, and is one of very few such structures found in Mesoamerica.

Central Plaza

A pathway from the entrance leads through the trees, across the moat, and to the backside of Structure IV, which has a profusion of decorative elements and openings. As tempting as it will be to clamber up it, there is much better access from the other side, at the end of your visit. Instead, continue through Becán's unique corbelled alley—a long covered passageway that functioned as a public street. It contains small niches that likely held images of deities, and where passersby might have paused to make small offerings.

Emerging onto the Central Plaza, the massive pyramids, Structures VIII and IX, loom to your right in the northeast corner of the plaza. Both can be climbed and afford spectacular views of the countryside. Structure IX, at 30 meters (98 feet) high, is the tallest structure at Becán; at the top is a platform with a

THE STATE OF CAMPECHE

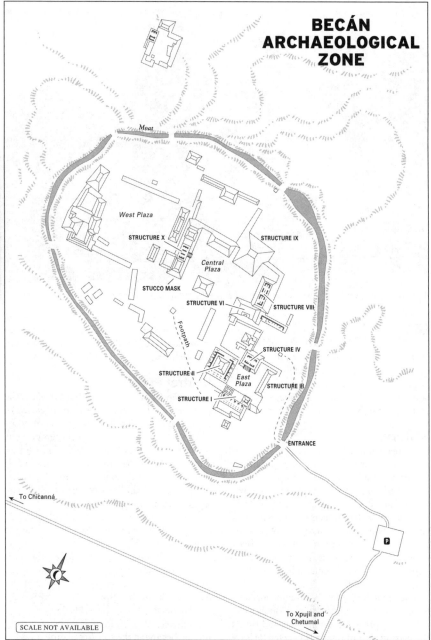

BECÁN ARCHAEOLOGICAL ZONE

Moat

West Plaza

STRUCTURE X

STRUCTURE IX

Central Plaza

STUCCO MASK

STRUCTURE VI

STRUCTURE VIII

Footpath

STRUCTURE IV

STRUCTURE II

East Plaza

STRUCTURE III

STRUCTURE I

ENTRANCE

To Chicanná

To Xpujil and Chetumal

SCALE NOT AVAILABLE

© AVALON TRAVEL PUBLISHING, INC.

huge mask on one end, and a shield-image on the other.

At the west end of the Central Plaza is Structure X. Though not as imposing as the two pyramids, many visitors find this one the site's most fascinating. Walking around the back, or west, side, you'll see that the structure contains several large central chambers (12 in all) and innumerable smaller rooms, spread over several levels and connected by way of winding staircases and passageways; there's even a hidden 2nd-floor patio on the south end. While many Maya structures gain complexity as new rooms and levels are added, Structure X's elegant design suggests it was planned from the start. The rooms are clearly residences, and some archaeologists speculate Structure X was a dormitory, of sorts, possibly for Becán's religious leaders. The Ball Court lies adjacent to the southern end of Structure X.

Be sure not to miss the beautiful and extremely well-preserved stucco mask on Structure X's southern exterior wall. Only recently uncovered, the mask may depict the sun god Kinichna. It has much of its original red paint and is protected by a pane of glass.

East Plaza

A short path leads through trees along the edge of the site to the East Plaza. The long imposing palace you see is Structure I. Its twin towers are much decayed, but still have remains of the impossibly steep staircases typical of the Río Bec style. Below, two levels of vaulted rooms are clearly more luxurious than the austere cells in Structure X; it's not hard to imagine Becán elite occupying these grand roomy chambers.

Structure I's back wall forms one side of the East Plaza. On the opposite side is Structure IV, the same building you encountered entering the site, albeit from the other side. Structure IV's staircase is well preserved, and a rope makes it even more climbable. At the top, look for narrow doorways on either side of the platform leading to spiral staircases down to musty rooms and passages in the structure's interior.

Back on the East Plaza, a staircase at the northeast corner (between Structures III and

THE STATE OF CAMPECHE

© LIZA PRADO

The elegant site of Becán is perfect for exploring or just enjoying a view of the countryside.

IV) leads down to the path you take to exit the site.

Getting There

Bécan is located five kilometers (3.1 miles) west of Chicanná, and seven kilometers (4 miles) west of Xpujil. The turnoff is well marked, and an access road of several hundred meters brings you to the entrance area.

XPUJIL ARCHAEOLOGICAL ZONE

Located on the western edge of the like-named town, Xpujil archaeological site (8 A.M.–5 P.M. daily, US$2.75) is small but well preserved. **Structure I** is the most famous of the few structures that have been excavated. It has three towers—a central one that is flanked by two smaller ones—and several false staircases. Built in classic Río Bec style, it is extraordinary because of the number of towers—most temples in the region only have two. On the back of the central tower, check out what's left of two huge stylized masks. The remaining buildings, **Structures II-IV** are believed to have been aristocratic residences.

EL HORMIGUERO ARCHAEOLOGICAL ZONE

Spanish for "The Anthill," El Hormiguero (8 A.M.–5 P.M. daily, US$2.75) is a remote site that few people visit. Although only a few structures have been excavated, it is most notable for **Structure II,** a dramatic building with two tall towers flanking an enormous monster mouth doorway. From there, a path leads visitors directly to the Central Group where the partially excavated **Structure V** looms before visitors.

Getting There

Located 22 kilometers (13 miles) south of Xpujil town, Hormiguero was, until recently, almost impossible to access without a heavy-duty four-wheel-drive vehicle and a lot of time. The road has improved significantly, and though it is still no autobahn, just about any car can get through as long as you go slowly and it hasn't been raining.

RÍO BEC ARCHAEOLOGICAL ZONE

The namesake site of this region is made up several scattered groups, and is currently being excavated. The architecture follows the region's dominate style, with high steep towers and tight-fitting stonework, but a lack of a central plaza and no evidence of a larger settlement suggest Río Bec was a getaway of sorts for the elite. Each group of structures may have functioned like a colonial-era hacienda, occupied by a privileged family and a small staff.

Getting There

Unfortunately, Río Bec is quite difficult to visit. You must have permission to enter the area, and the access road is rutted and overgrown; after a rain, it can be impossible to pass. The proprietors of Río Bec Dreams can arrange a tour of Río Bec, but plenty of advance notice is required.

BAT CAVES

At about Kilometer 107 on Highway 186 there is a small turnoff on the north side of the road, just big enough to pull your car off the road. From there, a couple of hundred meters of walking through the trees and up a small hill brings you to a huge sinkhole, at the bottom of which is a narrow cave opening. At dusk every night, hundreds of thousands of small black bats emerge from the cave in an endless whirling rush. Known locally as *la nube negra* (the black cloud), it is an incredible spectacle and unlike no other. At the height, you can feel the wind from their collective wings and winding upward flight—a few may even crash into you or stop for a rest on your pant leg. (No worries—they're completely harmless to humans, feeding mostly on insects). Although you may be able to find it on your own, it's better to stop in the morning at Río Bec Dreams and arrange for a guide (US$10–15).

XPUJIL TOWN AND AROUND

A small, dusty village, Xpujil is the only place in the Río Bec region with basic services for tourists. Not a particularly pleasant town, it's a convenient place to stay if you don't have a car. If you do have a rental, it's worth staying outside of town and coming in when you want to check your email or get your laundry washed.

Accommodations

Xpujil town has some basic, affordable hotels, but the area's best lodging options are a few kilometers west of town, near the ruins on Highway 186. If you're planning to visit Calakmul, consider spending at least one night near the site.

In Town: A short walk from the bus station, **Mirador Maya** (Av. Calakmul s/n, tel. 983/871-6005, US$32.50 s/d cabin, US$42 s/d with a/c) looks like a Girl Scout camp transplanted from the shores of an Alpine lake to a grubby lot in Xpujil overlooking the highway. The cabins themselves are dark with high A-frame ceilings but have fairly large bathrooms and a porch. Not a bad budget option—just make sure it has a working fan and good mosquito net. In the main building, there are two hotel rooms, which are significantly more comfortable—air-conditioning, cable TV, hot-water bathrooms, and good beds. A good option, especially if the electricity doesn't go out; if it does, the only ventilation you'll get is from a tiny window or the door.

On the same side of the highway a bit closer to town, **Hotel Calakmul** (tel. 983/871-6029, with private bath US$43 d, US$22 d with shared bath) has rooms of a little higher—and a little lower—standard. The better ones are small, clean, and comfortable, with air-conditioning, cable TV, and comforters with unicorns and tigers: very 3rd grade. The budget rooms are tiny wooden cabins perched incongruously at the end of the hotel parking lot; each has fan and *palapa* roof, and share recently renovated toilets and showers. The restaurant here is reliable, and open 6 A.M. to midnight.

Outside of Town: 【 **Río Bec Dreams** (Carr. Escárcega-Chetumal Km. 142, tel. 983/124-0501, www.riobecdreams.com, US$40 s/d jungalow, US$76–81 s/d cabin) is a good choice if you don't mind the sound of

an occasional truck passing late into the night. Four "jungalows"—small cabins with good screens and nice touches such as curtains, hand-painted sinks, and purified water—are set in the woods behind a well-tended jungle garden. These share outdoor bathrooms, which are kept spotlessly clean. Two new higher-end cabins with equally charming decor plus private tiled bathrooms, screened-in porches, and lots of space also are available. The hotel restaurant is one of the best in the area; owners Diane and Rick are extremely knowledgeable on the area, and give guided tours of the ruins.

Across from the ruins by the same name, **Chicanná Ecovillage** (Carr. Escárcega-Chetumal Km. 144, tel. 983/871-6075, chicanna@campeche.sureste.com, US$100 s with fan, US$114 d with fan) is the most comfortable hotel in the area. One- and two-story stucco villas rest on manicured grounds, with an inviting pool; rooms are spacious, with Maya-theme decor and modern amenities, except air-conditioning, as the hotel is mostly solar-powered. All also have a terrace or balcony with lounge chairs—a great place to relax after a day of ruin-hopping. It's not perfect—the beds are aging, the restaurant is overpriced, and you can count on only basic information and advice about the ruins—but given the challenges of running a high-end hotel in this neck of the woods, it's a real oasis.

Food

Like accommodations, the restaurant selection in and around Xpujil is pretty slim.

In Town: A classic Mexican *comedor* (eatery), 【 **Lonchería Lorena** (Av. Siluituc between Balakbal and Av. Becán, 7 A.M.–10 P.M. Mon.–Sat., US$1–2.50) is a tiny place offering Yucatecan specialties like *salbutes, empanadas,* and *tortas.* Breakfasts are particularly tasty.

A hotel restaurant, the **Mirador Maya** (tel. 983/871-6005, 7 A.M.–11 P.M. daily, US$3–6) serves standard Mexican fare—nothing too notable but it'll fill you up and it's open late. Popular with tour groups.

Just east of the post office, **Expendido de**

THE STATE OF CAMPECHE

Pan San Martín (Av. Calakmul s/n, 7 A.M.–10 P.M. Mon.–Sat.) sells fresh bread and pastries—perfect for a quick snack.

Outside of Town: 🎧 **Río Bec Dreams** (Carr. Escárcega-Chetumal Km. 142, tel. 983/124-0501, 7:30 A.M.–9 P.M. daily, US$4.50–8) offers the area's best meals, by far. The international menu varies according to what's fresh and available—think shrimp linguini, chicken curry, or English shepherds pie—but you can always count on excellent preparation, large portions and friendly service. For groups or special occasions, ask about arranging a full four- to five-course meal (US$23–33 per person). Box lunches also are available with advance notice, and are highly recommended for a long day at the ruins.

The **Chicanná Ecovillage** (Carr. Escárcega-Chetumal Km. 144, tel. 983/871-6075, 7 A.M.–10 P.M. daily, US$5–12) has a reliable though overpriced restaurant, with a large international menu.

Information and Services

As of this writing, there was no bank, ATM, or currency exchange agency in Xpujil. This is bound to change, but for now be sure to bring enough cash to make it through your visit, remembering that few places take credit cards. Otherwise, you may have to take an unexpected trip to Chetumal.

Hospitals: Xpujil Hospital Integral (Av. Siluituc between Balakbal and Av. Becan, tel. 983/871-7100) is a basic clinic with 24-hour emergency service.

Pharmacies: Farmacia Mérida (Av. Calakmul s/n, 7 A.M.–11 P.M. daily) is two doors down from the bus station.

Internet and Telephone: When there is electricity in town, the most reliable Internet place is **Internet La Selva** (across from the health clinic, Calle Becan s/n, 8 A.M.–3 P.M. and 5–10 P.M. Mon.–Fri., 9 A.M.–3 P.M. and 5–10 P.M. Sat., noon–8 P.M. Sun., US$1.50/hr.).

Next to the bus station, the **Caseta Telefónica Becán** (Calle Calakmul s/n, tel. 983/871-6133, 6 A.M.–10 P.M. daily) is a quiet place to make calls (US$0.56/minute to United States/Canada, US$0.90 rest of the world).

YOUR LICENSE, PLEASE

There are numerous military and police checkpoints in southern Campeche, especially east of Xpujil near the border with Quintana Roo. They typically are announced by orange pylons down the center lane, and large signs flanked by uniformed soldiers or officers. Drug smugglers are the main target, and most tourists are waved through (or simply ignored). The etiquette is to roll through slowly, coming to a full stop only if the officer signals you to do so. If you're stopped, you'll likely be asked for your driver's license and vehicle registration; the trunk or glove compartment of your car also may be searched. Friendly cooperation is the best way to get through these checkpoints as quickly as possible.

Post Office: The post office (Av. Calakmul s/n, 8 A.M.–2 P.M. Mon.–Fri.)—one man and his desk—is in a tiny building, next to a Western Union office.

Launderette: Lavandería Automática Calakmul (Av. Calakmul s/n, 7 A.M.–9 P.M. Mon.–Sat.) offers same-day service for US$1.40 per kilogram (2.2 pounds). Located near the western entrance to town, in a yellow clapboard house.

Getting There and Around

Having a rental car is all but essential to enjoy the ruins here. Without one, you'll either spend a lot of time waiting for rides, or a lot of money on taxi service, or both. Hitching is possible to and from Calakmul but not a sure thing.

Bus: The bus station (tel. 983/871-6027) is inside the Hotel Victoria, on the main drag in the center of town. You can catch buses east to Chetumal (US$5–7; two hours; 11:30 A.M.*, 2 P.M., 2:30 P.M.*, and 3 P.M.*) and to Cancún (US$27, seven hours; 6 A.M. and 10:45 A.M.), with stops in Tulum (US$20; five hours) and Playa del Carmen (US$23.50; six hours). Westbound, there's service to Campeche (US$12–13, five hours, 4 A.M., 6 A.M., 10:30 A.M., 1:45 P.M.* and 4:15 P.M.) and San Cristóbal de las Casas (US$29; six hours; 9:40 P.M.), with a stop in Palenque (US$21; five hours). An asterisk denotes first-class service.

Car: There's a **gas station** about five kilometers (three miles) east of Xpujil. It's open 24 hours when there's gas and electricity, and closed when either is out (a fairly common occurrence). Try filling up right when you arrive; if the station is closed, look for men selling gas from barrels near the entrance. It's more expensive, but worth the peace of mind.

Taxi: If you don't have a car, your best bet is to take a cab. **Private taxi service** is available at Mirador Maya hotel (tel. 983/871-6005). Round-trip to Calakmul and Balamkú for 1/2/3/4 people runs US$60/80/90/100; to Chicanná, Becan, and Xpujil US$30/40/45/50; and to Kohunlich and Dzibanché US$60/80/90/100. You'll get about the same rates from the drivers in town—look for them near the bus station.

ESCÁRCEGA

Escárcega is an unremarkable town at the junction of Highways 186 and 261. For tourists, it is mainly a gas stop for those headed east to the archaeological sites in the Río Bec area or north to Campeche City (150 km/93 mi). It has a reputation for being a rough-and-tumble place; true or not, there is little reason to linger here.

Accommodations and Food

There are two decent hotels on the main drag. The **Hotel Escárcega** (Av. Justo Sierra Méndez No. 87, tel. 982/824-0188, US$20 d with fan, US$32 d with a/c and TV) is closest to the bus station and has cheap, basic rooms. If you've got more to spend, head another 200 meters to **Gran Hotel Colonial** (Av. Justa Sierra Méndez at Calle 43, tel. 982/824-1908, US$30–32 d) where the rooms are generally better, and air-conditioning, cable T.V. and aqua-blue paint jobs are standard. Rooms facing the street have a small terrace, allowing in more light. Both hotels have off-street parking.

Hotel Escárcega has a modest restaurant, and there are a number of small-time eateries along the main drag.

Information and Services

There aren't many tourist services in this tiny town. The basics include:

Internet and Telephone: There is a no-name **Internet café** (Av. Hector Pérez Martínez at Calle 28, 9 A.M.–10 P.M. daily, US$0.90/hr.) south of the main road, near the Hotel Escárcega.

Launderette: A couple blocks west of the Internet café, there is a launderette (Av. Hector Pérez Martínez s/n, 6 A.M.–2 P.M. and 4–8 P.M. Mon.–Sat.) that charges US$2.75 per kilogram (2.2 pounds).

Getting There and Around

The **main bus terminal** (tel. 982/824-0144) is at the intersection of Highway 261 and Av. Justo Sierra Méndez; if you're coming from Campeche, it's just as you enter town. Always arrive a half-hour early—service here is *de paso* (mid-route), which means seats are limited and buses may come 15 minutes early or late.

Most travelers are headed to Campeche (US$9, 2.5 hours, six departures daily 8:30 A.M.–11:35 P.M.), Xpujil (US$8, two hours, 8:30 A.M., 12:35 P.M., and 2 P.M.), or Palenque (US$11.50, three hours, 12:15 am, 4 A.M., and 1 P.M.). There is also service to Chetumal (US$14, 4–4.5 hrs, nine departures 12:30 A.M.–11:55 P.M.) and Cancún (US$35, nine hours, eight departures midnight–noon, plus 7 P.M., and Mérida (US$19, 4.5 hours, eight departures 12:20 A.M.–5:20 P.M.)

The ADO buses don't stop en route, but those from the **second-class terminal** (Av. Justo Sierra Méndez and Calle 31, tel. 982/824-0498) can drop you at the Calakmul turnoff (US$3.75, 1.5 hrs) or the hotels just west of Xpujil (US$6, 2.5 hours); departures are at 7:45 A.M., 11:30 P.M., 1:30 P.M., 10:30 P.M., and 12:30 A.M.

There's a gas station—three actually—just down the main highway from the ADO terminal.

THE STATE OF TABASCO

The marshy Gulf state of Tabasco is not technically part of the Yucatán Peninsula. But as the birthplace of the Olmecs, the first advanced civilization in Mesoamerica, Tabasco represents an important piece of the region's historical puzzle. There are a few intriguing sights—museums in Villahermosa, nearby Maya ruins, and chocolate-producing haciendas—but the state remains well off the beaten track, so travelers with limited time often decide to spend it elsewhere. However, those who are intrigued by the little-understood Olmec people, or who are committed to seeing less-traveled Maya ruins, will find it's worthwhile to stop here for a few days.

PLANNING YOUR TIME

Three days are enough to visit Villahermosa and Comalcalco, the state's main destinations. In Villahermosa, spend the morning at Parque-Museo La Venta and the afternoon checking out sights in the Zona Remodelada, such as the Centro Cultural, Plaza de las Armas, and Torre del Caballero. The next day, hop on a *colectivo* to Comalcalco, where you easily can visit the ruins and a chocolate factory as a day trip. Spend your final day in the anthropology museum, admiring some of the Olmec, Toltec, and Maya artifacts found around the state. Spend the afternoon poking around downtown or, if you need a mall fix, head to Tabasco 2000.

© LIZA PRADO

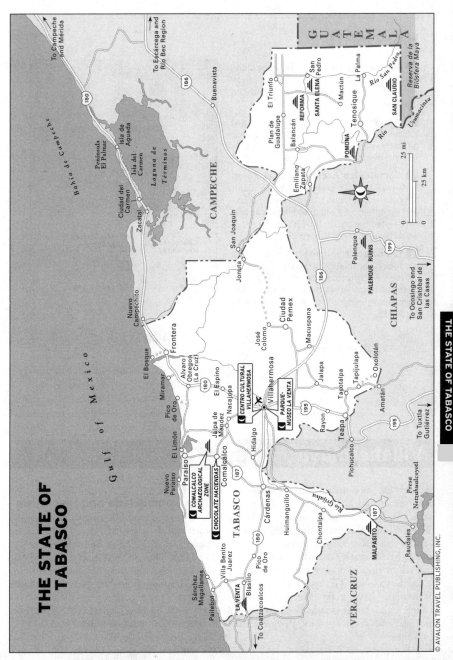

THE STATE OF TABASCO

© AVALON TRAVEL PUBLISHING, INC.

HIGHLIGHTS

(Parque-Museo La Venta: Huge stone heads from Mesoamerica's first civilization are highlights in this leafy park and zoo (page 367).

(Centro Cultural Villahermosa: Villahermosa's surprisingly hip cultural center features art exhibits in the foyer and a café with live music in back (page 369).

(Comalcalco Archaeological Zone: The Maya living in swampy Tabasco didn't have stone quarries, so they invented bricks and used them to build grand pyramids that have lasted the ages – the Third Little Piggy would have approved (page 375).

(Chocolate Haciendas: Tabasco is still producing chocolate 400 years after introducing it to Columbus. Tour a working chocolate plantation to see the process in action, from juicy green fruit to sweet brown candy (page 376).

LOOK FOR **(** TO FIND RECOMMENDED SIGHTS, ACTIVITIES, DINING, AND LODGING.

THE STATE OF TABASCO

Villahermosa

Spanish for "beautiful town," Villahermosa may not, at first glance, seem to deserve its name. Traffic snarls many of the streets and the buildings are plain compared to cities such as San Cristóbal and Mérida. Villahermosa's best feature is its lakes, which angle and elbow their way over much of the city. A few hotels—the Graham and Cencali in particular—have pretty lake views and enjoying a glass of lemonade by the water is a nice way to rest after visiting Parque-Museo La Venta.

SIGHTS
Zona Remodelada and Downtown
The narrow streets of the original town center, which are brick-paved and closed to traffic, are referred to as the **Zona Remodelada** or the **Zona Luz.** The tree-lined streets bring you past bustling shops and tiny cafés packed with locals. Just south of the Zona Luz, the **Plaza de Armas** is a pretty park surrounded by government buildings on a slight rise above the zone. It boasts the **Puente de Solidaridad**—a footbridge that spans the Río Grijalva and allows the residents of Colonia Las Gaviotas to cross

to the town center. Partway across the bridge, the **Torre del Caballero** (8 A.M.–5:30 P.M. daily, free) is a concrete lookout tower with a 211-step spiral staircase leading to a windy platform with fine views of the city and river.

◖ Parque-Museo La Venta

La Venta is one of the great Olmec communities, built on an island in the middle of the vast Río Tonolá marshland about 129 kilometers (80 miles) west of present-day Villahermosa. Archaeologists believe that it was founded around 900 B.C. and functioned primarily as a ceremonial center until it was abandoned around 300 B.C. The main structure was a 34-meter-high (111.5-foot-high) pyramid made of clay. The stunning cache of jade figurine burial offerings discovered there are now on display in Mexico City's Museo Nacional de Antropología. But La Venta is probably best known for the presence of massive stone heads measuring more than two meters (6.6 feet) tall and weighing more than 15 tons each. No one has yet figured out how the Olmecs managed to move these giant pieces of rock without the use of the wheel, since the raw material comes from an area almost 100 kilometers (62 miles) away. Frans Blom—an archaeologist famous for his work with the Lacondóns in eastern Chiapas—first investigated the ruins in 1925. It was the intrusion of the Pemex oil drills, however, that brought the Olmec ceremonial center back to national attention. A local poet named Carlos Pellicer Cámara arranged to have virtually the entire complex moved to a park on the outskirts of Villahermosa. There the artifacts were laid out in the precise configuration in which they were found.

Today, Pellicer Cámara's vision is the lovely **Parque-Museo La Venta** (Blvd. Adolfo Ruíz Cortines s/n, tel. 993/314-1652, 8 A.M.–4 P.M. Tues.–Sun., US$3), a combination outdoor museum and zoo that lies on the peaceful Laguna de las Ilusiones. A self-guided

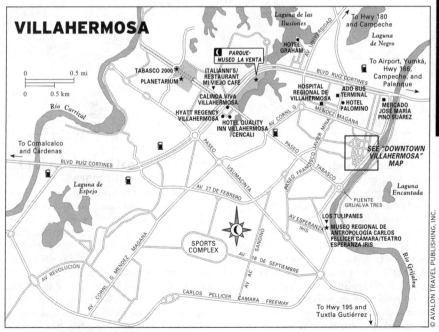

THE STATE OF TABASCO

© AVALON TRAVEL PUBLISHING, INC.

THE STATE OF TABASCO

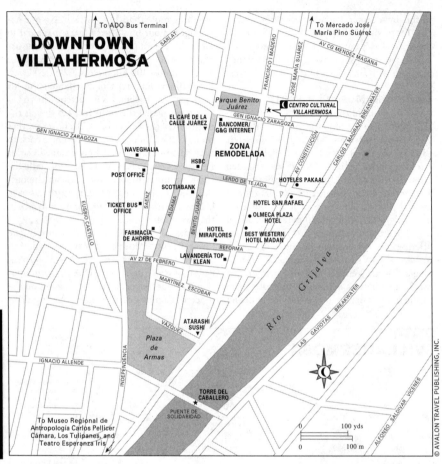

tour—brochures with explanations are available at the entrance—leads visitors through the thick trees and tropical foliage to numerous Olmec sculptures; in addition to the famous heads, look for large stones with finely carved deities and animals like dolphins and monkeys. If you have time—and the inclination—the park also presents a **sound and light show** at 7 P.M., 8 P.M., and 9 P.M. (US$9.50 pp, 1 hr), where visitors can admire the sculptures in the evening, which is an entirely different experience. Use the park entrance near the fountain, rather than the main one.

Museo Regional de Antropología Carlos Pellicer Cámara

As part of a larger complex known as the Center for Research of Olmec and Maya Cultures (CICOM), the Museo Regional de Antropología Carlos Pellicer Cámara (Av. Carlos Pellicer Cámara 511, tel. 993/312-6344, 9 A.M.–5 P.M. Tues.–Sun., US$3) is an aging but captivating museum with artifacts from Olmec, Toltec, and Maya archaeological sites. The pieces—pottery, clay figurines, stone carvings, and delicate pieces of carved jade—are impressive but, unfortunately, the signage

© LIZA PRADO

Parque-Museo La Venta has an excellent collection of Olmec sculptures.

doesn't seem to have been updated since the 1970s. Still, walking through the rambling museum is a fine complement to a visit to one of the region's ruins.

Yumká

Next to the airport, Yumká (Ranchería Las Barrancas s/n, tel. 993/356-0107, www.yumka .org, 9 A.M.–5 P.M. daily, US$4.75 adults, $2.50 children) is Villahermosa's attempt at an eco-park. Named after "the elf that watches over the plants and animals in between the wetlands and the jungle," Yumká is basically a glorified throwback to the *African Lion Safari* theme parks that were so popular in the United States in the 1970s. Divided into three sections—a guided walk through the jungle, a ride through the savanna on a tractor-pulled trolley, and a boat ride on a lagoon—visitors see monkeys, jaguars, hippos, giraffes, elephants, and birds. Between the tractor, the outboard motor, and the 747s taking off next door, however, it's not exactly an eco-adventure. The park offers shuttle ser-

vice on weekends and holidays only (US$1.50 pp, each way), departing from the entrance of Parque-Museo La Venta at 9 A.M., 10:30 A.M., noon, and 1:30 P.M. A taxi from downtown costs US$14–17.

ENTERTAINMENT AND EVENTS
⟨ Centro Cultural Villahermosa

Out of place on a busy downtown street corner, the Centro Cultural Villahermosa (Avs. Francisco Madero and Zaragoza, tel. 993/314-5552, 10 A.M.–8 P.M. Tues.–Sun., free) is a sleek, ultramodern building with a sloping glass facade and gleaming white walls inside and out. Counting the lustrous main lobby, there are seven exhibition spaces. A small theater also hosts occasional performances. Information about other expositions and cultural events around town is given here too. And if you just want a break from the heat, the café at the back has fresh coffee and good, light fare. There's live music, usually piano or guitar, most evenings 5–7 P.M.

ESCRITORÍO PÚBLICO

Not long after the conquest of the New World, there grew a need for the general populace to communicate through letters; loved ones moved away in search of work, business opportunities arose, officialdom required paperwork – the age of letter writing had arrived. Most people, however, were illiterate. As a result, a job was born: the *escritor público* (public writer). This person could be found in the central plaza, tucked under an archway of a main building. He sat at a table with ink, paper, and a sign *Escritorío Público* (public desk) with, perhaps, a drawing of a quill and scroll (after all, his clients couldn't read). For a coin or two, townspeople could have a letter written.

Today, this job is still very much in existence. Look around the main plazas. In small villages and large cities alike, you'll see people – now with typewriters – waiting at the ready for their next customer.

Tabasco 2000

This set of new buildings is developing into an impressive cultural center with a series of lovely fountains and walkways that make for a pleasant stroll. Along with Villahermosa's most modern mall with its polished marble floors and glass-enclosed shops, there are city and state government offices, a huge convention center, and a **planetarium** (tel. 993/316-3641). The planetarium's observatory closed years ago, but the Omnimax theater has shows every night but Monday; tickets are US$2.20. Cultural and art exhibits are often displayed in the foyer.

Teatro Esperanza Iris

Part of the same complex that houses the Museo Regional de Antropología Carlos Pellicer Cámara, the 1,300-seat Teatro Esperanza Iris (Av. Carlos Pellicer Cámara 511, tel. 993/314-4210) has regular dance, music, and theater performances. Check at the Centro Cultural Villahermosa or in the box-office window for upcoming events.

SHOPPING

Villahermosa is by no means a tourist's shopping mecca, but one shop definitely is worth noting: **Artesanías de Tabasco**—a state-run shop that sells some of the best handicrafts made in Tabasco. There are four stores around Villahermosa: inside Parque-Museo La Venta (Blvd. Adolfo Ruíz Cortines s/n, 993/315-3421, 9 A.M.–5 P.M. daily); the Museo Regional de Antropología Carlos Pellicer Cámara (Av. Carlos Pellicer Cámara 511, tel. 993/314-6058, 9 A.M.–5 P.M. Tues.–Sat.); Tabasco 2000 (Paseo Tabasco s/n, 2nd Fl., tel. 993/316-2822, 10:30 A.M.–8:30 P.M. daily); and at the airport (tel. 993/356-0196, 7 A.M.–9 P.M. Mon.–)Fri., 7 A.M.–8 P.M. Sat.–Sun.). If you prefer to shop online, check out their products at www.ifat.gob.mx.

If you need a mall fix, head to the sleek **Tabasco 2000** (Paseo Tabasco s/n, 10:30 A.M.–8:30 P.M. daily), a huge shopping center with large department stores, clothing boutiques, and a food court.

ACCOMMODATIONS

As one of the state's main commercial centers, Villahermosa's hotels are geared toward business travelers. The result is twofold: Budget hotel rates are inflated and the best rooms are taken early; while mid- to high-end hotels offer better-than-average services, such as business centers, good restaurants, and courtesy airport shuttles. Regardless of the category of hotel you choose, prices fall by about 25 percent on weekends. The best weekend deals are online—take a look before you head to town.

Under US$50

One of the first hotels in Villahermosa—and showing it—is the **Hotel San Rafael** (Av. Constitución No. 240, tel. 993/312-0166, US$10 s, US$14 d). This basic hotel offers relatively clean rooms with fans, private baths (cold water only), and a communal TV room. Ask for a room with a view of the river—they're quieter and feature balconies.

Directly in front of the ADO bus station, **Hotel Palomino** (Av. Francisco Javier Mina No. 222, tel. 993/312-8431, US$33.50 s/d with a/c) is a tolerable option if you've arrived on a late bus or need to catch an early-morning one. Don't expect much though—dark, clean rooms with cable TV are the best you'll find.

Just one block from the river, **Hoteles Pakaal** (Lerdo de Tejada No. 106, tel. 993/314-4648, US$37 s, US$42 d) offers decent rooms with air-conditioning, cable TV, and private bathrooms. Units on the upper floors are more spacious and get better sunlight. The beds are hit or miss—check a couple rooms before you commit to one.

Hotel Miraflores (Reforma No. 304, tel. 993/358-0470, toll-free Mex. tel. 800/234-0229, www.miraflores.com.mx, US$54 s, US$60 d) opens onto a pedestrian walkway in the heart of downtown, making it a bit quieter than most of the other hotels around. The rooms themselves are a bit dated, but they're spacious, clean, and have air-conditioning and cable TV—those facing the river have balconies and are especially sunny. The hotel also has wireless Internet in the lobby, parking, and a decent restaurant.

US$50-100

On a peaceful curve of the Laguna de las Ilusiones, the ◖ **Hotel Graham** (Rosendo Taracena s/n, tel. 993/312-7744, toll-free Mex. tel. 800/590-0554, www.hotelgraham.com.mx, US$60.50 s/d with a/c, US$80–98 suite with a/c) is an excellent option if you don't mind taking a taxi to and from city sights. Rooms are spacious, spotless, and have cable TV, telephones, and pleasant views of the lagoon. The hotel also features a small pool and a good restaurant.

Best Western Hotel Madan (Madero No. 408, tel. 993/314-0518, toll-free U.S./Canada tel. 800/780-7234, www.bestwestern.com, US$67 s/d with a/c) offers small but spotless rooms with cable TV and telephones. A sweeping *azulejo* staircase leads guests to their respective floors. Ask for a room in back for a more

restful stay—rooms near the front get lots of noise from the busy street and the (sometimes busier) hotel bar.

In the heart of the city center, the **Olmeca Plaza Hotel** (Av. Madero No. 418, tel. 993/358-0102, toll-free Mex. tel. 800/201-0909, www.hotelolmecaplaza.com, US$77–88 s/d with a/c, US$141 suite with a/c) offers rooms that feature comfortable pastel-colored furnishings, electronic door keys, satellite TV, small writing desks, and telephones. Executive floor rooms—with marble floors and thick glass shower walls—are on a separate floor. A small but very nice rooftop pool and a two-story gym are pluses. Be sure to ask about specials: Weekend rates are among the best around.

Over US$100

The understated and classy **Hotel Quality Inn Villahermosa Cencali** (Av. Juárez and Paseo Tabasco, tel. 993/313-6611, toll-free Mex. tel. 800/112-5000, www.qualityinnvillahermosa.com, US$90 s/d, US$106–145) has 161 rooms that occupy long low buildings with curved walkways and broad sloping clay roofs. A huge mural adorns the lobby and many of the rooms have nice views of Laguna de las Ilusiones. Rooms in the new wing are a bit nicer, but all are large and have modern furnishings, including air-conditioning. The hotel has a well-tended pool and a popular restaurant. Parque-Museo La Venta is a short walk away.

A gleaming lobby welcomes you at the ◖ **Calinda Viva Villahermosa** (Av. Adolfo Ruíz Cortínez at Paseo Tabasco, tel. 993/313-6000, toll-free Mex. tel. 800/711-5555, www.hotelescalinda.com.mx, US$85 s/d with a/c and buffet breakfast), where rooms are smallish but very nice. A welcoming garden-side pool, sunny restaurant, and fully equipped business center and gym are also at each guest's disposal. Parque-Museo La Venta and Tabasco 2000 are both a 10-minute walk away. Be sure to ask about weekly specials.

Next door, the **Hyatt Regency Villahermosa** (Av. Juárez at Paseo Tabasco, tel. 993/310-1234, www.villahermosa.regency.hyatt.com, US$135–160 s/d with a/c) has elegantly furnished rooms and five-star amenities, including a large swimming pool and patio area, two tennis courts, and a car-rental agency. For a bit more, the hotel's Regency rooms include continental breakfast and afternoon drinks along with a private lounge.

FOOD

No one could call Villahermosa a culinary hot spot, but it does have a few restaurants worth noting. There are also a number of good, cheap, no-name eateries downtown, especially on Calle Francisco Madero between Lerdo de Tejada Zaragoza and throughout the pedestrian-only zone.

Mexican

Near CICOM and the anthropology museum, **Los Tulipanes** (Carlos Pellicer Cámara 511, tel. 993/312-9209, 8 A.M.–10 P.M. Tues.–Sat., 8 A.M.–6 P.M. Sun., 1 A.M.–10 P.M. Mon., US$6–16) serves good if not spectacular regional food like baked fish and grilled chicken. The dining area is large and colorful, and there's live music every day but Monday, usually in the morning and the evening. It's a little hard to find: Take the wide passageway south of the theater toward the river.

Other Specialties

◖ **Italianni's** (Paseo Tabasco at Av. Ruíz Cortines, tel. 993/317-7258, 1–11 P.M. Mon.–Wed., 1 P.M.–1 A.M. Thurs.–Sat., 1–10 P.M. Sun., US$6–16) features well-prepared Italian fare in a relaxed, nice atmosphere. Many of the dishes—even salads and desserts—are designed for two people, so sharing is encouraged. The result is that you can have a varied meal for comparatively little money. (And since you're saving all that money, be sure to try a "watermelontini," "appletini," or another of the creative mixed drinks.)

Tucked into the northeast corner of the Plaza de Armas, ◖ **Atarashi Sushi** (Vasquez Norte 203, tel. 993/314-7025, noon–midnight daily, US$3–6) is a pleasant surprise, especially if you are getting tired of regional fare. Choose from about 20 different sushi rolls, all well-prepared and—with 10 hefty pieces—a good value. Two or three rolls, an order of veggie tempura, and some miso soup are more than enough for two. Other options include fried rice, noodles, and curry dishes.

Cafés and Bistros

Next door to Italianni's, **Restaurant Mi Viejo Café** (Paseo Tabasco at Av. Ruíz Cortines, 7 A.M.–midnight daily, US$4–12) is a classy but affordable place to eat, especially for breakfast or lunch. Morning specials vary from scrambled eggs to quiche Lorraine, and come with fresh-squeezed juice and cups of coffee. For lunch or dinner, try sandwiches, pasta, grilled chicken, or one of several cuts of beef.

Part of the Hotel Madan, **Restaurant Madan** (Av. Madero 408, tel. 993/312-1650, 7 A.M.–11 P.M. daily, US$3–6) is filled day and night with locals and visiting businesspeople huddled over never-ending cups of coffee. Try for a table by the front windows, where you can watch the action on the street. The *comida corrida* lunch special is a good deal, with soup, salad, entrée, dessert, and drink for US$3–4.

El Café de la Calle Juárez (Calle Juárez between Avs. Zaragoza and Lerdo de Tejada, tel. 993/312-3454, 7 A.M.–10 P.M. Mon.–Sat., 7:30 A.M.–9 P.M. Sun., US$2.50–5) is one of several cafés along Calle Juárez with smoky, air-cooled indoor seating and street-side outdoor seating. Like the others, this one serves good basic breakfast and lunch specials and is usually filled with old guys arguing politics and drinking coffee. Foreigners are almost as rare as women are, and the atmosphere is brusque but comfortable.

If you just need a break, the **Centro Cultural** (Av. Francisco Madero at Zaragoza, tel. 993/314-5552, 10 A.M.–8 P.M. Tues.–Sun, US$2–6) has an airy lobby café, with good coffee, light snacks, and pastries.

Groceries

The **Mercado José María Pino Suárez** (José María Pino Suárez at Av. Ruíz Cortines, 7 A.M.–6 P.M. daily) offers the freshest produce, dairy, and meats around. Check it out, even if just to experience the local market scene.

INFORMATION
Tourist Information
The state tourism board operates a tourist information booth at Parque-Museo La Venta (Blvd. Adolfo Ruíz Cortines s/n, tel. 993/314-1652, www.etabasco.gob.mx/turismo, 9 A.M.–3 P.M. daily) that generally is more helpful than the main offices near Tabasco 2000.

EnterARTE is a small glossy magazine published monthly by the state culture and recreation office. It has listings of events taking place at Villahermosa's many private galleries and public museums and cultural centers. You'll find complete listings of upcoming music, theater, and art shows, plus special events and lectures at local colleges, museums, and libraries.

Hospitals
PEMEX Hospital Regional de Villahermosa (Calle Gil at Calle Saenz, tel. 993/312-8718) is a busy public hospital with a 24-hour emergency room and pharmacy; expect lines.

Pharmacies
Farmacia Reforma (tel. 993/312-1438, 7 A.M.–10 P.M. daily) and **Farmacia de Ahorro** (tel. 993/315-6606, 7 A.M.–11 P.M. daily) are both on Avenida Reforma at the corner of Calle Saenz. Both have a large selection of medicines as well as toiletry items. The latter will deliver to your hotel until 10 P.M.

Police
Reach the police 24 hours a day by calling 066 from any public phone.

SERVICES
Money
In the Zona Remodelada, you'll find reliable ATMs at **Bancomer** (Av. Zaragoza at Parque Juárez, 9 A.M.–4 P.M. Mon.–Fri., 10 A.M.–2 P.M. Sat.) and **HSBC** (Calle Juárez at Av. Lerdo de Tejada, 8 A.M.–7 P.M. Mon.–Sat.).

Outside of downtown, **Tabasco 2000,** with its handful of ATMs, is your best bet.

Internet
Bustling **G&G Internet** (Av. Zaragoza at Parque Juárez, 8 A.M.–1 A.M. daily) has Internet access for US$1 an hour, while **Naveghalia** (Av. Lerdo de Tejada at Av. Zaragoza, 8 A.M.–3 A.M. daily) is smaller and less crowded, but slightly more expensive at US$1.25 an hour.

Post Office
The post office (Av. Saenz at Av. Lerdo de Tejada) is open 9 A.M.–5 P.M. Monday–Friday and 9 A.M.–1 P.M. Saturday.

Launderette
On the main drag downtown, **Lavandería Top Klean** (Av. Madero No. 303-A, tel. 993/312-2856, 8 A.M.–8 P.M. Mon.–Sat.) charges US$1.75 per kilogram (2.2 pounds) and provides same-day service if clothes are dropped off early.

Storage
The **ADO bus terminal** (24 hours daily) has luggage storage for US$1–1.50 an hour.

GETTING THERE
Considered a gateway to Central Mexico, Villahermosa is easily reached. A fine transportation network connects it with Mexico City, Chiapas, Guatemala, the Caribbean coast, and the rest of the Yucatán Peninsula.

Air
Villahermosa has a busy, compact airport (VSA, Aeropuerto Capitán Carlos Rovirosa Pérez) about 12 kilometers (7.5 miles) east of the city. Inside there is a bank with ATM and exchange services, a tourist information booth, a restaurant, and a few gift shops. Flights arrive daily from many cities in Mexico—including Mexico City, Mérida, and Tuxtla Gutiérrez—and there are often nonstop flights from Houston, Texas.

The following airlines service Villahermosa:

- **AeroCalifornia** (Tabasco 2000, Calle Via 3 No. 120, tel. 993/316-8000, toll-free Mex. tel. 800/237-6225, www.aerocalifornia .com);

- **AeroMar** (airport tel. 993/356-0360, toll-free Mex. tel. 800/237-6627, www.aeromar.com.mx);

- **Aeroméxico** (CICOM, Periferico Carlos Pellicer Cámara No. 511-2, tel. 993/316-6202, toll-free Mex. tel. 800/021-4010, www.aeromexico.com);

- **Aviacsa** (Tabasco 2000, Calle Via 3 No. 120, tel. 993/356-0133, toll-free Mex. tel. 800/006-2200, www.aviacsa.com);

- **Click Mexicana** (Tabasco 2000, Calle Via 3 No. 120, tel. 993/316-3132, toll-free Mex. tel. 800/502-2000, www.clickmx.com);

- **Continental** (toll-free Mex. tel. 800/900-5000, www.continental.com); and

- **Mexicana** (Tabasco 2000, Calle Via 3 No. 120, tel. 993/316-3132, airport tel. 993/356-0101, toll-free Mex. tel. 800/502-2000, www.mexicana.com).

Bus

The **ADO bus terminal** (Paseo Francisco Javier Mina at Calle Merino) is large and loud, with service to:

- Campeche, US$24.50, 6–7 hours, 10 departures 4:20 A.M.–12:50 P.M. and 7:20–11:45 P.M.

- Cancún, US$50–63, 12–13 hours, 5 A.M., 7:25 A.M., 4:10 P.M., and every 10–30 minutes 7:20–12:45 A.M. except 10–11:30 P.M.

- Chetumal, US$30, eight hours, 8:25 A.M. and six departures 4:10–11:55 P.M.

- Mérida, US$34–41, 8.5–9 hours, 18 departures 4:20 A.M.–12:50 P.M. and 8:45–1:45 P.M.

- Mexico City, US$48–65, 10–15 hours, 40-plus departures daily; check trip duration, which can vary significantly.

- Palenque, US$8, 2–2.5 hours, every 1–2 hours 5 A.M.–1:50 P.M., plus 4:40 P.M., 7:40 P.M., and 9:15 P.M.

- Playa del Carmen, US$47, 12 hours, 4:10 P.M., and every 10 minutes 7:20–9:40 P.M.

- San Cristóbal, US$18.50, seven hours, 9:30 A.M. and noon.

Near the ADO bus station and a block apart, **Comali Plus** (Calle Reforma at Calle Bravo) and **Transportes Torruco** (Calle Reforma at La Arboleda) provide identical service to and from Comalcalco. Vans accommodate 12 comfortably (or 14 uncomfortably), and leave every 20 minutes, 4:30 A.M.–9 P.M. daily (US$2.50, 45 minutes).

Car

Driving into Villahermosa is easy from both the north and the south. From Campeche and points east take Highway 186. From Campeche along the coastal route take Highway 180. From Veracruz along the coast take Highway 180 east. From San Cristóbal de las Casas and points south take Highway 199 to Highway 186. These all converge in Villahermosa.

GETTING AROUND

Navigating downtown Villahermosa on foot is easy, especially as several streets are pedestrian-only. You can conceivably walk from the large hotels to the downtown area, but it's a long haul.

Taxi

Around town, white *radio* taxis cost around US$2.50, while the yellow *colectivo* cabs (which may pick up several passengers along the way) cost around US$1.50. A taxi from the airport runs US$15—vouchers are sold at a booth near the main exit (airport cabbies don't accept cash).

Car Rental

Three car-rental agencies are inside the airport terminal and are open as early as the first flight and as late as the last flight: **Budget** (tel. 993/356-0118, toll-free Mex. tel. 800/700-1700, www.budget.com.mx), **Dollar** (tel. 993/356-0211, toll-free Mex. tel. 800/222-8524, www.dollar.com), and **Hertz** (tel. 993/316-4400, ext. 7960, toll-free Mex. tel. 800/709-5000, www.hertz.com.mx).

Comalcalco

Anything but charming, this dusty town is the gateway to the ruins at Comalcalco and to the chocolate haciendas. Just 45 minutes from Villahermosa, it is rare for tourists to stay the night. If you do, no worries, there's at least one decent hotel in town.

SIGHTS
◖ Comalcalco Archaeological Zone

Meaning "place of the house with the grills," Comalcalco (10 A.M.–5 P.M. daily, US$3) is set in the lush green hills of Tabasco's countryside. Evidence suggests the area was settled as early as 800 B.C., and may have formed part of the Olmec civilization, well to the west. It's primary Maya occupation began around A.D 250 and peaked around A.D. 750 or 800. Similarities between structures here and in Palenque suggest Comalcalco was an outpost of that great city.

Comalcalco is unique among the Maya archaeological sites because instead of using heavy cut stone, the Mayas built the structures using thousands of kiln-fired bricks. They bear a striking resemblance to modern-day bricks—in fact that is exactly what archaeologists used to restore some sections. The cores of the pyramids aren't piled rocks either, but packed earth. There was simply no stone in this marshy region to use.

Comalcalco's early residents built temples out of dirt mixed with oyster shells for strength and cohesion. The distinctive kilned bricks were developed A.D. 500–700 and were used to expand and elaborate the packed-dirt temples. Many of the bricks were incised with designs, including animals, humans, glyphs, and patterns, though for the most part the bricks themselves were covered in a thick layer of stucco painted red, blue, green, yellow, and black, which has long since eroded.

Temple I, the immense structure on the left as you walk in from the entrance, has the best remaining example of the stucco high relief that once covered most of the structures. Look for the animal figures along the pyramid's southeast corner as well as

THE STATE OF TABASCO

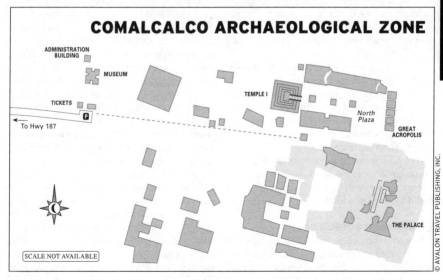

COMALCALCO ARCHAEOLOGICAL ZONE

ADMINISTRATION BUILDING

MUSEUM

TICKETS

To Hwy 187

TEMPLE I

North Plaza

GREAT ACROPOLIS

THE PALACE

SCALE NOT AVAILABLE

© AVALON TRAVEL PUBLISHING, INC.

Comalcalco is unique among Maya sites because its structures are made of brick instead of cut stone.

a molded skull about halfway up the main stairway. The facial features of these figures are unique, with thick, strangely shaped lips, somewhat resembling the colossal heads in La Venta, yet vastly different in style. Today, these valuable remnants of history are covered with glass and have been roofed over to deter further deterioration.

Opposite Temple I, the **Great Acropolis** sits 80 meters (262 feet) long and has a stucco mask of the Kinich Ahau, the sun god. To the right, walk up a hill to the **Palace,** which reveals a panoramic view of the countryside, including unexcavated mounds and a chocolate plantation in the distance.

A small but very interesting **museum** sits at the entrance to the site. Inside, you'll find excellent artifacts as well as a few human skeletons found by workers while excavating the site.

(Chocolate Haciendas

Tabasco is where cacao was first harvested and chocolate first brewed. Although chocolate manufacturers in other countries have eclipsed

Tabasco in terms of taste and quality, the state remains an important chocolate producer.

Traveling north on Highway 187, **Finca Cholula** (Carretera Comalcalco-Paraíso, tel. 933/334-3815, 9 A.M.–3 P.M. Tue.–Sun., US$2.75) is located about 500 meters (0.3 mile) past the turnoff to the ruins. It offers an interesting guided tour of its *finca* (plantation) and chocolate factory. The visit lasts about an hour, during which you'll stroll through the verdant fields, filled not only with cacao trees, but bananas, coffee plants, tall shade trees— cacao grows best in the shade—and even bee boxes and cinnamon trees. If you're lucky, you'll even spot some toucans or the resident troop of howler monkeys. Next, you'll visit the processing area, where the cacao seed is separated from the shell (which is composted and sold as fertilizer) and the sweet white fruit (used to make cacao liqueur) and then dried in the sun, toasted, ground up, mixed with cacao butter and sugar, and poured into candy molds. There's lots to taste and smell along the way, and you can buy various chocolate products at

CACAO

Although Christopher Columbus first discovered the cacao bean in 1502, it had been known – and coveted – in the Americas for centuries before that. The Aztecs believed that it had been given as a gift to humans by their god, Quetzalcoatl, to make a divine bitter drink. As legend goes, Quetzalcoatl scattered the seeds over Tabasco and in so doing, became lost at sea (perhaps not used to the winds off the Gulf?). He eventually reappeared in the Maya world, this time as the god Kukulcán, beans and all.

For Mayas, cacao was as precious as gold to the conquistadors; in fact, in some isolated villages it was used as currency until the 1840s. Today, it is enjoyed the world over as chocolate. An excellent source of energy, rich in vitamins, minerals, and antioxidants, cacao – in all of its culinary incarnations – just plain tastes good.

a cacao fruit – where chocolate begins

© LIZA PRADO

the end. Cacao trees produce fruit year-round, but the best time to visit is April–May and November–December, which are considered the peak harvest seasons.

If you haven't had your fill of chocolate by the end of the tour, the **Hacienda La Luz,** often referred to as **Wolter's** (next to the Tereno de la Fería, US$2.75), offers a similar, and equally popular, tour.

ACCOMMODATIONS AND FOOD

If you miss the last *combi* to Villahermosa, stay the night at **Hotel Plaza Broca** (Blvd. Adolfo López Mateos at Nicolas Bravo, tel. 933/334-4060, US$23.25 s, US$26–32.50 d). It offers simple but very clean rooms in the heart of town; all have air-conditioning, cable TV, telephone, and 24-hour hot water. With a private parking garage, this is one of the best deals around. Ask for a room in back, as the road in front can get loud.

Taco and hotdog stands rule in this town. While not the healthiest of options, these will definitely keep your belly full for the night. Look for them around the central plaza, just half a block from the *combi* station.

GETTING THERE

Bus

Near the ADO bus station in Villahermosa, **Comali Plus** (Calle Reforma at Calle Bravo) and **Transportes Torruco** (Calle Reforma at La Arboleda) provide identical service to and from Comalcalco. Van service runs every 20 minutes (4:30 A.M.–9 P.M. daily, US$2.50, 45 minutes). Passengers are dropped off and picked up in the center of Comalcalco.

Car

If driving from Villahermosa, head west on Highway 180 toward the city of Cárdenas. When you come to the junction with Highway 187, take it north to Comalcalco.

GETTING AROUND

Getting around downtown Comalcalco is easy on foot. Even though there's not much to look at, everything you might need—vans to Villahermosa, banks, hotels, taco stands—all are concentrated a few blocks from each other.

Once you're at the Comalcalco ruins, you also can walk to Finca Cholula. Its about a 10-minute walk from the ruins to the highway, where you turn right and walk another 10 minutes. The *finca* entrance is around the first large curve; take care walking along the highway as the shoulder is soft and the traffic is fast.

Bus

To head to the ruins or to the Finca Cholula by bus, take any bus headed north on Carretera Comalcalco-Paraíso (US$0.50, 10 minutes). Ask the driver to let you off at the *ruínas* or the Finca Cholula. Note that if you're heading to the ruins by bus, you'll get dropped off at

the turnoff to the ruins. It's another 10-minute walk to the entrance down a paved road. To return, a bus will probably pass before an empty cab does—flag down either on the highway.

Taxi

Taking a cab is the easiest of all options. A ride to or from the Finca Cholula or the ruins runs around US$3 from the center of town. For Hacienda La Luz (Wolter's), cabbing it is the best option, as it's a bit too far to walk and driving or taking a bus is confusing.

Car

If traveling by car to the ruins or Finca Cholula, continue north past the town of Comalcalco on Carretera Comalcalco-Paraíso. You'll see signs for the archaeological site and Finca Cholula near the outskirts of town.

THE STATE OF CHIAPAS

Chiapas is a place of high mountains, thick pine forests, and surprisingly chilly weather, quite different from the hot flat states of Yucatán, Quintana Roo, and Campeche. Chiapanecan Mayas are much more visible than their Yucatecan counterparts, not just for their bright traditional clothing (their hand-woven textiles make Chiapas the artistic hub of the region), but in their cultural and political clout. Yet the regions' history and culture are deeply intertwined, and, like the Yucatán, Chiapas offers travelers a rich array of sites and experiences, from the stunning Maya ruins of Palenque to the charming colonial city of San Cristóbal de las Casas. There are plenty of outdoor excursions as well, though you'll have to venture a bit off the beaten path. In short, travelers who enjoy the Yucatán Peninsula are all but guaranteed to *love* Chiapas.

PLANNING YOUR TIME

Five to seven days in Chiapas is enough to see the main highlights, though you can easily stay for weeks (and many people do just that). Budget one or two days for Palenque—one to see the ruins and museum, and another for a day trip in the surrounding area. San Cristóbal, five hours away, requires another three to four days—you'll want time to visit the sights, like museums and galleries, and to take a day trip (or two) to Sumidero Canyon and nearby indigenous villages. And leave some time to fall in love with San Cristóbal—to sit in the plaza, drink coffee, and soak up the atmosphere of this wonderful little city. Most people leave Chiapas wishing they had more time there, which is worth bearing in mind when you plan your trip.

© LIZA PRADO

HIGHLIGHTS

◖ **Palenque Archaeological Zone:** Palenque's rich history, graceful buildings, and well-preserved carvings and hieroglyphics, make it one of the most beautiful and important sites in the entire Maya world (page 382).

◖ **Yaxchilán Archaeological Zone:** Deep in the rainforest, you'll have one eye on delicate carvings and hillside temples and the other peeled for river crocs and howler monkeys (page 396).

◖ **Templo Santo Domingo:** This grand old church has a great *artesanía* market in front and an excellent museum and community folk art store in its former convent (page 407).

◖ **San Juan Chamula:** Tours of this autonomous indigenous village near San Cristóbal allow outsiders a peek into Maya life and customs without being intrusive or disrespectful (page 419).

◖ **ZOOMAT:** One of Latin America's best zoos, Tuxtla's ZOOMAT has jaguars, tapirs, armadillos, and every other mammal species found in Chiapas, housed in verdant modern enclosures (page 428).

◖ **Cañon del Sumidero:** Take a boat ride from Chiapa de Corzo through this winding river gorge with sheer walls more than a kilometer (0.6 miles) high (page 436).

LOOK FOR ◖ TO FIND RECOMMENDED SIGHTS, ACTIVITIES, DINING, AND LODGING.

In case you're wondering—most do—Chiapas is a peaceful and safe place to visit, though you should take some extra precautions such as not traveling at night (or getting involved in rowdy political demonstrations). And while Chiapas is firmly on the tourist route, prices here are still considerably lower than in most of the Yucatán Peninsula.

HISTORY

The earliest inhabitants of the Chiapas area are presumed to be the Olmecs. The Mayas settled here during the Preclassic period and during the Classic age created their most outstanding structures. Present-day Chiapas was occupied by many groups, most of whom spoke in Maya-derived tongues. The Choles inhabited the jungle; the Tojolabales lived in the plains between the valley of the Chiapas River and jungle; the Chiapanecans occupied the central part of the valley; the Mames lived along the coastal regions; the Zoques lived on the hillsides of the highlands; and the Tzotziles and Tzeltales cultivated the highlands. Today, the largest of these linguistic groups are the Tzotziles and Tzeltales, and they are familiarly referred to as the Chamulans, Zinacantecos, Oxchuqueros, and San Pedranos.

After the intrusion of the Spaniards in 1519 many years of fighting ensued. It was a fight that cost the Spanish dearly—conquistador Bernal Díaz described the native people here as "the most courageous warriors encountered in the New World." The first Spanish army, a mix of Spaniards and their indigenous allies, the Tlaxcaltecans, arrived in 1524 and were soon driven off by the Chiapanecans. In 1527, a Spanish army from Guatemala tried to take over but it too was sent running. Only in 1530, when Diego de Mazariegos arrived, were outsiders able to assume control of the area and,

as in all Spanish conquests, the natives were subjugated and made virtual slaves on their own land.

When Bartolomé de las Casas became bishop in 1544, he tried to abolish slavery and managed to convince the Spanish crown to provide legal protection for native people throughout the New World. For his efforts—only marginally successful—Bishop de las Casas was, and remains, held in great respect by the local indigenous peoples.

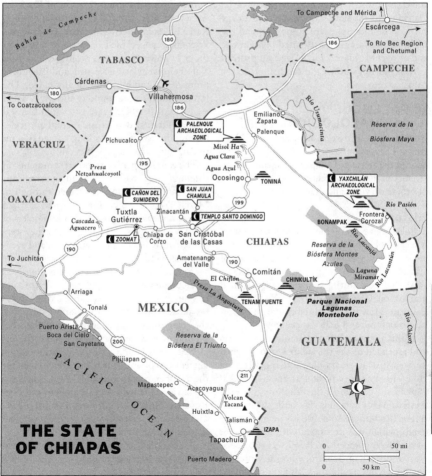

THE STATE OF CHIAPAS

Palenque Archaeological Zone and Town

The town of Santo Domingo de Palenque, usually just called Palenque, is eight kilometers (five miles) from the Palenque archeological zone. The town itself is rather nondescript, but it bulges at its seams with tourists here to visit the ruins. Avenida Juárez is the main drag, where you'll find the bus terminal, tour agencies, and other services, plus a number of no-frills hotels. For a bit more money, many travelers find the leafy neighborhood of La Cañada and the hotels along the road to the ruins to be more pleasant spots to spend the night. There's a small, little-used plaza at one end of Avenida Juárez, and a large sculpture of a Maya warrior's head (and the turnoff to the ruins) at the other.

◖ PALENQUE ARCHAEOLOGICAL ZONE

Palenque is a must-see on any itinerary of Maya ruins. The setting, on a lush green shelf at the edge of the Sierra de Chiapas forest, adds to the serenity of this noble archaeological compound of ornate carvings and graceful design.

History

Scholars have been able to decipher enough Maya glyphs to construct a reasonable genealogy of the Palenque kings, from the rule of Chaacal I (A.D. 501) to the demise of Kuk (A.D. 783). But it was during the reign of Lord Pakal and his son, Chan Bahlum (A.D. 615–701), that Palenque grew from a minor city to an important economic and political center.

K'inich Janaab Pakal was born in A.D. 603 and ascended to the throne in A.D. 615, when he was just 12 years old. During his long rule—he died in A.D. 684 at age 81—Pakal expanded Palenque's influence throughout the western Maya lowlands. He built the Temple of the Inscriptions to house his own elaborate tomb, which was decorated with deifications of his life and ancestors. Pakal was succeeded by his son, Chan Bahlum, who was noteworthy for having six digits on his hands and feet.

(To maintain the royal bloodline, Maya rulers often took relatives as their wives, eventually leading to birth defects. Pakal himself had a clubfoot, and some archaeologists believe his mother and father were siblings. Likewise, Pakal may have married his sister, leading to Chan Bahlum's defects.)

Chan Bahlum reigned for 18 years and built the temples of the Cross, Foliated Cross, and Sun to prove the preordination of his rule. After he died in A.D. 702, his younger brother, Kan Xul, took the reins of power. His rule was Palenque's apogee; the Palace was enlarged and the city's power reached its greatest extent. Kan Xul's heirs were less successful, and Palenque's prominence and glitter gradually faded. The last historical record found in the city is dated A.D. 799; it is a blackware vase from Central Mexico marked with crude hieroglyphs celebrating the accession of a king named 6 Cimi to Palenque's throne.

The earliest Spanish-recorded comments on Palenque were made by a Spanish army captain, Antonio del Río, who passed through in March 1785. (Two centuries earlier, Hernán Cortés came within a few dozen kilometers of the ruins but apparently never knew they were there.) Del Río drew maps and plans and eventually received a royal order to excavate the site for a year. But the Spaniard's "excavation" was amateur and brutish and led to the destruction of a number of structures. Captain del Río also broadcast wild and fantastic assumptions about the beginnings of the Mayas. It wasn't long before Europeans envisioned Palenque as the lost city of Atlantis or a sister civilization to the ancient Egyptians. A true picture of Palenque didn't emerge until the mid-1800s, when the American diplomat John L. Stephens and English artist Frederick Catherwood visited the site and wrote and drew realistic and detailed accounts of what they saw.

For detailed reports and photos of current and past archaeological digs, check out www .Mesoweb.com/palenque.

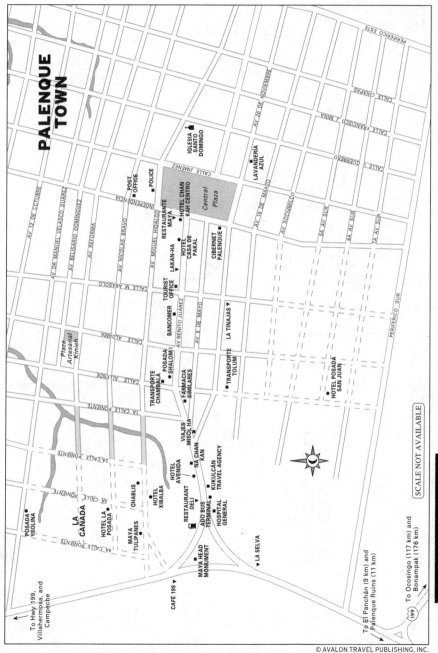

PALENQUE TOWN

To Hwy 199, Villahermosa, and Campeche

AV. 12 DE OCTUBRE
AV. DE MANUEL VELASCO SUAREZ
AV. BELISARIO DOMINGUEZ
AV. REFORMA
AV. NICOLAS BRAVO
AV. MIGUEL HIDALGO
AV. BENITO JUAREZ
AV. 5 DE MAYO
AV. 20 DE NOVIEMBRE
AV. 18 DE MARZO

CALLE INDEPENDENCIA
CALLE M. ABASOLO
CALLE ALDAMA
CALLE ALLENDE
1A. CALLE PONIENTE
2A. CALLE PONIENTE
3A. CALLE PONIENTE
4A. CALLE PONIENTE
CALLE JIMENEZ
CALLE CHIAPAS
CALLE FRANCISCO J. MINA
CALLE V. GUERRERO
AV. XOCHIMILCO
5A. AV. SUR
YA. AV. SUR
6A. AV. SUR
YA. AV. SUR
PERIFERICO SUR
PERIFERICO ESTE

POST OFFICE
POLICE
IGLESIA SANTO DOMINGO
RESTAURANTE MAYA
HOTEL CHAN KAH CENTRO
LAKAN-HA
HOTEL CASA DE PAKAL
CIBERNET PALENQUE
Central Plaza
LAVANDERIA AZUL
TOURIST OFFICE
BANCOMER
LA TINAJAS
POSADA SHALOM!
FARMACIA SIMILARES
TRANSPORTE CHAMBALA
TRANSPORTE TOLUM!
HOTEL POSADA SAN JUAN
Plaza Artesanal Kimoh
VIAJES MISOL-HA
HOTEL AVENIDA
NA CHAN KAN
KUKULCAN TRAVEL AGENCY
HOTEL XIBALBA
RESTAURANT DELI
ADO BUS TERMINAL
HOSPITAL GENERAL
CHABLIS
HOTEL LA POSADA
MAYA TULIPANES
POSADA YSOLINA
LA CAÑADA
MAYA HEAD MONUMENT
CAFÉ 199
LA SELVA

To El Panchán (9 km) and Palenque Ruins (11 km)
To Ocosingo (117 km) and Bonampak (176 km)
199

SCALE NOT AVAILABLE

© AVALON TRAVEL PUBLISHING, INC.

THE STATE OF CHIAPAS

THE STATE OF CHIAPAS

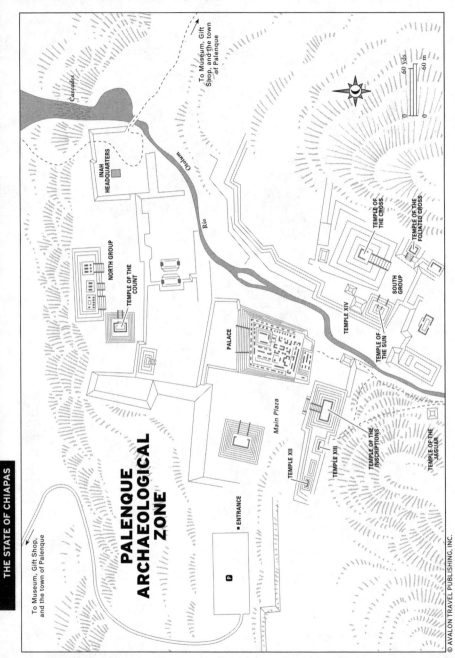

PALENQUE ARCHAEOLOGICAL ZONE

To Museum, Gift Shop, and the town of Palenque

Cascadas

To Museum, Gift Shop, and the town of Palenque

INAH HEADQUARTERS

Rio Otolum

NORTH GROUP

TEMPLE OF THE COUNT

PALACE

Main Plaza

ENTRANCE

P

TEMPLE XII

TEMPLE XIII

TEMPLE OF THE INSCRIPTIONS

TEMPLE OF THE JAGUAR

TEMPLE XIV

TEMPLE OF THE SUN

SOUTH GROUP

TEMPLE OF THE CROSS

TEMPLE OF THE FOLIATED CROSS

60 yds
60 m
0
0

© AVALON TRAVEL PUBLISHING, INC.

Temples XII and XIII

Through the entrance you follow a short road and a few steps up to Palenque's main plaza. The first two temples on your right are Temple XII and XIII. Temple XII is also known as Temple of the Skull—look for the carved stone skull about halfway up the steps. Temple XIII is just beyond. Both temples were the sites of major excavations in the early 1990s. In Temple XII, archaeologists discovered a long passageway leading from the top of the pyramid to a sarcophagus. Inside were the remains of an unidentified leader, plus several other bodies, most likely the leader's servants. The passage and tomb are at present off-limits to visitors. In Temple XIII, a maintenance worker discovered a loose stone, behind which archaeologists found a passageway and a massive tomb, painted a brilliant red inside and holding the remains of a woman. The tomb has few markings, so archaeologists have dubbed the deceased the "Red Queen." It seems likely that the woman was Pakal's mother, but that has not been proven.

Temple of the Inscriptions

Just beyond XIII you'll come to the Temple of the Inscriptions, also on your right. At the top of the 24-meter (78.7-foot) high pyramid is the temple, where magnificent tablets of glyphs tell the ancestral history of the Palenque rulers. It was toward the rear of the gallery that Mexican archaeologist Alberto Ruz L'Huillier first uncovered, in 1949, a secret stairway cleverly hidden under a stone slab. The stairs were intentionally jammed with rubble and debris, clearly to prevent access to whatever lay beneath.

It took Ruz three years to excavate the stairway, which descended in several sections all the way to ground level. At the foot of the stairs Ruz found another sealed passage, in front of which were clay dishes filled with red pigment, jade earplugs, beads, a large oblong pearl, and the skeletons of six sacrificial victims. A final large stone door was removed, and on June 15, 1952, Ruz made what many consider to be the greatest discovery of Maya archaeology: the untouched crypt of K'inich Janaab Pakal, or Lord Shield Pakal.

The centerpiece of the chamber is the massive sarcophagus, hewn from a single stone and topped by a flat, four-meter (13.1-foot) long, five-ton slab of stone. The slab is beautifully carved with the figure of Pakal in death, surrounded by monsters, serpents, sun and shell signs, and many more glyphs that recount death and its passage. The walls of the chamber are decorated with various gods, from which scientists have deduced a tremendous amount about the Palencanos' theology.

Working slowly to preserve everything in its pristine state, Ruz didn't open the lid of the sarcophagus for six months. It took a week of difficult work in the stifling, dust-choked room to finally lift the five-ton slab. On November 28, 1952, the scientists had their first peek inside. In the large rectangular sarcophagus they found another, body-shaped sarcophagus (a first in Maya history), within which was Pakal's skeleton, with precious jewelry and special accoutrements to accompany him on his journey into the next world. A jade mosaic mask covered the face, under which his own teeth had been painted red. (The mask was exhibited at the Anthropological Museum in Mexico City until December 24, 1985, when it was stolen along with several other precious historical artifacts. The mask was recovered in an abandoned house in Acapulco in 1989, mostly undamaged.)

The excavation of the Temple of the Inscriptions began a new concept in Maya archaeology. It was formerly believed that the pyramids had served a single function: to bring the temples at their summits closer to the heavens. But now it's known that pyramids were used as crypts for revered leaders as well. All of this bears a resemblance to the culture and beliefs of the Egyptians, and imaginative students of history have tried to link the two cultures—so far unsuccessfully.

The Temple of the Inscriptions and the passageway to Pakal's tomb were closed for many years, for fear of the erosion that thousands of hands and feet caused. It was reopened in

2006, amazingly enough, even as the directors of other major sites, including Uxmal and Chichén Itzá, restrict access to their most famous structures.

The Palace

Palenque's Palace is one of the most compelling structures among Maya ruins. Directly in front of you as you walk up the main pathway with the Temple of the Inscriptions on your right, the Palace occupies the unusually large space of a city block. The four-story tower, another rarity of the Classic Mayas, will immediately catch your eye. The top of the tower had collapsed by the time it was rediscovered, so the original height and appearance could only be guessed from the pattern of rubble. Archaeologists believe the tower was constructed to give a good view of the winter solstice (December 22), when the sun appears to drop directly into the Temple of the Inscriptions. It probably was also used to make astronomical calculations, an important part of Maya religious rites. The Palace has a large, sunken courtyard, surrounded by steps and adorned with excellent stone and stucco bas-reliefs. The large figures on the east side depict important prisoners captured in war. The entire Palace sits on a platform 10 meters (32.8 feet) high; stairs lead into a labyrinth of rooms and passageways that served as royal sleeping quarters.

South Group

Just east of the Temple of the Inscriptions, you come to the South Group, which includes the Temple of the Cross, the Temple of the Foliated Cross, and the Temple of the Sun, all built around a plaza on the edge of the jungle. The Temple of the Sun is the first of these, with tablets at the top depicting Lord Pakal and Chan Bahlum. The Temple of the Cross is the largest of the group and contains tablets of Chan Bahlum wearing the full paraphernalia of royalty after his accession and accompanied by the cigar-smoking God L, a lord of the underworld, in an owl-feather headdress. The small Temple of the Foliated

© LIZA PRADO

The Temple of the Cross is one of many magnificent structures at Palenque.

Cross against the jungle wall to the right holds more tablets celebrating the succession of Chan Bahlum. A team of Mexican archaeologists excavating the South Group found a major tomb at the base of the Temple of the Cross, containing the headless body of an official, perhaps the governor of a neighboring city, and 630 pieces of jade. They also found five perfectly preserved incense burners and some extremely fine ceramic figurines. One of these figurines, on display in the museum, is considered one of the finest Maya sculptures yet found; it depicts a man seated on a square bench. His head has been broken off, but his helmet, in the form of a bird, was found nearby.

East of these structures (behind the palace), you'll find a well-marked path that leads past several smaller structures down to the main road. You can also enter this way, but the path is steep in places and makes a much nicer descent than ascent. You may see some birds or even monkeys. The path opens onto the road a short distance from the museum.

Museum

After you see the ruins, be sure to leave time to visit Palenque's museum (10 A.M.–4:30 P.M. Tues.–Sun.), which contains some truly incredible stucco and stone sculptures, with explanations in English and Spanish. It's not huge—an hour will suffice—but definitely worth visiting; note that the museum is closed on Monday. Admission is included with the ticket into the ruins—be sure to hang onto it! A path from inside the ruins leads down the steep hill and rejoins the road near the museum.

Practicalities

The archaeological site is open 8 A.M.–5 P.M. daily (US$3.50). The museum is open 10 A.M.–4:30 P.M. Tue.–Sun. Guides can be hired at the entrance to the ruins; a basic tour lasts 1.5–2 hours (US$42–56) and is available in various languages.

Getting There

Local shuttle companies provide *combi* service to and from the ruins (every 10–15 minutes, 6 A.M.–6 P.M. daily, US$1). You can board at the depots across from the main bus terminal, at the Maya Head monument, or anywhere along the road to the ruins. Be aware that if you buy your bus ticket at the depot, the cashier may try to sell you a round-trip ticket. Don't bother—this saves no money and no time; on the contrary, it means you'll have to wait for a bus from that specific company when you're ready to leave.

There is parking at the ruins, although on busy days drivers end up parking well down the access road. A taxi between town and the ruins costs around US$5.

There is a national park service gate at the entrance to the ruins—a US$1 per person fee is changed to pass through, regardless of whether you're in a bus or car.

OTHER SIGHTS

The following sights are along the Río Tulijá, or the river *Yaks-Ha* (Blue Water), on the highway between Palenque and Ocosingo. The name is apt—the river's water has a striking blue-green hue, like the Caribbean but less transparent.

Getting There

Most travel agencies in Palenque offer a popular tour to these sister sights, typically spending 30 minutes at Misol Ha, an hour at Agua Clara, and four hours at the last and most dramatic, Agua Azul. Though it's a bit rushed, it's a convenient way to see the area in a day.

To visit the sights on your own, catch any **second-class bus** or *colectivo* headed to Ocosingo or San Cristóbal and ask to be dropped at the turnoffs (US$1.25–1.50). There is sometimes a truck waiting to ferry travelers from the highway to the park entrances (US$0.50–1), otherwise prepare to walk the 1.5–4 kilometers (0.9–2.5 miles). Note: Be sure to leave early and to head back to town by mid-afternoon, since you may have to wait a long time before a bus stops. It's not recommended that people travel (or wait!) on this road at night.

Misol Ha

Maya for "waterfall," Misol Ha (20 km/12.4 mi south of Palenque, 7 A.M.–6 P.M. daily, US$1.50) is definitely a waterfall, and a beautiful one at that, falling 30 meters (98.4 feet) into a shimmering pool. The fine spray in the air keeps everything cool and pleasant, and the swimming could hardly be better. Concrete stairs lead behind the waterfall and pool; visitors also can continue over some slippery rocks into a nearby cave. There's a small eatery on-site.

Agua Clara

Agua Clara (40 km/25 mi south of Palenque, 7 A.M.–6 P.M. daily, US$1.50) is a pretty spot where the Río Tulijá slows into a long, wide pool between sloping stone banks. It's a good place to appreciate the river's famous turquoise color. A long rope bridge spans the river from a high bluff, and one or two tourists usually dare each other into making the long, whooping plunge from the middle of the bridge into the water below.

THE STATE OF CHIAPAS

Agua Azul

Agua Azul (60 km/37 mi south of Palenque, 7 A.M.–6 P.M. daily, US$2) is the most famous stop on the route. Designated a national park in 1980, it has over 500 hefty waterfalls that crash and boil down several kilometers of limestone riverbed. When it's not a frothy white, the water is a distinctive blue. A few pools are even calm and large enough for swimming. Trails alongside the river lead far upriver and mostly are used by locals to carry wood, sweet potatoes, bananas, and other goods to and from tiny villages. As you climb higher, crossing rickety bridges and at some points just a log or two, there are beautiful views of the green valley below, criss-crossed by bluish brooks and rivers. The park also has a number of small eateries, snack shops, and places to change your clothes.

SHOPPING

Unremarkable shops line the main streets of Palenque selling postcards, T-shirts, and arts and crafts. They're good if you're running short on time or if you want something particularly kitschy to take home. There is, however, one place that stands out—the **Plaza Artesanal Kinich** (Calle Aldama at Av. Reforma, 10 A.M.–10 P.M. daily). Off the main drag, this indigenous market mostly sells the colorful fabrics and beautiful hand stitching that Chiapas is famous for. You'll also see some handcrafted toys, Maya replicas, and even a few Guatemalan goods. Take your time looking around—this is as good as it gets in this town.

ACCOMMODATIONS

The main reason to stay in town is to have easy access to the bus terminal and tour agencies, plus banks, Internet, and a wide selection of restaurants. Hotels here tend to be a bit run-down—adequate for a night or two but not especially pleasant. In the northwest corner of town, a neighborhood called La Cañada has a handful of good lodging options in a more secluded shady setting, if you don't mind the slightly longer walk into town. And on the road to the ruins are several higher-end hotels, and

a neighborhood called El Panchán, nestled in the forest, with eco-minded accommodations and a distinctly bohemian air.

In Town
UNDER US$50

Just a couple of blocks from the center of town, **Hotel Posada San Juan** (Allende at Av. Emilio Rabasa, tel. 916/345-0616, US$5 dorm, US$14–18.50 s/d with fan, US$32.50 s/d with a/c) offers an open-air mixed dorm that has twin beds, each with a futon-style pad. Sheets and communal lockers are provided (the reception holds the keys to the lockers). If you're looking for more privacy, the single/double rooms are basic but spotless. Be sure to ask for one at the back of the property since the *tortillería* in front is noisy in the morning.

Once you get past the dingy-looking lobby, **Hotel Avenida** (Av. Juárez 173, US$20 s/d with fan, US$35 s/d with a/c) opens onto a good-size, well-kept pool with a jungle backdrop. Rooms are simple but very clean and all have a television and screened windows. Many have porches looking out into the wilderness too. Just a block form the ADO bus station, this is a good value.

Posada Shalom I (Av. Juárez between Calles Allende and Aldama, tel. 916/345-0944, www.posadashalom.com, US$14 s, US$18.50 d, US$23 s with a/c, US$28 d with a/c) is in the heart of downtown and offers sparse, clean rooms with hot-water bathrooms and cable TV. Most have windows that open onto an interior hallway, so units are dark but quiet. If it's full, try its sister hotel, **Posada Shalom II** (Corregidora at Calle Abasolo, tel. 916/345-2641) which has almost identical prices and facilities.

In La Cañada district, **Hotel La Posada** (Av. Nicolas Bravo at Calle 3 Pte., tel. 916/345-0437, US$20 s/d with fan, US$30 s/d with a/c) is a clean and simple hotel. Its rooms are set far back from the road, away from the disco and restaurant noise that oppresses some of the neighboring hotels. Rooms on the 2nd floor are larger, though all have plenty of hot water and fans. Tables and chairs also are set out on a wide lawn in front of the rooms, where travelers often can be found relaxing.

On a quiet street behind La Cañada neighborhood is **◖ Posada Ysolina** (Av. Manuel Velasco Suarez 51, tel. 916/345-1524, US$21 s, US$23 d, US$25 s with a/c, US$28 d with a/c), where rooms are decorated with simple Mexican furniture, *talavera* tiles, and stenciled walls. Some have balconies and a couple even have bathtubs. Coffee and an assortment of breads are available each morning in the lobby. Worth every extra step it takes to get to the center of town.

Chablis (Calle Merle Green 7, La Cañada district, tel. 916/345-0870, US$50 s/d) offers 20 spacious and spotless rooms with cable TV, air-conditioning, and free wireless Internet. There also is a laid-back *palapa*-roofed lounge that is great for relaxing, reading, or—as the hotel name suggests—enjoying a glass of wine or two.

Across the street, **Hotel Xibalba** (Calle Merle Green 9, La Cañada district, tel. 916/345-0411, www.palenquemx.com/shivalva, US$28 s, US$32.50 d, US$37 s with a/c, US$35 d with a/c) is another excellent choice; rooms here are distributed in two buildings but all are cozy, clean, and comfortable. The ones in the Maya-temple-look-alike have A-frame ceilings on the 2nd floor and overlook a tropical forest. There's also an excellent restaurant on-site.

US$50-100

Hotel Chan Kah Centro (Av. Juárez at Independencia, tel. 916/345-0318, www.chan-kah.com.mx, US$55 s/d with a/c) is a reasonably clean and modern hotel offering acceptable though somewhat cramped accommodations. Some rooms have balconies overlooking the central plaza, which is nice for people watching. Be sure to confirm your stay before arriving—some readers have complained of lost reservations.

The best high-end choice in town, **◖ Maya Tulipanes** (Merle Green 6, La Cañada district, tel. 916/345-0201, www.mayatulipanes.com.mx, US$100 s/d) is a comfortable hotel offering excellent service and modern amenities, including air-conditioning and free wireless Internet,

all in a leafy forest setting. Rooms have tile floors, brightly colored walls, and good beds. A welcoming pool is in the center of the property as is a good restaurant—both bonuses. Tour groups often stay here but it doesn't seem to affect the service that independent guests receive. A fine choice, budget permitting.

Near the Ruins
UNDER US$50

At the far end of El Panchán district, **Rakshita's** (El Panchán, Carr. Ruínas Km. 4.5, tel. 916/100-6908, rakshita@yahoo.com, www.geocities.com/rakshita/Contact/contact.html, US$2 pp tent or hammock, US$6 dorm, US$12 s cabaña, US$15 d cabaña) is a New-Agey place in the middle of the jungle offering a wide range of accommodations—from a huge *palapa* to hang up your hammock to colorful cabañas with rustic private bathrooms. There's also a two-story yoga and meditation *palapa*, where free instruction is often given, a small massage hut next to a gurgling stream, a small pool, and a fantastic vegetarian restaurant. It's a great place to kick back for a day or two or three....

Named after the welcoming owner, **◖ Chato's Cabañas** (El Panchán, Carr. Ruínas Km. 4.5, www.elpanchan.com, US$12 s, US$15 d) offers clean cabañas of various sizes, all set deep in the jungle of El Panchán. All have private bath and fans. Be sure to ask for a newer cabaña, as the older ones are a bit worn. There's also a nice pool and a popular restaurant—Don Mucho—on-site.

Although it sounds like a Vegas casino, **Jungle Palace** (El Panchán, Carr. Ruínas Km. 4.5, www.elpanchan.com, US$2 pp tent or hammock, US$7.50 s with shared bathroom, US$9.50 d with shared bathroom) is a simple cabaña hotel offering 18 simple units in a manicured section of the jungle. Some have porches and hammocks—a definite plus. Hammock spaces under a *palapa* and camping spots also are available at the back of the property.

◖ Margarita and Ed (El Panchán, Carr. Ruínas Km. 4.5, tel. 916/341-0063, US$13 s cabañas, US$15 d cabañas, US$15–21 s/d,

US$15 s/d with kitchenette, US$28 s/d with a/c) is a good option if you like being in the wild but prefer the comforts of the modern world. Rooms are reminiscent of a mid-range hotel room in town—spotlessly clean, tile floors, decent beds, and fans or air-conditioning. Not much else. A couple of rustic cabañas also are available near the entrance.

Just one kilometer (0.6 miles) from the ruins, the sprawling **Maya Bell Trailer Park** (Carr. Ruínas Km. 5.5, US$3.50 pp tent or hammock, US$8–10 s/d shared bath, US$12 trailer, US$37 s/d, US$50 s/d with a/c) is a laid-back hippie-Rastafarian sort of place. Tents and hammocks are set up under *palapa* shelters on a small hillside, while trailers and spillover tents are on a large grassy area near the entrance. Shared bathrooms are kept relatively clean and there are basins and clotheslines for hand-washing clothes. Private rooms are surprisingly pleasant, with low comfortable beds and windows facing the grassy center. There's also a swimming pool on-site but it's kind of grubby and unappealing; it's best for relaxing on the side, a beer in hand, listening to guests play the bongo drums. There's also a decent restaurant on-site.

If El Panchán isn't quite your scene but you'd like to stay near the action, consider staying across the highway at **Cabañas y Camping Jaguar** (Carr. Ruínas Km. 4.5, www.elpanchan .com, US$2 pp tent, US$7.50 s with shared bathroom, US$9.50 d with shared bathroom, US$12 s, US$15 d). Although not as alluring as staying in the thick of the jungle, the cabañas are modern and comfortable and the cleared grounds offer spectacular stargazing.

OVER US$50

Set in a manicured jungle environment, the upscale 【 **Chan-Kah Resort Village** (Carr. Ruínas Km. 3, tel. 916/345-1134, toll-free Mex. tel. 800/714-3247, www .chan-kah.com.mx, US$141 casita with a/c) boasts 73 spacious *casitas,* each with stone-encrusted floors, porches, and views of the thick jungle or a gurgling creek—one even has a Maya ruin in its backyard! Ask for a casita toward the back of the property as these were

built more recently. There's a good restaurant on-site, a well-outfitted game room, and an impressive stone-floored pool too.

FOOD

As with hotels, Palenque has a large but not particularly inspiring selection of restaurants. With a few exceptions, expect standard Mexican dishes at moderate prices.

Mexican

In Town: Above a mini-mart and across from the bus terminal, you'd expect 【 **Restaurant Deli** (Av. Juárez s/n, tel. 916/345-2511, 7 A.M.–midnight daily, US$3–8) to sell hot dogs and Big Gulps. In fact, this bright eatery is surprisingly pleasant and an ideal spot for breakfast or lunch before a long bus ride—the pancakes with peach topping and the *huevos habañil* (eggs served with a habanero-cilantro sauce) are fantastic options. If you had a long day at the ruins, call for delivery, including snacks from the mini-mart.

Lakan-Ha (Av. Juárez between Calles Abasolo and Independencia, 7:30 A.M.–10 P.M. daily, US$3–10) is a breakfast favorite, with a variety of inexpensive combo plates, but it can be counted on for a decent, reasonably priced meal anytime. The pleasant dining room is on the 2nd floor, away from the hubbub on Avenida Juárez.

Restaurante Maya (Av. Independencia at Av. Hidalgo, tel. 916/345-0042, 7 A.M.–11 P.M. daily, US$4–12) is an old standby, with bright tablecloths and a mural on the back wall. Reputation lets it get away with somewhat inflated prices, but the location facing the plaza is good and the meals—standard chicken, fish, and beef dishes—reliable. A newer, brighter sister restaurant of the same name in La Cañada neighborhood has similar fare plus live marimba music most nights.

Near the Ruins: One of the nicest places around, **La Selva** (Carr. Ruínas Km. 0.5, tel. 916/345-0363, 8 A.M.–midnight daily, US$9–20) serves mostly traditional Mexican and seafood dishes under a high *palapa* roof. Items are a bit overpriced, but the classy atmosphere makes up for it. About a 10-minute walk from the Maya Head statue.

Other Specialties

In Town: Las Tinajas (Calle 20 de Noviembre at Calle Abasolo, 7:30 A.M.–10 P.M. daily, US$2–6) is one of the better options in town. In addition to standard fish, chicken, and beef dishes, there also are basic pastas, sandwiches, and salads. The main dining area is right on the corner with tables looking onto both streets. Portions are hefty—*jarras* (pitchers) of fruit drinks are a good deal for the very, very thirsty.

In La Cañada, the restaurant at **Hotel Xibalba** (Calle Merle Green 9, tel. 916/345-0411, 7 A.M.–11 P.M. daily, US$4–9) has thick wooden tables and high bright walls. A peaceful spot for breakfast, dinner is somewhat livelier, thanks to live marimba music at the restaurant across the street. Choose from a variety of vegetarian, Italian, and Mexican dishes, all well prepared and graciously served.

A boxy, modern structure, **Café 199** (Av. Juárez at the road to the ruins, 7 A.M.–11 P.M. daily, US$4–9) is a hip restaurant serving great mixed drinks and creative light fare, from sandwiches to crepes. Seating is open-air on the 1st floor, or in an understated indoor dining room upstairs.

Near the Ruins: Café Restaurante Don Mucho (El Panchán, Carr. Ruínas Km. 4.5, 9 A.M.–11 P.M. daily, US$3–10) is a popular spot in the jungle neighborhood of El Panchán. Italian and Mexican dishes line the menu, mostly homemade pastas, wood-oven pizzas, and *comida típica*. There's often live music and fire dancers too, which keeps the place busy between 9–11 P.M.

For excellent vegetarian food, head toward the ruins and **Rakshita's** (El Panchán, Carr. Ruínas Km. 4.5, tel. 916/100-6908, rakshita@yahoo.com, 7 A.M.–8 P.M. daily, US$2.50–4.50). A bohemian, jungle-enclosed restaurant specializing in light meals—eggs, sandwiches, salads—and creative juices. Live acoustic music also is played weekend nights.

INFORMATION

Tourist Information

The **tourist office** (Av. Juárez at Abasolo, 9 A.M.–9 P.M. Mon.–Sat., 9 A.M.–1 P.M. Sun.) hands out decent maps and can answer basic questions.

Hospitals

The Hospital General (Av. Juárez s/n, tel. 916/345-1443, 24 hours daily) is a large blue building just west of the bus station.

Pharmacies

Farmacia Similares (Av. Juárez at Calle Allende, tel. 916/345-2250) is open 24 hours daily.

Police

The police station (parque central, tel. 916/345-0141, 24 hours daily) is in the Palacio Municipal.

SERVICES

Money

Located on Avenida Juárez, **Bancomer** (8 A.M.–4 P.M. Mon.–Sat.) and **Banamex** (9 A.M.–4 P.M. Mon.–Fri.) have reliable ATMs and cash travelers checks.

Internet and Telephone

Check email and call home at **Cibernet Palenque** (Av. Independencia at Av. 5 de Mayo, 9 A.M.–11 P.M. daily). Internet costs US$0.90 an hour; calls run US$0.35 a minute to the United States and Canada, US$0.55 a minute to Europe.

Near the ruins, try El Panchán's no-name **Internet café** (Carr. Ruínas Km. 4.5, 9 A.M.–11 P.M. daily) for Internet (US$1.50/hour) and international calls (US$0.35/min to United States and Canada, US$0.52/min to Europe).

Post Office

The post office (Av. Independencia at Calle Bravo) is open from 9 A.M.–6 P.M. Monday–Friday and 9 A.M.–1 P.M. Saturday.

Travel Agencies

A great many travel outfits want your business. Almost all offer the same tours at pretty much the same prices. The most popular trips are to Misol Ha, Agua Clara, and Agua Azul (US$11 pp, 9 A.M.–4:30 P.M.); day trips to

Bonampak and Yaxchilán ruins (US$55 pp, 6 A.M.–7:30 P.M.); and two-day excursions to Bonampak, Yaxchilán, and the Lancandón forest (US$100 pp, including meals and lodging).

Tour operators also offer combination trips, such as a morning tour of Palenque ruins followed by an afternoon at Misol Ha and Agua Azul (US$10 pp). Convenient drop-off tours include spending the day visiting Bonampak and Yaxchilán, then taking a 25-minute boat ride to Betel, Guatemala, where a shuttle takes you to Flores (US$88 pp, including all transport and meals).

Reliable operators include **Na Chan Kan** (Av. Juárez next to Hotel Avenida, tel. 916/345-0263, nachan@tnet.net.mx, 8 A.M.–9 P.M. daily), **Viajes Misol Ha** (Av. Juárez 148 at Av. 20 de Noviembre 8, tel. 916/345-2271, 7 A.M.–9 P.M. daily), and **Kukulcán Travel Agency** (Av. Juárez 8 next to the ADO terminal, tel. 916/345-1506, 10 A.M.–6 P.M. daily).

Launderette

Lavandería Azul (Av. 20 de Noviembre between Calles Jiménez and Guerrero, tel. 916/345-2692, 8 A.M.–9 P.M. Mon.–Sat., 10 A.M.–3 P.M. Sun., US$1 per 1 kg/2.2 lbs for five-hr service, US$2 1 kg/2.2 lbs for two-hr. service).

In El Panchán, **Jungle Palace Lavandería** (El Panchán, Carr. Ruínas Km. 4.5, 7 A.M.–3 P.M. Mon.–Sat.) provides laundry service for US$2.50 per three kilograms (6.6 pounds).

Storage

Near the bus terminal, **Kukulcán Travel Agency** (Av. Juárez 8, tel. 916/345-1506, 10 A.M.–6 P.M. daily) charges US$0.25 an hour or US$4 a day.

GETTING THERE
Air

The tiny Palenque International Airport (PQM) is located about five kilometers (three miles) north of town; there was no regular passenger service there at the time of research.

Bus

The **ADO bus terminal** (Av. Juárez s/n, tel. 916/345-1344) is about 100 meters (328 feet) from the turnoff to the Palenque ruins. Destinations include:

- Campeche, US$20, 5–5.5 hours, take any Mérida bus

- Cancún, US$46–53, 12.5–13.5 hours, 5:20 P.M., 7:35 P.M., 8 P.M., 8:55 P.M., and 9 P.M.*

- Mérida, US$30, 7.5–8 hours, 8 A.M., 9 P.M., and 11:25 P.M.

- Mexico City, US$62, 10–11 hours, 6 P.M. (TAPO) and 9 P.M. (Norte)

- Ocosingo, US$6.50, 2.5 hours, take any San Cristóbal bus

- San Cristóbal, US$11, five hours, 6:25 A.M.*, 8:50 A.M., 9:30 A.M., 11:40 A.M. and 2:10 P.M.; the 11 P.M.–2 A.M. departures are not recommended for safety reasons.

- Villahermosa, US$8.50, 2–2.5 hours, 10 departures 7 A.M.–9 P.M.

An asterisk denotes first-class service.

Car

There are still no car rental agencies in Palenque; the nearest ones are Villahermosa, and the road from between the two cities (about 150 km/93 mi, two hours) is safe and pleasant. You can also rent in San Cristóbal de las Casas, about five hours away and more likely to be on your itinerary than Villahermosa. However, armed robberies have occurred on the Palenque-San Cristóbal highway, especially at night, so plan on driving during daylight hours only. Also, fill up whenever you can, as gas stations are few and far between.

GETTING AROUND

Palenque town is easy to navigate on foot. To get to the ruins or accommodations outside of town, *colectivos* shuttle between town and the ruins every 10–15 minutes 6 A.M.–6 P.M. (US$1); flag them down anywhere along the road. A private taxi costs about US$3.

The Río Usumacinta Valley

Visiting Yaxchilán and Bonampak archaeological zones used to be something of an adventure—a long, bumpy drive from Palenque into the heart of the lush forest, followed by a hike and boat ride through lands inhabited by reclusive Lacondón indigenous communities. Nowadays, paved roads have made it easy for travelers to make it to these sites on their own or with any number of tour agencies.

While the challenge of getting to the ruins certainly added to their mystique, Yaxchilán and Bonampak are no less impressive for being more accessible. Here visitors are treated to fantastic painted frescos, huge stelae, finely carved lintels, and plenty of howler monkeys and huge river crocs along the way.

Tours

Tour operators in Palenque offer one- and two-day tours to Bonampak and Yaxchilán. Day trips typically begin at 6 A.M. and include one hour at Bonampak, two hours at Yaxchilán, and lunch in Frontera Corozal before driving back to Palenque, arriving shortly after dark. Two-day trips include visits to both ruins plus a four-hour hike through the Lancandón forests with a local guide and overnighting in rustic cabañas.

In Frontera Corozal, **Escudo Jaguar** (tel. 555/329-0995, escudojaguar_hotel@yahoo .com.mx, www.chiapastours.com.mx/escudo jaguar) also offers tours and transport. Besides transporting day-trippers back and forth to Yaxchilán, it offers day-long and overnight excursions to several remote Maya ruins in the area, including Planchón de las Figuras, Altar de los Sacrificios, and Piedras Negras. Prices range from US$275 to US$500; ask in advance if goods and/or camping gear are included.

Getting There

The road between Palenque and Frontera Corozal has the reputation of being dangerous, with armed bandits stopping cars and even *combis* to rob their passengers. However, the problem seems to have diminished greatly, and it is no longer out of the question to visit the ruins by rental car or public transportation. You should still avoid driving at night, however.

BONAMPAK ARCHAEOLOGICAL ZONE

Bonampak is a modest site, but the possessor of some of the best ancient Maya murals ever discovered. The brilliant teal and red murals adorn the walls of a small innocuous temple partway up the steps of the city's main acropolis. The murals depict, among other things, sacrifices, ritual bloodletting, and violent battle scenes. The images shattered previous assumptions about the Maya, who had been portrayed by many researchers as a peace-loving civilization, in sharp contrast to Central Mexican indigenous groups and, of course, the Spanish colonizers.

History

Located in a fertile valley, it is near a small tributary of the Río Lacanjá, and with protective hills to one side. The earliest evidence of human occupation at Bonampak are ceramics dated to A.D. 100, and it reached its apogee in the Late Classic era (A.D. 600–800). Bonampak has a close and surprisingly amicable relationship with the nearby city of Yaxchilán, just 20 kilometers (12 miles) to the southeast. Bonampak's most notable leader—Chaan-Muan—was married to the sister of Yaxchilán's great king Shield Jaguar. The brothers-in-law joined forces in a war against an unknown third city in the 7th century. The battle is commemorated in a part of Bonampak's famous murals and lintels. Relatively little else is known about the city, however.

Much more ink has been dedicated to the scandal that arose around the site's discovery in the 1940s. An American conscientious objector—or draft dodger, depending on the telling—named Karl Frey was part of a team headed by filmmaker Giles Healy to find and document the ruins, which had been reported

THE STATE OF CHIAPAS

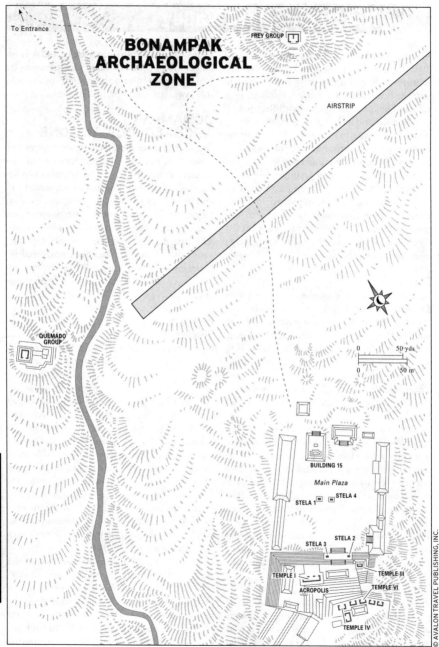

BONAMPAK
ARCHAEOLOGICAL
ZONE

To Entrance

FREY GROUP

AIRSTRIP

QUEMADO
GROUP

0   50 yds
0   50 m

BUILDING 15

Main Plaza

STELA 1   STELA 4

STELA 3   STELA 2

TEMPLE I   TEMPLE III

ACROPOLIS   TEMPLE VI

TEMPLE IV

© AVALON TRAVEL PUBLISHING, INC.

to archaeologists 40 years prior but never explored. The two had a falling out and the expedition was abandoned; later, in 1946, Frey succeeded in reaching the site, but evidently missed the murals. Healy made the trip several months later, discovered the murals—even the local Lacondón people seemed not to have known of their existence—and made headlines with his startling find. Frey spent years trying to convince the world he was the true discoverer, to no avail. He formed part of an ill-advised exploration team organized by the Mexican Fine Arts Institute in 1949—a joint Carnegie Institute and INAH exploration had already gone and returned with detailed maps and drawings—during which he drowned in the Río Lacanjá, reportedly trying to save a fellow team member after their canoe capsized.

Visiting the Ruins

Bonampak's murals are housed in **Temple I,** which stands on a low level of the **Acropolis,** a large stepped structure that backs onto a jungle-covered hill. In front of the Acropolis is a plaza with low buildings around the other three sides. Researchers believe that the story told through the murals should be read from left to right, from Room 1 to Room 3. The setting of Room 1's mural is the palace, where the child-heir is presented to the court and 336 days later is the focal point of a celebration with actors and musicians. Room 2 is set in the jungle and on a flight of stairs. These murals tell the story of a jungle battle, probably in honor of the heir, led by Chaan-Muan. This is considered the greatest battle scene in Maya art.

Next the scene moves to a staircase, where the captives are ritually tortured while Chaan-Muan watches from above. In Room 3 the setting is a pyramid, where costumed lords dance and a captive awaits his death. To the side, noblewomen ritually let their blood, while a pot-bellied dwarf is presented to the court. Anthropologists believe that the child-heir never ruled Bonampak, because there is evidence that the site was abandoned before the murals were even completed. The murals have faded with time and were damaged when the first researchers used kerosene to clean them—the kerosene brought out the colors but weakened the paints' adhesion and hastened the flaking and decay. The Museo Nacional de Antropología, in Mexico City, has a reproduction of how the murals likely looked in their full glory, and lesser copies are found in Tuxtla Gutiérrez and Villahermosa. But, though they are old and damaged, you still can't beat the originals.

When visiting Bonampak (and Yaxchilán) be sure to look at the beautifully carved scenes on the underside of the lintels (the slab of stone that forms the top of a doorway). Their location makes them easy to miss, but they are truly some of the best Maya relief carvings you'll see outside of a museum. In Bonampák, Lintel I shows Chaan-Muan holding a captive by the hair; Lintel II shows Itzanaaj B'alam doing the same; and Lintel III shows a figure, possibly Chan-Muan's father Knot Eye Jaguar, spearing a victim in the chest.

Practicalities

Bonampak is open 8 A.M.–5 P.M. daily; admission is US$3. There is no guide service, as most people come on guided tours from Palenque.

Accommodations and Food

Back along the highway, just a half hour from Palenque, **Valle Escondido** (Carretera Palenque-Frontera Corozal Km 61) is primarily a restaurant, but recently opened several basic but comfortable cabins. Prices were not yet established at the time of research, but the owner is well respected and rates are sure to be reasonable.

Getting There

From Palenque, **Transporte Chamoan** (Av. Miguel Hidalgo between Calles Allende and 1 Pte.) has *combis* that pass the turnoff to Bonampák en route to Frontera Corozal (US$4.50 to turnoff, two hours, every 30–90 minutes 5 A.M.–4 P.M.). The turnoff is at a community called San Javier; it's another four kilometers (2.5 miles) to the ruins, so definitely ask the driver if he'll drop you at the site's entrance. If he doesn't go for it (most won't)

THE STATE OF CHIAPAS

there's often a truck waiting to ferry people to the ruins (US$3.50 round-trip, with an hour at the site). Just be sure to return to the highway turnoff in time to catch a van onward to Frontera Corozal (US$1.50, 20 minutes, last one at 6 P.M.) or back to Palenque (last one at 5 P.M.).

◖ YAXCHILÁN ARCHAEOLOGICAL ZONE

The Yaxchilán ruins lie on the Río Usumacinta, Mexico's largest river and the border between Mexico and Guatemala. Archaeologists have found at least 35 stelae, 60 carved lintels, 21 altars, and five stairways covered with hieroglyphs here—a treasure trove for epigraphers. Yaxchilán's rulers were obsessed with venerating their dynasty as well as legitimizing their rule and endowed a major monument-carving operation to achieve these goals. In fact, it was Yaxchilán's hieroglyphs that provided much of the raw material that led to the deciphering of the Maya writing system.

History

Yaxchilán was a powerful city-state during the Classic era, ruled by the Jaguar dynasty, which traced its roots to A.D. 320 and a ruler named Yat B'alam (Jaguar Penis). The earliest recorded date at the site is from A.D. 435, and the first major monuments appeared early in the 6th century.

Yaxchilán's greatest ruler was Izamnaaj B'alam, or Shield Jaguar, who was born in A.D. 647 and ruled for more than six decades, A.D. 681–742, a remarkable feat for a man whose life expectancy would have been less than 40 years. He undertook numerous construction projects, including the construction of Structure 23 on the main plaza. Dedicated to his wife Lady Xoc, it is the only Maya temple known to have been built specifically in honor of a woman. But it may have more to do with politics than enlightenment; Shield Jaguar took a second wife, late in life, and named the son from that union, Bird Jaguar, heir to the throne. Building 23, which shows Lady Xoc conducting various noble rituals, may have been a way of appeasing her powerful family.

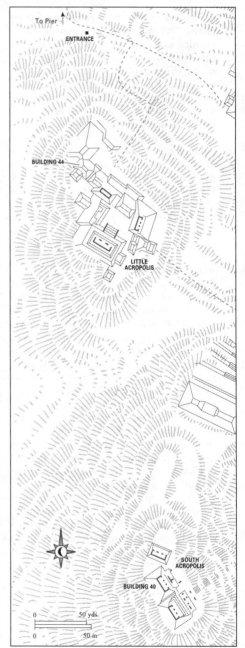

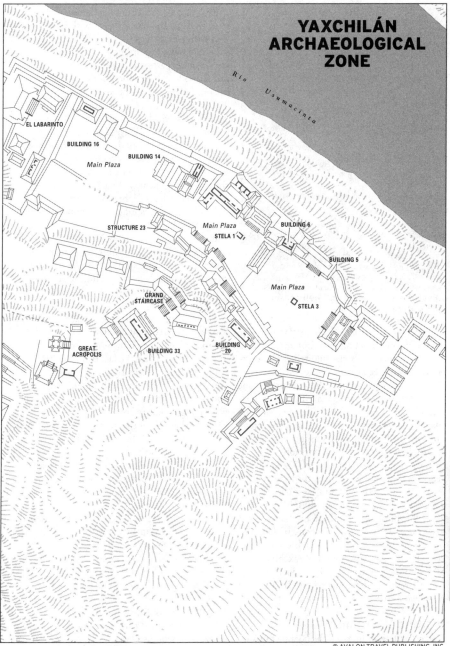

YAXCHILÁN
ARCHAEOLOGICAL
ZONE

Río Usumacinta

EL LABARINTO

BUILDING 16

BUILDING 14

Main Plaza

STRUCTURE 23

Main Plaza

STELA 1

BUILDING 6

BUILDING 5

GRAND
STAIRCASE

Main Plaza

STELA 3

GREAT
ACROPOLIS

BUILDING 33

BUILDING
20

© AVALON TRAVEL PUBLISHING, INC.

THE STATE OF CHIAPAS

one of the magnificent and well-preserved lintels at Yaxchilán

Bird Jaguar succeeded Shield Jaguar, and built numerous buildings, and immortalized his accomplishments in stelae and reliefs throughout the site, especially the impressive Structure 33. These were primarily military victories, but also included bloodletting, sacrificing captives, even prevailing in the Maya ball game. Most archaeologists interpret this obsessive self-aggrandizement as Bird Jaguar's attempts to shore up an otherwise shaky political position—indeed, he wasn't named king until A.D. 752, a full 10 years after his father's death. Bird Jaguar was the beginning of the end for the Jaguar dynasty, which lasted until about A.D. 800. Its last ruler, Ta-Skull, Bird Jaguar's grandson, constructed just two small, rather poorly constructed temples (Buildings 3 and 64) which contain the latest known date inscription at Yaxchilán, A.D. 808, commemorating a military victory. Yaxchilán gradually depopulated and by A.D. 900 had been returned to the jungle.

Visiting the Ruins

A steep path leads up from the boat pier to Yax-

chilán's ticket booth. Entering the site, the main road leads to the Main Plaza, with the Great Acropolis a long steep flight of stairs above. But instead of following the main road, consider taking the small path that cuts to your right up the hill to the **Little Acropolis.** It's a steep climb, but once there, the rest of your visit is downhill. The most important structure in this complex is Building 44, which was built by Shield Jaguar in celebration of his military successes.

Continue on the path to reach the **Great Acropolis** from the backside. It's a pleasant walk, and you may spot howler monkeys in the trees along the way. Around front, you'll be at the top of a long flight of stone stairs, and in front of one of Yaxchilán most notable structures, **Building 33,** with its intricate facade and soaring roof comb. Built by Bird Jaguar to celebrate himself—who else?—it includes incredibly fine lintels and panels depicting the ruler's accomplishments, including summoning his deceased ancestors in the midst of a ball game.

Descending the stairs, you'll reach the **Main Plaza,** a long rectangular plaza built alongside the river bank, framed by numerous structures and dotted with large stelae. **Building 20** and **Building 21** are to the right of the staircase as you reach the bottom; built by Shield Jaguar and Bird Jaguar, respectively, both have lintels portraying rituals related to the birth of heirs. On the other side of the staircase, **Building 23** is the famous temple built by Shield Jaguar and dedicated to Lady Xoc. This is where archaeologists discovered exquisitely carved panels portraying the noblewoman performing rituals, including drawing a thorny twine through her tongue.

At the west end of the main plaza is a complex called **El Labarinto** (The Labyrinth), so-named for its maze of vaulted passageways and chambers; it likely served as residential quarters. On the other side, the main path leads back through the trees to the boat landing.

Practicalities

The archaeological zone is open 8 A.M.–5 P.M. daily; admission is US$3.

Getting There

Yaxchilán is an hour down the Río Usumacinta from the town of Frontera Corozal. Long canoelike boats with sun covers and powerful outboard motors carry visitors down the river, often past huge river crocodiles sunning themselves on the banks, their mouths standing open.

FRONTERA COROZAL

This riverside border town is the jumping-off point for visiting the Yaxchilán ruins. Otherwise the town's main sight is the **Museo Comunitario Frontera Corozal** (8 A.M.–6 P.M. daily) a well-organized museum with three exhibition rooms. Displays include information on the area's history and culture, archaeological digs, and local flora and fauna. Signage in Spanish only.

Accommodations and Food

On the riverfront at the end of the main road, **Escudo Jaguar** (tel. 555/329-0995 ext. 8057, escudojaguar_hotel@yahoo.com.mx, www

.chiapastours.com.mx/escudojaguar, US$21 s/d with shared bath, US$23–33 s/d with private bath) has 15 pink *palapa* cabañas with private porches (say *that* five times fast) and six hotel-style rooms with shared bathroom. The units are simple but clean and have fans and screened windows. Camping (US$5 pp) is an option on the jungly grounds too, and the hotel has tents for rent. The hotel's **restaurant** (7 A.M.–8 P.M. daily, US$5–10) serves decent regional fare. The **Museo Comunitario Frontera Corozal** (8 A.M.–6 P.M.) has a good cheap restaurant on-site. It serves up reliable *comida corridas* (specials including soup, main dish, and drink) and good à la carte dishes.

Information and Services

At the time of research, there was no bank or ATM in town and no one accepted credit cards; bring enough cash to get you through your stay.

Getting There and Around

Transporte Chamoan (Av. Miguel Hidalgo between Calles Allende and 1 Pte.) provides

Keep your eyes peeled for crocodiles as you make your way down the river to Yaxchilán.

© LIZA PRADO

THE STATE OF CHIAPAS

combi service to Frontera Corozal (US$5, 2.5 hours, every 30–90 minutes 5 A.M.–4 P.M.) where you can walk to the river for boats to Yaxchilán. *Combis* return to Palenque 4 A.M.–5 P.M.

Two **boat cooperatives** (tel. 555/329-0885 ext. 8059) provide boat service along the Río Usumacinta from a pier at the end of the main road. To Yaxchilán ruins, it's a 50-minute boat ride there, and an hour back, with two hours at the site; you can stay longer, but you'll have to tip the boatman (even better, throw in a Coke and something to eat as well). Prices are fixed and non-negotiable: US$55 for 1–3 passengers, US$63 for four, US$76 for 5–7, and US$100 for 8–10). Getting there early gives you the best chance of being able to share a boat with other travelers or an arriving tour group. The boat cooperatives also provide one-way transportation to **Betel, Guatemala** (US$32.50 for 1–3 people, US$36 for four, and US$46 for 5–7, and US$50 for 7–10) where buses to Flores (near the archaeological site of Tikal) depart daily at around noon, 2 P.M., and 5 P.M.

Ocosingo

This small agricultural town is famous for three things: one, the impressive and oft-overlooked Maya ruins of Toniná, about 12 kilometers (7.5 miles) from town; two, as the site of the heaviest fighting during the Zapatista uprising in 1994 and more recently where numerous ranches were occupied by Zapatista soldiers; and three, the cheese. Yes, Ocosingo makes a mean cheese, from the tasty *doble crema* to the spicy spreadable *queso botanero.*

Surrounded by low hills and lush green vegetation, Ocosingo has an attractive plaza, a few decent places to stay and eat, Internet, and other services—and almost no tourists. While not a place to spend your whole vacation, it's worth a look. You could even stop on your way to San Cristóbal, store your bags at the bus terminal, spend a few hours at the ruins and museum, and be back in time to catch an afternoon bus. Better yet, get a hotel and enjoy this pleasant town for a night.

SIGHTS
Toniná Archaeological Zone

Meaning "House of Stone," Toniná (9 A.M.– 4 P.M. daily, museum closed Mon., US$3) is one of the best Maya archaeology sites that no one seems to know about. Easy to reach from both Palenque and San Cristóbal, it sees only a trickle of tourists.

Archaeologists believe Toniná was the last Classic Maya site, outlasting other cities by a century before finally being abandoned around A.D. 909. With the Maya world collapsing around them, it's not surprising that Toniná's rulers were obsessed with death and sacrifice, which is depicted in many of the inscriptions and carvings here. Unfortunately, there are no plaques (and only a few handwritten signs in Spanish) explaining the structures at the site.

Toniná's massive main structure rises 80 meters (262 feet) above the main grassy plaza, bustling with interweaving staircases, secondary temples, and well-preserved roof combs. Built on seven artificial terraces, it is not a true pyramid, but it is the highest pyramid-like structure known to have been built by the Classic Mayas. On the way up (or down if you just can't wait to get to the top) check out the labyrinthine palace, with winding passages and hidden doors and tunnels, and an excellent stucco mural depicting the end of the world.

Definitely leave time to visit the **museum,** which is one of the best at any Maya site. Opened in September 2002, it contains fantastic artifacts and carvings, including figures that were deliberately decapitated (which was probably done when the personage depicted was himself decapitated) and distinctive round obelisks marking important dates.

ACCOMMODATIONS

As the name suggests, **Hotel Central** (Av. Central 5, tel. 919/673-0024, US$18.50 s, US$20 d) is well located—in fact, it faces the central plaza. Rooms are small and simple but very clean. All have fans (no a/c), cable TV, and private bathrooms with hot water. Some rooms on the 2nd floor open onto a wide veranda overlooking the plaza, which is noisy in the mornings but great for people-watching in the afternoons.

Just around the corner, **Hospedaje y Restaurant Esmeralda** (Calle Central Nte. 14, www.ranchoesmeralda.net, tel. 919/673-0014, US$14 s with shared bathroom, US$17 d

---

ZAPATISTAS

On January 1, 1994, masked soldiers stormed government buildings in four cities in Chiapas, including San Cristóbal and Ocosingo. The soldiers were mostly indigenous peasants belonging to the **Ejército Zapatista de Liberación Nacional** (EZLN, Zapatista National Liberation Army). The Mexican army quickly responded and within a few days the Zapatistas, as they were known, had retreated to the hills. About 150 people, mostly Zapatistas, died in the uprising. The rebellion was launched on the day the North American Free Trade Agreement (NAFTA) took effect, which opponents (correctly) believed would lead to many peasants losing their livelihoods. The timing was not accidental – the seeds of the rebellion were planted much earlier.

The Zapatistas rose from eastern Chiapas, an area that has long tacked toward non-establishment leaders. Since the 1930s, the PRI, Mexico's long-time ruling party, nourished deep ties with indigenous leaders in western and northern Chiapas, mostly by rewarding loyalty with land and development programs. (Many indigenous communities did not support the Zapatista action, in part because of their historic ties to the PRI.) But these ties weren't formed in eastern Chiapas – at first because the area was ignored, and later because rural colonization programs of the 1970s made it more diverse and left fewer ethnic bonds for the PRI to exploit. The east also has many Protestants, which further alienated it from the mostly Catholic political elite.

By the 1980s, eastern Chiapas was an important base for anti-PRI peasant organizations. In 1982, facing a foreign debt of nearly US$100 billion, Mexico underwent an economic restructuring program that, among other things, cut vital agricultural subsidies to peasant farmers.

President Salinas de Gotari gutted even more programs, and in 1992 a constitutional amendment all but ended more than a half century of land-reform policies in Mexico. More and more farmers lost their land, and those who could, moved to squatter camps outside San Cristóbal and other cities. "But in eastern Chiapas, which has no major commercial centers and is largely inaccessible to road transport, the impoverished ha[d] no place to turn and little to lose by joining in the rebellion." (George A. Collier, *Cultural Survival Quarterly,* Spring 1994)

Zapatista attacks and raids continued intermittently. But the ruggedness of the region made a military campaign unappealing for the Mexican Army. The two parties finally negotiated a settlement in 1996 – known as the San Andrés Accords – but the government failed to fully implement the agreement and the situation remained tense, with more than 50,000 Mexican troops patrolling the remote Chiapas forests. There were sporadic raids and assassinations, and a major offensive by the army in 1999 uprooted thousands of ordinary Chiapanecans. Former President Fox had little success implementing real reforms; whether Mexico's current President Felipe Calderón can break the impasse remains to be seen.

Almost 15 years since launching the first salvo and little to show for it, the Zapatista movement struggles to maintain the world's focus and attention. In 2003, Zapatistas took over an eco-lodge operated by two Americans outside the city of Ocosingo. It was just one of scores of private ranches – several hundred by some counts – that rebels have occupied. However, most of the occupied land is going unused, and even Zapatista sympathizers wonder what the campaign is really achieving.

© LIZA PRADO

Most of Toniná's structures were built on one of its seven artificial terraces.

with shared bathroom, US$24 d with private bathroom) offers five large rooms in a remodeled historic home. Accommodations are simple and a little run-down but make up for it with homey touches such as Chiapanecan bedspreads, posters, and plants. The heart of the hotel is clearly in its restaurant and common areas, which are particularly inviting and have loads of tourist information.

Hotel Margarita (Calle 1 Pte. 9, tel. 919/673-0280, hotelmargarita@prodigy.net.mx, US$21 s, US$24 d, US$25 s with a/c, US$29 d with a/c, US$29 suite) offers ample rooms with two queen beds, fans, and cable TV. The one suite has a king-size bed and huge bathroom; it doesn't have air-conditioning, but is still a good value. Some rooms have nice views of the surrounding hills.

FOOD

Hospedaje Rancho Esmeralda (Calle Central Ote., 7 A.M.–10 P.M., US$4–10) has perhaps the best restaurant in town. A simple but varied menu—the chicken fajitas were quite

good—is served on large wooden tables in the hotel's homey common area. There's an honor bar with soda, beer, and liquor.

Restaurante El Desvan (tel. 919/673-0117, 7 A.M.–11 P.M. daily, US$4–10) is one of many simple restaurants around the central plaza. Most serve standard Mexican fare; here you also can get pizza.

Ocosingo is famous for its cheeses, which are produced locally in a half dozen or more varieties. **Quesos Santa Rosa** (1a Calle Ote. Norte s/n, tel. 919/673-0009, 8 A.M.–6 Mon. –Sat., until 1 P.M. Sun.) is a recommended shop just a block north of the plaza. If you can't decide which cheese to try, go for the tasty *doble crema* (double cream).

INFORMATION AND SERVICES
Pharmacies

Farmacias Similares (2a Calle Ote. Sur at 1a Sur Ote., tel. 919/673-1515, 8 A.M.–8 P.M. Mon.–Sat., 8 A.M.–2 P.M. Sun.) is directly behind the town church.

Money

Banamex (central plaza, 9 A.M.–4 P.M. Mon.–Fri.) has a 24-hour ATM.

Internet

You can't throw a Frisbee in Ocosingo without hitting an Internet café. There are two on the plaza and a half dozen on Calle Central Norte alone. All charge around US$0.75 an hour for Internet and are open roughly 8 A.M.–10 P.M. daily.

Post Office

The post office (2a Calle Ote. Nte. at 2a Av. Nte. Ote.) is open 8 A.M.–4:30 P.M. Monday–Friday.

Launderette

Near the plaza central, **Lavandería Espuma** (Av. 2 Norte s/n, 8 A.M.–9 P.M. Mon.–Sat., 8 A.M.–2 P.M. Sun.) charges US$0.90 per kilogram (2.2 pounds). Next-day service only.

Storage

The bus terminal has luggage storage for US$0.50 per half day.

GETTING THERE
Bus

Ocosingo's bus terminal (tel. 919/673-0431) is on the highway, about seven blocks from the center of town. Most departures are *de paso* (mid-route), so you should be sure to arrive a half hour early in case the bus arrives ahead of schedule. Destinations include:

- Palenque (US$6.50, 2.5 hours) 9:30 A.M., 1:30 P.M., 2:30 P.M., 4:50 P.M., 6 P.M.

- San Cristóbal (US$3.50, two hours) and Tuxtla Gutiérrez (US$7, four hours) 5:30 A.M., 7:30 A.M., 9 A.M., noon, 1:55 A.M., 3:45 A.M., and 4:25 P.M.

GETTING AROUND

Ocosingo is small enough that you easily can get around on foot. If you are coming or going to the bus station or are headed to Toniná, *combis* (vans) and taxis are your best option.

Combis

To get to Toniná, take a *combi* (US$1.60 each way) marked "Predio-Ruínas"; they leave from 3a Avenida Sur Oriente in the market. *Combis* leave whenever they are full, usually every 15–45 minutes. To return to town, catch the same *combi* back.

Taxi

Taxis between the bus terminal and town cost US$1.50. To the Toniná ruins, a cab runs about US$5.50 one way; arrange with the driver to pick you up after your visit.

San Cristóbal de las Casas

San Cristóbal de las Casas is a city of many layers, a place to delve into, not merely admire. It is wonderful old colonial town, easily one of Mexico's finest. Low colorful buildings with tile roofs and wrought-iron details line the narrow streets, their wooden doorways sometimes framed by exuberant bougainvillea vines. The shady central plaza is flanked by an elegant mustard-yellow cathedral that seems to glow in the setting sun. But San Cristóbal is more than just a pretty face. It has a strong indigenous presence, and residents from the numerous outlying villages come into the city to sell goods and crafts, to shop at the market, and to visit banks and NGO offices. The nonindigenous population tends to be progressive and bohemian, and the city boasts numerous art house theaters, funky cafés, and hip bars. With so many facets to explore, fascinating sights to take in, and welcoming places to spend the night, you'll find it easy—almost too easy—to extend your stay.

SIGHTS
Parque Central

The official name of San Cristóbal's leafy

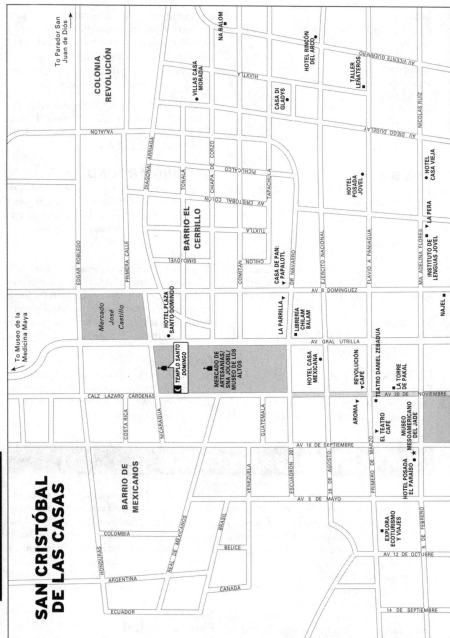

SAN CRISTÓBAL
DE LAS CASAS

To Parador San Juan de Diós →

COLONIA REVOLUCIÓN

BARRIO EL CERRILLO

BARRIO DE MEXICANOS

To Museo de la Medicina Maya →

Mercado José Castillo

NA BALOM

VILLAS CASA MORADA

HOTEL RINCÓN DEL ARCO

TALLER LEÑATEROS

CASA DI GLADYS

HOTEL POSADA JOVEL

HOTEL CASA VIEJA

LA PERA

INSTITUTO DE LENGUAS JOVEL

NAJEL

HOTEL PLAZA SANTO DOMINGO

TEMPLO SANTO DOMINGO

MERCADO DE ARTESANÍAS/ SNA JOLOBIL/ MUSEO DE LOS ALTOS

LA PARRILLA

LIBRERÍA CHILAM BALAM

HOTEL CASA MEXICANA

REVOLUCIÓN CAFÉ

TEATRO DANIEL ZEBADUA

LA TORRE DE PAKAL

AROMA

EL TEATRO CAFÉ

MUSEO MESOAMERICANO DEL JADE

HOTEL POSADA EL PARAÍSO

EXPLORA ECOTURISMO Y VIAJES

CASA DE PAN: PAPALOTL

VICENTE GUERRERO
NICOLAS RUIZ
AV DIEGO DUGELAY
MA ADELINA FLORES
FLAVIO A PANIAGUA
EJERCITO NACIONAL
DR NAVARRO
COMITÁN
CHILÓN
TUXTLA
TAPACHULA
AV CRISTÓBAL COLÓN
PICHUCALCO
CHIAPA DE CORZO
TONALÁ
DIAGONAL ARRIAGA
YAJALÓN
SIMOJOVEL
HUIXTLA
PRIMERA CALLE
EDGAR ROBLEDO
CALZ LÁZARO CÁRDENAS
COSTA RICA
NICARAGUA
GUATEMALA
VENEZUELA
ESCUADRÓN 201
28 DE AGOSTO
PRIMERO DE MARZO
5 DE FEBRERO
REAL DE MEXICANOS
BRASIL
COLOMBIA
HONDURAS
BELICE
ARGENTINA
CANADÁ
ECUADOR

AV B DOMÍNGUEZ
AV GRAL UTRILLA
AV 20 DE NOVIEMBRE
AV 16 DE SEPTIEMBRE
AV 5 DE MAYO
AV 12 DE OCTUBRE
14 DE SEPTIEMBRE

THE STATE OF CHIAPAS

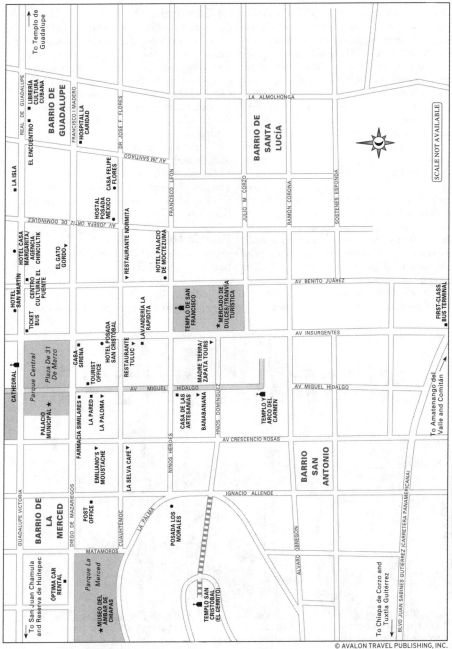

THE STATE OF CHIAPAS

© AVALON TRAVEL PUBLISHING, INC.

central plaza is Plaza de 31 de Marzo, but most people refer to it as the *parque central* (central park). During the colonial era, the plaza served several functions: a public market, a water-gathering spot (a large fountain supplied most of the town's water), and a place of punishment during the years of the conquest. Hundreds of years later in 1994, Zapatista rebels stormed the plaza and adjoining Palacio Municipal (City Hall), which was significantly damaged.

Today, although demonstrations by indigenous people and their supporters over squalid living and working conditions occasionally spill out onto the plaza, it's generally a tranquil place—green iron benches dot the wide walkways, large shade trees protect people from the sun, and a two-story kiosk serves up coffee drinks and light fare in the center of it all. Here and in front of the cathedral, expect to be approached by Chamulan women and children selling hand-woven bracelets, belts, and shawls. Their prices are unbelievably low, and even a small purchase seems greatly appreciated.

La Catedral

Constructed in 1528, San Cristóbal's cathedral sits on the north side of the central square. The facade is a standout, its bright yellow-ochre contrasting with 17th-century white mortared niches and geometric designs painted white, rust, and black. Inside, the nave and altar are decorated with fine religious art—don't miss the elaborately carved wooden pulpit. The cathedral and the plaza in front of it come to life during festivals and religious holidays, especially leading up to Easter and December 12 (Saint's Day for the Virgen of Guadalupe). The best photo ops are in the mid- to late afternoon, when the sun ignites the west-facing church in a brilliant display.

Palacio Municipal

On the west side of the central park, the Palacio Municipal (City Hall) has been rebuilt since the first stone was laid in 1863. Rebel troops led by Juan Ortega burned the original building to the ground during a skirmish

© LIZA PRADO

San Cristóbal's bright yellow cathedral is one of the most beautiful buildings in town. Capture it at sunset when its colors shine brightest.

between Royalists and Republicans. When construction of the present, newer building began, the city was still the capital of the state and the plan included a much larger edifice. But the capital was moved to Tuxtla Gutiérrez, and the planned capitalesque construction was never completed. Nevertheless, the final product is still attractive, with neoclassical columns, arches, and a large plaza in the rear where civic ceremonies are held. Demonstrations take place here occasionally, and this building bore the major damage during the Zapatista uprising in 1994.

Casa Sirena

One of the oldest buildings in San Cristóbal, Casa Sirena, literally, "Mermaid House" (Av. Insurgentes at Diego de Mazariegos), lies on the central plaza. Constructed in the mid-1500s, it is a lovely building where stylized versions of two serpent women and a sea nymph give the place its name. The insignia on the coat of arms (over the door) has been destroyed, so although the building often is claimed to have been the original home of Diego de Mazariegos, many believe it was built by another, Andrés de la Tobilla.

◖ Templo Santo Domingo

Built in 1547, the Templo Santo Domingo (Av. 20 de Noviembre near Nicaragua) is arguably the most impressive church of the many churches found in the city. It has a gorgeous baroque facade covered with intricately carved mortar, Solomonic columns, and statues tucked into ornate niches. The interior is equally impressive, its sensational pulpit covered in gold carvings and surrounded by countless *retablos* (religious paintings) that are offered in gratitude for answered prayers. It's not unusual to find an indigenous *curandera* (female healer) performing rituals inside the church: touching a patient with flowers, surrounding him with smoking copal, murmuring incantations, passing burning candles over and around his head and body, in front of the church altar.

In the church's courtyard, there's a daily outdoor *artesanía* market; in the attached ex-

convent, there's also an excellent weavers co-op and the Museo de los Altos de Chiapas.

Templo San Cristóbal (El Cerrito)

Every July 17, Catholic worshippers flock to the 17th-century church Templo San Cristóbal to honor its patron saint, San Cristóbal (Saint Christopher). And that's no easy task—the church is on a *cerrito* (small hill) and is reached by a steep set of about 240 steps. It's a nice place to visit at any time of the year, affording a panoramic view of town. If you're not up for the climb, there is a road on the other side of the hill; a cab to the top costs US$1.50.

Museo de Trajes Regionales

Anyone who is entranced with Chiapas's indigenous culture will enjoy a visit to the Museum of Regional Dress (Calle Guadalupe Victoria 38 at Av. 12 de Octubre, tel. 967/678-4289, by appointment only, US$2.50), a private collection of local resident Sergio Castro Martínez. Well-versed in the cultural history of Chiapas, Sr. Castro explains the cohesive role that clothes plays in each village, adding a few anecdotes and legends along the way. English and French spoken.

Museo de los Altos de Chiapas

The Museo de los Altos de Chiapas (Templo Santo Domingo, Av. 20 de Noviembre near Nicaragua, tel. 967/678-1609, 10 A.M.–5 P.M. Mon.–Sat., US$3) has interesting exhibits on pre-Hispanic customs and culture, the arrival of the Spanish, and ancient and contemporary Maya art (signage in Spanish only). Upstairs is a large temporary exhibit area—when we visited, there was a spectacular collection of handwoven textiles from various highland regions. The building itself, the former convent of the Templo Santo Domingo, is quite impressive, with high archways, wood floors, and thick stone and adobe walls.

Museo de la Medicina Maya

The Maya Medicine Museum (Av. Salomón González Blanco 10, Col. Morelos, tel. 967/678-5438, 10 A.M.–6 P.M. Mon.–Fri., 10 A.M.–5 P.M.

THE STATE OF CHIAPAS

Sat.–Sun., US$2) has creative exhibits on ancient and contemporary Maya medical practices, including a fascinating section on childbirth. There's a medicinal plant garden—products made from it are sold at a small pharmacy on-site. The museum is a project of OMIECH, an association of indigenous doctors in Chiapas; if you have an ailment, you can request a consultation while you're there (9 A.M.–2 P.M., Mon.–Fri. only). To arrive, walk north on Avenida General Utrilla until you see the museum; it's about a half-hour walk from the central plaza. A cab there costs about US$2.

Museo del Ámbar de Chiapas

The worthwhile Museo del Ámbar de Chiapas (Parque La Merced, Diego de Mazariegos near Matamoros, tel. 967/678-9716, www.museo delambar.com.mx, 10 A.M.–2 P.M. and 4–7 P.M. Tues.–Sun., US$2) has an extensive, beautiful collection of raw and sculpted amber, of various colors and qualities. There are displays on its mining, its use in pre-Hispanic societies, and how to distinguish it from glass and plastic imitations. While you're there, peek into the well-restored Ex-Convento de la Merced, dating from the 16th century.

Museo Mesoamericano del Jade

The overglorified Mesoamerican Museum of Jade (Av. 16 de Septiembre at Calle 5 de Febrero, tel. 967/678-1121, www.eljade.com, noon–8 P.M. Mon.–Sat., noon–6 P.M. Sun., US$3) is a small display in the Casa del Jade store. It is made up of jade reproductions of Maya masks and artifacts, including ones from Tikal, Copán, and the famous funerary mask of K'inich Janaab Pakal found in the Temple of the Inscriptions at Palenque. At the end is a large, rather underwhelming reproduction of Pakal's tomb.

Café Museo Café

The one-room Café Museo Café (Calle Mariá Adelina Flores between Avs. Belisario Domínguez and General Utrilla, tel. 967/678-7876, 9 A.M.–9:30 P.M. Mon.–Sat., US$2) tells the history of coffee in Mexico—from its introduction in the late 17th century to its boom in Chiapas under the dictatorship of Porfirio Díaz (1877–1911). At the end, visitors are gently prodded into a spacious café in the back; to its credit, it serves excellent coffee. The museum and café are run by Tuxtla-based COOPCAFE, an organization of small coffee producers.

THE STATE OF CHIAPAS

CHIAPANECAN AMBER

Amber comes from the sap of prehistoric pine trees, like the *succinifer,* that existed 40 to 50 million years ago. Over time, natural catastrophes altered the Earth's crust, burying these pine trees; this allowed the almost eternal process of petrification to occur, transforming the sap into amber.

Hard and brittle in form, amber typically is golden, although it can also be white, pink, red, wine, brown, or black. It can be opaque, transparent, or marbled, depending on its purity. Prehistoric insects sometimes are trapped in it à la *Jurassic Park* – a feature that dramatically raises the amber's value (these samples have enabled entomologists to classify almost 75 insect species from the Tertiary and Cretaceous periods).

In Chiapas, there is evidence of amber as early as 250 B.C. It was principally used by Mayas as an adornment – nose and lip rings, earrings, and necklaces. Certain groups even placed amber bracelets on their children to protect them from the "evil eye." Its distribution has helped determine the commercial routes of Maya traders across Mexico and Central America.

Today, Chiapas is the amber capital of Mexico and the world's third most important source after the Baltics and the Dominican Republic. Though it was first mined in northern Chiapas, new veins have been discovered. Unfortunately, it is almost always found in hard-to-reach places where landslides are a constant threat.

Museo Na Bolom

Located in the what once was the home of the photographer Gertrude Duby Blom and the archaeologist Frans Blom, the Museo Na Bolom (Av. Vicente Guerrero 33, tel. 967/678-1418, www.nabolom.org, 10 A.M.–6 P.M. daily, US$3.25) showcases the Bloms' interests: the preservation of the reclusive Lacondón Indians and the Chiapanecan rain forest. The rambling house itself is an extension of the museum, with room upon room of Maya artifacts, an impressive research library, and innumerable black-and-white photographs taken by Duby Blom. Guided tours of the museum and home are offered at 11:30 A.M. and 4:30 P.M. every day and include a film on the Bloms' work with the Lacandóns (English and Spanish, US$4). There also is an excellent gift shop and guest rooms.

City Tour

Get your bearings on a short city tour operated by **Tranvía Turística** (Av. Insurgentes at Calle Hermanos Domínguez, tel. 967/678-0525), a motorized trolley that makes a one-hour loop of San Cristóbal's key sights; a recorded explanation serves as the guide (Spanish and French only). Tours leave from the office (hourly, 10 A.M.–7 P.M., US$5 adults, $3 kids); a minimum of four passengers is required.

Regional Tours

Alex y Raul (tel. 967/678-9141, alexyraul@yahoo.com) has long offered the most highly recommended tours of San Juan Chamula, Zinacantán, and other indigenous villages. What started as a two-person operation has since grown to nearly a dozen guides, but it has not lost the balanced, insightful, and personalized quality that makes the tours so good. Day trips to San Juan Chamula and Zinacantán (US$14 pp) meet every day at 9:30 A.M. at the large wooden cross in front of the cathedral (Av. 20 de Noviembre at Calle Guadalupe Victoria).

Zapata Tours (upstairs from Madre Tierra restaurant, Av. Insurgentes 19-A at Calle Hnos. Domínguez, tel. 967/674-5152, www.zapatatours.com, 8:30 A.M.–8 P.M. daily) is run by a young Czech/Mexican couple and offers a

wide variety of appealing tours, from a popular horseback tour to San Juan Chamula and Zinacantán to a five-day, four-night trip excursion Yaxchilán, Bonampak, and Tikal. Other popular day trips go to Lagos de Montebello and Sumidero Canyon.

Agencia Chincultik (Calle Real de Guadalupe 34, tel. 967/678-0957, 9 A.M.–9:30 P.M. daily) is another recommended tour agency, offering many of the same one-day and multiday trips for essentially the same prices.

Explora Ecoturismo y Viajes (Calle 1 de Marzo 30 between Avs. 5 de Mayo and 12 de Octubre, tel. 967/678-4295, www.ecochiapas.com) offers tours ranging from one to six days that combine kayaking or river rafting, hiking in the rain forest, and visiting archaeological sites. All-inclusive tours average US$90 per day per person.

ENTERTAINMENT AND EVENTS
Bars and Live Music Venues

San Cristóbal has a vibrant nightlife and befitting the city's artsy progressive atmosphere, expect mostly small bars with live acoustic and rock music. Only a couple stay open past midnight, so don't wait too long to get your groove going.

Revolución Café (Av. 20 de Noviembre at 1 de Marzo) is a popular corner bar with a small bandstand in the window. Come for decent live rock starting around 9 P.M.

After Revolución Café closes, stagger a half block to **El Circo** (Av. 20 de Noviembre at 1 de Marzo) where live music, drum and dance show, and general late-night revelry don't pick up until 11 P.M. and continue well into the night.

With a good-size dance floor, **Latino's** (Diego de Mazariegos near Av. Juárez) is a good place to try out your merengue and salsa moves—live music most nights.

Other popular options include the urban-hip **Blue Bar** (Calle 1 de Marzo at Av. 16 de Septiembre), where salsa and reggae rule and **Zapata Vive** (Av. 5 de Mayo at Diego de Mazariegos), which is more of a locals scene.

Cinema

The large number of backpackers, researchers, and NGO workers in San Cristóbal has spawned several alternative cinema clubs, mostly showing art films, progressive documentaries, and a handful of Hollywood favorites.

Cine Club La Ventana (Av. Insurgentes 19, US$2) screens two movies on weeknights (6:15 and 8:30 P.M.) and three on weekends (5, 7, and 9 P.M.). Look for its monthly schedule at the tourist office and posted around town.

With a similar lineup, **Kinoki** (Calle Real de Guadalupe 20 between Avs. Utrilla and Belisario Domínguez, US$2) shows films Sunday–Thursday (6 and 8 P.M.) and Friday–Saturday (6, 8, and 10 P.M.).

Another good option is **Cinema El Puente** (Calle Real de Guadalupe at Av. Josefa Ortiz de Domínguez, tel. 967/678-3723, US$2) which screens two films every night but Sunday, usually at 4 P.M. and 8 P.M.

Theater

The imposing **Teatro Daniel Zebadua** (Av. 20 de Noviembre and Calle 5 de Febrero) regularly presents dramatic performances and cultural expositions. Tickets vary depending on the performance but typically run US$10–20.

Festivals

This is a very colorful city all year-round, but it comes to life on Catholic holidays, which indigenous communities celebrate with vigor. *Semana Santa* (Holy Week, leading up to Easter) is not only an important religious holiday but a big travel and vacation week for all Mexicans; San Cristóbal gets packed with indigenous faithful, local merchants, and visitors from Mexico City, Veracruz, and elsewhere. **December 12th** is Saint's Day for the Virgin of Guadalupe, which is celebrated with *peregrinaciones* (pilgrimages)— groups of churchgoers who run or walk for several days from surrounding cities to San Cristóbal's hilltop Church of Guadalupe. No matter what the holiday, expect firecrackers, paper streamers, marimba music, and lots of street food.

SHOPPING

Teeming with shops and markets, San Cristóbal is a place where the genius and beauty of Mexican art is on full display—handmade clothing, toys, textiles, amber jewelry—you'll be hard-pressed to leave without buying something. Bargaining is accepted, but be fair. Many artisans simply charge for the cost of the materials; their time often is given for free.

Markets

Every day the plaza surrounding Templo Santo Domingo hosts an **artesanía market** (8 A.M.–sunset) where you'll see row upon row of colorful *huipiles,* thick wool sweaters, embroidered placemats, woven belts, Zapatista dolls, dresses, and any number of handmade creations. Be sure to take a walk around the market before you buy—each step likely will reveal something unexpected.

Artesanía Boutiques

The state-run **Casa de las Artesanías** (Av. Miguel Hidalgo at Niños Héroes, tel. 967/678-1180, 9 A.M.–9 P.M. Mon.–Fri., 10 A.M.–9 P.M. Sat., 9 A.M.–3 P.M. Sun.) sells first-rate items from every corner of Chiapas—from amber jewelry to hand-painted toys. Salespeople are particularly helpful and often will share their knowledge about an item—the region it comes from, the process of creating it, and in some cases, even about the artist herself.

For some of the finest textiles around, visit **Sna Jolobil** (Templo Santo Domingo, Av. 20 de Noviembre near Nicaragua, 9 A.M.–2 P.M. and 4–6 P.M. Mon.–Sat.). Meaning "House of Weaving" in Tzotzil, Sna Jolobil is a profit-sharing co-op made up of 700 weavers from 20 Tzotzil- and Tzeltal-speaking villages in the highlands of Chiapas. Definitely worth a visit, these outstanding works of textile art are hard to resist. Prices are non-negotiable.

An indigenous women's co-op **Najel** (Belisario Domínguez between María Adelina Flores and Real de Guadalupe, tel. 967/674-0347, 10 A.M.–3 P.M. and 5–9 P.M. Tue.–Sat., noon–2 P.M. and 4–8 P.M. Sun.) is a boutique selling handcrafted textiles from neighboring villages. The artists

© LIZA PRADO

Templo Santo Domingo's outdoor *artesanía* market showcases the collective talent of Chiapanecan weavers and tailors.

themselves are often on hand to talk about their work; you're certain to leave in awe of their talent (and probably with an item or two).

Though specializing in Cuban books, **Librería Cultura Cubana** (Calle Real de Guadalupe between Diego Dugelay and Cristóbal Colón, 9 A.M.–2 P.M. and 4–6 P.M. daily) has an impressive Zapatista section: beautifully hand-stitched T-shirts, colorful handkerchiefs, and one-of-a-kind wall hangings—all with messages in support of the Zapatista cause.

Next door, **El Encuentro** (Calle Real de Guadalupe 63-A, 9 A.M.–8 P.M. Mon.–Sat., 5–8 P.M. Sun.) has a good selection of embroidered *huipiles,* ceremonial hats, and shawls. Beautiful bolts of woven cloth also are sold.

For high-end Lacondón *artesanía* and books, head to the gift shop at **Na Bolom** (Av. Vicente Guerrero 33, tel. 967/678-1418, 10 A.M.–6 P.M. daily). A bit off the beaten track, it's well worth a stop. The affiliated museum across the street is a treat in itself.

Bookstores

La Pared (Av. Miguel Hidalgo 2, tel. 967/678-

6367, 10 A.M.–2 P.M., 4–8 P.M. daily) is San Cristóbal's best source of English-language books, offering an excellent selection of new and used novels, Maya history and art books, textbooks for learning Spanish, and current travel guides and maps. There's also a book exchange.

Librería Chilam Balam (Av. General Utrilla and Calle Dr. Navarro, tel. 967/678-0486, 9:30 A.M.–8 P.M. daily) has a decent selection of guidebooks, maps, Maya and Mexican history books, and CDs. A number of titles are available in English, French, Italian, and German.

La Isla (Calle Real de Guadalupe at Av. Josefa Ortíz de Domínguez, 10 A.M.–2 P.M., 5–8 P.M. Mon.–Sat.) also carries English-language guidebooks and has a varied collection of CDs and new and used books, mostly in Spanish.

SPORTS AND RECREATION
Reserva de Huitepec

Just 3.5 kilometers (2.2 miles) from San Cristóbal, the Huitepec Reserve (9 A.M.–4 P.M. Tues.–Sun., US$1.50) is a 135-hectare (334-acre) cloud-forest on the side of an extinct volcano, where more than 80 species of birds

THE STATE OF CHIAPAS

have been identified. Several well-marked trails make for a pleasant morning hike. There also are guides on-site who can lead tours of the park (US$4 pp, 2.5–3 hours) or, with a day's notice, an early morning bird-watching tour (US$9.50 pp, 2.5–3 hours). To reserve a bird-watching tour, or for additional information, contact **Pronatura** (Av. Miguel Hidalgo 9, tel. 967/678-5000, www.pronatura-chiapas.org, 9 A.M.–4 P.M. Mon.–Fri.).

To get to the reserve, take a *colectivo* toward San Juan Chamula from the market on Avenida General Utrilla. Ask the driver to drop you off at Huitepec (US$0.35); from the turn-off, it's about 200 meters (656 feet) to the reserve entrance. To return, walk to the road and catch a *colectivo* headed back to town.

Workshops

Taller Leñateros (Calle Flavio A. Paniagua at Calle Huixtla, tel. 967/678-5174, www.taller lenateros.com. 9 A.M.–8 P.M. Mon.–Fri., 9 A.M.–2 P.M. Sat.) is an award-winning collective of more than 20 Maya men and women who create beautiful handmade paper products using materials such as flower petals, grass, vines, moss, recycled paper, and rags. There also is a gift shop on-site.

Spanish Classes

The highly regarded **Instituto de Lenguas Jovel** (Francisco Madero 45, tel. 967/678-4069, www.institutojovel.com) offers private and group courses, all taught by professionally trained, native Spanish-speaking instructors. Basic courses include 15 hours of instruction (US$130 pp group lessons, US$165 private lessons); home-stay students also receive seven nights' lodging with three meals per day (US$185 pp group lessons, US$240 private lessons). Specialized classes for professionals such as doctors, teachers, and social workers also are offered and include weekly visits to local hospitals, schools, and NGOs (US$70 pp extra per week). All rates include a workshop in either Mexican cooking or *artesanía*.

Operated out of the Centro Cultural El Puente, **El Puente Spanish Language School** (Calle Real de Guadalupe 55 at Av. Josefa Ortiz de Domínguez, tel. 967/678-3723, www.elpuente web.com) offers one-on-one Spanish lessons and can arrange home stays. A week package includes 15 hours of instruction (US$140); with home stay (including seven-night lodging and three meals per day) the rate is US$230. There also is a small restaurant, gallery, Internet café, and a movie house on-site.

ACCOMMODATIONS

San Cristóbal has plenty of lodging options, from great hostels to luxurious hacienda-type hotels; regardless of your budget, you're certain to find a charming place to stay, which surely will make leaving here that much harder.

Under US$25

Set in a converted colonial home, **◖ Hostel Posada México** (Dr. Felipe Flores 16, tel. 967/678-0014, www.hostellingmexico.com, US$6.50 dorm, US$9.50 s/d with shared bath, US$14 s/d with private bath) is one of the best hostels in southeastern Mexico. Dorms (mixed and single sex) and private rooms are very well kept—good mattresses, custom-made bunk beds, and clean hot-water bathrooms. Two common kitchens are open to all guests as is a cozy reading room, leafy courtyards, and two TV areas. Continental breakfast is included in all the rates.

A hipster hostel in need of a fresh coat of paint, **Casa Di Gladys** (Calle Cintalapa between Av. Diego Dugelay and Calle Huixtla, tel. 967/678-5775, casagladys@hotmail.com, US$5.50 dorm, US$10 s with shared bath, US$12–18 d with shared bath) has psychedelic murals, a common kitchen with two stoves, comfy lounge areas, and a rooftop hammock/barbecue area. Rooms are comfortable too—dorms hold just 3–5 twin beds and some private rooms have king-size beds.

The well-situated **Hotel San Martín** (Calle Real de Guadalupe 16, tel. 967/678-0533, hotelsanmartin@prodigy.net.mx, US$14 s, US$21 d) is a very simple, sparse hotel. Rooms have twin beds, tile floors, and clean private bathrooms—and that's about it.

US$25-50

The colonial 【 **Hotel Casa Margarita** (Calle Real de Guadalupe 34, tel. 967/678-0957, www.mundomaya.com.mx/casamargarita, US$35 s, US$45 d) has 25 modern and cozy rooms—all with private bath, hot water, cable TV, and parking. All open onto a sunny stone courtyard with whitewashed archways and tile walkways. Just a couple of blocks from the central plaza, this is an excellent option.

Hotel Posada Jovel (Flavio Paniagua 28, tel. 967/674-5415, www.mundochiapas.com/hotelposadajovel, US$11 s with shared bath, US$14 d with shared bath, US$23–30 s with private bath, US$28–35 d with private bath) is a solid option if you don't mind being a little off the beaten track. Rooms are sunny, attractive, and very clean, even the lower-end ones. Newer, more ample rooms are across the street in a renovated colonial building and are often filled with tour groups—be sure to call in advance if you'd like one of these. Be sure to check out the solarium—the views of the city are breathtaking.

A pleasing, rambling place, the **Hotel Palacio de Moctezuma** (Av. Juárez at Francisco Léon, tel. 967/678-0352, US$27 s, US$38 d) has a several small courtyards, a quiet sitting room, three gardens, and a fountain. Rooms are equally diverse—different sizes, ages, views, and decor—but all are clean and quiet—a rare commodity in this popular town. If your room doesn't have a view, be sure to check out the spectacular vista from the solarium.

Smack-dab in the middle of the action is the **Hotel Posada San Cristóbal** (Av. Insurgentes 3, tel. 967/678-6881, hotelsancristobal@hotmail.com, US$26 s, US$35 d). A beautifully renovated colonial hotel, it has spacious rooms with brick or wood floors, *talavera*-tiled bathrooms and colorful Chiapanecan bedspreads. Some have balconies overlooking the bustling street below. Be sure to set aside some time to enjoy a book in the 2nd-floor sitting area—with its rocking chairs and views of the piñata-filled courtyard, it's truly relaxing.

The cozy **Hotel Plaza Santo Domingo** (Av. Utrilla 35, tel. 967/678-6514, www.hotelplazasantodomingo.com, US$37 s, US$47 d) has quiet and clean rooms with comfortable beds; all also have cable TV and telephones. Some rooms on the top floor have great views of the neighboring Templo Santo Domingo too.

The childhood home of one of the owners, 【 **Hotel Posada El Paraíso** (Calle 5 de Febrero at Av. 16 de Septiembre, tel. 967/678-0085, www.hotelposadaparaiso.com, US$42 s, US$56 d) is a delightful hotel just steps from the central plaza. Completely renovated, the cozy rooms have textured ocher and blue walls, heavy wood beam ceilings, and Guatemalan bedspreads. Some also have handmade ladders that take guests to a loft with a twin bed—great if you're traveling with kids. Paraíso's restaurant also is considered one of the best in town.

One of the best values in town, 【 **Villas Casa Morada** (Av. Diego Dugelay at Chiapa de Corzo, tel. 967/706-3996, www.geocities.com/lacasamorada, US$40 studios, US$82 two-bedroom villas) has five charming studios and three two-bedroom condos with views of the surrounding mountains. Each comes complete with ironwork furniture, fully equipped *talavera*-tiled kitchen, telephone, free in-room Internet connection (BYO network cable), and wood-burning fireplace. The only downside is finding someone to rent you a room when the owner is away; be persistent, it's worth it.

US$50-100

One of the places you'll wish you could call home is 【 **Casa Felipe Flores** (Calle Dr. Felipe Flores 36, tel. 967/678-3996, www.felipeflores.com, US$87–107 s/d). A colonial-era gem, this home shines in every way; architectural nuances and beautiful folk art combine perfectly with lush courtyards and mountain views. Open the door to one of the five cozy guest rooms and you'll find fireplaces, high wood-beamed ceilings, and *talavera*-tiled bathrooms. The living room, with its rich fabrics, striking artwork, comfy couches, and—on cold nights—raging fire, will make you feel even more at home. In the evening, be sure to have a glass of wine with the charming owners—Nancy and David Orr—or, at the very least, make use of the honor bar tucked inside an antique chest. A hearty breakfast is included in the rate.

Partially built in the late 1800s, the **Hotel Rincón del Arco** (Ejercito Nacional at Av. Vicente Guerrero, tel. 967/678-1313, www.rincondelarco.com, US$47 s, US$56 d, US$74 suite) has 50 rooms, which are divided into two sections: a handful in the original building with antique furnishings and fireplaces, the rest in a modern section with comfortable, simple furnishings. Ask for one in the original building, preferably overlooking the expansive rose garden. If those are booked, opt for a modern one on the top floor—they have glorious views of the city.

Set in a lovely colonial home turned museum and research center, **(Na Bolom** (Av. Vicente Guerrero 33, tel. 967/678-1418, www.nabolom.org, US$60 s, US$80–100 d, US$110 suite) has beautifully appointed rooms showcasing the artwork of several different indigenous villages. The junior suites are stunning—with king-size beds, whirlpool bathtubs, and glorious views of the lush gardens, it's tough to leave. An inviting library is a great place to relax as is the dining room, where guests—often visiting scholars, social scientists, and travelers with a keen interest in the Maya—gather for family-style dinners. Rates include breakfast and a tour of the grounds.

Hotel Casa Mexicana (28 de Agosto at Av. Utrilla, tel. 967/678-0698, www.hotelcasamexicana.com, US$76 s, US$85 d, US$134–161 suite) is an upscale hotel in the heart of downtown. Set in a renovated colonial building, it has burnished terra-cotta colored walls and an atrium replete with tropical plants, palm trees, and a stone-edged pond. Original artwork leads to smallish modern rooms that are nicely appointed with hand-carved headboards and bright Chiapanecan bedspreads. The annex across the street has similar rooms.

The welcoming lobby of the **Hotel Casa Vieja** (Calle María Adelina Flores 27, tel.

967/678-6868, www.casavieja.com.mx, US$51 s, US$56 d) is a good indication of what you'll find inside: colonial-style rooms with wood-beam ceilings, hand-carved furniture, and *talavera*-tiled bathrooms. Although somewhat small, they're a lovely place to spend the night. The restaurant here is well recommended, especially for Sunday brunch.

Over US$100

Located on the edge of town, the 17th- and 18th-century buildings of **(Parador San Juan de Díos** (Calzada Roberta 16, tel. 967/678-1167, US$145–270 s/d) are now home to one of the finest hotels in San Cristóbal. The good-size rooms have an eclectic art collector's feel to them: antique Mexican furnishings, original oil paintings, and Persian rugs. Each different from the other, no room disappoints—they are breathtaking. Service is impeccable.

FOOD
Mexican

Emiliano's Moustache (Crescencio Rosas 7, tel. 967/678-7246, 9 A.M.–1 A.M. daily, US$3–9) has one of the best *comida corrida* deals in town: just US$4 for an appetizer, soup, entrée, dessert, beverage, and coffee (1–4:30 P.M. only). But just as many people come for the *tacos al pastor,* the tasty spiced meat sliced off a rotating spit and served with corn tortillas made fresh on the spot.

For good cheap eats, **(Restaurante Normita** (Av. Benito Juárez at Calle José Felipe Flores, 7 A.M.–11 P.M. daily, US$4–7) serves local specialties at a half-dozen tables. Low-key and friendly, locals and tourists stop in for *pozole,* squash flower quesadillas, and platefuls of cheese enchiladas.

Restaurante Tuluc (Insurgentes 5 at Calle Cuauhtémoc, tel. 967/678-2090, 7 A.M.–10 P.M. daily, US$3–10) has a dim, narrow dining area with indigenous crafts displayed at the entrance. It's a good lunch spot—the *comida corrida* includes a small mixed drink, bread and soup, an entrée (fish, chicken, or meat, usually served with rice), dessert and coffee. A couple of different *parrillada* specials include up to five different grilled meats, onions, and guacamole.

La Parrilla (Av. Belisario Domínguez at Calle Escuadron 201, tel. 967/674-6214, 2–11 P.M. Tues.–Sun., US$6–12) specializes, naturally, in *parrillada,* large metal plates of grilled meats served sizzling atop wooden boards and usually accompanied by a baked potato or grilled onions. Gnaw on steaks, smoked chicken, pork chops, and sausages, plus a half-dozen variations of *queso fundido* (melted cheese served with tortillas) and *chiles rellenos.*

Other Specialties

The airy front dining area of ◖ **La Paloma** (Av. Hidalgo 3 at Calle Cuauhtémoc, tel. 967/678-1547, 8 A.M.–midnight daily, US$4–10) has exposed beams and windows facing the street, while thick, green plants fill the garden area in back. Try the homemade raviolis, salmon fillet with wild mushroom, or the delicious squash flowers filled with cheese mousse and served with *huitlacoche* (black corn fungus, a Mexican delicacy).

El Gato Gordo (Calle Francisco Madero 28 at Av. Josefa Ortíz Domínguez, 1 P.M.–10:30 P.M. daily except Tues., US$2–5) boasts the cheapest lunch special in town: soup and main dish for US$2. The menu also includes crepes, standard Mexican dishes, and lots of vegetarian options. It has a full bar and great eclectic decor, with murals, posters, and drawings hanging from the walls and ceiling.

El Teatro Café (Calle 1 de Marzo at Av. 16 de Septiembre, tel. 967/678-3149, noon–10:30 P.M. Tues.–Sun., US$5–10) is a comfy, 2nd-floor restaurant around the corner from the theater. The menu has a mix of French, Italian, and Mexican options, including crepes, lasagna, and seasoned grilled meats. The daily special runs US$6–8 and includes a fresh salad, soup, main dish, and coffee.

The restaurant at ◖ **Hotel Posada El Paraíso** (Calle 5 de Febrero at Av. 16 de Septiembre, tel. 967/678-0085, 7 A.M.–11 P.M. daily, US$6–20) is one of San Cristóbal's best. Swiss chef and co-owner Daniel Suter's cheese and beef fondue is top-notch, Caesar salads are mixed right at your table, and the steak is the best in town. Simple but elegant wood tables make up the two small pleasant dining areas.

Light Fare

Madre Tierra (Av. Insurgentes 19 at Calle Hnos. Domínguez, tel. 967/678-4297, 8 A.M.–10 P.M. daily, US$5–10) is a San Cristóbal institution, serving quality food in a hip, progressive setting. The menu is mostly vegetarian, varying from gnocchi to spinach crepes, and includes fresh breads. The colonial-style dining room has heavy beams, high ceilings, and archways that lead to a lovely patio. At night, enjoy a couple **live bands** (mostly *trova,* world beat, and reggae), always followed by a couple of hours of salsa.

Located at the back of an irresistible bakery, the vegetarian ◖ **Casa de Pan: Papalotl** (Calle Dr. Navarro 10, tel. 967/678-5895, 8 A.M.–10 P.M. Tues.–Sun., US$3–7) is a bohemian affair with art on the walls, bougainvillea climbing one wall, and a peaked glass-and-wood ceiling. Breakfast includes homemade granola, whole-wheat muffins, and yogurt; lunch and dinner feature steamed rice and veggies, curried vegetable-filled *empanadas,* homemade soups, and quesadillas. There's often nightly live music from 8–10 P.M.

You'd be forgiven for thinking ◖ **La Pera** (Calle María Adelina Flores at Av. Cristóbal Colón, tel. 967/678-1209, 11 A.M.–11 P.M. Tues.–Sun., US$3–7) is named for the fruit—pear—but the name actually comes from the slang way of saying things are all right: *'ta pera* (it's cool). It's an apt name for this hip bar-restaurant-music venue. Stop in for an afternoon baguette or pasta dish in the chic dining rooms or the leafy courtyard. Or come at night, when you can enjoy beer specials and live music that usually starts around 8 P.M.

Literally a hole-in-the-wall, **Banabanana** (Av. Miguel Hidalgo between Calles Niños Héroes and Hnos. Domínguez, 9 A.M.–6 P.M. Mon.–Sat., US$2–5) has just five tables but the *tortas* and *liquados* are always made to order. Hamburgers, including soy burgers, go for US$2.50, or a bit more if you want fries. The walls are packed with posters of Frida Kahlo, Che Guevara, Maya ruins, and random landscapes.

Coffeehouses

Just off the pedestrian walkway, **Casa Raíz** (Calle Niños Héroes at Av. Miguel Hidalgo, tel. 967/674-6577, 1:30 P.M.–midnight Tues.–Sun.) has a bright spacious dining area and attractive stainless-steel tables and chairs. Besides a wide selection of coffees, the café has a good four-course lunch special for US$4. There's live jazz Fridays and Saturdays starting at 9:30 P.M. too.

Aroma (Av. 20 de Noviembre at 1 de Marzo, tel. 967/674-5783, 7 A.M.–11 P.M. daily) is a smaller coffeehouse at the other end of the pedestrian walkway, serving good coffee and cakes—try the raspberry cheesecake—at rustic wood tables and wrought-iron chairs.

La Selva Café (Av. Crescencio Rosas at Calle Cuauhtémoc, tel. 967/678-7244, 9 A.M.–11 P.M. daily) has 13 different types of coffee and a good breakfast special with yogurt, fruit, biscuit, and coffee for US$5.

Groceries

Many locals derive no small pride from the fact that their modest little city now has a **Chedraui** megastore (8 A.M.–10 P.M. daily). On the highway west of the bus terminal, the store even has a McDonald's next door.

Mercado José Castillo (7 A.M.–6 P.M. daily) is a sprawling public market with just about anything you could want, from great fresh fruit and vegetables to bootleg CDs and live turkeys. Worth a visit, even just to look.

INFORMATION
Tourist Information

Just off the central plaza, the **state tourist office** (Av. Hidalgo 1-B, tel. 967/678-6570, www.turismochiapas.gob.mx, 8 A.M.–8 P.M. Mon.–Fri., 9 A.M.–8 P.M. Sat., 9 A.M.–2 P.M. Sun.) has informative, English-speaking staff, and myriad brochures of local businesses and sights. It is considerably more helpful than the **city tourist office** (Palacio Municipal, tel. 967/678-0665, 9 A.M.–8 P.M. Mon.–Fri.).

Hospitals

Hospital la Caridad (Calle Francisco I. Madero 61 at Av. J. M. Santiago, tel. 967/678-0733) is open 24 hours daily.

Pharmacies

Farmacia Similares (Calle Diego de Mazariegos at Av. Miguel Hidalgo) is open 24 hours daily.

Police

The police (toll-free Mex. tel. 066) are available 24 hours daily.

SERVICES
Money

On the central plaza, **Banamex** (9 A.M.–4 P.M. Mon.–Fri., 10 A.M.–2 P.M. Sat.) and **Bancomer** (same hours) have 24-hour ATMs.

Internet and Telephone

San Cristóbal suffers no shortage of Internet cafés. Among many, **La Torre de Pakal** (10:30 A.M.–9 P.M. daily, US$1/hr.) and **PCS** (9 A.M.–9 P.M. daily, US$1/hr.) are reliable choices; they're located across the street from each other on Avenida 20 de Noviembre at Calle 5 de Febrero.

El Locutorio (Av. Belisario Domínguez at Calle Real de Guadalupe, tel. 967/674-0529, 8 A.M.–10 P.M. daily) has good Web-based phone service for rock-bottom prices to the United States and Canada (US$0.20/min.) and Europe (US$0.30/min.).

Post Office

The post office (8:30 A.M.–7 P.M. Mon.–Fri., 9 A.M.–1 P.M. Sat.) is on Avenida Ignacio Allende between Calles Cuauhtémoc and Diego de Mazariegos.

Immigration

The immigration office (Diagonal Hermanos Paniagua 2, tel. 967/678-0292, 9 A.M.–3 P.M.) is located just west of the town center.

Launderette

One of many launderettes around town,

SAN CRISTÓBAL BUS SCHEDULES

Departures from the **first-class bus terminal** (Av. Insurgentes s/n, tel. 967/678-0291) include:

DESTINATION	PRICE	DURATION	SCHEDULE
Campeche	US$29	11 hrs	take Mérida bus
Cancún	US$56-67*	17.5-18.5 hrs	12:15 P.M., 2:30 P.M., 3:45* and 3:50 P.M.
Chetumal	US$38-44*	12 hrs	take Cancún bus
Ciudad Cuauhtémoc	US$8	3 hrs	five departures 6:45 A.M.-5:30 pm
Comitán	US$3	1.5-2 hrs	every 30-90 min. 6:15 A.M.-8:45 P.M.
Mérida	US$42	14 hrs	6:20 P.M.
Mexico City	US$70-83*	13-14 hrs	every 30-60 min. 4:10 P.M.-7 P.M., plus 10:30 P.M.
Ocosingo	US$3.25	2 hrs	use Palenque bus
Palenque	US$11	5 hrs	nine departures 7:15 A.M.-11 P.M.
Tapachula	US$18	8 hrs	six departures 7:45 A.M.-12:05 A.M.
Tuxtla Gutiérrez	US$3	1 hr	every 15-60 min. 7:20 A.M.-10:45 P.M.
Villahermosa	US$18	7 hrs	11:20 A.M. and 11 P.M.

*Denotes first-class; not available on all departures.

First-class buses from San Cristóbal do not stop at Chiapa de Corzo. Instead, catch a Tuxtla-bound *colectivo* on the Carretera Panamericana, the main highway south of the center (US$2.50, 1.5 hrs).

THE STATE OF CHIAPAS

Lavandería La Rapidita (Av. Insurgentes between Calles Cuauhtémoc and Niñoes Héroes, tel. 967/678-8059, 8:30 A.M.–8 P.M. Mon.–Sat.) charges US$4 for 1–3 kilograms (2.2–6.6 pounds) and US$1.50 for each additional kilogram.

Storage
Store your bags at the **ADO bus terminal** (Av. Insurgentes at Carr. Panamericana, tel. 967/ 678-0291, 24 hours daily, US$1 per 12 hours).

GETTING THERE
Air
The new international airport just outside of Chiapa de Corzo has made arriving by plane fast and easy. San Cristóbal does have a small airport, but no commercial flights land there.

Bus
The **first-class bus terminal** (Av. Insurgentes at the Carr. Panamericana, tel. 967/678-0291) is seven blocks from the parque central. If you want to buy a ticket in advance but don't want to trek out to the station, tickets also are sold at **Ticket Bus** (Calle Real de Guadalupe 5, tel. 967/678-8503, 7 A.M.–11 P.M. Mon.–Sat., 9 A.M.–5 P.M. Sun.).

To go to Guatemala, **Agencia Chincultik** offers direct van service to Quetzaltenango/ Xela (US$23.50, seven hours), Panajachel (US$26, eight hours), and Antigua (US$37 pp, 10 hours). **Posada México** (Dr. Felipe Flores 16, tel. 967/678-0014) has the same service for similar prices. Both leave at 7 A.M. daily; reserve a day in advance. Otherwise, take a bus to Tapachula or Ciudad Cuauhtémoc, where you can cross and pick up a Guatemalan bus on the other side.

Car
Only 50 years ago you could figure a trip up the mountain from Tuxtla Gutiérrez to San Cristóbal was 12 hours by mule. In 2006, a long-awaited bridge and highway were completed, and then-President Fox was on hand for their official inauguration. The drive time was instantly cut in half, down to just over an hour.

From Palenque to San Cristóbal, figure 4– 5 hours on a winding road. You should never drive this road at night, due to occasional roadside robberies. Driving during the day is safe and beautiful, however.

GETTING AROUND
San Cristóbal is a very walkable city, and all but a couple of sights are easily reached on foot. For those places (or if you're just tuckered out) a taxi is your best option. Scores of cabs ply the streets and you can always find one parked at the central plaza; a ride around town costs US$1.75–2.50, depending on the distance. Rates go up slightly after midnight. If you need an early morning or late night ride, **Taxis de San Cristóbal** (tel. 967/678-0067) is a reliable option.

Car Rental
A car can be handy for visiting outlying areas, but bear in mind that tour agencies offer reasonably priced, guided tours to most of the places you're likely to visit with a car. Also, driving the narrow, crowded streets of San Cristóbal can be an adventure, and parking is a real problem. If you do rent a car, buy a good map and be extra cautious of pedestrians, bicycles, and animals along the roadside. Again, never drive at night.

Óptima Car Rental (Calle Diego de Mazariegos 39 across from Parque La Merced, tel. 967/674-5409, 9 A.M.–2 P.M., 4–7 P.M. Mon.– Sat., 9 A.M.–1 P.M. Sun.) rents various models of car; the least expensive is a VW bug at US$47 a day including taxes and insurance. Discounts available if you pay in cash.

Villages Around San Cristóbal

Numerous indigenous villages ring San Cristóbal, and extend deep into the mountains. Residents typically speak one of several Maya languages, and most continue to live by subsistence farming. Many villages practice traditional Maya forms of religion, land ownership, and self-government, independent from state and federal control. A few towns allow guides from San Cristóbal to bring small groups, and such tours are popular and highly recommended. Many travelers cringe at the idea of taking a tour to an indigenous village. But, seen another way, such tours are a way for villages to gain benefits from tourism, while retaining control over the number and nature of tour groups that come. For this reason, it is generally not recommended you drive or bike yourself to any of these places without a legitimate guide.

Taking Photographs

Cameras are viewed with considerable suspicion in most indigenous towns; if you must take pictures, be very discreet and always err on the side of caution, or in this case, respect. Landscape or village shots—not crowds of people—usually are fine. If you want to take a photograph of an indigenous person, ask permission first; if it's a child, ask one of their parents as well. And be prepared for the person to say no or to ask for money in exchange for a photo. Taking pictures inside of churches typically is not permitted; in some places, like San Juan Chamula, it is strictly prohibited and cameras can be confiscated by local officials if it's even out of its carrying case.

Getting There

You'll benefit most by visiting with a guided tour. Independent travelers are less common here, so you may have to explain yourself to curious town leaders. Do not plan to stay the night and know that towns beyond the most-visited ones tend to be very suspicious of strangers who just show up. Hiring a private guide is a good option, and something most tour operators also can arrange.

◖ SAN JUAN CHAMULA

With more than 10,000 residents, San Juan Chamula is the area's largest indigenous town; it also is the town that is most visited by outsiders, typically by tour from San Cristóbal. As with other villages, you will also learn immeasurably more with a guide than you can on your own.

Chamulan Dress

Chamulan women are noted for their beautiful weavings and are easily distinguished by their traditional dress—white *huipiles* with simple flowers embroidered around the necklines and

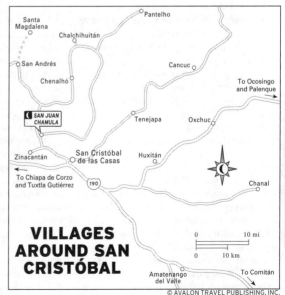

VILLAGES AROUND SAN CRISTÓBAL

© AVALON TRAVEL PUBLISHING, INC.

THE STATE OF CHIAPAS

© LIZA PRADO

a typical Chamulan home

thick black wool skirts cinched with red belts. Many women also wear sky-blue wool *rebozos* (shawls) that sometimes hide a baby tucked into its folds. These garments are hand-woven on a waist loom and generally are made of wool that has been carded by the women from animals raised on the family plot.

Chamulan men wear machine-made hats, Western-style pants and shirts, leather boots, and long, woolen tunics; most men wear white tunics and the village leaders wear black tunics. A man also wears a special official dress of authority during the time he serves on the town council.

Women and little girls are often barefooted—it is partly a question of money, but it also stems from a traditional belief that the earth makes females fertile through their feet. Tourists often are tempted to give indigenous people or children shoes, but some recipients experience such unsolicited charity as offensive; it's better to donate shoes—or better yet, money—to organizations with established relationships with indigenous communities (ask about recommended groups at San Cristóbal's state tourist office).

Saint John the Baptist Church

Along with the market in the central plaza, this colorful blue and white flowered church is the main attraction in San Juan Chamula and a deeply important place for villagers. Though it appears like any other church on the outside, there is no clergy here and the only standard Catholic ceremonies conducted are baptisms, when a priest is brought in for the occasion.

It is obvious from the moment you enter that it is no ordinary Catholic space. A rich aroma greets you as you walk in the door: a mixture of pine, flowers, incense, and candles. The floor is covered with pine needles, cut fresh from the forest and carried here every Saturday. The statues of the saints are dressed in many layers of brilliantly flowered clothes with mirrors hung around their necks. Most of the statues are now kept in glass boxes because villagers occasionally sought revenge when a request to the saint was not fulfilled. It wasn't unusual for

EL CARGO

At some point in his or her lifetime, every villager of San Juan Chamula – as in other indigenous communities – is expected to assume a religious *cargo*. Literally a "burden," in the case of Chamulans it also means a position of responsibility in the town's complex spiritual practices.

A cargo-holder's primary role sounds simple enough: to care for a wooden statue representing one of the many saints honored by Chamulans, usually for a term of one year. But this task is neither easy nor cheap. For starters, the statue has its own home, which the caretaker and his or her family move into for the duration of the term. The caretaker must supply the statue with a constant supply of fresh flowers and pine boughs, which must be cut in the mountains or bought in the market, along with other offerings. On saints' days and other special occasions, the caretaker must organize and host a huge celebration, providing food, soda, and alcohol for the entire village. Certain saints are more highly revered than others – caring for them earns a villager higher honor, but at greater expense.

All told *cargo* can cost its caretaker the equivalent of thousands or even tens of thousands of dollars, a staggering expense for someone who may earn less than five dollars a day. Cargo-holders often borrow the money and can spend years or a lifetime paying off the debt. Still, very few shirk their duty. When asked how he managed it, one cargo-holder shrugged and said, "Better to carry a burden for a year than for the rest of eternity."

ceremonies performed by people with the help of shamans for various daily or family matters. In addition to candles, ceremonies are conducted using chickens, eggs, a traditional homemade liquor called *posh* and—amazingly—Coca-Cola and Pepsi. An important means of ridding the body of bad spirits and energy is belching—*posh* once was used, but of course nothing is a better burp-inducer than Coke, which was quickly adopted by Chamulan shamans. Some may view this as corrupting, but it is one of innumerable instances in which indigenous people have of their own volition integrated the trappings of "modern" life into traditional practices. They are not, after all, blind to the world around them.

Festivals

Religious holidays are especially spectacular times to visit San Juan Chamula. **Carnaval** is one of the biggest celebrations and goes on for a week. **Fat Tuesday,** the day before Ash Wednesday, is especially colorful. **December 12th,** the Virgin of Guadalupe's saint day, also is a major event. During festivals, *cargo* holders, town leaders, shamans, and ordinary villagers all wear special ceremonial clothing, all different depending on the wearer's position but none without bright colors and exquisitely woven and embroidered designs. Solemn marches and special ceremonies are set against a backdrop of music, fireworks, and plenty of food and drink. A rich compelling scene—and you can't take even one photograph!

ZINACANTÁN

In nearby Zinacantán, life moves at a different pace. The town's main industry is growing and exporting flowers, and driving there you'll see large hothouses dispersed in hills and valleys. The Zinacantecans have been merchants since the early 1600s and still travel around the region selling their homegrown vegetables, fruit, and flowers. A growing tourism business also helps explain the town's relative prosperity.

Zinacantecan Dress

The traditional clothing worn by men is the most colorful in the area, and includes straw

an angry churchgoer to break a statue's finger off, turn the statue backward to face the wall, or even to take the statue outside and stick its head in the ground.

Hundreds of candles placed on the floor glow reverently in the dim light—red candles burn for someone who is ill, black candles announce death, but most are white and are part of detailed private

THE STATE OF CHIAPAS

hats, short white pants, and pinkish tunics decorated with bright embroidered flowers and fuchsia tassels. The women, on the other hand, wear dark skirts and white blouses trimmed with a minimum of color, topped with a beautiful blue *rebozo* (shawl).

Textiles

A stop in Zinacantán will include a visit to a weaver's home (in fact, some tours go *only* there, which is somewhat of a disappointment). Zinacantec textiles are noted for their colorful embroidery in flamboyant reds, pinks, purples, and blues. The work is done outdoors in a family yard with most of the women attached to a waist loom. They create tablecloths, bedspreads, placemats, and of course the men's tunics.

SAN ANDRÉS LARRAINZAR

This Tzotzil-speaking municipality consists of about 54 villages with 17,000 inhabitants scattered across the highlands. A few of the more well-known villages are Santa Marta, Santa Magdalena, and San Santiago. It is an impoverished region with little economic activity, and although Larrainzars voted to outlaw bars in certain towns, alcoholism remains a serious problem. San Andrés was and remains an important Zapatista stronghold and was the location of peace talks after the 1994 uprising.

Textiles

As elsewhere, weaving is an important part of life and a source of additional income. Larrainzar women do all the weaving and are well known for threading colored bits of yarn into the warp and weft of their back-strap looms to create special designs. One product is the brocade, an ancient design that incorporates traditional symbols such as the snake, diamond, flower, and monkey. The background color is usually bright red with many colors woven in.

South of San Cristóbal

AMATENANGO DEL VALLE

The Carretera Panamericana (Hwy. 190) rolls past the small pottery-making village of Amatenango del Valle. Passersby are treated to an incredible display of classic Tzeltal Maya artisanship—most notable are the rustic clay doves, some tiny, some measuring over one meter (3.3 feet) in height. All of the objects are made without a wheel. Pieces made from natural gray clay are sun-dried and then fired in an aboveground open fire rather than in a kiln. The pottery is not as durable as some, but the pieces are a wonderful souvenir if you can get them home.

A number of San Cristóbal–based tour operators stop here on the way to or from the Lagunas de Montebello, but if you are driving it is easy enough to visit on your own. Driving past town, you'll see jars, doves, and other pieces set up right on the highway's shoulder. If you stop, the owner of the particular collection of pieces typically will come running out. You can try asking to see the artist's workshop—not all artisans are open to this (or are working at the moment you pull up)—but it makes for an interesting few minutes. As elsewhere, refrain from taking pictures.

COMITÁN

A great base for exploring the nearby Lagunas de Montebello, Comitán itself is a pleasant place to spend a day. Built on a hill, Comitán has steep inclines leading to the shady central plaza. Colonial buildings make up the center of town and services—hotels, restaurants, Internet, banks—are just footsteps from one another.

Sights

The small **Museo Arqueológico de Comitán** (Calle 1 Sur Ote. between Av. Rosario Castellanos and Av. 2 Ote. Sur, tel. 963/632-5760, 9 A.M.–6 P.M. Tues.–Sun., free) traces the history of the Maya in Chiapas. With excellent artifacts, especially those found in tombs, it is definitely worth a stop. Signage in Spanish only.

Servicios Aéreos San Cristóbal (tel. 963/632-4662, www.chiapastours.com.mx/serviciosaereos) offers scenic flights and aerial tours of the region, including a five-hour trip to Yaxchilán and Bonampak ruins (US$785, 4–5 passengers).

Accommodations

The bright and sunny **Hotel San Francisco** (Av. 1 Ote. Norte between Calles 1 and 2 Norte Ote., tel. 963/632-0194, US$9 pp) offers clean rooms that are situated around two courtyards—one is part of a remodeled colonial home, and the other is a modern motel-style annex. They're small but all have private hot-water bathrooms—at US$9, it's a great deal if you're traveling solo. A good place to meet other travelers.

Facing the central plaza, the basic **Hotel Delfín** (Av. Central Sur 21, tel. 963/632-0013, US$22 s, US$28 d) has wood-paneled rooms with private hot-water bathrooms and cable TV—those on the 2nd floor have exposed wood beams. With the park right outside, it's hard to go wrong.

For something nicer, head to the colonial **Posada El Castellano** (Calle 3 Norte Pte. between Avs. Central and 1 Sur Pte., tel. 963/632-0117, www.posadaelcastellano .com.mx, US$34 s, US$37 d). This charming hotel has 22 rooms with tile floors, sparkling bathrooms, cable TV, and phones. All units surround a sunny courtyard with a gurgling fountain. Breakfast included for stays of more than one night.

Food

Overlooking the central plaza, **Helen's Enrique** (Av. Central 19, tel. 963/632-1730, 8 A.M.–midnight daily, US$3–6) offers a good variety of dishes; the food is nothing special but it's filling. Especially good if you're tiring of tacos but don't want to spend too much.

For mouthwatering pizza, head to **La Alpujarra** (central plaza, Av. Central between Calles 1 Norte Pte. and 1 Sur Pte., tel. 963/632-2000, 8 A.M.–midnight daily, US$5–14). Pies come loaded with all the fixin's. If in doubt, try the Rebollon Chiapaneco, which comes oozing with mozzarella, olives, capers, and green peppers. Sandwiches, pastas, and tacos also offered.

As soon as you step into **Matisse** (Av. 1 Pte. Norte 14, tel. 963/632-5172, 2 P.M.–midnight Tues.–Sat., 2–6 P.M. Sun., US$8–16) you'll feel as if you've walked into an upscale Manhattan restaurant. With streamlined furnishings, sparse decor, billowing fabrics, and skylights, it is the epitome of ultrachic. The class extends to the food—Italian gourmet—with a number of pasta and meat dishes to choose from. An excellent choice for a night out on the town.

Mercado Primero de Mayo (Av. 2 Ote. Norte at Calle Central Ote., 6 A.M.–5 P.M. daily) sells fresh foods and breads. A good place to stock up if you're planning to head to the lake region.

Information and Services

Tourist Information: Just a few doors north of the Palacio Municipal is the **tourist office** (Calle Central Ote. 6, tel. 963/632-4047, 9 a.m.–7 p.m. Mon.–Fri., 9 a.m.–2 p.m. Sat.–Sun.). Along with a fistful of area maps and brochures, you'll also get lots of personalized attention.

Pharmacies: Farmacia del Ahorro (Calle 1 Sur Ote. at Av. Central Sur, tel. 963/632-7777, 7 a.m.–11 p.m. daily) is on the central plaza.

Money: Just off the central plaza, **Bancomer** (Av. Rosario Castellanos at Calle 1 Sur Pte., 8:30 a.m.–4 p.m. Mon.–Fri.) has two ATMs.

Internet and Telephone: Cyber@dictos Internet (Calle 1 Norte Pte. between Avs. Central and Rosario Castellano, 9 a.m.–9 p.m. daily) has reliable Internet. To call home, try **Caseta Maguis** (Calle 1 Sur Pte. between Avs. Central and 1 Pte. Sur, 963/632-6713, 9 a.m.–9 p.m. Mon.–Sat., 9 a.m.–8 p.m. Sun.).

Post Office: The **post office** (Av. Central Sur between Calles 2 and 3 Sur Pte.) is open 9 a.m.–3 p.m. Monday–Friday.

Consulates: At the time of research, citizens of the U.S., Canada, and E.U. did not need visas to enter Guatemala. Be sure to double-check this, as Guatemalan visa requirements may have changed by the time you read this.

Launderette: Lavandería Express (Av. 1 Sur Pte. at Calle 3 Norte Pte., 9 a.m.–2 p.m. and 4:30–8 p.m. Mon.–Fri., 9 a.m.–5 p.m. Sun., US$0.90 per 1 kg/2.2 lbs) offers next-day service only.

Getting There

Comitán's modern bus terminal (Av. Belisario Domínguez, tel. 963/632-0980) is several blocks from the city center. Departures include:

- Ciudad Cuauhtémoc, US$5, 1.5 hrs, 8:35 A.M., 9:35 A.M., 1:20 P.M., 3:45 P.M., and 7:20 P.M.

- Palenque, US$16.50, 6.5–7 hours, 2 P.M. and 9:15 P.M., or connect via San Cristóbal.

- San Cristóbal, US$3, 1.75 hours, take any Tuxtla Gutiérrez bus.

- Tapachula, US$14, six hours, seven departures 9:35 A.M.–1:55 A.M.

- Tuxtla Gutiérrez, US$6.50, three hours, every 30–60 min. 7 A.M.–10:40 P.M., plus 5:30 A.M. and 11:40 P.M.

For bus service to the Lagunas de Montebello see *Getting There and Around* in that section.

Car

Just 76 kilometers (47.2 miles) from San Cristóbal, Comitán is an easy drive on Highway 190. Be sure to fill your gas tank before you leave town—gas stations are far and few between in this part of the state.

BETWEEN COMITÁN AND LAGUNAS DE MONTEBELLO
Tenam Puente Archaeological Zone

Some 15 kilometers (9.3 miles) south of Comitán is Tenam Puente (9 A.M.–4 P.M. daily, US$3), a Maya city-state that reached its height around A.D. 1000—after the Mayas abandoned the Petén region. While not particularly glorious, the site, with its large numbers of buildings, is popular among tour groups from San Cristóbal.

Chinkultic Archaeological Zone

On the road to the Lagunas de Montebello, Chinkultic (8 A.M.–5 P.M. daily, US$3) is a little-visited site that dates to A.D. 600 and was abandoned by A.D. 1200. Partially excavated, this site's principal structures (Structures A, B, C, and D) afford spectacular views of a cenote and the region beyond. The ball court once held a unique bas-relief of a ballplayer; this artifact now rests in the National Museum of Anthropology in Mexico City.

Hotel Parador Santa María

Hotel Parador Santa Maria (Carr. Trinitaria-Lagunas de Montebello Km. 22, tel. 963/632-5116, www.paradorsantamaria.com.mx, US$135 s/d) is a remodeled hacienda with a small religious art gallery (US$1.50), a pleasant outdoor restaurant (8 A.M.–6 P.M. daily, US$6–15), and eight rooms. Although appointed with admittedly beautiful colonial antiques and oil paintings, accommodations are somewhat sparse and feel more like museum exhibits than hotel rooms. Nevertheless, this is by far the nicest place to stay in the lakes region. Leave the door open to your room—the green fields and mountain view give the place a little life.

LAGUNAS DE MONTEBELLO NATIONAL PARK

About an hour's drive from Comitán (51 km/31.7 mi), is the beautiful Lagunas de Montebello National Park (8 A.M.–sunset daily, US$2 pp). Set in the middle of the Lacandón Forest, the lakes cover more than 33,670 square kilometers (13,000 square miles) and reflect colors as varied as pale blue, lavender, deep purple, and reddish black—a lush and stunning place. The 22 lakes are easily accessible to visitors and while you can see a few of them from your car, the best way to see the region is by boat, horseback, or foot.

© LIZA PRADO

Twenty-two lakes are easily accessible in the Lagunas de Montebello National Park.

Practicalities

The **visitors center** at Lake Pojoj has a handful of simple eateries and restrooms. It also is where you can book a boat ride (US$15–35) and horseback tour (US$13–15).

Lake Tziscao

One of the largest and most accessible lakes in the region is Lake Tziscao. Just a few kilometers off the main highway, a dirt road leads to it and its namesake village, where there are a handful of rustic hotels. By far, the best place to stay around here are the lakeside cabañas at **Hotel Tziscao** (tel. 963/633-5244, US$9 pp with private bath). The plywood rooms are simple, clean, and have terraces. Avoid the hotel rooms in the main building—they're pretty sketchy. If this place is full, the cabañas next door at

Playa Escondida (no phone, US$2 pp camping, US$6 pp with shared bath) are tolerable.

Getting There and Around

Bus: In Comitán, **Transportes Montebello** (2 Av. Sur Pte. between 2 and 3 Calle Sur Pte.) has daily combi service to the visitors center on Lake Pojoj. Departures are every 20 minutes 6 a.m.–6 p.m. daily (US$2.50, 30 minutes).

Car: A rental car is the easiest way to explore the lake region—you'll have the freedom to stop where you want and you'll never have to wait by the side of the road for a combi to stop.

Taxi: A one-way cab ride from Comitán costs around US$20. For a day of sightseeing, ask the taxi driver to name his price and then bargain hard.

THE STATE OF CHIAPAS

Tuxtla Gutiérrez

Tuxtla Gutiérrez is a busy modern city of more than a half-million residents, a world apart from the colonial cities and indigenous villages most travelers associate with Chiapas. Hotels, government buildings, museums, and parks are of mostly contemporary design—even the main cathedral is a modern-day revision of the original colonial church. That said, Tuxtla does have a one of the best zoos in Latin America, a decent museum, and easy access to Cañon del Sumidero and the colonial village of Chiapa de Corzo.

ORIENTATION

Tuxtla's numbered street grid can be confusing at first, but you'll quickly figure it out. The main thing to remember is that *avenidas* (avenues) run *oriente–poniente* (east–west), while *calles* (streets) run *norte–sur* (north–south).

SIGHTS
Plaza Cívica

The Plaza Cívica stretches across Avenida Central and includes the central plaza and many government buildings. The plaza sometimes serves as

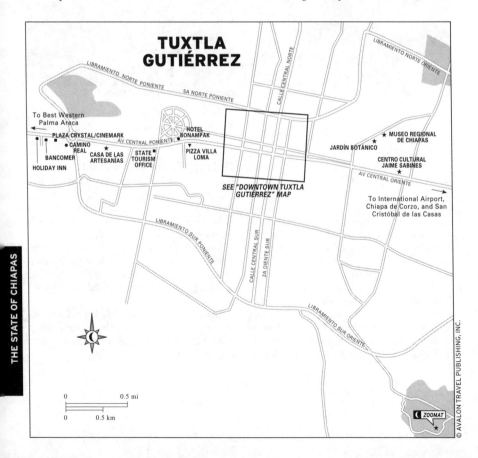

© AVALON TRAVEL PUBLISHING, INC.

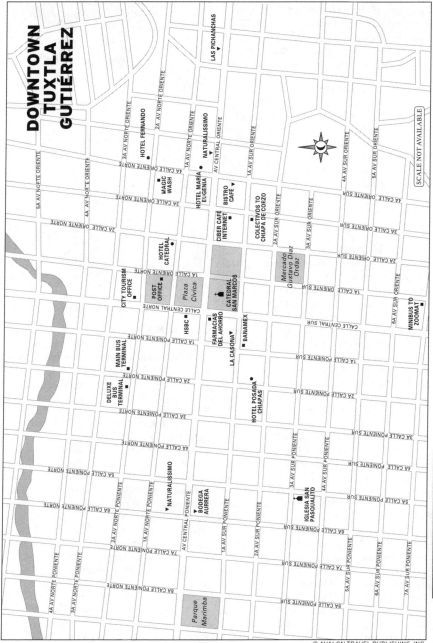

DOWNTOWN
TUXTLA
GUTIÉRREZ

SCALE NOT AVAILABLE

LAS PICHANCHAS ▼

HOTEL FERNANDO ■

NATURALISSIMO ●

HOTEL MARIA EUGENIA ●

MAGIC WASH ■

BISTRO CAFÉ ▼

CIBER CAFÉ INTERNET ■

COLECTIVOS TO CHIAPA DE CORZO

Mercado Gustavo Díaz Ordaz

HOTEL CATEDRAL ●

CITY TOURISM OFFICE ■

POST OFFICE ■

Plaza Cívica

CATEDRAL SAN MARCOS ✝

HSBC ■

FARMACIAS DEL AHORRO ■

LA CASONA ▼

BANAMEX ●

MINIBUS TO ZOOMAT ■

MAIN BUS TERMINAL

DELUXE BUS TERMINAL

HOTEL POSADA CHIAPAS ●

NATURALISSIMO ▼

BODEGA AURRERA ■

IGLESIA SAN PASQUALITO ♦

Parque Marimba

5A AV NORTE ORIENTE
4A AV NORTE ORIENTE
3A AV NORTE ORIENTE
2A AV NORTE ORIENTE
1A AV NORTE ORIENTE
AV CENTRAL ORIENTE
1A AV SUR ORIENTE
2A AV SUR ORIENTE
3A AV SUR ORIENTE
4A AV SUR ORIENTE
5A AV SUR ORIENTE

4A CALLE ORIENTE NORTE
3A CALLE ORIENTE NORTE
2A CALLE ORIENTE NORTE
1A CALLE ORIENTE NORTE
CALLE CENTRAL NORTE
1A CALLE ORIENTE SUR
2A CALLE ORIENTE SUR
3A CALLE ORIENTE SUR
4A CALLE ORIENTE SUR

1A CALLE PONIENTE NORTE
2A CALLE PONIENTE NORTE
3A CALLE PONIENTE NORTE
4A CALLE PONIENTE NORTE
5A CALLE PONIENTE NORTE
6A CALLE PONIENTE NORTE
7A CALLE PONIENTE NORTE
8A CALLE PONIENTE NORTE

CALLE CENTRAL SUR
1A CALLE PONIENTE SUR
2A CALLE PONIENTE SUR
3A CALLE PONIENTE SUR
4A CALLE PONIENTE SUR
5A CALLE PONIENTE SUR
6A CALLE PONIENTE SUR
7A CALLE PONIENTE SUR
8A CALLE PONIENTE SUR

6A AV NORTE PONIENTE
5A AV NORTE PONIENTE
4A AV NORTE PONIENTE
3A AV NORTE PONIENTE
2A AV NORTE PONIENTE
1A AV NORTE PONIENTE
AV CENTRAL PONIENTE
1A AV SUR PONIENTE
2A AV SUR PONIENTE
3A AV SUR PONIENTE
4A AV SUR PONIENTE
5A AV SUR PONIENTE
6A AV SUR PONIENTE
7A AV SUR PONIENTE

© AVALON TRAVEL PUBLISHING, INC.

THE STATE OF CHIAPAS

a gathering place for protests and sit-ins; violent altercations are extremely rare, even as the demonstrations have become more frequent since the 1994 Zapatista uprising. At all other times, the plaza is placid and relaxing, both day and night.

Catedral San Marcos

On the south end of the Plaza Cívica, the Catedral San Marcos is a brilliant white building with modern lines—a stark beauty. Its German-made clockwork mechanism (a carillon with 48 bells) sends 12 carved apostles in and out of the tower every hour to a medley of international tunes. The church was originally built in the second half of the 16th century as a Dominican convent. Today the on the central section of the front arch remains.

Parque Marimba

Just a 15-minute walk from the central plaza, Parque Marimba (Av. Central Pte. between 8 and 9 Calle Pte.) makes a great place to people watch, enjoy live music, and dance. Shade trees and walkways encircle a large attractive kiosk where every night musicians play songs that usually involve a marimba in one way or another. Regardless of the beat, most people—young and old—dance. You definitely don't have to be an expert to join in, and visitors and foreigners are warmly welcomed. Concerts begin at 7 P.M. and last two to three hours.

Museo Regional de Chiapas

The Regional Museum of Chiapas (9 A.M.–4 P.M. Tues.–Sun., US$3) has fascinating exhibits and artifacts—and less-impressive signage—that walk visitors through Chiapanecan history, from the Protoclassic era to the present. The upper floor has a good exhibit on the colonial and republican era, including a fine collection of Chiapanecan art. On your way to the entrance, check out the busts of some of the country's most important leaders on the walkway known as **Calzada de Los Hombres Ilustres** (Avenue of Illustrious Men). After the museum, stop in the neighboring *jardín botánico* (botanical garden), a cool, relaxing place to wander and relax.

© LIZA PRADO

Remodeled several times, Tuxtla's Catedral San Marcos was originally built in the 16th century.

ZOOMAT

Possibly Tuxtla's most visited site is its impressive city zoo, the **Zoológico Regional Miguel Álvarez del Toro** (ZOOMAT, tel. 961/614-4700, 8:30 A.M.–5 P.M. Tuesday–Sunday, US$2, Wed.–Sun., free Tues.). Known as ZOOMAT, it occupies a 100-hectare (247-acre) swath of forest where a 2.5-kilometer (1.6-mile) trail leads visitors past every species of animal found in Chiapas. Housed in large enclosures, there are jaguars, pumas, and little *tigrillos;* beautiful macaws, birds of prey, and the elusive, much-revered quetzal; and unusual creatures such as tapirs, otters, and anteaters. An interesting innovation of the zoo is the *Casa Nocturna,* where artificial lighting has led various nocturnal creatures to think day is night and night is day. Once your eyes adjust, you can watch them going about their business—a lot more interesting than seeing them asleep.

To get to ZOOMAT, take the R-60 minibus (US$0.50, 30 minutes) from the corner of 7 Avenida Sur Oriente and 1 Calle Oriente Sur; from the central plaza, a cab costs around US$5.

ENTERTAINMENT AND EVENTS

Live Music

Parque Marimba (Av. Central Pte. between 8 and 9 Calle Pte.) is the best place to go for live, traditional music and a bit of low-key dancing and people watching. Restaurants **Las Pichanchas** (Av. Central Ote. at 7 Calle Ote.) and **La Casona** (1 Av. Sur Pte. 134 at Calle Central Sur) also have nightly music and dance shows.

Art and Cultural Performances

A beautiful building set on lush grounds, the **Centro Cultural Jaime Sabines** (12 Ote. Norte at Av. Central, tel. 961/612-5198, www.coneculta chiapas.gob.mx/jaimesabines, 10 A.M.–9 P.M. Mon.–Sat.) often hosts dance and dramatic performances, as well as concerts and art exhibits. Call or stop by for a schedule of events.

Bars and Discotheques

Tuxtla's nightclub scene is very much a locals one, where people dress to impress. Best on weekends and after midnight, these were the hottest clubs when we were in town: **Piña's and Charlies** (Blvd. Belisario Domínguez 871, tel. 961/602-5388, 9 p.m.–3 a.m. Tues.–Sat., cover US$3) where reggae rules; **Zhio** (Blvd. Belisario Domínguez 1081, tel. 961/615-7533, 9 p.m.–3 a.m. Thurs.–Sat., cover US$5) for techno; and **Sky** (Blvd. Las Fuentes s/n, 9 p. m.–3 a.m. Thurs.–Sat., cover US$3) where the DJ mixes it up.

Auto Races

Tuxtla Gutiérrez is the traditional starting point for an annual **Carrera Panamericana,** or Pan Am road rally (www.panamrace.com), the last open road race of its kind in the world. Using vintage racecars, two-person teams cover some 3,000 kilometers (1,864 miles) from Tuxtla to the Texas border. The race is typically held the third week of October and draws close to 100 teams and their support squads, from professional roadsters to amateur stock car junkies. The start of the race is sometimes moved to Veracruz and Oaxaca, but if you happen to be in Tuxtla when the race is starting you can join locals in admiring scores of racing cars lined up on Avenida Central Poniente awaiting the big start.

Cinema

Cinemark (Blvd. Belisario Domínguez at Oro Ferraro, tel. 961/615-2969, US$4.25 general, US$2.75 before 3 P.M., US$2.50 Wednesday) is located in the Galería Boulevard, next to Plaza Crystal.

SHOPPING

Tuxtla is an excellent place to shop if you are looking for car parts, a washing machine, or tight disco clothes. It definitely is not a mecca of Chiapanecan handicrafts, but rather a place to get last-minute T-shirts or machine-made knockoffs of indigenous products. The one exception is the fantastic **Casa de las Artesanías** (Blvd. Belisario Domínguez 2035, tel. 961/614-1833, 10 A.M.–8 P.M. Mon.–Sat. and 10 A.M.–3 P.M. Sun.), where there's a little of everything Chiapanecan: fine embroidery, wooden carvings, pottery, leather products, jewelry, and coffee.

If the mall is more your style, head to **Plaza Crystal** (Blvd. Belisario Domínguez at Oro Ferraro, 10 A.M.–9 P.M. daily). There are plenty of department stores, upscale clothing boutiques, and a decent food court.

ACCOMMODATIONS

Tuxtla has plenty of lodging options in the budget and high-end ranges, but not many for mid-range travelers.

Under US$50

In the thick of downtown, **Hotel Posada Chiapas** (2 Calle Pte. Sur between 1 and 2 Calles Sur Pte., tel. 961/612-3354, US$19 s/d, US$28 s/d with a/c) offers boxy but spotless rooms with cable TV. While all open onto a sunny courtyard, few get much sunlight from their one window. If you don't mind that, it's a good choice.

Just a block from the central plaza, the popular **Hotel Catedral** (1 Calle Norte Ote. 367, tel. 961/613-0824, US$22 s with fan, US$26 d with fan) offers ample and spotless rooms with cable TV. Be sure to ask for a room in back since the busy street in front makes for a short night's rest.

Hotel Fernando (2 Calle Norte Ote. at 4 Calle Ote. Norte, tel. 961/613-1740, US$19.50 s with fan, US$25 d with fan) has good-size rooms, cable TV, and great views of the city from the top floor. Check out a couple of rooms before signing in—some have saggy beds and others smell a little musty.

US$50-100

Hotel María Eugenia (Av. Central Ote. 507, tel. 961/613-3767, toll-free Mex. tel. 800/716-0149, www.mariaeugenia.com.mx, US$65 s with a/c, US$74 d with a/c) is the only official four-star hotel in the center of town. The stars, however, are hanging on by a thread. The rooms are out of date, the pool is neglected, and the hallways—though gleaming—have no decor. What it does have is a great location, nice views of the city from the 5th floor, and a decent restaurant. The hotels near the old airport are far better but if you want to be near the action, this is your best bet.

Walking distance to Parque Marimba, **Hotel Bonampak** (Blvd. Belisario Domínguez at 14 Calle Pte. Norte, tel. 961/602-5916, toll-free Mex. tel. 800/507-7177, www.hotelbonampak .com.mx, US$71–81 s/d with a/c) offers rooms that are overwhelmed by white furniture and flower-print decor—you'll feel transported to the 1970s. Somewhat basic for the price tag, but at least there's cable TV, a nice pool, and a popular coffee shop on-site.

◖ Best Western Palma Areca (Blvd. Belisario Domínguez Km. 1080, tel. 961/617-0000, toll-free Mex. tel. 800/500-0102, www .hotelarecas.com.mx, US$62 s/d with a/c, US$73 suite) is set back from the road with rooms that open onto a manicured garden and a nice lap pool; all are ample, nicely appointed, and have cable TV and in-room phones. Check the website before you book—it often has specials.

Over US$100

Hands down the best place to stay in this town is the **◖ Camino Real** (Blvd. Belisario Domínguez 1195, tel. 961/617-7777, toll-free Mex. tel. 800/901-2300, www.caminoreal .com/tuxtla, US$160–250 s/d with a/c). This modern architectural beauty sits on a hill overlooking Tuxtla. The luxurious rooms have the finest in amenities and incredible views. Services include a full-service spa and gym, illuminated tennis courts, and a business center. A rock-inlaid pool with a waterfall is the centerpiece and an excellent restaurant (open 24 hours) overlooks it.

The Moorish-style **Holiday Inn** (Blvd. Belisario Domínguez Km. 1081, tel. 961/617-1000, toll-free U.S. tel. 888/465-4329, www .holiday-inn.com/tuxtla, US$96–140 s/d with a/c) offers comfortable rooms with the amenities you'd expect: cable TV, phones, and air-conditioning. A large and inviting pool is in the center of the complex and a good restaurant faces it. There's also a travel agency, car rental office, and a business center. While a ways from the center of town, this makes a restful base for your visit.

FOOD
Mexican

Tuxtla's best-known restaurant is **◖ Las Pichanchas** (Av. Central Ote. at 7 Calle Ote., tel. 961/612-5351, noon–midnight daily, US$6–15) with a lively courtyard dining area that is decorated with local pottery and colorful *papel picado* (tissue paper streamers). The menu has a good sampling of regional dishes; try an assortment of tamales and an appetizer plate with local cheeses and sausages. For the complete experience, come during a performance: marimba 2:30–5:30 P.M. and 8:30–11:30 P.M. daily, *ballet folklórico* 9–10 P.M. daily.

Closer to the central plaza, **La Casona** (1 Av. Sur Pte. 134 at Calle Central Sur, tel. 961/612-7534, 7 A.M.–11 P.M. daily, US$4–10) has a similar concept, with colorful Mexican tablecloths and wrought-iron chairs. Mexican fare is mixed with some international options, so you can order either chicken mole or chicken cordon bleu. Enjoy live marimba music 2–6 P.M. Monday–Saturday and 10 A.M.–6 Sunday.

Other Specialties

Just a short walk from Parque Marimba, **Pizza Villa Loma** (Av. Central Pte. 1357 at 13 Calle Pte., tel. 961/618-1705, noon–midnight daily, US$5–13) is considered the best pizzeria in town. Pizza connoisseurs will be underwhelmed, but it still makes a decent pie. Live classical guitar most weekend evenings.

Naturalissimo (tel. 916/613-9648, 8 A.M.–9 P.M. daily, US$2–6) is a rare, but emerging, trend in Mexico: a whole food store and good vegetarian restaurant. There are two locations: Avenida Central Oriente at 4 Calle Oriente, and 6 Calle Poniente Norte at Avenida Central Poniente. The menu is identical at both and includes mostly soy-based dishes like hamburgers and *tacos al pastor*. There also are deluxe shakes (US$2) made with various fruit and veggie juices—everything from beets to papaya. The setting is a bit sterile, but it's a nice alternative.

The **Bistro Café** (4 Calle Ote. Sur between Av. Central and 1 Av. Sur, tel. 961/600-0745, 1–10 P.M. Mon.–Sat., US$2.50–6) is a San Francisco–style café with great coffee, crepes, *tortas,* and other light fare. A great place for an end-of-the-day cappuccino and piece of chocolate cake too.

The restaurant at the **Hotel María Eugenia** (Av. Central Ote. 507, tel. 961/613-3767, 7 A.M.–11 P.M. daily, US$4–10) isn't exactly scintillating, but it serves a variety of reliable meals, from pasta and quesadillas to grilled meat and fish fillets. The breakfast buffet is a bit pricey (US$8) but includes made-to-order eggs, pancakes, sausage, yogurt, and cereal.

Groceries

Bodega Aurrera (Av. Central Pte. at 6 Calle Pte., 8 A.M.–10 P.M. daily) is a huge supermarket with produce, canned food, and much more.

In the center of town, the **Mercado Gustavo Díaz Ordaz** (1 Calle Ote. Sur at 3 Calle Sur Ote., 6 A.M.–6 P.M. Mon.–Sat. and 6 A.M.–3:30 P.M. Sun.) has mountains

of bright fruits and vegetables, rows of live chickens, flower peddlers, shoemakers, bicycle repair shops—you name it, you'll probably find it here. Be sure to try a cold glass of *tazcalate,* a sweet drink made from local chocolate, cinnamon, and *pinole* (roasted corn) before you leave.

INFORMATION
Tourist Information

The **city tourism office** (Calle Central Norte at 2 Av. Norte, tel. 961/612-5511, 9 A.M.–8 P.M. Mon.–Fri., 8 A.M.–1 P.M. Sat.) has friendly, helpful staff.

The **state tourism office** (Av. Belisario Domínguez at 15 Calle Pte. Norte, 1st Fl., tel. 961/602-5269, toll-free Mex. tel. 800/280-3500, 8 A.M.–9 P.M. Mon.–Fri., 9 A.M.–3 P.M. Sat.) also has a knowledgeable staff but is a bit far from the center. There also is a tourist information booth (9 A.M.–3 P.M. Tues.–Sun.) at the zoo.

Hospitals

Hospital Sanatorio Rojas (2 Av. Sur Pte. 1487, tel. 961/602-5138) has 24-hour emergency services.

Pharmacies

Farmacias del Ahorro (Av. Central at Calle Central, no phone) is right across from the *catedral* and open 24 hours.

Police

There is no police station near the center area, but officers usually patrol the area on foot. For emergency assistance, call toll-free 066.

SERVICES
Money

HSBC (Calle Central Norte between Av. Central and 1 Av. Norte, 8 A.M.–7 P.M. Mon.–Sat.) is near the central plaza and has an ATM.

Near the outlying hotels, **Bancomer** (10 A.M.–5 P.M. Mon.–Fri. and 10 A.M.–2 P.M. Sat.) has an ATM. Look for it across from the Plaza Crystal mall.

Internet and Telephone

Tuxtla's center area has a plethora of small Internet cafés, especially along Avenida Central and 2 Avenida Norte Oriente. **Ciber Café Internet** (3 Calle Ote. Sur between Calle Central Ote. and 1 Av. Sur, 8:30 A.M.–9 P.M. Sun.–Thurs., until 6 P.M. Fri., US$0.45/hr.) is one that's centrally located.

Tel Centro (2 Av. Norte at 2 Calle Ote., tel. 961/612-7187, 10 A.M.–10 P.M. daily) places national and international calls for about the same rate as at public phones.

Post Office

The post office (9 A.M.–5 P.M. Mon.–Fri., 9 A.M.–1 P.M. Sat.) is on the Plaza Cívica.

Immigration

The immigration office (tel. 961/614-3288, 9 A.M.–1 P.M. Mon.–Fri.) is on Libramiento Norte Oriente near Paso Limón.

Travel Agencies

For plane tickets and local tours, try **Viajes Kali** (Av. Central Ote. 507, tel. 961/611-3175, 8 A.M.–8 P.M. Mon.–Fri., 8 A.M.–4 P.M. Sat., 9 A.M.–2 P.M. Sun.), located in the Hotel María Eugenia.

Launderette

Magic Wash (4 Calle Ote. Norte at 2 Av. Norte, tel. 961/615-2480, 8 A.M.–7:30 P.M. Mon.–Fri., 8 A.M.–2 P.M. Sat.) charges around US$3.25 per load, or about 3 kilograms (6.6 pounds).

Storage

Rápidos del Sur (2 Calle Ote. at 2 Av. Norte) is a second-class bus line right next to the first-class OCC/ADO terminal; luggage storage is US$0.50 every 12 hours.

GETTING THERE
Air

Opened in 2006, Tuxtla's brand-new **Aeropuerto Internacional Angel Albino Corzo** (TGZ, tel. 961/615-0537) is located 35 kilometers (21 miles) east of town. Airlines serving it include: **Click Mexicana** (toll-free Mex. tel. 800/112-5425, www.clickmx.com); **Mexicana** (Blvd. Belisario Domínguez 1748, tel. 961/612-5771, toll-free Mex. tel. 800/502-2000, www.mexicana.com), and **Aviacsa** (Av. Central Pte. 160, tel. 961/611-2000, toll-free Mex. tel. 800/006-2200, www.aviacsa.com).

Bus

The **main first-class bus terminal** (2 Av. Norte and 2 Calle Pte., tel. 961/613-5995, ext. 2431) has ADO and OCC service, plus an ATM, mini-mart, and Telmex Internet terminal. The **deluxe-service terminal** (tel. 961/612-1639, ext. 2421) has ADO-GL and UNO service and is just across 2 Calle Poniente from the main terminal.

Colectivos to Chiapa de Corzo (US$0.75, 30 minutes) leave every 10–15 minutes 5 A.M.–10 P.M. daily from the corner of 3 Calle Oriente Sur and 1 Avenida Sur Poniente.

Car

Rental cars start at around US$45–55/day for a compact VW or Chevy. Some agencies in town include **Budget** (Blvd. Belisario Domínguez 2510, tel. 961/615-0672, 8 A.M.–1 P.M. and 4–7 P.M. Mon.–Sat.) and **Hertz** (Hotel Camino Real, Blvd. Belisario Domínguez 1195, tel. 961/615-5348, 8 A.M.–8 P.M. Mon.–Sat., 9 A.M.–5 P.M. Sun.).

GETTING AROUND

Tuxtla's downtown area is a decent size but not so big that you can't get around by foot. A walk from the Plaza Cívica to Parque Marimba will take about 15–20 minutes—taking a *colectivo* there and back is always an option too.

Bus

Colectivos (public minibuses) serve some of Tuxtla's outlying destinations, including the zoo and the malls. Route 1 is also handy, running the length of Avenida Central.

Taxi

Taxi fares range US$2–5, depending on how far you are going. Drivers do not use meters, so agree on a price beforehand.

TUXTLA GUTIÉRREZ BUS SCHEDULES

Departures from the **main first-class bus terminal** (2 Av. Norte and 2 Calle Poniente, tel. 961/613-5995, ext. 2431) and the **deluxe service terminal** (tel. 961/612-1639, ext. 2421) include:

DESTINATION	PRICE	DURATION	SCHEDULE
Campeche	US$37	12.5 hrs	5 P.M.
Mérida	US$46-60	14-15 hrs	5 P.M. and 6 P.M.*
Mexico City-Norte	US$65-77*	12-13 hrs	13 departures 4:30 P.M.-11:50 P.M.
Oaxaca	US$28-34*	10 hrs	11:30 A.M., 7:30 P.M., 9:30 P.M.*, and 11:55 P.M.
Palenque	US$14-17*	6 hrs	seven departures 6 A.M.-11:55 P.M.
San Cristóbal	US$3	1 hr	every 5-30 min 4:40-10:55 A.M. and every 30-60 min. noon-11:55 P.M.
Tapachula	US$17	6.5-8 hrs	every 30-60 minutes 3:50 A.M.-12:30 A.M.
Villahermosa (via Puente)	US$19-21*	4-5 hrs	seven departures 5 A.M.-11:45 P.M.

*Denotes first-class; not available on all departures.

Around Tuxtla Gutiérrez

CHIAPA DE CORZO

This quiet colonial town between Tuxtla and San Cristóbal is best known as the jumping-off point for boat tours through Cañon del Sumidero, a winding, must-see canyon whose 1,000-meter (3,281-foot) walls will lodge a crick in your neck in no time. But Chiapa de Corzo is also the purported birthplace of marimba, and boasts a couple of good museums and a popular annual festival.

History

Generations before the Spanish conquest, the area of present-day Chiapa de Corzo was inhabited by indigenous people who immigrated from what is now Nicaragua. Those early Chiapanecos were fierce and courageous warriors, and it took the better-armed Spanish two brutal invasions—the first in 1524 led by Luís Marin and the second in 1528 by Diego Mazariegos—to conquer them. On April 3,

MARIMBA

Marimba is truly the sound and soul of Chiapas, the instrument that accompanies virtually every important event and celebration. An early version of the instrument was brought to the Americas on Spanish ships by enslaved Angolans. Its cheerful tone and music spread and was adapted over the centuries, and has come to be highly revered in Chiapas, Guatemala, and elsewhere.

Today, Chiapas produces some of the world's finest marimbas. In Chiapa de Corzo – considered the birthplace of the modern marimba – the instruments are constructed from *hormiguillo,* known as the "singing wood," which gives the marimba a rash, brilliant sound. Sticks made from the strong but flexible *guisisil* wood are wrapped at one end with natural rubber to make mallets that fly across the keys. And the marimba is no longer the lesser stepsister of concert instruments – it lacks only two octaves to equal the range of a concert piano, and more and more scores are being written for the marimba by classical and popular musicians around the world.

1528, the conquered Chiapaneco village was named Villa Real and dedicated under a large ceiba tree.

Like most early Spanish settlements, Villa Real was given as an *encomienda* (royal commission) to the conqueror, in this case Mazariegos. This arrangement made vassals of the Chiapanecos, who built the city under squalid living and working conditions. Fortunately, Bishop Bartolomé de las Casas began agitating for a change in the indigenous people's conditions. By 1552 the *encomienda* was dismantled, and the city was renamed Villa Real Corona. It changed names another half-dozen times until 1888, when the city adopted its current name in honor of the revered president of the municipality, Ángel Albino Corzo.

Sights

The centerpiece of Chiapa de Corzo is **La Pila,** the largest colonial fountain in Chiapas and certainly among the most impressive. Built in 1562, it is an elegant Moorish-style structure in the shape of the Spanish crown; it is built from red bricks cut in an unusual diamond shape. When it was used, La Pila provided the village's main water supply and was a place to do laundry and come together for important social events. Today, it is a well-touristed sight and has informational plaques around it with a thumbnail history of the city.

Catedral Santo Domingo is a huge white building that stands just up the hill from the Embarcadero. Its massive 4,546-kilogram (10,000-pound) bell was cast in gold, silver, and copper in 1576, and when it tolls, can be heard for miles around. The **Ex-Convento Santo Domingo,** which now serves as a cultural center, was built in 1554 in the usual design of the friars, with tile floors, thick walls, and broad archways edging once-lovely patios. Today, a few of the rooms on the 2nd floor house an excellent gallery and museum, the Museo de Laca.

Inside the Ex-Convento Santo Domingo, the impressive **Museo de Laca** (10 A.M.–5 P.M. Tues.–Sun., free) exhibits Chiapa de Corzo's stand-out lacquer ware, a craft brought by the Spanish and improved upon by native Chiapanecans. There are beautiful examples of this precision art—from tiny, delicate jewelry boxes to enormous wood chests, each covered with bright colors and intricately hand-painted designs. There's also an unrelated exhibit with an extensive collection of Mexican ceremonial masks—don't miss it, it's truly spectacular.

As the name suggests, the **Casa-Museo de la Marimba** (Av. Independencia 36, tel. 961/616-0012, donations accepted) is a museum all about marimbas. It is run out of the home of the Nandayapas, a family of world-renown marimba artisans and musicians. They are creators of perhaps the country's finest marimbas, still patterned from the 100-year-old templates of the first generations of their family. Their marimbas come in all sizes, the larg-

La Pila is the largest colonial fountain in Chiapas.

est being the concert-size instrument, which is 2.4 meters (eight feet) long and has a range of 6.5 octaves. If you time it right, admission includes a tour of the museum and a concert (noon Fri.–Sun.).

Templo y Mirador de San Gregorio was built on the hill in the middle of town. The ruins of this 17th-century church evoke the one-time wealth and import of Chiapa de Corzo; it has three naves and walls that echo the influences of Muhadin, Renaissance, and baroque architecture. Not a great deal is left today, just a few walls and fine arches, but the view of the town remains as impressive as ever.

Entertainment and Events

Chiapa de Corzo's biggest celebration—the **Festival de San Sebastián**—takes place January 8–22 every year. Boys and men dress in colonial Spanish garb, and wear pink-skinned, mustachioed masks made from wood and topped with bright bushy yellow hair, known as *parachicos*. They carry rattles and perform in dances and processions in the city center. Most

say the masks represent an ailing Spanish boy who was cured long ago by Saint Sebastian, and whose mother threw a huge celebration *para el chico* (for the boy), from which today's term is derived.

It is a special—and popular—time to be in Chiapa de Corzo; reserve your hotel well in advance if you can. For those who don't get a hotel room (most don't), the buses to and from Tuxtla run late into the night.

Accommodations

There are few overnight visitors to Chiapa de Corzo, but with the growing attraction of Chiapas and its natural beauties, this small town is keeping up.

A long way from California, but right on the plaza, the colonial **Hotel Los Ángeles** (Av. Julian Grajáles 2, tel. 961/616-0048, www.losangeleschiapas.com, US$18 s, US$20 d, US$5 extra for a/c) offers spotless rooms with private hot-water bathrooms and cable TV. Bright bedspreads make them feel that much more inviting.

THE STATE OF CHIAPAS

Down the block, the **Hotel Posada Real** (Av. Julian Grajáles 192, tel. 961/616-1015, hotelposadareal@hotmail.com.mx, US$18.50 s/d, US$23 s/d with a/c) is slightly more up-scale. Rooms are large and have gleaming tile floors, air-conditioning, and cable TV.

The nicest place in town is **La Ceiba** (Av. Domingo Ruiz 300, tel. 961/616-0389, US$60 s/d with a/c), three blocks west of the plaza. In a colonial building, it has an Old World look but New World amenities; each of the rooms has a private bathroom and cable TV, plus there's a welcoming pool and a lush garden.

Food
Centro-Nutricional (Calle Mexicanidad, 7 A.M.–9 P.M. daily, US$1.50–5) whips up great *liquados* (fruit shakes) and good basic meals, such as quesadillas, empanadas, and scrambled eggs, mostly served on disposable dishes. Outdoor tables are in a pretty corridor facing the central plaza.

Information and Services
Tourist Information: Just off the central plaza is the **state tourism office** (Av. Domingo Ruiz at 5 de Febrero, 8 A.M.–4 P.M. Mon.–Fri.); it also staffs an **information desk** (Calle 5 de Febrero 1, 9 A.M.–3 P.M. Tues.–Fri.) inside a nearby *artesanía* shop.

Pharmacies: Farmacia Esperanza (Calle 21 de Octubre between Calles Mexicanidad and Tomás Cuesta, tel. 961/616-0454, 7 A.M.–11 P.M. daily) is one of several pharmacies near the central plaza.

Money: You'll find reliable ATMs at **Bancomer** (Calle Mexicanidad, 8:30 A.M.–4 P.M. Mon.–Fri.) on the central plaza.

Internet and Telephone: Turbonet Xtreme (Calle Mexicanidad 11-A, tel. 961/616-0004, 8 A.M.–10 P.M. daily, US$0.75/hour) is a block north of the central plaza.

Getting There
From Tuxtla Gutiérrez, *colectivos* leave for Chiapa de Corzo (US$1, 30 minutes) every 10–15 minutes 5 A.M.–10 P.M. daily from the corner of 3 Calle Oriente Sur and 1 Avenida Sur Poniente. Passengers are dropped off on the north side of Chiapa de Corzo's central plaza. To return to Tuxtla, catch the bus headed the other direction on the opposite side of the street.

❰ CAÑON DEL SUMIDERO
The Río Grijalva was formerly a roaring series of rapids; it eventually cut its way through stone to form the narrow Cañon del Sumidero (Sumidero Canyon). In 1981, the river was harnessed with the construction of the **Chicoasén Dam,** one of Mexico's largest; the tranquil waterway that resulted now serves as a favorite recreational area for locals and foreigners alike.

In Chiapa de Corzo, a painting in the ex-Convento Santo Domingo portrays an infamous story associated with the canyon: Early in the conquest, an indigenous community was invaded by Spanish troops. They fought fiercely, but could not defeat their better-armed opponents. Facing defeat, men and women, some holding their children, jumped from the canyon walls to their deaths rather than be captured.

Visiting Cañon del Sumidero
Chiapa de Corzo is the main starting point for **boat trips** through the Cañon del Sumidero. A two-hour boat ride (US$10 pp, 9 A.M.–4 P.M. daily) starts at the Embarcadero (end of Calle 5 de Febrero), downhill from the central plaza. Boats leave when they are full (12–16 people); although afternoon trips are especially beautiful, you're more assured of a trip and have less waiting time if you arrive between 9 A.M.–noon, especially in low season.

The boat motors an hour downriver to the dam and an hour back. Along the way, you'll pass below towering stone walls—your driver/guide should point out the highest spot, a sheer drop of more than one kilometer (0.6 mile). In the walls and along the water's edge, you'll see interesting rock formations, caves, waterfalls (during the rainy season), and an ever-changing vista of plants and trees. In one area, a wispy waterfall has created a beautiful forma-

© LIZA PRADO

A boat trip is the best way to enjoy the breathtaking views of the Cañon del Sumidero.

tion of moss and plants that looks like a huge Christmas tree.

An alternative way to see the canyon is by **car.** A road follows the 14-kilometer (8.7-mile) gorge and has five lookout points—**La Ceiba, La Coyota, Las Tepehuajes, El Roblar,** and **Los Chiapas**—all offering spectacular views.

Another option is to spend the day at the **Cañon del Sumidero Parque Ecoturístico** (tel. 961/600-6712, www.sumidero.com, US$20–30). Located on the river just before you reach the dam, the park includes a number of moderate- to low-impact outdoor activities, including kayaking, rappelling, zip lines, and hiking on interpretive trails. There's a restaurant and a small zoo on-site too. Admission includes the boat trip through the canyon; there are additional fees for most of the activities inside.

CAVE AND VILLAGE LOOP

A number of caves and indigenous villages can be visited near Tuxtla Gutiérrez; it's a pleasant drive, exploring the countryside and its ham-

lets. You'll need a car to travel the loop and a guide to take you into the caves (do not venture into any caves alone!). Ask at the Tuxtla tourist offices for recommended guides.

Visiting the Loop

Headed south from Tuxtla, Highway 195 crosses a broad agricultural region known as **La Frailesca.** After about 18 kilometers (11.2 miles), you'll reach the pleasant little town of **Suchiapa,** a former stronghold of Chiapanecan indigenous people. The town has a pleasant plaza with a 16th-century church, Iglesia San Esteban.

Another 30 kilometers (18.6 miles) down Highway 195 is a small sign and turnoff to **Grutas de Guaymas** (Guaymas Caves). Continue on this unpaved single-track road for approximately 14 kilometers (8.7 miles); along the way there are chestnut trees, orchids, bromeliads, and delicate ferns.

The entrance to the Grutas de Guaymas is hidden by coffee trees but once you're led in, you'll find an untouched cave containing beautiful stalactites and stalagmites. After you've had your fill, ask your guide to take you to nearby caves of **Belén, El Nilar, La Calavera, El Jaragual, El Encanto,** and **Grutas de Cristal.**

Once you come up for air, return to Highway 195. There are a series of small- to medium-size villages that grew out of worker settlements around former haciendas. **Villaflores** was created for workers of the Santa Catalina hacienda—the hacienda is long gone, but the town

is now the area's agricultural hub, producing mainly corn and cattle. Beyond Villaflores are more hacienda-born towns, including **Villa Corzo** and **San Pablo Buenavista,** which has remains of the old hacienda buildings.

From San Pablo Buenavista, turn onto Highway 230 to **Revolucíon Mexicana,** where the road leads to Highway 157 north to Chiapa de Corzo—a cutoff before Chiapa de Corzo crosses the Santo Domingo river and reconnects with Highway 190 back to Tuxtla.

The Pacific Coast

From Tuxtla, Highway 190 takes travelers through the **Valley of Cintala,** an area where sprawling haciendas used to stand. Some, like Las Cruces and La Valdiviana still have the remains of beautiful chapels and tall chimneys. Crossing the imposing **Sierra Madre,** the road winds through the dramatic pass of La Sepultura and eventually reaches the town of Tonalá and Highway 200. Running parallel to the coast, this highway runs north towards Oaxaca all the way to Tapachula, the border with Guatemala.

PUERTO ARISTA

Though a popular getaway for Chiapanecans from Tonalá and Tuxtla, the beaches and facilities at Puerto Arista aren't exactly glorious. This one-street town has a handful of basic hotels and simple *palapa* restaurants. The beach itself is ashy volcanic sand and the surf can be quite heavy, but it makes a mellow place to kick back for a day or two. For swimming, head to the nearby fishing village of **Boca de Cielo,** which sits across from a long sand-spit, creating a small, protected lagoon.

The best place to stay in town is **Hotel Arista Bugambilia** (main street, 994/600-9044, US$60–70 s/d with a/c) with small but clean rooms right on the beach. A leafy garden with a well-tended pool in the middle is a plus. There's a good beachside restaurant and gated parking too.

For eats, walk down the main drag and see what looks appealing—fresh seafood is the specialty everywhere.

PIJIJIAPÁN

Farther south on Highway 200, the town of Pijijiapán is a settlement that was founded more than 1,000 years ago. Once a trading post for the regional indigenous groups—Olmecs, Nahuas, Aztecs, Mixes, and Zoques—today, it is a whimsical town dotted with red tile roofs and crayon-colored houses. It's a nice place to spend a morning, wandering around.

About 1.5 kilometers (one mile) west of town are the archaeological remnants of **La Retumbadora,** a collection of three large granite rocks with Olmec carvings. Dating to 1200–900 B.C., the largest is **Los Soldados** (the Soldiers), which has a group of indigenous warriors represented on it.

RESERVA DE LA BIOSFERA EL TRIUNFO

Located in the peaks of the Sierra Madre, El Triunfo Biosphere Reserve is a mountainous cloud-forest reserve that straddles the international border between Mexico and Guatemala. Extending over 750,000 acres (300,000 hectares), it contains myriad streams, waterfalls, and lush tropical flora. A bird-watchers paradise, two of the rarest in Latin America—the Homed Guan and the Azure-rumped Tanager—have been spotted among the almost 400 bird species here. The memorable Resplendent Quetzal, with its brilliant colors and superlative tail feathers up to 76 centimeters (30 inches), also occasionally is seen.

To access the park, enter through the town of Mapastepec off Highway 200. A trip for hardy hikers, it's about a 13-kilometer (eight-mile) climb up the side of a dormant volcano to the reserve; there are no roads and the trails are often muddy because of the misty conditions. There is a basic campground and cabin within the park. Since it's best to have a guide or park ranger lead you—ask for recommendations at one of Tuxtla's tourist information office before heading into the reserve.

TAPACHULA

A sweaty bustling city, Tapachula is Mexico's main border town with Guatemala. Far from charming, there's not much reason for travelers to come here other than to leave the country. And the only reason to stay overnight is if you've arrived too late to cross the border during the day.

Accommodations and Food

With hundreds of people crossing the border everyday, there are plenty of hotels and restaurants in town. Solid choices include:

The boutiquey **◖ Casa Mexicana** (8a Av. Sur at 2a Calle Pte., tel. 962/626-6605, www .casamexicanachiapas.com, US$50 s with a/c, US$60–70 d with a/c) offers artsy rooms in a luxurious colonial setting. The 10 rooms are decorated slightly differently but all have original art and antique furnishings as well as air-conditioning and cable TV. They open onto a leafy garden with a welcoming pool. Wireless Internet and private parking also are available.

The colorful **Hotel Los Portales** (8a Av. Norte 19, tel. 962/626-4050, US$37 s/d with a/c) has simple sunny rooms with spotless bath-

rooms and air-conditioning (a must!). Breakfast included in the rate.

For food, head to the central park, **Parque Hidalgo** (8a Av. Norte between Calles 1 and 5 Pte.), which is lined with Mexican restaurants. If in doubt, head to **Los Comales** (south side of the central park, tel. 962/626-2405, 24 hours daily, US$3–8), which specializes in *tamales* and *pozole*.

Information and Services

Most traveler services can be found on or near Parque Hidalgo: the **tourist office** (9 A.M.– 3 P.M. and 6–9 P.M. Mon.–Fri.), several 24-hour **pharmacies, banks** with ATMs, and **Internet cafés.**

The **immigration office** (Av. 14 Norte 57, tel. 962/626-1263) is open 9 A.M.–1 P.M. Monday–Friday.

The **Guatemalan Consulate** (Calle 2 Ote. 33, tel. 962/626-1252) is open 9 A.M.–5 P.M. Monday–Friday.

Getting There and Around

As a major border town, Tapachula has an extensive public transportation system.

Air: The **Tapachula International Airport** (TAP, tel. 962/626-4189) is located about 18 kilometers (11 miles) south of the city on the road toward Puerto Madero. It is serviced by **Aviacsa** (toll-free Mex. tel. 800/006-2200, www.aviacsa.com) and **Aeroméxico** (toll-free Mex. tel. 800/021-4010, www.aero mexico.com).

Bus: The bustling **first-class bus station** (Calle 17 Ote. at Av. 3 Norte) has extensive bus service to destinations throughout Mexico, including Tuxtla Gutiérrez, San Cristóbal, Villahermosa, and Mexico City. **TICA** bus line (tel. 962/626-2880, www.tica bus.com) also offers international bus service to **Guatemala City** (five hours, twice daily, US$15) from here.

BACKGROUND

The Land

The history of the Yucatán Peninsula is deeply intertwined with its unique geology and ecology. From the ancient Maya to modern-day tourism, the land and its resources have shaped the course of Yucatecan events. And the Yucatán, in turn, has helped shape the course of Mexican history, from being the stage upon which the early Spanish conquest was conducted to helping rescue a moribund Mexican economy in the 1980s. An understanding of the Yucatán Peninsula's land, ecology, culture, and politics is vital to understanding the region today.

The Yucatán Peninsula spans some 113,000 square kilometers (70,215 square miles) in southeastern Mexico, and is made up of three states: Yucatán, Campeche, and Quintana Roo. It has more than 1,600 kilometers (994 miles) of shoreline, with the Caribbean Sea to the east and the Gulf of Mexico to the north and west. To the southwest are the Mexican states of Tabasco and Chiapas, and directly south are the countries of Belize and Guatemala.

Geologically, the Yucatán Peninsula is a flat shelf of limestone, a porous rock that acts like a huge sponge. Rainfall is absorbed into the ground and delivered to natural stone-lined sinks and underground rivers. The result

© GARY CHANDLER

CHICXULUB CRATER

Sixty-five million years ago, a meteorite more than 10 kilometers wide (6.2 miles) collided with the Earth. It was traveling at 20 kilometers per second (12.4 miles per second) and at the time of impact, its temperature was 18,000°C (32,432°F) – three times that of the sun's surface. The massive meteor created a colossal crater – more than 2.5 kilometers (1.6 miles) deep and about 200 kilometers (124.3 miles) in diameter – the largest and best-preserved crater on Earth. It caused volcanoes to erupt, the planet to tremble, and tidal waves more than 500 meters (0.3 miles) high. This monumental movement, in turn, sent millions of tons of pulverized rock into Earth's atmosphere, plunging it into darkness. The lack of sun eventually led to the demise of more than 70 percent of all living things on the planet, including the dinosaurs.

All very interesting, but why mention it in a guidebook to the Yucatán? Because this is where the meteor hit – in what is today the coastal town of Chicxulub, just east of Progreso. In 1981, scientists from PEMEX (Mexico's national petroleum company) were drilling in the Yucatán Peninsula when they discovered gravitational anomalies near the town of Chicxulub. The scientists took core samples and soon concluded that the meteor that had changed the face of the planet crashed in the Yucatán. It provided an explanation as to why the limestone-covered peninsula had eroded so dramatically, creating a ring of caves and cenotes in numbers found nowhere else on Earth. In 1991, UNAM (the National Autonomous University of Mexico) in cooperation with NASA confirmed the theory.

The Yucatán Peninsula is well known as one of the richest parts of the world; what many do not know, however, is that life as we know it began here.

is that the Yucatán has virtually no surface water, neither rivers nor lakes. (It also has very few hills.) The geology changes as you move south, and the first sizable river—the Río Hondo—forms a natural boundary between Belize and Mexico.

GEOGRAPHY
The Coast
The northern and western coasts are bordered by the emerald waters of the Gulf of Mexico. Just inland, the land is dotted with lagoons, sandbars, and swamps. The east coast is edged by the turquoise Caribbean and the glorious islands of Isla Cozumel, Isla Mujeres, and Isla Contoy lie just offshore. Along the coast runs the Mesoamerican Reef, the second-longest coral reef in the world.

Cenotes
Over the course of millennia, water that seeped below the Yucatán's porous limestone shelf eroded a vast network of underground rivers and caves. When a cave's ceiling wears thin, it may eventually cave in, exposing the water below. The Maya called such sinkholes *dzo'not,* which Spanish explorers recorded as *cenotes.* Most cenotes are extremely deep, and interconnected by way of underground channels. A cenote's surface may be near ground level, but more often it is much farther down, as much as 90 meters (295 feet) below. In those cases, the Maya gathered water by carving stairs into the slick limestone walls or by hanging long ladders into abysmal hollows that lead to underground lakes.

CLIMATE
The weather in the Yucatán falls into a rainy season (May–October) and a dry season (November–April). Travelers to the Yucatán Peninsula in the dry season will experience warm days, occasional brief cold storms called *nortes,* and plenty of tourists. In the rainy season, expect spectacular storms and hot, muggy days. The region is infamous

for its heat and humidity in May and June, which hovers around 90°F *and* 90 percent humidity.

Hurricane season runs July–November with most activity occurring mid-August– mid-October. Though tropical storms are common this time of year, full-fledged hurricanes are relatively rare. If one is bearing down, don't try to tough it out. Head inland immediately.

Flora

Quintana Roo's forests are home to mangroves, bamboo, and swamp cypresses. Ferns, vines, and flowers creep from tree to tree and create a dense growth. The southern part of the Yucatán Peninsula, with its classic tropical rainforest, hosts tall mahoganies, *campeche zapote,* and *kapok*— all covered with wild jungle vines. On topmost limbs, orchids and air ferns reach for the sun.

TREES
Palms
A wide variety of palm trees and their relatives grow on the peninsula—tall, short, fruited, and even oil-producing varieties. Though similar, various palms have distinct characteristics:

- Royal palms are tall with smooth trunks.

- Queen palms are often used for landscaping and bear a sweet fruit.

- Thatch palms are called *chit* by Mayas, who use the fronds extensively for roof thatch.

- Coconut palms—the ones often seen on the beach—produce oil, food, drink, and shelter and are valued by locals as a nutritious food source and cash crop.

- Henequen is a cousin to the palm tree; from its fiber come twine, rope, matting, and other products. Because of its abundance, new uses for it are constantly sought.

Fruit Trees
Quintana Roo grows sweet and sour oranges, limes, and grapefruit. Avocado is abundant and the papaya tree is practically a weed. The mamey tree grows full and tall (15–20 meters/49–65 feet), providing not only welcome shade but also an avocado-shaped fruit, brown on the outside with a vivid, salmon-pink flesh that tastes like a sweet yam. The *guaya* is another unusual fruit tree and a member of the litchi nut family. This rangy evergreen thrives on sea air and is commonly seen along the coast. Its small, green, leathery pods grow in clumps like grapes and contain a sweet, yellowish, jellylike flesh—tasty! The calabash tree provides gourds used for containers by Mayas.

Other Trees
The ceiba (also called *kapok*) is a sacred tree for the Mayas. Considered the link between the underworld, the material world, and the heavens, this huge tree is revered and left undisturbed—even if it sprouts in the middle of a fertile cornfield.

When visiting in the summer, you can't miss the beautiful *framboyanes* (royal poinciana). When in bloom, its wide-spreading branches become covered in clusters of brilliant orange-red flowers. These trees often line sidewalks and plazas and when clustered together present a dazzling show.

FLOWERS
While wandering through jungle regions, you'll see numerous plants that have vexed amateur botanists the world over. Here in their natural environment, these plants thrive in a way unknown to windowsills at home: Crotons exhibit wild colors, *pothos* grow 30-centimeter (11.8-inch) leaves, the philodendron splits every leaf in gargantuan glory, and common morning glory creeps and climbs for miles over bushes and trees. You'll also be introduced to many delicate strangers in this tropical world: the exotic white and red ginger, plumeria (sometimes called frangipani)

© LIZA PRADO

Seventy-one species of orchids are found in the Yucatán Peninsula.

with its wonderful fragrance and myriad colors, and hibiscus and bougainvillea, which bloom in an array of bright hues. In fact, keeping jungle growth away from the roads, utility poles, and wires is a constant job for local authorities because the warm, humid air and ample rainfall encourage a lush green wonderland.

Orchids

Orchids can be found on the highest limbs of the tallest trees, especially in the state of Quintana Roo. Of the 71 species reported on the Yucatán Peninsula, 80 percent are epiphytic, attached to host trees and deriving moisture and nutrients from the air and rain. Orchids grow in myriad sizes and shapes: tiny buttons spanning the length of a half-meter-long (two-foot) branch, large-petaled blossoms with ruffled edges, or intense, tiger-striped miniatures.

Fauna

Many animals found nowhere else in Mexico inhabit the Yucatán Peninsula's expansive flatlands and thick jungles. Spotting them can be difficult, though with patience and a skilled guide, not impossible.

LAND MAMMALS
Nine-Banded Armadillos

The size of a small dog and sporting a thick coat of armor, this peculiar creature gets its name from the nine bands (or external "joints") that circle the midsection and give the little tank some flexibility. The armadillo's keen sense of smell can detect insects and grubs—its primary food source—up to 15 centimeters (6 inches) underground, and its sharp claws make digging for them a cinch. An armadillo also digs underground burrows, into which it may carry a full bushel of grass to make its nest, where it will sleep through the hot day and emerge at night. Unlike armadillos that roll up into a tight ball when threatened, this species will race to its burrow, arch its back, and wedge in so that it cannot be pulled out. The tip of the Yucatán Peninsula is a favored habitat for its scant rainfall; too much rain floods the burrow and can drown young armadillos.

Giant Anteaters

A cousin of the armadillo, this extraordinary animal measures two meters (6.6 feet) from the tip of its tubular snout to the end of its bushy tail. Its coarse coat is colored shades of brown-gray; the hindquarters are darker in tone, while a contrasting wedge-shaped pattern of black and white decorates the throat and shoulders. Characterized by an elongated head, long tubular mouth, and extended tongue (but no teeth), it can weigh up to 39 kilograms (86 pounds). The anteater walks on the knuckles of its paws, allowing its claws to remain tucked under while it looks for food.

Giant anteaters are found in forests and swampy areas in Mexico and through Central and South America. It is mainly diurnal in areas where there are few people but nocturnal in densely populated places. Its razor-sharp claws allow it to rip open the leathery mud walls of termite and ant nests, the contents of which are a main food source. After opening the nest, the anteater rapidly flicks its viscous tongue in and out of its small mouth opening. Few ants escape.

Tapirs

South American tapirs are found from the southern part of Mexico to southern Brazil. A stout-bodied animal, it has short legs and a tail, small eyes, and rounded ears. The nose and upper lip extend into a short but very mobile proboscis. Tapirs usually live near streams or river, which they use for daily bathing and as an escape from predators, especially jaguars and humans. Shy and placid, these nocturnal animals have a definite home range, wearing a path between the jungle and their feeding area. If attacked, the tapir lowers its head and blindly crashes off through the forest; they've been known to collide with trees and knock themselves out in their chaotic attempt to flee.

Peccaries

Next to deer, peccaries are the most widely hunted game on the Yucatán Peninsula. Two species of peccaries are found here: the collared javelina peccary and the white-lipped peccary. The feisty collared javelina stands 50 centimeters (20 inches) at the shoulder and can be one meter (3.3 feet) long, weighing as much as 30 kilograms (66 pounds). It is black and white with a narrow, semicircular collar of white hair on the shoulders. The name *javelina* (which means "spear" in Spanish) comes from the two tusks that protrude from its mouth. This more familiar peccary is found in the desert, woodlands, and rainforests, and it travels in groups of 5–15. The white-lipped peccary is reddish brown to black and has an area of white around its mouth. Larger than the javelina, it can grow to 105 centimeters (41 inches) long, and is found deep in tropical rainforests living in herds of 100 or more. Peccaries often are compared to the wild pigs found in Europe, but in fact they belong to entirely different families.

Felines

Seven species of cats are found in North America, four in the tropics. One of them—the jaguar—is heavy chested with sturdy, muscled forelegs. It has small, rounded ears and its tail is relatively short. Its color varies from tan and white to pure black. The male can weigh 65–115 kilograms (143–254 pounds), females 45–85 kilograms (99–187 pounds). The largest of the cats on the peninsula, the jaguar is about the same size as a leopard. Other cats found here are the ocelot and puma. In tropical forests of the past, the large cats were the only predators capable of controlling the populations of hoofed game such as deer, peccaries, and tapirs. If hunting is poor and times are tough, the jaguar will go into rivers and scoop up fish with its large paws. The river also is one of the jaguar's favorite spots for hunting tapirs, when the latter comes to drink.

SEALIFE
Coral Reefs

The spectacular coral reefs that grace the peninsula's east coast are made up of millions of tiny carnivorous organisms called polyps. Individual polyps can be less than a centimeter (0.4 inch) long or up to 15 centimeters (6 inches) in diameter. Related to the jellyfish and sea anemone, coral polyps capture prey with tiny tentacles that deliver a deadly sting.

Reef-building polyps have limestone exoskeletons, which they create by extracting calcium from the seawater. Reefs are formed as generation after generation of polyps attach themselves to and atop each other. Different species attach in different ways, resulting in the many shapes and sizes of ocean reefs: delicate lace, trees with reaching branches, pleated mushrooms, stovepipes, petaled flowers, fans, domes, heads of cabbage, and stalks of broccoli. Though made up of individual polyps, coral structures function like a single organism, sharing nutrients through a central gastro-vascular system. Even in ideal conditions, most coral grows no more than five centimeters (2 inches) per year.

Reefs are divided into three types: barrier, atoll, and fringing. A barrier reef runs parallel to the coast, with long stretches separated by narrow channels. The Mesoamerican Reef extends 250 kilometers (155 miles) from the tip of Isla Mujeres to Sapodilla Cay in the Gulf of Honduras—only the Great Barrier Reef in Australia is longer. An atoll typically formed around the crater of a submerged volcano. The polyps begin building their colonies along the lip of the crater, forming a circular coral island with a lagoon in the center. The Chinchorro Bank, off the southern coast of Quintana Roo, is the largest coral atoll in the northern hemisphere, measuring 48 kilometers long and 14 kilometers wide (30 miles by 9 miles) long. A fringing reef is coral living on a shallow shelf that extends outward from shore into the sea.

Fish

The Yucatán's barrier reef is home to myriad fish species, including parrot fish, candy bass, moray eels, spotted scorpion fish, turquoise angelfish, fairy basslets, flame fish, and gargantuan manta rays. Several species of shark also thrive in the waters off Quintana Roo, though they're not considered a serious threat to swimmers and divers. Sport fish—sailfish, marlin, and blue fin tuna—also inhabit the outer Caribbean waters.

Inland, anglers will find hard-fighting bonefish and pompano in the area's lagoons, and those snorkelers and divers looking to float through caves will find several species of blind fish in the crystal-clear waters of cenotes. These fish live out their existence in dark underground rivers and lakes and have no use for eyes.

Sea Turtles

Tens of thousands of sea turtles of various species once nested on the coastal beaches of Quintana Roo. As the coast became populated, turtles were severely over-hunted for their eggs, meat, and shell, and their numbers began to fall. Hotel and resort developments have hastened the decline, as there are fewer and fewer patches of untrammeled sand for turtles to dig nests and lay their eggs. The Mexican government and various ecological organizations are trying hard to save the dwindling turtle population. Turtle eggs are dug up and reburied in sand on safe beaches; when the hatchlings break through their shells, they are brought to a beach and allowed to rush toward the sea in hopes of imprinting a sense of belonging there so that they will later return to the spot. In some cases the hatchlings are scooped up and placed in tanks to grow larger before being released into the open sea. The government also is enforcing tough penalties for people who take turtle eggs or capture, kill, sell, or imprison these animals.

Manatees

The manatee—or the sea cow, as it is often called—is a creature of immense proportions

Once prevalent on Mexico's Caribbean coast, manatees are now rarely seen outside of reserves or eco-parks.

© LIZA PRADO

with gentle manners and the curiosity of a kitten. Large numbers of this enormous animal once roamed the shallow inlets, bays, and estuaries of the Caribbean. Images of them are frequently seen in the art of the ancient Mayas, who hunted them for their flesh. In modern times, the population has been reduced by the encroachment of people in the manatees' habitats along the river ways and shorelines. Ever-growing numbers of motorboats also inflict deadly gashes on the inquisitive, surface-feeding creatures. Nowadays it is very rare to spot one; Punta Allen and Bahía de la Acensión have the most sightings.

At birth the manatee weighs 30–35 kilograms (66–77 pounds); it can grow up to four meters (13.1 feet) long and weigh more than a ton. Gray with a pinkish cast and shaped like an Idaho potato, it has a spatulate tail, two forelimbs with toenails, pebbled coarse skin, tiny sunken eyes, and numerous fine-bristled hairs scattered sparsely over its body. The head of the mammal seems small for its gargantuan body, and its preproboscidean lineage includes dugongs (in Australia), hyrax, and elephants. The manatee's truncated snout and prehensile lips help push food into its mouth. The only aquatic mammal that survives entirely on plants, the manatee grazes on bottom-growing grasses and other aquatic vegetation. It eats as much as 225 kilograms (496 pounds) per day, cleaning rivers of oxygen-choking growth. It also is unique among mammals in that it constantly grows new teeth—to replace worn ones, which fall out regularly. Posing no threat to any other living thing, it has been hunted for its oil, skin, and flesh.

BIRDS

Since a major part of the Yucatán Peninsula is still undeveloped and covered with trees and brush, it isn't surprising to find exotic, rarely seen birds all across the landscape. The Mexican government is beginning to realize the great value in this treasure of nature and is making efforts to protect nesting grounds. In addition to the growing number of nature reserves, some of the best bird-watching locales are the archaeological zones. At dawn and dusk, when most of the visitors are absent, the trees that surround the ancient structures come alive with birdsong. Of all the ruins, Cobá—with its marshy-rimmed lakes, nearby cornfields, and relatively tall, humid forest—is a particularly good site for birders. One of the more impressive birds to look for here is the keel-billed toucan, often seen perched high on a bare limb in the early hours of the morning. Others include *chachalacas* (held in reverence by the Mayas), screeching parrots, and, occasionally, the ocellated turkey.

Flamingos

At the northern end of the peninsula, the reserve at Río Lagartos plays host to thousands of long-necked, long-legged flamingos during the nesting season (June–August). They begin arriving around the end of May, when the rains begin. This homecoming is a breathtaking sight: a profusion of pink/salmon colors clustered together on the white sand, or sailing across a blue sky, long, curved necks straight in flight, the flapping movement exposing contrasting black and pink on the undersides of their wings. The estimated flamingo population on the Yucatán Peninsula is 30,000. This wildlife refuge, called El Cuyo, protects the largest colony of nesting American flamingos in the world.

Many of these flamingos winter in Celestún, a small fishing village on the northwest coast a few kilometers north of the Campeche-Yucatán state border. Celestún lies between the Gulf of Mexico and a long tidal estuary known as La Ciénega. Since the disruption of Hurricane Gilbert, a flock of flamingos has found a new feeding ground near Chicxulub.

Quetzals

Though the ancient Mayas made abundant use of the dazzling quetzal feathers for ceremonial costumes and headdresses, they hunted other fowl for food; nevertheless, the quetzal is the only known bird from the pre-Columbian era and is now almost extinct. Today, they are still found (though rarely) in the high cloud forests of Chiapas and Central America, where they thrive on the constant moisture.

Estuary Havens

Estuaries play host to hundreds of bird species. A boat ride into one of them will give you an opportunity to see a variety of wintering ducks from North America, blue-winged teals, northern shovelers, and lesser scaups. You'll also see a variety of wading birds feeding in the shallow waters, including numerous types of heron, snowy egret, and, in the summer, white ibis. There are 14 species of birds endemic to the Yucatán Peninsula, including the ocellated turkey, Yucatán whippoorwill, Yucatán flycatcher, orange oriole, black catbird, and the yellow-lored parrot.

REPTILES

Although reptiles thrive in Yucatán's warm, sunny environment, humans are their worst enemy. In the past, some species were greatly reduced in number because they were hunted for their unusual skin. Although hunting them is now illegal in most countries, a few black marketers still take their toll on the species.

Caymans

Similar in appearance to the crocodile, the cayman is a part of the crocodilian order. Its habits and appearance are similar to those of crocodiles with the main difference being in its underskin. The cayman's skin is reinforced with bony plates on the belly, making it useless for the leather market. (Alligators and crocodiles, with smooth belly skin and sides, have been hunted almost to extinction in some parts of the world.)

Several species of cayman frequent the brackish inlet waters near the estuaries of Río Lagartos (whose name means "River of Lizards"). They are broad-snouted and often look as though they sport a pair of spectacles. A large cayman can be 2.5 meters (8.2 feet) long and very dark gray-green with eyelids that look swollen and wrinkled. Some species have eyelids that look like a pair of blunt horns. They are quicker than alligators and have longer, sharper teeth. Skilled hunters, cayman are quick in water and on land, and will attack a person if cornered. The best advice you can heed is to give the cayman a wide berth when you spot one.

Iguanas

This group of American lizards—family Iguanidae—includes various large plant-eaters seen frequently in Quintana Roo. Iguanas grow to be one meter (3.3 feet) long and have a blunt head and long flat tail. Bands of black and gray circle its body, and a serrated column reaches down the middle of its back almost to the tail. The young iguana is bright emerald green and often supplements its diet by eating insects and larvae.

The lizard's forelimbs hold the front half of its body up off the ground while its two back limbs are kept relaxed and splayed alongside its hindquarters. When the iguana is frightened, however, its hind legs do everything they're supposed to, and the iguana crashes quickly (though clumsily) into the brush searching for its burrow and safety. This reptile is not aggressive—it mostly enjoys basking in the bright sunshine along the Caribbean—but if cornered it will bite and use its tail in self-defense.

From centuries past, recorded references attest to the iguana's medicinal value, which partly explains the active trade of live iguana in the marketplaces. Iguana stew is believed to cure or relieve various human ailments such as impotence.

Other Lizards

You'll see a great variety of other lizards in the peninsula; some are brightly striped in various shades of green and yellow, others are earth-toned and blend in with the gray and beige limestone that dots the landscape. Skinny as wisps of thread running on hind legs, or chunky and waddling with armorlike skin, the range is endless and fascinating.

Be sure to look for the black anole, which changes colors to match its environment, either when danger is imminent or as subterfuge to fool the insects that it preys on. At mating time, the male anole puffs out its bright-red throat-fan so that all female lizards will see it.

Coral Snakes

Two species of coral snakes, which are related to the cobra, are found in the southern part of the Yucatán Peninsula. They have prominent rings around their bodies in the same sequence of red, black, yellow, or white and grow to 1–1.5 meters (3.3–4.9 feet). Their bodies are slender, with no pronounced distinction between the head and neck.

Coral snakes spend the day in mossy clumps under rocks or logs, emerging only at night. Though a coral snake bite can kill within 24 hours, chances of the average tourist being bitten by a coral (or any other) snake are slim.

Tropical Rattlesnakes

The tropical rattlesnake (*cascabel* in Spanish) is the deadliest and most treacherous species of the rattler. It differs slightly from other species by having vividly contrasting neckbands. It grows 2–2.5 meters (6.6–8.2 feet) long and is found mainly in the higher and drier areas of the tropics. Contrary to popular myth, this serpent doesn't always rattle a warning of its impending strike.

INSECTS AND ARACHNIDS

Air-breathing invertebrates are unavoidable in any tropical locale. Some are annoying (gnats and no-see-ums), some are dangerous (black widows, bird spiders, and scorpions), and others can cause pain when they bite (red ants); but many are beautiful (butterflies and moths), and *all* are fascinating.

Butterflies and Moths

The Yucatán has an abundance of beautiful moths and butterflies. Of the 90,000 types of butterflies in the world, a large percentage is seen in Quintana Roo. You'll see, among others, the magnificent blue morpho, orange-barred sulphur, copperhead, cloudless sulphur, malachite, admiral, calico, ruddy dagger-wing, tropical buckeye, and emperor. The famous monarch also is a visitor during its annual migration from Florida. It usually makes a stopover on Quintana Roo's east coast on its way south to the Central American mountains where it spends the winter.

Environmental Issues

SIAN KA'AN BIOSPHERE RESERVE

With the growing number of visitors to Quintana Roo and the continual development of its natural wonders, there's a real danger of decimating the wildlife and destroying the resources that are vital to the Maya inhabitants. In 1981, authorities and scientists collaborated on a plan to stem that threat. The plan, which takes into account land titles, logging, hunting, agriculture, cattle ranching, and tourist development—and which local people feel comfortable with—culminated in the October 1986 establishment of the Reserva de la Biósfera Sian Ka'an, part of UNESCO's World Network of Biosphere Reserves. Inside, visitors will find hundreds of species of birds including the ocellated turkey, great currasow, parrots, toucans, roseate spoonbill, jabiru stork, and 15 species of herons, egrets, and bitterns. Land mammals also are in abundance: jaguars, pumas, ocelots, margays, jaguarundis, spider and howler monkeys, tapirs, as well as white-lipped and collared peccaries. In the lagoons and ocean you're also sure to see crocodiles, a myriad of turtles (green, loggerhead, hawksbill, and leatherbacks), and maybe even a manatee or two. Needless to say, this is an environmentally rich part of the region and one worth visiting.

CONSERVATION

Among the top concerns of environmentalists in Mexico is deforestation, which has accelerated with Mexico's burgeoning population. Slash-and-burn farming is still widely practiced in remote areas, with or without regulation. In an effort to protect the land, environmentalists are searching for alternative sources of income for locals. One is to train them to become guides by teaching them about the flora and fauna of the region as well as English. While not solving the problem, it does place an economic value on the forest itself and provides an incentive for preserving it.

Another focus is the plight of the palm tree. The palm is an important part of the cultural and practical lifestyle of the indigenous people of Quintana Roo—it is used for thatch roofing and to construct lobster traps. However, the palms used—*Thrinax radiata* and *Coccothrinax readii*—are becoming increasingly rare. Amigos de Sian Ka'an together with the World Wildlife Fund are studying the palms' growth patterns and rates; they are anticipating a management plan that will encourage future growth. Other environmental projects include limiting commercial fishing, halting tourist development where it endangers the ecology, and studying the lobster industry and its future. A number of other worthwhile projects are still waiting in line.

History

ACROSS THE BERING LAND BRIDGE

People and animals from Asia crossed the Bering land bridge into North America in the Pleistocene epoch about 50,000 years ago, when sea levels were much lower. As early as 10,000 B.C., Ice Age humans hunted woolly mammoth and other large animals roaming the cool, moist landscape of Central Mexico. The earliest traces of humans in the Yucatán Peninsula are obsidian spear points and stone tools dating to 9,000 B.C. The Loltún caves in the state of Yucatán contained a cache of extinct mammoth bones, which were probably dragged there by a roving band of hunters. As the region dried out and large game disappeared in the next millennia, tools of a more settled way of life appeared, such as grinding stones for preparing seeds and plant fibers. The epic human trek south continued until only

STEPHENS AND CATHERWOOD

The Maya ruins of the Yucatán Peninsula were all but unknown in the United States and Europe until well into the 19th century. Although Spanish explorers and colonizers had occupied the peninsula for more than two centuries, conflicts with local Mayas and Catholic antipathy for all things "pagan" probably account for the Spaniards' lack of research or even apparent interest. To be fair, the immensity of the task was surely daunting – by the time the Spanish reached the Yucatán in the early 1500s, the majority of sites had been abandoned for at least 300 years, and in some cases double or triple that. Many were piles of rubble, and those still standing were mostly covered in vegetation. Just getting to the sites was a task in itself.

Between 1839 and 1841, an American explorer and diplomat named John Lloyd Stephens and an English artist and architect named Fredrick Catherwood conducted two major explorations of the Maya region, including present-day Yucatán, Chiapas, and Central America. Stephens, an amateur archaeologist, kept a detailed account of their travels and the ruins they visited, while Catherwood made incredibly precise drawings of numerous structures, monuments, hieroglyphs, and scenes of peasant life. They published their work in two volumes, made a sensation in the United States and Europe, and awakened outside interest in ancient Maya civilization. Their books now are condensed into a single, very readable volume, *Incidents of Travel in Yucatan* (Panorama Editorial, 1988), available in English and in many bookstores in the Yucatán. It makes for fascinating reading, not only for the historic value but also as a backdrop for your own travels through the Yucatán.

3,000 years ago, however, when, anthropologists say, people first reached Tierra del Fuego, at the tip of South America.

ANCIENT CIVILIZATION

Between 7,000 and 2,000 B.C., society evolved from hunting and gathering to farming; corn, squash, and beans were independently cultivated in widely separated areas in Mexico. Archaeologists believe that the earliest people we can call Mayas, or proto-Mayas, lived on the Pacific coast of Chiapas and Guatemala. These tribes lived in villages that might have held more than 1,000 inhabitants and made beautiful painted and incised ceramic jars for food storage. After 1,000 B.C. this way of life spread south to the highlands site of Kaminaljuyú (now part of Guatemala City) and, through the next millennium, to the rest of the Maya world. Meanwhile, in what are now the Mexican states of Veracruz and Tabasco, another culture, the Olmecs, was developing what is now considered Mesoamerica's first civilization. Its influence was felt throughout Mexico and Central America. Archaeologists believe that before the Olmecs disappeared around 300 B.C., they contributed two crucial cultural advances to the Mayas: the Long Count calendar and the hieroglyphic writing system.

LATE PRECLASSIC PERIOD

During the Late Preclassic era (300 B.C.–A.D. 250), the Pacific coastal plain saw the rise of a Maya culture in Izapa near Tapachula, Chiapas. The Izapans worshipped gods that were precursors of the Classic Maya pantheon and commemorated religious and historical events in bas-relief carvings that emphasized costume and finery.

During the same period, the northern Guatemalan highlands were booming with construction; this was the heyday of Kaminaljuyú, which grew to enormous size, with more than 120 temple-mounds and numerous stele. The earliest calendar inscription that researchers are able to read comes from a monument found at El Baúl to the southwest of Kaminaljuyú; it has been translated as A.D. 36.

EARLY CIVILIZATIONS AND MAYA TIMELINE

PERIOD	YEAR
Paleoindian	before 7000 B.C.
Archaic	7000-2500 B.C.
Early Preclassic	2500-1000 B.C.
Middle Preclassic	1000-300 B.C.
Late Preclassic	300 B.C.-A.D. 250
Early Classic	A.D. 250-600
Late Classic	A.D. 600-925
Early Postclassic	A.D. 925-1200
Late Postclassic	A.D. 1200-1530

In the Petén jungle region just north of the highlands, the dominant culture was the Chicanel, whose hallmarks are elaborate temple-pyramids lined with enormous stucco god-masks (as in Kohunlich). The recently excavated Petén sites of Nakbé and El Mirador are the most spectacular Chicanel cities yet found. El Mirador contains a 70-meter (230-foot) tall temple-pyramid complex that is the tallest ancient structure in Mesoamerica. Despite the obvious prosperity of this region, there is almost no evidence of Long Count dates or writing systems in either the Petén jungle or the Yucatán Peninsula just to the north.

EARLY CLASSIC PERIOD

The great efflorescence of the southern Maya world stops at the end of the Early Classic period (A.D. 250–600). Kaminaljuyú and other cities were abandoned; researchers believe that the area was invaded by Teotihuacano warriors extending the reach of their Valley of Mexico–based empire. On the Yucatán Peninsula, there is evidence of Teotihuacano occupation at the Río Bec site of Becán and at Acanceh near Mérida. You can see Teotihuacano-style costumes and gods in carvings at the great Petén city of Tikal and at Copán in Honduras. By A.D. 600, the Teotihuacano empire had collapsed, and the stage was set for the Classic Maya eras.

LATE CLASSIC PERIOD

The Maya heartland of the Late Classic period (A.D. 600–900) extended from Copán in Honduras through Tikal in Guatemala and ended at Palenque in Chiapas. The development of these city-states, which also included Yaxchilán and Bonampak, almost always followed the same pattern. Early in this era, a new and vigorous breed of rulers founded a series of dynasties bent on deifying themselves and their ancestors. All the arts and sciences of the Maya world, from architecture to astronomy, were focused on this goal. The Long Count calendar and the hieroglyphic writing system were the most crucial tools in this effort, as the rulers needed to recount the stories of their dynasties and of their own glorious careers.

During the Late Classic era, painting, sculpture, and carving reached their climax; objects such as Lord Pakal's sarcophagus lid from Palenque are now recognized as among the finest pieces of world art. Royal monuments stood at the center of large and bustling cities. Cobá and Dzibilchaltún each probably contained 50,000 inhabitants, and there was vigorous intercity trade. Each Classic city-state reached its apogee at a different time; the southern cities peaked first, with the northern Puuc region cities following close behind.

By A.D. 925 nearly all of the city-states had collapsed and were left in a state of near-abandonment. The Classic Maya decline is one of the great enigmas of Mesoamerican archaeology. There are a myriad of theories—disease, invasion, peasant revolt—but many researchers now believe the collapse was caused by a combination of factors, including overpopulation, environmental degradation, and a series of devastating droughts. With the abandonment of

Among their many talents, the Maya were master artists.

© LIZA PRADO

the cities, the cultural advances disappeared as well. The last Long Count date was recorded in A.D. 909 and many religious customs and beliefs were never seen again.

EARLY POSTCLASSIC PERIOD

After the Puuc region was abandoned—almost certainly because of a foreign invasion—the center of Maya power moved east to Chichén. During this Early Postclassic era (A.D. 925–1200), the Toltec influence took hold, marking the end of the most artistic era and the birth of a new militaristic society built around a blend of ceremonialism, civic and social organization, and conquest. Chichén was the great power of northern Yucatán. Competing city-states either bowed before its warriors or, like the Puuc cities and Cobá, were destroyed.

LATE POSTCLASSIC PERIOD

After Chichén's fall in 1224—probably due to an invasion—a heretofore lowly tribe calling themselves the Itzá became the Late Postclassic

(A.D. 1200–1530) masters of Yucatecan power politics. Kukulcán II of Chichén founded Mayapán A.D. 1263–1283. After his death and the abandonment of Chichén, an aggressive Itzá lineage named the Cocom seized power and used Mayapán as a base to subjugate northern Yucatán. They succeeded through wars using Tabascan mercenaries and intermarrying with other powerful lineages. Foreign lineage heads were forced to live in Mayapán where they could easily be controlled. At its height, the city covered 6.5 square kilometers (four square miles) within a defensive wall that contained more than 15,000 inhabitants. Architecturally, Mayapán leaves much to be desired; the city plan was haphazard, and its greatest monument was a sloppy, smaller copy of Chichén's Pyramid of Kukulcán.

The Cocom ruled for 250 years until A.D. 1441–1461, when an upstart Uxmal-based lineage named the Xiu rebelled and slaughtered the Cocom. Mayapán was abandoned and Yucatán's city-states weakened themselves in a series of bloody intramural wars that left them hopelessly divided when it came time to face the conquistadors. By the time of that conquest, culture was once again being imported from outside the Maya world. Putún Maya seafaring traders brought new styles of art and religious beliefs back from their trips to Central Mexico. Their influence can be seen in the Mixtec-style frescoes at Tulum on the Quintana Roo coast.

SPANISH ARRIVAL AND CONQUEST

After Columbus's arrival in the New World, other adventurers traveling the same seas soon found the Yucatán Peninsula. In 1519, 34-year-old Hernán Cortés sailed from Cuba against the wishes of the Spanish governor. With 11 ships, 120 sailors, and 550 soldiers he set out to search for slaves, a lucrative business with or without the government's blessing. His search began on the Yucatán coast and would eventually encompass most of Mexico. However, he hadn't counted on the ferocious resistance and cunning of the Maya Indians. It

© LIZA PRADO

Monuments of the conquistadors are reminders of the region's brutal past.

took many decades and many lives for Spanish conquistadors to quell Maya resistance, despite a huge advantage in military technology, including horses, gunpowder, and metal sword and armor. Francisco de Montejo, who took part in Cortés's earlier expedition into central Mexico, spent 1528–1535 trying to conquer the Yucatán, first from the east at Tulum and later from the west near Campeche and Tabasco, but was driven out each time. Montejo's son, also named Francisco de Montejo "El Mozo" (The Younger), took up the effort and eventually founded the city of Campeche in 1546 and Mérida in 1542. From those beachheads, the Spanish conquest slowly spread across the peninsula.

Economic and religious oppression were central to the conquest too, of course. The Xiu indigenous group proved an important ally to the Spanish after its leader converted to Christianity. And in 1562, a friar named Diego de Landa, upon learning his converts still practiced certain Maya ceremonies, became enraged and ordered the torture and imprisonment of numerous Maya spiritual leaders. He also gathered all the religious artifacts and Maya texts—which he said contained "superstitions and the devil's lies"—and had them burned. It was a staggering loss—at least 27 codices—one that Landa later seemed to regret and attempted to reconcile by writing a detailed record of Maya customs, mathematics, and writing.

The Caste War

By the 1840s, the brutalized and subjugated Mayas organized a revolt against Euro-Mexican colonizers. Called the Caste War, this savage war saw Mayas taking revenge on every white man, woman, and child by means of murder and rape. European survivors made their way to the last Spanish strongholds of Mérida and Campeche. The governments of the two cities appealed for help to Spain, France, and the United States. No one answered the call. It was soon apparent that the remaining two cities would be wiped out. But just as the governor of Mérida was about to begin evacuating the city, the Mayas picked up their weapons and walked away.

Attuned to the signals of the land, the Mayas knew that the appearance of the flying ant was the first sign of rain and signaled the time to plant corn. When, on the brink of the Mayas' destroying the enemy, the winged ant made an unusually early appearance, the Indians turned their backs on certain victory and returned to their villages to plant corn.

Help came immediately from Cuba, Mexico City, and 1,000 U.S. mercenary troops. Vengeance was merciless. Mayas were killed indiscriminately. Some were taken prisoner and sold to Cuba as slaves; others left their villages and hid in the jungles—in some cases, for decades. Between 1846 and 1850, the population of the Yucatán Peninsula was reduced from 500,000 to 300,000. Quintana Roo along the Caribbean coast was considered a dangerous no-man's land for almost another 100 years.

Growing Maya Power

Many Maya Indians escaped slaughter during the Caste War by fleeing to the isolated coastal forests of present-day Quintana Roo. A large number regrouped under the cult of the "Talking Cross"—an actual wooden cross that, with the help of a priest and a ventriloquist, spoke to the beleaguered indigenous fighters, urging them to continue fighting. Followers called themselves Cruzob (People of the Cross) and made a stronghold in the town of Noj Kaj Santa Cruz, today Carrillo Puerto. Research (and common sense) suggest the Mayas knew full well that a human voice was responsible for the "talking," but that many believed it was inspired by God.

Close to the border with British Honduras (now Belize), the leaders of Noj Kaj Santa Cruz began selling timber to the British and were given arms in return. At the same time (roughly 1855–1857), internal strife weakened the relations between Campeche and Mérida, and their mutual defense as well. Maya leaders took advantage of the conflict and attacked Fort Bacalar, eventually gaining control of the entire southern Caribbean coast.

Up until that time, indigenous soldiers simply killed the people they captured, but starting in 1858 they took lessons from the colonials and began to keep whites for slave labor. Women were put to work doing household chores and some became concubines, men were forced to work the fields and even build churches. (The church in Carrillo Puerto was built largely by white slaves.)

For the next 40 years, the Maya people and soldiers based in and around Noj Kaj Santa Cruz kept the east coast of the Yucatán for themselves, and a shaky truce with the Mexican government endured. The native people were economically independent, self-governing, and, with no roads in or out of the region, almost totally isolated. They were not at war as long as everyone left them alone.

The Last Stand

Only when President Porfirio Díaz took power in 1877 did the Mexican federal government began to think seriously about the Yucatán Peninsula. Through the years, Quintana Roo's isolation and the strength of the Mayas in their treacherous jungle had foiled repeated efforts by Mexican soldiers to capture the Indians. The army's expeditions were infrequent, but it rankled Díaz that a relatively small and modestly armed Maya force had been able to keep the Mexican federal army at bay for so long. An assault in 1901, under the command of General Ignacio Bravo, broke the government's losing streak. The general captured a village, laid railroad tracks, and built a walled fort. Supplies arriving by rail kept the fort stocked, but the indigenous defenders responded by holding the fort under siege for an entire year. Reinforcements finally came from the capital, the Mayas were forced to retreat, first from the fort and then from many of their villages and strongholds. A period of brutal Mexican occupation followed, lasting until 1915, yet Maya partisans still didn't give up. They conducted guerrilla raids from the tangled coastal forest until the Mexican army, frustrated and demoralized, pulled out and returned Quintana Roo to the Mayas.

But beginning in 1917 and lasting to 1920, influenza and smallpox swept through the Maya-held territories, killing hundreds of thousands of Indians. In 1920, with the last of their army severely diminished and foreign gum-tappers creeping into former Maya territories, indigenous leaders entered into a negotiated settlement with the Mexican federal government. The final treaties were signed in 1935, erasing the last vestiges of Maya national sovereignty.

LAND REFORMS

Beginning in 1875, international demand for twine and rope made from henequen, a type of agave cactus that thrives in northern Yucatán, brought prosperity to Mérida, the state capital. Beautiful mansions were built by entrepreneurs who led the gracious life, sending their children to school in Europe, cruising with their wives to New Orleans in search of new luxuries and entertainment. Port towns were developed on the gulf coast, and a two-kilometer (1.2-mile) wharf named Progreso was built to accommodate the large ships that came for sisal (hemp from the henequen plant).

The only thing that didn't change was the lifestyle of indigenous people, who provided most of the labor on colonial haciendas. Henequen plants have incredibly hard, sharp spines and at certain times emit a horrendous stench. Maya workers labored long, hard hours, living in constant debt to the hacienda store.

Prosperity helped bring the Yucatán to the attention of the world. But in 1908, an American journalist named John Kenneth Turner stirred things up when he documented the difficult lives of the Indian plantation workers and the accompanying opulence enjoyed by the owners. The report set a series of reforms into motion. Felipe Carrillo Puerto, the first socialist governor of Mérida, helped native workers set up a labor union, educational center, and political club that served to organize and focus resistance to the powerful hacienda system. Carrillo made numerous agrarian reforms, including decreeing that abandoned haciendas could be appropriated by the government. With his power and popularity growing, conservatives saw only one way to stop him. In 1923, Felipe Carrillo Puerto was assassinated.

By then, though, the Mexican Revolution had been won and reforms were being made throughout the country, including redistribution of land and mandatory education. Mexico entered its golden years, a 40-year period of sustained and substantial growth dubbed "The Mexican Miracle," all the more miraculous because it took place in defiance of the worldwide great Depression. In the late 1930s, President Lázaro Cárdenas undertook a massive nationalization program, claiming the major electricity, oil, and other companies for the state, and created state-run companies like PEMEX, the oil conglomerate still in existence today. In the Yucatán, Cárdenas usurped large parts of hacienda lands—as much as half of the Yucatan's total arable land, by some accounts, most dedicated to the growing of henequen—and redistributed it to poor farmers.

The economic prosperity allowed the ruling Institutional Revolutionary Party, or PRI, to consolidate power, and before long it held every major office in the federal government, and most state governments as well. The Mexican Miracle had not ameliorated all social inequalities—and had exacerbated some—but the PRI grew increasingly intolerant of dissent. Deeply corrupt, the party—and by extension the state—resorted to brutal and increasingly blatant repression to silence detractors. The most notorious example was the gunning down of scores of student demonstrators—some say up to 250—by security forces in 1968 in Mexico City's Tlatelolco plaza. The massacre took place at night, and by morning the plaza was cleared of bodies and scrubbed of blood, and the PRI-led government simply denied that it ever happened.

The oil crisis that struck the United States in the early 1970s was at first a boon for Mexico, whose coffers were filled with money from pricey oil exports. But a failure to diversify the economy left Mexico vulnerable; as oil prices stabilized, the peso began to devalue. It had fallen as much as 500 percent by 1982, prompting then-president López Portillo to nationalize Mexico's banks. Foreign investment quickly dried up and the 1980s were dubbed *la década perdida* (the lost decade) for Mexico and much of Latin America, a time of severe economic stagnation and crisis. In September 1985, a magnitude 8.1 earthquake struck Mexico City, killing 9,000 people and leaving 100,000 more homeless. It seemed Mexico had hit its nadir.

Yet it was during this same period that Cancún began to take off as a major vacation destination, drawing tourism and much-needed foreign dollars into the Mexican economy. The crises were not over—the implementation of the North American Free Trade agreement (NAFTA) in 1994 was met simultaneously by a massive devaluation of the peso and an armed uprising by a peasant army called the Zapatistas in the state Chiapas—but Mexico's economy regained some of its footing. A series of electoral reforms implemented in the late 1980s and through the 1990s paved the way for the historic 2000 presidential election, in which an opposition candidate—former Coca Cola executive Vicente Fox of the right-of-center PAN—defeated the PRI, ending the latter's 70-year reign of power. Fox was succeeded in 2006 by another PAN member, Felipe Calderón Hinojosa, in an election in which the PRI finished a distant third. However, the election was marred by allegations of fraud and weeks of post-election demonstrations. President Calderón's priority list for the early part of his term include expanding the job market, encouraging foreign investment (including for new tourism projects in the Yucatán and elsewhere), and combating the country's persistent drug and gang problem.

Government

Mexico enjoys a constitutional democracy modeled after that of the United States, including a president (who serves one six-year term), a two-house legislature, and a judiciary branch. For 66 years (until the year 2000) Mexico was controlled by one party, the so-called moderate Partido Revolucionario Institutional, or Institutional Revolution Party (PRI). A few cities and states elected candidates from the main opposition parties—the conservative Partido de Acción Nacional (PAN) and leftist Partido de la Revolución Democrática (PRD)—but the presidency and most of the important government positions were passed from one hand-picked PRI candidate to the next, amid rampant electoral fraud.

Indeed, fraud and corruption have been ugly mainstays of Mexican government for generations. In the 1988 presidential election, PRI candidate Carlos Salinas Gortari officially garnered 51 percent of the vote, a dubious result judging from polls leading up to the election and rendered laughable after a mysterious "breakdown" in the election tallying system delayed the results for several days.

Salinas Gortari ended his term under the same heavy clouds of corruption and fraud that ushered him in—he is in hiding somewhere in Europe, accused of having stolen millions of dollars from the federal government during his term. That said, Salinas pushed through changes such as increasing the number of Senate seats and reorganizing the federal electoral commission that helped usher in freer and fairer elections. He also oversaw the adoption of NAFTA in 1993, which has sped up Mexico's manufacturing industry but seriously damaged other sectors, especially small farmers, many of whom are indigenous.

The 1994 presidential election was marred by the assassination in Tijuana of the PRI candidate Luis Donaldo Colosio, the country's first major political assassination since 1928. Colosio's campaign manager, technocrat Ernesto Zedillo, was nominated to fill the candidacy and eventually elected. Zedillo continued with reforms, and in 2000, for the first time in almost seven decades, the opposition candidate officially won. PAN candidate Vicente Fox, a

© LIZA PRADO

Government offices in the region's cities are often architecturally distinct.

businessman and former Coca-Cola executive from Guanajuato, took the reigns promising continued electoral reforms, a stronger private sector, and closer relations with the United States. He knew U.S. President-elect George W. Bush personally, having worked with him on border issues during Bush's term as governor of Texas. Progress was being made until the terrorist attacks of September 11, 2001, pushed Mexico far down on the U.S. administration's priority list. With Mexico serving a term on the U.N. Security Council, Fox came under intense pressure from the United States to support an invasion of Iraq. He ultimately refused—Mexican people were overwhelmingly opposed to the idea—but it cost Fox dearly in his relationship with Bush. The reforms he once seemed so ideally poised to achieve were largely incomplete by the time Fox's term ended.

The presidential elections of 2006 were bitterly contested, and created—or exposed—a deep schism in the country. The eventual winner was PAN candidate Felipe Calderón Hinojosa, a former Secretary of Energy under Fox. His main opponent, Andrés Manuel López Obrador, is a former mayor of Mexico City and member of the left-leaning PRD. Though fraught with accusations and low blows, the campaign also was a classic clash of ideals, with Calderón advocating increased foreign investment and free trade, and López Obrador assailing the neo-liberal model and calling for government action to reduce poverty and strengthen social services. Both men claimed victory after election day; when Calderón was declared the winner, López Obrador alleged widespread fraud and called for a total recount; his supporters blocked major thoroughfares throughout the country for weeks. The Mexican Electoral Commission did a selective recount and affirmed a Calderón victory; the official figures set the margin at under 244,000 votes out of 41 million casts, a difference of just one-half percent. Calderón's inauguration was further marred by legislators fist-fighting in the chamber, and the new president shouting his oath over jeers and general ruckus.

Calderón was confronted with a number of thorny problems upon inauguration, including a protest in Oaxaca that had turned violent, and spiraling corn prices which in turn drove up the cost of tortillas, the most basic of Mexican foods. While addressing those issues, he pressed forward with promised law and order reforms, raising police officers' wages and dispatching the Mexican military to staunch rampant gang and drug-related crime in cities like Tijuana and Monterrey. He also launched a First Employment program, giving incentives to companies who hire first-time job seekers, including students and women who have never worked outside of the home.

Economy

OIL

The leading industry on the Yucatán Peninsula is oil. Produced by the nationally owned PEMEX, the oil industry is booming along the Gulf Coast from Campeche south into the state of Tabasco. Most of the oil is shipped at OPEC prices to Canada, Israel, France, Japan, and the United States. Rich in natural gas, Mexico sends the United States 10 percent of its total output. Two-thirds of Mexico's export revenue comes from fossil fuels. As a result, peninsula cities are beginning to show signs of financial health.

FISHING

Yucatecan fisheries also are abundant along the Gulf Coast. At one time fishing was not much more than a family business, but today fleets of large purse seiners with their adjacent processing plants can be seen on the Gulf of Mexico. With the renewed interest in preserving fishing grounds for the future, the industry could continue to thrive for many years.

TOURISM

Until the 1970s, Quintana Roo's economy amounted to very little. For a few years the chicle boom brought a flurry of activity up and down the state—it was shipped from the harbor of Isla Cozumel. Native and hardwood trees have always been in demand; coconuts and fishing were the only other natural resources that added to the economy—but neither on a large scale.

With the development of an offshore sandbar—Cancún—into a multimillion-dollar resort, tourism became the region's number-one moneymaker. The development of the Riviera Maya (extending from Cancún to Tulum)—and now, the Costa Maya (south of Sian Ka'an)—only guaranteed the continued success of the economy. New roads now give access to previously unknown beaches and Maya structures. Extra attention is going to archaeological zones ignored for hundreds of years. All but the smallest have restrooms, ticket offices, gift shops, and food shops.

People and Culture

PAPEL PICADO

Mexicans are famous for their celebrations – whether it's to honor a patron saint or to celebrate a neighbor's birthday, partying is part of the culture. Typically, fiestas feature great music, loads of food, fireworks, and brightly colored decorations, often including *papel picado* (literally, diced paper).

Dancing at the slightest breeze, *papel picado* is tissue paper cut or stamped with a design that is appropriate for the occasion: a manger scene at Christmas, church bells and doves for a wedding, skeletons in swooping hats for Day of the Dead. Once cut, row upon row of *papel picado* is strung across city streets, in front of churches, or in people's backyards.

After the celebration, few are inclined to take down the decorations. Eventually, all that's left are bits of colored paper blowing in the wind, the cord that it was hung on, and the memories of the fine fiesta.

DEMOGRAPHY

Today, 75–80 percent of the Mexican population is estimated to be mestizo (a combination of the indigenous and Spanish-Caucasian races). Only 10–15 percent are considered to be indigenous peoples. For comparison, as recently as 1870, the indigenous made up more than 50 percent of the population. While there are important native communities throughout Mexico, the majority of the country's indigenous peoples live in the Yucatán Peninsula, Oaxaca, and Chiapas.

RELIGION

The vast majority of Mexicans are Roman Catholic, especially in the generally conservative Yucatán Peninsula. However, a vigorous evangelical movement gains more and more converts every year.

LANGUAGE

The farther you go from a city, the less Spanish you'll hear and the more dialects of indigenous languages you'll encounter. The government estimates that of the 10 million indigenous people in the country, about 25 percent do not speak Spanish. Of the original 125 native languages, 70 are still spoken, 20 of which are classified as Maya languages, including Tzeltal, Tzotzil, Chol, and Yucatec.

Although education was made compulsory for children in 1917, this law was not enforced in the Yucatán Peninsula until recently. Today, schools throughout the peninsula use Spanish-language books, even though many children do not speak the language. In some of the rural schools, bilingual teachers are recruited to help children make the transition.

ART

Mexico has an incredibly rich colonial and folk-art tradition. While not art for the people who make and use it, traditional indigenous clothing is beautiful and travelers and collectors are increasingly able to buy it in local shops and markets. Prices for these items can be high, for the simple fact that they are hand-woven and can literally take months to complete. Mérida has shops filled with pottery, carving, and textiles from around Yucatán state.

HOLIDAYS AND FESTIVALS

People in Mexico take their holidays seriously—of their country, their saints, and their families. You'll be hard-pressed to find a two-week period when something or someone isn't being celebrated. On major holidays—Christmas, New Year's Day, and Easter—be prepared for crowds on the beaches and ruins. Be sure to book your hotel and buy your bus tickets well in advance; during holidays, the travel industry is saturated with Mexican travelers.

In addition to officially recognized holidays, villages and cities hold numerous festivals and celebrations: patron saints, birthdays

REGIONAL HOLIDAYS AND CELEBRATIONS

Jan. 1: **New Year's Day**

Jan. 6: **Día de los Reyes Magos** (Three Kings Day – Christmas gifts exchanged)

Feb. 2: **Virgen de la Candelaria** (religious candlelight processions light up several towns)

Feb. 5: **Flag Day**

Feb./March: **Carnaval** (seven-day celebration before Ash Wednesday)

March 21: **Birthday of Benito Juárez** (President of Mexico for five terms; born in 1806)

March 21: **Vernal Equinox in Chichén Itzá** (a phenomenon of light and shadow displays a serpent slithering down the steps of El Castillo)

May 1: **Labor Day**

May 3: **Day of the Holy Cross** (Dance of the Pigs' Head performed in Celestún, Carrillo Puerto, and Hopelchén)

May 5: **Battle of Puebla** (aka **Cinco de Mayo;** celebration of the 1862 defeat of the French)

May 20-30: **Jipi Festival** (Becal's celebration of the jipijapa plant, used in making *jipi* hats)

Early July: **Founding of Ticul**

Sept. 16: **Independence Day** (celebrated on the night of the 15th)

Sept. 27-Oct. 14: **El Señor de las Ampollas** (religious celebration in Mérida)

Oct. 4: **Feast Day of San Francisco de Asisi** (religious celebrations in Conkal and Telchac Puerto)

Oct. 12: **Columbus Day**

Oct. 18-28: **El Cristo de Sitilpech** (religious celebration in Izamal – the height is on the 25th)

Nov. 1-2: **All Souls' Day and Day of the Dead** (church ceremonies and graveside parties in honor of the deceased)

Nov. 20: **Día de la Revolución** (celebration of the beginning of the Mexican Revolution in 1910)

Dec. 8: **Feast of the Immaculate Conception** (religious celebrations in Izamal and Celestún)

Dec. 12: **Virgen de Guadalupe** (religious celebration in honor of Mexico's patron saint)

Dec. 25: **Christmas** (celebrated on the night of the 24th)

of officials, a good crop, a birth of a child. You name it, and it's probably been celebrated. Festivals typically take place in and around the central plaza of a town with dancing, live music, colorful decorations, and fireworks. Temporary food booths are set up around the plaza and typically sell tamales (both sweet and meat), *buñuelos* (sweet rolls), tacos, *churros* (fried dough dusted with sugar), *carne asada* (barbecued meat), and plenty of beer.

ESSENTIALS

Getting There

For centuries, getting to the Yucatán Peninsula required a major sea voyage to one of the few ports on the Gulf of Mexico, only to be followed by harrowing and uncertain land treks limited to mule trains and narrow paths through the tangled jungle. Today, the peninsula is easily accessible. Visitors arrive every day via modern airports, a network of good highways, excellent bus service, or by cruise ship. From just about anywhere in the world, the Yucatán is only hours away.

AIR

The main international airports on the Yucatán Peninsula are in **Cancún** and **Mérida;** another is reportedly being built in Tulum. Most travelers use the Cancún airport—it's well located for those vacationing in the Caribbean as well as for those traveling inland. Fares typically are cheaper here than to any other airport in the region.

Travelers who are planning to spend their entire time inland, often choose to fly to Mérida instead—the city itself is an important destination and it's close to many of the area's key sights and archaeological ruins.

Similarly, many travelers who only will be visiting **Isla Cozumel,** fly directly there—it's often more expensive than landing in Cancún but avoids the time and hassle of traveling from

© LIZA PRADO

the mainland to the island (more time to dive and to enjoy the island!).

There also are airports in **Chetumal, Villahermosa, Tuxtla Gutiérrez,** and **Tapachula,** which are typically used for domestic travel. However, for travelers planning to spend most of their time in Campeche, Tabasco, or Chiapas, they may be most convenient.

Departure Tax

There is a US$36 departure tax to fly out of Mexico—most airlines incorporate the tax into their tickets, but it's worth setting aside some cash just in case.

BUS

The Yucatán's main interstate bus hubs are Mérida and Cancún, with service to and from Mexico City, Veracruz, Oaxaca, and other major destinations in the country. There also are buses between Chetumal and cities in Belize and Guatemala. Travel agencies and tour operators in San Cristóbal and Palenque offer van service to various cities in Guatemala, including Flores, Quetzaltenango, Panajachel, Antigua, and Guatemala City.

CAR

Foreigners driving into Mexico are required to show a valid driver's license, and title, registration, and proof of insurance for their vehicle. Mexican authorities do not recognize foreign-issued insurance; Mexican vehicle insurance is available at most border towns 24 hours a day and several companies also sell policies over the Internet. Do not cross the border with your car until you have obtained the proper papers.

CRUISE SHIP

Increasing numbers of cruise ships stop along Mexico's Caribbean coast every year, some carrying as many as 5,000 people. Many sail out of Miami and Fort Lauderdale, stopping at Key West before continuing to Punta Venado (Riviera Maya), Isla Cozumel, and Mahahual.

Prices are competitive and ships vary in services, amenities, activities, and entertainment. Pools, restaurants, nightclubs, and cinemas are commonplace. Fitness centers and shops also make ship life convenient. To hone in on the type of cruise you'd like to go on, research options on the Internet, in the travel section of your local newspaper, and by contacting your travel agent.

If your budget is tight, consider traveling standby. Ships want to sail full and are willing to cut their prices—sometimes up to 50 percent—to do so. Airfare usually is not included. Note: Once you're on the standby list, you likely will have no choice of cabin location or size.

NEIGHBORING COUNTRIES

Cancún is an important international hub, not only for tourists from North America and Europe but for regional flights to Central America and the Caribbean. In southern Quintana Roo, Chetumal is the gateway to Belize and there's a direct bus to Flores, Guatemala. Most travel to Guatemala, however, is through Chiapas, from the towns of San Cristóbal and Palenque.

Travel agencies can book tours to Belize, Guatemala, and Cuba, though its relatively easy to arrange a trip yourself. Most travelers do not need prearranged visas to enter either Belize or Guatemala, but they may have to pay an entrance fee at the airport or border. Call the respective consulates for additional information.

Note: The U.S. government prohibits most ordinary travel to Cuba by U.S. citizens—technically, Americans without permits are not allowed to spend money in Cuba, and hefty fines against Americans traveling there are being levied. Nevertheless, tens of thousands of Americans travel to Cuba every year, a large share of them via Cancún. Most Cancún travel agencies sell plane tickets to Cuba; Americans are issued a separate paper visa that Cuban officials stamp instead of their passport. Needless to say, most American travelers manage to lose that visa before getting onto a plane back to the United States. Remember you won't be able to use any U.S.-based credit cards, debit cards, or travelers checks in Cuba—take plenty of cash as Cuba can be shockingly expensive. Don't count on any help from the U.S. State Department if you have problems.

Getting Around

AIR

Although budget airlines like Click Mexicana are starting to appear on the Mexican airline scene, flying domestically is still relatively expensive. The Yucatán is no exception. Once you factor in the check-in process, security, and baggage claim, there are very few flights within the region that make sense travel-wise, unless your time is incredibly tight. And if that is the case, you may as well see what you can do by car or bus and start planning a return trip.

BUS

Mexico's bus and public transportation system is one of the best in Latin America, if not the Western Hemisphere, and the Yucatán Peninsula bus system is no exception. ADO and its affiliate bus lines practically have a monopoly, but that has not made bus travel any less efficient or less affordable. Dozens of buses cover every major route many times per day, and even smaller towns have frequent and reliable service.

Buses come in three main categories. **First-class**—known as *primera clase* or sometimes *ejecutivo*—is the most common and the one travelers use most often. Buses have reclining seats and TVs where movies are played on long trips. First-class buses make some intermediate stops but only in large towns. The main first-class lines in the Yucatán are ADO and OCC (primarily serving Chiapas).

Deluxe class—usually called *lujo* (luxury)—is a step up; they often are slightly faster since they're typically nonstop. The main deluxe line is ADO-GL, which costs 10–25 percent more than regular ADO. ADO-GL buses have nicer seats and better televisions (even more recent movies!). Sometimes there are even free bottles of water in a cooler at the back. Even nicer are UNO buses, which often charge twice as much as

© LIZA PRADO

Ferries and catamarans stand side-by-side at Isla Mujeres's small dock.

regular ADO. UNO offers cushy, extra-wide seats (only three across instead of four), headphones, and usually a light meal like a sandwich and soda.

Second-class—*segunda clase*—are significantly slower and less comfortable than first-class buses, and they're not all that much cheaper. Whenever possible, pay the dollar or two extra for first-class. Second-class buses are handy in that you can flag them down anywhere on the roadside, but that also is precisely the reason they're so slow. In smaller towns, second-class may be the only service available, and it's fine for shorter trips. The main second-class lines in the Yucatán are Mayab, Oriente, Noreste, and ATS.

For overnight trips, definitely take first-class or deluxe. Not only will you be much more comfortable, second-class buses are sometimes targeted by roadside thieves since they drive on secondary roads and stop frequently.

Wherever bus service is thin, you can count on there being frequent *colectivos* or *combis*—vans or minibuses—that cover local routes.

They can be flagged down anywhere along the road.

FERRY

Ferries are used to get to and from the region's most visited islands, including Isla Mujeres (reached from Cancún), Isla Cozumel (reached from Playa del Carmen), and Isla Holbox (reached from Chiquilá). Service is safe, reliable, frequent, and affordable.

CAR

As great as Mexico's bus system is, a car is the best way to tour the Yucatán Peninsula. Most of the sights—ruins, deserted beaches, haciendas, caves, cenotes, wildlife—are well outside of the region's cities, down long access roads, or on the way from one town to the next. Having a car also saves you the time and effort of walking or the cost of cabbing to all those "missing links"; it allows you to enjoy the sights for as long or as little as you choose.

If you're here for a short time—a week or less—definitely get a car for the simple

Busy but orderly city streets are typical in the region.

© LIZA PRADO

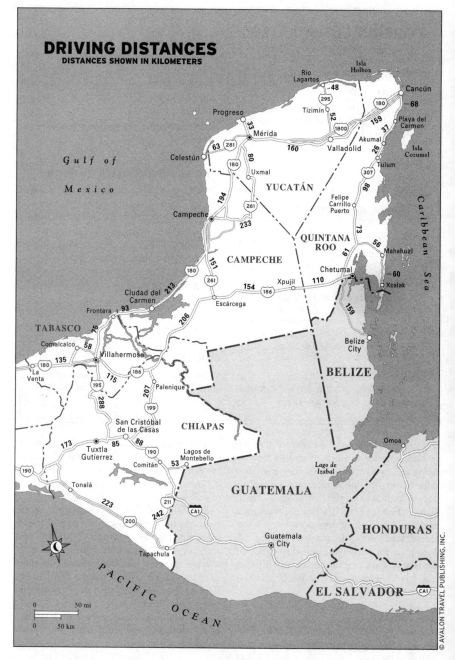

DRIVING DISTANCES
DISTANCES SHOWN IN KILOMETERS

© AVALON TRAVEL PUBLISHING, INC.

FOREIGN CONSULATES

Foreign consulates and consular agencies in the region include:

BELGIUM

- Cancún: Plaza Protical, Av. Tulum 192, Local 59, S.M. 4, tel. 998/892-2512, 10 A.M.-2 P.M. Monday–Friday.

BELIZE

- Cancún: Av. Nader 34, S.M. 2-A, tel. 998/887-8417, 9 A.M.-1 P.M. Monday–Friday.

- Chetumal: Av. Armada de México 91, tel. 983/832-1803, 9 A.M.-1 P.M. Monday–Friday.

- Mérida: Calle 53 between Calles 56 and 58, tel. 999/928-6152, 9 A.M.-1 P.M. Monday–Friday.

CANADA

- Cancún: Plaza Caracol, Blvd. Kukulcán Km. 8.5, Local 330, tel. 998/883-3360, 9 A.M.-5 P.M. Monday–Friday. In case of an emergency, call the embassy in Mexico City at toll-free Mex. tel. 800/706-2900.

CUBA

- Cancún: Pecari 17, S.M. 20, tel. 998/884-3423, 9 A.M.-1 P.M. Monday–Friday.

- Mérida: Calle 42 between Calles 1-D and 1-E, tel. 999/944-4216, 8:30 A.M.-1:30 P.M. Monday–Friday.

FRANCE

- Cancún: France no longer has a consulate in Cancún.

- Mérida: Calle 33-D between Calles 62-A and 72, tel. 999/925-2886. (Appointment only.)

GERMANY

- Cancún: Punta Conoco 36, S.M. 24, tel. 998/884-1898, 9 A.M.-noon (by telephone until 1:30 P.M.) Monday–Friday.

GREAT BRITAIN

- Cancún: Royal Sands Resort, Blvd. Kukulcán Km. 13.5, tel. 998/881-0100, 9 A.M.-5 P.M. Monday–Friday.

GUATEMALA

- Chetumal: Av. Héroes de Chapultepec 356, tel. 983/832-3045, 9 A.M.-5 P.M. Monday–Friday.

reason that you'll have the option of seeing and doing twice as much. If renting for your entire vacation isn't feasible money-wise, consider renting in choice locations: a couple of days in Mérida to see the Puuc Route, a few in Campeche to see the Río Bec archaeological zones, and a couple of days to explore the less-accessible parts of Quintana Roo. You also may want a car for a day in Cozumel to check out the island. Cars aren't necessary to visit Cancún, Isla Mujeres, Mérida, or San Cristóbal de las Casas.

Car Rental

International rental chains like Hertz, Budget, and Avis sometimes have good online specials but otherwise they tend to be much more expensive than local shops. Mexican car rental agencies may have an older fleet; it is rare, however, that travelers are tricked or mistreated.

Regardless of where you rent, be sure to ask about the insurance policy: Is it partial or full? How much is the deductible? Does it offer a zero-deductible plan? Note: you will be asked to leave a blank credit card imprint, ostensibly to cover the deductible if there is any damage. Be sure that this is returned to you when you bring back the car.

Before renting, be sure to have the attendant review the car for existing damage—definitely accompany him on this part and don't be shy

- Comitán: Calle 1 Sur Poniente at Av. 2 Poniente Sur, tel. 963/632-2669, 9 A.M.-5 P.M. Monday-Friday.

- Tapachula: Calle 2 Oriente 33, tel. 962/626-1252, 9 A.M.-5 P.M. Monday-Friday.

ITALY

- Cancún: Parque Las Palapas, Alcatraces 39, Retorno 5, S.M. 22, tel. 998/884-1261, 9 A.M.-2 P.M. Monday-Friday.

NETHERLANDS

- Cancún: Cancún International Airport, 2nd floor, tel. 998/886-0070, 9 A.M.-2 P.M. Monday-Friday.

- Mérida: Calle 64 between Calles 47 and 49, tel. 999/924-3122, 9 A.M.-5 P.M. Monday-Friday. (Appointment only.)

SPAIN

- Cancún: Oasis Cooperativo, Blvd. Kukulcán Km. 6.5, tel. 998/848-9900, 10 A.M.-1 P.M. Monday-Friday. MAY MOVE

- Mérida: Calle 8 between Calles 5 and 7, tel.

999/984-0181, 9:30 A.M.-1 P.M. Monday-Friday.

SWITZERLAND

- Cancún: above Rolandi's restaurant, Av. Cobá 12, Local 214, tel. 998/884-8446, 8 A.M.-3 P.M. Monday-Friday.

UNITED STATES

- Cancún: Plaza Caracol, Blvd. Kukulcán Km. 8.5, Local 323, tel. 998/883-0272, 9 A.M.-2 P.M. Monday-Friday. The after-hours contact number is 044-998/845-4364, but should be used *only* for serious emergencies involving an American citizen, e.g., death, arrest, or a major crime such as kidnapping, assault, rape, or murder. Officials look extremely unkindly on any nonemergency calls made to this phone number.

- Isla Cozumel: Main plaza, Villa Mar shopping center, 2nd floor, tel. 987/872-4574, after-hours emergency tel. 044-987/876-0624, noon-2 P.M. Mon.-Fri.)

- Mérida: Paseo de Montejo at Av. Colón, tel. 999/925-5011, 8:30 A.M.-5:30 P.M. Monday-Friday.

about pointing out every nick, scratch, and ding. Other things to confirm before driving off include:

- There is a spare tire and a working jack.

- All doors lock and unlock, including trunk.

- All windows roll up and down properly.

- The proper—and current—car registration is in the car.

- The amount of gas—you'll have to return it with the same amount.

- There is a 24-hour telephone number for the car rental agency in case of an emergency.

Highways and Road Conditions

Driving in Mexico isn't as nerve-racking as you might think. The highways are in excellent condition and even secondary roads are well maintained. There are a few dirt and sand roads—mostly along the Costa Maya, in the Sian Ka'an Biosphere Reserve, and to some of the lesser-visited archaeological sites in Campeche.

The main **highways** in the region are Highway 307, which runs the length of Mexico's Caribbean coast; Highway 180, the thoroughfare that links Cancún, Mérida, and Campeche City; Highway 186, which crosses the southern portion of the Yucatán Peninsula and leads travelers to Campeche's Río Bec region and

Villahermosa; and Highways 195, 190, and 200 which criss-cross the state of Chiapas.

In the entire region, there are only two **toll roads,** both sections of Highway 180: Between Mérida and Cancún (US$28) and between Campeche City and the town of Champotón (US$4.25). They're not cheap, but they can shave off a bit of travel time. Good if you're in a rush, otherwise you're better off taking secondary roads, which pass through picturesque countryside and by indigenous villages.

Off the highways, the biggest hazard are *topes*—speed bumps. They are common on all roads and highways, save the toll roads. They vary in size, but many are big and burly and hitting them at even a slow speed can do a number on you, your passengers, and your car. As soon as you see a sign announcing an upcoming town or village, be ready to slow down. By the same token, few roads have much of a shoulder—watch for people and animals on the roads, especially around villages but even in places you don't expect.

If you break down or run out of gas on a main road during daylight hours, stay with your car. *Los Ángeles Verdes* (The Green Angels, toll-free Mex. tel. 078 or 800/903-9200), a government-sponsored tow truck and repair service, cruise these roads on the lookout for drivers in trouble. They carry a CB radio, gas, and small parts and are prepared to fix tires. If you have a cellular phone—or happen to be near a pay phone—call your car rental agency; the Green Angels are a great backup. If you are on a remote road and don't have a phone, you're better off walking or hitching a ride to the nearest town.

Driving Scams

Most travelers have heard horror stories about Mexican police and worry about being taken for all their money or being trundled off to jail without reason. While it is true that there is corruption among the police, they don't target tourists; foreigners are, after all, the economic life blood of the region—the police don't want to scare them away.

As long as you are a careful and defensive driver, it is very unlikely you'll have any interaction with the police. Most travelers who are pulled over actually have done something wrong—speeding, running a stop sign, turning on red. In those situations, remain calm and polite. If you have an explanation, definitely give it; it is not uncommon to discuss a given situation with an officer. Who knows, you may even convince him you're right—it's happened to us!

Of real concern are gas station attendants. Full service is the norm here—you pull up, tell the person how much you want, and he or she does the rest. A common scam is for one attendant to distract you with questions about wiper fluid or gas additives while another starts the pump at 50 or 100 pesos. Before you answer any questions, be sure the attendant "zeroes" the pump before starting.

HITCHHIKING

Hitchhiking is not recommended for either men or women. That said, it sometimes can be hard to know what is a private vehicle and what is a *colectivo* (shared van). If there's no bus terminal nearby, your best bet is to look for locals who are waiting for public transportation and see which vans they take.

TOURS

Regional travel agents and tour operators offer a vast range of organized trips. You pay extra, of course, but all arrangements and reservations are made for you: from guides and transportation to hotels and meals. Special-interest trips also are common—archaeological tours, hacienda and convent routes, bird-watching and dive trips. Ask around, surf the Internet, and you'll find a world of organized adventure.

Visas and Officialdom

PASSPORTS

Gone are the days you can zip down to Mexico with just your driver's license and birth certificate. Since January 2007, all **U.S. citizens** returning from Mexico (and elsewhere) by air are required to have a passport. The same will apply to those re-entering by land or sea starting in 2008. **Canadians** may travel to Mexico without a passport; they simply need an official photo I.D. and proof of citizenship, such as an original birth certificate. All **other nationalities** must have a valid passport.

VISAS AND TOURIST CARDS

Citizens of most countries, including the United States and Canada and members of the E.U. do not need to obtain a visa to enter Mexico. Foreigners, however, are issued a white tourist card when they enter, with the number of days that they are permitted to stay in the county written at the bottom, typically 30–60 days. If you plan to stay for more than a month, politely ask the official to give you the amount of time you need; the maximum stay is 180 days.

Hold onto your tourist card! It must be returned to immigration officials when you leave Mexico. If you lose it, you'll be fined and may not be permitted to leave the country (much less the immigration office) until you pay.

To extend your stay up to 180 days, head to the nearest immigration office a week *before* your tourist card expires. Be sure to bring it along with your passport. There, you'll pick up several forms and fill them out, go to a bank to pay the US$22 processing fee, make photocopies of all the paperwork (including your passport, entry stamp, tourist card, and credit card), and then return to the office to get the extension. For every extra 30 days requested, foreigners must prove that they have US$1,000

available, either in cash, travelers checks, or simply by showing a current credit card. The process can take anywhere from a couple hours to a week, depending on the office.

CUSTOMS

Plants and fresh foods are not allowed into Mexico and there are special limits on alcohol, tobacco, and electronic products. Archaeological artifacts, certain antiques, and colonial art cannot be exported from Mexico without special permission.

Above all, do not attempt to bring marijuana or any other narcotic in or out of Mexico. Jail is one place your trusty guidebook won't come in handy.

Returning home, you will be required to declare all items you bought in Mexico. Citizens of the United States are allowed to re-enter with US$800 worth of purchases duty-free; the figure varies by country.

CONSULATES

The consulates in Cancún, Mérida, and Chetumal handle passport issues (replacing a lost one, adding pages, etc.) and can help their citizens if they are in a serious or emergency situation, including hospitalization, assault, arrest, lawsuits, or death. They usually do not help resolve common disputes—with tour operators or hotels, for example.

UNDERAGE TRAVELERS

In the United States, anyone under 18 traveling internationally without *both* parents or legal guardians must present a signed, notarized letter from the parent(s) staying at home granting permission to leave the country. This requirement is aimed at preventing international abductions, but it causes frequent and major disruptions for vacationers.

Food

Considered among the most distinct cuisines of the country, Yucatecan food reflects the influences of its Maya, European, and Caribbean heritage. Some of the most popular menu items follow:

Cochinita Pibil: pork that has been marinated in achiote, Seville orange juice, peppercorn, garlic, cumin, salt, and pepper, wrapped in banana leaves, and baked. Typically served on weekends only.

Dzoto-bichay: tamales made of *chaya* (a leafy vegetable similar to spinach) and eggs. It comes smothered in tomato sauce.

Empanizado: slices of pork or chicken that has been breaded and fried. This is often served with salad, rice, and beans.

Panucho: handmade tortilla stuffed with refried beans and covered with shredded turkey, pickled onion, and slices of avocado. Like a *salbute* plus!

Papadzules: hard-boiled eggs chopped and rolled into a corn tortilla. It comes smothered in a creamy pumpkin-seed sauce.

Poc-Chuc: slices of pork that have been marinated in Seville orange juice and coated with a tangy sauce. Pickled onions are added on the side.

Salbute: handmade tortilla covered with shredded turkey, pickled onion, and slices of avocado. Served hot and fast.

Sopa de Lima: turkey-stock soup prepared with shredded turkey or chicken, fried tortilla strips, and lemon juice.

CHILE PEPPERS

It's almost a given that at some point you'll bite into a seemingly innocent quesadilla, or dip a chip into a cute little bowl of salsa, and end up with a raging fire in your mouth. A wide variety of chile is used to spice food in the Yucatán, and throughout Mexico. Some are quite mild, even sweet, while others can make you sweat just sniffing them. (In all chiles, the seeds are the hottest part.) Many waiters are kind enough to warn you if a sauce or dish is *pica mucho* (stings a lot). Here are some of the chiles you may encounter on your trip:

- **Pimiento** (bell pepper): benign

- **Chile dulce** (sweet pepper – small, pumpkin-shaped, and light green): benign

- **Güero** (light-skinned – long, light green): mildly hot

- **Chile seco** (dried pepper – comes in *pasilla* and *Ancho* varieties: mildly hot

- **Poblano** (medium-size, dark green): ranges from mild to very hot

- **Serrano** (small torpedo-shaped peppers, typically green or red): medium hot

- **Puya** (small, thin, red peppers): hot

- **Jalapeño** (small to medium-size, hard and green, often pickled): hot

- **Chipotle** (medium and rust-colored, often dried): hot

- **Morita** (smoked and red): very hot

- **Piquín** (tiny, red, torpedo-shaped): extremely hot

- **De árbol** (literally, "from a tree" – long, red, thin): extremely hot

- **Habanero** (bulbous, small, typically green, orange, or yellow): five-alarm fire

If you take a wrong bite, you'll find some quick relief in a glass of milk, a bite of banana, a pinch of salt, or a glass of beer. *Buen provecho!*

© LIZA PRADO

Seafood is king of the menu in this part of Mexico.

Tips for Travelers

THE BEACH

Topless and nude sunbathing are not customary on Mexican beaches, and are rarely practiced in Cancún and other areas frequented by Americans and Canadians. However, on beaches popular with Europeans, especially Playa del Carmen and Tulum, it is more commonplace. Wherever you are, take a look around to help decide whether baring some or all is appropriate.

PHOTOGRAPHING LOCALS

No one enjoys having a stranger take his or her picture for no good reason. Indigenous people are no different. The best policy simply is not to take these photographs unless you've asked the person's permission—and they've agreed—first.

OPPORTUNITIES FOR STUDY AND EMPLOYMENT

While it may never approach neighboring Guatemala for the sheer number of Spanish schools, the Yucatán Peninsula has a variety of options for travelers who want to learn the language. Cancún, Isla Mujeres, Playa del Carmen, Mérida, and San Cristóbal all have schools or private instruction available. All also are well positioned to maximize travelers' enjoyment of the area's richness, whether its beaches, Maya ruins, colonial cities, or indigenous villages.

WOMEN TRAVELING ALONE

Solo women should expect a certain amount of unwanted attention, mostly in the form of whistles and catcalls. It typically happens as they walk down the street and sometimes comes from the most unlikely sources—we saw a man dressed as Bozo the clown turn mid–balloon animal to whistle at a woman walking by. Two or more women walking together attract much less unwanted attention, and a woman and man walking together will get none at all (at least of this sort—street vendors are a different story). While annoying and often unnerving, this sort of attention is almost always completely benign, and ignoring it is definitely the best response. Making eye contact or snapping a smart retort only will inspire more attention. Occasionally men will hustle alongside a woman trying to strike up a conversation—if you don't want to engage, a brief *hasta luego* or *no gracias* should make that clear. If it really gets on your nerves, carrying a notebook—or creating the appearance of working—reduces the amount of unwanted attention greatly.

GAY AND LESBIAN TRAVELERS

While openly gay women are still rare in Mexico, gay men are increasingly visible in large cities and certain tourist areas. Mérida has a fairly large gay community, of which a number of expat hotel and guesthouse owners are a prominent part. Cancún and Playa del Carmen both have a visible gay presence and a number of gay-friendly venues. Nevertheless, many locals—even in large cities—are not accustomed to open displays of homosexuality and may react openly and negatively. Many hotel attendants also simply don't understand that two travel companions of the same gender may prefer one bed—in some cases they will outright refuse to grant the request. Some couples find it easier to book a room with two queen-size beds and just sleep in one.

TRAVELERS WITH DISABILITIES

Mexico has made many improvements for the blind and people in wheelchairs—many large stores and tourist centers have ramps or elevators. A growing number of hotels have rooms designed for guests with disabilities, and there are two museums in the region—the Museo de las Estelas (Campeche City) and the Museo Regional de Antropología Carlos Pellicer Cá-

mara (Villahermosa)—that have high-quality replicas of Maya artifacts that visually impaired travelers can hold and touch. That said, Mexico is still a hard place to navigate if you have a disability. Smaller towns are the most problematic, as their sidewalks can be narrow and even some main streets are not paved. Definitely ask for help—for what Mexico lacks in infrastructure, its people make up for in graciousness and charity.

SENIOR TRAVELERS

Seniors should feel very welcome and safe visiting the Yucatán. Mexico is a country that affords great respect to its *personas de la tercer edad,* literally "people of the third age," and especially in the tradition-minded Yucatán Peninsula. But as anywhere, older travelers should take certain precautions. The Yucatán, especially Mérida and the surrounding area, is known to be extremely hot and humid, especially May–July. Seniors should take extra care to stay cool and hydrated. Exploring the Maya ruins can also be hot, not to mention exhausting. Bring water and snacks, especially to smaller sites where they may not be commonly sold. Travelers with balance or mobility concerns should think twice about climbing any of the pyramids or other structures. They can be deceptively treacherous, with steps that are steep, uneven, and slick.

Cancún, Playa del Carmen, and Mérida all have state-of-the-art hospitals, staffed by skilled doctors, nurses, and technicians, many of whom speak English. Most prescriptions medications are available in Mexico, often at discount prices. However, pharmacists are woefully under trained and you should always double-check the active ingredients and dosage of any pills you buy here.

TRAVELING WITH CHILDREN

The Yucatán Peninsula is a great place to take kids, whether youngsters or teenagers. The variety of activities and relative ease of transportation help keep everyone happy and engaged. Cancún and the Riviera Maya are especially family-friendly, with several different eco- and water parks, miles of beaches, and (if all else fails!) plenty of malls with movie theaters, arcades, bowling, minigolf, aquariums, and more. Perhaps best of all, Mexico is a country where family is paramount.

TRAVELING WITH IMPORTANT DOCUMENTS

Make several copies of your passport, tourist card, and airline tickets. Whether you're traveling solo or with others, leave a copy with someone you trust at home. Store one copy in a separate bag and if you have a travel companion, give a copy to him. Be sure to carry a copy of your passport and tourist card in your purse or wallet instead of the originals, which can be left in the hotel safe or locked in your bag; they're a lot more likely to be lost or stolen on the street than taken by hotel staff. When you move from place to place, carry your passport and important documents in a travel pouch, always under your clothing. Write down your credit card and ATM numbers and the 24-hour service numbers and keep those in a safe place.

Health and Safety

SUNBURN

Common sense is the most important factor in avoiding sunburn. Use waterproof and sweatproof sunscreen with a high SPF. Re-apply regularly—even the most heavy-duty waterproof sunscreen washes off faster than it claims to on the bottle (or gets rubbed off when you use your towel to dry off). Be extra careful to protect parts of your body that aren't normally exposed to the sun and give your skin a break from direct sun every few hours. Remember that redness from a sunburn takes several hours to appear—that is, you can be sunburned long before you *look* sunburned.

If you get sunburned, treat it like any other burn by running cool water over it as long and as often as you can. Do not expose your skin to more sun. Re-burning the skin can result in painful blisters that can easily become infected. There are a number of products designed to relieve sunburns, most with aloe extracts. Finally, be sure to drink plenty of water to keep your skin hydrated.

HEAT EXHAUSTION AND HEAT STROKE

The symptoms of heat exhaustion are cool moist skin, profuse sweating, headache, fatigue, and drowsiness. It is associated with dehydration and commonly happens during or after a strenuous day in the sun, such as visiting ruins. You should get out of the sun, remove any tight or restrictive clothing, and sip a sports drink such as Gatorade. Cool compresses and raising your feet and legs helps too.

Heat exhaustion is not the same as heat stroke, which is distinguished by a high body temperature, a rapid pulse, and sometimes delirium or even unconsciousness. It is an extremely serious, potentially fatal condition and victims should be taken to the hospital immediately. In the meantime, wrap the victim in wet sheets, massage his arms and legs to increase circulation, and do not administer large amounts of liquids. Do not give liquids if the victim is unconscious.

DIARRHEA

Diarrhea is not an illness itself, but your body's attempt to get rid of something bad in a hurry; that something can be any one of a number of strains of bacteria, parasites, or amoebae that are often passed from contaminated water. No fun, it is usually accompanied by cramping, dehydration, fever, and of course, frequent trips to the bathroom.

If you get diarrhea, it should pass in a day or two. Anti-diarrheals such as Lomotil and Imodium A-D will plug you up but don't cure you—use them only if you can't be near a bathroom. The malaise you feel from diarrhea typically is from dehydration, not the actual infection, so be sure to drink plenty of fluids—a sports drink such as Gatorade is best. If it's especially bad, ask at your hotel for the nearest *laboratorio* (laboratory or clinic) where the staff can analyze a stool sample for around US$5 and tell you if you have a parasitic infection or a virus. If it's a common infection, the lab technician will tell you what medicine to take. Be aware that medicines for stomach infection are seriously potent, killing not only the bad stuff but the good stuff as well; they cure you but leave you vulnerable to another infection. Avoid alcohol and spicy foods for several days afterward.

A few tips for avoiding any stomach problems include:

Only drink bottled water. Avoid using tap water even for brushing your teeth.

Avoid raw fruits or vegetables that you haven't disinfected and cut yourself. Lettuce is particularly dangerous since water is easily trapped in the leaves. Also, as tasty as they look, avoid the bags of sliced fruit sold from street carts.

Order your meat dishes well done, even if it's an upscale restaurant. If you've been to a market, you'll see that meat is handled very differently here.

INSECTS

Insects are not of particular concern in the Yucatán, certainly not as they are in other parts of the tropics. Mosquitoes are common, but are not known to carry malaria. Dengue fever, also transmitted by mosquitoes, is somewhat more common, but still rare. Some remote beaches, like Isla Holbox and the Costa Maya, may have sand flies or horseflies, but they have been all but eliminated in the more touristed areas. Certain destinations are more likely to be buggy, like forested archaeological zones and coastal bird-watching areas, and travelers definitely should bring and use insect repellent there, if only for extra comfort.

CRIME

The Yucatán Peninsula is generally quite safe, and few travelers report problems with crime of any kind. Cancún is the one area where particular care should be taken, however. You may find illicit drugs relatively easy to obtain, but bear in mind that drug crimes are prosecuted vigorously in Mexico (especially ones involving foreigners), and your country's embassy can do very little to get you off. Sexual assault and rape have been reported by women who attend nightclubs, sometimes after having been slipped a "date rape" drug. While the clubs are raucous and sexually charged by definition, women should be especially alert to the people around them, and wary of accepting drinks from strangers. In all areas, common-sense precautions are always recommended, such as taking a taxi at night (especially if you've been drinking) and avoiding flashing your money and valuables, or leaving them unattended on the beach or elsewhere. Utilize the safety deposit box in your hotel room, if one is available; if you rent a car, get one with a trunk so your bags will not be visible through the window.

Information and Services

MONEY
Currency
Mexico's official currency is the *peso,* divided into 100 *centavos.*

Exchange Rates
At the time of research, US$1 was equal to MP$10.8, while the Canadian dollar exchanged at MP$9.5, and the Euro at MP$14.0.

ATMs
Almost every town in the Yucatán Peninsula has an ATM and they are without question the easiest, fastest, and best way to manage your money. The ATM may charge a small transaction fee (US$1–2.50 typically) and your home bank may as well, but you don't lose any more than you would by buying travelers checks and then exchanging them for a fee or at a bad rate.

Travelers Checks
With the spread of ATMs, travelers checks have stopped being convenient for most travel, especially in a country as developed as Mexico. If you do bring them, you will have to exchange them at banks or a *casa de cambio* (exchange booth).

Credit Cards
Visa and MasterCard are accepted at all large hotels and many medium and small ones, upscale restaurants, main bus terminals, travel agencies, and many shops throughout Mexico. American Express is accepted much less frequently. Some merchants tack on a 5–10 percent surcharge for any credit card purchase—ask before you pay.

Cash
It's a good idea to bring a small amount of U.S. cash, on the off-chance your ATM or credit cards suddenly stop working; US$200 is more than enough for a two-week visit. Stow it away with your other important documents, to be used only if necessary.

Tax
A 12 percent value-added tax (*IVA* in Spanish) applies to hotel rates, restaurant and bar tabs, and gift purchases. When checking in or making reservations at a hotel, ask if tax has already been added. In some cases, the tax is 17 percent.

Bargaining
Bargaining is common and expected in street and artisans' markets, but try not to be too aggressive. Some tourists derive immense and almost irrational pride from haggling over every last cent, and then turn around and spend several times that amount on beer or snacks. The fact is, most bargaining comes down to the difference of a few dollars or even less, and earning those extra dollars is a much bigger deal for the artisan than spending them is to most tourists.

Tipping
While tipping is always a choice, it is a key supplement to many workers' paychecks. In fact, for some, the tip is the *only* pay they receive. And while dollars and euros are appreciated, pesos are preferred. (Note: Foreign coins are useless in Mexico since moneychangers—whether banks or exchange houses—will not accept them.) Average gratuities in the region include:

- Archaeological zone guides: 10–15 percent if you're satisfied with the service; for informal guides (typically boys who show you around the site) US$0.50–1 is customary.

- Gas station attendants: around US$0.50 if your windshield has been cleaned, tires have been filled, or the oil and water have been checked; no tip is expected for simply pumping gas.

- Grocery store baggers: US$0.30–0.50.

- Housekeepers: US$1–2 per day; either left daily or as a lump sum at the end of your stay.

- Porters: about US$1 per bag.
- Taxi drivers: Tipping is not customary.
- Tour guides: 10–15 percent; and don't forget the driver—US$1–2 is typical.
- Waiters: 10–15 percent; make sure the gratuity is not included in the bill.

MAPS AND TOURIST INFORMATION
Maps

An excellent source of maps of Cancún, Isla Cozumel, and other places on the Riviera Maya and beyond is www.cancunmap.com. Providing detailed city and area maps, virtually every building and business is identified, most with a short review, plus useful information like taxi rates, driving distances, ferry schedules, and more. Maps cost around US$8–10.

Otherwise, maps can be hard to come by in the Yucatán Peninsula. The tourist office is always a good place to start, where maps are distributed to tourists free of charge. Car-rental agencies often have maps and many hotels create maps for their guests of nearby restaurants and sights.

Tourist Offices

Most cities in the Yucatán have a tourist office, and some have more. Some tourist offices are staffed with friendly and knowledgeable people and have a good sense of what tourists are looking for—the city tourism office in Mérida is one of the best. At others, you'll seriously wonder how the people there were hired. It is certainly worth stopping in if you have a question—you may well get it answered, but don't be surprised if you don't.

Film, Photography, and Video

It's easy to find 35mm film in Mexico, but you can probably buy it for less at home. If you do bring your own film, do not send it through the X-ray machine at the airport or in your checked luggage (most of which is also X-rayed). Instead, ask the security officers to hand-inspect your film, both exposed and unexposed rolls. The modern machines are not supposed to hurt 400-plus-speed film or lower, but it's better to be safe than to risk coming home with 10 rolls of faded or grainy shots.

Digital cameras are as popular in Mexico as they are everywhere else, but memory sticks and other paraphernalia are still prohibitively expensive. Bring what you think you'll need, including a few blank CDs and a USB cable to download photos—most Internet cafés allow you to download and burn photos, but may not have the CD or cable.

Video is another great way to capture the color and movement of the Yucatán. Be aware that all archaeological sites charge an additional US$3 to bring in a video camera; tripods are often prohibited.

COMMUNICATIONS AND MEDIA
Postal Service

Mailing letters and postcards from Mexico is neither cheap nor necessarily reliable. Delivery times vary greatly, and letters get "lost" somewhat more than postcards. Letters (under 20 grams) and postcards cost US$1 to the United States and Canada; US$1.20 to South America; and US$1.35 to the rest of the world.

Telephone

Ladatel—Mexico's national phone company—maintains good public phones all over the peninsula and country. Plastic phone cards with little chips in them are sold at most mini-marts and supermarkets in 30-, 50-, 100-, and 200-peso denominations. Ask for a *tarjeta Ladatel*—they are the size and stiffness of a credit card, as opposed to the thin cards used for cell phones. Insert the card into the phone, and the amount on the card is displayed on the screen. Rates and dialing instructions are inside the phone cabin. At the time of research, rates were US$0.10 a minute for local calls, US$0.40 a minute for national calls, and US$0.50 a minute for calls to the United States and Canada.

To dial a cellular phone, you must dial 044 and the area code, then the number. Note that calling a cell phone, even a local one, costs the

USEFUL TELEPHONE NUMBERS

TRAVELER ASSISTANCE

- Emergencies: 060 or 066

- Green Angels: 078 or 800/903-9200

- Directory Assistance: 044

LONG-DISTANCE DIRECT DIALING

- Domestic long-distance: 01 + area code + number

- International long-distance (United States only): 001 + area code + number

- International long-distance (rest of the world): 001 + country code + area code + number

LONG DISTANCE COLLECT CALLS

- Domestic long-distance operator: 02

- International long-distance operator (English-speaking): 09

the most expensive was US$7 per hour. The vast majority, however, charge US$0.85–1 per hour. Most places also will burn digital photos onto a CD—they typically sell the blank CD, but travelers should bring their own USB cable. Expect to pay US$2–3 a burn, plus the computer time. Many Internet shops also offer telephone and fax service.

Newspapers

The main daily newspapers in the Yucatán Peninsula are *El Diario de Yucatán, Novedades Quintana Roo,* and *Voz del Caribe.* The main national newspapers are also readily available, including *Reforma, La Prensa,* and *La Jornada.* For news in English, you'll find the *Miami Herald Cancún Edition* in Cancún and occasionally in Playa del Carmen, Isla Cozumel, and Mérida.

Radio and Television

Most large hotels and a number of midsize and small ones have cable or satellite TV, which usually includes CNN (though sometimes in Spanish only), MTV, and other U.S. channels. AM and FM radio options are surprisingly bland—you're more likely to find a good *rock en español* station in California than you are in the Yucatán.

WEIGHTS AND MEASURES
Measurements

Mexico uses the metric system, so distances are in kilometers, weights are in kilograms, gasoline is sold by the liter, and temperatures are given in Celsius. See the chart at the back of this book for conversions from the Imperial system.

Time Zone

The Yucatán Peninsula, Tabasco, and Chiapas are in the same time zone—U.S. Central Standard Time. Daylight Savings Time is recognized April–October.

Electricity

Mexico uses the 60-cycle, 110-volt AC current common in the United States. Bring a surge protector if you plan to plug in a laptop.

same as a domestic long-distance telephone call (US$0.40/min.).

A number of Internet cafés offer inexpensive Web-based phone service, especially in the larger cities where broadband connections make this sort of calling possible. Rates tend to be slightly lower than those of Ladatel, and you don't have to worry about your card running out.

Beware of phones offering "free" collect or credit card calls; far from being free, their rates are outrageous.

Internet Access

Internet cafés can be found in virtually every town in the Yucatán Peninsula. Prices vary—the cheapest we saw was US$0.45 per hour,

RESOURCES

Maya Glossary

MAYA GODS AND CEREMONIES

Acanum protective deity of hunters

Ahau Can serpent lord and highest priest

Ahau Chamehes deity of medicine

Ah Cantzicnal aquatic deity

Ah Chuy Kak god of violent death and sacrifice

Ahcit Dzamalcum protective god of fishermen

Ah Cup Cacap god of the underworld who denies air

Ah Itzám the water witch

Ah kines priests that consult the oracles and preside over ceremonies and sacrifices

Ahpua god of fishing

Ah Puch god of death

Ak'Al sacred marsh where water abounds

Bacaboob supporters of the sky and guardians of the cardinal points, who form a single god, Ah Cantzicnal Becabs

Bolontiku the nine lords of the night

Chac god of rain and agriculture

Chac Bolay Can butcher serpent living in the underworld

Chaces priests' assistants in agricultural and other ceremonies

Cihuateteo women who become goddesses through death in childbirth

Cit Chac Coh god of war

Hetzmek ceremony when the child is first carried astride the hip

Hobnil Bacab bee god, protector of beekeepers

Holcanes warriors charged with obtaining slaves for sacrifice

Hunab Ku giver of life, builder of the universe, and father of Itzámna

Ik god of the wind

Itzámna lord of the skies, creator of the beginning, god of time

Ixchel goddess of birth, fertility, and medicine; credited with inventing spinning

Ixtab goddess of the cord and of suicide by hanging

Kinich face of the sun

Kukulcán quetzal-serpent, plumed serpent

Metnal the underworld, place of the dead

Nacom warrior chief

Noh Ek Venus

Pakat god of violent death

Zec spirit lords of beehives

FOOD AND DRINK

alche inebriating drink, sweetened with honey and used for ceremonies and offerings

ic chili

itz sweet potato

kabaxbuul heaviest meal of the day, eaten at dusk and containing cooked black beans

kah pinole flour

kayem ground maize

macal a root

muxubbak tamale

on avocado

op plum

p'ac tomatoes

put papaya

tzamna black bean

uah tortillas

za maize drink

ANIMALS

acehpek dog used for deer hunting
ah maax cal prattling monkey
ah maycuy chestnut deer
ah sac dziu white thrush
ah xixteel ul rugged land conch
bil hairless dog reared for food
cutz wild turkey
cutzha duck
hoh crow
icim owl
jaleb hairless dog
keh deer
kitam wild boar
muan evil bird related to death
que parrot
thul rabbit
tzo domestic turkey
utiu coyote

MUSIC AND FESTIVALS

ah paxboob musicians
bexelac turtle shell used as percussion instrument
chohom dance performed in ceremonies related to fishing
chul flute
hom trumpet
kayab percussion instrument fashioned from turtle shell
Oc na festival where old idols of a temple are broken and replaced with new ones
okot uil dance performed during the Pocan ceremony
Pacum chac festival in honor of the war gods
tunkul drum
zacatan drum made from a hollowed tree trunk, one opening is covered with hide

ELEMENTS OF TIME

baktun 144,000-day Maya calendar
chumuc akab midnight
chumuc kin midday
chunkin midday
haab solar calendar of 360 days plus five extra days of misfortune, which complete the final month
emelkin sunset

kaz akab dusk
kin the sun, the day, the unity of time
potakab time before dawn
yalhalcab dawn

NUMBERS

hun one
ca two
ox three
can four
ho five
uac six
uuc seven
uacax eight
bolon nine
iahun 10
buluc 11
iahca 12
oxlahum 13
canlahum 14
holahun 15
uaclahun 16
uuclahun 17
uacaclahun 18
bolontahun 19
hunkal 20

PLANTS AND TREES

ha cacao seed
kan ak plant that produces a yellow dye
ki sisal
kiixpaxhkum chayote
kikche tree trunk that is used to make canoes
kuche red cedar tree
k'uxub annatto tree
piim fiber of the cotton tree
taman cotton plant
tauch black zapote tree
tazon te moss

MISCELLANEOUS WORDS

ah kay kin bak meat-seller
chaltun water cistern
cha te black vegetable dye
chi te eugenia, plant for dyeing
ch'oh indigo
ek dye
hadzab wooden swords

halach uinic leader
mayacimil smallpox epidemic
palapa traditional Maya structure constructed without nails or tools
pic underskirt
ploms rich people

suyen square blanket
xanab sandals
xicul sleeveless jacket decorated with feathers
xul stake with a pointed, fire-hardened tip
yuntun slings

Spanish Glossary

Many of the following words have a socio-historical meaning; others you will not find in the usual English-Spanish dictionary.

abarrotería grocery store
alcalde mayor or municipal judge
alfarería pottery
alfarero, alfarera potter
andando walkway or strolling path
antojitos native Mexican snacks, such as tamales, *chiles rellenos*, tacos, and enchiladas
artesanías handicrafts, as distinguished from *artesano, artesana* a person who makes handicrafts
audiencia one of the royal executive-judicial panels sent to rule Mexico during the 16th century
ayuntamiento either the town council or the building where it meets
bienes raices literally "good roots," but popularly, real estate
birria pit-barbequed goat, pork, or lamb – especially typical of Jalisco
boleto ticket, boarding pass
caballero literally, "horseman," but popularly, gentleman
cabercera head town of a municipal district, or headquarters in general
cabrón literally a cuckold, but more commonly, bastard, rat, or S.O.B.; sometimes used affectionately
cacique chief or boss
calandria early 1800s-style horse-drawn carriage, common in Guadalajara
camionera central central bus station
campesino country person; farm worker
canasta basket of woven reeds, with handle

casa de huéspedes guesthouse, often operated in a family home
caudillo dictator or political chief
charro, charra gentleman cowboy or cowgirl
chingar literally, "to rape," but is also the universal Spanish "f- word," the equivalent of "screw" in English
churrigueresque Spanish baroque architectural style incorporated into many Mexican colonial churches, named after José Churriguera (1665-1725)
científicos literally, scientists, but applied to President Porfirio Díaz's technocratic advisers
cofradía Catholic fraternal service association, either male or female, mainly in charge of financing and organizing religious festivals
colectivo a shared public taxi or minibus that picks up and deposits passengers along a designated route
colegio preparatory school or junior college
colonia suburban subdivision/satellite of a larger city
Conasupo government store that sells basic foods at subsidized prices
correo post office
criollo person of all-Spanish descent born in the New World
cuadra Huichol yarn painting, usually rectangular
Cuaresma Lent
curandero, curandera indigenous medicine man or woman
damas ladies, as in "ladies room"
Domingo de Ramos Palm Sunday
ejido a constitutional, government-sponsored form of community, with shared land ownership and cooperative decision making

encomienda colonial award of tribute from a designated indigenous district

estación ferrocarril railroad station

farmacia pharmacy or drugstore

finca farm

fonda food stall or small restaurant, often in a traditional market complex

fraccionamiento city sector or subdivision

fuero the former right of clergy to be tried in separate ecclesiastical courts

gachupín "one who wear spurs"; a derogatory term for a Spanish-born colonial

gasolinera gasoline station

gente de razón "people of reason"; whites and mestizos in colonial Mexico

gringo once-derogatory but now commonly used term for North American whites

grito impassioned cry, as in Hidalgo's *Grito de Dolores*

hacienda large landed estate; also the government treasury

hidalgo nobleman; called honorifically by "Don" or "DoÑa"

indígena indigenous or aboriginal inhabitant of all-native descent who speaks his or her native tongue; commonly, but incorrectly, an Indian *(indio)*

jardín literally garden, but often denoting a town's central plaza

jejenes "no-see-um" biting gnats, especially around San Blas, Nayarit

judiciales the federal or state "judicial," or investigative police, best known to motorists for their highway checkpoint inspections

jugería stall or small restaurant providing a large array of squeezed vegetable and fruit *jugos* (juices)

juzgado the "hoosegow," or jail

larga distancia long-distance telephone service, or the *caseta* (booth) where it's provided

licenciado academic degree (abbr. Lic.) approximately equivalent to a bachelor's degree

lonchería small lunch counter, usually serving juices, sandwiches, and *antojitos* (Mexican snacks)

machismo; macho exaggerated sense of maleness; person who holds such a sense of himself

mescal alcoholic beverage distilled from the fermented hearts of maguey (century plant)

mestizo person of mixed European/indigenous descent

milpa native farm plot, usually of corn, squash, and beans

mordida slang for bribe; literally, "little bite"

palapa thatched-roof structure, often open and shading a restaurant

panga outboard launch *(lancha)*

Pemex acronym for Petróleos Mexicanos, Mexico's national oil corporation

peninsulares the Spanish-born ruling colonial elite

peón a poor wage-earner, usually a country native

petate a mat, traditionally woven of palm leaf

plan political manifesto, usually by a leader or group consolidating or seeking power

Porfiriato the 34-year (1876-1910) ruling period of president-dictator Porfirio Díaz

pozole popular stew, of hominy in broth, usually topped by shredded pork, cabbage, and diced onion

presidencia municipal the headquarters, like a U.S. city or county hall, of a Mexican *municipio*, county-like local governmental unit

preventiva municipal police

pronunciamiento declaration of rebellion by an insurgent leader

pueblo town or people

puta derogatory term for women, as in whore, bitch, or slut

quinta a villa or country house

quinto the royal "one-fifth" tax on treasure and precious metals

retorno cul-de-sac

rurales former federal country police force created to fight *bandidos*

Semana Santa pre-Easter holy week

Tapatío, Tapatía a label, referring to anyone or anything from Guadalajara or Jalisco

taxi especial private taxi, as distinguished from taxi colectivo, or shared taxi

telégrafo telegraph office, lately converting to high-tech

telecomunicaciones, or **telecom**, offering telegraph, telephone, and public fax services

tenate soft, pliable basket, without handle, woven of palm leaf

vaquero cowboy

vecinidad neighborhood

vinchuca "kissing" or "assassin" bug

yanqui Yankee

zócalo town plaza or central square

Abbreviations

Av. *avenida* (avenue)

Blv. *bulevar* (boulevard)

Calz. *calzada* (thoroughfare, main road)

Fco. Francisco (proper name, as in "Fco. Villa")

Fracc. *Fraccionamiento* (subdivision)

Nte. *norte* (north)

Ote. *oriente* (east)

Pte. *poniente* (west)

s/n *sin número* (no street number)

Spanish Phrasebook

Whether you speak a little or a lot, using your Spanish will surely make your vacation a lot more fun. You'll soon see that Mexicans truly appreciate your efforts and your willingness to speak their language.

PRONUNCIATION

Spanish commonly uses 30 letters—the familiar English 26, plus four straightforward additions: ch, ll, ñ, and rr, which are explained in "Consonants," below.

Once you learn them, Spanish pronunciation rules—in contrast to English—don't change. Spanish vowels generally sound softer than in English. (Note: The capitalized syllables below receive stronger accents.)

Vowels

a *like ah, as in "hah": agua AH-gooah (water), pan PAHN (bread), and casa CAH-sah (house)*

e *like eh, as in "hem:" mesa MEH-sah (table), tela TEH-lah (cloth), and de DEH (of, from)*

i *like ee, as in "need": diez dee-EHZ (ten), comida ko-MEE-dah (meal), and fin FEEN (end)*

o *like oh, as in "go": peso PEH-soh (weight), ocho OH-choh (eight), and poco POH-koh (a bit)*

u *like oo, as in "cool": uno OO-noh (one), cuarto KOOAHR-toh (room), and usted oos-TEHD (you); when it follows a "q" the u is silent; when it follows an "h" or has an umlaut, it's pronounced like "w"*

Consonants

b, d, f, k, l, m, n, p, q, s, t, v, w, x, y, z, and *ch* pronounced almost as in English; *h* occurs, but is silent.

c *like k as in "keep": cuarto KOOAR-toh (room), Tepic the-PEEK (capital of Nayarit state); when it precedes "e" or "i," pronounce c like s, as in "sit": cerveza sehr-VEH-sah (beer), encima ehn-SEE-mah (atop).*

g *like g as in "gift" when it precedes "a," "o," "u," or a consonant: gato GAH-toh (cat), hago AH-goh (I do, make); otherwise, pronounce g like h as in "hat": giro HEE-roh (money order), gente HEN-teh (people)*

j *like h, as in "has": Jueves HOOEH-vehs (Thursday), mejor meh-HOR (better)*

ll *like y, as in "yes": toalla toh-AH-yah (towel), ellos EH-yohs (they, them)*

ñ *like ny, as in "canyon": año AH-nyo (year), señor SEH-nyor (Mr., sir)*

r *is lightly trilled, with your tongue at the roof of your mouth like a very light English d, as in "ready": pero PEH-roh (but), tres TREHS (three), cuatro KOOAH-troh (four).*

rr *like a Spanish r, but with much more emphasis and trill. Let your tongue flap. Practice with burro (donkey), carretera (highway), and Carrillo (proper name), then really let go with ferrocarril (railroad).*

Note: The single exception to the above is the pronunciation of *y* when it's being used as the Spanish word for "and," as in "Eva y Leo."

In such case, pronounce it like the English ee, as in "keep": Eva "ee" Leo (Eva and Leo).

Accent

The rule for accent, the relative stress given to syllables within a given word, is straightforward. If a word ends in a vowel, an n or an s, accent the next-to-last syllable; if not, accent the last syllable.

Pronounce *gracias* GRAH-seeahs (thank you), *orden* OHR-dehn (order), and *carretera* kah-reh-TEH-rah (highway) with the stress on the next-to-last syllable.

Otherwise, accent the last syllable: *venir* veh-NEER (to come), *ferrocarril* feh-roh-cah-REEL (railroad), and *edad* eh-DAHD (age).

Exceptions to the accent rule are always marked with an accent sign: (á, é, í, ó, or ú), such as *teléfono* teh-LEH-foh-noh (telephone), *jabón* hah-BON (soap), and *rápido* RAH-pee-doh (rapid).

BASIC AND COURTEOUS EXPRESSIONS

Most Spanish-speaking people consider formalities important. Whenever approaching anyone, do not forget the appropriate salutation–good morning, good evening, etc. Standing alone, the greeting *hola* (hello) can sound brusque.

Hello. *Hola.*
Good morning. *Buenos días.*
Good afternoon. *Buenas tardes.*
Good evening. *Buenas noches.*
How are you? *¿Cómo está Usted?*
Very well, thank you. *Muy bien, gracias.*
Okay; good. *Bien.*
Not okay; bad. *No muy bien; mal.*
So-so. *Más o menos.*
And you? *¿Y usted?*
Thank you. *Gracias.*
Thank you very much. *Muchas gracias.*
You're very kind. *Muy amable.*
You're welcome. *De nada.*
Good-bye. *Adios.*
See you later. *Hasta luego.*
please *por favor*
yes *sí*
no *no*
I don't know. *No sé.*

Just a moment, please. *Un momentito, por favor.*
Excuse me, please (when you're trying to get attention). *Disculpe or Con permiso.*
Excuse me (when you've made a mistake). *Lo siento.*
Pleased to meet you. *Mucho gusto.*
How do you say...in Spanish? *¿Cómo se dice...en español?*
What is your name? *¿Cómo se llama Usted?*
Do you speak English? *¿Habla Usted inglés?*
Is English spoken here? *¿Se habla inglés?*
I don't speak Spanish well. *No hablo bien el español.*
I don't understand. *No entiendo.*
My name is . . . *Me llamo...*
Would you like . . . *¿Quisiera Usted...*
Let's go to . . . *Vamos a...*

TERMS OF ADDRESS

When in doubt, use the formal *Usted* (you) as a form of address.

I *yo*
you (formal) *Usted*
you (familiar) *tu*
he/him *él*
she/her *ella*
we/us *nosotros*
you (plural) *ustedes*
they/them *ellos* (all males or mixed gender); *ellas* (all females)
Mr., sir *señor*
Mrs., ma'am *señora*
miss, young lady *señorita*
wife *esposa*
husband *esposo*
friend *amigo* (male); *amiga* (female)
boyfriend; girlfriend *novio; novia*
son; daughter *hijo; hija*
brother; sister *hermano; hermana*
father; mother *padre; madre*
grandfather; grandmother *abuelo; abuela*

TRANSPORTATION

Where is...? *¿Dónde está...?*
How far is it to...? *¿A cuánto está...?*
from...to . . . *de...a...*
How many blocks? *¿Cuántas cuadras?*

Where (Which) is the way to...? *¿Dónde está el camino a...?*
the bus station *la terminal de autobuses*
the bus stop *la parada de autobuses*
Where is this bus going? *¿Adónde va este autobús?*
the taxi stand *la parada de taxis*
the train station *la estación de ferrocarril*
the boat *el barco or la lancha*
the airport *el aeropuerto*
I'd like a ticket to . . . *Quisiera un boleto a...*
first (second) class *primera (segunda) clase*
round-trip *ida y vuelta*
reservation *reservación*
baggage *equipaje*
Stop here, please. *Pare aquí, por favor.*
the entrance *la entrada*
the exit *la salida*
the ticket office *la taquilla*
(very) near; far *(muy) cerca; lejos*
to; toward *a*
by; through *por*
from *de*
the right *la derecha*
the left *la izquierda*
straight ahead *derecho; directo*
in front *en frente*
beside *al lado*
behind *atrás*
the corner *la esquina*
the stoplight *el semáforo*
a turn *una vuelta*
here *aquí*
somewhere around here *por aqui*
right there *allí*
somewhere around there *por allá*
street; boulevard *calle; bulevar*
highway *carretera*
bridge *Puente*
toll *cuota*
address *dirección*
north; south *norte; sur*
east; west *oriente (este); poniente (oeste)*

ACCOMMODATIONS
hotel *hotel*
Is there a room? *¿Hay cuarto?*

May I (may we) see it? *¿Podría (podríamos) verlo?*
What is the rate? *¿Cuál es la tarifa?*
Is that your best rate? *¿Es su mejor precio?*
Is there something cheaper? *¿Hay algo más económico?*
a single room *un cuarto sencillo*
a double room *un cuarto doble*
double bed *cama matrimonial*
twin bed *cama individual*
with private bath *con baño privado*
hot water *agua caliente*
shower *ducha*
towels *toallas*
soap *jabón*
toilet paper *papel higiénico*
blanket *cobija*
sheets *sábanas*
air-conditioned *aire acondicionado*
fan *abanico; ventilador*
key *llave*
manager *gerente*

FOOD
I'm hungry *Tengo hambre.*
I'm thirsty. *Tengo sed.*
menu *carta; menú*
order *orden*
glass *vaso*
fork *tenedor*
knife *cuchillo*
spoon *cuchara*
napkin *servilleta*
soft drink *refresco*
coffee *café*
tea *té*
drinking water *agua pura; agua potable*
carbonated water *agua mineral*
bottled uncarbonated water *agua sin gas*
beer *cerveza*
wine *vino*
milk *leche*
juice *jugo*
cream *crema*
sugar *azúcar*
cheese *queso*
snack *antojito; botana*

breakfast *desayuno*
lunch *almuerzo or comida*
daily lunch special *comida corrida*
dinner *cena*
the check *la cuenta*
eggs *huevos*
bread *pan*
salad *ensalada*
fruit *fruta*
mango *mango*
watermelon *sandía*
papaya *papaya*
banana *plátano*
apple *manzana*
orange *naranja*
lime *limón*
fish *pescado*
shellfish *mariscos*
shrimp *camarones*
meat (without) *(sin) carne*
chicken *pollo*
pork *puerco*
beef; steak *res; bistec*
bacon; ham *tocino; jamón*
fried *frito*
roasted *asada*
barbecue; barbecued *barbacoa; al carbón*

SHOPPING

money *dinero*
money-exchange bureau *casa de cambio*
I would like to exchange traveler's checks. *Quisiera cambiar cheques de viajero.*
What is the exchange rate? *¿Cuál es el tipo de cambio?*
How much is the commission? *¿Cuánto cuesta la comisión?*
Do you accept credit cards? *¿Aceptan tarjetas de crédito?*
money order *giro*
How much does it cost? *¿Cuánto cuesta?*
What is your final price? *¿Cuál es su último precio?*
expensive *caro*
cheap *barato; económico*
more *más*
less *menos*

a little *un poco*
too much *demasiado*

HEALTH

Help me please. *Ayúdeme por favor.*
I am ill. *Estoy enfermo.*
Call a doctor. *Llame un doctor.*
Take me to . . . *Lléveme a...*
hospital *hospital; clinica medica*
drugstore *farmacia*
pain *dolor*
fever *fiebre*
headache *dolor de cabeza*
stomachache *dolor de estómago*
burn *quemadura*
cramp *calambre*
nausea *náusea*
vomiting *vomitar*
medicine *medicina*
antibiotic *antibiótico*
pill; tablet *pastilla*
aspirin *aspirina*
ointment; cream *pomada; crema*
bandage *venda*
cotton *algodón*
sanitary napkins *Kotex*
birth control pills *pastillas anticonceptivas*
contraceptive foam *espuma anticonceptiva*
condoms *preservativos; condones*
toothbrush *cepillo de dientes*
dental floss *hilo dental*
toothpaste *pasta de dientes*
dentist *dentista*
toothache *dolor de dientes*

POST OFFICE AND COMMUNICATIONS

long-distance telephone *teléfono de larga distancia*
I would like to call . . . *Quisiera llamar a...*
collect *por cobrar*
person to person *persona a persona*
credit card *tarjeta de crédito*
post office *correo*
letter *carta*
stamp *estampilla, timbre*
postcard *tarjeta postal*
air mail *correo aereo*

registered *registrado*
money order *giro*
package; box *paquete; caja*
string; tape *cuerda; cinta*

AT THE BORDER

border *frontera*
customs *aduana*
immigration *migración*
tourist card *tarjeta de turista*
inspection *inspección; revisión*
passport *pasaporte*
profession *profesión*
marital status *estado civil*
single *soltero*
married; divorced *casado; divorciado*
widowed *viudado* (male); *vuidada* (female)
insurance *seguro*
title *título*
driver's license *licencia de manejar*

AT THE GAS STATION

gas station *gasolinera*
gasoline *gasolina*
unleaded *sin plomo*
fill it up, please *lleno, por favor*
tire *llanta*
tire repair shop *vulcanizadora*
air *aire*
water *agua*
oil; oil change *aceite; cambio de aceite*
grease *grasa*
My...doesn't work. *Mi...no sirve.*
battery *batería*
radiator *radiador*
alternator *alternador*
generator *generador*
tow truck *grúa*
repair shop *taller mecánico*
tune-up *afinación*
auto parts store *refaccionería*

VERBS

Verbs are the key to getting along in Spanish. They employ mostly predictable forms and come in three classes, which end in *ar, er,* and *ir.* Note that the first-person *(yo)* verb form is often irregular.

to buy *comprar*
I buy, you (he, she, it) buys *compro, compra*
we buy, you (they) buy *compramos, compran*
to eat *comer*
I eat, you (he, she, it) eats *como, come*
we eat, you (they) eat *comemos, comen*
to climb *subir*
I climb, you (he, she, it) climbs *subo, sube*
we climb, you (they) climb *subimos, suben*

to do or make *hacer*
I do or make, you (he she, it) does or makes *hago, hace*
we do or make, you (they) do or make *hacemos, hacen*
to go *ir*
I go, you (he, she, it) goes *voy, va*
we go, you (they) go *vamos, van*
to go (walk) *andar*
to love *amar*
to work *trabajar*
to want *desear, querer*
to need *necesitar*
to read *leer*
to write *escribir*
to repair *reparar*
to stop *parar*
to get off (the bus) *bajar*
to arrive *llegar*
to stay (remain) *quedar*
to stay (lodge) *hospedar*
to leave *salir* (regular except for *salgo,* I leave)
to look at *mirar*
to look for *buscar*
to give *dar* (regular except for *doy,* I give)
to carry *llevar*
to have *tener* (irregular but important: *tengo, tiene, tenemos, tienen*)
to come *venir* (similarly irregular: *vengo, viene, venimos, vienen*)

Spanish has two forms of "to be." Use *estar* when speaking of location or a temporary state of being: "I am at home." "*Estoy en casa.*" "I'm sick." "*Estoy enfermo.*" Use *ser* for a permanent state of being: "I am a doctor." "*Soy doctora.*"

Estar is regular except for *estoy*, I am. *Ser* is irregular:
to be *ser*
I am, you (he, she, it) is *soy, es*
we are, you (they) are *somos, son*

NUMBERS

zero *cero*
one *uno*
two *dos*
three *tres*
four *cuatro*
five *cinco*
six *seis*
seven *siete*
eight *ocho*
nine *nueve*
10 *diez*
11 *once*
12 *doce*
13 *trece*
14 *catorce*
15 *quince*
16 *dieciseis*
17 *diecisiete*
18 *dieciocho*
19 *diecinueve*
20 *veinte*
21 *veintiuno*
30 *treinta*
40 *cuarenta*
50 *cincuenta*
60 *sesenta*
70 *setenta*
80 *ochenta*
90 *noventa*
100 *cien*
101 *cientiuno*
200 *doscientos*
500 *quinientos*
1,000 *mil*
10,000 *diez mil*
100,000 *cien mil*
1,000,000 *millón*
one half *medio*

one third *un tercio*
one fourth *un cuarto*

TIME

What time is it? *¿Qué hora es?*
It's one o'clock. *Es la una.*
It's three in the afternoon. *Son las tres de la tarde.*
It's 4 A.M. *Son las cuatro de la mañana.*
six-thirty *seis y media*
a quarter till eleven *un cuarto para las once*
a quarter past five *las cinco y cuarto*
an hour *una hora*

DAYS AND MONTHS

Monday *lunes*
Tuesday *martes*
Wednesday *miércoles*
Thursday *jueves*
Friday *viernes*
Saturday *sábado*
Sunday *domingo*
today *hoy*
tomorrow *mañana*
yesterday *ayer*
January *enero*
February *febrero*
March *marzo*
April *abril*
May *mayo*
June *junio*
July *julio*
August *agosto*
September *septiembre*
October *octubre*
November *noviembre*
December *diciembre*
a week *una semana*
a month *un mes*
after *después*
before *antes*

Adapted from Bruce Whipperman's *Moon Pacific Mexico.*

Suggested Reading

The following titles provide insight into the Yucatán Peninsula and the Maya people. A few of these books are more easily obtained in Mexico, but all of them will cost less in the United States. Most are nonfiction, though several are fiction and great to pop into your carry-on for a good read on the plane, or for when you're in a Yucatecan mood. Happy reading.

Beletsky, Les. *Travellers' Wildlife Guides: Southern Mexico* Northampton: Interlink Books, 2007. A perfect companion guide if you plan on bird-watching, diving/snorkeling, hiking, or canoeing your way through your vacation. Excellent illustrations.

Coe, Andrew. *Archaeological Mexico: A Traveler's Guide to Ancient Cities and Sacred Sites.* Emeryville: Avalon Travel Publishing, 2001.

Coe, Michael D. *The Maya.* New York: Thames and Hudson, 1993. A well-illustrated, easy-to-read volume on the Maya people.

Coe, Michael D. *Breaking the Maya Code.* New York: Thames and Hudson, 1992, 1999. A fascinating account of how epigraphers, linguists, and archaeologists succeeded in deciphering Maya hieroglyphics.

Cortés, Hernán. *Five Letters.* Gordon Press, 1977. Cortés' letters to the king of Spain, telling of his accomplishments and justifying his actions in the New World.

Davies, Nigel. *The Ancient Kingdoms of Mexico.* New York: Penguin Books. An excellent study of the preconquest of the indigenous peoples of Mexico.

De Landa, Bishop Diego. *Yucatán Before and After the Conquest.* New York: Dover Publications, 1978. This book, translated by William Gates from the original 1566 volume, has served as the basis for all the research that has taken place since.

Díaz del Castillo, Bernal. *The Conquest of New Spain.* New York: Penguin Books, 1963. History straight from the adventurer's reminiscences, translated by J. M. Cohen.

Fehrenbach, T. R. *Fire and Blood: A History of Mexico.* New York: Collier Books, 1973. Over 3,000 years of Mexican history, related in a way that will keep you reading.

Ferguson, William M. *Maya Ruins of Mexico in Color.* Norman: University of Oklahoma Press, 1977. Good reading before you go, but too bulky to carry along. Oversized with excellent drawings and illustrations of the archaeological structures of the Maya.

Franz, Carl. *The People's Guide to Mexico.* Emeryville: Avalon Travel Publishing, 2002. A humorous guide filled with witty anecdotes and helpful general information for visitors to Mexico. Don't expect any specific city information, just nuts-and-bolts hints for traveling south of the border.

Greene, Graham. *The Power and the Glory.* New York: Penguin Books, 1977. A novel that takes place in the 1920s about a priest and the anti-church movement that gripped the country.

Heffern, Richard. *Secrets of the Mind-Altering Plants of Mexico.* New York: Pyramid Books. A fascinating study of many substances, from ancient ritual hallucinogens to today's medicines that are found in Mexico.

Laughlin, Robert M. *The People of the Bat.* Smithsonian Institution Press, 1988. Maya tales and dreams as told by the Zinacantán Indians in Chiapas.

Maya: Divine Kings of the Rain Forest. Könemann, 2006. A beautifully compiled book of essays, photographs, and sketches relating to the Maya, past and present. Too heavy to take on the road but an excellent read.

McNay Brumfield, James. *A Tourist in the Yucatan.* Tres Picos Press, 2004. A decent thriller that takes place in the Yucatán Peninsula; good for the beach or a long bus ride.

Meyer, Michael and William Sherman. *The Course of Mexican History.* Oxford University Press. A concise, one-volume history of Mexico.

Nelson, Ralph. *Popul Vuh: The Great Mythological Book of the Ancient Maya.* Boston: Houghton Mifflin, 1974. An easy-to-read translation of myths handed down orally by the Quiche Maya, family to family, until written down after the Spanish conquest.

Riding, Alan. *Distant Neighbors.* Vintage Books. A modern look at today's Mexico.

The Rise and Fall of the Maya Civilization. Norman: University of Oklahoma Press, 1954. One man's story of the Maya. Excellent reading.

Sodi, Demetrio M. (in collaboration with Adela Fernández). *The Mayas.* Mexico: Panama Editorial S.A. This small pocketbook presents a fictionalized account of life among the Mayas before the conquest. Easy reading for anyone who enjoys fantasizing about what life *might* have been like before recorded history in the Yucatán.

Stephens, John L. *Incidents of Travel in Central America, Chiapas, and Yucatán.* 2 vols. New York: Dover Publications, 1969. Good companions to refer to when traveling in the area. Stephens and illustrator Frederick Catherwood rediscovered many of the Maya ruins on their treks that took place in the mid-1800s. Easy reading.

Thompson, J. Eric. *Maya Archaeologist.* Norman: University of Oklahoma Press, 1963. Thompson, a noted Maya scholar, traveled and worked at most of the Maya ruins in the 1930s.

Webster, David. *The Fall of the Ancient Maya.* New York: Thames and Hudson, 2002. A careful and thorough examination of the possible causes of one of archaeology's great unsolved mysteries—the collapse of the Classic Maya in the 8th century.

Werner, David. *Where There Is No Doctor.* Palo Alto, California: The Hesperian Foundation, 1992. This is an invaluable medical aid to anyone traveling not only to isolated parts of Mexico but to any place in the world where there's not a doctor.

Wolf, Eric. *Sons of the Shaking Earth.* University of Chicago Press, 1962. An anthropological study of the indigenous and mestizo people of Mexico and Guatemala.

Wright, Ronald. *Time Among the Maya.* New York: Weidenfeld and Nicolson, 1989. A narrative that takes the reader through the Maya country of today with historical comments that help put the puzzle together.

Internet Resources

www.campeche.gob.mx
Official website of the Campeche state tourism authority.

www.cancunmap.com
An excellent source of detailed maps of the Riviera Maya.

www.cancuntips.com.mx
The online version of Cancún's main tourist magazine, with tons of listings, travel tips, and tourist resources.

www.la5ta.com
The online version of a hip Playa del Carmen

magazine, with nightlife, restaurants, art, and culture listings.

www.locogringo.com

Privately operated website with extensive business listings for Playa del Carmen and other areas on the Riviera Maya.

www.mayayucatan.com

Official website of the Yucatán state tourism authority.

www.mesoweb.com

Detailed website relating to Mesoamerican cultures, including detailed reports and photos of past and current archaeological digs.

www.sedetur.qroo.gob.mx

Official website of the Quintana Roo state tourism authority.

www.turismochiapas.gob.mx

Official website of the Chiapas state tourism authority.

www.visitetabasco.com

Official website of the Tabasco state tourism authority.

www.yucatantoday.com

Website of the helpful monthly tourist magazine of the same name. Based in Mérida but contains coverage of all of Yucatán state.

Index

A

Acancéh ruins: 283-284
Acrópolis (Ek' Balam): 319
Agua Azul: 388
Agua Clara: 387
Ah Kim Pech: 328
airplane wreck, Cozumel: 106
air travel: 461-462, 463
Aktun Chen: 169
Akumal: 167-174
Akumal Ecological Center: 169
alligator feedings (Cobá village): 201
Amatenango del Valle: 422
amber: 408
anteaters: 444
ants, leaf-cutter: 200
aquariums, interactive: 27, 45
arcades (Cancún): 49
archaeological sites: Acancéh ruins 283-284;
    Balamkú 354-355; Becán 357-360;
    Calakmul 348-354; Cancún 38-39;
    Chacchoben 219; Chicanná 355-356;
    Chichén Itzá 304-313; Chinkultíc 424; Cobá
    197-202; Comalcalco 375-377; Cozumel
    107-109; Dzibanché 225-226; Dzibilchaltún
    290-291; Edzná 344-347; Ek' Balam
    319-322; El Hormiguero 360; El Rey 38;
    Isla Jaina 347-348; itinerary for visiting
    22-23; Ixchel Ruins 74; Izamal 300; Kabah
    269-271; Kinichná 225-226; Kohunlich 225;
    Labná 272-274; La Venta 367; Loltún caves
    274-275; Mayapán 286; Muyil 202; Oxkintok
    283; Palenque 21, 382-387; Pijijiapán 438;
    Punta Laguna 200; Río Bec 360; Tenam
    Puente 424; Toniná 400; touring 187; Tulum
    182-185; Uxmal 263-269; Xcambó 297;
    Xpujil 360; Yamil Lu'um 39
architecture: Izamal 298; La Catedral de San
    Ildefonso 236; La Catedral (San Cristóbal
    de las Casas) 406; Los Palacios Gobernales
    238; Muna church 282; Museo de la
    Arquitectura Maya 330
Arch of Kabah: 271
Arch of Labná: 273
armadillos: 443-444
art classes: 79
Arte Maya: 276
artesanía, crafts and: general discussion 459;
    Campeche City 335; Cancún 44; Chiapan
    textiles 388, 407, 419, 421, 422; Isla Mujeres

76-77; Izamal 301; Mérida 246; Pacheco,
    Fernando Castro 238; Playa del Carmen
    144; pottery 276, 422; sacred art 240; San
    Cristóbal de las Casas 410-411; Templo Santo
    Domingo 407; traditional clothing 247-248;
    Tulum 187; Villahermosa 370; workshop
    collectives 412
Ascension Bay: 203
ATMs: 475
ATV tours: 118, 134
auto racing: 429

B

Bacalar Lagoon: 220-224
Balamkú Archaeological Zone: 354-355
Balankanche Caves: 309
Baluarte Nuestra Señora de la Soledad: 330
Baluarte San Francisco: 331
Baluarte San Juan: 331
banana boats: 45, 166
bargaining: 475
baseball: 42, 94
bat caves: 360
Batería de San Luis: 332
beaches: ettiquete for 471; public access to
    32-33
Becán Archaeological Zone: 22, 357-360
birds: 324, 446-447
bird-watching: Aviario Xaman-Ha 143; Celestún
    287-288; Cobá 197, 200; eco-adventure
    25; El Triunfo Biosphere Reserve 438-439;
    flamingos 24-25, 287-288, 296-297,
    323, 324, 447; Isla Contoy 89; Isla
    Holbox 89, 93; Isla Pájaros 91; kayak-in
    tours 187; Laguna Bacalar 221; Parque
    Nacional Arrecife Alacranes 293; Reserva
    de Huitepec 411-412; Río Lagartos 323;
    Sian Ka'an Biosphere Reserve 202, 203;
    Uaymitún Reserve 296-297
boating: 436
Bonampak Archaeological Zone: 21, 23,
    393-396
bookstores: Campeche City 336; Cancún
    44; Chetumal 226; Mérida 247; Playa del
    Carmen 144; San Cristóbal de las Casas 411
Boulevard Bahía (Chetumal): 225
bowling (Canún): 49
bullfights: Cancún 41; Mérida 245
bus travel: 462, 463-464
butterflies: 448

C

cacao: 376, 377
Café Museo Café: 408
Calakmul Archaeological Zone: 21, 22, 348-354
Calcehtok caves: 25, 283
calesa tours (Isla Cozumel): 112
Campeche, state of: 327-363; archaeological overview 22; Campeche City 328-344; Edzná 344-347; highlights 329; maps 328; regional overview 16; Río Bec region 348-363; Santa Rosa de Xtampák 347; trip planning 327
Campeche City: 328-344; accommodations 336-338; dining 338-340; El Malecón 336; history 328-330; maps 330, 332; services 340-341; shopping 335-336; sights 21, 330-334; tourist info 340; transportation 341-344
Cancún: 29-69; accommodations 50-56; beaches 45; dining 56-61; entertainment 40-43; excursions from 29; highlights 30; history 30-32; maps 31, 34-37; marriages in 62; recreation 45-50; regional overview 14; services 61-64; shopping 44-45; sights 32-40; tourist info 61-63; transportation 65-69; trip planning 30
Cañon del Sumidero: 436-437
Caracol: 308
cargo, religious: 421
Carillo Puerto: 206-209
Carnaval: 111
car racing: 429
Carrera Panamericana: 429
car travel: 462, 464-468
Casa de la Cultura: 79
Casa de Montejo: 238-239
Casa-Museo de la Marimba: 434
Casa Sirena: 407
cash: 475
Caste War: 206, 207, 453-454
Castillo Reef: 109
Catedral San Marcos: 428
Catedral Santo Domingo: 434
Catherwood, Fredrick: 450
caves: Aktun Chen 169; Balankanche Caves 309; Calcehtok 283; Grutas de Guaymas 437; Hacienda San Antonio Chalanté 301; Loltún 25, 274-275; Misol Ha 387; Río Bec bat 360; Sumidero Canyon area 437-438; Tecoh 286
caymans: 447
CEDAM (Conservation, Ecology, Diving, and Archaeology Museum): 161, 162

Celestún: 24, 286-290
cenotes: general discussion 186, 441; Aktun Chen 169; Cenote Azul 26, 221; Cenote Cristalina 26; Cenote Sagrado Azul 309; Cenotes de Cuzamá 284-285; Cenote Tankah 175; Cenote Tza Ujun Kat 285-286; Cenote Zaci 315; Chichén Itzá 307-308; children's swimming 27-28; diving 24; Dzitnup 315; Hacienda San Antonio Chalanté 301; Hidden Worlds 26, 186; snorkeling 46; Tulum 186-187
Central Plaza, Cozumel: 103
Centro Cultural Villahermosa: 369
Centro Ecológico Akumal (CEA): 169
Chacchoben Archaeological Zone: 219
Chamulan dress: 419-420
checkpoints, police: 362
Chetumal: 224-231
Chiapa de Corzo: 433-436
Chiapas, state of: 379-439; amber 408; archaeological overview 23; Cañon del Sumidero 436-437; highlights 380; history 380-381; indigenous villages 419-422, 437-438; maps 381; Ocosingo 400-403; Pacific coast 438-439; Palenque 382-392; regional overview 17; Río Usumacinta Valley 393-400; San Cristóbal de las Casas 403-418; textiles 388, 407, 419-420; trip planning 379; Tuxtla Gutiérrez 426-432
Chicanná Archaeological Zone: 22, 355-356
Chichén Itzá: 304-313; accommodations 309-311; dining 311-312; itinerary for visiting 20, 22, 28; maps 305; transportation 312-313
Chicoasén: 436
Chicxulub Crater: 296, 441
Chicxulub Puerto: 296
children, traveling with: 27-28, 472
chile peppers: 470
Chinchorro Bank: 27, 216
Chinkultíc Archaeological Zone: 424
chocolate: 376, 377
Chunkanan cenotes: 284-285
cinema: Cancún 42; Isla Cozumel 112; Mérida 245; Playa del Carmen 144; San Cristóbal de las Casas 410
city walls, Campeche: 330
climate: 441-442
clothing: Chamulan 419-420; Chiapan 388; Larrainzar 422; Museo de Trajes Regionales 407; to pack 19; traditional 247-248; Zinacantecan 421-422
coastal geography: 441
Cobá: 22, 197-202

Codz Poop: 269-270
coffee museum: 408
Colombia: 107
Comalcalco: 23, 375-378
Comitán: 422-424
conch shells: 131
conservation, environmental: 449
consulates: foreign 466-467; Mexican 469
Convento de San Antonio de Padua: 300
cooking classes (Mérida): 248
coral reefs: 103-107, 445
coral snakes: 448
Costa Maya: see La Costa Maya
Cozumel: see Isla Cozumel
credit cards: 475
crime: 474
Croco Cun Zoo: 132
cruises: 462
Cuba, travel to: 462
cuisine: 470
cultural performances: Campeche City 334;
    Isla Cozumel 112; Villahermosa 369
culture, people and: 459-460
currency: 475
customs: immigration 469; social 471

D

demography: 459
Destilería Sisal Tour: 301
diarrhea: 473-474
dining: 470-471
disabilities, travelers with: 472
discos: 41, 76, 242, 335, 429
diving: see scuba diving
documents, travel: 469, 473
dolphins, swimming with: Cancún 47; Dolphin
    Discovery 78; Playa del Carmen 146; Puerto
    Aventuras 161; Xcaret Eco-Park 147
Domingo en Mérida: 240, 241
Dovecote, the: 267
Duby Blom, Gertrude: 409
Dzibanché Archaeological Zone: 225
Dzibilchaltún: 290-291
Dzitnup cenotes: 315
Dzul-Ha: 106

E

eco-adventure itinerary: 24-25
economy: 458
eco-parks: Cancún 47; Isla Cozumel 116; Parque
    Garrafón 78-79; Sumidero Canyon 437;
    Tulum 188; Xcaret Eco-Park 147; Yumká 369
eco-tours: Celestún 288; Isla Contoy 74-75;
itinerary 24-25; jungle tours 49; Laguna
    Bacalar 221; Mérida 244; Playa del Carmen
    147; Río Lagartos 323; Sian Ka'an Biosphere
    Reserve 187, 203
Edzná Archaeological Zone: 22, 344-347
Ek' Balam: 22, 28, 319-322
El Caracol: 109
El Castillo: 306
El Cedral: 108
El Cerrito: 407
El Conejo: 300
El Cristo de las Ampollas: 236
El Hormiguero Archaeological Zone: 360
El Malecón: 336
El Mirador (Labná): 273
El Mirador (Sayil): 271-272
El Palacio (Labná): 273
El Rey Archaeological Zone: 23, 38
El Triunfo Biosphere Reserve: 438-439
El Trono: 319
employment abroad: 472
environmental issues: 131, 449
Escárega: 363
estuaries: 447
exchange rates: 475

F

family trip itinerary: 27-28
fauna: general discussion 443-448; Calakmul 351;
    Cobá 200; Sian Ka'an Biosphere Reserve 202
felines: 444
ferries: 86-87, 464
festivals: general discussion 459-460; Cancún
    Jazz Festival 42; Carnaval 111; Chiapa de
    Corzo 435; Festival de El Cedral 311-312;
    Festival de Jazz 335; Festival Histórico
    de Campeche 335; Fiesta de San Joaquín
    221; Mérida 242; Orange Festival 281;
    San Cristóbal de las Casas 410; San Juan
    Chamula 421
film, camera: 476
Finca Cholula: 376
fish: 445
fishing: Akumal 170; Ascension Bay 203;
    Cancún 47-48; economy 458; Isla Cozumel
    117; Isla Holbox 89, 94; Isla Mujeres 79; Playa
    del Carmen 147; Puerto Morelos 134; Sian
    Ka'an Biosphere Reserve 187; Xcalak 217
flamingos: general discussion 324, 447;
    Celestún 287-288; eco-tours with 24; Río
    Lagartos 323; Uaymitún Reserve 296-297
flora: general discussion 442-443; Cobá 200;
    Sian Ka'an Biosphere Reserve 202

flowers: 442
food: 470
foreign consulates: 466-467
forts, Campeche: 331
fountain shows (Campeche): 335
Francesa, Allanza: 112
Frontera Corozal: 399-400
fruit trees: 442
Fuerte de San Miguel: 331
Fuerte San Felipe Bacalar: 220-221

G

Galería de Arte Juanita Canche de Manzanero: 276
gardens: 132, 331
gay and lesbian travelers: 472
gear: 19
geography: 14-17, 440-442
geology: 296, 440-441
golf: Cancún 48; Isla Cozumel 117; Mérida 248; Playa del Carmen 147; Puerto Aventuras 162
Governer's Place (Uxmal): 266
government: 456-458
Gran Plaza (Edzná): 345
gratuities: 475
Great Ball Court (Chichén Itzá): 307
Great Pyramid: Kabah 271; Uxmal 267
Group of a Thousand Columns (Chichén Itzá): 308
Grutas de Guaymas: 437
guayaberas: 246, 247, 301

H

haciendas: general discussion 275; chocolate 376; Hacienda Mundaca 72; Hacienda San Antonio Chalanté 301, 303; Hacienda San Pedro Nohpat 275; Hacienda Santa Rosa 275; Hacienda Tabi 275-276; Hacienda Temozón 275; Hacienda Yaxcopoil 282
hammocks, Yucatecan: 133
Hard Rock Cafe: 40
health: 473-474
heat stroke: 473
Hecelchakán: 348
henequen: 301, 455
Hidden Worlds: 26, 186
hieroglyphics, deciphering: 181
history: 449-456; Caste War 207; Zapatistas 401; *see also* Maya culture; *specific place*
hitchhiking: 468
holidays: see festivals

horseback riding: Cancún 49; Hacienda San Antonio Chalanté 301; Isla Cozumel 117; Lagunas de Montebello National Park 425
horse-drawn carriage rides: 112, 300
Hotel Parador Santa María: 424
House of the Turtles: 267
huipiles: 246, 247, 301, 410, 411
Hurricane Isadora: 323
Hurricane Wilma: 102

I

Iglesia de Balam Nah: 207
Iglesia de San Mateo: 279
Iglesia y Ex-Convento San Bernardino de Siena: 315
iguanas: 448
insects: 448, 474
insurance, diving: 116
international travel: 462
Internet access: 477
Isla Contoy: 74-75
Isla Cozumel: 98-128; accommodations 118-122; beaches 109-111; dining 122-125; entertainment 111-112; highlights 99; history 99-101; maps 100-101, 104-105; recreation 114-118; regional overview 14; scuba diving 26, 103-107; services 125-126; shopping 113; sights 103-111; transportation 126-128; trip planning 99
Isla de la Pasión: 92
Isla Holbox: 89-97; accommodations 94-95; beaches 91; dining 95-96; history 89; recreation 92-94; services 96-97; shopping 92; sights 90-92; transportation 97
Isla Jaina: 347-348
Isla Mujeres: 69-88; accommodations 79-83; dining 83-85; entertainment 76; history 69; maps 70, 72-73; orientation 69; recreation 77-79; services 85-87; shopping 76; sights 71-75; transportation 86-88
Isla Pájaros: 91
Itzamatul: 300
Ixchel Ruins: 74
Izamal: 21, 24, 298-304

JK

jade museum: 408
jaguars: 444
Jardín del Arte: 40
jazz: 40, 335
jungle tours: 49
Kabah Archaeological Zone: 269-271
Kabul: 300

Kinich Kak Moo: 300
Kinichná Archaeological Zone: 225
kiteboarding: Cancún 46; Chicxulub Puerto 296; Isla Cozumel 116; Isla Holbox 91, 93; Mahahual 211; Playa del Carmen 146; Tulum 188
Kohunlich Archaeological Zone: 23, 225

L

La Bandera: 77
Labná Archaeological Zone: 272-274
La Casa de Arte Popular Mexicano: 39-40
La Catedral de San Ildefonso: 236
La Catedral (San Cristóbal de las Casas): 406
La Costa Maya: 209-219; Chacchoben Archaeological Zone 219; Mahahual 209-215; Xcalak 215-219
La Frailesca: 437
Laguna Bacalar: 220-224
Lagunas de Montebello National Park: 424-425
Laguna Yal-Ku: 167
La Hacienda Xcanatún: 275
La Iglesia (Cobá): 199
Lake Tziscao: 425
Landa, Fray Diego de: 280
land mammals: 443-445
language: 459
La Pila: 434
La Playa (Progreso): 292
La Rodonda: 321
Las Gemelas: 322
Las Pinturas Group: 200
La Torre Escénica: 40
La Venta: 367
leaf-cutter ants: 200
lesbian and gay travelers: 472
lighthouses: Isla Mujeres 74; Playa del Carmen 142; Progreso 292; Punta Molas 111
light shows: Campeche City 331; Chichén Itzá 308; Uxmal 267-268
lizards: 448
locals lounges (salones familiares): 242
Loltún caves: 25, 274-275
Los Langosteros: 42
Los Palacios Gobernales: 238

M

Macanxoc Group: 200
Mahahual: 209-215; accommodations 211-213; dining 214; recreation 27, 210-211; transportation 215
malls: 44-45, 370
manatees: 445-446
Manzanero, Amerando: 276
Maracaibo: 107
marimba: 434
marinelife: 445-446
marriage, in Cancún: 62
massage: Akumal 170; Cancún 50; Isla Cozumel 118; Isla Mujeres 79; Playa del Carmen 148; Tulum 189; Xpu-Há 166
Maya culture: Caste War 206, 207; collapse of 352; Fray Landa's destruction of 280; hieroglyphics 181; history 450-454; modern-day 419; Museo de la Arquitectura Maya 330; Museo de la Cultura Maya 224; Museo de la Medicina Maya 407-408; Museo Regional Antropología e Historia 239; nationalism 207; see also archaeological sites; specific place
Mayapán Archaeological Zone: 286
measurements: 477
Media Luna: 77
Mercado 20 de Noviembre: 281
Mérida: 235-263; accommodations 249-253; city layout 235-236; dining 253-256; entertainment 240-245; maps 235, 236-237, 264, 287; recreation 248-249; services 256-258; shopping 245-248; sights 20, 236-240; signs 239; tourist info 256; traditional clothing 247-248; transportation 258-263
Misol Ha: 387
money: 475
monkeys: general discussion 350; eco-adventures with 25; Punta Laguna 200
mountain biking: 187, 188
movies: see cinema
Muna: 283
murals: 281, 393
Museo Arqueológico de Comitán: 422
Museo Comunitario Frontera Corozal: 399
Museo Comunitario (Izamal): 300
Museo de Arte Sacro en Yucatán: 240
Museo de Historia Natural: 240
Museo de Laca: 434
Museo de la Canción Yucateca: 239-240
Museo de la Ciudad (Chetumal): 224
Museo de la Ciudad (Mérida): 239
Museo de la Cultura Maya: 224
Museo de la Isla de Cozumel: 103
Museo del Ámbar de Chiapas: 408
Museo de la Medicina Maya: 407-408
Museo de la Piratería: 221
Museo de los Altos de Chiapas: 407
Museo de Pueblo Maya: 290-291

Museo de Trajes Regionales: 407
Museo MACAY: 239
Museo Mesoamericano del Jade: 408
Museo Na Bolom: 409
Museo Regional Antropología e Historia: 239
Museo Regional de Antropología Carlos Pelicar
    Cámara: 368
Museo Regional de Chiapas: 428
Museo San Roque: 315
Museo Sub-Acuatico CEDAM: 161
music, live: Campeche Plaza weekends 334;
    Cancún 40-41; Chetumal 226; Cozumel
    112; Festival de Jazz 335; Isla Mujeres
    76; marimba 434; Mérida 240; Museo de
    la Canción Yucateca 239-240; Parque
    Marimba 428; San Cristóbal de las Casas
    409-410; Tuxtla Gutiérrez 429
Muyil Archaeological Zone: 202

NO

newspapers: 477
nightclubs (Cancún): 42-43
Nohoch Mul: 199
Nohoch-Ná: 346
Noj Kaj Santa Cruz: 206
Nunnery, Chichén Itzá: 308
Nunnery Quadrangle: 266
Ocosingo: 400-403
oil economy: 458
Olmec culture: 367
orchids: 443
Osario: 308
Oxkintok Archaeological Zone: 283
Oxkutzcab: 280-282

P

Paamul: 160-161
Pacheco, Fernando Castro: 238
packing: 18-19
Palace of the Archbishop: 238
Palacio Municipal (San Cristóbal de las Casas):
    406
Palacio Municipal (Valladolid): 315
Palancar reef: 107
Palenque: 382-392; accommodations 388-
    390; dining 390; itinerary for visiting 23;
    maps 383-384; transportation 392
palms: 442
papel picado (diced paper decorations): 459
Paraíso: 106
parasailing: 45, 162, 166
Parque Central (San Cristóbal de las Casas): 403
Parque Ecoarqueológico Ik Kil: 309

Parque Ecológico Punta Sur: 26, 116
Parque Garrafón: 47, 78-79
Parque Las Palapas: 27, 40
Parque Los Artesanos: 40
Parque Marimba: 428
Parque-Museo La Venta: 367
Parque Nacional Arrecife Alacranes: 293
Parque Nacional Chankanaab: 26, 117
Parque Zoológico del Centenario: 245
partying, in Cancún: 42-43
Paso de Cedral: 107
passports: 469
Paz, Leonardo: 281
peccaries: 444
people and culture: 459-460
peppers, chile: 470
performing arts: Campeche City 334; Cancún
    41; Mérida 240; San Cristóbal de las Casas
    410; Teatro Esperanza Iris 370; Tuxtla
    Gutiérrez 429
photography: 419, 471, 476
pier, Progreso: 292
Pijijiapán: 438
Pinacoteca del Estado Juan Gamboa Guzmán:
    240
pirates: 221
Pisté: 304-313
planetariums: 370
plantlife: 442-443
Playa Ballenas: 38
Playa Bonita: 110
Playa Caracol: 33
Playa Chac-Mool: 27, 33
Playa del Carmen: 139-159; accommodations
    149-153; dining 153-155; entertainment
    143-144; maps 140-141; recreation 145-149;
    services 156-158; shopping 144; sights 20,
    139-143; transportation 156-159
Playa Delfines: 38
Playa El Faro: 142
Playa Lancheros: 71
Playa Marlín: 33
Playa Norte: 71
Playa Palancar: 109
Playa Rasta: 110
Playa San Francisco: 109
Playa Tankah: 175
Playa Tortugas: 110
Playa Tukán: 26, 142
Playa Xcalacoco: 138-139
Plaza Cívica (Tuxtla Gutiérrez): 426
Plaza de la Independencia: 236
Plaza de Toros: 41

Plaza la Bandera: 226
postal service: 476
pottery: Amatenango del Valle 422; Ticul 276
prehistory: 449
Progreso: 291-295
public writer *(escritorio público):* 370
Puerto Arista: 438
Puerto Aventuras: 161-165
Puerto de Tierra: 331
Puerto Morelos: 130-138; accommodations 134-136; beach 130-132; dining 136-137; maps 132; recreation 134; scuba diving 26, 132-133; shopping 133
Punta Allen: 202-206
Punta Bete: 138-139
Punta Laguna: 200
puppet theaters: 245
Puuc Route: 21, 263-282; itinerary for visiting 22; Kabah 269-271; Labná 272-274; Loltún caves 274-275; maps 264; Oxkintok 282; Oxkutzcab 280-282; Santa Elena 278-280; Sayil 271-272; Ticul 276-278; Uxmal 263-269; Xlapak 272
Pyramid of the Magician: 263-269

QR

Quadrangle of the Birds: 266
Queen Conch: 131
quetzals: 447
Quinta Avenida: 139
Quintana Roo: 198-231; archaeological sites 22-23; Carillo Puerto 206-209; Chetumal 224-231; Cobá 197-202; highlights 179; La Costa Maya 209-219; Laguna Bacalar 220-224; maps 180; Punta Allen 202-206; regional overview 15; Sian Ka'an Biosphere Reserve 202-206; trip planning 178
radio: 477
Rancho Loma Bonita: 49
rattlesnakes: 448
reefs, coral: 445
regional overviews: 14-17
religion: 421, 459, 460
rental cars: 466-467
reptiles: 447-448
Reserva de Huitepec: 411-412
Reserva de la Biosfera El Triunfo: 438-439
Reserva Ecológica de los Petenes: 287
Revolucíon Mexicana: 438
Río Bec Archaeological Zone: 360
Río Bec region: 348-363; Balamkú 354-355; Calakmul 348-354; Chicanná 355-356; Escárega 363; Xpujil town 360-363

Río Lagartos: 323-324
Río Tulijá: 387
Río Usumacinta Valley: 393-400
Riviera Maya: 129-177; Akumal 167-174; highlights 130; maps 131; Paamul 160-161; Playa del Carmen 139-159; Playa Xcalacoco 138-139; Puerto Aventuras 161-165; Puerto Morelos 130-138; Punta Bete 138-139; regional overview 15; Tankah Tres 175-177; trip planning 129; Xpu-Há 165-166
Ruínas de Acancéh: 283-284
Ruta Puuc: see Puuc Route

S

safety: 33, 473-474
sailboarding: 146
sailing: 146, 170
Saint John the Baptist Church: 420-421
salt extraction: 286
San Andrés Larrainzar: 422
San Cristóbal de las Casas: 403-418; accommodations 412-414; dining 414-416; entertainment 409-410; maps 404-405; recreation 411-412; shopping 410-411; sights 21, 403-409; transportation 417-418
San Felipe: 325-326
San Gervasio: 23, 107-108
San Juan Chamula: 419-421
San Miguel de Cozumel: 98, 101
San Pablo Buenavista: 438
Santa Elena: 278-280
Santa Rosa de Xtampák: 347
Santa Rosa Wall: 106
Santo Domingo de Palenque: 382-392
Santuario de la Cruz Parlante: 207
Sayasol: 347
Sayil Archaeological Zone: 271-272
scams, driving: 468
scenic drives: 437
scenic flights: 147, 423
scenic views: 40
scuba diving: Akumal 169-170; Cancún 46; CEDAM (Conservation, Ecology, Diving, and Archaeology Museum) 161, 162; choosing dive shops 115; insurance 116; Isla Cozumel 103-107, 114-115; Isla Holbox 92-93; Isla Mujeres 77-78; itinerary 26-27; Mahahual 210-211; Paamul 160; Playa del Carmen 145; Puerto Aventuras 161; Puerto Morelos 132-133, 134; Tankah Tres 175; Tulum 187; Xcalak 216; Xpu-Há 165-166
sculpture gardens: 74
sealife: 445-446

seasons, best travel: 18
sea turtles: 72-74, 89, 169, 445
senior travelers: 472
services: 475-477
sharks: 77
Sian Ka'an Biosphere Reserve: 187, 202-206, 449
Sierra Madre: 438
sisal: 301, 455
skydiving: 147
Sleeping Shark Cave: 77
snakes: 448
snorkeling: Akumal 170; Cancún 46; eco-tours 24; Isla Cozumel 103-107, 115-116; Isla Holbox 92-93; Isla Mujeres 77; itinerary 26-27; Mahahual 210-211; Paamul 160; Playa del Carmen 146; Puerto Aventuras 161; Puerto Morelos 132-133, 134; Sian Ka'an Biosphere Reserve 187; Tankah Tres 175; Tulum 188; with whale sharks 90-91; Xcalak 216; Xpu-Há 165-166
social norms: 471
Spanish conquest: 452-453
Spanish language classes: Cancún 50; Isla Mujeres 79; Mérida 248; Playa del Carmen 148; San Cristóbal de las Casas 412
spiders: 448
Stephens, John Lloyd: 450
stucco frieze, Balamkú: 354-355
student travelers: 471
Suchiapa: 437
Sumidero Canyon: 436-437
sunburn: 473
surfing: 47
surf warnings: 33

T
Tabasco, state of: 364-378; archaeological sites 23; Comalcalco 375-378; highlights 366; maps 365; regional overview 17; trip planning 364; Villahermosa 366-374
Tabasco 2000: 370
Tankah Tres: 175-177
Tapachula: 439
tapirs: 444
taxes: 475
Teatro Cancún: 41
Teatro Esperanza Iris: 370
Tecoh caves: 286
Telchac Puerto: 297-298
telephones: 476
television: 477
temperatures: 441

Temple of Kukulcán: 306
Temple of the Columns: 270
Temple of the Cross: 386
Temple of the Descending God: 184
Temple of the Frescoes: 184
Temple of the Inscriptions: 385
Temple of the Jaguars: 307
Temple of the Seven Dolls: 290
Temple of Warriors: 308
Templo San Cristóbal (El Cerrito): 407
Templo Santo Domingo: 407
Templo y Ex-Convento de San Francisco: 281
Templo y Mirador de San Gregorio: 435
Tenam Puente Archaeological Zone: 424
tennis: 48, 162
textiles: see clothing
theft: 474
Ticul: 276-278
time zone: 477
tipping: 475
Tizimín: 326
Toniná: 23, 400
Tormentos: 106
Tortugranja: 72
tourist cards: 469
tourist economy: 458
tourist information: 476
tours: general discussion 468; Bonampak 393; Calcehtok caves 283; Campeche City 334-335; Celestún 287-288; Cenotes de Cuzamá 284-285; Chacchoben Archaeological Zone 219; Destilería Sisal Tour 301; Edzná Archaeological Zone 346; indigenous villages of Chiapas 409; Mérida 242-245; Muyil Archaeological Zone boat 203; Punta Laguna 200; San Cristóbal de las Casas 409; scenic flights 423; Sian Ka'an Biosphere Reserve 187; Sumidero Canyon boat 436; Yaxchilán 393; see also specific place
transportation: 461-468; police checkpoints 362; see also specific place
travelers checks: 475
trees: 442-443
trip planning: 18-19
Tulum: 181-197; accommodations 189-194; beaches 25, 185; dining 194-195; highlights 179; itinerary for visiting 23; maps 180, 182, 190; recreation 187-189; regional overview 15; services 195-197; transportation 196, 197; trip planning 178
Tunich: 106
Tuxtla Gutiérrez: 426-432
Tzompantil: 307

UV

Uaymitún Reserve: 296-297
Ultrafreeze: 77
underage travelers: 469
UNESCO sites: Calakmul 348-354; Sian Ka'an Biosphere Reserve 202-206
Uxmal Archaeological Zone: 21, 22, 263-269
Valladolid: 27, 313-319
Valley of Cintala: 438
vegetation: 442-443
Villa Corzo: 438
Villaflores: 438
Villahermosa: 366-374
visas: 469
volunteering: 211

W

wakeboarding: 47
waterfalls: 387, 388
water parks: 47, 116
waterskiing: 47
wave runners: 45
weather: 18, 441
whale sharks: 89, 90-91
windsurfing: 296
women travelers: 471-472
writing, deciphering Maya: 181

XY

Xcalak: 27, 215-219
Xcambó: 297
Xcaret Eco-Park: 27, 47, 147
Xel-Ha: 47
Xlapak Archaeological Zone: 272

Xpu-Há: 165-166
Xpujil Archaeological Zone: 21, 360
Xpujil town: 360-363
Yalahua Spring: 92
Yal-Ku: 167
Yamil Lu'um Archaeological Zone: 23, 39
Yaxchilán Archaeological Zone: 21, 23, 396-399
Yaxcopoil: 283
Yucab: 106
Yucatán, state of: 232-326; archaeological overview 22; Celestún 286-290; Chichén Itzá 304-313; Dzibilchaltún 290-291; Ek' Balam 319-322; highlights 233; Izamal 298-304; maps 234; Mérida 235-263; Progreso 291-295; Puuc Route 263-282; regional overview 16; Río Lagartos 324-325; San Felipe 325-326; Tizimín 326; trip planning 232; Valladolid 313-319
Yucatecan hammocks: 133
Yumká: 369

Z

Zacpol: 347
Zama: 71
Zapatistas: 401
Zinacantán: 421-422
Zona Hotelera (Cancún): accommodations 51-53; beaches 32-38, 34-35; dining 56-61; entertainment 41; geography 32; maps 34-35; nightclubs 42-43
Zona Hotelera (Tulum): 183, 190
Zona Remodelada (Villahermosa): 366
ZOOMAT: 428
zoos: 132, 428, 437

Acknowledgments

**To Eva Quetzal Chandler,
the love of our lives.**

Thank you first and foremost to the many, many residents of the Riviera Maya and Yucatán Peninsula, most of whose names we never learned, who helped us in the course of updating this book. From friendly bus drivers to helpful shop owners to patient hotel receptionists, they made this project possible and have our sincere gratitude.

Particular people we met along the way deserve special mention and thanks. In Mérida, we are grateful to Sophi and Daniel of Hotel Marionetas, Nicole and Nelson at Hotel MedioMundo, and John at Ángeles de Mérida. We have long turned to Kristine and Santiago at Flycatcher Inn in Santa Elena for sound advice about the Puuc Route and beyond, and to Diane and Rick at Río Bec Dreams outside of Xpujil for similar help and insight into the Río Bec region.

In Quintana Roo, we are indebted to Bob Rodríguez of Casa Colonial in Isla Cozumel, Curtis and Ashley at Villa La Bella in Isla Mujeres, and Rosy Besomi of La Bambina II in Isla Holbox. Along the Costa Maya, our many thanks to Carol and Alan at Hotel Balamkú, Carolien and Jan at Hotel Maya Luna, and Margo and Robert at Sin Duda.

We are fortunate to have—and extremely grateful to receive—such excellent editorial and production support from everyone at Avalon Travel Publishing. Thanks to Grace Fujimoto for sending us off on the right foot, Kevin McLain for his gentle and able shepherding during the research and writing, and Naomi Adler Dancis for her sharp editing. Thank you to Kevin Anglin and the cartography department for their excellent work on the maps, and Stefano Boni and others in the production department for making this book look so great. Thank you to Sarah Juckniess for navigating us through Avalon's administrative waters, and to Hannah Cox for arranging all those book talks and radio interviews, and for generally making us feel famous.

We'd like to extend, once again, a special acknowledgment to Chicki Mallan, who, with husband and photographer Oz Mallan, wrote the first seven editions of this book—a remarkable achievement. Her dedication, experience, and enduring love for the Yucatán region are a model for any would-be travel writer.

Finally, and above all, thank you to our families and friends for their unwavering love and support: Mom and Dad Prado, Mom and Dad Chandler, Ellen, Elyse, Joey and Sue and the little one, Katy and Kyle and their little one, Brian and Becky and their little *two*—it's been a productive couple of years!—Dave, Javier, Debbie, Owen, Sammy, Tío Miguel, Kelly, Dan, Kaitlyn, TJ, Beatriz, Rich, Scott, Lulu, and Rukaiyah.

www.moon.com

For helpful advice on planning a trip, visit www.moon.com for the **TRAVEL PLANNER** and get access to useful travel strategies and valuable information about great places to visit. When you travel with Moon, expect an experience that is uncommon and truly unique.

HANDBOOKS | METRO | OUTDOORS | LIVING ABROAD

MAP SYMBOLS

▬▬▬ Expressway	【 Highlight	✗ Airfield	⚓ Golf Course
▬▬▬ Primary Road	○ City/Town	✗ Airport	℗ Parking Area
▬▬▬ Secondary Road	◉ State Capital	▲ Mountain	◤ Archaeological Site
▪▪▪▪ Unpaved Road	◉ National Capital	✛ Unique Natural Feature	♟ Church
▬ ▬ ▬ Trail	★ Point of Interest		
⋯⋯⋯ Ferry	• Accommodation	⊱ Waterfall	⊗ Gas Station
⊢⊢⊢ Railroad	▼ Restaurant/Bar	▲ Park	◠ Glacier
▬▬▬ Pedestrian Walkway	▪ Other Location	🕇 Trailhead	◫ Mangrove
▥▥▥ Stairs	Λ Campground	⛷ Skiing Area	▭ Reef
			▭ Swamp

CONVERSION TABLES

$°C = (°F - 32) / 1.8$
$°F = (°C \times 1.8) + 32$
1 inch = 2.54 centimeters (cm)
1 foot = 0.304 meters (m)
1 yard = 0.914 meters
1 mile = 1.6093 kilometers (km)
1 km = 0.6214 miles
1 fathom = 1.8288 m
1 chain = 20.1168 m
1 furlong = 201.168 m
1 acre = 0.4047 hectares
1 sq km = 100 hectares
1 sq mile = 2.59 square km
1 ounce = 28.35 grams
1 pound = 0.4536 kilograms
1 short ton = 0.90718 metric ton
1 short ton = 2,000 pounds
1 long ton = 1.016 metric tons
1 long ton = 2,240 pounds
1 metric ton = 1,000 kilograms
1 quart = 0.94635 liters
1 US gallon = 3.7854 liters
1 Imperial gallon = 4.5459 liters
1 nautical mile = 1.852 km

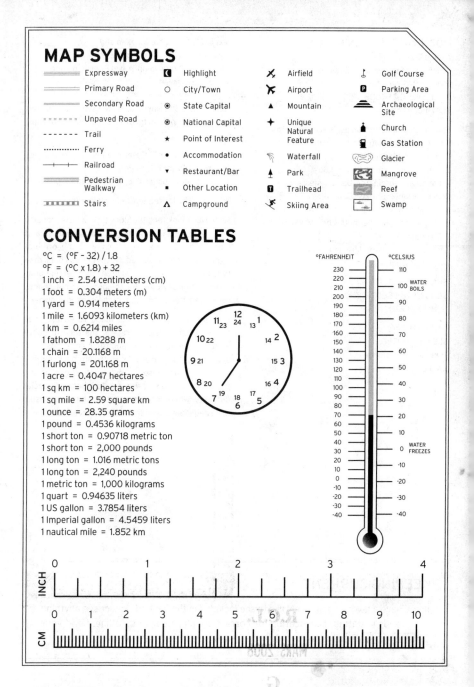

MOON YUCATÁN PENINSULA

Avalon Travel Publishing
a member of the Perseus Books Group
1400 65th Street, Suite 250
Emeryville, CA 94608, USA
www.moon.com

Editors: Naomi Adler Dancis, Grace Fujimoto
Series Manager: Kathryn Ettinger
Copy Editor: Mary Miller
Graphics Coordinator: Stefano Boni
Production Coordinator: Darren Alessi
Cover Designer: Stefano Boni
Map Editor: Kevin Anglin
Cartographers: Kat Bennett, Chris Markiewicz,
    Suzanne Service
Cartography Director: Mike Morgenfeld
Indexer: Rachel Kuhn

ISBN-10: 1-56691-781-6
ISBN-13: 978-1-56691-781-0
ISSN: 1098-6707

Printing History
1st Edition – 1986
9th Edition – October 2007
5 4 3 2 1

Text © 2007 by Chicki Mallan and
    Avalon Travel Publishing, Inc.
Maps © 2007 by Avalon Travel Publishing, Inc.
All rights reserved.

Some photos and illustrations are used by permission
and are the property of the original copyright
owners.

Front cover photo: © Cosmo Condina/Getty Images
Title page photo: © Liza Prado
Interior photos: pages 4–8, © Liza Prado

Printed in the United States by Malloy, Inc.

Moon Handbooks and the Moon logo are the property
of Avalon Travel Publishing. All other marks and
logos depicted are the property of the original
owners. All rights reserved. No part of this book may
be translated or reproduced in any form, except brief
extracts by a reviewer for the purpose of a review,
without written permission of the copyright owner.

Although every effort was made to ensure that
the information was correct at the time of going
to press, the author and publisher do not assume
and hereby disclaim any liability to any party for any
loss or damage caused by errors, omissions, or any
potential travel disruption due to labor or financial
difficulty, whether such errors or omissions result
from negligence, accident, or any other cause.

KEEPING CURRENT

If you have a favorite gem you'd like to see included in the next edition, or see anything
that needs updating, clarification, or correction, please drop us a line. Send your
comments via email to feedback@moon.com, or use the address above.

RCL

MARS 2008

G